River

Pg.113

ITALY, GREECE & ASIA MINOR

T H R A C E

Byzantium
(Constantinople)

M A C E D O N I A

SAMOTHRACE

P H R Y G I A

LEMNOS

Mount Olympus

Troy

Pergamon

CHIOS

Thermopylae ✕
Orchomenos

Ephesus Tralles

Delphi

Thebes
Eleusis

Mara-
thon

SAMOS

Priene

Sicyon

Athens

ANDROS

C A R I A

Corinth

SALAMIS

Miletus

Olympia

Mycenae

AEGINA

DELOS

Halicarnassus

Argos

Tegea

Tiryns

Epidaurus

Bassae

Sparta

Chidus

RHODES

MELOS

Cythera

CRETE

Candia

Phaistos Knossos

ARTS AND IDEAS

Vermeer. *The Artist in His Studio*. Oil on Canvas. 52⅛" x 43¼". *c.*1665–1670. Kunsthistorisches Museum, Vienna

ARTS
and IDEAS

William Fleming

SYRACUSE UNIVERSITY

HENRY HOLT AND COMPANY · NEW YORK

CONTENTS

v

F O R E W O R D

THIS INTERPRETIVE STUDY is designed to fulfill the need for a book that will present the major periods of Western art through a series of representative masterpieces drawn from the fields of architecture, sculpture, painting, literature, and music. It hopes to suggest relationships among the various modes of expression—relationships based on the fact that groups of artists lived and worked at a certain time, in a common geographical location, and shared a world of ideas, even though they responded to them individually and used different techniques.

The Chronologies, which appear at the beginning of each chapter, are in the nature of programs, listing at a glance the background of important events against which the drama of each period is to be played, as well as the cast of characters who will be making their appearance. The introductory sections follow in the nature of curtain raisers, which attempt to capture something of the social spirit of the time as well as to highlight some of the dominant issues that motivated its activities. The succeeding sections, like the several acts of a drama, then present the architectural, sculptural, pictorial, literary, and musical expressions of the period in such a way that each will give glimpses into the creative dynamics of that society. The architectural monument, for instance, far from being a mere mass of brick and mortar, becomes a framework for its ordered life. The sculptural and pictorial embellishments take on the character of concrete embodiments of that society's hopes and fears; while the literary and musical forms are the stylized patterns of its traditions, activities, and objectives. The final section, or epilogue, of each chapter will then be in the nature of a style synthesis, designed to bring the separate arts into a demonstrable relationship that falls within the scope of the history of ideas.

Each phase is set in a time and place where the cultural dynamics have reached climactic proportions; where the lines of influence converge and point to an inner unity; and where the productivity can provide a representative cross section of an important period. Athens thus becomes the setting of the Hellenic Style, Pergamon of the Hellenistic, and Trajan's reign that of the Roman Style; while together they combine as different aspects of the Classical Period. Part Two is concerned with the Medieval Period, and Ravenna provides the scene of the Early Christian and Byzantine styles, the Abbey of Cluny of the Monastic Romanesque,

Normandy of the Feudal Romanesque, and Chartres of the Gothic. An Italian panorama (Chapter 8) then leads into the Florentine and Roman phases of the Renaissance; while Venice, the Escorial, Versailles, Amsterdam, and London become the settings for the various facets of the Baroque. A northern European panorama (Chapter 16) then leads toward the various styles of the Revolutionary Period, which extends from the late 18th century to the present time, where a final panoramic view of current developments in the arts (Chapter 20) will be found.

Any valid approach to the arts must be based on the dual nature of the work of art itself, which is at once both an organized whole and a historical fact. In one case, by the process of analysis, it can be reduced to its component parts for the purpose of study; in the other, by means of synthesis, it can be fitted into the whole picture of the period that produced it. The artist must start with the creative vanishing point of the void and proceed to select, place together, build up, and grow. Thus from the singular the procedure is toward the plural, from unrelatedness to relatedness, and eventually to the order and unity of a style. Many artists within a period must inevitably share certain ideas while working together in one place and within a given time span. Pericles, Phidias, Socrates, Sophocles, and Euripides, as contemporaries within a single half-century, surely shaped as well as shared many of the thoughts and views current in the Athens of their day. They likewise participated in the life of their time in all its aspects. Whether the artist be reformer or conformer, revolutionist or evolutionist, prophet of things to come or nostalgic dreamer of past golden ages, his own contemporary society and its ideas is his point of departure. Techniques by which artists—whether architect, sculptor, painter, writer, or musician—produce their works will always differ radically. However, the end result of their labors, springing as it does from the same social source and in turn addressed to it, must have a certain unity. When these aesthetic phenomena are viewed as an interrelated whole, it begins to be possible to speak of a *style*, which might be defined as a synthesis of the outgrowth of man's changing ideas as expressed in the symbolic language of the arts and consisting of certain features shared by them all. The arts thus become a language in symbols and images by which man communicates his ideas of order and the meaning of life in perceptual rather than conceptual terms. The artist, then, is one who gives blood transfusions to the cold logic of reality in the world of events, and breathes into disembodied abstract principles the breath of life and the warmth of humanity.

A positive approach can thus be based on the triple concept of *time, place,* and *idea*. A given group of artists, while working in their separate fields,

are an integral part of a society, living and moving within a certain geographical and temporal center, and collaborating to a greater or less
extent. The closer the coincidence, of course, the closer the relationship.
Composite works of art, such as cathedrals or operas, are always collaborative in nature and must to a considerable extent have mutual influences.
Liturgical demands, for instance, must be taken into account in a cathedral's architectural design, and the sculptural and pictorial embellishments
must fit themselves into the plan and iconography of the building. Hence
in one period of *time*, and in one *place*, the arts of architecture, sculpture,
liturgy, and music can share a common constellation of *ideas* in relation
to the contemporary social order and its cultural aspirations.

Humanistic understanding can acquire a deeper meaning as the striving
of other men and societies is observed within our own time, and still
greater insight is possible through the historical dimension when kinship is
established with the creative revelations of other peoples and cultures
across the centuries. The arts in their natural relationship become, then,
the study of people reflected in the ever-changing images of man as he
journeys across historical time, as he lives and expresses his attitudes toward
himself, his fellow men, and the universe, and as he strives toward his
ideals in the ceaseless effort to create significant meanings for life.

The ultimate objective is thus the understanding of self and society
through knowledge of the manifold human values revealed in the infinite
ways man expresses the various facets of his nature through visual, verbal,
and tonal imagery. As the separate works of art build up into the syntheses
of style periods, the image of man emerges as a means of grasping comparative differences. What, for instance, was Classical man striving for? How
does he differ from Byzantine man? What changing constellations of
ideas lead to Medieval man? What are the distinguishing marks of Monastic
man? Of Feudal man? In what images does Renaissance man reveal himself? How are the contrasting images of the aristocratic and bourgeois
ideals of man reflected in the arts of the 18th century? What is the nature of
Romantic man? Of Machine Age man?

A high degree of selectivity is, of course, necessary. The material that
can be presented within a work of these proportions could not possibly
aim at inclusiveness. The book, therefore, is intended not so much as a
history of the arts as it is a sequence of stylistic and historical studies within
common geographical, temporal, and ideational contexts, related in
method and theme, and distilling the essence of the arts and ideas of selected periods from the work of several outstanding figures who are seen
moving against the background of their time. Instead of mentioning every-

thing, as in the survey method, or using the extensive approach replete with origins, influences, rises, growths, developments and declines, this study will try to provide a more intensive investigation of a limited number of monuments and bring them into a working relationship so that they will appear as living episodes in the historical cavalcade of Western culture.

At this point a word is in order to the teachers who, like the author, are engaged in the presentation of introductory courses in the arts. Now that works of art, dramatic productions, symphony concerts, and operatic performances, which formerly were rare and remote experiences, have, through the mediums of photography, sound recordings, radio, and television, become everyday household experiences, the process of "reading" in our time has acquired a far broader meaning than ever before. How important it is, then, to make these experiences an articulate part of the student's education by fitting them into the general framework of the humanities.

The principle followed in this book has been to reduce technical terminology to a minimum. The index, it will be found, includes many features of a glossary indicating the pages where definitions of unfamiliar terms are to be found, as well as figure references which illustrate the case in point. It likewise lists all works of art by title as well as by artist; and, in addition, buildings also appear under their respective cities. Another objective has been to confine the discussions mainly to those works of art that are actually presented in evidence. Owing to the exigencies of space and time, however, the latter is far more feasible in the case of the visual illustrations than with literary quotations and musical examples. However, with standard editions of the classics on library shelves, and with the surprising currency of recordings in the case of music, the supplementary material needed for outside study and classroom use should be quite readily available. Inevitably in the book, it will be found that a favorite picture or a reference to an important play, poem, or piece of music is missing; but with the growing wealth of audio-visual aids in college collections, the material in the text can easily be supplemented by slides, readings, and recordings in the manner most congenial to the individual instructor. The value of the book as a text will therefore be that of providing focal points, like the hubs of wheels to which the teacher can add spokes reaching outward in any desired direction, and that of revealing a fruitful approach, with free scope allowed for the introduction of additional material for comparative purposes. It is hoped, therefore, that this method will demonstrate a manner of thinking and a way of grouping data within style periods so that valid syntheses can be achieved.

The heartfelt gratitude of the author must be expressed to all those whose help has made it possible for these pages to see the light of day. Many years have gone into the preparation of this project; and many more would doubtless have drifted by had it not been for a timely grant for study and research during its later stages by the Fund for the Advancement of Education. That corporation, however, is not to be understood as approving by virtue of its grant any of the statements or views expressed herein. Specific acknowledgments to the many individuals and organizations who have contributed to this volume will be found in appropriate places, such as in the captions below the illustrations, as well as in the text, the footnotes and the index.

As John Dewey has so pungently put it—there is no immaculate conception of ideas. Just as a man's social education starts within the family circle, beginning with parents, continuing with brothers, sisters, and friends, and is eventually completed with wife and children, so his intellectual life is initiated by his teachers, enriched by his colleagues and others who make up the extended family of a professional life, and ultimately comes around to its beginning with the students who teach their teachers far more than they ever realize.

As these concentric circles of one's horizons continue to widen, they encompass the happy band of archeologists whose diligent digging over the centuries has uncovered piece by piece the parts of the cultural jigsaw puzzle that make it possible to reconstruct the images of past periods. Encircled in this band are also the museums and their staff members who collect and preserve these precious pieces of the past in order to make them available in the present. The next zone of this expanding circle embraces the scholars who unlock the rich storehouses of their knowledge via the books and monographs that shed so many rays of light on the darker regions of history. Included here are the editors who prepare the manuscripts, the publishers who print them, and the librarians who catalogue and store them so that they may readily find their way into the hands of readers. In this ring are also the embassies, consulates, tourist offices, and information services who facilitate travel so that the original monuments of their respective countries may be studied at first hand, and who make photographs of their national treasures available. Finally surrounding this whole round disk in the manner of a glowing aureole is always the inspired work of the great artists whose creative contributions throughout the ages have illuminated not only their own periods, but shine through well into our own time to illuminate the lives of all those who have eyes to see, the ears to hear, and the minds to understand.

Syracuse University   W. F.
January 1955

PART 1

||

THE CLASSICAL
PERIOD

CHRONOLOGY: Athens, Latter Half of 5th Century B. C.

General Events

B. C.		
	480	Persians under Xerxes invaded Greece and occupied Athens
	479	Persians defeated by Athenians in Battle of Marathon
		Acropolis buildings in ruins
	c.461	Pericles (490–429) became political leader of Athens
	454	Delian Treasury transferred to Athens
	447 – 432	Parthenon built by Ictinus and Callicrates
		Parthenon sculptures executed under Phidias
	437 – 432	Propylaea built by Mnesicles
	431	Peloponnesian War between Athens and Sparta began
	429	Death of Pericles
	423	Temple of Athena Nike built by Callicrates
	421 – 409	Erechtheum built and Erechtheum sculptures executed
	404	Athens fell to Sparta—end of Athenian Empire
	c.350	Praxiteles executed *Hermes and the Infant Dionysus*
A. D.	150 – 180	Pausanias wrote description of Greece

Philosophy

c.582–c.507	Pythagoras
500 – 428	Anaxagoras
469 – 399	Socrates
427 – 347	Plato
384 – 322	Aristotle

History

484 – 425	Herodotus
471 – 399	Thucydides

Sculpture

c.490–c.432	Phidias
c.475–c.450	Myron flourished
c.460–c.420	Polyclitus active
c.360–c.330	Praxiteles active

Painting

c.480–c.430	Polygnotus
440	Apollodorus, the "shadow painter" flourished

Drama and Music

525 – 456	Aeschylus
496 – 406	Sophocles
480 – 406	Euripides
c.444 – 380	Aristophanes

1

||||||||||||||||||||||||||||||||||||||||||||||||||||||||||||||||||||||||||||||||||||||||||||||||||||||||||||||||||||||||||||||||||||||||||||||||||

THE HELLENIC STYLE

ATHENS, 5th CENTURY B. C.

An unparalleled constellation of events, circumstances, men, and ideas presided over the cultural climax that took place in Athens in the latter half of the 5th century B. C. A long line of historical developments, a few fortuitous happenstances, the multiple birth of human genius, and the capacity for inspired thinking were some of the signs of the times that pointed toward the culmination which took place in this small city-state on the shores of the Aegean Sea.

Earlier in the century the decisive victory over the Persians in the battle of Marathon had prepared the way for much that was to follow. The subsequent rise of their city to a pre-eminent position as the center of the defensive Delian League assured the Athenian citizens of a surplus of funds in the city treasury. Their Persian enemies had conveniently brought about the destruction of their archaic buildings—which their own religious tradition probably would not have allowed them to do. With the site for their new temples and civic buildings thus cleared, they very sensibly decided upon a new building program rather than a reconstruction of the former edifices. By a fortunate circumstance the marble material needed for the vast architectural and sculptural enterprises was found in the newly discovered quarries of Mount Pentelicus, a bare ten miles away, while formerly marble had to be brought by ship over the Aegean Sea. The Athenian aristocracy had inherited a tradition in which it was their high duty to support such public activities as dramatic festivals and athletic contests. Their political leaders, as well as their poets and artists, had listened to the wisdom and wit of Anaxagoras, the philosopher who taught that the universe was ruled by a supreme mind which, through the processes of reason, imposed an external geometry on the chaotic forces of nature; and that man, by the exercise of his own rational powers, could likewise give form and order to his more human world.

Athens, like so many other ancient cities, had developed around an *acra*, or hill, which at first was a military vantage point and later a site for palaces, temples, and civic buildings (Fig. 1:1). When such a hill served as a refuge in time of peril, a seemingly hopeless situation might have been turned, by some fortunate circumstance, into a glorious victory. Later this seemingly miraculous turn of events would then become associated with the divine intervention of a god or goddess, and the hilltop fortress in the popular mind would become a divinely favored place. Thereafter the particular deity would be adopted as a local patron and a suitable monument eventually crown the *acra*, just as the kingly diadem often came to adorn the brow of the warrior responsible for the heroic deeds. The *polis*, or citizenry, thus were able to look with pride toward their *acropolis*, which became the common center where such buildings as their assembly place, theater, official residences, sanctuaries, and temples were located.

The Athenian acropolis was the site of the palace of Erechtheus, the early hero and legendary king. Homer seems to be describing the process of its shift from a military citadel and royal residence to a religious shrine when he wrote in his *Odyssey:* "Therewith grey-eyed Athene departed over the unharvested seas, and left pleasant Scheria, and came to Marathon and wide-wayed Athens, and entered the house of Erechtheus." [1] Throughout the years of prehistory the acropolis was never static but the scene of constant human activity, and the buildings on it were a reflection of the changing fortunes of the people. This process continued until, by the end of the 5th century B. C., the hill had become the dwelling place only of divine beings and a sanctuary especially sacred to the goddess Athena, protectress of the city.

Not far from the base of the acropolis was the *agora*, or market place, where merchants gathered to sell their wares. This busy square, however, served not only as a setting for the active commercial life of the city but also as a place for the meeting of minds. On a typical day Socrates could be heard carrying on one of his philosophical feuds with the Sophists, whom he called the retailers of knowledge—for, as Plato so aptly pointed out, the merchandising there was "partly concerned with food for the use of the body, and partly with the food of the soul which is bartered and received in exchange for money." [2] These intellectual opportunists were clever manipulators of public opinion, who knew all the tricks of their trade and who did not hesitate to use false reasoning if it gained them the end they were

Fig. 1:1. *The Acropolis*, Athens (Courtesy Royal Greek Embassy)

seeking. In his disputations Socrates was able to point out how this sophistry was really a matter of quibbling on the surface over words rather than penetrating more profoundly into the deeper world of ideas. By puncturing some of their pomposities with the sting of his wit and showing how they were primarily concerned with turning knowledge to their own personal purposes rather than pursuing truth for its own sake, Socrates gained his immortal reputation as the "gadfly of Athens."

In the hollow space carved out of the southeastern slope of the acropolis was the horseshoe-shaped theater of Dionysus where the annual dramatic festivals were held. Here, more than 2000 years before the birth of Shakespeare, the entire free citizenry of Athens gathered together with their priests, magistrates, and families to enjoy plays that mirrored their world in dramatic form. Through their applause each year they picked the winner of the coveted prize that was won no less than 13 times by Aeschylus, the founder of the heroic Greek tragedy and principal poet of the Periclean period. Sophocles, his successor, humanized this dramatic form by introducing more action and a greater suppleness of language, while Euripides, last of the great Greek tragic poets, spanned the limits of dramatic tension and endowed his plays with such passion and pathos that they reached into the innermost recesses of the human spirit. After the great period was past, the comedies of Aristophanes proved that the Athenians could still indulge in the luxury of laughter.

Above the theater on the rocky plateau of the acropolis itself was the site where the temples were constructed. Under Pericles, the enlightened statesman, it was the place of ceaseless efforts of countless builders, sculptors, painters, and craftsmen. As the buildings rose stately in size and fair of form, the workmen, according to Plutarch, were "striving to outvie the material and the design with the beauty of their workmanship, yet the most wonderful thing of all was the rapidity of their execution. Undertakings, any one of which singly might have required, they thought, for their completion, several successions and ages of men, were every one of them accomplished in the height and prime of one man's political service." [3] Pericles had the wisdom to foresee that the unity of a people could rest on philosophical idealism and artistic expression as well as on military might and material prosperity. The city thus became one whose acknowledged wealth was in its dramatists and poet-musicians, such as Aeschylus, Sophocles, and Euripides; in its architects, such as Ictinus, Callicrates, and Mnesicles; in its sculptors, such as Myron, Polyclitus, and Phidias; and in its painters and craftsmen, such as Polygnotus and Callimachus.

Here then was both the material and spiritual treasury of the Athenian people, the place which held their worldly gold reserves as well as their religious and artistic monuments. The work continued with unabated enthusiasm until by the end of the century the acropolis had become a sublime setting, worthy of the goddess of wisdom and beauty, and the pedestal that proudly bore the shining temples dedicated to her.

ARCHITECTURE

The Acropolis and the Propylaea

The life of the Athenian citizen was not centered in his modest home so much as it was in the open market places and public buildings of the city. Towering above these was always the supreme meeting place, the acropolis, where the citizens re-created themselves, commemorated their heroes, and worshiped their gods. Accessible only from the slope on the western side, the acropolis presented a difficult climb, and the upward path was never an easy one. In a comedy by Aristophanes a chorus of old men, bearing olive branches to kindle the sacred fires, chant as they mount the hill: "But look, to finish this toilsome climb only this last steep bit is left to mount. Truly, it's no easy job without beasts of burden and how these logs do bruise my shoulder!" [4]

The sacred way led from the heart of the city to the summit of the hill, where entrance was made through the majestic Doric and Ionic columns of the Propylaea (Fig. 1:2). This imposing structure was conceived as a fulfillment of the need for a suitable gateway to the center of the acropolis. It was in the form of a spacious portal with wings on either side stretching for an over-all width of approximately 156 feet. The outer portico consisted of six Doric columns, with the two in the center spaced more widely than the others so as to allow passage for chariots on ceremonial occasions. Pedestrians could enter from the sides into an open vestibule where the interior columns were of the slender Ionic order, permitting greater height and more open space. Here a place was provided where pilgrims could be seated on stone benches and the populace could gather on festive days before the gates were opened. According to Pausanias who wrote a description of the building in the second century A. D., the enclosed room on the left was a picture gallery. Opposite the entrance colonnade the structure was closed off by a solid wall with five portals corresponding to the intercolumniation of the façade.

The Athenians took greater pride in this structure than in any of their other buildings. It was entirely of white Pentelic marble except for the occasional use of black Eleusinian stone for contrasting effects in the frieze and other embellishments. Pausanias especially singled out the white marble ceiling for admiration when he said: "in the size and beauty of the stones [it] remains supreme even to my time." It was also remarkable in the fact that it pointed directly toward the colossal bronze statue of Athena Promachos (Champion), and that its axis paralleled that of the Parthenon. This was an exception to the usual self-containment of Greek buildings before the Hellenistic Period, and possibly found justification in the architectural canons of the time because of the Propylaea's function as an entrance way rather than as a completely independent unit.

Through the portals of the Propylaea the visitor entered upon the center of the sacred area. Standing amid the revered monuments of gods and heroes was the great statue of Athena Promachos—said to have been cast by Phidias from the bronze shields of defeated Persian enemies—the tip of whose gleaming spear guided the homecoming sailors over the sea toward Athens. On the right was the majestic Parthenon and on the left, the graceful Erechtheum. Practically in a single stroke, the Athenians here had brought to the highest point of development two distinct building

Fig. 1:2 (above). *The Acropolis*, Athens, Restored (Martin L. D'Ooge. *The Acropolis of Athens*. New York, Macmillan, 1909. Plate IX)

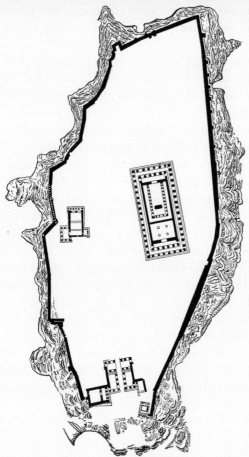

Fig. 1:3 (left). *Plan* of the Acropolis. Lower right, Temple of Athena Nike; lower center, the Propylaea; upper right, the Parthenon; upper left, the Erechtheum

Fig. 1:4. Ictinus and Callicrates. *Parthenon. c.*228′ x 104′, columns 34′ high. 447–432 B. C. Athens (Courtesy Royal Greek Embassy)

traditions, the Doric in the Parthenon and the Ionic in the Erechtheum. That the two should be combined as in the Propylaea, and enshrined separately in these twin temples on either side of the acropolis, was an architectural reflection of the fact that the city was the place where the Dorian people of the western Greek mainland and the Ionians of the coast of Asia Minor across the Aegean Sea lived together in peace and harmony and through the generations had become one people.

The Parthenon

The plan and appearance of the Parthenon (Fig. 1:4) was in no way revolutionary but, rather, the culmination of a long, slow evolutionary process. The conception of the typical Greek temple grew out of that of an enlarged and idealized house conceived as the dwelling place of the god. The interior was a windowless room called the *cella*, in which the cult statue was placed. The cella was surrounded on the exterior by rows of columns, called a *colonnade*; and entrance to the interior was made through a *portico*, or porch, faced with columns. The building principle is one of extreme simplicity that consisted merely of setting up a series of vertical *posts* for the support of a horizontal member, called the *lintel*. The gravitational pressure of the lintel, and all that was above it, was grounded through the posts. When the lintels had the strength of marble, the superstructure could be increased and the *intercolumniation*, or space between the supporting posts, could be widened. The history of Greek temple architecture is largely the evolution and refinement of this post-and-lintel system, which permitted the architect a steadily increasing freedom. Although the terms *Doric* and *Ionic* are usually used to distinguish the type of columns, more accurately they refer to the rules that determined the proportions and relationships of the parts to the whole of the building. At the end of the 5th century B. C. another order of Greek architecture was added, the *Corinthian*, which varied from the Ionic principally in the more elaborately carved capitals of the columns.

In keeping with the dual purpose of the building, the plan of the Parthenon (Fig. 1:3) was one with a double cella. The larger one on the east end was to house the new cult statue by Phidias, and that on the west was to serve as the treasury. It was the latter that technically was called the Parthenon, or chamber of the virgin goddess; later the name was given to the whole building. The outer walls of these interior sections were decorated by a continuous frieze running around each of the four sides. A peristyle of free-standing columns, spaced far enough outward from the cella walls to permit a passageway, completely enclosed the building. Along its 228 feet of length were 17 columns on each side, and because there were eight along the 104-foot width in front and back, the Parthenon is called octastyle. The number of columns used on the ends, however, was determined by the size of the building rather than by any rigid rule, six being the usual number, while some temples had as many as 10 and 12. Between the portals of the two interior chambers on either end, and inside the exterior colonnade, were six smaller columns that formed the inner porticos. Like the usual Doric building (Fig. 1:5), the temple proper stood on a platform made up of three steps, the top of which is called the *stylobate*. The columns rested directly on this top step without any other base and seemed to spring directly from it.

The objective thought of the period was well exemplified by its architects, because the plan for each building was as clear and logical as a geometrical proposition. Each structure was a self-contained unit, and in order to preserve the proper proportion of parts to the whole, the measure adopted was that of the *module*, which was equal to one half the average diameter of the columns at their base. In working out the proportion of the smaller details, the module was subdivided into parts or minutes. As worked out in the Parthenon, the height is 14 modules and 6 parts. The columns themselves occupy 11 modules, or $34\frac{1}{2}$ feet of this height, while the portion above was 3 modules and 6 parts (Fig. 1:6). The columns appear to be of a single piece of marble, but they were actually constructed of sections called drums, so carefully fitted together and held by square wooden plugs in the

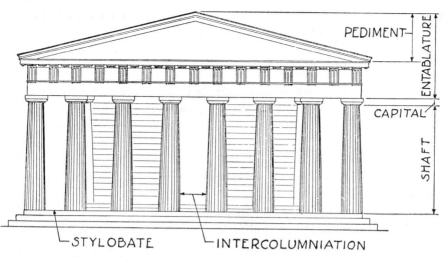

PEDIMENT

ENTABLATURE

CAPITAL

SHAFT

STYLOBATE   INTERCOLUMNIATION

Fig. 1:5. *Doric Temple Façade*. Drawing by W. D. Richmond

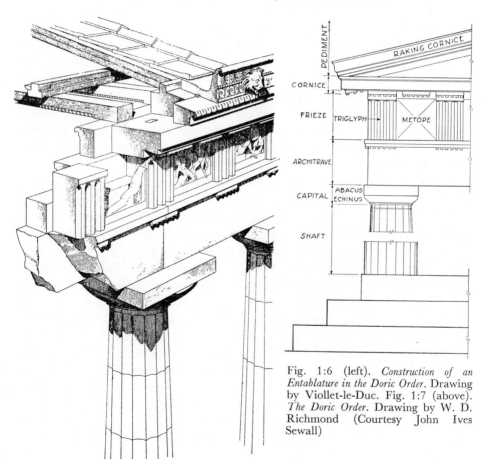

PEDIMENT

RAKING CORNICE

CORNICE

FRIEZE   TRIGLYPH   METOPE

ARCHITRAVE

CAPITAL   ABACUS
           ECHINUS

SHAFT

Fig. 1:6 (left). *Construction of an Entablature in the Doric Order*. Drawing by Viollet-le-Duc. Fig. 1:7 (above). *The Doric Order*. Drawing by W. D. Richmond (Courtesy John Ives Sewall)

center that the joinings are scarcely visible. The outer surface of the columns have 20 grooves, called flutes, which formed concave channels from the bottom to the top of the shaft. The purpose of this fluting is two-fold, the first being to correct an optical illusion. When seen in the direct sunlight a series of ungrooved round columns will appear flat. The fluting provides shadows in all lighting so that the round appearance is main-tained. The second is an aesthetic one, that of providing a number of graceful curves pleasing to the eye. By thus adding to the number of vertical lines the visual rhythm is increased, and the eye is also led upward toward the sculpture of the entablature.

Far from maintaining a rigid mathematical regularity, the columns show a great number of subtle variations from the norm. One of the most striking is the departure of the shafts from a straight line by curving slightly out-ward as they rise, reaching their greatest deviation about one third of the way above the stylobate, then gradually tapering toward the top. This curving is called *entasis* and constitutes a tempering of mathematical correctness in order to give the appearance of life and elasticity to the columns, which thus seem to give slightly under the weight they carry. Furthermore, the corner columns seem dark when viewed against the sky, while those between seem light when seen against the dark cella. If all were equal in diameter those on the ends would appear thinner. The architect has consequently corrected this optical distortion by increasing the diameter of the corner columns and by spacing them closer at the ends, thus pro-moting the appearance of stability at these important points.

The capital of the Doric column is in three parts, the *necking*, the *echinus*, and the *abacus*. (Fig. 1:7). The purpose of any capital is to mediate between the vertical shaft of the column and the horizontal entablature above. The necking is the first break in the upward lines of the shafts, though the fluting continues up to the outward flare of the echinus. This, in turn, leads to the abacus, a block of stone which squares the circle, so to speak, and smoothly effects the transition between the lower and upper members. Everything above the columns is referred to as the *entablature*. Immediately above the abacus is the undecorated *architrave*, a series of rectangular blocks that are the lintels of the construction. These stretch horizontally from the center of one column to that of its neighbor around the entire building and support the *frieze, cornice,* and *pediment*. The first element of the design to make use of decoration is the frieze, which in this case is made up of alter-nating *triglyphs* and *metopes*. The rectangular triglyphs are so named be-cause of their three vertically indented channels. They are the weight-bearing members, and by rule one is placed above each column, and one in the middle of the interval between. The regularity provided by the sameness of the triglyphs alternates with the differently carved relief panels of the metopes. This regularly repeated visual rhythm results in a harmonious pattern, which exemplifies the classical principle of balancing equally the opposites of unity and variety. The frieze is protected from the elements by the eavelike projection of the cornice; and a second cornice, called the *raking cornice*, rises from the sides to an apex in the center. The triangular space thus enclosed, which recedes all the way back to the wall of the cella, is called the *pediment*. The lower cornice forms a platform on which free-standing sculpture can be placed to climax the decorative scheme; and the pediment as a whole completes the design of the façade.

The entire Parthenon was of white marble except for such details as the timbered roof underneath the marble tiles, and the doors with their frames. The fine-grained Pentelic stone, because of the presence of minute quantities of iron, was originally slightly cream-colored. By the process of oxidation, as it weathered through the centuries, its patina deepened richly, varying from the color of honey to its present yellowish brown. A good part of the design, as originally conceived, depended on the use of color in the members above the architrave, which were painted. From Pausanias it is known that the triglyphs were tinted dark blue and that parts of the molding were red. The sculptured parts of the metopes were left white, but the backgrounds were painted. In the frieze along the cella wall the reins of the horses were bronze additions that have disappeared in the course of time. The draperies of the free-standing sculptures of the pediments were painted; and the facial features, such as the eyes, lips, and hair, were done in natural tints.

For sheer technical skill the work as a whole is astonishing. No mortar was used anywhere, and every block was fitted together with such precision as to defy detection. If this were all, however, it would still be just a case of skillful engineering. The Parthenon goes far beyond the technical execution, however, and becomes a work of art through the infinite care expended both on its design as a whole and on the minute details of its parts. The appearance of a balance between vertical and horizontal elements is certainly the impression the architects strove to create. However, on careful analysis there is not a straight line to be found anywhere in the entire design. It is psychologically rather than mathematically correct—which is to say, that a system of curved lines is made to compensate for the optical aberrations of the human eye. The construction is thus carried out on a subjective basis in order, paradoxically, to achieve the ideal of objectivity. The entasis of the columns has already been pointed out. In addition to this, the stylobate on which they rest and the entablature above them, while giving the appearance of straight lines, actually have a slightly upward and outward curve. From the corners they rise toward the center on the façade side about 2¾ inches, and on the long sides about 4 inches, in order to counteract the impression of sagging. The axes of the columns and the walls of the cella tilt slightly inward to avoid the feeling of top-heaviness. That this was intentional and not accidental is known from the writings of the Roman architect Vitruvius, who apparently had access to the book on the Parthenon by one of its architects, Ictinus. Owing to the fact that the foundations rested on rock and that construction was in marble, the accuracy of the measurements is assured. By all these variations from mathematical exactness, the architects succeeded in avoiding frigidity and harshness and thus gave the design a quality associated with living forms.

Pericles' great building program began with the Parthenon in 447 B. C. Only ten short years later this temple was dedicated during the Panathenaic festival in honor of the patron goddess of the city, to house both the magnificent gold and ivory cult statue of her by the hand of Phidias and the treasure of her city and its allies. The latter was listed in the ancient inscriptions as consisting of bullion, gold and silver articles, precious stones, musical instruments, and such trophies of war as weapons and armor.

The Parthenon would be standing today, with only the usual deteriorations due to the passage of time, were it not for an unfortunate disaster in the late seventeenth century. At that time a Turkish garrison was using the building for an ammunition dump, and during a siege by the Venetians a random bomb ignited the gunpowder stored there, blowing out the center section. From that time on the Parthenon has been a noble ruin. However, even today after numerous partial restorations, its harmonious system of relationships can be apprehended even in a casual viewing. Its success rests on a humanizing of the experience of space so that in its geometry such visual facts as interval, repeated patterns, spatial progressions, and distances are all brought within optical grasp and intellectual comprehension. By its incomparable proportions and reserved poise it remains one of the imperishable achievements of the mind of man.

The Erechtheum

After Athena was so handsomely housed in her new temple, the city fathers felt that the other deities who had shared the acropolis with her in former times should not be neglected. Hence a new building in the Ionic order (Fig. 1:8) was undertaken about a decade after the completion of the

Fig. 1:8. Mnesicles (?). *Erechtheum*, View from the South. *c*.421–409 B. C. (Clarence Kennedy)

Parthenon. It was described in the city records as "the temple in the acropolis for the ancient statue." [5] This old image was believed to have fallen from the sky, and the site of the previous temple before the Persian occupation was the traditional place where their early king, Erechtheus, dwelled. As recounted by Homer: "And they that possessed the goodly citadel of Athens, domain of Erechtheus the high-hearted, whom erst Athene daughter of Zeus fostered when Earth, the grain giver, brought him to birth;—and she gave him a resting-place in Athens in her own rich sanctuary; and there the sons of the Athenians worship him with bulls and rams as the years turn in their courses. . . ." [6] The site was also the legendary spot where Athena and Poseidon had their famous contest over the possession of the land of Attica and the honors of the city of Athens. As they sought to assert their claims, Poseidon raised his trident and struck a rock, whereupon a horse, his gift to man, sprang out. A spring of salt water also gushed forth to commemorate the great event. When Athena's turn came she brought forth the olive tree, and the gods awarded her the victory. Later Erechtheus, whom she protected, tamed the horse and made him useful to man. The precinct on the acropolis where all these miraculous occurrences took place had the sacred olive tree, the salt spring, and the mark of Poseidon's trident on a rock; and the new temple had to be planned to house them. It also had to be designed as a place for the worship of Athena, Erechtheus, and some minor deities—and, whether from love or fear, Poseidon also was included.

The irregular site and the need for the various sanctuaries all to be within one building explain the strangeness of the plan, which is as complex as that of the Parthenon was simple (Fig. 1:3). Its interior was made up of four rooms for the various altars of the gods. In addition there was a

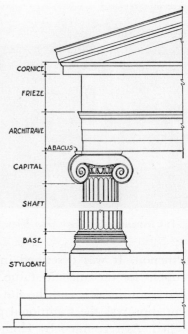

Fig. 1:9 (left). Mnesicles (?). Erechtheum, *North Porch. c.*421–409 B. C. (Courtesy Royal Greek Embassy). Fig. 1:10 (right). *The Ionic Order.* Drawing by W. D. Richmond

subterranean corridor that contained Poseidon's salt water spring and the mark of his trident, while out of doors on the west was an enclosure for Athena's olive tree. The rectangular interior section is on two levels, one 10½ feet higher than the other, measuring altogether about 37 feet wide and 66 feet long. Projecting outward from three of the sides were porticos, each of different dimensions and design. That on the east has a row of six Ionic columns, almost 22 feet in height, giving the building on that side the appearance of an Ionic hexastyle temple. The north porch (Fig. 1:9) has the same number of Ionic columns, but with four in front and two on the sides; while the smaller porch on the south (Fig. 1:11) has six sculptured maidens, the famous Caryatids, upholding the architrave.

Unlike Doric columns, those of the Ionic order (Fig. 1:10) are more slender and have their greatest diameter at the bottom. Their shafts rest on a molded base instead of directly on the stylobate, and they have 24 instead of 20 flutings. Most striking of all, however, they have a different type of capital. Those of the north porch are among the finest examples of their kind in existence (Fig. 1:9). Just below the fluting and above the base molding they have a band carved with a delicate design. At the top the necking of the shaft is embellished with a wider band that uses a beautiful leaf pattern. Above this is a band with the egg-and-dart motive, while next come the characteristic scrolls or volutes, and finally a thin abacus that is molded with a smaller version of the egg and dart. These columns support a plain architrave; a continuous frieze, rather than one with the Doric triglyphs and metopes; and, above it, a shallow pediment without sculpture. Behind the columns the broad doorway into the cella (Fig. 1:13) has a stone frame which has been called the most superb in Greek architecture.[7] The door is framed with a series of receding planes that seem to invite entry. On the lintel above, successive bands of carved ornamentation tastefully combine the honeysuckle, bead-and-reel, egg-and-dart, and leaf-and-tongue patterns without appearing overelaborate. A similar combination of motives is also found on the decorative band that runs around the cella (Fig. 1:14).

The small porch on the west is perhaps the most striking because of its use of human figures as columns (Fig. 1:12.) It is smaller than the other porticos, measuring only some 10 by 15 feet. Above the three steps rises a parapet 6 feet high on which the six caryatids, about one and one half times larger than life, are standing. On their heads they carry a cushionlike echinus carved with the egg and dart on which an abacus and the architrave rest. In order to avoid the appearance of overburdening them, the

Fig. 1:11 (left). Erechtheum, *Caryatid Porch*. Fig. 1:12 (right), Caryatid Porch, *Side View* (Courtesy Royal Greek Embassy)

Fig. 1:13 (left). Erechtheum, *North Door* (Courtesy Royal Greek Embassy). Fig. 1:14 (right). *Decorative Band* from Erechtheum, showing Honeysuckle, Bead-and-Reel, Egg-and-Dart, and Leaf-and-Tongue motives (Walter Hege)

frieze and pediment are omitted. In spite of the fact that they have been exposed to the elements for 2500 years, they are as well preserved as any originals of the 5th century B. C. Grouped as if in a procession, with four in front and two on the sides, the figures infer a stately forward motion from the manner in which their weight is carried. The three on one side have their right legs bent as if stepping forward, while those on the other side incline their left legs in the same manner. They give the impression of being solid enough to carry their weight without yielding under it; and, while strict symmetry is preserved, there is no hint of stiffness. The handling of the draperies harmonizes with the architectural function of the figures, with the folds of their skirts resembling the fluting of columns. This helps to give the impression of strength below; while above, the treatment becomes increasingly transparent and plastic. The long locks of hair strengthen their neck lines, thus giving a greater feeling of stability at a point which might otherwise have seemed weak.

It is perhaps possible to go one step beyond the structural and aesthetic purpose, and attribute a meaning to the use of the human figure in connection with this temple. Pausanias makes reference to certain "maidens who bear on their heads what the priestess of Athena gives them to carry." [8] It is conjectured that they were related in some way to the ritual of the temple, just as in the case of the cella frieze of the Parthenon. A fragment from an older frieze shows a priestess leading a procession in which four maidens bear a long chest on their heads. Since Erechtheus, their warrior king, according to tradition, was buried in the temple, and since the building bears his name, the caryatids may be related to a ceremony in honor of the heroic dead. At any rate, the folds of the garments and position of the legs show them as if moving in a dignified procession and not merely as architectural members bearing the weight of the architrave.

The temple as a whole has been considered the high point of Ionic architecture. Mnesicles, the designer of the Propylaea, is generally thought to have been its architect, and the flexibility he showed in solving the difficult problems of its design demonstrates eloquently the adaptability of the Hellenic style. Partly because of the difficulties in reconciling the different religious demands, and partly because of the change in the public taste in the latter part of the century, the architect had to sacrifice the harmony of the whole in order to emphasize the ornamental details, which were here carried out with a finish and delicacy unsurpassed in any other Greek building.

SCULPTURE

The crowning glory of the Parthenon was a series of sculptures made up of the following groups. First, the high-relief panels of the metopes, alternating with the triglyphs in the Doric frieze; next, the free-standing sculptures of the east and west pediments; then, the continuous frieze on the four outer walls of the cella; and, finally, the great cult statue of Athena inside the cella. All the sculpture was intimately bound up with the architectural design and hence should not be judged apart from it. Not only did it serve the purpose of relieving the austerity and cool logic of the architectural design, but its flowing lines and broken masses gave just the right contrast to the formal vertical and horizontal rhythms of the building as a whole. Fully conscious of its purpose, Phidias never overstepped the boundaries of simplicity and judicious restraint; and his design consequently kept the sculpture always what it was originally intended to be—an architectural embellishment. It existed in balanced proportion to the building as a whole and did not attempt to divert the attention from the total structure and become separated from it as a thing in itself. In this respect his design was completely in harmony with the taste and spirit of his times. Since the decorated parts of a building in the Doric order are all above the architrave, the Parthenon sculptures are designed to be seen from about 35 feet below and at a certain distance outward. A fundamental falsification results from viewing and photographing them from the eye level in museums, where the lighting is so completely different from that originally intended. Out of context their function and purpose as part of a temple must be imagined.

The workmanship of the sculpture reveals the unevenness of quality common to all projects that depend on the efforts of a large corps of crafts-men. Some show the hand of a master, others are the routine products of artisans. The scheme of the whole was doubtless designed by Phidias him-self, but since everything except the pediment sculptures was completed in a ten-year period, it is certain that he had a whole school of trained assist-ants working from his sketches. Some samples in each group may have been executed by him as models, and the best of them are sometimes attributed to him. However, the only work known definitely to have been completed by his hand was the cult statue of Athena Parthenos, which has long since disappeared except for copies made in later times. In spite of these qualifica-tions and shortcomings, the Parthenon sculptures as a whole constitute one of the most distinguished chapters in the history of that art. The fact that the metopes were begun first and were surpassed by the cella frieze, and that both in turn were eclipsed by the greater excellence of the pedimental sculptures, the last to be completed, shows significantly that the work aimed at no dead perfection as such. Since it evolved continuously, it represented a will toward improvement and perfection rather than any final crystallization. The sculptures, however, have a timeless beauty all their own, and that this quality was recognized by the ancients also is attested to by Plutarch, who wrote: "For every particular piece of his [Phidias'] work was immediately, even at that time, for its beauty and elegance, antique; and yet in its vigour and freshness looks to this day as if it were just executed." [9]

The metopes of the Doric frieze which alternate with the triglyphs are done in such high relief that the figures are almost in the round. There were 92 of them in all with 32 along the sides and 14 on each end. Those on the south side are the only ones preserved. Unlike the triglyphs, which were solid blocks of marble designed to carry the weight of the superstruc-ture, the metopes were separate panels, which were carved below and placed in the frieze afterward. The choice of high relief was undoubtedly determined by their location on the building. The carving of the figures had to be bold enough to be seen from the ground level and also to stand out sufficiently so as not to be subordinated by the architecture. To main-tain the necessary balance, the deep carving was designed to take full advantage of the bright Athenian sunlight. Furthermore, the panels are composed in such a way that their figures give a dominantly diagonal accent so as to contrast with the vertical lines of the architrave below and the cornice above. Relating the story of the battle of the Lapiths and Centaurs, their subject matter provides a sense of movement, which helps to balance the more static architectural lines. One of the best realized of the extant examples is thought to have been carved by Phidias himself (Fig. 1:15). The broad sweeping curves of the mantle draped on the arms of the Lapith make a fine contrast to the expressive angularity of the Centaur beside him.

The key to the iconography of the pediment sculptures has been provided by Pausanias, who said that the eastern pediment had to do with the birth of Athena, while that on the west pediment told of the strife between Athena and Poseidon over the patronage of the land of Attica. More remains of the eastern pediment are extant; and, from ancient vase paintings and a 17th-century drawing made shortly before the building was destroyed, the missing parts and the relationship of the surviving figures have been fairly conclusively established. While completely missing, the central figure below the apex of the roof undoubtedly was Zeus, father of the gods. On one side probably stood Hephaestus who, according to the

Fig. 1:15. Phidias (?). *Centaur and Lapith*, Metope from the Parthenon. Marble. 3' 11" x 4' 2". 447–441 B. C. British Museum, London

myth, was supposed to have cloven the head of Zeus with an axe, so that
Athena, fully grown and fully armed, could spring forth. Thus it must have
been the goddess herself who stood on the other side of Zeus. The action
of the remaining figures radiated outward toward each of the sides. The
action of the story, like that of the classical dramas, was compressed into
the span of a single day. This was symbolized through appropriate figures,
and those at the extreme ends, therefore, are Helios, god of the sun, rising
from the foaming sea in a chariot drawn by four horses, and Selene, goddess of the moon descending below the horizon. The identification of the
other figures is more problematic, and many theories have been offered
as solutions. The older theory that they represented Attic heroes, accounts
for the usual identity of the recumbent male figure as Theseus (Fig. 1:16).
Another solution, however, seems more plausible. Since the mythological
action takes place on Mount Olympus, legendary dwelling place of the
gods, the figures must represent either Olympian deities or personifications
of natural phenomena, such as mountains, rivers, and so on. This figure,
then, would be the personification of Mount Olympus. Facing Helios, the
rising sun god, he reclines easily on a rock over which a panther's skin and
his mantle are spread. The folds cascade gently down the sloping surface
in a series of plastic lines that harmonize with those of the figure. His relaxed pose seems to indicate that in keeping with the earliness of the hour
he is just awakening. Because this is one of the rare originals of this period
whose head is preserved intact, it is possible to form a judgment of the
work as a whole. It is a figure full of the potential strength of one not yet
fully conscious of his power. The body is molded with freedom and grace
by a sculptor who likewise has just begun to achieve complete mastery of
his medium. The facial expression is impersonal yet thoughtful and quietly

expressive. He seems to be as yet unaware of the event that has transpired in the center of the composition.

Just behind him seated on two chests are the feminine figures that are usually identified as Demeter and Persephone (Fig. 1:17). In keeping with the previous theory, however, they would be the Horae sitting at the gate of Mount Olympus, where they opened and closed the entrance to the eternal cloud which surrounded its summit. One is seated in a relaxed manner, while the other turns toward the approaching figure of Iris, the messenger, who bears the news of the miraculous birth to the waiting world. The three figures are grouped as an episode in the composition and form a significant part of the whole. The rich flow of their drapery conveys their function and meaning more eloquently than any speculation on their exact identity. The more static lines of the figure farthest to the left reveal that she is just beginning to be aware of the coming messenger. The upward sweep of her garments lead the eye toward the center figure who is turning around toward Iris. The contrary direction of the folds of Iris' costume show her drawing near with such rapid motion that the wind blows her costume into undulating folds. The eloquent manner in which the sculptor tells his story of haste and excitement reveals a high degree of mastery.

The usual identification of the three figures on the far right as the Three Fates (Fig. 1:18)—symbolizing the past, present, and future, who were thought to be present at all births—is somewhat uncertain. However, again the postures and flowing draperies make clear their relation to the whole composition. The figure nearest the center, aware of what has happened, is just about to rise, while the one in the middle is turning toward her. The reclining figure at the far right, still in repose, is as unaware of the event as was her counterpart, Mount Olympus, on the other side. Like the feminine group on the other side these figures also constitute a unified episode, and their relationship to the whole is likewise made clear in the subtle design achieved by the opulent lines of their flowing robes. This linear

Fig. 1:16 (far left). Parthenon, East Pediment, *Mount Olympus* (?), or *Theseus* (?). 5′ 8″ long. Fig. 1:17 (center left). *The Horae and Iris* (?), or *Demeter, Persephone, and Iris* (?). Seated figures 4′ 10½″ high, standing figure, 5′ 8″ high. Fig. 1:18 (left). *The Three Fates* (?). Marble. 447–432 B. C. British Museum, London

pattern, and the manner in which it brings out the different parts of the splendid bodies beneath, is a miracle of grace and beauty.

Perhaps the most remarkable aspect of the whole composition is the admirable manner in which each of the figures fills its assigned space. To fit such a variety of figures into a triangle from the central apex outward to the acute side angles, and at the same time to maintain an appearance of naturalness and ease, is a feat of design calling for the highest degree of skill. Even the smallest details, such as the heads of the horses on either side, are so handled that they contribute to the whole. The one on the left, the rising steed of Helios, springs upward with a mighty leap, while the beautifully modeled one on the other side inclines his head gently downward, his energies spent. The varied postures, rich plastic modeling, and flowing lines connect all the figures with a motion so unified that even though the climactic ones in the center are missing, the meaning is quite clear.

The frieze carved in low relief around the outer walls of the cella was a continuous band about 3¼ feet wide and over 500 feet long. While the other sculptures deal with mythological subjects, this frieze, by a representation of the Athenian festival in honor of their patroness, introduced into the iconography of a temple subjects familiar to the people of the city. It represents the Pan-Athenaic, or All-Athenian, procession that took place each year in August. Through the naturalness of the way in which the scene is presented, it is a faithful panoramic reflection of the life and aspirations of the Athenian people of the 5th century B. C. The course of the procession moved along the sacred highway through the city and up the western slope of the acropolis through the Propylaea. After a pause for regrouping in the area before the west façade of the Parthenon, it then continued more slowly in parallel lines along the north and south sides, and finally all the participants gathered in front of the east entrance.

The scene depicted on the west side is one of bustle and confusion as the riders ready their mounts and make final preparation for the equestrian procession (Fig. 1:19). At the northwest corner stands the single figure of the marshal who directs the cavalcade. Around the corner on the north side some horsemen are still engaged in preparation and are to follow the others who have already started. Ahead are those in chariots; farther on are young men leading the sheep and cows for the sacrifice; and toward the front are youths carrying water jars on their shoulders. Similiar subjects are shown along the south side, while both lines converge as the procession continues around the east side. Moving toward the center are rows of matrons bearing sacrificial implements and other offerings that are to be

Fig. 1:19. Parthenon, West Frieze, *Horsemen*. Marble. *c*.40″ high. 447–441 B. C. British Museum, London

Fig. 1:20. Parthenon, East Frieze, *Seated Gods*. Marble. *c*.40″ high. 447–441 B. C. British Museum, London (Courtesy Royal Greek Embassy)

Fig. 1:21. Parthenon, Frieze, *Old Men Carrying Olive Branches*. Marble. *c*.40″ high. 447–441 B. C. British Museum, London (Courtesy Royal Greek Embassy)

accepted by the magistrates and priests. At the head of the procession are the chosen maidens who have woven the saffron and purple tinted *peplos*, or sacred mantle, which is to drape the image of the goddess. The central group shows the peplos being folded up by the priest. In panels directly above the entrance, flanking the center but still a part of the frieze, are two groups of seated deities who, as guests of Athena, calmly contemplate the brilliant spectacle and bestow their Olympian approval upon it. The panel, generally thought to depict Poseidon, Apollo, and Artemis (Fig. 1:20), is in an almost perfect state of preservation, and its beauty of execution is a proper tribute to the Olympian personalities who honor the city by their presence.

Such was the brilliant spectacle with its panorama of sacrificial animals, spirited youths, graceful girls, dignified elders, and venerable old men carrying olive branches (Fig. 1:21). All were in life and motion bearing appropriate offerings to the deities, who presided over their individual destinies as well as those of their city and state. The part shown here was but the beginning phase of the great festival, which continued later with equestrian sports, chariot racing, and such other athletic contests as wrestling and discus throwing. In the theater at the base of the acropolis competing poets and rhapsodists rivaled each other in recitations of verses from Homer and others; musical contests were held; the Pyrrhic dance took place; and the festival in which dramatists competed for prizes awarded by popular acclaim was held.

The placement of the frieze along the top of the cella wall meant that it would be seen in the half-light reflected upward from the marble pavement below. The shadows thus fell upward, and to protect the clarity of the design, the shallow relief carving was done so that the lower parts projected outward less than the upper parts. Color and metal additions also aided in promoting the definition of the pattern as a whole. The time and place of the procession were known to every citizen, hence there is no attempt to make any suggestion of its location in the background. It must be kept in mind that the presentation here is that of one great and colorful scene, and there is no attempt to relate a narrative sequence or to tell any story. It is also interesting to note that the parade was arranged so that it moved along the sides toward the east paralleling the living procession as it passed along its way on the feast day, thus giving the participants as they glanced upward a feeling of identification with their historical tradition. The careful balance between parts and the whole can be understood when it is pointed out that about 600 figures are included without crowding the composition, and that the perspective is handled so well that four or more horsemen can be shown riding side by side without confusing the planes. Furthermore, there is sufficient variety in the manner of placing and handling the figures so that the impression of monotony is skillfully avoided.

The only one of the sculptures known definitely to have been executed by the hand of Phidias himself was the cult statue of Athena Parthenos that was placed within the sanctuary of the cella. He is said to have preferred marble but to have yielded to the desires of the citizens who wished to honor their patroness only with the most precious of materials—gold for the helmet and armor and ivory for the hands and face. The copies that survive can give only a faint idea of what the original was like. Its height of almost 42 feet including the pedestal was, of course, quite out of proportion to the interior of such a room, but it was designed to be seen outside the temple and at a considerable distance. Only the priests and priestesses had access to the windowless interior and the doors were kept closed except on feast days. When opened, the rays of the morning sun penetrated deeply into the interior of the cella and gave sufficient light for the populace which gathered in front of the temple to see the goddess clearly.

In appraising works of this sort one can easily overlook the fact that what is now seen in the light of criticism were once idols before which people made sacrifices, recited prayers, and chanted hymns; and as they gazed upward they identified the figure before them with the divinity it represented. The unique quality of Phidias' conception was that, unlike previous cult statues, his Athena was a revelation of beauty as such. That he was so credited by ancient writers is brought out in the following quotation from Quintilian to the effect that its "beauty is such that it is said to have added something even to the awe with which the god was already regarded: so perfectly did the majesty of the work give the impression of godhead." [10]

A certain continuity in the Parthenon sculptures as a whole is discernible by starting with the metopes, all of which have to do with various mythological and semihistorical struggles. Those on the east apparently represented the primeval battle of the gods and giants for control of the world; on the south, the Lapiths, oldest Greek inhabitants of Thessaly, are pitted against the half-human centaurs; on the north the Homeric epic of the fall of Troy is told; and finally on the west the Greeks and Athenians battle against the ferocious Amazons, who symbolized their Asiatic enemies. Each represents a stage in the advance of civilization against the forces of chaos and barbarism. In the east pediment the allegory of the birth of Athena, goddess of wisdom, is related, while in the west pediment the story turns to that of the rivalry of Athena, as the personification of intellect, and Poseidon, as patron of maritime trade and commerce. This is essen-

Fig. 1:22 (above left). *Athena*. Relief from the Acropolis. Marble. *c*.18″ high *c*.445 B. C. Acropolis Museum, Athens. Fig. 1:23 (above right). *Goddess Tying Her Sandal*. Relief from balustrade of the Temple of Athena Nike. Marble. 42″ high. *c*.410 B. C. Acropolis Museum, Athens (Courtesy Royal Greek Embassy)

Fig. 1:24. Callicrates (?). *Temple of Athena Nike*. Pentelic Marble. 18½′ x 27′. *c*.423 B. C. (Courtesy Royal Greek Embassy)

tially the struggle between two ways of life—that of the pursuit of culture and wisdom on one side and of material wealth on the other. In the Pan-Athenaic procession on the exterior cella walls, the citizens of the then-contemporary Athens celebrate the victory of Athena as they approach her sacred temple. The climax of the festival came as the portals of the temple were opened and the rays of the rising sun fell upon the gleaming gold and ivory image of the goddess. She then shone forth as the divine embodiment of the eternal truth, goodness, and beauty for which the favored faithful of her city were striving. With her help the forces of civilization, represented by the Greeks, had been delivered from tyranny and had triumphed over the ignorance of the barbarians. By depicting mythological episodes in which she was involved, the sculptures emphasized the bond between the goddess herself and the citizens of the city which enjoyed her protection. Through this iconographical plan, united as it was with the architectural form of the temple as a whole, the Parthenon became the living symbol of the unity of the aspirations of the people and those of their goddess.

The tremendous distance the art of sculpture had come during this half-century period is graphically illustrated when two reliefs from the acropolis are compared. The so-called *Mourning Athena* (Fig. 1:22) dates from about 455 B. C., while the *Goddess Tying Her Sandal* (Fig. 1:23) is from a balustrade that was built about 408 B. C. to surround the exquisite Ionic temple of Athena Nike (Fig. 1:24). It can be observed how the noble restraint of the former has yielded to the informal treatment of the latter. The dignified calm of Athena has melted into the gracefully relaxed posture of the goddess whose sandal has come untied. Whatever rigidity there was in the perpendicular lines of the earlier example has yielded in the later instance to the freely flowing lines of the drapery, which transparently reveal the curves of the beautiful body beneath.

The contrast is even more apparent when an example of Hellenic sculpture in the round is placed beside one from the following century. The bronze original of Polyclitus' *Doryphorus*, or *Spear Bearer*, is now known only through routine Roman copies, such as that in the Naples Museum (Fig. 1:25), while Praxiteles' *Hermes and the Infant Dionysus* (Fig. 1:26), which postdates Polyclitus' work by about 90 years, is almost certainly an original. Polyclitus, a contemporary of Phidias, is known from ancient sources to have worked out a theory of mathematical proportions for the portrayal of the human figure. While its exact nature remains a subject of speculation, his canon is known to have rested on the assumption that the beauty of the body depended on the orderly relationship of its parts to each other and these, in turn, to the whole. Just as the Parthenon had its

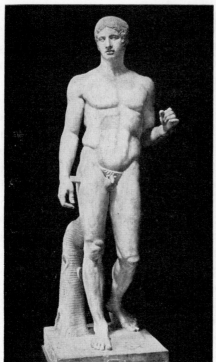

Fig. 1:25 (left). Polyclitus. *Doryphorus* (Spear Bearer). Roman copy in marble after the original bronze of *c*.440 B. C. 7′ high. National Museum, Naples (Alinari). Fig. 1:26 (right). Praxiteles. *Hermes and the Infant Dionysus*. Marble. 7′ 8″ high. *c*.350 B. C. Museum, Olympia (Courtesy Royal Greek Embassy)

module derived from a unit of the building, so Polyclitus took his module from a part of the body itself. Whether it was the head, the cubit (length of the forearm), or the palm (distance from wrist to fingertips) is not known, but it apparently varied from statue to statue. Once adopted, however, it had to be carried through, and all the dimensions had to be multiples or fractions of the module. In the case of the *Doryphorus*, the unit appears to be the head, which is one seventh the height of the whole—or, put the other way round, the figure is seven heads high. The beauty of the surface treatment of Polyclitus' bronze original can be supplied only by an act of the imagination, while with the *Hermes* of Praxiteles it can be seen to some extent even in a photograph. As Hermes rests his weight on one foot, the relaxed stance throws his body into the familiar S-curve. If Praxiteles was thinking in arithmetical terms, he disguised it so successfully that his observers are unaware of it. In spite of the natural walking posture of the *Doryphorus*, the figure still has something of the strength and stiffness of archaic sculpture, while under Praxiteles' masterly hand, the *Hermes* has all the ease and grace of a living being.

MUSIC

The word *music* today usually carries with it the connotation of a fully
mature and independent art. It must be remembered, however, that such
contemporary institutions as symphony concerts, chamber music, and solo
recitals, where the focus is more exclusively on the medium of abstract
sound, are relatively modern. The word is still used to cover the union of
sound with many other elements as in the case of popular songs, dance
music, military marches, and church music. Music is also found in combination with words as in the drama, with dancing as in the ballet, and with
all the arts as in the opera. In ancient Greece the word in its broadest sense
meant any of the arts and sciences that came under the patronage of the
muses. These imaginary maidens were the daughters of the heavenly Zeus
and the more earthly Mnemosyne; and like them, music was considered
to be a creation half divine and half human. Since Zeus in the ancient
conception was the creator, and Mnemosyne, as her name implies, the
symbol of memory, the muses and their arts were the result of the union of
the creative urge and memory. This was simply a fanciful way of saying
that music was remembered inspiration. As the Greek civilization progressed, the muses gradually increased until they reached nine in number,
and the arts and sciences over which they presided included almost all the
intellectual and inspirational disciplines that sprang from the fertile minds
of this highly creative people. The principal concerns of the muses were
lyric poetry, tragic and comic drama, choral dancing, and song. Astronomy
and history were also included; but curiously enough, there were no muses
for the visual arts, even though the Greeks excelled in architecture, sculpture, and painting.

Music was placed by Plato and others in opposition to gymnastic or
physical pursuits, and its meaning in this sense was as broad as our use of
liberal arts or culture. The Greeks also used music more narrowly in the
sense of the tonal art. It was always, however, intimately bound up with
poetry, drama, and the dance and was usually found in their company. At
one place in the *Republic* Socrates asks: "And when you speak of music, do
you include literature or not?" And the answer was in the affirmative.
Thus, while it is known that the Greeks did have independent instrumental
music apart from its combination with words, the evidence points to the
fact that the vast body of their music was connected with literary forms.
This does not imply, of course, that it lacked a distinct identity or that it
was swallowed up by poetry, but rather that it had an important and hon-

ored part in it. Plato, for instance, inquires: "And I think that you must
have observed again and again what a poor appearance the tales of the
poets make when stripped of the colours which music puts upon them, and
recited in simple prose. . . . They are like faces which were never really
beautiful, but only blooming; and now the bloom of youth has passed away
from them?" [11] Greek music must therefore be considered primarily in its
union with literature. The clearest statement of this is again found in the
Republic where it is pointed out that "melody is composed of three things,
the words, the harmony (by which is meant the melodic intervals), and
the rhythm." In discussing the relative importance of each, it is stated that
"harmony and rhythm must follow the words." [12] The two arts are thus
united in the single one of prosody, and it is well to keep in mind that this
conception of the role and function of music is not only valid for the period
of Greco-Roman antiquity, but for the Middle Ages as well. Our knowledge
of Greek music must be gleaned from a variety of sources, such as occasional
literary references, poetry and drama, visual representations of musical
instruments and music-making in sculpture and painting, theoretical
treatises, and some very fragmentary surviving examples of the music
itself.

Music in both its broad and narrow sense was closely woven into the
fabric of the emotional, intellectual, and social life of the ancient Greeks;
and the art was considered by them to have a fundamental connection with
the well-being of individuals personally as well as that of the social and
physical environment in which they lived. Surely no more eloquent tribute
to the power of art in public affairs has ever been made than that quoted
by Socrates to the effect that music is so fundamentally related to government that "when modes of music change, the fundamental laws of the
State always change with them." [13] The importance attached by the
Greeks to the role of music in health and life is found in certain linguistic
images that are still in current use. To them a happy person was like a
well-tuned lyre. When the body and soul were in a proper state of attunement, a person was well and health thus meant being in a harmonious
condition. Muscles, when the body was in good form, were said to have
the proper tone, and physicians today still speak of a quality of "muscular
tonus." When individuals were too tense they were said to be "high
strung"; or when too relaxed or depressed, they were "low" and needed a
"tonic" to tone or tune them up. When things reached a really critical
state, the patient was said to be all "unstrung." Still another Greek word
connected with health was *katharsis*, which Aristotle used in reference to
the function of art as a purging of the emotions through the experience of
music and the drama.

Lyric poetry to the Greeks meant verse actually sung to the accompaniment of the lyre. When a situation elicits from us a profound emotional response, we still speak occasionally as the ancients did of a "tugging at the heart strings." The Greeks had an elaborate theory that connected their musical modes, or scales, and certain moods or emotions with which they were specifically associated. We too find a relationship between various moods and our major and minor modes, though not apparently with such precision as the ancients did. Education for young people in Greece consisted of a balanced curriculum of music for the soul and gymnastic for the body. We still adhere to the broad principle of building a sound mind in a sound body as a kind of ideal in education. Even the welfare of the soul after death had musical overtones, since immortality to many Greeks meant being somehow in tune with the cosmic forces, and being at last able to hear the "music of the spheres." All these notions had to do with the idea of the physical nature being somehow in harmony with the metaphysical, and the soul being an attunement of the body.

The most important Greek contribution to the development of Western music is—and probably always will remain so—the discovery of the mathematical ratios of the melodic intervals and the subsequent establishment of the rational basis for musical theory. When all the separate sources of information are combined, however, it is possible to glean from them at least a faint notion of what Greek music was actually like. From them it is apparent that its highest development undoubtedly was found in its union with the drama. The great 5th-century dramatists were composers as well as poets, and the nearest parallel to their art in our time is that of the opera. In this medium music is still found, as it was then, in such a wide variety of forms and combinations as orchestra numbers, ballet scenes, vocal quartets, trios, solo arias, and recitatives. The Athenian dramatist was by tradition responsible for the music, the training of the chorus, and the staging of the play as well as for writing the book. In addition to all this, he often played one of the roles himself. The great dramatists were therefore composers as well as poets, actors, playwrights, and producers.

In reconstructing the Greek drama in our imaginations, we must try to put ourselves in the place of a Greek audience to whom the drama was a lively aural and visual experience of choral singing and dancing, of vocal and instrumental music, as well as of dialogue and dramatic sequence. When we read such a play as the *Suppliants* of Aeschylus, it is as if we were seeing only the libretto of an opera to which all the music, dances, and stage directions are missing. It is so clearly a lyric drama that the music itself must have been the principal means by which the poet conveyed his meaning. Euripides' *The Bacchae*, on the other hand, has far greater intrinsic dramatic substance, but even here the emotional intensity of the individual scenes often rises to such a pitch that music had to take over where the words left off; just as when a person is so overcome with feeling that words fail, and he resorts to inarticulate sounds and gestures.

The weight of the musical expression fell primarily on the chorus, which was the original basis of the dramatic form and from which all the other elements of the drama evolved. We have at last realized, said Nietzsche in his analysis of Greek drama, "that the scene, together with the action, was fundamentally and originally conceived only as a *vision*, that the only reality is just the chorus, which of itself generates the vision and speaks thereof with the entire symbolism of dancing, tone, and word." [14] The chorus performed both in stationary position and in motion, accompanied by mimetic gestures as it circulated about the orchestra. This part of the theater meant literally a dancing place, and the choral songs, dances, and group recitatives took place in this section around the altar of Dionysus. The forms of the choruses were metrically and musically very elaborate and were written with such variety and invention that repetitions either within a single play, or even in other plays by the same author, were very rare. In *The Bacchae*, each chorus differs in meter, in the metrical arrangements of the strophes and antistrophes, and in the alternation of groups of varying sizes which sing responsorially with the soloists.

Interestingly enough, the sole surviving relic of Greek music from this century is a fragment of a choral *stasimon*, or stationary chorus, from Euripides' *Orestes*, which was produced in Athens only three years before *The Bacchae*.[15] All the Greek manuscripts come down through the ages from the hands of medieval scribes who omitted the musical notation of the earlier copies because it was no longer comprehensible to them. In this instance the musical notation was included, but all that is left is a single sheet of papyrus which has become perforated with age. From ancient accounts it is known that the music of Euripides differed considerably from that of his predecessor Aeschylus and his contemporary Sophocles. Euripides was educated in the "new" music by Timotheus, while Sophocles received his instruction from the rival musician Lampros who was of the conservative type. The new music was considered more ornate and was criticized because it was so complex that the words were unintelligible. The text was thus on its way to becoming as of little consequence as that of an opera chorus of today, while traditionally it had dominated the music. Evidence to support this claim is found in the literary content of Euripidean choruses, which sometimes have little or no direct connection with the action.

Fragmentary though this scrap of evidence is, these few notes from Euripides' *Orestes* are enough to tell their own story. Since the intervals called for are in half and quarter tones, it means that Euripidean choruses were musically complex enough to demand highly skilled singers. The mode is mixolydian, which is described by Aristotle in his *Politics* as being "mournful and restrained." The words that accompany the fragment perfectly express this sentiment, and when properly performed, it still conveys this mood. Other than this single relic of choral recitative, the music of the century must remain mute to our ears, and we can only echo the words of Keats in his "Ode on a Grecian Urn": "Heard melodies are sweet, but those unheard are sweeter."

DRAMA

In approaching Greek drama, one must remember that a presentation always coincided with a religious festival, and that its forms were composed of elements drawn from mythological lore, epic poetry, patriotic pageantry, and pleasant recreation. Without the modern access to books, the Athenians experienced their plays only in oral presentations. In reading a Greek drama, therefore, the imagination must supply the missing qualities associated with a live theatrical production—poetic declamation, the eloquence of spoken dialogue, the rhythms of choral singing and dancing, the surprises of scenic spectacle, and the unfolding of a plot. Only in this way can such complex works of art be appreciated and understood in the context of the popular art form it was in ancient times.

The scope of Greek drama was tremendous, running a gamut from majestic tragedy of heroic proportions, through the pathos of melodrama in its original sense of drama with melody, and subtle satires, or satyr plays, all the way to the riotous Aristophanic comedies. The implications of the early Aeschylean tragedy were strongly ethical, showing clearly that the drama was still identified in his mind with theological thought. The forms of Sophocles' plays were distinguished by their impeccable craftsmanship, while their lofty content was based on the course of human destiny as seen in the light of the inexorable moral law of the universe.

In some ways the works of Euripides may not be as typical of the Hellenic style as those of either Aeschylus or Sophocles, but his influence on the subsequent development of the drama, both in Hellenistic and later times, was incalculably greater. *The Bacchae*, the last of his 92-odd plays, was written at a time when the darkness of disillusionment was descending on Athenian intellectuals toward the end of the disastrous Peloponnesian war, and it was performed posthumously in Athens about 405 B. C. Like most masterpieces it is atypical in some respects, while in others it seems to stem out of the deepest traditional roots of the theater's origin. Despite some inner inconsistencies and a certain elusiveness of meaning, it has all the formal perfection and grandeur of utterance of the loftiest tragedies. The strange wild beauty of the choruses, the magic of its poetry, and the complex interplay between the human and divine wills endow it with all the necessary ingredients of the theater at its best.

As is the custom in Greek tragedy, the plot of *The Bacchae* is based on a myth. In this instance Euripides has chosen one with particular appropriateness to the theater and the drama, since the origin of both centered in the feast of Dionysus, the Bacchus of Roman mythology, who was the god of wine and revelry. The beginnings of the dramatic form were deeply rooted in the religious ritual associated with his cult, which gradually evolved from the practice of certain magic rites into a vehicle for powerful creative expression. The theater itself was always located in a precinct sacred to the god Dionysus; his altar occupied the center of the orchestra around which the chorus performed, and all who gathered around it paid tribute to the god by their presence. The specific function of the chorus, according to Nietzsche, was to conjure up the divine vision in which it "beholds its lord and master Dionysus . . . [and] sees how he, the god, suffers and glorifies himself." [16]

The *prologue* supplied the introductory material pertinent to the situation that was to be developed in the course of the play. In this case Dionysus himself appears and declares to the audience in the sonorous phrases of Euripides:

> Behold, God's Són is come unto this land
> Of Thebes, even I, Dionysus, whom the brand
> Of heaven's hot splendour lit to life, when she
> Who bore me, Cadmus' daughter Semele,
> Died here . . .
> > There by the castle side
> I see her place, the Tomb of the Lightning's Bride . . .
> > > > (Lines 1–8) [17]

The Athenian audience of 405 B. C., when the play was first performed, needed only such an allusion to bring to mind the entire mythological background of the drama. Since those of the 20th century are not so well equipped, the myth must be recounted at this point. Zeus, so the myth goes, had destined his son by Persephone, Dionysus, to be his successor as the lord of the world. As the youth was roaming the earth a primitive race of giants, the wicked Titans, lured the young god into their power, tore him to pieces, and devoured him. Athena, however, rescued his heart and brought it to Zeus, who determined to save the young god by reincarnating him. At that time Zeus was enamored of a beauteous earthly maiden of noble family, Semele, daughter of Cadmus, King of Thebes. The jealousy of Hera was aroused as usual, and her revenge consisted of persuading Semele to beg Zeus to reveal himself to her in the full majesty of his godhead, knowing that she would thereby be burned by the heavenly fire. Zeus, after having vowed to grant Semele her wish, appeared to her as a stroke of lightning, and Semele was consumed in one incandescent flash. In order to save her prematurely born child Dionysus, and to deceive Hera, Zeus transferred him to his thigh, and the new god was eventually born in a mysterious second birth.

Zeus meanwhile had destroyed the Titans with a thunderbolt and created man from their ashes. The duality of human nature was thus symbolized by the substance from which men were created, the ashes of the Titans being responsible for their grossly physical nature; but, since the Titans had eaten the divine flesh of Dionysus, mankind had an immortal spark as well. To the cult this meant that the soul or divine essence was imprisoned in the tomb of the body, and salvation lay in the release of the soul from the bonds that confine it. Purification was made through participation in the mysteries that revealed how the soul could be restored eventually to its divine origin. The second birth of Dionysus was the essence of his cult, and mortals by performing his rites could likewise be reborn. At first these mysteries probably included human sacrifice; later, a bull, the form in which the god was slain, was torn to pieces in a re-enactment of the first death of Dionysus. At the sacrificial feast, the raw flesh of the animal was devoured to effect a symbolic union with the god. In a later phase the "blood" of the grape was substituted for that of the animal, and wine was used to induce the state of ecstasy, literally a stepping out from the body, which effected the sought-for separation of the divine from the physical element of human life. There is an allusion to this in the play, where Cadmus relates that Dionysus

> found the liquid shower
> Hid in the grape. He rests man's spirit dim
> From grieving, when the vine exalteth him.
> He giveth sleep to sink the fretful day
> In cool forgetting. Is there any way
> With man's sore heart, save only to forget? (278–283)

At this stage the ritual included wine, dancing, and music as the means of achieving ecstasy. As a chorus of maidens in the play expresses it,

> Will they ever come to me, ever again,
>> The long long dances,
> On through the dark till the dim stars wane?
> Shall I feel the dew on my throat, and the stream
> Of wind in my hair? Shall our white feet gleam
>> In the dim expanses?   (863–868)

Later this aspect of the cult was further refined, and ecstasy was brought on by the inspiration of music, poetry, and the drama. This transition was probably the result of a religious reformer by the name of Orpheus, who had such great influence that the cult subsequently bore his name. The Orphic connection is also recalled in the course of the drama when the chorus sings:

> Oh, where art thou? . . .
>
> .   .   .   .
>
> In the elm-woods and the oaken,
>> There where Orpheus harped of old,
> And the trees awoke and knew him,
>> And the wild things gathered to him,
> As he sang amid the broken
>> Glens his music manifold?   (562–566)

A still further step was taken by Pythagoras, a philosopher and reformer of the Orphic cult. Through the discovery of the mathematical basis of the musical intervals, he speculated that the universe was constructed on harmonic principles, and that the planets made a concert of musical sounds as they whirled in their orbits. Hence melody unaided also might bring on the state of ecstasy; and when it does, the votary may then hear the music of the spheres. This doctrine has endured in Western thought and poetry up to the present time, and perhaps none has expressed it more beautifully than Shakespeare did in a passage (Act V, Sc. I) from *The Merchant of Venice:*

> . . . look, how the floor of heaven
> Is thick inlaid with patines of bright gold:
> There's not the smallest orb which thou behold'st
> But in his motion like an angel sings,
> Still quiring to the young-eyed cherubins;
> Such harmony is in immortal souls;
> But, whilst this muddy vesture of decay
> Doth grossly close it in, we cannot hear it.

The discovery that is almost universally attributed to Pythagoras laid the basis for the foundation of Western musical theory by demonstrating that musical intervals rest on mathematical ratios. This can easily be seen when a tuned string is stopped off exactly in the middle. The musical interval between the tone of the unstopped string and the one which is equally divided will then be the octave, and the mathematical ratio will be 1:2. Similarly if the string is divided into three equal parts, the musical interval between its tone and the one divided into two parts will be the fifth, and the ratio for it is 2:3. Also by comparing the tone of the triply divided string with one divided into four parts, the interval will be the fourth and the ratio 3:4. Hence mathematically 1:2 equals the octave; 2:3, the fifth; 3:4, the fourth; 8:9, the whole tone, and so on. Music to Pythagoras and his followers was thus synonymous with order and proportion, and rested on a demonstrably rational basis. This tremendous discovery seemed to be a key that might unlock the secrets of the universe, which, they reasoned, might likewise be reduced to numbers and be constructed according to the principles of a musical scale. This idea found its way into all aspects of the intellectual life of Greece, and even Plato built up a conception of the cosmic harmony of the world on these musical principles in his *Timaeus*. It is possible that the architects also incorporated these laws into the proportions and designs of their buildings. The Roman architect Vitruvius, for instance, was thoroughly familiar with Greek musical theory.

Plato then carries it one step farther when he says: "as the eyes are designed to look up at the stars, so are the ears to hear harmonious motions; and these are sister sciences." [18] He then proceeds to the most abstract and rational of all interpretations of Orphism, the dialectical method, which is the meaning of his dictum that philosophy "is the noblest and best of music." [19] Thus the ultimate stage in the progressive refinement of the means of attaining ecstasy is reached. Throughout, the emphasis was more and more on reason, although the mystical element even in Plato's thought was never absent. Euripides, in *The Bacchae*, is concerned with the earlier pre-Pythagorean stage of the cult's development, and the rites as he described them consisted of wine, revelry, dancing, and the participation in secret mysteries in ceremonial costume. Animal symbolism is still a strong element, as the fawn skin was worn; and it is interesting to recall that in the century before the play was written, the prize for winning the choral contest in the Dionysian festival was a goat's head. A sculptural relief found at Patras near Athens (Fig. 1:27) gives a vivid visual interpretation of the Orphic dances.

To return now to the Prologue, Dionysus, whose earthly mother was a

Fig. 1:27. *Dionysian Procession*. Fragments of a sarcophagus found
at Patras, Greece. National Museum, Athens (Alinari)

princess of Thebes, finds himself, like most prophets, without honor in his
own land. "And now I come to Hellas," he proclaims, "having taught all
the world else my dances and my rite of mysteries, to show me in men's
sight manifest God" (lines 19–22). Pentheus, grandson of Cadmus and son
of Agave, the sister of Semele, fears that the influence of the cult may prove
subversive and thus gnaw at the very roots of society. As King of Thebes,
he determines to take some action, and his first weapon is the use of reason.
He consequently puts forth a less-exalted and more-prosaic explanation of
the birth of Semele's child Dionysus. The whole legend, he says, is a ruse
to cover up her affair with a lover who was undoubtedly more human than
divine. This explanation infuriates the god who declares:

> I cry this Thebes to waken; set her hands
> To clasp my wand, mine ivied javelin,
> And round her shoulders hang my wild fawn-skin.
> For they have scorned me whom it least beseemed,
> Semele's sisters; mocked my birth, nor deemed
> That Dionysus sprang from Dian seed.
> My mother sinned, said they; and in her need,
> With Cadmus plotting, cloaked her human shame
> With the dread name of Zeus; for that the flame
> From heaven consumed her, seeing she lied to God.
>
> . . .
>
> Thus shall this Thebes, how sore soe'er it smart,
> Learn and forget not, till she crave her part
> In mine adoring; thus must I speak clear
> To save my mother's fame, and crown me here
> As true God, born by Semele to Zeus.   (22–47)

The stage is thus set for the conflict between the human and divine, between the natural and supernatural, and between a rational world view and one colored by all the mysterious emotional excitement of the unknown forces of the universe. As Dionysus leaves, a white-robed chorus of 15 bacchae, or bacchantes, enters to perform the first of the choral sections, which alternate with the dramatic action of the *episodes* and separate the several parts into what would correspond to the acts of a modern play. They are in ceremonial costume, some bearing the mystic wand, the thyrsus; and others have musical instruments sacred to the cult, the timbrels, or round drums similar to tambourines, and the *auloi*, wind instruments like a double oboe. They chant a choral song that goes:

> The wild orb of our orgies,
> Our timbrel; and thy gorges
> Rang with this strain; and blended Phrygian chant
> And sweet keen pipes were there. (124–127)

The mystic rites are vividly described by the same group in their second *stasimon:*

> Girt with garlands and with glee,
> First in Heaven's sovranty?
> For his kingdom, it is there,
> In the dancing and the prayer,
> In the music and the laughter,
> In the vanishing of care,
> And of all before and after;
> In the God's high banquet, when
> Gleams the grape-blood, flashed to heaven:
> Yea, and in the feasts of men
> Comes his crownèd slumber; then
> Pain is dead and hate forgive! (380–390)

The dramatic action centers around the conflict between the wills of king and god; and Pentheus, foredoomed in this unequal contest and the victim of his own one-sidedness, emerges in the process as one of the heroes of Greek tragedy. By his unwillingness to recognize the force of the emotional factor in human psychology, he brings about his own downfall. In a remarkable scene Pentheus confronts his divine antagonist, but mortal reason proves to be no match for the adroit power of the god. He is induced to go to the mountains in order to witness the rites for himself. Since, however, only women may see the mysteries, Pentheus is persuaded to don female attire. Now entirely in the hands of his adversary, degraded and incapable of decision, he is led away to the secret places where:

> The Maenad maidens sate; in toil they were,
> Busily glad. Some with an ivy chain
> Tricked a worn wand to toss its locks again;
> Some, wild in joyance, like young steeds set free,
> Made answering songs of mystic melody.   (1056–1060)

Through a messenger we learn that Pentheus was delivered over to the frenetic female furies. Persuaded that he was some sacrificial animal, they literally tore him to pieces, and his own mother claims his head as her festive prize.

>   'Twas his mother stood
> O'er him, first priestess of those rites of blood.
> . . . But she, with lips a-foam and eyes that run
> Like leaping fire, with thoughts that ne'er should be
> On earth, possessed by Bacchios utterly,
> Stays not nor hears . . .
>   . . . and the torn flesh cried,
> And on Autonoe pressed, and all the crowd
> Of ravening arms. Yea, all the air was loud
> With groans that faded into sobbing breath,
> Dim shrieks, and joy, and triumph-cries of death.
> And here was borne a severed arm, and there
> A hunter's booted foot; white bones lay bare
> With rending; and swift hands ensanguinèd
> Tossed as in sport the flesh of Pentheus dead.   (1113–1138)

The grisly *climax* is consummated by the entrance of Agave bearing the head of her own son on the point of her thyrsus, believing it to be the prize of the revels, the head of a lion. In the words of the messenger who announces her return: "She bears in triumph . . . her own broken heart!" Her father Cadmus gradually brings her back to consciousness and the blood-curdling truth dawns upon her. The will of the god has thus been done, and in solitary glory he views the human wreckage as he pronounces the Epilogue:

> Thus speaketh Dionysus, Son confessed
> Of no man but Zeus!—Ah, had ye seen
> Truth in the hour you would not, all had been
> Well with ye, and the Child of God your friend!   (1342–1345)

When all the actors have left, the chorus intones the final *stasimon*, after which it makes its solemn *exodus*:

> There be many shapes of mystery.
> And many things God makes to be,
>   Past hope and fear.
> And the end men look for cometh not,
> And a path is there where no man thought.
>   So hath it fallen here.   (1387–1392)

The key to the interpretation of the drama is found in the contest between the rational and irrational elements in the human psychological
constitution. The conflict between the known and the unknown in this
intensely human situation is treated by Euripides symbolically as the interplay between human and divine elements. He deals with the phenomenon
of a proselytizing cult eager to make converts, something which was entirely outside the dignified Olympic religious tradition. This was something
new in Greek experience, a shocking revelation, and Euripides organizes
his play in order to bring the full implications of it to the eyes and ears of
his audience. In his view, reason attempts to explain events on a demonstrable cause-and-effect basis; but the phenomena which can be reduced to
such terms are always so small in comparison to those which are unknown
and probably even unknowable. The Orphic mysteries were attempting
to come to terms with these invisible aspects of experience and in so doing
were able to attain for the initiates certain fleeting moments of joy and a
sense of harmony with the cosmic forces. Their indifference to reason, however, left the way open to self-delusion and emotional excesses that were
dangerous both to self and society. They loved so violently and hated so
furiously that the most basic human relationships, including in this case
the love of a mother for her son and the mutual respect which held a noble
family together, were swept away in a flood of blind passion.

Pentheus, on the other hand, desiring to rule in the light of reason,
neglected to take into account the forces of emotion and enthusiasm in
human affairs. He is also blind to the fact that such cults actually flourish
under repression, and if handled unwisely can shake the social order to
its foundations. Euripides, through the example of Pentheus, seems to be
saying that man does not live by reason alone; and if he would be a ruler,
the emotional factor in human relations must be taken into account. Even
though Dionysus and emotionalism triumph at the end, it does not, however, imply an endorsement by Euripides or that he has seen the futility of
the use of rationalism in human affairs. The conclusion can only be that
pure reason and violent emotionalism must both be curbed, and some way
devised whereby these polar extremes can be harmonized by some golden
mean. Euripides thus strongly suggests that the power of man's reason is

too weak and his knowledge too limited for him to depend on this alone; and if he does, like Pentheus, he will eventually be destroyed. Euripides makes it equally clear, however, that blind emotionalism is just as dangerous as rigid reason. Both lead to intolerance and the destruction of the balance and harmony in human society without which individual happiness is impossible. While offering no specific solution, it is clear that neither intolerant reason nor blind belief is the answer. Euripides thus leaves the problem unresolved, but in the tradition of Greek drama the moral basis is strongly implied.

From this specific example some judicious generalizations about Greek drama as a whole can be made. First of all, the play is a satisfactory whole in Aristotle's sense because it fulfills the three necessary conditions of form— that is, it has a beginning, a middle, and an end. It also coincides with the Aristotelian definition of tragedy as "an imitation of an action that is serious, complete, and of a certain magnitude; in language embellished with each kind of artistic ornament, the several kinds being found in separate sections of the play; in the form of action, not of narrative; with incidents arousing pity and fear, wherewith to accomplish its *katharsis* [purgation] of the emotions." [20] Furthermore for Aristotle, tragedy must be composed of six necessary elements which he ranks in the following order: Plot, "the arrangement of the incidents"; Character, "that which reveals moral purpose"; Thought, "where something is proved to be or not to be"; Diction, "the metrical arrangement of the words"; Song, "melody holds the chief place among the embellishments"; and finally Spectacle.

The sequential arrangement of *The Bacchae* is typical with its orderly procession of *prologue*, six choral *stasima* framing in the five dramatic *episodes*, and concluding with the *epilogue* and *exodus*. The conflict between the *protagonist* and his superhuman *antagonist* rises to its *climax* in the middle episode. Through the proper tragic necessity his inevitable downfall comes because he carries the seeds of his own destruction within his breast. After this turning point the well-planned *anticlimax* resolves the action once more back into a state of equilibrium. Like the best of Greek tragedies it is short, direct, and without subplots; and all the violence takes place elsewhere while the audience is informed of it by means of a messenger. The triple unities of classical drama are present as well, since the time element is kept within the bounds of one day, the place always remains the same, and the action is continuous. The chorus, as the most stylized element, provides the necessary relief after the intensity of the dramatic scenes; makes its commentary on the action; and supplies the music and dancing. *The Bacchae* is also a problem play that allows ample scope for speculation and reflection, and each of the characters is a blend of both the good and bad elements inherent in human nature. They were undoubtedly taken from the types familiar in the Athens of the dramatist's time, and their views reflected some of the political, social, and religious situations of the time. The drama unfolds, however, in mythological and symbolic terms, since the necessary conditions of tragedy can be fulfilled only when some noble figure—one "highly renowned or prosperous" as Aristotle puts it—is brought to grief through some flaw in his own psychological make-up and by some inevitable stroke of fate. The reasons for this must gradually be made apparent to the audience through the process of "causal necessity." A common man's woes might bring about a pathetic situation, but not a tragic one in the classical sense. When a virtuous hero is rewarded, or the evil designs of the villain receive their just deserts, there is obviously no tragic situation. When a blameless man is brought from a fortunate to an unfortunate condition, or when an evil person rises from misery to good fortune, there is likewise no tragedy because the moral sense is outraged. Such was Euripides' last play and final legacy to Athens. Its grandeur and beauty rise above all these technical and critical considerations, and *The Bacchae* emerges as a powerful and moving work of art, capable of taking its place unblushingly at the side of the architecture and sculpture of the Parthenon and Erechtheum as one of the highest achievements of the century.

IDEAS

The three principal ideas that permeated so many aspects of Athenian life and thought, and through which the separate arts find their unity and relationship, are humanism, rationalism, and idealism.

Humanism

The idea of humanism provides the first key to the understanding of Greek art. Any humanistic point of view is, of necessity, based on the premise that life here and now is somehow good and is meant to be enjoyed. This attitude is in direct contrast to the asceticism of the Middle Ages, which held the only real good to be in the world beyond and the joys of life to be the snares of the devil. The Greek attitude is well expressed in a remark of their legendary athletic hero Achilles, who said he would rather be the slave of the humblest living artisan than reign as king over the shades of the underworld. For the Greeks, then, the subject of their art and the object of their studies was man and his environment. The latter part of the 5th century B. C., while the political star of his city was in the ascendancy, was an era of confidence and security for Athenian man. The state itself—meaning the people as a whole—became the principal patron of the arts;

and the citizen took delight in draping his national wealth in golden garlands around Athena's neck, where it could be seen, enjoyed, and admired in the designs of Phidias, instead of burying it in some classical Fort Knox.

Politically and socially his life was a balance between the forces of an aristocratic conservatism and a liberal individualism, which were maintained in equilibrium by the democratic institutions of his society. His art reflects a gravitational pull between this aristocratic tradition, which resisted change and emphasized austerity, stylization, and restraint; and that of the new dynamic liberalism, which opposed it with emotionalism, a desire for faithfulness to nature, and a tendency toward more elaborate forms of decoration. The genius of Phidias was that he was able to achieve a golden mean between these oppositions, and the incomparable Parthenon and its sculptures was the result. Greek architecture humanized the experience of space by organizing it so that it was neither too complex nor too grand to be fully comprehended by the mind. The simplicity and clarity of Greek construction was always evident to the eye, and the humanistic sense was enhanced by bringing the indefiniteness of man's spatial environment within his intellectual grasp. Greek architecture as a whole thus imposed a concept of order on the chaos of space, and by so doing rendered it clearly intelligible.

Particularly congenial to this humanistic mode of thought was the art of sculpture. The anthropomorphic aspect of the Greek religion embraced the conception of the gods as idealized human beings without the usual human limitations, and of all historical periods they were probably the most successful in capturing the godlike image in human form. With the human body as a point of departure such divinities as Apollo and Athena appeared as idealized images of perfect masculine and feminine beauty. Equally imaginative were the deviations from the human norm, such as the goat-footed Pan, the half-human half-horse centaurs, and the myriads of other fanciful creatures with which they populated their countryside and personified the forces of nature. The Greeks were more thoroughly at home in the physical world than any of the later Christian peoples who based their beliefs on a dualistic separation of flesh and spirit. Their greatest pride was in the beauty and agility of the human body at the peak of its development. This interest was not only aesthetic but had functional aspects as well, since the strength of their athletes in the hand-to-hand combat of their mode of warfare was both useful and necessary to the preservation of their state. Just as we figuratively flex our muscles on occasion by exhibiting our tanks, atomic artillery, and jet planes, they paraded the beautifully developed bodies of their athletes at the peak of their strength and dedicated them to the service of the city. In addition to their studies in reading, literature, and music, they were trained from childhood for combat in the competitive Athenian and Pan-hellenic games. The nude body in action was a fact of daily experience, and the sculptor had ample opportunity to observe its proportions and musculature in a wide variety of postures. The result is embodied in such well-known examples as the *Discobolus*, or *Discus Thrower*, by Myron, as well as in the many statues of athletes attributed to Polyclitus. The rendition of the undraped male body reached a high point of accuracy and clarity in the 5th century, but it remained for the succeeding one to do the same for the female form.

From sculpture it is but a step further to the dance and drama where the expressive medium is the human body in movement. These arts fell within the broad meaning of the word music, and their humanistic connection was emphasized in the education of youth, because, as Plato says, "rhythm and harmony find their way into the inward places of the soul, on which they mightily fasten, imparting grace, and making the soul of him who is rightly educated graceful." [21] Just as architecture humanized the perception of space, so the arts of the dance, music, poetry, and drama humanized the experience of time. The triple unities of time, place, and action observed by the dramatists brought the temporal flow within intelligible limits. The essential humanism of Greek drama lay in such of its aspects as the creation of distinctive human types; the role of the chorus as a collective human commentary on the individual actions of gods and heroes; its concern with human problems that transcended the particular and became universally applicable; and above all, the creation of tragedy, in which the great individual is shown rising to the highest estate and plunging to the lowest depths, thereby revealing the ultimate limits of human experience. In sum, all the arts of Greece became the generating force by which Athenian man consciously or unconsciously felt himself identified with his fellow citizens. Through the medium of the arts, human experience is raised to its highest level; through participation in their refining fire, the individual was able to see his world more clearly in the light of universal values. By heightening his awareness of the true human significance of life, they helped Athenian man to dip into the entire rhythmic stream of living, creative elements that swirled about him.

Rationalism

In all human societies rational forces must coexist with the irrational; and while in Athens the ordering of the state and its activities in the light of reason seems to have been somewhat stronger than in other times and places, it does not mean that the opposite tendency was not present and active. Space as such was never very real to the Greeks, and our modern

concept of a nation as a territorial—that is, spatial—unit did not exist
for them. A nation that thought of itself in terms of a city-state was not
likely to be concerned with arbitrary lines on a map. This was at once the
power and weakness of Athens. Its influence depended upon intellectual
prestige, and its tendency to rely on the power of persuasion allowed rival
states to rise and undermine its influence. Except for a will to resist the
encroachments of barbarians, there was a curious absence of military dynamics in the Athenian mind, and consequently no real desire to conquer
foreign regions and push their frontiers outward. Time also seemed unreal
to them, and they measured it merely as the interval between events. Their
unconcern with a precise historical past was indicated both in the imperfection of their calendar and in the fact that their historians were really
chroniclers of almost contemporary events. Their geometry was designed
to measure static rather than moving bodies, and their visual arts followed
by emphasizing the abiding qualities of poise and calm. The spatial and
temporal unity of their drama was opposed to the continuous narrative
style of later periods. All these separate phenomena seem primarily to set
certain arbitrary limits that can be comprehended readily by the mind
and hence are aspects of rationalism.

The qualities of balance, clarity, and simplicity that the Greeks set up
as standards of excellence in all the arts depended upon the selective faculty
of a well-ordered mind. As Plato put it, "beauty of style and harmony and
grace and good rhythm depend on simplicity,—I mean the true simplicity
of a rightly and nobly ordered mind and character." [22] Plato's attitude
toward the arts that did not meet these specifications was highly critical,
and he was suspicious that works of art tended sometimes to be more the
product of divine madness than of rule or reason. He was disturbed, for
example, by such architectural refinements as the entasis of columns, and
the tilting of walls for the purpose of creating the appearance of perfection
by carefully calculated distortions. Since only the world of mathematics
seemed fixed and logical, and the world of appearances was deceptive, as
proved by such illusions as the case of a straight stick appearing bent when
thrust into water, the architect, to Plato, was one who sometimes ministered
to the deficiencies rather than the strengths of human nature. "Thus," he
writes, "every sort of confusion is revealed within us; and this is that weakness of the human mind on which the art of conjuring and of deceiving by
light and shadow and other ingenious devices imposes, having an effect
like magic." [23] The philosopher was well aware that such calculations also
entered into the designs of other visual artists, and he points out that "in
works either of sculpture or painting, which are of any magnitude, there is
a certain degree of deception; for if artists were to give the true proportions

of their fair works, the upper part, which is farther off, would appear to be out of proportion in comparison with the lower, which is nearer; and so they give up the truth in their images and make only proportions which appear to be beautiful, disregarding the real ones." [24] Furthermore, that which is true of the deviations of visual lines applies also to the variations in the rhythms of recited poetry and performed music. If mathematical regularity prevails, the result is dull and mechanical. In music, pitch must also waver slightly in order to sound lifelike and interesting. This Plato also felt to be irrational, and he felt that the only hope was for "the arts of measuring and numbering and weighing [to] come to the rescue of human understanding." [25] It follows that the excellence or inferiority of the several arts then depend upon the manner in which they make use of mathematical principles.

The influence of Pythagorean number theory permeates all the arts and imparts to each a certain internal coherence of its own. Just as the harmony of the Parthenon depended on the module taken from the Doric columns, so Polyclitus derived his proportions for the human body from the mathematical relationships of its parts. In a similar fashion, the melodic lines in music were based on the subdivisions of the perfect intervals that were derived from the mathematical ratios of the fourth, fifth, and octave. So also were the choral sections of the Greek drama constructed of intricate metrical units that added up to the larger parts on which the unity of the drama depended. In none of these cases, however, was a cold crystallization the desired effect. In the architecture of the Hellenic style, the statues of Polyclitus, the dramas of Aeschylus, Sophocles, and Euripides, and the dialogues of Plato, the rational approach was used principally as a dynamic process to suggest ways to solve a variety of aesthetic and human problems.

In spite of the suspicions of the philosophers, Greek architecture in retrospect turns out to be a high point in the rational solution to building problems. The post-and-lintel system of construction as far as it goes is eminently reasonable and completely comprehensible. All structural members fulfill their logical purpose, and nothing is hidden or mysterious. The orderly principle of repetition on which its designs are based is as logical in its way as one of Euclid's propositions or Plato's dialogues. It accomplishes for the eye what Plato was trying to achieve for the mind. Sculpture likewise avoided the pitfalls of rigid mathematics but nevertheless adopted rules valid to its peculiar needs. The Greek concept of the human body, as exemplified in the canon of Polyclitus (Fig. 1:25), was based at this time on a rational analysis of the whole and its related parts. The unity was maintained by subordinating these parts and not allowing any one of them to dominate. When the body is thus conceived as a whole the head becomes only one of the expressive elements. Too much emotion in a facial expression, for instance, would throw the composition out of balance. The impassive faces of statues and the use of masks by the actors were designed to preserve this balance, to aid in the projection of types rather than individuals, and to prevent violent feeling in a single part from destroying the harmony of the whole. The prevalence of architectural sculpture at this time is also based on a rational view. A free-standing statue always begs the question, What is it doing there? As architectural embellishment, however, sculpture has a perfectly logical place in the scheme of things, and does not otherwise have to justify its existence.

Rational and irrational elements were present in both the form and content of Greek drama just as they were in the architecture of the time. In the Parthenon the structurally regular triglyphs were interspersed between panels showing centaurs and other mythological creatures. The theme of these sculptures was the struggle between the Greeks as champions of enlightenment and the forces of darkness and barbarism. In the drama the rational Apollonian dialogue existed alongside the inspired Dionysian chorus. However, even in the Dionysian chorus the composition of intricate metrical schemes and the orderly and complex arrangements of the parts partake of rationalism and convey the dramatic content in highly orderly form. In the dialogue the action of the episodes must by rule lead inevitably and inexorably toward the predestined end, just as the lines and grouping of the figures must in a composition like the east pediment of the Parthenon. In the union of mythological and rational elements, tragedy could mediate between intuition and rule, the irrational and rational, the Dionysian and Apollonian principles.

In the Hebraic and Christian traditions, mortal error lay in transgressions of the moral law, but to the Greeks original sin was a lack of knowledge. The tragedy of Oedipus, in Sophocles' drama *Oedipus the King*, was his ignorance that did not permit him to know that he was murdering his father, marrying his mother, and begetting children who were also his own brothers. His downfall therefore came through his ignorance, and his fate was the price he had to pay for it. In *The Bacchae* the general theme was the conflict between the known and the unknown. Agave was led to murder her own son because she voluntarily surrendered her reason to an irrational cult. Her son Pentheus' downfall came because his reason was not strong enough to comprehend the emotional and irrational forces that motivated the lives of the members of his family and his subjects. In order to bring these factors under control they first had to be understood, and therefore he lacked the wisdom and tolerance necessary in a successful ruler. The entire Greek philosophical tradition concurred in the assumption that, without knowledge and the free exercise of the faculty of reason, there is no ultimate happiness for mankind.

It was also the Greeks who first realized that music, like the drama and other arts, was a mean between the divine madness of an inspired musician such as Orpheus and the solid mathematical basis on which the art rested acoustically. The element of inspiration had to be tempered by an orderly theoretical system that could demonstrate mathematically the arrangement of its melodic intervals and metrical proportions. Finally it should always be remembered that the chief deity of the city was Athena, goddess of knowledge and wisdom. Even a cult religion like that of Dionysus, through the Orphic and Pythagorean reforms, tended constantly in the direction of increased rationalism and abstract thought. While Athena, Dionysus, and Apollo were all born out of a myth, their destinies found a common culmination in the supreme rationalism of Socrates and Plato who eventually concluded that philosophy was the highest music.

Idealism

Running through all aspects of Athenian art and life was the idea that physical beauty and spiritual beauty were related, and that both somehow were intimately bound up with the moral order of the universe. The art of the Greeks was based on the conviction that if the subjective balance of body and spirit could be brought into harmony with the objective order of the real and ideal worlds, the result would enable man to scale the heights of moral grandeur. The Socratic theory of education, expressed in the balance between gymnastic for the body and music for the soul, was designed as a curriculum leading toward this end. The rulers of the state should also be guided by this principle, and Aristotle's definition of politics as the highest ethics was the political parallel of this theory. The Greek temple, the nobly proportioned sculptural figures, the hero of epic and tragedy, and the orderly relationships of the melodic intervals in music are one and all the embodiments of this ideal. Politician, priest, philosopher, poet, artist, and teacher all shared a common responsibility in trying to bring it closer to realization. As Socrates said: "Let our artists rather be those who are gifted to discern the true nature of the beautiful and graceful; then will our youth dwell in a land of health, amid fair sights and sounds, and receive the good in everything; and beauty, the effluence of fair works, shall flow into the eye and ear, like a health-giving breeze from a purer region, and insensibly draw the soul from earliest years into likeness and sympathy with the beauty of reason." [26]

If the real and ideal worlds are considered in the extreme sense to represent blind chaos as opposed to divine order, the proper course for man to

steer is one that leads from the actual toward the ideal. Through the cultivation of the humanistic disciplines the chaotic forces of man's existence
can be subdued and a seemingly unattainable perfection can be brought
closer. The process is based upon an optimistic world view, since in recognizing human limitations it nevertheless sets perfection as a goal. Plato's
Republic is, of course, an intellectual exercise in projecting an ideal state.
The author fully realizes that one did not exist in fact and probably never
would, but this did not lessen the value of the activity. "Would a painter
be any the worse," he asks, "because, after having delineated with consummate art an ideal of a perfectly beautiful man, he was unable to show
that any such man could ever have existed? . . . And is our theory a
worse theory because we are unable to prove the possibility of a city being
ordered in the manner described?" [27] The distinguishing characteristics of
idealism in art are clearly recognized by Aristotle when he says: "it follows
that we must represent men either as better than in real life, or as worse,
or as they are. It is the same in painting. Polygnotus depicted men as
nobler than they are, Pauson as less noble, Dionysius drew them true to
life. . . . So again in language, whether prose or verse unaccompanied by
music. Homer, for example, makes men better than they are; Cleophon as
they are; Hegemon the Thasian, the inventor of parodies, . . . worse
than they are." He also applies the same standard to drama pointing out
that "Comedy aims at representing men as worse, Tragedy as better than
in actual life." [28] In the visual arts the distinction, then, is between making
an idealized image, a realistic image, and a caricature; and it is clearly
implied that the one with which the true artist should concern himself is
the ideal. The Greek temple was thus an idealized dwelling place, and its
proportions were designed by the architects as a place fit for an idealized
being. By the logical interrelation of its lines, planes, and masses, it achieves
something of permanence and stability strongly in contrast with the ephemeral and haphazard state of nature. In the same spirit the sculptors avoided
representing the human being in infancy or old age, since these extremes of
immaturity and postmaturity implied incompleteness or imperfection and
hence were incompatible with the projection of ideal types. The range of
representations extends from athletes in their late teens; through images of
Hermes, Apollo, and Athena, who are conceived in their early maturity;
to Zeus, father of the gods, who appears as the fully developed patriarch in
all the power of mature manhood. It must also be remembered that few
of their subjects were intended to represent human beings as such. The
majority were fashioned to represent gods, who, if they were to be cast in
human form, must have bodies of transcendent beauty.

In some way even the intangible tones of music participated also in the ideal world by reason of the mathematical relationships on which they are based. A melody, therefore, had something more permanent than its fleeting nature might indicate. One of the main functions of the drama was to create ideal types, and while the typical was always opposed to the particular, yet somehow it arose from it. The interpretation of this interplay was assigned to the chorus, and the drama as a whole shared with the other arts the power of revealing how the permanent could be derived from the impermanent; how the formula could be extracted from the process of forming; an abiding quality distilled from the state of universal flux; the type found in the many particular cases; and the archetype in the types.

Conclusion

Athenian man could look backward historically or around him geographically without the slightest envy of any other human society. He did not attribute omnipotence either to his gods or rulers. He thought of his deities as immortal in the sense that they did not die; as being more powerful than himself, possessing more perfect bodies, and having better means of transportation. But they had limitations and hence needed man's help in bringing about a better world. Athenian man was, therefore, a proud being with a secure place in the living universe, sharing responsibility for direction of his world with the gods. He was also thoroughly at home in the realm of ideas, words, visual symbols, and tones. Through them he created the arts by which he was able to identify himself with his fellow citizens in striving toward well-defined, superindividual but humanistic ends.

The Socratic notion of truth, for instance, was not brought down from a mountain, or imposed from above by either god or man; it was evolved with practice and effort by the application of rational principles, in a dialectical, or give-and-take, process. Since his arts were addressed to other reasonable beings, they were more persuasive if they possessed the qualities of balance, order, and proportion than if they attempted to impress by the ponderous massiveness of a pyramid or the colossal height of a projected tower of Babel. His idealism found expression in a trinity made up of the eternal verities of truth, beauty, and goodness, each in its way a facet of the ideal oneness attainable by the mind of man. The approach to these ideals was not through mystical rites but through the processes of dialectics, aesthetics, and ethics. Through these avenues he could discern on the distant horizon an intellectual, beautiful, and moral living space, broad enough to insure the indefinite expansion of his institutions and arts into a sphere of excellence seldom equalled and never excelled by men before or since. Such, then, was the remarkable configuration of historical, economic, and artistic events that led to this unique flowering of culture.

C H A P T E R

||||||||||||||||||||||||||||||||||||||||||||||||||||||||||||||||||||||||||||||||||||||||||||||||||||||||||||||||||||||||

CHRONOLOGY: Pergamon, 2d Century B. C.

General Events

B. C.		
323	Death of Alexander the Great (356–323 B. C.)	
283 – 263	Philetaerus, military governor of Pergamon, established the Attalid dynasty	
263 – 241	Eumenes I, son of Eumenes the Brother of Philetaerus	
241 – 197	Attalus I	
	Assumed title of king after great victory over the Gauls of Galatia	
	Patron of the First School of Pergamene sculpture, which commemorated his victory over the Gauls	
222	Attalus I made alliance with the rising Roman power at a time when the fortunes of his kingdom were at a low ebb	
197 – 159	Eumenes II	
	Patron of the Second School of Pergamene Sculpture; founder of Pergamene Library	

c.180	Eumenes II commissioned the Great Altar of Zeus to celebrate his victory over the Gauls
	Power and glory of the city and kingdom of Pergamon at its height
159 – 138	Attalus II
	Patron of painting
	Material prosperity of the kingdom at its peak
146	Roman conquest of Greece
138 – 133	Attalus III
133	Pergamon willed to Rome by Attalus III
129	Pergamon organized as a Roman Province in Asia Minor

Philosophy

c.341–c.270	Epicurus, founder of Epicureanism
c.336–c.264	Zeno of Citium, founder of Stoicism
c.320	Aristoxenus of Tarentum, musical theorist, flourished

2

THE HELLENISTIC STYLE

PERGAMON, 2d CENTURY B. C.

Like the earlier city of Athens, Pergamon developed around its *acra*, which at first was a military stronghold and afterward the residence of its rulers and a sanctuary. The Pergamene acropolis was a geographical site with even greater natural advantages than that of Athens, and it played a significant role in the growth of the city. The town that grew around it was far enough from the Aegean Sea to assure its safety from a surprise naval attack, yet at the same time close enough to its harbor to permit the development of a thriving export trade. The fertile plain, formed by the confluence of three rivers, was easily defensible from the hill; and the city itself, surrounded as it was by the wide sea on one side and high mountains and precipitous ravines on the others, was impregnable except from its southern approach. Here, in a situation of unusual beauty, grew the city that was to play such an important role in the Hellenistic period.

As Greece moved away from the small but democratically enlightened city-state as its basic political unit—first to the larger and more autocratic form of kingdoms, then, finally, to the empire of Alexander the Great— its culture became progressively more and more cosmopolitan. With its great centers separated as widely as Syracuse on the island of Sicily, Alexandria on the banks of the Nile, and the cities of Asia Minor on the east coast of the Aegean, the thought and attitudes of the time became more varied and international in scope. The historical period covers the two centuries between the death of Alexander in 323 B. C. and the Roman conquest of Greece in 146 B. C. While the cultural leadership still belonged to the cities of the Greek mainland, the changes wrought by the conquered countries and peoples brought about a mixture of Greek and native influences. Hence the distinction is drawn between the earlier Hellenic and the later Hellenistic worlds.

In the Asia Minor region significant art centers developed at Antioch, Halicarnassus, Ephesus, on the island of Rhodes, and especially at Pergamon. The unique position held by the latter was largely owing to the energy and political sagacity of the Attalid kings, whose early recognition of the rising power of Rome led to an advantageous alliance with the city of the future. Pergamon was thus both an important center of civilization in its own right, and one of the principal bridges over which the Greek tradition passed into the Roman Empire.

The art of Greek city planning can be traced from about the middle of the 5th century B. C., when a broad strip of land was set aside as a processional highway at Athens. On holidays this thoroughfare was used as a ceremonial approach to the temples on the acropolis and as a means of facilitating the gathering of large crowds for games and spectacles; in daily life it was used as a road to and from the market place. Besides the thoughtful arrangement of buildings on the acropolis and this highway, planning in the city of Athens went no further. Its entire residential district was a haphazard collection of modest houses facing on crooked and narrow streets, which were dull and dusty by day and dark and damp by night. Even in the hallowed precinct of the acropolis, the buildings were planned separately with more attention paid to their individual logic and aesthetic fitness than to their relationship as a group. Each building, therefore, had a stately perfection of its own and existed independently rather than communally.

Aristotle mentions that Pericles commissioned Hippodamus to design a residential section for Piraeus, the port of Athens, which had a geometrical plan with wide streets crisscrossing one another at right angles. At the time it was apparently more of an exception than a rule, but with the rapid growth of new cities during the Hellenistic period the situation was reversed. When Polybius was describing the layout of a Roman military encampment about 150 B. C., he wrote that it was "four-sided and equal-sided, while details of its street planning and its general arrangement are precisely parallel to those of a city." [1] From this it is evident that he was comparing it with the normal plan of a Greek city of his time. A little later St. John was describing his ideal city, the new and heavenly Jerusalem, which was surrounded by a great wall with twelve gates, three on each side. "And the city," he wrote, "lieth foursquare, and the length is as large as the breadth" (Rev. 21:16).

Instead of allowing for the irregularities of nature and taking advantage of normal ground contours, the Hellenistic attitude, as seen in the plan of Priene, involved the imposition of a preconceived geometrical scheme on the site. In this Asia Minor city, which is not far from Pergamon, the streets ran due north and south and were crossed by others running east and west, thus enclosing square blocks for houses very much in accordance with many modern cities. So rigidly was this gridiron pattern carried out that some of the steep hilly streets could by negotiated only by precipitous stairways. While the residential sections of the ancient city of Pergamon have not yet been excavated, it is inferred that they must have followed some such regular system. Under Eumenes II the city reached its largest extent, and the thick wall he built around it enclosed over 200 acres of ground—more than four times the territory included by his predecessor. A system of ducts brought in an ample water supply from the nearby mountain springs. This system, the greatest of its kind before the Roman aqueducts, was on a sufficient scale to provide for the needs of a large metropolitan area whose population has been estimated at about 120,000.

The main entrance to Pergamon was from the south through an impressive arched gateway topped by a pediment with a triglyph frieze. Traffic was diverted through several vaulted portals that led into a square, where there was a fountain for the refreshment of travelers. From here the road led past the humbler dwelling places toward the large lower market place, which bustled with the activities of peddlers and hucksters of all sorts. This market was built in the form of a large open square surrounded on three sides by a two-story colonnade enclosing rows of rooms that served for shops. Moving onward, the road went past buildings that housed the workshops and mills in which pottery, tiles, and textiles were produced. Homes of the wealthier citizens were located on promontories off the main streets overlooking the rest of the city. At the foot of the acropolis another square opened up, which could boast of the large city fountain and a fine view.

Rising almost 1000 feet above the surrounding countryside was the acropolis, a commanding citadel that ranked among the most imposing in the Greek world. Up the slopes of the hill, on a system of rising levels supported by massive retaining walls and fortifications, were the buildings and artifacts that gave the city its reputation as a second Athens. By ingenious use of its natural contours, the Pergamenes had developed settings for a number of buildings, which were not only outstanding as individual entities but which, by means of connecting roadways, ramps, and open courtyards, were grouped into a harmonious whole. Here on a succession of rising levels were gymnasiums, athletic fields, temples, assembly places, public squares, wooded groves, and an amphitheater. Above them all, flanked by watch towers, barracks, arsenals, storage houses, and spacious gardens, stood the royal residence. Thus in one concentrated location were grouped the places where the people of Pergamon carried on their civic business, recreated themselves, honored their king, and worshiped their gods.

ARCHITECTURE

On the three lowest of these artificially created terraces of the Pergamene acropolis were a series of open grounds, enclosed by colonnades and buildings, which comprised a triple gymnasium—one for each general age level. The spacious outdoor areas included a playground for boys, an athletic field, and a race course. Provision was also made for baths and indoor sports. And, as the educational center of the city, the gymnasium included classrooms and lecture halls as well. At various points sculptured figures of youths in attitudes associated with sports were found in niches. On marble pedestals stood statues of such mythical heroes as Asclepius, son of Apollo and physician of the gods, and of Hygeia, his daughter, who was guardian of the health of growing youths. Nearby was a small temple dedicated to one of the patron deities of sports, possibly Hermes, the fleet-footed messenger of the gods, or Heracles, mythological paragon of strength. Statues of Nike, goddess of victory, altars for votive offerings, and the names of prominent athletes who won the contests held at Olympia and other Greek centers have also been found there. Such Hellenistic gymnasiums were the prototypes of the later Roman baths.

Along the hillside above the gymnasium a ramp ascended to the next level on which the upper agora, or market place, was located. This open square, surrounded by porticos, served both as an assembly place and a market where such merchandise as pottery and textiles were sold.

The three remaining terraced levels, as can be seen in the restorations (Fig. 2:1), were grouped around the crest of the hill. Together they formed a stately semicircle running from the south at the lower left, where stood the Altar of Zeus, to the northern plateau on the top, where the palace of the kings was located. Midway is the precinct sacred to Athena, where her temple and the great Pergamene library were found, and in the crescent-shaped ravine below was the theater.

Through the propylon, which can be seen below center of the lower restoration, entrance was made to the wide marble-paved terrace at the left on which stood the Great Altar of Zeus. Dating from about 180 B. C., this artistic triumph of the Eumenian period shared with such monuments

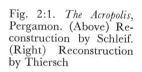
Fig. 2:1. *The Acropolis,* Pergamon. (Above) Reconstruction by Schleif. (Right) Reconstruction by Thiersch

as the pyramids, the hanging gardens of Babylon, the Parthenon, the temple of Artemis at Ephesus, the lighthouse at Alexandria, the mausoleum at Halicarnassus, and the Colossus of Rhodes, the distinction of being one of the Seven Wonders of the ancient world. Since both the structure and sculptures of this building are of major importance, it will be discussed in detail in the following section.

The next level, which is about 80 feet above the altar, was approached by means of ramps and stairways. This was the precinct dedicated to Athena Polias, patroness of Pergamon. The shrine of this goddess, who sprang fully armed from the head of Zeus, can be seen in the restoration hovering appropriately enough immediately above the altar dedicated to him. It is a graceful hexastyle temple, simple in structure, with six Doric columns at each end and ten on the sides. Above these ran a triglyph frieze with blank metopes and two sculptured pediments. In the courtyard at the side of the temple were placed the monuments and trophies commissioned by Eumenes' father, Attalus I, to celebrate his victories over the Gauls. The temple itself dates back to the founder of the dynasty and was built about the time of Alexander the Great. The L-shaped colonnade which framed it on two sides, however, was contemporary with the great altar and thus falls within the reign of Eumenes II. It was a two-story affair, with Doric columns 17 feet in height on the ground level, and those of the Ionic order continuing onward 11 feet above. Besides its function as a framework for the temple and courtyard, it formed the frontispiece of the great library of Pergamon. Behind the colonnade on the second-story level were the four rooms, totaling about 145 feet in length and 47 feet in width, in which the most precious part of the library was housed. It was symbolically appropriate that the library should be located in the precinct of Athena and thus be associated with the goddess of reason, contemplation, and wisdom. On its collective stone shelves, some of which are still extant, rested the ancient scrolls that have been estimated to have numbered about 200,000 volumes in the time of the Attalids. The Pergamon library ranked with that of Alexandria as one of the two greatest libraries of antiquity. Later, after the major portion of the Alexandrine collection of 500,000 volumes had been burned in an uprising against Caesar, Antony presented the entire library of Pergamon to Cleopatra as a gift.

One of the principal industries of the city, incidentally, was that of the preparation of the skins of sheep and calves for writing purposes. The product was called by the Romans *pergamena*, from which are derived our English words *pergameneous* and *parchment*. Thus the very name of the city, as well as one of its main products, was synonymous with writing materials and books. Parchment still continues to be identified with scholarship and learning in the traditional sheepskins of college diplomas. A great commercial as well as scholarly rivalry raged in ancient times over the comparative merits of Alexandrian papyrus, or paper, and the Pergamenian sheepskin, or parchment. Owing to its greater enduring powers, posterity has overwhelmingly endorsed the superiority of parchment.

Below the Athena precinct on a spacious terrace stood the theater (Fig. 2:2), which was constructed under Eumenes II about 170 B. C. It had a flat circular section known as the orchestra, in the middle of which was a small altar dedicated to Dionysus. The section known as the auditorium rose 122 feet up the slope of the hill in a series of semicircular curves. The 78 tiers of stone seats were sufficient to accommodate some 10,000 spectators. From the auditorium the audience overlooked the orchestra toward the proscenium, a rectangular stage in the form of a portico or temple façade. Since the principal action of the play took place in the

Fig. 2:2. *Theater at Pergamon*, Auditorium. *c*.170 B. C.

orchestra, this scenery building performed the function of enclosing this space, and acted as a sounding board to facilitate the audibility of the actors. Its higher level also provided the space for the appearances of the gods in the course of the drama. Above this building the audience could catch a glimpse of the gleaming Aegean Sea beyond which lay the historic shores of the Greek peninsula.

Glancing upward from the orchestra, the principal groups of acropolis buildings could be seen spreading out like a fan. On the right was the great altar, in the center the temple of Athena and the library, and on the plateau at the left were the fortifications and buildings of the royal palace. Just as the Attalid kings dominated the life of their city and constituted the apex of the social pyramid of their kingdom, their royal residence crowned the highest point in their capital city. Later, when the realm came under the domination of Rome, the royal palace was replaced by a large Corinthian temple in honor of the Emperor Trajan. From their hilltop summit the kings of Pergamon could survey much of their rich domain. From the mountains to the north came the silver and copper that furnished them with the metal for their coins—so necessary in promoting trade and paying their soldiers. From the same region came also their supplies of pitch, tar, and timber—so much in demand for the building of ships—as well as the marble for their buildings and sculptures. A panorama thus unfolded around them, starting with the heights of Mount Ida and the surrounding range (down whose slopes flowed the streams that watered the fertile valleys and broad plains), all the way to the bright waters of the shining Aegean.

The residence generally referred to as the royal palace was in actuality a loose constellation of small buildings set amid wooded groves and gardens, which shifted from time to time with the changing fortunes and dignities of the kings. At its grandest it was, in view of the proverbial wealth of the Attalids, a comparatively modest residence no more pretentious than some of the better houses of Pompeii. The group included units of living rooms opening out into peristyle halls, courtyards surrounded by porticos, rooms devoted to the dynastic cult, a barracks for the royal guard, a treasury, and various storerooms for goods, grain, and arms. Bound by the long cultural tradition in the building of their temples, the Hellenistic architects were most inventive in such secular structures as these.

Unfortunately all the important examples of Hellenistic domestic architecture have perished with the ravages of time. Since they constituted but a link in the unbroken evolutionary chain of Mediterranean architecture, it is not difficult to reconstruct them on the basis of later models. From the excavations made of this group at Pergamon, it is clear that such royal residences as this, in addition to others at Alexandria and Antioch, were the prototypes for the future villas of the wealthy Romans. Outlines and fragments of the palace group have been sufficiently identified to clarify the successive stages of these buildings under the various Attalid kings. A faint idea of the decorative scheme of the palace at the time of Eumenes II can be seen in the two mosaic panels which were found there (Fig. 2:11).

This residential group apparently followed a plan similar to that of the palace of the Ptolemies at Alexandria, which was renowned as the epitome of Mediterranean luxury. The Attalids by later standards lived comparatively simply in view of their vast wealth. "Rich as an Attalid" was the phrase used by Horace long after their rule was over; and along with that of Croesus, their family name was used widely as a synonym for fabulous riches. Their love of display took on the more external form of the great public buildings they erected and in the ostentatious gifts they made to cities, such as Athens and Rome. More important to the Attalid kings than the size and luxury of their dwelling was the close link with the temples of the gods that the location afforded. Both symbolically and practically their residence was located here in order to dominate the city that spread out below them. From there all eyes would be attracted to the magnificent group of edifices, thus causing the populace to look upward both psychologically as well as actually toward the place of the kings and gods who ruled over their lives.

The planning of the town thus cleverly promoted the idea of the mon-archy towering above it. There, topographically as well as politically, stood the king, aloof from his people and associated with the gods. Even while living he was accorded some divine prerogatives, such as a cult statue with perfumed grain burning on an altar before it and an annual celebration in his honor. This semidivine status was connected with his right to rule and served the practical social purposes of commanding obedience to his laws; facilitating the collection of taxes, often under the guise of offerings to the gods; and uniting the cosmopolitan groups of races and factions who lived under him. Assisting in this deification process were the intellectuals and artists he attracted to his court, whose works were regarded by the multi-tude with awe. The vast impressiveness of the architecture and sculpture was enough to overwhelm native and foreigner alike.

Certain architectural advancements are apparent in such domestic buildings as the palace and also in the modifications that were made here in the basic Greek building system. From excavations in and around the city substantial evidence has been accumulated that in this Hellenistic city a significant departure was made from the post-and-lintel construction of the earlier period. Examples have been found in the arched city gates and in underground tombs dating from the time of Eumenes II. These show quite unmistakably that the principle of arch-and-vault construction was both understood and widely practiced. Thus, architecturally as well as culturally Pergamon forms the link between the Greek and Roman periods. In general, however, the architecture stayed with the traditional forms in the case of temples, which tended more and more toward greater delicacy and ornateness. The columns became thinner and taller; greater elegance, a love of luxury and decoration for its own sake were in the ascendancy over dignity and restraint.

The pomp and theatrical display that was the tenor of Hellenistic life was a distinct departure from the simplicity and nobility of the more austere 5th century. Grandeur became the grandiose, and many of the monuments were built with the idea of glorifying the reign of a king who thought of himself in superhuman terms. The accent was away from the abstract idealism and universality of the earlier period and was moving toward the aggrandizement of a single individual. Such was the picture of the brilliant city of Eumenes II, one of the most beautiful of the Greek world, filled literally with thousands of statues, sculptured reliefs, painted murals, and books and peopled with philosophers, athletes, writers, scholars, and artisans living a life of luxury and devoted to the pursuit of pleasure.

SCULPTURE

While sculptural works of all kinds are known to have existed in profusion throughout the city of Pergamon, the examples that claim the attention of posterity were located on two of the terraces of the acropolis. In the Athena precinct just below the palace, bounded by the temple on one side and the portico of the library on the others, was a spacious courtyard in which Attalus I erected the sculptural monuments celebrating his victories. The groups he commissioned were in place during the last quarter of the 3d century B. C. On the terrace below, a generation later in the first quarter of the 2d century B. C., his son and successor Eumenes II built the Altar of Zeus (Fig. 2:5) with its great frieze. Historically the two periods have been distinguished as the First and Second schools of Pergamon, but since they were separated by less than half a century, it is possible that some of the same sculptors may have worked on both projects. The bronze originals of the First School have all disappeared and can be studied only in the marble copies made by later Hellenistic or Roman artists. Owing to the fortunate results of the late 19th-century German excavations, many of the sculptures from the Second School may be seen in the originals.[2]

The principal works of the First School were two large monuments in bronze, each of which was composed of many figures. One commemorated the victories of Attalus over the neighboring Seleucid kingdom, but only a few details of this group survive. The other honored his earlier and greater victory over the strange wild tribes of Gauls, who swept down from Europe across the Hellespont into the region north of Pergamon. From this province, which was called Galatia after them, they were a constant threat to the Greek cities lying to the south. While his predecessor had bought them off by paying tribute, Attalus I refused this expedient and met their subsequent invasion with an army. The great battle was fought about 30 miles to the east of his city, and the outcome was decisive enough to drive back the Gauls for a generation. The consequences were felt far and wide, and all the cities and kingdoms of the Greek world breathed a little easier.

The ferocious Gauls had inspired such general terror that their defeat was associated in the popular mind with something of a supernatural character. The name of Attalus was everywhere acclaimed as *Soter* (Savior), and after incorporating the lands he had gained into a unit, he assumed the title of king. Thereafter, as King Attalus the Savior, he continued to capitalize on his fortunes by embarking on a program of beautifying his city with the services of the best available Greek artists. Sharing the same patroness, Pergamon proudly began to bear the appellation of a second Athens, and its ruler that of a political and cultural champion of Hellenism over the barbarians. Not content with adding to the renown only of his own city, Attalus made donations of treasure and works of art to other Greek centers, especially Athens. There he paid his tribute to the ancient capital by erecting on its acropolis a monument celebrating the four great Greek victories—that of the gods over the giants; the early Greeks over the Amazons; the 5th-century Athenians over the Persians; and, of course, his own over the Gauls—thus linking his kingdom more closely with the long unbroken chain of Greek culture. The copies and fragments of struggling giants, dead Amazons, wounded Persians, and dying Gauls that have been found all over the Mediterranean region testify to the fame of this group. It is a curious commentary on the taste and temper of these times that replicas only of the unfortunate victims were made, while the proud victors, probably riding in triumph on horseback, apparently held no interest. At Pergamon, however, Attalus' monument was devoted solely to the occasion in which he was the winner. It was a large collective group that rested on a circular platform some 10 feet in diameter. In the center rose a cylindrical base, about 7 feet high, on which were placed the victorious Pergamenes and their leader, while their vanquished opponents were found below on three lower steps which radiated outward from it. Parts of the monument are to be seen in numerous museums, the two most famous of which are the *Dying Gaul*, and the *Gaul and His Wife*.

The *Dying Gaul* (Fig. 2:3)—often erroneously called the *Dying Gladiator* because it was the inspiration of Byron's poem of that name—is a fine example of Hellenistic pathos. The mortally wounded warrior has agonizingly dragged himself out of the thick of the battle to struggle alone against death to the last. His dying eyes are fixed on the ground where the trumpet he has sounded for aid and other pieces of his equipment are lying. He supports himself weakly with one arm, proud and defiant to the end, while his life's blood is slowly flowing out of the gaping wound in his side. The anguished expression in the handsome face is portrayed with an intensity not hitherto encountered in Greek art. The strong but rude musculature of his powerful body, so different from that of the supple Greek athletes, mark him as a barbarian. Further contrast is found in his hair, which is greased so heavily that it is almost as thick as a horse's mane; in the moustache, which was never worn by the Greeks or Romans; and in the collar of twisted gold worn around his neck. All these carefully recorded details show the interest of the period in individuals as such, in racial distinctions, and, above all, in the artist's desire to awaken the sympathies of

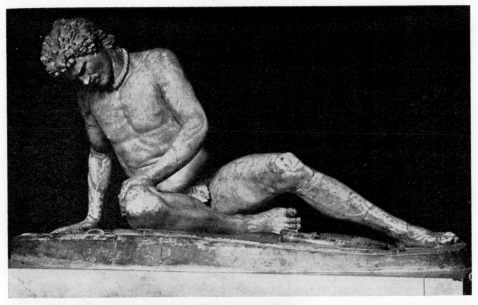

Fig. 2:3. *Dying Gaul*. Marble. 6′ 3″ long. Roman copy after Bronze original of *c.*225 B. C. Capitoline Museum, Rome (Anderson)

Fig. 2:4. *Gaul and His Wife*. Marble. Roman copy after Bronze original of *c.*225 B. C. Terme Museum, Rome (Alinari)

the observer. The sculptor thus invites by the process of empathy the involvement of the observer in the situation. The contemporary audience would have felt both attraction and repulsion toward such a subject and hence would have experienced a strong emotional reaction. The litter of the battlefield beside him, as well as other realistic details, is not used so much for their own sake as to convey a sense of immediacy in the experience of the beholder. At the same time the observer was invited to look beyond the physical wounds and behold the real inner conflict in the wounded spirit of the proud warrior, which is seen in his reluctance to accept his fate. The use of this type of realism helps to convey the essential spiritual anguish of defeat.

The expressive impact of the *Gaul and His Wife* (Fig. 2:4) is no less strong. The custom of the Gauls was to take their women and children with them on their campaigns. Realizing his defeat, and too proud to be taken a slave, he has just killed his wife and is looking apprehensively over his shoulder at the approaching enemy as he plunges his sword into his own neck. The mood of despair is heightened by the sweeping lines of the woman's drapery, which droops downward in deep folds and casts dark shadows. In both these surviving representations strong feeling is aroused by the noble figures who stare death so courageously in the face.

To the Second School of Pergamon are assigned all the works that fall within the reign of Eumenes II, the master builder under whom Pergamon achieved the highest point of its power and glory. Like his father before him, he too had his victories over the Gauls, and he continued the tradition of erecting votive works with the Altar of Zeus (Fig. 2:5). It is at once the greatest single monument of the city and one of the few top-ranking works of the Hellenistic period. It too was intended to glorify the position of the king and to impress the entire Greek world with his contribution to the cause of Hellenism in the struggle against the barbarians. Because of the assiduous efforts of the German excavators, it is possible to appraise the work of this period from the originals. Beginning in 1878, piece by piece each fragment was painstakingly unearthed, diligently investigated, and after a half-century of study, the entire monument was reassembled and reconstructed in the Pergamon Museum in Berlin, where it stood until the beginning of World War II. Famed throughout the ancient world, it is even mentioned in the Revelation of St. John (2:13) when he refers to Pergamon as the place "where Satan's seat is." Undoubtedly the reference was prompted by the resemblance of the structure to an immense throne and by the statuary of the frieze depicting mythological deities and such fabulous creatures as the enormous serpents.

While the principal interest is focused on the sculpture, the building itself has also a claim to architectural importance. It should be pointed out that to speak of the whole as being the altar is inaccurate. The altar was actually the comparatively small platform on which the flesh of the sacrificial animals and other offerings were burned. It was located in the open inner court which was approached by the broad front stairway. Only a few fragments of this altar remain; and the structure which enclosed it, as seen in the Berlin restoration, is technically called a *temenos*. The sacrificial altar, then, stood on a huge solid podium, 18 feet high, 120 feet wide, and 112 feet long. The inner court was surrounded by an Ionic colonnade that extended outward beyond the court to flank the stairway with projecting tongues on either side. Above the colonnade was a friezeless entablature with a dentil range underneath the roofing, and crowning the whole was a series of free-standing statues of gods and mythological animals placed at various points along the outer edges of the roof. Around the outside of the platform below were four steps, above which was the most noteworthy aspect of the whole structure—the great frieze, over 7 feet in height with figures in high relief. It ran continuously around the entire podium and extended inward on either side of the stairway, diminishing in height as the steps rose (Fig. 2:6). It was framed below by a molding and above by a second dentil range under a ledge that projected far enough over the frieze to protect it from the elements.

The structure reveals a distinct difference from the 5th-century concept of space and spatial movement against a plane. In the earlier period the altar was placed outside the temple and the ritual took place against the background of the exterior colonnades. The Hellenistic concept of space, by way of contrast, shows an interest in depth. In the case of the Altar of Zeus the spectator looked not toward a flat background but toward the interior of the courtyard that enclosed the altar. The wider space between the columns also invited the eye into the interior, whereas the closer intercolumniation of the 5th century promoted the continuity of the plane. Since the Hellenistic concept uses the same structural members as the previous Greek style, it is more an evolution from the 5th century than a departure. The columns, entablatures, and interior walls, consistent with the Greek tradition, clearly define the spatial limits, and there is as yet no hint of the unbounded or infinite.

The general effect produced by the Altar of Zeus as a whole is that of a traditional Greek temple—the Parthenon, for example—turned upside down. The simple dignity of the Doric temple depended upon its structural integrity. In a very logical manner the architrave and frieze rested on the

Fig. 2:5. *Altar of Zeus*, Pergamon. Marble. 120′ wide, 112′ long. Podium, including Frieze, 18′ high. *c.*180 B. C. Pergamon Museum, Berlin (Marburg)

columns, which served as supports for all the upper members. Part of its
harmonious effect depended on the fact that all its structural organization
was apparent and visible. Here at Pergamon, however, the traditional
structure is inverted. Since the frieze is considered more important, it appears below, where it can be apprehended more easily at the eye level;
above it, for the sake of tradition, appears the colonnade without any
visible structural purpose. Hence it is clear that structurality as a guiding
principle has yielded to decoration for its own sake, and the art of architecture has in effect given way to that of sculpture. In the case of the
Parthenon the decorative frieze is included to give some variety to what
might otherwise have been a monotonous unity. The Altar of Zeus, on the
other hand, with the overwhelming variety of a frieze almost 450 feet long,
needs a colonnade to preserve the unity. The quiet Greek architectural
drama, in other words, has now become an architectonic melodrama.

The subject of the frieze is the familiar one of the Gigantomachy, or battle
of the gods and giants. The usual frieze, even in Hellenistic times, included
only the 12 Olympian deities battling against the giants, which was quite
enough to populate the allotted space. The unprecedented length of this
frieze, however, demanded a correspondingly larger number of figures. It
seems certain that the scholars of the library must have been called upon
to compile a complete catalogue of divinities in order to have enough to
fill the colossal length and breadth of space in such a frieze. The attributes
of the gods, their attendants, and the objects associated with them were
provided as visual footnotes, so to speak, so that they could be identified.
To the average citizen of Pergamon this pantheon must have seemed quite
bewildering, as many of the depicted deities were beyond his range of
knowledge. The situation had to be remedied by placing the names of the
figures above their heads like labels, an expedient which proved of inestimable value in their reconstruction and interpretation. Further intellectual
influence is found in the allegorizing of the ancient themes. Literal belief
in the gods as such was pretty much a thing of the past, and the local
scholars and Stoic philosophers had already interpreted them as personifications of the forces of nature. In contrast to the almost morbid preoccupation with pain in the earlier Pergamene sculpture, the action of the gods
against the giants is carried out in this case with dispatch and abandon.
The mood is lightened and the giants are slain with something approaching
gaiety. The reaction of the viewer is correspondingly one of wonder and
admiration for the marvelous ingeniousness of the gods and the fantastic
variety of their weapons and modes of warfare, instead of sympathy for
their victims. The great mythological battle also alludes to the war be-

tween the Pergamenes and the Gauls, but it is now told in symbolic terms, and the Pergamenes have become superhuman figures, while the Gauls are grotesque monsters. Instead of the frank realism of the previous generation, the tale is told in a sweeping composition that uses a visual language of extreme grandiloquence.

On the inner part of the podium, facing the stairs, the action begins with the divinities of the earth who are summoned forth to take part in the great struggle which is to decide the overlordship of the world. Zeus and his fellow gods are locked in mortal conflict with his father Chronus, who is supported by the wicked titans. Moving outward along the tongue parallel with the stairs, the action proceeds along the south. This side, which was exposed to the brightest sunlight, depicted the giants as forces of darkness in conflict with the spirits of light. Here Helios, the sun god, is shown as a charioteer drawn by four horses. Fighting with him are Hemera, the winged goddess of day, her brother Aether, the goddess of the moon and others. With this side the transition is made to the realm of the sky, and around the corner on the east, as the climax of the composition, the Olympian deities themselves are found. First among them is Hecate, accompanied by her dog who is biting off a piece of a giant. Next is Artemis, the heavenly huntress, who fells her foe with one of her arrows. Then comes Zeus himself to whom the altar was dedicated. He is depicted with Heracles, the father of Telephus who was the legendary founder of Pergamon. In keeping with his Olympian stature, Zeus is the only one who is opposed by three titans. In a series of four slabs (Fig. 2:7), his powerful figure, wrapped in his swirling mantle, is seen in the second, where he is standing back in order to smite all three at once with his spear and thunderbolts. While most of his arm is missing, the hand is seen in the upper left corner of the panel. The giant in the lower left has been overcome by a thunderbolt, pieces of which have pierced his thigh. It is depicted as a pointed spear with a handle ending in acanthus leaves. The second giant is on his other side quavering before the blow falls, his body tense with terror. In the slab to the right Porphyrion, king of the giants, is shown from the back. From his animal ears to his serpent legs, he is a fearsome sight as he shields himself with a lion's skin both from Zeus' eagle above him and from the thunderbolts.

Nearby was the fine group depicting the part played by Athena, the protectress of the city (Fig. 2:8). Her figure is shown in the second slab, with a shield on her left arm while her right hand grasps a winged giant by the hair. Invulnerable in his native earthly haunts, she pulls him upward so that he loses his strength, and her faithful serpent can inflict the

Fig. 2:6. Altar of Zeus, Detail, *West Bastion*, *c.*180 B. C. Pergamon Museum, Berlin (Titzenthaler)

Fig. 2:7. Detail of Frieze. *Zeus Hurling Thunderbolts*. Marble. 7′ 10″ high. Pergamon Museum, Berlin (Staatliche Bildstelle)

Fig. 2:8. Detail of Frieze. *Athena Slaying a Giant*. Marble. 7′ 10″ high. Pergamon Museum Berlin (Staatliche Bildstelle)

Fig. 2:9. Detail of Frieze. *Styx* (?) *Throwing Jar of Snakes*. Marble. 7′ 10″ high. Pergamon Museum, Berlin (Altertümer von Pergamon)

mortal wound. The snake is shown coiling around him and sinking its fangs into the giant's chest. A moment of pathos is provided by his gesture pleading for the help of his mother, the earth goddess Ge, or Gaea. Even though she is on the side of the gods, the eyes of the earth mother implore Athena to spare the life of her rebellious son. Ge's attributes are seen in the horn of plenty she carries in her left hand, a cornucopia filled with the rich fruits of the earth—apples, pomegranates, and grapes with vine leaves and a pine cone. Over her hovers the goddess Nike, symbolizing the fact that Athena is ever victorious. Among Athena's other attributes are seen the serpents that were sacred to her, two of which extend themselves around her waist as a girdle.

From this climax in the sky, the action on the shadowy north side gradually descends into the realm of the water spirits, who drive the fleeing giants around the other corner of the stairway into the sea where they drown. Here are the representations of marine animals, water nymphs, various sea gods, and personifications of the rivers of Greece. Among the latter is a goddess who is generally identified as Styx (Fig. 2:9), the spirit of the river that separates the realm of the living and the dead. In her hand is a jar of snakes which she is about to hurl against her adversary. It is possible that reference is made here to an incident in a naval battle in which the fleet of Eumenes II was opposed by that of the famous Hannibal. The Carthaginians resorted to a unique method of warfare by collecting poisonous snakes, packing them in terra cotta jars, and hurling them onto the decks of the Pergamene ships. Finding their vessel filled with writhing serpents, the sailors jumped overboard and swam for the shore. This historical episode, while not very flattering to local pride, was nevertheless in keeping with the theme of the frieze. At any rate this fine figure, with her flowing drapery and vigorous attitude, is one of the best realized of the entire frieze. Around the face of the west side and up the stairs are other creatures of the sea. The tumultuous action thus opens and closes on the terrestrial plane, starting on the other side of the stairway with the divinities of the land and ending here with those of the sea. They are separated by the expanse of the wide steps, as well as their roles at the beginning and the end of the dramatic conflict.

The frieze as a whole is a technical *tour de force* of the first magnitude. The skillful high-relief carving alone indicates the presence of virtuoso sculptors. While the names of a dozen of these sculptors have been found inscribed around the molding underneath the frieze, the name of the master designer remains unknown. In the case of the Parthenon frieze there were metopes depicting action alternating with triglyphs which arrested it, while here there is more than 400 feet of continuous action. The unity does not depend on a regular rhythm of points of motion alternating with those of repose, but in the continuity of the movement itself. It is a minor miracle how all these intensely struggling forms can be represented with such dynamic force without at the same time flying off in all directions. Of necessity, the whole breaks down into smaller groups that are united by the means of the coiling snakes. As a plastic device they can be made to fill any empty space with some plausibility. Furthermore, they can be shown in any position and thus become the connecting element of the composition by leading the eye from one group to another. Winding in and out and around, they help to impart the sensation of continuous writhing motion.

The imaginative and emotional range encompassed by the frieze is enormous. The forms of the giants, for instance, vary from those which are entirely human and closely resemble the Gallic types of the earlier period, to monsters with enormous wings, animal heads, snaky locks, long tails, and serpentine legs. They recall the profusion of grotesque prehistoric creatures who inhabited the primordial world. Their wild unkempt appearances intensify their uncontrolled cries of pain. As a consequence the reaction of the contemporary audience must have ranged from curiosity and wonder to fear and terror. A sense of horror at the spectacle of such bestialized forms must have melted to sympathy when the earth mother pleads for the life of her unruly offspring and then into laughter at the antics of the clumsy and inept giants. By contrast the gods would have commanded admiration; while they have lost their traditional serenity, they still have everything well under control.

Decorating the inner wall of the colonnade, and facing the court where the altar stood, was a smaller and less-pretentious frieze carved in low relief. It is generally referred to as the Telephus frieze, since it told the story of that mythical founder of the city who was claimed as an ancestor by the Attalids. The extant remains are so severely damaged that they do not hold the aesthetic interest of the great frieze. Dating from the last years of the reign of Eumenes II, its principal claim to fame lies in the telling of its legend in a series of episodes that follow in chronological sequence and shift accordingly in geographical location. The narration of the myth is handled in the manner of an epic poem, and its composition and design show unmistakable signs of literary influence.

The action is cyclical and moves against a variable background which includes outlines of mountains, rocks, trees, and such architectural details as columns and pilasters. By these means the changes of scene are indicated. The pictorial backgrounds, which were both carved and painted, are a clear attempt to use perspective and are thus designed to convey the impression of depth, with the human figures in the foreground moving against an architectural or landscape background. It is the earliest known example of such treatment and points in the direction of the later Roman narrative friezes, such as that on the Column of Trajan (Fig. 3:22). By attempting to overcome the previous limitations of unified space and time, the art of sculpture was on its way to becoming more pictorial. The large frieze had prevented the breaking down of its subject matter into episodes by connecting the groups visually by means of the coiling serpents and the avoidance of a specific background, which would have suggested temporal and spatial differentiations. In the Telephus frieze, however, unity in time is broken down by the sequence of biographical events from early youth to manhood; and unity in space, by a richly varied background. The art was thus brought closer to the psychological experience of the observer and hence becomes yet another aspect of the growth of realism.

In the work of the Second School, especially in the great frieze, the element of pathos is again accented. It is not created so simply and directly as in the examples from the earlier period, but it tends to be reduced to a formula, put on the stage, and done with sweeping motion, theatrical gesticulations, and histrionic posturings. The functional strength of the Dying Gaul has become the Herculean power of the professional strong man who is more at home in the circus than on the battlefield. The ferocious attitudes, wildly fluttering drapery, massive muscles, scenes of violence, and general stress and strain, all produce the effect of a colossal spectacle, and therefore tend to command more awe than sympathy. Yet, as in good theater, opposites are skillfully juxtaposed, such as the graceful figure of Styx and the other beautiful feminine forms found in the midst of the bloody battlefield.

The simple realism of the First School has become exaggeration. The overdeveloped muscles of some of the figures are anatomically correct, but they sometimes seem more like the specimens of a scientific inquiry than the believable creations of artists. Details of the costumes, such as the sandals and shoes, are expertly handled. Embellishments, such as buckles, are polished so as to resemble metal; textiles are carved with deep folds in order to convey the quality of silk; and saddles are made to simulate the texture of leather. There is thus no doubt about the complete mastery the artists had of their medium. In the Telephus frieze the veins in the leaves and their various shapes distinguish plane trees, for instance, from oaks. The classical unity of place and time, in which an entire drama unfolds in one location and within the span of a day, conveys a sense of aesthetic satisfaction, but it is nevertheless stylized and unreal. Human experience involves both time sequences and shifts of locale, hence their inclusion in the Telephus frieze brought it, as a work of art, closer to reality.

Previously in the case of the whole structure of the Altar of Zeus, it was pointed out that the perception of depth entered into the architectural composition with the eye being drawn into an enclosed interior. In the case of the sculpture the eye does not move only from side to side, as in a plane, but is constantly led back and forth into spatial depth. The marble background is no longer a solid boundary but dissolves into atmosphere. To escape the plane, some of the figures of the great frieze are in such high relief as to be almost in the round, others even step outward from the frieze and support themselves by kneeling on the edge of the steps (Fig. 2:6). The heavy shadows cast by the high-relief carving further intensifies this effect. While it is known that the frieze was painted in vivid color, it is not certain whether the background of the large frieze was done with painted landscapes. There is no doubt about the smaller Telephus frieze, which was definitely intended to be so painted. At any rate the logical coloring for the Olympian section of the great frieze would have been blue to suggest the sky, a color which would have promoted the effect of recession in depth. Thus the two-dimensional plane of the Hellenic style was expanded here into a three-dimensional composition in depth, which promoted the perception of forward and backward movement.

A general comparison with the Athenian art of the 5th century B. C. brings out an impression of discord rather than harmony; a magnitude which overwhelms rather than dimensions that can be contained and comprehended; a wild emotionalism in the place of controlled action and reaction; virtuosity triumphing over dignified refinement; melodrama superseding drama; variety in ascendance over unity. The Athenian culture, in short, placed its trust in man; the Hellenistic period, in superman. No longer the master of his fate, Hellenistic man is now engulfed in the storms and stresses of grim circumstances beyond his control.

PAINTING, MOSAICS, AND THE MINOR ARTS

Owing to the enduring qualities of stone, more sculptural works from ancient times have come down to us intact and in greater quantity than works in any other form. Buildings were torn down for their materials and replaced by others. Statues in bronze, precious metal, and ivory were intrinsically too valuable to survive as such. The libraries of antiquity have either been burned, or their books have disintegrated in the course of time, so that they come down through the ages only in imperfect copies made by medieval scribes or as quotations in other volumes. The musical notation contained in ancient manuscripts was not understood by these copyists and eventually was omitted altogether. Mosaics, pottery, and other such works were either broken up or carried off by conquerors and collectors. Of all the major visual arts in antiquity, however, painting has suffered most from the ravages of time, and the number of surviving examples is sufficient to give only a hint of what this art must have been at its best. Because of this situation, it is easy to gain the impression that sculpture was the most important of all the arts. Literary sources, however, attest to the effectiveness and the high esteem in which painting was held by the ancients. The fame of individual painters and the expressions of critical praise for their works make it clear that it was considered on at least as high a plane as architecture and sculpture.

Two renowned painters were known to have been active in Athens during the 5th century B. C. One was Polygnotus who worked out the principles of perspective drawing, so that his pictures created the illusion of three dimensions and the recession of planes in depth. Apollodorus, "the shadow painter," was the other, who was famed for his use of light and shade and the finer gradations of color. Pausanias described some murals of Polygnotus, which were in the Propylaea at Athens and elsewhere, and gave longer and more detailed accounts of them than he did of the sculptures on the acropolis. He also mentions many paintings at Pergamon and describes an especially famous one of the Three Graces. This example, as well as most of the other murals which once adorned the walls of the temples and palaces there, has disappeared in the course of time. The influence of these mural painters, however, survives to a limited extent in the copies that were made of their masterpieces, and in the vase painting which was done by ceramic craftsmen in imitation of their methods. The latter is, however, only a by-product of the main art and must be considered the work of artisans rather than that of independent artists.

From the excavated fragments at Pergamon, we know that walls were frequently painted with pictorial panels, and with streaks of various colors in imitation of marble, that realistically recall the textures of stone. Other scattered pieces found in such places as the markets, the interiors of temples, and the palace reveal that the Pergamene painters loved bright colors, such as yellows, pinks, and greens, which they contrasted with deep reds, blues, and browns. The designs of the palace paintings used motives of actual animals, such as lions and charging bulls, and imaginary ones, such as tritons and griffins. Interiors of rooms were often decorated with painted imitations of sculptural friezes; and walls, especially of small rooms, were painted with panels, columns, and pilasters, which cast realistic shadows in order to create the illusion of spaciousness. The writers of antiquity also attest to paintings drawn from such literary sources as scenes from the *Odyssey* and the like. It is also known that Hellenistic painting often dealt in genre scenes drawn from daily life.

While Attalus I and Eumenes II were both closely identified with the great sculptural developments of their times, their successor Attalus II was primarily interested in painting. He acquired a large collection by purchase and by sending his artists to various centers to copy famous works that he could not buy. An inscription reveals that Eumenes II sent artisans to Delphi to assist in the repair of its theater; and that Attalus II in 140–139 B. C. dispatched three painters to restore a famous painting there, possibly one which he had previously caused to be copied.

By far the best-preserved examples of ancient painting come from Herculaneum and Pompeii, where the tidal mud of the sea and the protective ashes of Mount Vesuvius enclosed them for almost 2000 years. The taste of both places was Hellenistic in orientation, and the proximity of Herculaneum to the dominantly Greek city of Naples would certainly have accounted for this. The well-to-do patrons of such a settlement preferred the tried-and-true traditional subjects; more often than not, they commissioned copies of famous paintings rather than original works. In the basilica near the forum of Herculaneum, a series of large-scale murals on mythological subjects dating from the 1st century A. D. have been found. In one of these, *Hercules Finding His Infant Son Telephus* (Fig. 2:10), both the subject and its treatment point to a Pergamene original. The two cities had an ancestral connection, since Telephus was the legendary founder of Pergamon, and Herculaneum bore the name of the mythological strong man who was his father. Furthermore, one of the sculptured panels of the Telephus frieze of the Altar of Zeus uses the same scene, and the subject was also known to have existed there as a mural painting.

In the Herculaneum picture the infant Telephus is shown in the lower right amid wild animals and being suckled by a doe. He is pointed out to Hercules, who is depicted as a rather gross figure standing like a bronze statue in a relaxed posture. The place is Arcadia, personified by the cold and pompous laurel-crowned woman. While the subject and general handling so far were undoubtedly dictated by tradition, the painter had a bit more freedom with his minor figures and background subjects. Behind Arcadia is the playful figure of a youthful satyr with a shepherd's crook,

Fig. 2:10. *Hercules Finding His Infant Son Telephus.* Fresco from Herculaneum. 1st century A. D. Probably a copy of Pergamene original of 2d century B. C. National Museum, Naples (Alinari)

blowing on the panpipes; while the basket of fruit at Arcadia's side adds a skillfully executed still life to the composition. The coloring is in dark tones, with a predominance of reddish brown occasionally relieved with lighter blues and greens. The folds of the drapery of the statuesque feminine figure are treated in the manner of relief sculpture, while the powerful musculature of Hercules' body is projected in the three-dimensional manner of sculpture in the round. The planes are clearly defined, and the light and shade effects relate the style to that of the high-relief Pergamene sculpture.

Since sculpture itself was also painted in vivid colors, and sometimes landscapes were even painted in the backgrounds of reliefs, it is apparent that the two arts were closely identified in the Hellenistic mind, and that they should perhaps be thought of more as complementary arts than as completely independent media. Paintings were obviously more adaptable and convenient for interiors, while the resistance of stone to weather and time made marble reliefs better for out-of-doors. From the extant evidence it is clear that the visual intention and expressive effect of both arts were closely associated, and that neither could claim supremacy to the exclusion of the other.

Among the minor arts mosaics were highly esteemed in Pergamon and were widely used for the pavement of large interiors. Besides the usual geometrical and floral patterns they included in their subjects mythological episodes, landscapes, and genre scenes. Copies of many of the more famous Pergamene designs have been found at Pompeii, and examples found in other centers indicate that they were used as models by the Romans for the two succeeding centuries. According to Pliny the Elder, the most renowned mosaicist of antiquity, Sosus, was active at Pergamon. Widely copied in Roman times, a well-known design for a dining-room floor there was attributed to him. It consisted of representations of odd pieces of food, such as vegetables, fruit, fish, and a drumstick and other scraps of chicken, lying scattered around on a white background. A whimsical touch was added by a mouse starting to eat a nut.

A splendid mosaic design representing one of the finest known Hellenistic examples of the art has been found in the palace of Eumenes II (Fig. 2:11). In a room 28 feet square the entire floor was covered with mosaic. Running around the center section of the square design was a border about a yard wide. The plain bands and those with the geometrical patterns used bits of marble in colors of black, dark gray, red, yellow, and white. They enclose a frieze consisting of a floral pattern of great complexity which, in the 40 feet that have been found, shows no repetition. Colored flowers, exotic lilies, vine leaves, and various fruits are each treated with delicate shading against a black background. In some places grasshoppers can be seen feeding on acanthus leaves, while in others small boys are playing among the vines. The central portion is almost entirely missing except for the signature of the artist. With disarming informality, it is represented as appearing on a piece of tan-colored parchment. Three of the corners appear as if held down by red sealing wax in the same manner as a royal decree might have been posted on a wall. The other corner curls up loosely and casts a shadow on the floor. It reads: "Hephaiston made it"; and the fact that it is so signed indicates that it was the work of an artist of high repute.

In its crafts Pergamon was justly noted for its textiles, particularly its woolen fabrics, carpets, and curtains. A special brocaded cloth with interwoven gold threads, which bore the name *vestes Attalicae*, was famous all over the ancient world. Its name indicates that it was manufactured in the royal mills and that it was a monopoly of the kings. Their scientists were known for certain chemical discoveries used in the making of perfumes and especially for the development of mineral dyes that produced the rich coloration of the textiles. The city was also known for its metalware, such as its silver bowls, medallions, bronzes, and coins. Owing to the precious

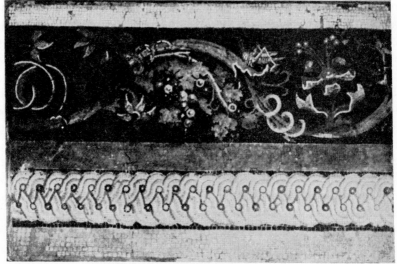

Fig. 2:11. *Mosaic from the Palace of Eumenes II.* 2d century B. C. (Altertümer von Pergamon)

material used, very few pieces have survived; but from those which have, it is evident that they were the work of craftsmen who were highly skilled in the art of embossing, or chasing, the metal so as to produce beautiful designs in low relief. The art of gem engraving, such as cameos and miniature-carved portraits on precious stones, was widely practiced at Pergamon and many fine examples survive.

Pergamon was also known as a ceramic center. The clay of the region was apparently well adapted to the making of everything from bricks and tiles to pottery of all sorts. A type of the latter, known as Pergameneware, probably originated here and was distinguished by its bright varnished surfaces in colors of rich reds with variations in coral, orange, and brownish shades. Designs on its bowls, plates, saucers, and drinking cups included the wave, tongue, and egg-and-dart patterns with leafy garlands of ivy, laurel, and oak leaves. A type of red glazed pottery vases with applied designs in relief seems to have been a unique Pergamene creation. The decorative patterns were made separately in molds, then attached to the vases, colored, and baked in the kiln. Terra-cotta figurines, varying from a few inches to a full foot in height, were made here in considerable quantity. The usual reproductions of famous statues as well as those depicting mythological figures have been found, but in general the heroic subjects were left to the large monuments. The figurine medium, being particularly adaptable to informal treatment, was used largely for genre scenes, such as children playing, mothers nursing their young, intoxicated satyrs, and grotesque old men going to market with their wares. The subjects, which were often humorously treated, sometimes even ludicrously, had a distinctly human appeal. In common with the practice of the time, artisans and craftsmen traveled about between various centers, and those trained in Pergamon were in wide demand and enjoyed a particularly high reputation.

MUSIC

Pergamon, as a city near that part of northern Asia Minor known as Phrygia, was identified with the musical tradition of that region, which had its own characteristic idioms, modes, rhythms, scales, and instruments. As early as the 5th century B. C. the Greeks in Athens were divided in their musical views and tastes as to the relative merit and propriety of their native Dorian tradition and the increasing influences coming from foreign centers. In particular the wild and exciting music of Phrygia was in the ascendancy and was constantly gaining in popular favor. The melodies in the Phrygian mode apparently induced strong emotional reactions, and the introduction of a musical instrument called the Phrygian pipe had a similar effect in inflaming the senses. This was a double-reed instrument with a peculiarly penetrating sound, somewhat like the modern oboe, and properly known as the *aulos* when used singly, and the *auloi* when the player used a double version of the instrument. In the English versions of ancient Greek works it is erroneously translated as the flute.

The Dorian music, on the other hand, was associated with such stringed instruments as the lyre and cithara, the latter of which is inaccurately rendered as the harp. Both the aulos in the Phrygian music and the lyre and cithara in the Dorian were used principally to accompany the songs, melodies, and choruses in these modes and, to a lesser extent, were played independently by skilled players as solo instruments. Lyre-playing in particular was associated in the Dorian tradition with the Apollo cult, and the Greeks attributed to this body of music the quality of *ethos*, or ethical character; while the aulos, as the instrument of Dionysus, was associated with a sensuous quality conducive to enthusiasm. To the Athenians this meant a division in their aspirations and ideals, one instrument and mode of singing being associated with clarity, restraint, moderation, and order, the other showing the strong desire for emotional excitement and the arousing of passions.

The resultant division of opinion was crystallized in the many sculptural representations of the musical contest between the Olympian Apollo and the Phrygian satyr Marsyas. According to an ancient myth, Athena was the inventor of the aulos. One day as she was playing, however, she accidentally caught sight of her reflection in a pool of water. So displeased was she with the facial grimaces it caused her to make while playing that she threw it away in disgust. Marsyas, one of the Sileni, happened to come along, found it, and was so enchanted by its ravishing sounds that he challenged Apollo himself, the immortal patron of the muses, to a contest. The god chose to play on the dignified lyre, won the contest easily, and proved once again that mortals are no match for the gods. As a punishment he had his challenger flayed alive.

A 5th-century version of the myth attributed to Myron shows Athena, calm and disposed, disdainfully throwing away the instrument which distorted her fine features, while Marsyas, seeing her do so, makes a gesture of surprise. A 4th-century relief from Mantineia of the school of Praxiteles (Fig. 2:12) represents the contest in progress. On one side, calmly awaiting his turn, is the seated Apollo poised with his lyre; while on the other, Marsyas is ecstatically blowing on the auloi. Between them is the judge standing by patiently but with a knife in his hand. The Pergamene versions left out the contest and showed the victorious Apollo on one side, the unfortunate loser in the center strung up by his wrists to a tree, and to his left the crouching figure of a Scythian slave (Fig. 2:13), who is whetting his knife with keen anticipation. The choice of the punishment as the part of the myth to be represented, and the evident enjoyment with which this Hellenistic artist tackled his sinister subject, was obviously designed to tear the emotions of his audience to shreds.

The disapproval of Phrygian music shown by the punishment of Marsyas must have reflected the official attitude. Yet the power and popularity of the aulos, and the Phrygian melodies associated with it, grew constantly. One measure of its hold on the people is found in the attitude of the philosophers who were concerned with maintaining balance and order in the state. Plato, for instance, would admit neither aulos makers nor aulos players into his ideal state, because he considered the instrument "worse than all the stringed instruments put together." He was most emphatic about his preference for "Apollo and his instruments to Marsyas and his instruments." But even the complex stringed instruments must go, and those retained are only the simple lyre and cithara for use in the city, and the pipe to keep the shepherds happy in the country. But while he rejects the aulos he makes a curiously human concession in retaining the Phrygian melodies. The two musical modes allowed in the ideal state were the Dorian, which he calls the "strain of necessity," and the Phrygian, which is the "strain of freedom." The first was "warlike, to sound the note or accent which a brave man utters in the hour of danger and stern resolve"; clearly a type of military music is implied by this. However, maintaining such heroic resolve at all times was apparently too much to expect even of the citizen of his Utopia, and he therefore allows the Phrygian music "to be used by him in times of peace and freedom of action, when there is no pressure of necessity." [3]

Aristotle, while agreeing for the most part in his musical views with Socrates and Plato, took exception to this point, and said: "The Socrates of the *Republic* is wrong in retaining only the Phrygian mode along with the Dorian, the more so because he rejects the flute [aulos]; for the Phrygian is to the modes what the flute [aulos] is to musical instruments—both of them are exciting and emotional. Poetry proves this, for Bacchic frenzy and all similar emotions are more suitably expressed by the flute [aulos] and are better set to the Phrygian than to any other mode." [4] It must be pointed out that Aristotle did not reject the Phrygian mode altogether, but only in the case of the education of youth. For this he strongly recommended only the Dorian music since it was the "gravest and manliest." The Phrygian might produce too much enthusiasm, while the Dorian was more likely to result in a "moderate and settled temper."

Fig. 2:12. *Contest of Apollo and Marsyas*. Marble. 38¼″ high. *c.*350 B. C. Slab from Manteneia, Greece. National Museum, Athens (Alinari)

Fig. 2:13 (left). *Slave Sharpening Knife*. Marble. Uffizi, Florence. Fig. 2:14 (right). *Satyr Playing the Scabellum*. Marble. Uffizi, Florence

In spite of the philosophers and their dire warnings, the stimulating Phrygian music made rapid headway, and in Hellenistic times it was the dominant musical style. The calm, simple, and dignified Dorian tradition, which Plutarch called the age of "beautiful music," was a thing of the past, and the wilder, more frenzied strains of Phrygia had taken its place. Their effects can readily be seen in the sculptural representation of a *Satyr Playing the Scabellum* (Fig. 2:14). The satyr cult was a Phrygian phenomenon, and this as well as other satyr types have been traced to a Pergamene origin. Holding the clashing metal scabellum, or cymbals, in his hands and stamping on a castenetlike percussion instrument attached to one foot, the satyr is performing an orgiastic dance with wild abandon. The physical tension seen in the lines of the torso reflects the frenzied Dionysian rhythm which seems to electrify his whole body. This image of youthful passion makes it easy to understand why the austere thinkers felt that the music which produced such a reaction lacked ethos or moral character.

Pergamon was, of course, one of the cities where this music originated, and the Greeks freely acknowledged the geographical connection by ascribing its creation to Olympos, the son of Marsyas the Phrygian. While historical facts about the actual musical life of Pergamon are few, it is known that here, as in other Hellenistic centers, the practice of music was accorded a high place in the arts. Both boys and girls received musical instruction in their educational institutions and sang hymns as they marched in processions and participated in religious observances. The curriculum included the teaching of musical notation and the chanting of poetry to the accompaniment of the cithara. The chief educator of the city, the gymnasiarch, was also expected, among his other duties, to arrange for the appearances of visiting poets and musicians.

The Hellenistic era was one of increasing professionalism in activities that had previously been performed by free citizens as part of their public duties and honors. Participation in athletic contests and performances of certain dances, which earlier had been done only by those of noble birth, were taken over by specialists who often commanded high fees for their services. Professional associations, known as the Dionysiac *technites*, had a membership made up of stage managers, actors, mimes, dancers, and musicians who participated in theatrical productions. These groups functioned as guilds or unions, and the master craftsmen accepted talented apprentices who understudied them. The Attalids and other Hellenistic monarchs promoted and protected these societies with an eye toward improving and maintaining the quality of their theatrical and musical performances.

While evidence of musical activity at Pergamon is quite sketchy, Tralles, one of the cities of the Pergamene kingdom, provides some general information and one of the best musical examples of antiquity. Less than 100 miles from Pergamon as the crow flies, Tralles was a subject-city of the Attalids, who maintained a residence there which usually was occupied by the high priest of the city as their representative. This Phrygian town was saved from the threat of defeat and enslavement at the hands of the Gauls by the victory of Eumenes II in 168 B. C. The cities of the region were so grateful for their deliverance that they instituted an annual gymnastic and musical festival at Tralles in honor of the Pergamene king. One of these was the Panathenaea, which honored Athena as the protectress of Pergamon; another was the Eumenaia, which feted the monarch himself. From inscriptions it appears that the Eumenaia at Tralles was principally a musical contest.

At Tralles, in the latter part of the 19th century, a tombstone was unearthed that had an inscription of some four lines of poetry accompanied by clear musical notation. It was an epitaph inscribed on a slab of stone by a man named Seikolos for the grave of his wife Euterpe. On transcription it turned out to be the words and music of a short but presumably intact tune in the Phrygian mode from the 2d century B. C. After hearing about the wild and orgiastic character of Phrygian music, this short song which survives from this period will seem to be a model of sobriety. The mood in fact is more melancholy than intoxicating, and since it was carved on a tombstone, it may also have had something of this character to the Greeks.

The *Skolion* of Seikolos (2d or 1st century B.C.)   (After Kunkel)

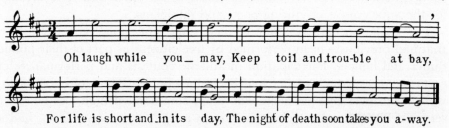

Oh laugh while   you__ may, Keep   toil and trou-ble   at bay,

For life is short and in its   day, The night of death soon takes you a-way.

This delightful little song, well over 2000 years old, was of a popular type known as a *skolion*, or drinking song, which was sung after dinner by the guests themselves as the cup was passed around for toasts and libations to the gods. The word *skolion* is derived from the Greek meaning zigzag and referred to the manner in which the lyre and cup were passed back and forth, crisscrossing the table as each of the reclining guests sang in his turn.

The simplicity of this example marks it as the type of song expected to be in the social repertory of every acceptable guest, rather than one of the more elaborate ballads intended to be sung by professional entertainers. In spirit and mood it is not unlike the familiar Auld Lang Syne, and the occasions on which it was sung would parallel those when we sing the venerable Scottish air. The substance of the words is the universal one of eat, drink, and be merry for tomorrow we die, which expresses a convivial philosophy of the Epicurean type. Technically it is in the Phrygian mode with the upper and lower extremes falling on e' and e, thus spanning an octave. The tone most often stressed is a, which thus becomes the mean between the higher and lower reaches of the melody and consequently functions as its tonal center.

IDEAS

Many striking differences are to be noted between the Hellenistic approach and that of the earlier Hellenic style. Since one is Greek and the other a combination of Greek and regional influences, the contrast is not one between polar extremes but rather that of a shifting of the balance off center, as in a pair of scales which first tilts one way then the other. The broad humanism so much in evidence in the Athens of the 5th century B. C. becomes the individualism of Pergamon three centuries later; the noble Hellenic idealism is inundated by a wave of realism, with the desire to present the world in terms more closely approximating that of immediate experience; and the rugged rationalism of Socrates yields to the erudition of scholars who concentrate conservatively on the accumulation of the factual bases of knowledge rather than embark on new intellectual adventures. The tendencies which underlie the various art enterprises and productions of Pergamon in particular and the Hellenistic period in general, then, are to be found in a pattern of interrelated ideas, of which individualism, realism, and erudition are the component parts.

Individualism

One of the strongest characteristics of the period—and its influence pervades all aspects of Hellenistic life, thought, and art—is individualism. In philosophy it is found in the desire for contemplation and self-reflection; in science, in the use of the empirical method. In social thought it is seen in the tendency toward personal hero worship, which began during the reign of Alexander the Great and continued to be felt in the fascination the personalities of courtly society had for the popular mind. In government it assumed the form of an evolution toward autocracy; in literature, of the interest in biography; in architecture, of the lavish display of monuments and temples glorifying individual patrons. In sculpture there is an accent on individual and racial differences; and in the arts of the theater and music, the rising spirit of professionalism and virtuosity.

The arduous mental gymnastics that had characterized the dialectical method of Socrates and Plato were replaced by the contemplation of pleasure, especially that which came from a peaceful state of mind. Pleasure, according to Epicurus, the founder of the school, consisted of "freedom from trouble in the mind and from pain in the body." [5] The noble idealism of Socrates and Plato thus gave way to a sort of rational hedonism, based, however, on the fact that mental processes are a necessary accompaniment to the pursuit of pleasure. This Epicurean philosophy found ready acceptance in the rich and flourishing cities of Asia Minor. The architects took special interest in domestic dwellings; painters and mosaicists were concerned with the lavish pictorial embellishment of the houses of the well-to-do; sculptors chose genre scenes from daily life; and fine craftsmen, metal workers, potters, and the like all worked to contribute to the life of luxury and ease enjoyed by a frankly pleasure-loving people.

The Hellenistic artist was more interested in exceptions than in rules, in the abnormal than the normal, in types rather than archetypes, in diversity rather than unity, and in action rather than abstraction. He saw the physical peculiarities which set the individual apart from his fellows more than those which united him with others. Even the gods were personalized rather than generalized, and the choice of subjects from daily life showed his increased preoccupation with the transitory more than with the permanent. He was also more concerned with environmental influences on man than with man's being able to transcend his environmental limitations. The Hellenistic artist also recognized the complexity of life and gave his attention to rendering subtle shades of feeling and to representing the infinite variety of the world of appearances. Hence even individual facial expressions are made to reflect reactions to immediate circumstances and thus to enhance the art of portraiture.

After the 5th century B. C. the arts entered upon a new and more intense emotional orientation. This emphasis on pathos, especially in the feeling for spiritual anguish and physical pain, was still another facet of individualism. Joy and serenity are social emotions that can be shared by all, but sorrow and pain separate the individual from his fellows and project the thoughts inward toward the self. It is an old variation on the theme—laugh and the world laughs with you, weep and you weep alone. The artists turned from

Fig. 2:15. *Laocoön*. Marble. *c*.50 B. C. Vatican Museum, Rome (Anderson)

the ideal of self-mastery to one of self-expression, from the concealment of inner impulses to outbursts of feeling—in short from ethos to pathos. It was said of Pericles, for example, that he was never seen laughing, and that even the tragic death of his son did not alter his dignified calm. A strong contrast to this Olympian attitude is provided by the late Hellenistic *Laocoön* group (Fig. 2:15). The balance between mind and body, the harmony of opposites, the search for the golden mean, are all replaced by a reveling in feeling for its own sake. What is lacking in self-restraint and regard for the limitations of the medium, however, is amply made up for in the vigor of the treatment and the virtuosity of the execution.

The preoccupation of the Pergamene artists with such painful and agonizing subjects as the defeated Gauls and the punishment of Marsyas show the deliberate intention of involving their audience in a kind of emotional orgy. Misfortune here becomes something that can be enjoyed by the fortunate, and they are invited to participate in the situation with a kind of morbid satisfaction rather than rise above it. As La Rochefoucauld said: "We all have strength enough to endure the misfortunes of others." In the spirit of the Stoic philosophy, life and its suffering was something to be endured with a sort of grim satisfaction, which was tantamount to a certain form of enjoyment. The artists of the Great Altar frieze, for instance, show an incredible inventiveness in the ways and means they found for the gods to inflict pain and death. The composition approaches an almost-encyclopedic inclusiveness in respect to the various modes of combat on the part of the gods, and the capacity for physical suffering on the part of the giants. Nothing like it in art appears again until the Romanesque Last Judgments and Dante's *Inferno*.

Realism

The 5th-century belief in an underlying unity of knowledge and the permanent and abiding quality of values produced the poise of its figures and the impassivity of their facial expressions. Hellenistic knowledge of the fleeting nature of things, the transitoriness of values, and the ephemeral nature of experience was responsible for the motional and emotional tensions that characterize its art. The distance between the ideal and the real was closer to the experience of Hellenistic man than its proximity. The unbridgeable gap between the unattainable serenity of the world of the aspirations and the frustrations of the world of matter in which he lived was the real fact of his experience. Hellenistic thought was therefore based on the conviction that the abstract and the ideal were not so important a part of experience as the real and the concrete. Hellenistic realism accordingly used for its material the substance of individual experience and individual differences. Such realism took variety more than unity into account, and the demands it made on the techniques of the artist were tremendous. In this desire to render the truth of nature as they saw it, there was a feeling for all aspects of life, multiplicity of motion, and the quality of individual character. The decline of idealism in favor of realism was thus not necessarily the result of decadence, as is so frequently stated; rather it was a matter of the placing of man's activities in a new light, a re-examination of his goals, and a redefinition of basic human values.

The complexities of life were so well understood by the Hellenistic artist that he made no attempt to reduce them to an artificial simplicity. The writhing forms of the Great Altar frieze reveal many of the tortured con- flicts and contradictions of Hellenistic man. He portrayed his gods as projections of his own psychological problems. This attitude can also be noted in the fact that the individual is not only aware of his surroundings but inextricably involved with and conditioned by them. The tendency of the earlier Greek period had been to isolate him as much as possible. This is true in each of the visual arts. In the Athenian architecture of the 5th century B. C., each building, however well in harmony with its site, was an independent unit, and the architects were little concerned with its precise relation to nearby buildings. Indeed, to have admitted that one structure was dependent upon another in a group would have diminished its status as a self-contained whole and thus rendered it incomplete by their stand- ards. On the Athenian acropolis, for instance, each temple had its own axis and its independent formal existence—in keeping with the conception that each separate work of art must be a logical whole made up only of the sum of its own parts. Only such concessions to nature as were necessary for structural integrity were made. To man alone belonged the power of creating symmetrical form and balanced proportion, and the perfection of each building had to stand as a monument to the mind of man, and as such to rise above its material environment rather than be bound by it. Hel- lenistic architecture moved away from the isolated building in the ideal sense of its being a self-contained whole toward a realistic recognition that nothing is complete in itself but must always exist as part of an interrelated pattern. City planning is therefore in this sense a form of realism, and Hellenistic buildings were considered in their relation to the community as a whole. In the case of the Pergamene acropolis the relationship of each building was carefully calculated not only in regard to its natural surround- ings but to its place in the group.

In sculpture the members of each group are likewise conditioned by their environment, and man is portrayed as an integral part of his sur- roundings. In such reliefs as the Telephus frieze, the natural background places him constantly in reference to specific locations. The tendency to- ward higher relief, the increased use of light and shade, the suggestion of depth, the allowance for movement in more than one plane, and the tend- ency for sculpture to become more pictorial—all serve to illustrate the changes in the art. In earlier sculpture there was a marked preference for showing the individual as subordinate to his position. A warrior, for in- stance, was portrayed as a well-developed physical specimen, and his face and body bore little relation to any one personality. He could be identified by a spear or shield and as a consequence was more a member of a class than a personage in his own right. The Hellenistic desire to render men as unique personalities and not as abstractions necessitated the acquisition of a masterly technique capable of reproducing such particular physical characteristics as the twist of a mouth, wrinkles of the skin, physical blemishes, and individualized expressions of the facial features. Faces, furthermore, had to appear animated and lifelike, so that a realistic portrait could be successful and its subject distinguished from all others. Fidelity to nature also meant the meticulous rendering of the details of the anatomy. Like a scientist the sculptor observed with precision all the details of the human body, until the Hellenistic virtuoso sculptor was capable of conveying every nuance of the flesh. In all the works the human being is seen in relation to the forces which shape his character and mold his flesh, and all the minute physical and psychological conditions which vary the bodies and minds of men, women, and children were taken into account. Yet the end result was managed so that the dignity and status of the art was maintained by rising above the letter of realism in order to portray the spirit of the subjects represented. This emphasis on realism appealed greatly to the forthright Roman conquerors of Greece, and it is highly likely that this very quality was responsible for the ultimate preservation of these Pergamene sculptures.

Erudition

A reputation for learning had a direct bearing on the political purposes of the Pergamene dynasty. The more renowned their capital became for its intellectual and cultural enterprises, the higher its prestige in the Greek world grew. A striking illustration is provided by the career of the brother of Eumenes II who eventually succeeded him as Attalus II. As a skillful general, he was invaluable to the Pergamene government. Yet at the conclusion of a successful war, he spent five years studying philosophy at the academy in Athens. Furthermore, the proudest boast of the Attalids in the wake of their military victories was always that they were the saviors of Hellenism from the benighted barbarians. This claim, of course, had to be fortified by the development of their capital as a center of arts and letters so that it could be hailed as a second Athens. To advertise the cultural achievements of his realm, Eumenes II appointed his librarian, Crates of Mallos, who was famed as a grammarian, to the highest diplomatic post of the kingdom, that of ambassador to Rome. The lasting impression Crates made in that capital was said to have fanned the flames of humanistic learning there and to have been instrumental in whetting the Roman appetite for more knowledge about the great authors of the Greek world.

Under the influence of Socrates and Plato, Athenian thought had become more abstract, and the stress was put on the dialectical method as the means to truth and knowledge. At Pergamon and other Hellenistic centers, the emphasis was more on scientific research and invention, which was better served by the empirical method. The *a priori*, or deductive, method of Platonism was in reality a daring, optimistic form of thought that was designed to make a clean break with the past. The Hellenistic use of *a posteriori*, or inductive, reasoning, which derived truth from a large accumulation of facts, was more in keeping with the spirit of research. Here also the materialistic philosophy of the Epicureans entered the picture. In his explanations of natural phenomena, Epicurus had tried to eliminate all the supernatural elements which had formerly been attributed to the intervention of the gods. By so doing, he laid the basis for the scientific materialism that was such a productive aspect of Hellenistic research. Creativity, however, tended to be diminished by this emphasis on research, especially when it was accompanied by a growing spirit of antiquarianism. This attitude predisposed the literary life of Pergamon more to historical pursuits than to creative writing as such, and erudition eventually became a substitute for inspiration.

After establishing the library, Eumenes II gathered about him many of the outstanding Greek scholars of his day. They were dedicated to the task of preserving the literary masterpieces of bygone days, making critical editions of the works of ancient poets and dramatists, selecting material for anthologies, cataloguing collections, copying manuscripts, writing grammatical treatises, and compiling dictionaries. In their scholarly endeavors they upheld the works of the ancients above the writers of their own time, and as a consequence their literary production began to be addressed more to other scholars than to the people at large. Such a restricted audience of cultivated readers could not be supplied by Pergamon alone but had to be sought for all over the scattered Greek world. By mutual consent the pure and majestic Attic Greek of Pericles, Euripides, and Plato became their "common dialect," and the artificial medium of communication between the cultured classes. With this emphasis on a tongue that was no longer spoken, the living language in which writers could address their fellow citizens began to be regarded as a vulgar local dialect.

This scientific attitude found brilliant expression in the musical field by the development of the theoretical basis of that art. While philosophers and mathematicians of the earlier period had made many discoveries and had had brilliant insights into the nature of music, it remained for the Hellenistic mind to systematize them and construct a rational and coherent science of music. Under Aristoxenos of Tarentum, a disciple of Aristotle, and under Euclid, the theory of music reached a formulation so complete and comprehensive that it became the foundation for Western music. While it is impossible to go into the intricacies of the Greek musical system here, one should keep in mind that it was in this field more than any other that a lasting musical contribution was made.

The influence of the library and its scholars was felt in the visual arts as well. The magnitude of the design of the Great Altar frieze demanded the collaboration of scholars, and the completeness of the undertaking shows evidence of the spirit of research. It is, in fact, a catalogue of mythology, which even includes the obscure names of the individual giants. The labeling of the figures of the frieze in the manner of visual footnotes and annotations contrasts markedly with that of the Parthenon. At that time any Greek would have recognized the principals in the cast, and the supporting members were left to the imagination since they served mainly in the aesthetic capacity of filling in the extra space. As in the case of literature, the Hellenistic visual arts no longer stemmed from the experience of a local community by deriving their spirit and substance from the spoken word and the common religious experience. They were addressed, on the contrary, to an educated class who were sophisticated enough to understand it. The theory of art for art's sake therefore took over.

Like his literary colleagues the sculptor and painter were confronted for the first time with a museum filled with noted works from the glorious past that commanded increasing admiration from his contemporaries. In their zeal for collection, the Attalid kings had even carried on extensive excavations which brought to light many works that the 5th century had thought it better to bury. Fortunately this spirit of looking to a past golden age was not carried to the point of entirely excluding contemporary creative activity. Many artists of the time, however, had to devote their energies to making copies of famous works of the past, such as those by Myron, Phidias, and others, which were placed in the halls of the great library.

The interest of the patrons extended also to the historical and critical aspects of the visual arts, just as it had done in the case of literature and music. This had the positive result of formulating aesthetic standards and the setting up of critical criteria so necessary in the evaluation process. In the earlier period artists did not enjoy the high social position they had in Pergamon and other Hellenistic cities at this time. Hence the theorizing about taste and the development of aesthetic judgment proved that now, in contrast with the earlier period, their products were at last worthy of the attention of the highest intellectual and social circles. The collector became a judge and connoisseur, and hence engendered a state of mind in which standards of value and aesthetic expression were regarded as important intellectual pursuits.

With the literary talents being diverted into the editing of manuscripts, scholars delving into the history of the past, art collectors digging for buried treasure, and musicians writing theoretical treatises, Pergamon was well on its way toward becoming an archive and a museum. This antiquarianism was bound in time to lead artistic developments into a stylistic eclecticism and to reduce aesthetic procedures to academic formulas and rules—all of which is symptomatic of artistic hardening of the arteries, and the eventual decline of the creative powers. When, therefore, in 133 B. C. Attalus III willed his kingdom to Rome, he was actually presenting that city with a living museum. The vast art holdings of the Attalids were soon on their way to Italy where the interest and admiration they commanded, when they were shown in public exhibitions, were destined to have a powerful effect on the taste of the Roman people.

CHAPTER

CHRONOLOGY: Rome, Early 2d Century A. D.

General Events

B. c.100 – 44 Julius Caesar
29 – 19 Vergil wrote the *Aeneid*
27 – 14 Augustus reigned
c.16 Maison Carrée at Nîmes

A. D.

c.50 Pont du Gard at Nîmes
54 – 68 Nero reigned
79 Eruption of Mount Vesuvius
Destruction of Pompeii and Herculaneum
81 Arch of Titus, Rome
82 Colosseum, Rome, finished
c.93 Quintilian wrote the *Institutes of Oratory*
96 – 180 Antonine Age
96 – 98 Nerva reigned
98 – 117 Trajan reigned
Roman Empire reached its greatest extent
c.100 Suetonius wrote the *Lives of the Twelve Caesars*
100 Pliny the Younger delivered his *Panegyric* to Trajan before the Roman Senate
101 – 102 Trajan's First Dacian Campaign
105 – 106 Trajan's Second Dacian Campaign

110 Via Traiana built between Benevento and Brindisi
Baths of Trajan built
113 Forum of Trajan completed except for Basilica Ulpia and Trajan's Temple
Column of Trajan
114 Arch of Trajan at Benevento
117 – 138 Hadrian reigned
120 – 124 Pantheon, Rome
138 – 161 Antoninus Pius reigned
c.150 "House of Diana" at Ostia
161 – 180 Marcus Aurelius Antoninus reigned
217 Baths of Caracalla completed

Literature

B. c.106 – 43 Cicero
c.96 – 55 Lucretius
70 – 19 Vergil
65 – 8 Horace
43 – A. D.17 Ovid
A. D.35 – 95 Quintilian
c.40 – c.102 Martial
c.46 – c.120 Plutarch
c.55 – c.117 Tacitus
c.60 – c.140 Juvenal
c.62 – c.113 Pliny the Younger
c.100 Suetonius flourished

3

⎮⎮

THE ROMAN STYLE

ROME, 2d CENTURY A. D.

"If a man were called upon to fix the period in the history of the world during which the condition of the human race was most happy and prosperous," wrote Gibbon in the 18th century, "he would, without hesitation, name that which elapsed from the death of Domitian to the accession of Commodus." [1] With due allowance for the classical enthusiasm that led him to undertake his immense scholarly labors, the great historian nevertheless brings many cogent arguments to the support of his conviction that the Golden Age of the world was attained during the 2d century of the Christian era, when "the Empire of Rome comprehended the fairest part of the earth and the most civilized portion of mankind." [2] This benign state of affairs he attributed to the Roman genius for law and order, their cultivation of tolerance and justice, and their capacity for wise government. His whole vast book, *The Decline and Fall of the Roman Empire*, therefore, became a kind of classical *Paradise Lost* and a colossal postscript to the splendors of the Antonine Age.

A proud monument, the Arch of Trajan at Benevento (Fig. 3:1), recalls some of this vanished grandeur by proclaiming the virtues and accomplishments of the first of the great emperors of Gibbon's chosen period. It was erected by the Roman Senate to celebrate the completion of the Via Traiana, a 200-mile highway over the mountains, linking Rome with the large port of Brindisi. The Senate chose this way to honor a singular achievement in engineering as well as the chief engineer of their Empire. Such a gateway, marking as it did the start of the long road toward the East, must have challenged Roman imaginations to envisage that which lay beyond and must have reminded them that their city was not a self-

99

Fig. 3:1. *Arch of Trajan*, A. D. 114. Benevento (Anderson)

Fig. 3:2. Arch of Trajan, Detail, *Sacrifice of Trajan*. A. D. 114. Benevento (Anderson)

Fig. 3:3. Arch of Titus, Detail, *Spoils of Jerusalem*. A. D. 81. Rome (Anderson)

contained unit. The Roman awareness that their individual destinies as well as those of their city and state were closely bound up with the surrounding territories found its logical expression in just such a monument. Among ancient city-states Rome was unique in its solution of the problem of how to maintain its municipal integrity and at the same time manage a far-flung empire. In evolving the institutions by which this political unity could be made compatible with such wide human diversity, the Romans achieved their greatest social distinction.

Such arches usually marked the conclusion of a successful military campaign, by which distant barbarian tribes were subdued or some new civilized people was brought into the Roman orbit. In the case of the Arch of Titus in Rome, the returning conqueror, together with his army, a train of captives, and the trophies of war, passed through the arch with the plaudits of the multitudes ringing in his ears. In keeping with this martial theme, the sculptural panels on one side of the passageway of the arch show Titus after his conquest of Palestine, driving his chariot in the grand procession, preceded by the goddess Roma and followed by Senators and representatives of the Roman people. On the other side are servants bearing the seven-branched golden candelabra and the sacred trumpets he had plundered from the temple at Jerusalem (Fig. 3:3).

Though Trajan's Arch was modeled architecturally after that of Titus (even to the extent of repeating the attached columns of the Composite Order on its face), it differs from it iconographically by celebrating the arts of peace rather than those of war. The sculptural reliefs that so liberally cover its surface were arranged in characteristic Roman fashion so as to inform and instruct as well as to delight the eye. On the side toward the town of Benevento (Fig. 3:1), which was also the one toward Rome, the panels deal with Trajan's domestic policy. He is seen making land grants in the newly conquered Danube region to the veterans of his wars; standing in the midst of prosperous merchants who were favored by his building a new harbor for them at Ostia, the port of Rome; and receiving the acclamation of the Senate and people in the Roman Forum. Across the lintel moves a triumphal procession, and on either side of the keystone hover spirits who hold the banners and crown of victory in their hands. Above, Jupiter, Juno, and Minerva, known in Roman mythology as the Capitoline Triad, are seen extending their welcome to the Emperor. As a gesture of approval, Jupiter is about to turn over his thunderbolt to Trajan, a recognition of his great power as well as a sign that the adulation of the emperor was gradually replacing the worship of the old Olympian deities. This group is placed next to the inscription, which adds to Trajan's usual string of titles that of *Optimo*, the best, which is said to have pleased him especially since he shared it only with Jupiter himself.

On the side toward the country are the scenes having to do with his foreign policy. Germany is seen taking the oath of allegiance; various Oriental rulers are sending tributes through their envoys; and Trajan is establishing state-sponsored benefits for the relief of poor children. Above, a figure symbolizing Mesopotamia is paying him homage, and the divinities of the Danube territory are welcoming the Emperor. The inside passage of the archway is similarly decorated. One side shows a group of happy, well-fed children and their parents, all grateful for the benefits bestowed upon them. On the other, Trajan is participating in a sacrificial observance before setting out on the new highway for his Eastern conquests (Fig. 3:2). While all the panels are based on separate episodes, they find a unity in their constant repetition of the imperial personage. Variety is achieved by means of shifting the human and geographical environment. The changes of place are indicated partly by the activities and partly by the backgrounds, which indicate a setting in Rome by some familiar buildings, a country place by some trees, or remote localities by exotic river gods. The subject matter is obviously propaganda for imperial rule, even to the extent of sometimes showing Trajan as a figure of superhuman size, but the restrained manner of its presentation keeps this aspect from becoming too blatant. The sculpture itself is technically well handled, though there is a tendency to accent linear detail at the expense of unity and repose.

While an edifice of this type was nonutilitarian in purpose, the arch form that it exemplifies points to the building principle which underlies the Roman achievements in architecture. With the arch they constructed their vaults and domes that carried architecture forward well into modern times. The fact that Trajan's Arch was built in a provincial town south of Rome on the road to and from the great centers of the East—Athens, Pergamon, Alexandria, Ephesus, and Antioch—also serves as a reminder of the route by which the heritage of the classical Mediterranean world became a part of Western cultural tradition. By military conquest, by annexation, by inheritance, and by voluntary action, all the proud old city-states and kingdoms one by one became a part of greater Rome. Likewise all the ideas, institutions, and art forms of this vast region were sifted through the ingenious Roman mind, and, together with notable contributions of her own, Rome gradually achieved a culmination of culture, expressed in her literature, architecture, and sculpture, that could compare favorably with the political eminence of her great empire.

ARCHITECTURE

The Forum of Trajan

Shortly after his accession as emperor in A. D. 98, Trajan began a grandiose project in Rome, the construction of a new forum. Just as the empire had grown in his time to its greatest extent, so the population of Rome itself had risen to more than one million inhabitants, thus giving rise to the need for larger and more imposing public buildings. The old Forum Romanum of the Republic had long been inadequate, and several extensions had been undertaken in the early years of the Empire. The ambitiousness of Trajan's Forum can be measured by the fact that it was the equal of all the previous forums combined, and that it brought the total area covered by them to over 25 acres. Needless to say, its magnificence was in every way comparable to its size. Trajan entrusted the project to Apollodorus, a Greek architect-engineer from Damascus, who was famous for the construction of a bridge over the widest part of the Danube during the second Dacian campaign. From the fact of his Greek origin it must not be inferred that the choice of Apollodorus represented a Hellenistic bias on the Emperor's part. All other known architects in Rome at this

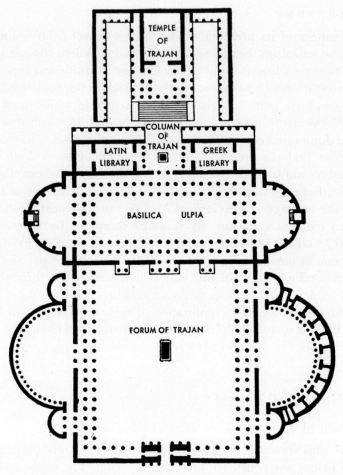

TEMPLE
OF
TRAJAN

COLUMN
OF
TRAJAN

LATIN
LIBRARY

GREEK
LIBRARY

BASILICA   ULPIA

FORUM OF TRAJAN

Fig. 3:4 (above). Forum of Trajan, Rome. *Plan* (Based on Helen Gardner. *Art Through the Ages*. New York, Harcourt, Brace, 1948. p. 177. By permission). Fig. 3:5 (below). Forum of Trajan. *Northeast Exedra and Market Hall*. A. D. 113

time, including those who collaborated on the project, were Romans, and Apollodorus was thoroughly conversant with the current Roman building tradition.

A forum is actually a specifically Roman conception, consisting as it does of a system of open courtyards and buildings all grouped with a specific relationship to each other. A glance back at the plan of the Athenian acropolis (Fig. 1:3) will show how little the Parthenon and Erechtheum were related to each other. No part of a forum, however, existed in isolation, and in this instance everything was conceived from the beginning on a large scale and with an eye to symmetry. From the plan (Fig. 3:4) it can be seen that the whole was bisected equally by a central axis that ran its entire length from the center of the arched gateway, through the middle of the square, the entrance to the basilica whose axis is at right angles to it, onward to the base of the column, and finally up the steps of the temple and on to the altar at the back.

Originally a forum was an open city square, serving as a combined market and meeting place. By degrees the buildings around it became administrative in nature with space provided for political centers, law courts, triumphal arches, commemorative monuments, and temples. Its origin has been sought by various historians in the city plans of smaller Roman settlements, in Roman military camps, and domestic dwellings. All are agreed on one point, however, that it is a specific Roman institution since no comparable units have been found in Greek centers or elsewhere. Because the Senate met in the Roman Forum, and the area was the center of heated political debates, a forum has since become associated with parliamentary bodies and a meeting of minds.

The problems confronting Apollodorus in the case of the Forum of Trajan were by no means simple. Clearing such a large space in a densely populated city meant the demolishing of many blocks of houses. His site, moreover, was the valley between the Quirinal and Capitoline hills. If the usual interpretation of the inscription on the base of Trajan's column is accepted, that monument was erected "to show posterity how high rose the mountain levelled by the Emperor." In practical terms this would mean that more than 100 feet was cut off the base of the Quirinal and carted away to make room for the courtyard and basilica. The remaining part was then terraced as a site for the market buildings, which extended up the hillside.

Entrance to the forum was made through a majestic triple archway into the large paved quadrangle, which was enclosed on three sides by a wall and colonnade and on the fourth by the Basilica Ulpia, whose entrances corresponded with those of the archway. Standing in the exact center was

Fig. 3:6. *Column of Trajan and the Ruins of the Basilica Ulpia.* Marble. Column 97' high. Spiral Frieze 656' long. Rome

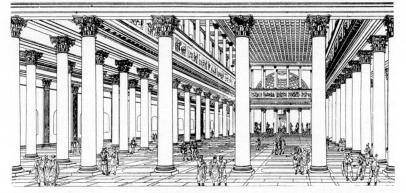

Fig. 3:7 (above). Basilica Ulpia, *Reconstruction of Interior.* A. D. 113. Fig. 3:8 (below). Court Surrounding Base of Trajan's Column, *Reconstruction.* Rome

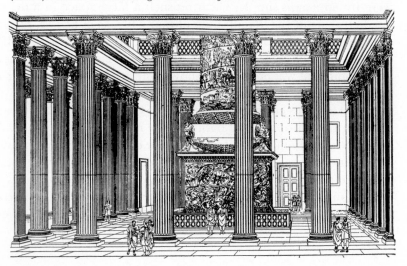

an impressive bronze portrait of Trajan on horseback. Though the statue is no longer extant, it is known to have been similar to the surviving bronze equestrian portrait of Marcus Aurelius (Fig. 3:9). With the baton of command firmly in his hand, this last of the Antonine emperors sits astride his splendid mount with an equilibrium worthy of the patient Stoic philosopher, and the thoughtful mien of the author of the widely read book of *Meditations*. Flanking the square on the east and west sides were semicircular *exedrae* outlined by tall Doric columns. Similar in shape were the mercantile units that were built upward into the two hills. The best preserved are those on the Quirinal side, which were six stories in height and constructed of brick (Fig. 3:5). There were more than 150 booths including those on the forum floor, for the selling of vegetables, fruit, and flowers; above were large vaulted halls where wine and oil were stored; spices and imported delicacies were sold on the third and fourth floors; the fifth was used to distribute food and money out of the imperial treasury; and on top was a market where fish were kept in ponds supplied by fresh water from one of the city's aqueducts.

Adjacent to the open square (Fig. 3:4) was the Basilica Ulpia, of which only the rows of broken columns now mark the site (Fig. 3:6). The term *basilica* was applied rather generally to large public buildings and is approximately equivalent to the modern use of the word *hall*, referring to a place for meetings. Since court sessions were also held in such places, the term *hall of justice* is likewise related to one of its functions. As an architectural form, the basilica represents a culmination of the long Mediterranean building tradition that can be traced backward through domestic structures and the Greek temples to the Egyptian hypostyle hall. The tradition was carried forward through the Christian basilicas, which differed from their Roman prototypes in such details as having the main entrance on one of the short ends.

The vast rectangular interior of the Basilica Ulpia (Fig. 3:7), named for Trajan's family, was marked by a double colonnade that ran completely around the building, supporting a balcony and a second tier of columns, which in turn supported the beams of the timbered roof. This large central hall served as a general meeting place as well as a business center. The semicircular apses, possibly roofed over with hemispherical vaults and set apart from the central hall by screens or curtains, housed the courts of law. The decorative scheme of the building included the lavish use of polychrome marbles. The steps at the entrances were of *giallo antico* stone, and the flanking columns were of matching yellow marble. The exterior and interior walls were liberally faced with varicolored marble panels, while the floor was done in rich mosaic patterns. In the double colonnade the shafts of the columns on the ground floor were of red granite, while their Corinthian capitals were carved from white stone. Pausanias' description of the "roof of bronze" probably meant that the decorative scheme had been completed with some form of metal embellishments.

Beyond the basilica were two libraries, one for Greek and the other for Latin books, separated by a courtyard that enclosed the base of Trajan's Column (Fig. 3:8), the sculpture of which will be discussed later in this chapter.

After Trajan's death his adopted son and successor, Hadrian, built at the end of the main axis of the Forum the Corinthian temple that climaxed the grand design. Architecturally it was a large-scale version of the Maison Carrée (Fig. 3:15) at Nîmes in southern France. Like other Roman temples of this type, Trajan's temple and the Maison Carrée rested on podiums and had porticos in the front, which were much more prominently featured than those in Greek temples. The well-preserved example at Nîmes like-wise shows only the columns of the portico standing free, while the rest are attached to the cella, indicating that they were needed less for structural strength than for embellishment.

The process of deifying the emperors and building temples to them had begun as early as the reign of Augustus. The type of statue that stood in such temples can be seen in the *Portrait of Augustus* (Fig. 3:10), which was found near Prima Porta. He stands in the imposing attitude of an imperator addressing his troops. Carved on the cuirass, or metal breastplate of his armor, are scenes in low relief recounting the outstanding achievements of his reign and pictures of the gods and goddesses who conferred their favors upon him. At his side is a cupid astride a dolphin, which alludes to the divine origin of the Julian family. Vergil, the principal poet of his period, traced Augustus' ancestry all the way back to Aeneas, the legendary founder of Rome, whose father was the mortal Anchises but whose mother was none other than the immortal Venus herself. Much of the Roman religion was a family affair, honoring the living *pater familias* as well as the nearer and more remote ancestors. A room in every household was set aside for this purpose, and the custom was responsible for a whole genre of sculpture, such as the portrait bust of an *Unknown Roman* (Fig. 3:11). In contrast to the generalized and somewhat idealized portrait of Augustus as the states-man and imperator, the unpretentious portrait of this ordinary citizen is remarkably realistic. Both, however, served essentially the same purpose— one as the image of the father of a family in a simple household, the other for the veneration of a great man in a temple.

Fig. 3:9 (left). *Equestrian Statue of Marcus Aurelius.* Gilded Bronze. A. D. *c.*175–180. Heroic size. Piazza del Campodoglio, Rome (Alinari).

Fig. 3:10 (below left). *Augustus.* Found at Prima Porta. Marble. 6′ 8¼″ high. B. C. *c.*13. Vatican Museum, Rome (Alinari). Fig. 3:11 (below right). *Unknown Roman.* Terra Cotta. Life size. 1st century B. C. Museum of Fine Arts, Boston

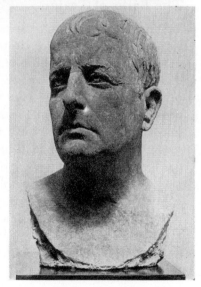

The paternalistic emperors were felt to deserve the universal reverence of the whole Roman family, since they were considered *pater patriae*, or fathers of their country. Erecting a temple to a distinguished emperor was not unlike the spirit evidenced in the building of the Washington Monument or the Lincoln Memorial in our own national capital. Certain days were set aside for the offering of food and drink in the simpler family ceremonies; on the day for honoring the emperor, the rites at his temple were more formal, occasionally including animal sacrifice, a procession, festivities, and amusements. Religion to the Romans thus represented the tradition and continuity of the family and, in the larger sense, the history and destiny of Rome itself.

With the exception of this temple, the Forum of Trajan was completed in the Emperor's lifetime and was dedicated by him for the use of the people of Rome in A. D. 113. The whole, then, is made up of parts consisting of the triumphal entrance archway, the courtyard and its equestrian statue, the mercantile buildings, the Basilica Ulpia, two libraries, a monumental column, and the temple. It all adds up to an architectural composition on a grand scale, designed to accommodate a hierarchy of activities beginning with a shopping center and place to transact business, continuing with a general meeting place and the halls of justice, moving on to places for quiet contemplation, study in the libraries and the reading of history in visual form on the column, and, finally, coming to rest in the precinct for the veneration of the Emperor and the worship of their Roman gods.

The Baths of Trajan

While the forums took care of the more serious pursuits of his people, Trajan never forgot that circuses were often as important as bread in promoting the general welfare of his volatile subjects. One of every emperor's duties, in fact, was to make provision for public amusement out of his private purse. Only the very wealthy could afford entertainment in their own homes, so the people as a whole had to look for their recreation outside. To this end the many baths, theaters, amphitheaters, arenas, and stadiums had been built all over the city. The variety they encompassed has never been surpassed, and even to this day the highest praise that can be given to an elaborate public festival is to call it a Roman holiday.

Trajan added to the already-existing public baths a large establishment that was also built by Apollodorus. Besides the hot, cold, and tepid swimming pools there were many other facilities, such as dressing rooms, gymnasiums, restaurants, bars, and shady walks. Guests could also listen to public lectures, read in one of the libraries, or stroll about the galleries

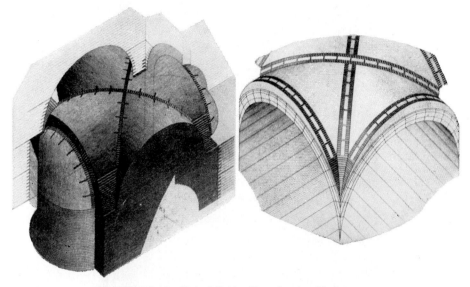

Fig. 3:12. *Groined Vaults.* Drawing by Choisy

where statuary and paintings were exhibited. Favored as places to exhibit the booty and souvenirs carried off during foreign conquests, the baths have provided the sources where much ancient statuary has been found, including the *Laocoön* (Fig. 2:15), a notable discovery in the early 16th century. They were, in short, people's palaces where the sociable citizenry could enjoy together the things that only the rich could afford separately.

The ruins of the Thermae (Baths) of Trajan are not in so good a state of preservation as the later baths of Caracalla and Diocletian. However, enough about them is known to establish a clear picture of what they were like. Only a degree smaller than the later examples, their facilities were on a comparable scale. The large central hall was the earliest known instance of the use of concrete cross vaulting, the principle of which can be studied in Figure 3:12. In this respect it was similar to the central hall of the Baths of Caracalla (Fig. 3:13), which measured 183 feet in length with an open space between the walls of 79 feet. It can be seen here that the barrel vault which runs lengthwise is three times intersected at right angles by shorter vaults extending across the width of the room. Besides spanning larger interior spaces, this method of construction had the additional advantage of allowing for ample lighting through the clearstory windows, which were provided with thin strips of translucent yellow marble in lieu of glass. When erecting such places as the Union Station in Washington, D. C., and the Pennsylvania and Grand Central terminals in New York City, modern

Fig. 3:13 (above). Baths of Caracalla. *Great Hall*, Restored by Spiers. A. D. 211–217. 183′ long, 79′ wide, 108′ high (W. J. Anderson and R. P. Spiers. *Architecture of Ancient Rome*. London, B. T. Batsford, 1927. Plate XLIX). Fig. 3:14 (below). *Colosseum*. Long axis 620′, Short axis 513′, height 160′. A. D. 75–82. Rome (Courtesy Italian State Tourist Office)

architects could find no better precedents among large secular structures than these Roman imperial baths, and the resemblance is quite obvious. These baths did not serve only to entertain; they had important hygienic advantages as well. With the habit of daily bathing in fresh water, the people of a major city have probably never been so clean before or since.

The Colosseum, Aqueducts, and Apartment Houses

Other places, such as the Colosseum (Fig. 3:14) which dates from the late 1st century, were the scene of more garish forms of mass amusement, such as the gory gladiatorial contests between men and wild beasts. The oval form of the Colosseum covers about 6 acres and could seat about 50,000 spectators at one time. Around its circumference run some 80 archways, which served so efficiently as entrances and exits that the entire bowl could be emptied in a matter of minutes. The Roman talent for organization is not only evident here in such practical respects but extends to the structure and decorative design as well. Three architectural orders are combined in the successive stories of the same building. The attached columns on the lower range are the "home-grown" Roman variation of the Doric, known as the Tuscan; those on the second tier are Ionic; on the third, Corinthian; while on the fourth, which rises to a height of 157 feet, are found flat Corinthian pilasters. The corbels, or sockets, for the poles over which a canvas awning was stretched to protect the spectators from sun and rain, can also be plainly seen at this point. The building material was a concrete made by mixing broken pieces of brick, small rocks, volcanic dust, lime, and water. It could be poured into molds of any desired shape and when dry was as hard as natural stone. The exterior was originally covered with marble facing, and the entire structure would be in good condition today had it not been used as a quarry for building materials right up to the 18th century. In spite of this, the Colosseum is still probably the most imposing ruin to survive from Roman times, and its popularity as a proto-type can be seen in the numerous football stadiums that grace so many college campuses today.

In order to assure an ample water supply for the baths that bore his name, Trajan found it necessary to improve on the old system of aqueducts and to add a new one 35 miles long that is still in use today. One of the most beautiful examples of these Roman aqueducts is the Pont du Gard at Nîmes (Fig. 3:16), which survives from the 1st century A. D. A system of underground and open concrete channels were constructed to bring water from its mountain source to the town some 25 miles away. Functioning on the principle of gravity, the ducts were sloped in the desired direction,

Fig. 3:16. *Pont du Gard.* 880' long, 155' high. A. D. *c.*50. Nîmes, France (Courtesy French
Government Tourist Office)

Fig. 3:17 (left). Roman Apartment House at Ostia. *Ruins.* 2d century A. D. Fig. 3:18 (right). *Restored* by Gismondi

and in this instance, the water was carried almost 300 yards across the valley at a height of more than 160 feet. The graceful lower range of arches support a bridge that is still in use, while the upper series of large and small arches supported the water channel.

The most ambitious of Trajan's civil engineering projects, however, was the construction of a port at Ostia about 15 miles from Rome. The actual port was a complicated system of breakwaters and canal connections with the Tiber River and was useful for export and import trade as well as for an anchorage for the Roman fleet. The town rapidly grew into one of the most important commercial centers of the 2d century, and recent excavations have uncovered some of its warehouses, theaters, baths, and many other public and private buildings. Of major interest are the ruins of apartment houses that reveal the type of multiple-family dwelling place in use at this time both in Ostia and in Rome. In contrast to the more leisurely and rambling Mediterranean country villas found at Pompeii, the so-called House of Diana (Fig. 3:17) shows a close-knit, economically spaced, well-planned building of five stories, which has a strikingly modern look. Because the house was located on a street corner, the ground floor had rows of shops along two sides. The second floor provided small apartments for the shopkeepers and their families, and each apartment was connected by separate steps to the shops below. In the reconstruction drawing (Fig. 3:18) two entrances can be seen on the right. One led into the center courtyard, which provided light for the inner rooms and where there was a fountain; the other led to a staircase, which gave access to the upper floors. The most desirable apartments would have been those with the balconies on the third floor. In the time of Constantine, two centuries later, Rome was known to have had almost 50,000 of such apartment houses, some of which rose as high as eight stories. Compared with these multiple-dwelling units, there were only about 1700 private town houses.

The Pantheon

With their highly developed sense of social organization, the Romans hit upon the idea of a pantheon as a place for all the gods. This religious conception was an interesting extension of their political experience, and the Olympian deities were considered in this context as a sort of supersenate who legislated on such cosmic matters as thunderstorms and earthquakes and on other odd matters that were outside the jurisdiction of the otherwise efficient and conscientious Roman senators and emperor. To house their divine deliberations, and to afford well-intentioned Romans the opportunity of propitiating them on the proper occasions, the temple known as the Pantheon had been built. After the earlier structure was destroyed by fire, Hadrian undertook its reconstruction about A. D. 120 (Fig. 3:19). The boldness of its design as well as its masterly execution mark it as one of the marvels of Roman engineering.

Unlike the soldierly Trajan, his successor was more a man of thought than of action. He took delight in disputations with philosophers and is known to have prided himself on his architectural acumen. No definite records exist to show what specific role he played in any particular building, but his architects, in deference to their imperial patron, showed their discretion by failing to claim any personal credit for their labors. The most famous architect of Trajan's reign, Apollodorus, is known to have continued his career under Hadrian, and since the Pantheon represents a kind of culmination of Roman engineering skill, it is generally thought to be mainly his work.

The builders first constructed a cylindrical base whose walls are 20 feet in thickness. Eight large recesses were left in it, one to allow for the entrance vestibule, and the others to provide niches for the statuary. To furnish support for the massive dome, a system of relieving arches and abutments were embedded in the wall to discharge its great weight. The concrete for the dome was poured in adjoining sections; and as it dried, it became one solid mass of stone, thus justifying its description as an artificial monolith. Entrance is made through the octastyle Corinthian portico that measures a little over 100 feet in width. Such a huge structure could easily have been just an overwhelming mass of brick and concrete. Its solid exterior proportions actually do very little to relieve this general impression, but the fact that it was conceived primarily as an interior (Fig. 3:20), enclosing a definite space, rather than as the solid mass which surrounds it, saves the day. The Pantheon's geometry is based on the union of a cylinder and hemisphere, with the interior diameter and the height of the dome both

Fig. 3:19 (above). *Pantheon.* Portico 101' wide, 59' high. A. D. 120–124. Rome (Anderson).
Fig. 3:20 (below). Pantheon, *Interior.* Diameter 142', height 140'. Engraving by Piranesi.
Metropolitan Museum, New York

being about 140 feet. The clarity of form achieved by the visible equality
of horizontal and vertical dimensions, as well as by the simplicity of its
design, is evident even to the casual eye. The satisfying sense of spatial
proportion it imparts, and the harmonious impression its interior provides,
is based on this concord of applied scientific skill and aesthetic feeling.
In the Pantheon the Romans advanced architecture to the place where it
began to be conceived in the sense of significant interiors. The inner surface
of the dome is characterized by indented panels, known as coffers, which
served the dual purpose of diminishing the weight of the dome and furnish-
ing the basis for its decoration. In the center of each coffer was a gilded
bronze star, a motive introduced possibly to relate the dome symbolically
to the sky. The sole source of light is the single, 29-foot-round opening in
the middle of the dome. This *oculus*, or eye, as it was called, most likely was
interpreted as an allusion to the all-seeing eye of heaven. Streaming downward through it was a shaft of light sufficient to bathe the whole interior
with brightness. The effect, however, was definitely one of increasing the
sense of clarity rather than of imparting an air of mystery.

What is seen today is but the bare skeleton denuded of its former rich
and colorful covering. The bronze plates of the portico ceiling, the gilded
bronze tiles that covered the entire exterior of both the drum and the
dome, the polychrome marbles that faced the interior walls, and the monumental statues of the gods have all disappeared in the course of time. In
spite of these systematic mutilations, the Pantheon is still the best-preserved
single building that survives from the ancient world, as well as the oldest
structure of large proportions with its original roof intact. It has been able
to hold its own as one of the world's most impressive domed buildings in
spite of such outstanding competition as Hagia Sophia in Constantinople,
St. Peter's in Rome (Fig. 10:18), and St. Paul's in London (Fig. 15:4). Its
descendants are legion—the Villa Rotunda (Fig. 11:6), Thomas Jefferson's
home at Monticello, the rotunda he designed for the University of Virginia,
the Pantheon in Paris, certain features of the Capitol rotunda in Washington, D. C., and the Low Memorial Library at Columbia University in New
York, to name but a few of them.

The Roman Architectural Contribution

The Roman contribution to architecture was fourfold: (1) building for use,
(2) emphasizing verticality, (3) designing significant interiors, and (4) developing and extending the arch as a building principle. In the first case,
Roman architecture is marked by a shift in emphasis from religious buildings to the civil-engineering projects that had such an important bearing

on the solution of the practical problems of the day. This does not mean that the Romans neglected their shrines and temples or that they lacked religious feeling. As in the 19th and 20th centuries, however, the main architectural expression is to be found in secular rather than religious structures. In this category come the basilicas, aqueducts, roads, bridges, even the sewer systems, which so admirably served the utilitarian purposes of the Romans.

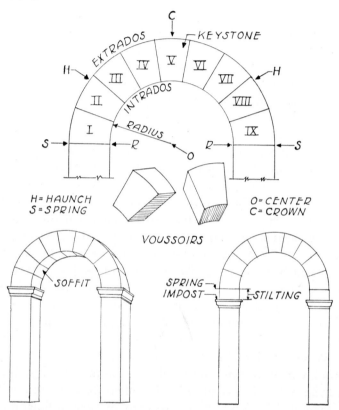

Fig. 3:21. *Elements of a True Arch.* Drawing by W. D. Richmond (Courtesy John Ives Sewall)

Second, by their technical advances they were able to increase the height of their buildings in proportion to the growing size of their large structures. The six-story mercantile buildings of Trajan's Forum, which ran up the Quirinal hillside, are an impressive demonstration of the practical advantages of such verticality, which allowed the combination of many small shops into a single structure in a crowded city location. The multifamily apartment houses in Ostia and Rome are other cases in point. In less practical instances, the trend is seen in the additional height that imparts such pleasing spatial proportions to the halls in the Baths of Trajan and Caracalla as well as the Pantheon, which were all made possible by the methods of cross vaulting and the dome.

Third, the enclosing of large units of interior space was made necessary by the expansion of the city's population. The direction of architectural thought in meeting this need can easily be seen by contrasting a Greek agora, or market place, with the Forum of Trajan; a Hellenistic theater with the Colosseum; or the Parthenon with the Pantheon. Special attention to space composition and the problems of lighting are in evidence in the planning of such interiors as those of the Basilica Ulpia, the Pantheon, and the halls of the great baths. In all instances the increasing Roman aware-ness of the value, tangibility, and reality of the spatial medium is dis-cernible.

Lastly—and perhaps most important of all—was the Roman exploitation of the possibilities inherent in the arch as a building principle to implement the above objectives. The construction of a true arch by means of the wedge-shaped blocks known as *voussoirs* can be seen more easily in Figure 3:21 than explained in words. When such arches are placed side by side in a series, the resulting arcade can be used for such structures as aqueducts and bridges, as seen in the Pont du Gard (Fig. 3:16). When placed in a series from front to back, the result is a barrel vault, also called a tunnel vault, which can be seen in the Arch of Trajan at Benevento (Fig. 3:1), and which was used to roof over interiors. When two such half-cylindrical vaults intersect each other at right angles, as seen in Figure 3:12, the result is referred to as a cross vault or groined vault. This is the principle which is used so advantageously in the central halls of the Baths of Trajan and Caracalla. When a series of arches span a given space by intersecting each other around a central axis, the result is a dome, as exemplified in the Pantheon (Fig. 3:20). In greatly oversimplified form, these constitute the technical principles that underlie the Roman architectural achievement.

SCULPTURE

The Spiral Frieze of Trajan's Column

To commemorate Trajan's victories in the two campaigns against the Dacian people who inhabited the lower Danube region, a monumental column was erected in his Forum by the Senate and people of Rome. It was placed in a small court opening off from the Basilica Ulpia between the two libraries. Its base (Fig. 3:8) was originally surrounded by a colonnade that supported an upper gallery from which better views of the sculptures could be obtained. The width of the column varies from 12 feet at the base of its shaft to 10 feet at the top. As a whole it rose to a full height of 128 feet, including the 18-foot base, the 97-foot shaft, and a 13-foot colossal statue of Trajan made of gilded bronze, which originally stood at the top. The latter has long since disappeared and has been replaced by one of St. Peter. Inside the column is a circular staircase which winds upward to the top and is lighted by small windowlike slits cut into the frieze. According to tradition, Trajan chose the monument as his burial place, and his ashes were placed somewhere beneath it. The column itself is of the Doric order and is constructed in several sections of white marble. Its surface is entirely covered by a spiral band, carved in low relief, which winds around it from the bottom to the top in twenty-three revolutions. Reading from left to right, the story of the two Dacian campaigns unfolds in a continuous frieze about a yard wide and 218 yards long in which more than 2500 human figures make their appearance, in addition to horses, boats, vehicles, and equipment of all kinds.

The hero of the story is, of course, the soldierly Trajan, who is shown fulfilling his imperial mission as the defender of Rome against the encroachments of the barbarians. The Empire was always willing to include any people who accepted the values of Mediterranean civilization, but it could tolerate no challenge. When an important kingdom was founded in Dacia, Trajan regarded it as a threat and set out accordingly to bring it under Roman control. While it took two campaigns to do the job, the lasting result of this Romanizing process is shown by the fact that one of the nations of the region still calls itself Rumania. Trajan's brilliance as a commander was well known, and on this and other similar monuments his reputation certainly did not suffer for lack of advertisement. In the frieze he is invariably present and is consistently portrayed as a resolute figure in complete command of the situation at all times. Sharing top billing with their general is the Roman army; and their opposite numbers are found in the Dacian king Decebalus, who appears as Trajan's antagonist, and his barbarian hordes, who play opposite the Roman legions.

The beginning of the campaign is placed on the banks of the Danube in a Roman encampment guarded by sentries and supplied by boats (Fig. 3:22). As they set forth across a pontoon bridge, a river god personifying the Danube rises from a grotto and lends his support by holding up the bridge. From this point onward the action moves with singular force and directness toward the inevitable climax, the triumph of Roman arms. The ensuing scenes show the Emperor holding a council of war; clad in a toga

Fig. 3:22. Column of Trajan, Reliefs on the Lower Part of Shaft. *Trajan's Campaign against the Dacians*. Marble. A. D. 113 (Alinari)

pouring a libation to the gods; and standing on a tribunal as he addresses his troops. The army is shown pitching a camp on enemy soil; burning a Dacian village; and in the midst of battle. At the psychological moment Jupiter appears in the sky, throwing bolts of lightning at the enemy and dispersing them in all directions. The aftermath of the battle is then shown with the soldiers crowding around Trajan and holding up the decapitated heads of the enemy for his approval; surgeons are seen caring for the wounded; and winged victory makes her appearance.

At the making of peace Trajan is shown seated in judgment on the left and the still-defiant Decebalus is standing on the far right in front of the wall of the Roman camp. Between them are the representatives of the vanquished people prostrating themselves before their conqueror and imploring him for mercy. Here the protagonist and antagonist of the drama confront each other directly in a single scene in the middle of the frieze, which serves as an interim summary of the action up to this point. On this occasion Trajan made a lenient peace which gave the king of the Dacians his chance to regather his forces, thus making a second campaign inevitable. At the conclusion of the story near the top of the column, Decebalus is shown falling on his sword; his head is brought to Trajan as a trophy; the barbarians take refuge across a river; and finally a personification of Night is seen hovering over a desolate landscape.

The scenes are designed to promote the continuous flow of action as smoothly as possible. For reasons of clarity the scenes have to be differentiated, and the artist does this through some 90 separate appearances of Trajan, which always signal a new activity. Other devices employed are an occasional tree, to set off one scene from another, and new backgrounds that are indicated in some places by a mountain, in others by a group of buildings, and so on. The comparison of this type of spiral relief has aptly been made with the form of the unfolding papyrus scrolls that the educated Romans were accustomed to read. Trajan is known to have written an account of his Dacian campaigns, much as Julius Caesar had done in the case of his Gallic wars, but the document was lost. Since commentaries on this bit of history are so fragmentary, the column has become one of the principal sources of information about it. The impression the viewer receives is so vivid that he feels almost as if he had experienced the campaign with Trajan.

The reliefs have a definite affinity to literature in their manner of telling a story by the process of visual narration. The methods that the Romans used in such cases have been distinguished as "the simultaneous" and "the continuous." The first is the same as that used by the Greeks in the east pediment and frieze of the Parthenon, for instance, where all the action takes place at a given moment that is frozen into sculptural form. The simultaneous or isolating method thus observes the classical unities of time, place, and action. The continuous or cyclic method was developed by the Romans for just such a series of scenes as Trajan's wars. The unity of action is obtained by the telling of a life story, or it can be broadened to include a couple of military campaigns, as in this instance. The unities of time and place are sacrificed as far as the whole composition is concerned but are preserved in the separate scenes. While the origin of this continuous style is still a matter of scholarly dispute, none has challenged the effective use the Romans made of it. Its spirit is close to their keen interest in historical and current events, and its value for the purposes of state propaganda is obvious.

Despite the direct narrative content, the style is not realistic. For his effects, the artist depended upon as carefully a worked out set of symbols as the writers of epics have done in the case of words. The use of a series of undulating lines, for instance, indicates the sea; a jagged outline on the horizon stands for a mountain; a giant rising up out of the water represents a river; a wall can mean either a city or a camp; and a female figure whose

draperies are folded in the shape of a crescent moon informs the observer
that it is night. In such a symbolic process, liberties with perspective inevitably occur, and it is quite usual to find a man taller than a wall and an
important figure, such as that of the Emperor, much greater in size than
those around him. This technique does not preclude such clearly recognizable things as the banners of certain Roman legions as well as the details
of their shields and armor. But there is a sharp stylistic differentiation between the approach in this case and the obvious realism of the relief on
the Arch of Titus (Fig. 3:3). The Trajan frieze points unmistakably in the
direction of the pictorial symbolism employed by early Christian and
medieval artists, who doubtless were influenced by it.

Much of the work will seem crude if placed beside the sculpture of the
Hellenistic style produced during the same period. But this relief is clearly
and intentionally an example of Roman popular art, and as such it was
addressed to that large segment of the populace which was not accustomed
to getting its information and enjoyment from books. Its location between
two libraries also indicates a recognition that history could come from
pictorial sources as well as from Greek and Latin scrolls. The elegant and
placid forms of Greek gods were not apt to arouse the emotions of those
Romans who sought amusement in the gladiatorial contests held in the
Colosseum. While the educated minority could admire the virtues of
dignity and restraint in their sculpture, the vast majority had to be aroused
by just such an energetic direct-action story as this, and one which involved
people like themselves. Viewed in this light, the work is fresh, original, and
astonishingly alive.

The artist who designed the frieze was clearly a master of his medium,
who was able to depict with ease in extremely low relief whole armies,
pitched battles, and the surrounding land and seascapes. The care in
execution is consistently carried out, and, even though the reliefs at the
top were almost completely out of view, the workmanship remains the
same. Standing in its prominent location from Trajan's time to ours, the
column has had incalculable influence on later art. The continuous mode
of visual narration was taken over directly into the catacomb paintings of
the early Christians; was continued in illuminated manuscripts, religious
sculptures, and the stained glass of the Middle Ages; and can still be found
going strong in the comic strips of daily newspapers. Even the motion
picture owes a certain debt to the technique worked out here in the 2d
century A. D. In this book examples of the direct influence of this narrative
mode include the mosaics relating the story of Christ in the church of

Sant' Apollinare Nuovo in Ravenna (Figs. 4:4 through 4:6); the Bayeux Tapestry, which tells the story of the Norman conquest of England (Figs. 6:1 through 6:4); Giotto's frescoes on the life of St. Francis of Assisi (Figs. 8:3 through 8:6); Michelangelo's Sistine Chapel ceiling murals (Figs. 10:9 through 10:16); and the studious duplication of it made under Napoleon for the Place Vendôme in Paris (Fig. 17:5).

LITERATURE AND MUSIC

While the time of Trajan could boast of no writers of the caliber of Cicero, Lucretius, Vergil, or Horace, it could at least point with pride to some of its eminent men of letters. Quintilian, author of the famous textbook known as the *Institutes of Oratory*, had influenced directly or indirectly a group of writers including Pliny the Younger, a persuasive orator and graceful letter writer; Tacitus, the historian; Juvenal, the satirist; and Suetonius, who was responsible for the gossipy but informative *Lives of the Twelve Caesars*. Plutarch, though a Greek, must also be listed among the major writers of the period, especially for his perceptive series of biographies of Greek and Roman statesmen, the *Parallel Lives*.

A very vivid picture of the life of a Roman of the patrician class is found in the correspondence of Pliny the Younger. As a senator and holder of important offices under Trajan, he enjoyed a wide acquaintance with many men of affairs. As a man of means he was able to enjoy all the refinements of a style of living that was highly luxurious even by modern standards. His civic duties required him to pass much of his time in Rome, but, like so many others of his class, he preferred to live in more rural surroundings. His country estates extended from one end of the Italian peninsula to the other, and he took special pride in the beautiful villas he built on them. Two that he was especially fond of were located on Lake Como. One he called Tragedy because it commanded a grand view from its lofty situation; the other he named Comedy because it was more intimately built on the lakeshore and more conducive to sport. "You may fish yourself," he wrote to a friend, "and throw your line out of your room, and almost from your bed, as from a boat." [3]

Pliny's descriptions of his villa near Florence and another near Ostia are so detailed that architects have been able to reconstruct them with considerable exactness. The pleasures available at his Tuscan estate included hunting, supervising the farming, strolling about in gardens, exercising and playing games in the gymnasium, banqueting, and swimming, for which there were no less than three pools including a warm one in the sun and a cool one in the shade. Pliny was not one to neglect the pleasures of the mind, which in his case included reading in his extensive library, conversing and corresponding with stimulating friends, and collecting objects of art that took his fancy. His enthusiasm for the latter pursuit is expressed in one of his letters. "I have lately purchased with a legacy that was left me, a statue of Corinthian bronze," he informed a friend. "It represents an old man in a standing posture. The bones, the muscles, the veins, and wrinkles are so strongly expressed, that you would imagine the figure to be animated." [4]

Because of the Ciceronian eloquence he had developed as a pupil of Quintilian, Pliny was chosen by the Senate to make the welcoming speech on the occasion of Trajan's first arrival in Rome after his accession as emperor. The *Panegyric* he delivered was a veritable triumphal arch of flowery oratory. His later correspondence with Trajan, when he was governor of the distant province of Bithynia, is as businesslike and direct as the speech to the Senate was ornate and devious. Pliny wrote to his superior with a proper note of deference, and Trajan's replies were always terse and right to the point. In a typical exchange Pliny asked whether it would be advisable to rebuild the baths in one of the towns under his jurisdiction. The complete text of Trajan's reply was as follows: "If the erecting a public bath will not be too great a charge upon the Prusenses, we may comply with their request; provided, however, that no new tax be levied for this purpose, nor any of those taken off which are appropriated to necessary purposes." [5]

The practice of poetry and music enjoyed higher favor among the educated Romans than dabbling in the visual arts. Suggesting a plan for a building or some of the details of its decorative design was all right for a landowner, but from there on it was the architect's and carpenter's business. With sculpture and painting, a wealthy man could make an imposing impression as a collector, but the actual chiseling and daubing was something for artisans and slaves. When it came to the writing of verse or singing to the accompaniment of the lyre, however, amateurs abounded in the highest ranks of society right up to the emperors themselves. While Trajan's recreations seem to have been as strenuous as some of his military activities, those of his immediate successors included literary and musical pursuits. Hadrian, for instance, wrote poetry in both Greek and Latin, but it remained for the last of the Antonines, Marcus Aurelius, to make an enduring reputation for himself as a writer and philosopher. Hadrian, Antoninus

Fig. 3:23. *Gladiatorial Contest*, showing Orchestra with Hydraulic Organ, Trumpet, and Horn Players. Mosaic from Zliten, Tripolitania. A. D. *c.*70 (Courtesy Salvatore Aurigemma)

Pius, and Caracalla were proficient on the cithara and hydraulic organ. Their musical prowess, however, was not destined to put that of their famous predecessor, Nero, into the shade.

While much is known about Roman literature, there is a dearth of exact information on the nature of Roman music. Since no actual examples survive, the only available sources are occasional literary references; sculptures, mosaics, and wall paintings, which show music-making situations; and some of the musical instruments themselves. From these it is clear that the Romans heard a great deal of music, and that no occasion, public or private, was complete without music of some kind.

A mosaic showing a small Roman instrumental ensemble performing in an amphitheater during a gladiatorial contest has been found in some recent excavations at Zliten in North Africa (Fig. 3:23). One musician is shown playing the long, straight brass instrument known as the *tuba*, or trumpet; two others are playing the circular *cornu*, or horn; while still another is seated at the *hydraulus*, or water organ. Equipped with a rudimentary keyboard and stops, this highly ingenious instrument worked on the principle of forcing air compressed by two water tanks through a set of bronze pipes. Some of these instruments were 10 feet high, and they were used mainly in open-air arenas where their tone must have resembled that of the calliopes, once so popular in old-fashioned circus parades. Other Roman instruments included the *tibia*, which was a version of the Greek *aulos*, or reed pipe; the panpipes, principally a rustic instrument; and the metal plates known as cymbals which were clapped together by the hands, or sometimes attached to the feet.

In keeping with the Roman idea of grandeur, the size of their instruments was greatly increased. Marcellinus described a performance in which hundreds of players took part, some of whom were said to have performed on "lyres as big as chariots." Owing to their usefulness in warfare, an ever-increasing volume of sound was demanded of wind instruments. Battle signals were relayed by means of trumpet calls, and the larger the legions, the bigger and brassier became the sound. This is borne out by Quintilian, who asks a typical rhetorical question, then proceeds to answer it with a characteristic flourish: "And what else is the function of the horns and trumpets attached to our legions? The louder the concert of their notes, the greater is the glorious supremacy of our arms over all the nations of the earth." [6] The large audiences accustomed to gather in amphitheaters also played a part in the stepping up of the volume of individual instruments and in the development of sizable vocal and instrumental ensembles. Writing in the 1st century A. D., Seneca notes that the size of the vocal and instrumental ensembles was such that there sometimes were more singers and players in the arena than in the audience. Soloists would obviously be lost in such vast surroundings, and it is not unusual to come across descriptions of large groups of singers accompanied by wind instruments of various kinds and the hydraulic organ.

Quintilian also points out some of the practical applications of music to the art of oratory. He particularly emphasizes the development of the voice because "it is by raising, lowering, or inflexion of the voice that the orator stirs the emotions of his hearers." He then cites the example of one of the great speakers of the past who had a musician standing behind him while making his speeches, "whose duty it was to give him the tones in which his voice was to be pitched. Such was the attention which he paid to this point even in the midst of his most turbulent speeches, when he was terrifying the patrician party." [7]

Literary sources point to a high degree of musical activity in Rome during the 2d century A. D. From the number of Greek-trained singers, instrumentalists, and mimes who were active, it is clear that the Greek tradition was still very much alive. In its more austere forms, however, Greek art could have appealed only to the aristocratic minority. Hence like so many other Greek artistic practices, music was adapted to the needs and uses of a large cosmopolitan center which embraced a great variety of tastes. Pliny casually mentions what the entertainment in a cultivated household would

Fig. 3:24. Dioskourides of Samos. *Street Musicians*. Mosaic from Herculaneum. *c*.100 B. C. National Museum, Naples (Alinari)

have been like, when he chides one of his friends for not appearing at a dinner to which he had been invited. After describing the menu he missed, he tells him that he was to have been "entertained either with an interlude, the rehearsal of a poem, or a piece of music," [8] whichever his guest preferred. Music was also a part of every theatrical performance, and, while the Roman drama omitted the chorus that the Greeks had stressed, its dialogue was interspersed with songs accompanied by the *tibia*. Such musical portions, however, were not composed by the dramatists as they had been in the Athenian tradition, but were delegated to specialists in this field. In addition to the use of trumpets for signaling, the importance of choruses and bands for military morale was not overlooked, and a functional type of military music also existed. In addition, there was the popular ensemble music which was played at games and contests; and some strolling street musicians can be seen performing in Figure 3:24.

The fact that not a single note of any of this music is in existence today points to the fact that Roman music was primarily a performing art. While the practicing musicians may very well have composed their own songs and pieces, or made variations on traditional tunes, none seems to have been concerned with committing them to paper—and if one had done so, the church fathers would have seen to it that these pagan melodies were committed to the flames. So, like the folk music that existed only in oral tradition until the advent of modern notation and recording devices, the art died with the people who practiced it.

IDEAS

As a part of the main stream of classical culture, Roman civilization shared many of the basic ideas that produced the Hellenic and Hellenistic styles. Significantly the Romans widened the scope of the arts to include not only works that were aimed at the connoisseur level but those that carried broad mass appeal as well. The two ideas, then, that differentiate the Roman from the earlier aspects of the classical styles and that dominate the Roman expression in the arts, are the genius for organization and the frank spirit of utilitarianism, evidenced in their conception of the arts as a means to popular enjoyment and the solution of practical problems.

Organization

The Roman ability to organize is shown in the consistent application to the building up of a systematic world order, which embraced a unified religion, a unified body of laws, and a unified civilization. Military conquest was, to be sure, one of the means employed; but the allowance of a maximum of self-government to subject peoples, a wide latitude to local customs, even to tribal and cult religions, is proof of the Romans' psychological realism and toleration. Their promotion of external unity did not imply internal uniformity, and their recognition of this fact was at the root of their success as administrators. With this ability to organize their religious, legal, social, and governmental institutions, it is clear that their greatest contribution in the arts would lie in the direction of architecture. This organizational spirit, moreover, is revealed most decisively in their undertaking of large public-works projects, such as the building of roads, ports, aqueducts, and the like. It is also seen in their manner of grouping buildings on a common axis, as in the Forum of Trajan, which was so directly in contrast to the

Hellenic idea of isolated perfection; in the organization of business activities in common centers, and the various forms of recreation in the baths; in the technical application and development of all the possibilities of construction by means of the arch; in the combination of the Ionic and Corinthian capitals to form the Composite order, their only distinctive contribution to the classical orders of architecture; in the use of three orders on the exterior of the same building, as in the Colosseum where Tuscan-Doric columns are found on the first story, Ionic on the second, and Corinthian on the third; in the development of the multifamily apartment house; in the attention given to the efficient assembling and dispersing of large numbers of people in such buildings as the Colosseum; in the invention of a supermarket, such as the six-storied example in Trajan's Forum; and finally, in the erection of a supertemple for all the gods, as in the Pantheon.

The same organizational spirit is reflected in the expansion of interior space as in the Basilica Ulpia, the Pantheon, and the great halls of the baths in order to accommodate ever larger numbers of people. The Greek idea had been to define space in planes, and the exteriors of their temples were designed as backdrops for processions and religious ceremonies. Those who worshiped Athena at the Parthenon were concerned primarily with its external colonnade, not the interior. Space in this sense was defined but not organized, but in the Pantheon interior space was enveloped and made real. To the Greeks, space always remained a formless void, but the Romans recognized the possibilities of three-dimensional space, enclosed it, and endowed it with significant form. Among the many ways they sought to enhance this spatial feeling are a sensitivity to scale; a tendency to design buildings in related structural units; an exploitation of color by the use of polychrome marbles, which livened interiors and which added to the perception of depth; a use of illusionistic wall paintings to suggest the third dimension; and an increased attention given to lighting problems. All this the Romans accomplished without sacrificing the classical clarity of form. The same feeling, furthermore, is carried over into sculpture where the tangibility of the spatial environment is reflected in the backgrounds of reliefs by means of buildings and landscapes which suggest depth, whereas the 5th-century B. C. Grecian style consciously omitted any such frame of reference. In addition to this, the organization of time into a temporal continuum, as in the cyclical series presented on the Column of Trajan, shows a new concept of sequential order translated into the pictorial medium.

Still another facet of this Roman organizational ability is found in the allowance for a wide range of taste in the arts. There were styles which

appealed to the educated few and those which held the attention of the
untutored populace of the middle and lower classes. In one case it was
directed to the eye and ear of the connoisseur, and in the other it was
frankly popular in its appeal. The conservative tastes of the first group
harkened back to the tried-and-true values of Greek art; hence they
either collected antique statuary and paintings, or they commissioned new
works to be executed in the older style. In extolling the virtues of his newly
acquired Corinthian statuette, Pliny the Younger wrote: "It is small, but
pleasing, and finely executed, at least, if I have any taste." [9] Such a piece
would have held little interest for the majority, who needed something
more like a large bronze equestrian statue or a monumental triumphal
arch to capture their attention. In Trajan's Forum due allowance was made
for this variety of taste, with the Greek and Latin libraries placed on either
side of a court and a column in between, where the story of Trajan's
campaigns was related in a carefully worked out language of symbols
designed to awaken the curiosity of the multitude.

The disdain of the conservative group for popular art was well stated by
Athenaeus, a Greek scholar and teacher who resided in Rome about A. D.
200. He championed the virtues of the older cultural tradition and frequently made unflattering comparisons between the higher standards of
the past and those that prevailed in his day. "In early times," he wrote,
"popularity with the masses was a sign of bad art; hence, when a certain
aulos-player once received loud applause, Asopodorus of Phlius, who was
himself still waiting in the wings, said 'What's this? Something awful must
have happened!' The player evidently could not have won approval with
the crowds otherwise. . . . And yet the musicians of our day set as the
goal of their art success with their audiences." [10] Just as in the case of
architecture, sculpture, and painting, the Romans were heirs to the Greek
musical tradition. The ancient theories survived in philosophical speculation, and Greek music teachers were employed by preference in the homes
of the wealthy. The only musical compositions to survive from this period,
for instance, are three hymns by Mesomedes, a Greek musician attached to
Hadrian's court. Those who cultivated this more austere style still felt
that music was meant to educate and elevate the mind, but the popular
taste lay in quite another direction.

The music-making that Athenaeus and his conservative group scorned
was obviously the very kind that the majority of Romans enjoyed at their
public festivals, military parades, games, sporting contests, races, and to
some extent the theater. The modern parallel would be the cleavage that

exists between audiences interested in chamber music, symphony concerts, and the opera, and those attracted by bands at football games, Broadway musicals, and Hollywood films. What the Romans accomplished here was broadening the base of the appeal of the arts and gearing them to a number of different types of audience. They thus succeeded in providing for the entertainment of a large city population, just as their buildings and civil-engineering projects took care of their physical needs.

Utilitarianism

In referring to the administrations of the last two Antonine emperors, Gibbon declared that "their united reigns are possibly the only period of history in which the happiness of a great people was the sole object of government." [11] The basis of this claim is to be found in the way the Romans managed to steer a middle course between the Scylla of Greek theoretical abstractions about the nature of an ideal state and the Charybdis of religious speculation on the joys of the world to come, that was to characterize the subsequent Christian phases of the Empire. Speculation on the eternal verities could edify the mind, but the understanding of human behavior was rewarded by more immediate advantages. In the late Antonine Age, Rome had reached an equilibrium based on an acceptance of the Stoic doctrine of "live and let live," and the Epicurean idea of pleasure as an index to the highest good. The transfer of these individualistic doctrines to the forms and policies of a government meant a high degree of tolerance on one side, and a recognition that the standard of excellence in either a law or a work of art was whether it would bring the greatest good to the greatest number. The construction of elegantly proportioned temples was therefore not so important as the building of a new hospital or an aqueduct. Maintaining a luxurious private palace was secondary to that of providing people's palaces such as the public baths and theaters. A private collection of sculpture was subordinate to public exhibitions in city squares and galleries where the statues could be seen and enjoyed by many. A play, poem, or piece of music that awakened only the sensibilities of the cultured minority did not rank so high on this scale as those that were applauded by the multitude. In short, the practical arts were favored over the decorative arts; material goods superseded more remote spiritual blessings; and utility was in the ascendance over abstract beauty, though it must be remembered that the two are not mutually exclusive.

Since the Romans were concerned less with ideal forms, it was by no means accidental that their greatest successes were in the arts of government rather than in the fine arts. As Vergil said in the *Aeneid:* "Let others melt and mold the breathing bronze to forms more fair . . . or trace with pointed wand the cycled heaven, and hail the constellations as they rise; But thou, Oh Roman, learn with sovereign sway to rule the nations." [12] As might be expected the art which was most congenial to Roman aspirations was that of architecture, especially in its utilitarian aspects as found in the field of civil engineering. Building a 200-mile highway over the mountains, moving part of a hill over 100 feet high to make way for a forum, providing a sewer system for a city of over one million inhabitants, bridging the Danube at its widest point, perfecting new building materials such as brick and concrete—all these were taken in stride.

When it came to sculpture, the Romans saw that its subject matter served the purposes of the state by extolling the virtues and deeds of the emperors. Such epic poems as the *Aeneid* performed a similar service in the literary medium; and, as Quintilian said, the loud sounds of the brass instruments proclaimed the glory of Roman arms. Other applications of this utilitarianism are found in the brilliant exploitation of such technical devices as the arch and the vault. Their success in solving such practical problems as the bringing of water from great distances and the like is proved by the number of roads and bridges which are still serving their purpose to this day. In sculpture the application of the continuous-narrative method to the telling of a story was progressive in that it promoted the sense of continuity in the temporal dimension, and that it anticipated later Christian and secular pictorial forms. The development of such a practical form of verbal communication into the art of letter-writing, beginning with Cicero and continuing with the younger Pliny, was the literary facet of the same idea. Finally, when Quintilian pointed out how the art of melody could be applied to oratory by the use of a pitch pipe to give the speaker a more persuasive tone, the cycle is complete.

Effective as this utilitarianism was, it was purchased at the price of a conflict between structure and decoration; extrinsic and intrinsic values; and the purposive and nonpurposive aspects of art. The Romans built and decorated well, but the two, somehow, failed to achieve a harmonious coexistence. This is well illustrated by the somewhat hollow claim of Augustus, who proudly boasted that he found Rome a city of brick and left it a city of marble. Actually Rome was still a city of brick and concrete under an Augustan marble veneer. Both materials need no apology nor even a disguise, as proved by the rhythmical grace of the functional arches of the Pont du Gard. Hence it was in no way necessary to imply that Roman structures were solid marble like the Parthenon. As a whole, then, Roman architecture was at its best when it stuck to its frank utilitarianism, undertook vast engineering projects, and successfully solved the practical problems of construction.

Conclusion

Older cultural centers, such as Athens and Pergamon, were so far off the beaten track that not until the archeological discoveries of the 19th century did their more austere classical purity exert any appreciable influence on the forms of Western art. All intervening phases of classicism, such as those associated with the Renaissance, Baroque, and the 18th-century Neo-classical movement, were associated with adaptations of some aspects of the Roman style. With the establishment of the Roman building methods, the course of Western architecture was firmly set, and it steered in sub-stantially the same direction until the technological discoveries of the 19th and 20th centuries. It must therefore be emphasized once more that Rome was the gateway through which all the styles, forms, and ideas of Mediter-ranean civilization passed by in review. After being transformed by the process of selectivity, and with flashes of genuine originality, into a uniquely Roman configuration, they proceeded onward through the arch into medi-eval culture by way of the new capitals of Byzantium in the east and Ravenna in the west. When Rome declined as the center of world empire, it still remained the capital of Christendom. As the object of pilgrimages, its architectural, sculptural, and literary monuments were bound to exert a massive influence on the rulers, people, and artists who gravitated at one time or another toward the city. Because of this enduring pre-eminence during all subsequent phases of Western culture, no important city exists without a bit of Rome in it. The list of later buildings derived directly from Roman antecedents would read like an encyclopedia of architecture. To set but a few of those in New York City alone beside their models, one could mention the triumphal arch built in Washington Square to honor the centenary of the first president's inauguration and the Arch of Titus; the High Bridge across the Harlem River and the aqueduct of Claudius; the concourse of the Pennsylvania Station and the Baths of Caracalla; and the Low Memorial Library at Columbia University and the Pantheon. It is therefore with full justification that Rome has been and still continues to be called the Eternal City.

PART 2

THE MEDIEVAL
PERIOD

CHAPTER

4

THE EARLY CHRISTIAN
AND BYZANTINE STYLES

RAVENNA, 6th CENTURY

Many an old Roman coin bears the inscription *Ravenna Felix*—happy Ravenna. If happiness in a city means peace and tranquillity, long periods of security and consistent prosperity, this inscription is certainly a misnomer. If, on the other hand, the definition of municipal bliss includes hardship and struggle, sudden turns in fortune, healthy growth, climactic maturity, several centuries of marriage to a glamorous Oriental city and culture, a building program of unparalleled brilliance, a long slow period of declining years, the confident knowledge of leaving behind a distinguished memory, and bequeathing to posterity a rich treasure of works of art, then Ravenna must be reckoned among the happiest of cities.

Ravenna began life as a minor Roman provincial town, solitary amidst swamps and marshes, remote and inaccessible except from the sea, and it would have been a reckless prophet who dared to predict that one day she would be greater, more populous and resplendent than Rome itself. In her early days Ravenna saw Caesar setting forth to cross the nearby Rubicon River on his way to found the greatest empire the world has ever seen. In her maturity she was the center and setting of the three-way struggle for parts of that empire by the remnants of Rome in the west, the rising power of Constantinople in the east, and the vigorous push of the Gothic kingdoms in the north. In her declining years she witnessed such diverse events as Charlemagne entering as a conqueror, Giotto painting murals, Paolo making love to Francesca, and Dante finishing his *Divine Comedy*.

It was to Ravenna that the Emperor Honorius repaired in the early years of the 5th century when he was under the constant harassment of the northern barbarians. After the city of Rome fell to them, Ravenna held out until the year 476 when Odoacer finally succeeded in entering the all but impregnable city. Surrounded on the east by the Adriatic Sea, on the north and south by the Po River delta, Ravenna could be entered only through a narrow land corridor running through swamps. It was here that the beleaguered Roman forces could retire and regroup with full natural protection. By thus providing the necessary refuge for land armies, the port from which they could be supplied by the Eastern Empire, and a stable location where the business of government could be carried on, Ravenna's future was assured.

An early visitor to the city has left a word picture of how it appeared in the 5th century. "There your ears are pierced by the mosquito of the Po," he wrote, "and a talkative mob of frogs is always croaking around you. Ravenna is a mere marsh where all the conditions of life are reversed, where walls fall and waters stand, towers flow down and ships squat, invalids walk and their doctors take to bed, baths freeze and houses burn, the living perish with thirst and the dead swim about on the surface of the water, thieves watch and magistrates sleep, priests lend at usury and Syrians sing psalms, merchants shoulder arms and soldiers haggle like hucksters, greybeards play at ball and striplings at dice, and eunuchs study the art of war and the barbarian mercenaries study literature." [1] On this unpromising site Roman emperors, Gothic kings, and Byzantine overlords constructed a mighty if somewhat fantastic city. New aqueducts brought in greater water supplies; part of the river was diverted into canals, which passed through the streets, bringing merchandise and food in periods of peace and forming protective moats in time of war. A harbor for the Roman Adriatic fleet was constructed, and the new city of Classe grew up about it.

Mere geography in this case tells us no more than the boards of a theater do about a play; and Ravenna was the stage on which the decisive political, military, religious, and artistic events of a century and a half of world drama were played. More than the sea stretched between Ravenna and Constantinople in the east; there were higher mountains than the Apennines separating her from Rome, and far more than the Alps stood between her and the northern barbarian tribes. The metaphysical barriers were even more dense and impassable than the mountain ranges and the sea. This was an age beset by doctrinal disputes centering around the nature of the Trinity, especially with Christ as the second person of the Trinity. Was his nature all divine, all human, or both? The Gothic tribes had been converted to Christianity by the followers of Arius of Alexandria (d. 336), who denied the existence of the Trinity. The Arians held that since Christ was created by God the Father, he was subordinate and hence not of one substance with Him. While they believed that Christ was the noblest of all created beings, he was essentially human rather than divine. In Constantinople the monophysites held that Christ, as the incarnated Word, was of one divine nature only, and hence not human in the usual sense. The Roman Catholic position was a middle ground between the two extremes, holding that since the Word was made flesh, Christ was a full member of the Trinity and possessed both divine and human natures. While such theological controversies seem remote to later times, they were of sufficient intensity in the early days of Christianity to shake empires, depose kings, and cause decades of war.

With Ravenna the new seat of the Roman Empire of the West, the Pope, as Bishop of Rome, had historical precedent on the side of his claim to supremacy, whereas the Bishop of Ravenna had the weight of political authority since he was nearer to the center of power. The rivalry had to be settled by a decree from the Emperor Justinian, recognizing the precedence of the Bishop of Rome over all priests. Thus while Ravenna produced no original heresies or political crises strictly of her own making, the conflicts of the Empire all centered within her walls. For a considerable time she succeeded in maintaining an uneasy equilibrium between the Arian Goths in Italy, the monophysites in the east, and Roman Catholicism. Politically this meant the balance between the Arian Gothic kingdom, the Byzantine Empire of the East, and the remnants of the disintegrating Roman Empire of the West. The struggle was among different minds and among different ways of life, all jockeying for position within the great and sprawling territories formerly constituting the Roman Empire.

Here in Ravenna the marriage between East and West was consummated and eventually dissolved. Here the remarkable confluence of Roman, Gothic, and Byzantine elements bore rich artistic fruit. The last flowering of imperial Rome took place under Galla Placidia. In the Ostrogothic kingdom of Theodoric, Latin and Teutonic forces were fused for three decades. After Theodoric's death the struggle to bring Ravenna and Italy within the Byzantine orbit was triumphantly accomplished by the Emperor Justinian through the military prowess of Belisarius and the political sagacity of Archbishop Maximian. Most of the monuments which represent this play of forces between the worlds of the north, east, and west rose in Ravenna during the first half of the 6th century. It is thus because of the abundance of artistic progeny produced by this marriage of the Orient and the Occident, rather than in the endless theological disputations and the violent fluctuations of her political and military fortunes, that Ravenna can truly be called happy.

ARCHITECTURE AND MOSAICS

When Ravenna replaced Rome as the capital of the Western Empire, she had to undergo a rapid transformation from her status as a minor provincial town to that of a major metropolis. When she was taken over as the center of his Ostrogothic kingdom, Theodoric wrote to an official in Rome: "I wish my age to match the preceding ones in the beauty of its buildings," thus showing that he had equally ambitious plans for the city. Later when Ravenna was joined to the dominions of the Byzantine Empire, Justinian could not afford to be outdone by his predecessors, and he continued to make notable architectural contributions of his own. As a capital city with a cosmopolitan population, Ravenna contained at one time specimens of every important architectural type of its period, secular as well as sacred. Each foreign embassy, for instance, had to build not only a palace for its delegation but also a church. Differences of creed created the need for appropriate architectural settings for each religious practice. Consequently there were Jewish synagogues and a profusion of Christian churches to provide theaters for the various eastern liturgies of Antioch, Alexandria, and Constantinople, as well as a dozen varieties of Western usages. If all these buildings had survived, Ravenna would now be a complete museum of the Mediterranean architecture of the 5th and 6th centuries. All but a few fragments of the secular buildings, however, have perished with the passage of time; but a representative cross section of its religious structures remains that is capable not only of conveying a clear idea of the distinctive building types of the time, but, more broadly, of constituting an adequate cultural index of this important transitional period between the classical and medieval worlds.

The Mausoleum of Galla Placidia, which survives from the latter days of the Western Roman Empire, is the earliest known example of a church or chapel built in the form of the equal-winged Greek cross. Two Early Christian oblong basilicas, Sant' Apollinare Nuovo and Sant' Apollinare in Classe, illustrate the adaptation of one of the Roman public building forms for Christian worship. Two domed octagonal baptistries, one for the use of the Roman Orthodox and the other for Arian Christians, provide the link between Roman bathing habits and Christian baptismal practices. A circular tomb built for Theodoric and the Byzantine church of San Vitale point to the continuation of classical buildings of the central type. All these examples, furthermore, fall conveniently within the span of time that corresponds with the period of Ravenna's greatness.

Sant' Apollinare Nuovo

Theodoric's building program for the city included a church for his own sect, the Arian Christians, but when construction began it had the dual purpose of providing a chapel adjacent to his new palace and an Arian cathedral for the city. According to the original inscription, the church was dedicated by Theodoric to "Our Lord Jesus Christ." After Justinian's conquest it was rededicated to St. Martin of Tours, the arch enemy of the Arian heresy, and it was then known as San Martino in Cielo d'Oro, because of its golden roof which was later destroyed. In the middle of the 9th century, when the nearby city of Classe was threatened by a Saracenic invasion, the relics of St. Apollinare were transferred from his church there, and once more the church was rededicated, this time as the "new St. Apollinare." This saint, according to tradition, was a friend and disciple of St. Peter in Antioch and is believed to have been appointed by St. Peter as the city's first bishop.

The form of Sant' Apollinare Nuovo is that of the oblong Early Christian basilica type. As a glance at the floor plan (Fig. 4:1) will show, it is divided by twin rows of 12 columns each into a wide nave and two narrower side aisles. The simple plan is without a transept and terminates in a semi-circular apse the width of the nave. The form is thus closely allied with that of the large public buildings of the imperial Roman period, such as the Basilica Ulpia (Figs. 3:4 and 3:7).

The older temples had proved unadaptable for Christian purposes, not only because of their pagan associations but because of the cramped space allotted to their interiors. Since Christianity was a religion that demanded the active participation of all its members, sufficient space to accommodate large numbers had to be provided. While the Altar of Zeus at Pergamon had, in effect, turned the older Greek temple upside down, the Christian basilica may be said to have turned it outside in, with the colonnade, frieze, and pediment all oriented toward the interior. This shows, of course, a fundamental change in spirit. In Greek temples, the worshipers had gathered around outdoor altars, and the cella interiors were plain rooms designed principally to house the cult statue. Hence the decorative elements of these classical structures were found mostly on the outside. The early Christians, however, remained almost entirely indifferent to the exteriors of their buildings; but in contrast to the external severity, the church interiors were just as elaborately designed and as richly adorned as their means would permit.

The prototype for many Early Christian churches is Old St. Peter's, which

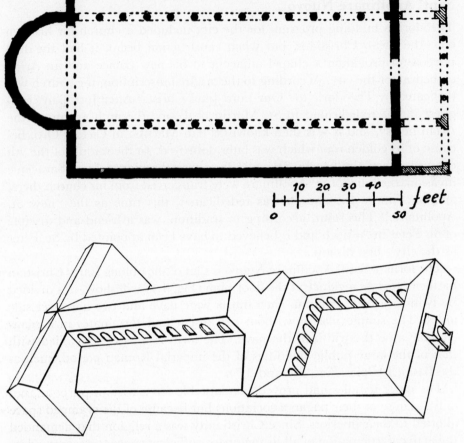

Fig. 4:1 (top). Sant' Apollinare Nuovo, *Plan*. (Nikolaus Pevsner. *An Outline of European Architecture*. London, John Murray, 1949. p. 3. By permission). Fig. 4:2 (above). *An Early Christian Basilica with Atrium*. Schematic drawing by Henry Tisdall (Courtesy John Ives Sewall)

was built on Vatican Hill by Constantine. As the see of Rome, St. Peter's naturally became the object of all Christian eyes, and its influence on subsequent church plans can hardly be overestimated. Sant' Apollinare Nuovo was one of the many smaller buildings modeled after it; and, like its model, it was approached through a type of open courtyard called the *atrium* (Fig. 4:2). Architecturally this was a unit derived from the old Roman private house, and served to enclose the façade of a church by means of a colonnade and a portico. It thus functioned as a protection to the church from street noises, as a place for the instruction of converts, and as an enclosure for the fountain that was used for the ceremonial washing of hands before entering the church. The old atrium of Sant' Apollinare Nuovo has long since disappeared, and its present façade, portico, apse, and bell tower all belong to much later periods. The nave, however, remains intact (Fig. 4:3).

Entrance to the church is through the western portals, and it is an important fact that Early Christian basilicas are literally "oriented"—that is, turned toward the east. The basilica interior, like that of its Roman secular counterpart, is a rectangular hall, oblong in shape and about twice as long as it is wide. A colonnade running lengthwise on either side divides the space into three parts, with that in the center about twice the width of the side aisles. Vertically the center section rises higher than those on the side, thus allowing for rows of clearstory windows on either side to provide light and ventilation. Roofed over with timber, this main part of the basilica was known as the *nave*, a word derived from the Latin *navis*, or ship, which symbolically transported the believers safely to the haven, or heaven, of salvation.

Like all Early Christian basilicas, Sant' Apollinare Nuovo gives the impression of being a shelter from the outside world. Perhaps this is so partly

Fig. 4:3. *Sant' Apollinare Nuovo*, Interior of Nave. *c*.493–526. Ravenna (Alinari)

because in the early days the Christians were a persecuted sect and partly because Christianity is a mystery religion. The Early Christian basilica, therefore, provided no windows from which the outside world could be seen. Those of the clearstory are too high and deeply set to allow even a glimpse of the sky. The inner radiance of the spirit was sought more than the light which emanated from natural sources. Since true illumination could come only from within, the architecture had to allow for the necessary closed interior space in which the Christian mysteries could be enacted. The oblong basilica, with its long colonnades leading the eyes as well as the movements of the faithful toward the altar, was thus ideal for the processional aspects of the liturgy, and it has substantially remained so up to the present time. In the early rites of the Western Church, the congregation approached the altar first in the Offertory procession, then once again for the Communion service. When the Offertory procession was abolished in the Eastern Church, the oblong basilica became obsolete there, and the domed central type church was found to be better adapted to its more static liturgy. The difference between the Churches of the East and the West in this respect became that between a contemplative and an active form of worship.

Still other spatial divisions had to be set aside for the enactment of the Christian mysteries. Between the nave and the sanctuary is the arch through which the faithful pass on their way to the altar. Both because of its architectural resemblance to the older Roman imperial structures, and because of its liturgical significance as the point through which the procession must pass, it was called a *triumphal arch* and was usually adorned with either frescoes or mosaics. A space for the choir was designated, and some columns or a screen were used to set aside a space for the *presbyterium*—literally, a place for the elders. The climax of the building was, of course, the high altar, which was placed in the apse where it was enframed by a half dome on which heavenly scenes were represented.

In addition to its architectural interest, the mosaics in its nave would in themselves be sufficient to assure Sant' Apollinare Nuovo a place among the world's most notable buildings. In the Early Christian period the three-dimensional art of sculpture was minimized, since it still had lingering overtones from the graven images of pagan idols. The earliest buildings were decorated mostly with mural paintings in fresco, but as the new religion acquired prestige and the wealth to employ the finest artists, mosaic work gradually replaced the murals. The mosaic medium lends itself unusually well to the representation of the abstract subjects demanded by the iconography of the period.

The mosaics of Sant' Apollinare Nuovo are of two styles, the earlier

Fig. 4:4. Sant' Apollinare Nuovo. *Mosaic Panels. c.*520

being those done under Ostrogothic rule, while the later date from the time of Byzantine dominance. The examples commissioned by Theodoric are clearly of Roman workmanship. The letter in which he requested the services of mosaicists from Rome is still extant. "Send us from your city," he wrote through his secretary Cassiodorus, "some of your most skillful marble-workers, who may join together those pieces which have been exquisitely divided, and, connecting together their different veins of color, may admirably represent the natural appearance." [2]

The composition as a whole is symmetrical, with both side walls divided into three zones (Fig. 4:4). Above the nave arcade and below the clearstory windows, a wide and continuous mosaic band runs the entire length of the nave in the manner of a frieze. From *Theodoric's Palace* on one side and from the *City of Classe* on the other, two long processions of martyred saints move majestically toward the altar. The second zone occupies the space between the clearstory windows, where representations of unidentified prophets and saints are found. Above the clearstory windows is a series of panels that tell of Christ's parables and miracles on one side, and of his passion and resurrection on the other. The mosaics of the upper and middle zones are intact from the time of Theodoric, while only a part of the lower frieze dates from his time.

Fig. 4:5. Sant' Apollinare Nuovo. *Last Supper*. Mosaic. *c*.520

Fig. 4:6. Sant' Apollinare Nuovo. *Good Shepherd Separating the Sheep from the Goats*. Mosaic. *c*.520 (Anderson)

The scenes in the upper zone are the most complete representation of the life of Christ in Early Christian art. Their simplicity and directness is entirely different in spirit from the more remote and symbolic treatment evident in the later Byzantine examples. Different cultural and theological viewpoints are reflected in the two types of mosaics, with the Arian examples emphasizing Christ's worldly life and human suffering, while the more symbolic Byzantine panels accent his divinity and remoteness from the mundane sphere.

The two scenes on opposite sides nearest the altar are the *Marriage at Cana* and the *Last Supper* (Fig. 4:5). Their appropriateness in this location is obvious, since both refer to the institution of the Eucharist. In one Christ changed the water into wine as his first miracle, while at the Last Supper he changed the wine into his blood which was to be shed for the salvation of man. This interesting representation of the Last Supper shows the disciples reclining in the manner of a Roman banquet.

Beyond the *Marriage at Cana* on the miracle side is the *Good Shepherd Separating the Sheep from the Goats* (Fig. 4:6), an incident alluding to the Last Judgment. Here Christ appears youthful and unbearded with blue eyes and brown hair, while on the passion side of the nave he is more mature, with a beard and blond hair. On both sides he is depicted with the cruciform halo with a jewel on each of the arms of the Cross, thus distinguishing him from the saints and angels. His dignified demeanor and purple cloak, as well as the fact that he is always attended by a disciple, tend to show him in the royal light of majesty. This series of episodes is told with a clarity and dramatic quality that make it outstanding in the history of Western art. Its only equals are to be found later in Romanesque sculpture and the frescoes of Giotto.

In the great mosaic frieze on either side of the entrance of Sant' Apollinare are representations of the old city of Ravenna and that of Classe, which date from Theodoric's time. In the picture of the port city, the crescent-shaped harbor is shown between two lighthouses, with three Roman galley ships riding at anchor. Above the city walls some of the ancient buildings are discernible. The procession of female saints is shown as issuing from the city gate. On the opposite side, the words "City of Ravenna" are inscribed above a gateway. Adjacent to it is a representation of *Theodoric's Palace* (Fig. 4:4). The word "Palatium" appears here above the central arch of the façade where originally a portrait of Theodoric was to be found. Vestiges of heads and hands in other places show that members of his court were also portrayed. When the Gothic kingdom came to an end, these effigies had to be replaced by the textile curtains seen there

Fig. 4:7. Sant' Apollinare Nuovo. *Procession of Virgins*. Mosaic. *c*.560 (Alinari)

at present. Above the palace are the buildings identified with Theodoric's reign. Among them appears the roof of Sant' Apollinare, and adjacent to it is the dome of the Arian Baptistry. The others are no longer identifiable.

From these two cities issue the saintly processions which move toward the altar. In accordance with the early church custom, the congregation was divided according to the sexes, with the women gathering on the left and the men on the right. The processional frieze reflects this practice, and on the left a line of 22 virgins are being led by the Three Wise Men to the throne of the Virgin Mary, who is holding the Christ Child on her lap. Arrayed in the splendor of their white tunics and richly bejeweled golden mantles, they carry their crowns of martyrdom in their hands as offerings to be laid at the feet of Christ. The saints (Fig. 4:7) are all identified by inscriptions above their heads, but only St. Agnes is shown with her attribute, the lamb. The eye is carried forward by the folds of their garments as the virgins tread a path strewn with flowers and lined with palm trees laden with heavenly fruit. Similarly identified on the opposite side are the 25 male martyrs being led by St. Martin into the presence of Christ, who is seated on a lyre-backed throne.

On both sides, the saints are ineffably serene, with no traces of their earthly suffering in evidence. The palm trees that alternate with the figures signify both their martyrdom and the fact that the scene is enacted in Paradise. The gold backgrounds contrast with the blue ones of the earlier mosaics above. Such gold backgrounds were known in Roman times, but they were not widely used until the 6th century. Stylistically they indicate richness and grandeur; symbolically they refer to heaven. Their shimmering quality reflects light with greater luminosity than blue, and the gold color imparts a visual liveliness to a scene that otherwise seems somewhat static. In considering the composition as a whole, one notes that the simplicity of the earlier Roman examples contrasts strongly with the more elaborate treatment of those from the Byzantine period. In spite of the fact that they represent two different styles, however, they blend remarkably well into a unified group, with the later work providing a fitting decorative climax to the pageantry as a whole.

Mosaics, in order that their full potentialities be realized, must be placed properly in regard to light. The myriad of small surfaces constitutes an ideal medium for the reflection of light whether it emanates from the sun or from artificial interior sources. The placement therefore involves careful planning on the part of the mosaicist, who must calculate both the source of the light and the position of the viewers. Sometimes the whole surface as well as the individual *tesserae* must be slanted slightly in order to produce the desired effect. Mosaics are especially well adapted to dimly lit interiors, and they are capable of evoking a mood all their own, quite different from that of fresco painting or stained glass. The mysterious spell they cast affords a maximum of stimulation to the imagination. Capable as they are of catching even the faintest ray of candle light, they can convey the impression of a light which emanates from within the church rather than from without.

In an age conditioned to look beyond the world of reality, the mosaic medium was thus ideal for conjuring up visions of the other world and directing the thoughts toward the invisible world of the spirit. Even though they are essentially a pictorial art, mosaics are more closely allied with architecture than either sculpture or painting. While the latter, except in the case of frescoes, are detachable, a mosaic is for all intents and purposes the surface of the floor or wall itself. Reproductions of mosaics unfortunately can give only a slight impression of their true value and beauty. Their shimmering, constantly changing color is all-important, and even more than sculpture and painting they need to be seen in the original architectural settings for which they were designed.

Fig. 4:8 (above). San Vitale. *Exterior of Apse.* *c.*526–547. Ravenna (Alinari). Fig. 4:9 (below).
Plan (Nikolaus Pevsner. *An Outline of European Architecture*. London, John Murray, 1949. p. 7.
By permission)

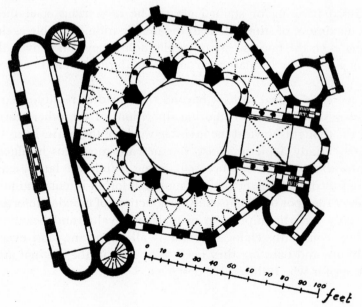

San Vitale

In the short span of a little more than a year, the death of Theodoric, the accession of Justinian as emperor in Constantinople, and the laying of the foundation stones of the church of San Vitale took place. According to the methods of statecraft valid in those times, the building of a new church was the logical first step in the assertion of Justinian's power in Italy. While Theodoric's successors continued to rule in Ravenna, the power and prestige of the great king was a thing of the past. In order to demonstrate the weakening of Gothic power and the ascendancy of his own, Justinian's building had to surpass in magnificence anything undertaken by Theodoric, which meant specifically the great palace and Sant' Apollinare Nuovo. At first Justinian's hold on the capital of the West was so uncertain that the project languished for a considerable period. Eventually it became necessary for him to use force, and the invasion of Italy was begun and later climaxed by the entrance of his military deputy, Belisarius, into the city in the year 540. Thereafter the construction of San Vitale proceeded apace, and the church was ready for its dedication by Archbishop Maximian some seven years later.

The unadorned exterior of San Vitale (Fig. 4:8) shows plainly that it was constructed in the old Roman tradition of baked bricks with concrete cores. From the architectural point of view it constitutes a highly developed example of a centralized church, and as such it differed radically from those of the oblong basilica type. Yet, as the ground plan (Fig. 4:9) clearly shows, it had all the usual features of the basilica with a narthex entrance, nave, aisles, and a triumphal arch leading into a sanctuary that included an apse and two side chambers. The striking difference is that, while the oblong basilica has an axis running horizontally through the center of the church separating it lengthwise into two equal halves, buildings of the central type have a vertical axis rising from the center upward to the middle of the dome. Moving from the central space outward, the shape of the aisles would make the building a complete octagon except for the addition of the oblong narthex on one side and an apse on the other. The two side chambers on either side of the apse are usually associated with Eastern churches, and their presence at San Vitale points to the fact that it was designed as a theater for the Byzantine liturgy. The northern chamber was designated as the *prothesis*, which indicates its use as the place where the Communion bread and wine were prepared for the altar. In the Eastern usage, particularly in Syria, the sacrificial aspect of the Mass assumed greater prominence. On the table of the *prothesis* the sacramental bread was "wounded, killed, and buried" before it made its appearance on the altar, where it became symbolically the resurrection of the body. The southern chamber is called the *diakonikon* and served as the vestry as well as a place to store the sacred objects used in the service.

While the ancestors of the oblong basilica were found in Roman domestic and public buildings, the centralized church type can be traced to Roman bath houses and tombs. Surviving examples of both are found in Ravenna itself in its two baptistries and Theodoric's mausoleum. The eight-sided Christian baptistry is derived from that part of a pagan Roman bath known as the *frigidarium*, or cold-water pool. With the Romans the pool was frequently octagonal, and with the Christians it was practically always so. Since the pool occupied the center of the structure, the building that housed it logically assumed the octagonal shape. The baptistry is thus clearly a bath house; and with the absence of the need for an altar, the central type was a natural and satisfying solution to the liturgical needs of the ceremony.

The Arian Baptistry, now known as Santa Maria in Cosmedin, was built in Theodoric's time in the same style as the earlier Baptistry of the Orthodox. The small size of the baptistries is appropriate, since the sacrament is a personal and family affair rather than one that calls for the presence of a large congregation. Both are domed structures whose chief interest is focused on the fine mosaics which are encrusted on their walls. Both have similar representations of the baptism of Christ on the interior surfaces of their cupolas. That of the Arian Baptistry (Fig. 4:10) shows the ceremony being performed by St. John, while the River Jordan is personified as an old man in the manner of the ancient pagan fluvial gods. Around this central scene are the Twelve Apostles who move processionally toward the throne of Christ. Just as the virgins and martyrs re-enacted the Offertory procession above the nave arcade of Sant' Apollinare Nuovo, the Apostles here mirror the baptismal rites on a higher and more transcendental level. Just as they grouped themselves around the center where Christ was being baptized above, so the clergy, family, and sponsors gathered about the font below for the baptism of some Christian. Here still another instance is found where the iconography of the decorative scheme reflects the liturgical activity that took place within the walls of the building.

Besides the baptistries Ravenna also provides an example of another type of early centralized structure in Theodoric's tomb (Fig. 4:11), which dates from about 520. Built with blocks of hewn stone, the lower story is a ten-sided crypt, while the upper part is a circular chapel. The whole is surmounted by a shallow dome, a huge monolith 107 feet in circumference,

Fig. 4:10. Baptistry of the Arians. *Baptism of Christ and Procession of the Twelve Apostles.* Mosaic. Early 6th century. Ravenna (Alinari)

carved from a single piece of Istrian marble. The ancient preference for the circular form of mausoleum can be explained partly by its symbolism. Immortality was frequently expressed by the image of a serpent biting its tail—that is, a living creature whose end was joined to its beginning. Serpents were also used in ancient healing practices, and the symbolism is still to be found in the insignia of the Army Medical Corps. A fine example of the Hellenistic type of round mausoleum, known as a *tholos*, can be found at Epidaurus. Another prototype is provided by Hadrian's colossal tomb on the banks of the Tiber in Rome.

Fig. 4:11. *Tomb of Theodoric*. *c*.520. Ravenna (Courtesy Italian State Tourist Office)

The idea of a church built in the form of a tomb is not such a gloomy thought as one might at first think. In the Christian sense, a church was a symbolic representation of the Easter sepulchre, which reminded all of the resurrection of Christ. In his memory they were dedicated to martyrs and saints who were believed to be partaking of the heavenly life with him, just as the faithful hoped that they themselves would one day be doing. The ancient Orphic cult had stressed the idea of the body being the tomb of the spirit, and the same symbolism was carried over into Early Christian times. Hence death and resurrection were associated as aspects of one and the same idea, and the martyr's death was thus his mystical union with Christ. Indeed, the altar itself is a tomb or repository for the sacred relics of the saint to whom the church is dedicated. Early altars in the catacombs were actually sarcophagi which served also as Communion tables. Thus, in the rites of the church, not only was the earthly past of Christ, his Apostles, saints, and martyrs commemorated, but, at the same time, the glorious, heavenly future was anticipated.

The centralized spatial composition of the church of San Vitale revolves in the manner of a wheel, with its vertical axis functioning as a hub. The Pantheon (Fig. 3:20) was one of the clearest examples of the central-type structure, which consisted of a dome in the shape of a half sphere resting on cylindrical walls. In this case there is still another adaptation of a pagan architectural form to Christian uses. Centralized plans, however, have always run into certain problems in connection with the liturgy. With the structural accent of the building converging on the axial center underneath the dome, this point would be the logical spot for the altar. Christian usage, however, frowns upon the congregation being placed behind the altar. At San Vitale, therefore, an apse was appended in the east for the altar, thus in effect dividing the architectural and liturgical climaxes of the edifice.

One of the prime advantages of a centralized structure of this type lies in the fact that all the separate structural members are unified by the dome, and that the eye is able to perceive this unity at a glance. On the interior of San Vitale (Fig. 4:12) the dome and its supports are in evidence, and the structure is therefore self-explanatory. Psychologically this equilibrium is important in producing a restful effect, which stands in direct contrast to the restless interiors of Gothic cathedrals. The dynamic urge of the latter depends partly on the fact that the external buttressing is not apparent. Indeed, the dome of San Vitale is an interior fact only, because on the outside the octagonal base on which it rests is continued upward and roofed over.

One of the principal contributions of the architects of this period came from their persistent preoccupation with the problem of balancing domes over square or octagonal understructures. The Romans had found one solution in the case of the Pantheon, but in Ravenna examples of two other solutions by later architects are found. The exquisite little mausoleum of Galla Placidia, which dates from about the year 440, was built in the form of a Greek cross. Its dome rests on pendentives—that is, on four concave spherical triangles of masonry—which mediate between the square structure below and the round dome above (Fig. 4:13). It was this solution that was to receive such triumphant expression in the great dome of Hagia Sophia in Constantinople, which was built under Justinian less than a century later. The Ravenna baptistries exemplify the same pendentive solution, except that in their case the domes rest on octagonal understructures. Another solution for the dome problem, stemming from the same early period, is found in a baptistry in Naples in which a dome rests on an octagonal base by means of squinches—that is, on a series of small

Fig. 4:12. San Vitale, *Interior*. *c*.526–547. Ravenna (Anderson)

Fig. 4:13 (left). *Pendentives*. Fig. 4:14 (right). *An Arched Squinch*. Drawings by W. D. Richmond (Courtesy John Ives Sewall)

apsidal vaults inserted between the angles of the octagonal wall (Fig. 4:14). This was the method used for the doming of San Vitale. The eight piers of the arcaded central room below rise upward and culminate in an octagonal drum on which, by means of the squinches, the dome rests. In order to keep the load as light as possible, a most ingenious method was devised for the dome of San Vitale, that of embedding hollow earthenware pots in the masonry. Between the aisles below and the dome above is a vaulted triforium gallery running around the church and opening into the nave. This gallery, which was called the *matronaeum*, was intended for the use of women, who were more strictly segregated in the Byzantine than in the Roman rites.

In the apse of San Vitale, facing the altar from opposite sides, are two panels in mosaic that portray the leading figures of the early Byzantine rule in Ravenna. On one Emperor Justinian appears in the midst of his courtiers (Fig. 4:15), while on the other, facing him as an equal, is Empress Theodora in all her sovereign splendor (Fig. 4:16). It is significant that this finest extant portrait of the great Emperor should be in mosaic rather than in the form of a sculptured bust, a bronze effigy on horseback, or a colossal statue. It is just this medium which could best capture the unique

Fig. 4:15. San Vitale. *Emperor Justinian and His Courtiers*. Mosaic. *c*.547 (Anderson)

spirit of his life and times. Concerned as he was with the codification of Roman law, presiding at religious councils, and reconciling divergent political points of view, Justinian based his rule on the manipulation of legal and theological formulas as well as on naked military might. He is therefore represented as a symbol of unity between the spiritual force of the Church on one hand and the temporal power of the state on the other.

Preceding Justinian in the procession are the clergymen, among whom only Archbishop Maximian is specifically identified by name. His pectoral cross is held up as an assertion of his power as the spiritual and temporal lord of Ravenna. On the Emperor's other side are his courtiers and honor guard holding their jeweled swords aloft. The shield with its Chrismon insignia points to the status of the soldiers as defenders of the faith. The Chrismon was a widely used monogram of the time, made up of the Greek

Fig. 4:16. San Vitale. *Empress Theodora and Her Retinue.* Mosaic. *c.*547 (Alinari)

letters Chi (X) and Rho (P), which together form the abbreviation of Christ. Somewhat more allegorically, the letters become a combination of the Cross and the shepherd's crook, which symbolize the Savior's death and pastoral mission. In the center stands the Emperor himself, clothed in all his magnificence and crowned with the imperial diadem. The observer is left in no doubt whatsoever that he is in the presence of no ordinary royal personage but rather one who could sign his name augustly to the preface of his *Digest of Laws* as the Emperor Caesar Flavius, Justinianus, Alamannicus, Francicus, Germanicus, Anticus, Alanicus, Vandalicus, Africanus, Pious, Happy, Renowned, Conqueror and Triumpher, ever Augustus.

On her side the Empress Theodora, richly bejeweled and clad in the imperial purple, is seen as she is about to make her entry into the church from the narthex. Possibly because of her humble origin as the daughter of the feeder of the bears at the circus of Constantinople, Theodora appears more royal than the king. Her offering recalls the dictum of the contemporary historian Procopius, who said that she fed the geese of the devil while on the stage and the sheep of Christ when she sat on the throne. The Offertory motive is also carried out on the hem of her robe where figures of the Three Wise Men, the first bearers of gifts to Christ, are embroidered. Since they also were from the east, this may have been a subtle attempt to gain the good graces of the people of Ravenna for their Oriental rulers.

These two portrait murals are particularly precious since they are among the few surviving visual representations of the vanished glories of Byzantine courtly ceremonials. The regal pair appear as if participating in the Offertory procession at the dedication of the church, which took place in the year 547, though neither of them was actually present on that occasion. Such ceremonial entries were a part of the elaborate Byzantine liturgy, and both the Emperor and Empress are shown as the bearers of gifts. On his side Justinian is carrying the gold paten, which was used to hold the Communion bread at the altar, while Theodora is presenting the chalice which contains the wine. Since their munificence was responsible for the building, decoration, and endowment of San Vitale, the allusion is to gifts of gold as well.

In keeping with the rigid conventions of Byzantine art, all the heads must appear in one plane. Those of Justinian and Theodora, however, are distinguished by their halos, which in this case allude not only to their awesome power but to a carry-over of the semidivine status assumed by the earlier Roman emperors. Even though they are moving in a procession, they are portrayed frontally in the manner of imperial personages accustomed to receiving the homage of their subjects. In spite of the stylized medium, the eye can follow the solemn train as it moves in dignified cadence by means of the linear pattern made by the folds of the garments. The elegant costumes and other draperies add generally to the richness of the scene, emphasizing by their designs the lavish luxury of their Oriental origin.

Together with the other mosaics that cover the surface of the triumphal arch, the presbyterium, and the apse, the interior of San Vitale presents the appearance of a jewel box. In addition to the mosaics there are many carved alabaster columns, polychrome marble wall panels, and decorative sculptural details. The capitals of the columns are carved with a profusion of intricate patterns, such as the one seen in Figure 4:17. The influence of San Vitale on subsequent Western European architecture dates from the

Fig. 4:17. San Vitale, *Byzantine Capital*. *c*.547. Ravenna (Alinari)

time of Charlemagne's conquest. So impressed was he with this church that he not only adopted its plan for his imperial chapel at Aachen, but carried off at least half of its original marble and mosaic decorations as well. When the harmonious proportions of the building as a whole are compounded with the rich optical effects of the mosaics, polychrome marbles, and ornamental sculptures, San Vitale, as the Western counterpart of Hagia Sophia in Constantinople, becomes the architectural climax of the interval between the classical and medieval periods.

SCULPTURE

From its high status as a major art in Greco-Roman times, sculpture declined to a point where it occupied a comparatively modest place in the hierarchy of Early Christian arts. Instead of constituting a free and independent medium, it became more of an adjunct to the architectural and liturgical forms of Christianity. Even its classical three-dimensionality was in eclipse, and the art tended to become increasingly pictorial and symbolic in Early Christian usage. When statuary moved indoors, its placement in regard to light and shade underwent a radical change. Since it was usually placed against a wall, it was intended to be seen from one angle only.

Sculpture in the round, therefore, became increasingly rare and was replaced more and more by relief panels. With the influence on Christian thinking of such Old Testament dictums as that of the First Commandment which forbade the making of "graven images," it was in some ways remarkable that the art survived at all. The close proximity in time and place to the pagan religions also served to channel Christian visual expression in other directions.

The art, however, showed sufficient vitality and plastic adaptability to save it from extinction. It began to assume new forms and identify itself with new purposes. In the new frame of reference, architectural sculpture—capitals of columns, decorative relief panels, carved wooden doors, and, to some extent, statues in niches—continued with appropriate modifications. The principal emphasis, however, began to shift toward objects associated with the new form of worship, such as altars, pulpits, pierced marble screens, and carved ivory reliefs. Smaller things, such as precious metal boxes for relics, lamps, censers, communion chalices, and patens all with delicately wrought designs, began to ally the former grand classical art more closely with that of the jeweler.

One of the strongest influences on Early Christian design was the new orientation of thought in the direction of symbolism. As long as the religions of Greece and Rome were anthropomorphic, sculpture had flourished with representations of the gods in idealized human forms. However, in Christian terms, how could the sculptor represent the Trinity, the Holy Ghost, the salvation of the soul, or the idea of redemption through participation in the Eucharistic sacrifice? How could the new allegorical interpretations of the Scriptures be embodied in concrete form? The solution could come only through use of parables and symbols. The Christian idea of immortality, for instance, was rendered through the Biblical scenes of deliverance, such as that of Noah from the flood, Moses from the land of Egypt, Job from his sufferings, Daniel from the lion's den, the children from the fiery furnace, and Lazarus from his tomb. One of the most frequent of all was the story of Jonah. Jesus had said: "For as Jonas was three days and three nights in the whale's belly; so shall the son of man be three days and three nights in the heart of the earth" (Matthew 12:40). This story therefore became a representation of the resurrection, hence it was frequently carved on Christian sarcophagi. Since a whale was beyond his ken, the sculptor used the classical sea monster known as the hippogriff to illustrate this old Hebrew legend, which had become in Christian terms the symbol of the resurrection of Christ. Such a case is typical of the adaptation of ancient pictorial forms and ideas to the new purposes.

Rare examples of sculpture in the round are found in such representations as that of a shepherd carrying a sheep on his back. The subject was a fairly frequent one in Hellenistic and Roman genre sculpture. In the new meaning, however, it is the Good Shepherd; the sheep is the congregation of the faithful; and when a jug of milk is included it refers to the Eucharist. Birds, when so treated, also become symbols, with the dove representing the Holy Spirit, the peacock standing for Paradise, and so on. The Cross is seldom found in the earlier phases, since it recalled a type of punishment used for the lowest type of criminal. Instead, the Chrismon symbol already seen on the shield of Justinian's soldiers was most frequently used. A fish, or the Greek word for it, *Icthys*, is often found as a reference to Jesus making his disciples fishers of men. The letters of the word also constituted an abbreviation for Jesus Christ Son of God, Savior. Such symbols and lettered inscriptions caused sculpture to assume the aspect of engraved designs on stone surfaces, which carried special meaning and mystical significance to the initiated.

Capitals of columns departed from the unity and regularity of the classical orders and began to show all sorts of variations. This tendency had begun with the early phases of Christian art, when materials for new churches had to be assembled from the parts of ancient buildings which had fallen into disrepair or disuse. Sant' Apollinare in Classe has a variation of the Roman Corinthian order in its so-called wind-blown acanthus capitals, while still another variety is found at Sant' Apollinare Nuovo. Far greater complexity and variety appear, however, in those of San Vitale, which are more distinctly Byzantine in style. Some of these elaborately carved foliated patterns are found with eagle's or ram's heads in the corners, or with such intricate arabesque designs as that seen in Figure 4:17.

One of the chief forms of Early Christian sculpture is that of carved stone sarcophagi. The custom of burial above ground was carried over from late Roman times, and a special Christian impetus came from the desire for interment within the sacred precincts of the church. The relics of saints reposed in the altar; tombs of bishops and other dignitaries were housed in the church; while the sarcophagi of laymen were usually placed outside in the atrium. Survivals of this latter custom continue well into modern times with burials taking place in churchyards.

Ravenna provides numerous examples of these sarcophagi, and a type was established when a monopoly on their production was granted to a single firm by Theodoric. They are distinguished from those of Roman workmanship by barrel-shaped rather than flat lids, and by a tendency toward more purely symbolic figures rather than pictorial representations.

Fig. 4:18. *Sarcophagus of Archbishop Theodore*. 5th Century. Sant' Apollinare in Classe, Ravenna (Alinari)

A fine example is provided by the sarcophagus of Archbishop Theodore (Fig. 4:18). The center shows the combination of the Chrismon symbol with that of the first and last letters of the Greek alphabet, Alpha and Omega. These are likewise a reference to Christ, taken from his statement that he was both the beginning and the end. Their inclusion here on a tomb is a reference to the end of earthly life and the beginning of the heavenly one. Flanking the symbol are two peacocks symbolizing Paradise, while behind them on either side a graceful vine pattern is found, in which the birds feeding on grapes refer symbolically to Communion. The inscription reads in translation, "Here rests in peace Archbishop Theodore." Above this are repetitions of the same monogram as below, which are surrounded here by the conventional laurel wreaths symbolizing immortality.

By far the most impressive single example of sculpture from this period is the chair which is thought to be that of Maximian (Fig. 4:19), the Archbishop portrayed at the side of Justinian in the mosaic panel in San Vitale. Such an archepiscopal throne is technically called a *cathedra*, and the church in which it is housed is therefore called a cathedral. It is also referred to by the Latin word for chair, *sedes*, from which is derived the term *see*, meaning the seat of a bishop. Originally it meant simply a chair denoting high position. Roman senators used such chairs on public occasions, and modern political figures still campaign for "a seat in the Senate." Both Jewish rabbis and Greek philosophers taught from a seated position, hence the reference

Fig. 4:19. *Throne of Archbishop Maximian.* Ivory Panels on Wooden Frame. *c.*546–556. Palace of the Archbishop, Ravenna (Alinari)

in colleges to "a chair of philosophy or history." When the bishops addressed their congregations from such a chair, they were said to be speaking *ex cathedra*.

The present example is constructed with a wooden frame which originally was covered entirely with ivory panels. From the fact that the sides as well as the back are as elaborately covered as the front, it was clearly not intended to remain in one place. During the service the bishop was seated in the presbyterium either at the side or behind the altar. Since his words would have been inaudible from this location, his chair was brought forward at the proper time to a place where he could conveniently be both seen and heard.

The work here consists of a composition made up of ivory plaques, carefully joined together and delicately carved. Originally there were 39 different pictorial panels, some of which told the Old Testament story of

167

Fig. 4:20. Throne of Archbishop Maximian, *Detail of Side.* Ivory. *c.*546–556. Palace of the Archbishop, Ravenna (Anderson)

Joseph and his brethren, and the others the story of Jesus. According to the most recent research, it was probably commissioned by Maximian on the occasion of a visit to Constantinople, and its workmanship shows the influence of artists from Alexandria. On the front panel, below Maximian's monogram, is a representation of St. John the Baptist flanked on either side by the Evangelists (Fig. 4:19). The Baptist holds a medallion on which a lamb is carved in relief, while the Evangelists hold their traditional books. One of the side panels that tells the story of Joseph is seen in Figure 4:20. When the two are compared, the workmanship reveals certain inconsistencies. In order to tell his story with compelling force, the carver of the Joseph panel lapses into some crudities of execution. But in both cases the decorative borders with their complex foliated designs are carved with great skill, inventiveness, and high technical competence. While sculpture is not the outstanding Byzantine art, such intricate tracery and arabesque patterns become its unique feature. Since ivory does not make monumentality either possible or desirable, such details, when handled with a jeweler's precision, are perhaps more satisfying than the work as a whole.

MUSIC

From the writings of Theodoric's learned ministers Boethius and Cassiodorus, some knowledge can be gained about the status of musical thought
in the Ravenna of the 6th century. Like the writings of the church fathers
and other men of letters of the time, however, they reveal much about the
theoretical aspects of the art and very little about its actual practice. Boethius was an indefatigable translator of philosophical and scientific treatises
from the original Greek into Latin, among which were no less than 30
books by Aristotle alone. When he fell from favor and was imprisoned, he
wrote his *Consolations of Philosophy*, which became one of the most influential
books of the Middle Ages. Called by Gibbon "a golden volume not unworthy of the leisure of Plato or Tully," the book later found its way into
English via the translations of Alfred the Great and Chaucer. Boethius'
was a universal mind, capable of discoursing on anything from the mechanical principles of water clocks to astronomy.

Boethius' treatise on music became the common source of most medieval
tracts on the subject; and thus, in transmitting the best of ancient Greek
musical theory, it became the foundation stone of Western musical thinking. Like the ancients before him, Boethius ascribed to the notion that "all
music is reasoning and speculation," and hence more closely allied with
mathematics than with the auditory art that music today is considered to
be. He divided music into three classes, the first of which was the "music
of the universe," by which he meant the Greek doctrine of the music of the
spheres and the unheard astronomical "music" of planetary motion. The
second was "human music," which referred to the attunement of the mind
and body, or the rational and irrational elements of the human constitution, in the manner of the Greek harmony of opposites. The third was
instrumental music and song, of which he had the philosopher's usual low
opinion, considering only the theoretical aspects of the art as pursuits
worthy of a gentleman and scholar. The only true "musician" in his opinion was one "who possesses the faculty of judging, according to speculation
or reason, appropriate and suitable to music, of modes and rhythms and of
the classes of melodies and their mixtures . . . and of the songs of the
poets." [3]

Cassiodorus also wrote in a similarly learned vein after he had retired
from public life to the haven of his monastery at Vivarium. But while he
was still embroiled in the affairs of Theodoric's kingdom, he was constantly
called upon to solve every conceivable administrative problem. Among

these was a request from Clovis, king of the Franks, for a *citharoedus*—that is, a singer who accompanied himself on the stringed instrument of the classical lyre type known as the cithara. In his search for such a musician, Cassiodorus turned to his fellow senator Boethius, who was in Rome at the time. His letter first launches into a flowery discourse on the nature of music, which he describes as the "Queen of the senses." It continues with interminable discussions about its curative powers, how David cast out the evil spirit from Saul, the nature of the modes, the structure of the Greek scale system, and the history of the art. Then he comes to the lyre, which he calls "the loom of the Muses," and after going off on a few more tangents, he finally gets to the point. "We have indulged ourselves in a pleasant digression," he says, making the understatement of the millenium, "because it is always agreeable to talk of learning with the learned; but be sure to get us that *Citharoedus*, who will go forth like another Orpheus to charm the beast-like hearts of the Barbarians. You will thus obey us and render yourself famous." [4]

This rare document is the only source on the state of secular music in the Ravenna of the 6th century, and it tells little about the capacities and duties of such a musician. It is clear, however, that this type of bardic poet-singer still existed at that time, though apparently so scarce that Cassiodorus had to send to Rome and seek the advice of the most eminent musical authority of the time. It is to be inferred also that such professional poet-musicians were active at Theodoric's court, otherwise the request from Clovis would not have been addressed to him. It is also known that Theodoric's exploits, together with those of the other heroes of the migration period, found their way into the fables and songs of the Gothic peoples, undoubtedly through the medium of just such musicians.

Knowledge about the church music of Ravenna at this time is even more conjectural and must be inferred from a variety of sources. From the writings of the church fathers it is evident that great importance was attached to music in connection with divine worship. The problem, however, was to separate a proper body of church music from the rude folk musical idioms on one hand, and from the highly developed but pagan art music of Rome on the other. From St. Paul and Pliny the Younger, in the first and second centuries respectively, it is known that the earliest Christian music sounded very much like the ancient Jewish singing of psalms. A fragment of an Early Christian hymn from the latter part of the third century was recently found at Oxyrhynchos in North Africa. From the Greek text and ancient musical notation, it is possible to establish its stylistic connection with the late Hellenistic musical tradition in much the same way as the Hellenistic visual arts merged into the Byzantine style. [5]

Hebrew, Greek, and Latin sources thus provided the basis for Early Christian music just as they had done in the cases of theology and the visual arts. Out of these heterogeneous elements, and with original ideas of their own, the Christians of the Eastern and Western churches gradually worked out a synthesis over the centuries, which resulted in a musical art of great power and beauty. The 6th century witnessed the culmination of many early experimental phases; and at its close, the Western form of the art found official codification in the body of music known as the Gregorian Chant. In its various transmutations and restorations, as well as in its theoretical aspects, this system has remained the official basis of Roman church music up to the present time. Closely related forms are still in use throughout Christendom, and free adaptations of its melodies have enriched the hymn books of nearly every Christian denomination.

Knowledge about the Arian liturgy, such as that which was practiced at Sant' Apollinare Nuovo during Theodoric's reign, is very obscure, since all sources were destroyed when the orthodox Christians gained the upper hand and stamped out the Arian heresy. From a few derogatory comments, however, it is known that hymn and psalm singing by the congregation as a whole were among their practices. Arius, the founder of the sect, was accused of insinuating his religious ideas into the minds of his followers by means of hymns that were sung to melodies derived from drinking songs and theatrical tunes. Such hymns were frowned upon in Orthodox circles because they were too closely allied with popular music. Furthermore, the Arian way of singing them was described as loud and raucous, indicating that they must have grated on the ears of the more civilized Roman Christians.

The popularity of these musical practices, however, was such that the Arians were making too many converts. So in the spirit of fighting fire with fire, St. Ambrose, the Bishop of Milan where the Arians were strong, made a compromise by introducing hymn and psalm singing into the Orthodox church service. A first-hand account of it is contained in a passage from St. Augustine's *Confessions*. In the 4th century, when Bishop Ambrose was engaged in one of his doctrinal disputes with the Byzantine Empress Justina, he and his followers at one point had to barricade themselves in a church for protection. "The pious people kept guard in the church, prepared to die with their bishop," wrote St. Augustine. "At the same time," he continues, "was it here first instituted after the manner of the Eastern Churches, that hymns and psalms should be sung, lest the people should wax faint through the tediousness of sorrow: which custom being retained from that day to this, is still imitated by divers, yea, almost by all thy congregations throughout other parts of the world." [6] The practice spread widely and was incorporated into the Roman liturgy in the following century. Since Ravenna was the neighboring see to that of Milan, the musical practices there must have been very similar.

Aeterne rerum Conditor   Hymn of St. Ambrose (After Dreves)

Some half-dozen hymns have been attributed to the authorship of St. Ambrose. Whether he also composed the melodies is not so certain, but they at least date from his time. From the example of *Aeterne rerum Conditor* (above), it can be seen that the extreme simplicity and metrical regularity of these vigorous Ambrosian hymns made them especially suitable for congregational singing. The singing of psalms was also an Arian practice that was taken over at the same time into the Ambrosian liturgy. The mosaics of Sant' Apollinare Nuovo show files of male and female saints on opposite sides of the nave arcade. Below them the men of the congregation were grouped on one side, while the women and children gathered on the other, thus forming two choirs. The psalms were sung in two ways, antiphonally and responsorially. When the two choruses sang alternate verses, then joined together in a refrain on the word *Alleluia*, the practice is referred to as antiphonal psalmody. When the celebrant chants one verse as a solo, and the choirs perform the next in unison, it is called responsorial psalmody. Both were widespread practices in the Western church including Ravenna.

Since Sant' Apollinare Nuovo and San Vitale were designed for different purposes, it follows that their music must also have differed. As a part of the Byzantine liturgy, the music heard at San Vitale would have been like that of the cathedral of Constantinople. As in the West, congregational singing was included there at first, but with the abandonment of the Offertory procession, congregational singing was gradually replaced by that of a professional choir. In his *corpus juris* Justinian made provision for a staff at Hagia Sophia which included over 100 lectors and a choir of 25 singers. The professional status of the latter is attested to by the fact that they are expressly enjoined in the same document from singing in public theaters. The lectors, as leaders of worship, also chanted the service; hence with this large group, it is clear that church music there had already attained the status of a highly developed art. Music for congregational singing must always be kept relatively simple, and only with a truly professional group can all the rich potentialities of the art be explored and developed.

Since the church of San Vitale, like that of Hagia Sophia in Constantinople, was also under the direct patronage of the emperor, and since both constituted a part of Justinian's grand design, the matter of providing for a group capable of performing the music of the Byzantine liturgy could hardly have been overlooked. The principal difference between the music of the Eastern and Western churches is that between a contemplative and an active attitude. The contemplative aspect of the Eastern liturgy is illustrated by a remark of St. John Chrysostom, who said that "one may also sing without voice, the mind resounding inwardly, for we sing not to men, but to God, who can hear our hearts and enter into the silences of the mind." [7] This attitude contrasts strongly with that of St. Ambrose who said in connection with the participation of the congregation in song: "If you praise the Lord and do not sing, you do not utter a hymn. . . . A hymn, therefore, has these three things: song and praise and the Lord." [8]

Ambrosian *Alleluia* of Byzantine Origin   (After Wellesz)

In a static form of worship greater rhythmic freedom is possible, while the chant which accompanies a procession must have some degree of metrical regularity. The singing of a virtuoso professional choir, furthermore, implies an elaborate and highly developed art, while the practice of congregational singing means the avoidance of technical difficulties. The difference, then, is that between the sturdy Ambrosian hymn (page 172), and the *Alleluia* of Byzantine origin (page 173). Such Byzantine music had a distinctive style of its own, comparable in this respect to that of the visual arts. The elaborate melismas of the latter example would have been heard at San Vitale and at other Byzantine churches at the end of the 6th century. It was precisely such excessively florid Alleluias that were ruled out by the Gregorian reform.

IDEAS

After these colorful works have passed by individually in review, those that share the same circumstances of patronage, a common geographical origin, and a similar ideational pattern combine themselves into stylistic groups. Since all the arts of the period were enlisted in the service of either the Ostrogothic kingdom, the Byzantine Empire, or the Church of Rome, the question of their purpose is of paramount importance in determining the forms of architecture, the iconography of the mosaics, the designs of the sculpture, and the modes of the music. The styles were all religiously oriented, all were Christian, and each of the arts lived, moved, and had its being within the all-embracing arms of mother Church. The two ideas that grow out of the various church viewpoints, and in which the arts of the time found their unity, are authoritarianism and mysticism.

Authoritarianism

Ravenna in the 6th century was the scene of a three-way struggle between a barbarian king, who was a champion of Roman culture; a Byzantine emperor, who claimed the prerogatives of the past golden age; and a Roman pontiff, who had little military might but a powerful claim based on the apostolic succession. As the conflict shaped up, it was among an enlightened secular liberalism, a theocratic traditionalism, and a new spiritual institution with a genius for compromise. In the course of the century, the Gothic kingdom was vanquished by the Byzantine Empire. However, after a brief period of domination, the power of the East crumbled; and the political and military weakness that followed became the soil which nurtured the growth of the new Rome. By the end of the century, Pope Gregory the Great had succeeded in establishing the papacy as the authority which was eventually to dominate the medieval period in the West.

The principle of authority was by no means foreign to the nature of Christianity. The religion came to maturity in the final phase of the Roman

Empire, and as the official state religion under the protection of the emperors, Christianity acquired an authoritarian character. Roman Christian philosophers, such as Boethius and Cassiodorus, cited the authority of Plato and Aristotle on all matters. Theologians accepted the authority of the Scriptures and the commentaries on them by the early Church fathers. The thought of the period was expressed in constant quotations and re-quotations, interpretations and reinterpretations of ancient Hebrew, Greek, Latin, and Early Christian authors. No one was willing or able to assume complete authority in his own right; on all issues each had to cite ancient precedents for his position. The intellectual climate produced by this patristic type of thinking paved the way for the mighty struggle for political and spiritual authority. The question was only what form the authority was to assume, and who would exercise it.

Justinian, who claimed the authority of the old Roman emperors, lived in an atmosphere so static and conservative that the words *originality* and *innovation* were used at his court only as terms of reproach. In paying such a high price for unity, Byzantine civilization purchased only a blanket uniformity. The principal creative energies of Byzantine man, however, were channeled into aesthetic expression, largely because they had no other place to go. Only in art was any variety and freedom to be found. Here again, however, the art of both Church and state were under the sole patronage of the emperor. It was thus all the more remarkable that such a flowering as that which produced Hagia Sophia in Constantinople and San Vitale in Ravenna could have taken place. In both instances the methods of construction were experimental, and the solution of the architectural and decorative problems were remarkably uninhibited and daring.

The Byzantine concept of authority is embodied in both the architectural and decorative plan of San Vitale. The central type of church, with its sharp hierarchical divisions which set aside a place for men and women, clergy and laity, aristocrat and commoner, is admirably suited to convey the principle of imperial authority. The vertical axis culminated in a dome which overwhelmed Byzantine man by reminding him, when he is in the presence of the Supreme Authority, of his humble place in the scheme of things. The august portraits in the sanctuary showed him that outside the clergy, only the emperor and empress and those who occupy the top rungs of the social ladder may approach the altar of God. He may not even presume to bring forward his gifts to the altar in the Offertory procession. Since all material things come within the province of Caesar, the exalted duty of making the offering is his alone. Byzantine man, furthermore, was not even allowed to raise his voice with those of his fellow men in God's praise, as it was also the emperor's prerogative to provide a chorus of qualified musicians whose privilege this was. The attitude of reverence was not only due to God alone but to His viceroys on earth. The imperial portraits left no doubt about that. The majesty of God was felt through the infinite power of government. Through the solemn rituals of sacred and courtly ceremonies, both spiritual and secular authority were imposed on Byzantine man from above. His place in this world as well as in the cosmic hereafter was inexorably determined; and his human dignity was in proportion to the blandness of his acceptance of the unified ideal of one Christian empire with one church, one emperor, and one body of laws.

Sant' Apollinare Nuovo as the typical Western form of the basilica, on the other hand, indicated a contrasting conception of both God and man. As the twin rows of columns on either side of the nave march forward, they carry the eyes and activities of the faithful with them. The approach to the sacred precincts is encouraged rather than forbidden, and even the gift of the widow's mite is acknowledged above in one of the mosaic panels. Just as the congregation had gone forth from the doors of their homes to the house of the Lord, the processions of saints in the mosaics had likewise moved out of the gates of the twin cities of Classe and Ravenna. The rites they attended were not so incomprehensible and fearsome but that every-one could have the dignity of ministering to the Lord. The spatial divisions of the oblong basilica, to be sure, still allowed for differences of status, such as that of men and women, choir and clergy. The allowance for all to participate in the sacred service, however, modified the authoritative con-cept, so that it was essentially a spiritual principle rather than that of the overwhelming might of a theocratic state.

By exercising his power to offer gifts and maintaining his active partici-pation, Western man saw that the concept of authority was kept on a spiritual level, and he thus retained a certain individual freedom which Byzantine man had surrendered to his rulers. Sant' Apollinare Nuovo and San Vitale thus are the reflections of two contrasting images of man. The oblong basilica was designed for active spatial and temporal movement, while the domed central-type church indicated Byzantine man's passive acceptance of the role of spectator. In one case the horizontal axis, by inviting forward movement, placed man in a progressive relation to space; in the other, the vertical axis, by pointing upward, tended to check physical movement and divert the energies toward stationary contemplation. The mosaics of Sant' Apollinare Nuovo, in addition to the processions, depict the life story of Christ in narrative form, while those in San Vitale are confined to individual representations of separate scenes without any sequential arrangement and are designed to dazzle by their impressive splendor. The music of Sant' Apollinare Nuovo was written for congregational participation and had a metrical regularity conducive to marching, while that of San Vitale was highly complex, melismatic, and had an assymetrical cadence which minimized bodily motion.

Mysticism

The art of the 6th century in Ravenna, like that of other important centers such as Constantinople and Rome, represents in all its aspects a bridge between the ancient Greco-Roman and medieval worlds. While some of the ancient grandeur remained, the accent on symbolism laid the foundation for the new style. Many of the older forms were carried over and reinterpreted in a new light. The Roman bath house, for instance, became the Christian baptistry; and the public basilica was redesigned for church purposes. Mosaics, which were used for Hellenistic and Roman pavements, became the mural medium for pictorial expression. The shepherd of classical genre sculpture became symbolically the Good Shepherd. Classical bird and animal motives became symbols for the soul and spiritual realm. Music became a reflection of the divine unity of God and man; and the classical lyre, because of its stretched strings on a wooden frame, was reinterpreted by St. Augustine as a symbol of the crucified flesh of Christ. Orpheus by means of its sounds had descended into the underworld and overcome death. Christ is therefore frequently represented as playing on the lyre, and at Sant' Apollinare Nuovo he is seated on a lyre-backed throne.

The concept of space turned from the limited classical three-dimensional representation of reality to an infinite Christian two-dimensional symbolic world. Invisible things outranked in importance those that could be seen with the eyes. While classical man had regarded his world objectively from without, Early Christian man contemplated his subjectively from within. While natural science had been the foundation stone of ancient philosophy, symbolic theology became that of the Christian philosophical viewpoint. While the Greek drama had reached its climax step by step with remorseless logic, the Christian drama, kindled by the fires of faith, arrived at its mystical climax by intuitive means. The denial of the flesh and the conviction that only the soul can be beautiful, doomed classical bodiliness and exalted abstraction.

What sometimes seems to be a crude technique in contrast to the high quality of classical craftsmanship is partly owing to the new orientation in which the artists are no longer attempting to convey a natural image of the real world. Elegance of linguistic as well as pictorial expression was considered too close to pagan aberrations for comfort. Civilized Roman men of letters, for instance, chafed at the comparative roughness of the Hebrew scriptures. St. Jerome, when he went into the wilderness to translate the Bible, took along with him a copy of his beloved Cicero. Such weakness, however, he attributed to his sinful nature. St. Augustine, as a grammarian, loved the noble Latin of Vergil and the beautiful classical melodies; such "moral lapses" caused him bitter self-recrimination. The fervent congregational singing of the untutored faithful, no matter how unrefined it sounded, was morally preferable to the higher virtuosity of pagan musical sophistication. The Church fathers, who were among the highly educated few, had the difficult task of adapting the older theological, philosophical, artistic, and musical forms to the needs of their congregations, whose ranks included former slaves, artisans, and unlettered barbarians. The result was a technical decline from the high standards of classical craftsmanship in the arts and letters due to the lowering of the relative literacy of those to whom the new visual and verbal vocabularies were addressed. This was an age of transition from one cultural frame of reference to another. The fact that all the arts survived and acquired in the process an astonishing new vitality is all-important.

The great creation and the all-inclusive medium shaped during this period to convey this other-worldly vision was the liturgy. The thought, action, and sequence of the rites of Constantinople, Ravenna, Rome, and other centers determined to a large extent the architectural plans, the iconography of the mosaics, and the forms of the sculpture and music. At this time the fruits of generations of contemplative and active lives gradually ripened into mature structures. The content of centuries of theoretical speculation united with the practical efforts of countless generations of writers, builders, decorators, and musicians to produce the Byzantine liturgy in the East and the synthesis of Gregory the Great in the West. Removed from its primary religious association and seen in a more detached aesthetic light, the liturgy as a work of art embodies a profound and dramatic insight into the deepest longings and highest aspirations of the human spirit.

During the 6th century the controversy still raged as to whether Christ's nature was essentially human or divine. The more the Eastern view emphasized Christ's divinity, the more remote he became. One of the prayers of St. John Chrysostom, for instance, begins: "O Lord, our God, Whose power is inconceivable and glory incomprehensible, Whose mercy is immeasurable and tenderness to man unspeakable. . . ." Such a conception makes any attempt to comprehend the divine essence by reason or direct representation highly presumptuous. Hence the mosaics of San Vitale weave such abstract symbols as that of the Chrismon into a rich arabesque of florid designs. Strict symmetry and other means are employed to raise the representations out of the plane of reality, and thus widen the immeasurable gulf between divinity and humanity. The dim lighting, the golden glow of the mosaics, the mysterious symbols whose meaning it was the privilege of the initiated to contemplate—all helped conjure up this unfathomable and invisible divinity. The most sacred rites took place behind carved alabaster screens; the choirs sang softly back of embroidered curtains. The words addressed from Maximian's carved ivory chair took on a superhuman impressiveness. All these in concert conveyed the mystical idea and awakened the vision of eternity in the minds of the beholder.

The Western position was eventually settled by a compromise upholding Christ's dual nature as both human and divine, but Western thought continued to accent his role as the sufferer and Savior of humanity. The more this aspect was accented, the more approachable and comprehensible the figure of Christ became. This is the side that finds expression in the mosaics of Sant' Apollinare Nuovo, especially in those which recount the parables and miracles as well as the passion, death, and resurrection of the historical Christ.

The Early Roman Christian and Byzantine styles therefore evolved in response to the need for new verbal, visual, and auditory modes of expression. In both cases there was a shift from the forms designed to represent the real world to those capable of conjuring up other-worldly visions. Through the poetry of language, the choreographic patterns of step and gesture, and the exalted melodies of the chant, this gripping drama of humanity embodied in the liturgy was enacted in sublime theaters that were furnished with a full panoply of stage settings, decor, costumes, and props created by the inspired hands of the finest craftsmen and artists of the time. The liturgy is, moreover, a continuous pageant lasting not only for a few hours, but unfolding with constant variation during the continuous sequence of solemn and joyful feasts through the weeks, months, and seasons of the calendar year, the decades, centuries, and millennia.

C H A P T E R

CHRONOLOGY: Cluny, Late 11th and Early 12th Centuries

526 St. Benedict founded the first Western European monastery at Montecassino in Italy

910 Abbey of Cluny in Burgundy, France, founded by William the Pious, Duke of Aquitaine

927 – 942 Odo was Abbot of Cluny
Reputed author of musical treatises, including the *Enchiridion musices*

962 Otto the Great crowned as Holy Roman Emperor in Rome

994 – 1049 Odilo was Abbot of Cluny

1000–1150 Approximate dates of the High Romanesque Period

1049–1109 Hugh of Semur was Abbot of Cluny

1050 Death of Guido of Arezzo (*c*.995–*c*.1050)
Author of important musical treatises
Inventor of staff notation

1050 Approximate high point of the Holy Roman Empire
Beginning of the ascendancy of papal power

1066 William, Duke of Normandy, conquered England
Reigned as King of England 1066–1087

1072 Death of St. Peter Damian

1073–1085 Pontificate of Gregory VII (Hildebrande)

1077 Emperor Henry IV bowed to Pope Gregory VII at Canossa; Hugh of Semur acted as intermediary

1088–1099 Pontificate of Urban II, the Cluniac Pope

1088–1130 Building of the Great Third Church at Cluny
1088 Third Church begun under Hugh of Semur
1095 Apse dedicated by Pope Urban II
1120 Church finished
1125 Nave vaults partially collapsed
1131 Church dedicated by Pope Innocent X

1095 Urban II preached the First Crusade

1096–1120 Building of the Abbey Church of La Madeleine at Vézelay
1096 Abbey Church at Vézelay begun
1104 Original Romanesque Choir and transept dedicated
1110 Nave finished
1120 Narthex begun
Nave revaulted after fire
1130 Approximate date of the Tympanum over the central portal of narthex
1132 Narthex dedicated
1170 Approximate date of Chapter Room at Vézelay
1180 Approximate date of the Gothic Choir

1098 Cistercian Order founded and opposed the Order of Cluny; St. Bernard of Clairvaux was its principal spokesman

1109 Pontius became Abbot of Cluny on the death of Hugh of Semur

1122 Peter the Venerable became Abbot of Cluny

5

THE MONASTIC
ROMANESQUE STYLE

THE MONASTERY AT CLUNY, LATE 11th AND EARLY 12th CENTURIES

The most distinctive framework devised by the early Middle Ages for its picture of life was the monastery. The life of ancient Athens and Pergamon had culminated in the constellations of their acropolis buildings, while that of Rome had been realized in forums and civil-engineering projects. Constantinople and Ravenna had evolved the cathedral and palace as the Church and state sides of a theocratic social order. The medieval way of life, however, led directly to the monastery, and the largest and grandest of them all was the French abbey of Cluny in the late 11th and early 12th centuries. In the plan shown in Figure 5:1, Kenneth J. Conant has reconstructed it at the point when it reached the pinnacle of its power and fame.

Like other monasteries, it was a miniature world in itself, containing an entire cross section of the society of its time. Within its walls men of contemplation could be found along with men of action; those who were world-weary dwelled side by side with those who knew little of life beyond the cloister; and saints brushed shoulders with criminals who sought refuge from prosecution at the hands of secular authorities. Those who were drawn toward the vocation of a monk were firm believers in the seeming paradox contained in Christ's words: "For whosoever will save his life shall lose it: but whosoever will lose his life for my sake, the same shall save it" (Luke 9:24). By taking the triple vows of poverty, chastity, and obedience,

181

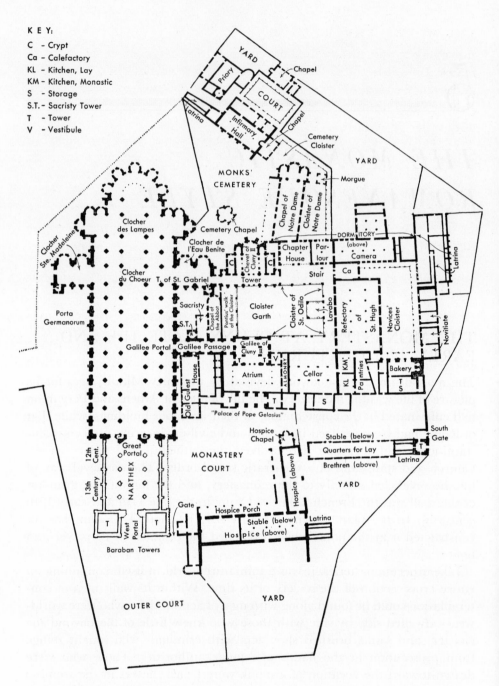

KEY:

C – Crypt
Ca – Calefactory
KL – Kitchen, Lay
KM – Kitchen, Monastic
S – Storage
S.T. – Sacristy Tower
T – Tower
V – Vestibule

Fig. 5:1. Abbey of Cluny, *Plan c.*1135. By K. J. Conant (Courtesy Mediaeval Academy of America)

the monk automatically renounced such worldly pursuits as personal material rewards, the pleasures of the senses, the satisfactions of family life, and even the exercise of his own free will. According to the Rule of St. Benedict, the founder of Western monasticism, a monk "should have absolutely not anything; neither a book, nor tablets, nor a pen—nothing at all. For indeed it is not allowed to the monks to have their own bodies or wills in their power." Through this renunciation of all worldly desires, the monk sought a higher life in the realm of the spirit, which can be summed up most completely in the words of St. Paul: "I live; yet not I, but Christ liveth in me" (Gal. 2:20). In order to realize such other-worldly aims, segregation from the secular world had to be effected, and a special way of life found.

Historically, the monastic idea took root in the West during the days which followed the decline and fall of the Roman Empire. The founding of a monastery at Vivarium by Cassiodorus can be cited as a case in point. After the collapse of his political aims under the Ostrogothic kingdom of Theodoric and his successors, Cassiodorus sought a spot off the beaten track where he and the group of idealists he gathered around him could preserve some of the remaining values of classical life and learning. His literary interests were generally incorporated into the monastic movement, and all through the Middle Ages the monasteries were centers of learning in which the only libraries, schools, and hospitals were to be found. The value of hard work was stressed in the Benedictine Rule, which prescribed an average of six or seven hours a day of manual labor. In the early stages this meant literally toiling in the fields and tending the flocks, but with the growth in the ranks and the accumulation of land and treasure by the monastic communities, something like a division of labor took place. At Cluny, for instance, the singing of psalms, the recitation of prayers, and the reading and copying of manuscripts were all construed as the proper work of a monk. According to the feudal practice of the time, the actual agricultural pursuits were delegated to peasants and serfs who worked under the direction of lay brothers.

When Cluniac life had to be defended from the criticism of the stricter order of Cistercians, Peter the Venerable, abbot of Cluny during the first part of the 12th century, found it necessary to write: "It is more noble to set one's hand to the pen than to the plow, to trace divine letters upon the page than furrows upon the fields. Sow on the page the seed of the word of God, and when the harvest is ripe, when your books are finished, the hungry readers shall be satisfied by an abundant harvest." [1] In order to live such a life, a monastery had to be planned so that the monks would have all that was necessary both for their bodily subsistence and spiritual sustenance. The objective was to be as independent of Caesar as possible, so as to render their all unto God.

The Benedictine Rule did not prescribe the exact form that any of the monastic buildings should take. Each abbey was nominally independent and could solve its problems according to its needs, the contours of its site, and the extent of its resources. Tradition, in such cases, often operated as rigidly as rules, and with local variations most monasteries adhered to a common pattern. Allowing for its exceptional size and the complexities brought about by its being the mother house of a great order, the plan of Cluny is fairly typical.

Since the life of a Cluniac monk was one of almost constant religious observances, alternating with periods set aside for contemplation, the soul of the monastery was in its abbey church and its heart was in its cloister. The church served primarily as the scene of the ceaseless devotional activities of the monks day and night throughout the year, and only secondarily as a shrine for the pilgrimages that were made to revere the relics of the saints, which were exhibited there at certain seasons. The monk's day was punctuated by the sequence of the Regular Hours that were sung in the abbey church. These holy offices consisted of prayers and canticles appropriate to each time of day and night together with the singing of entire psalms. Matins took place before dawn with Prime coming just after sunrise, and Tierce two hours later. Solemn High Masses were celebrated after both Prime and Tierce, the latter being in commemoration of the dead and the Mass that all the brothers except those who were ill were expected to attend. Sext and None followed after Tierce at approximately three hour intervals; Vespers came at sundown, Compline at nightfall, and both Nocturn and Vigils in the course of the night. Since so much of the daily ritual took place at night or early in the morning in the unheated church, the monk had to dress in warm woolen robes, and in the winter he was provided with fur-lined boots. The Cluniac habit had a leather belt, heavy sleeves which could serve as hand muffs, a cowl which could become a hood, and a cape for extra warmth and protection from the elements.

Next in importance to the church services was the provision for the contemplative life that found its focal point in the cloister. In the plan it will be found typically in the center of the abbey and south of the nave of the church, with the other monastic buildings clustering around it. The usual cloister was an open quadrangular garden plot, called the garth, which was enclosed by a covered arcade on all four sides. The somewhat irregular shape of the cloister at Cluny at this time was due to the ambitious building program necessitated by the rapid growth of the monastery. The old 11th-century cloister of Abbot Odilo next to the refectory was retained. After the abbey's great new third church was ready, however, the nave of the older second church was demolished to make way for an enlargement of the cloister. The choir and narthex of the old church can still be seen in the plan on the east and west sides of the extended cloister. It was here that the monks found the creative solitude they needed for the inward life as they walked to and fro in all kinds of weather, reading the Scriptures and other books from the adjacent library, pondering on the meaning of the symbolic sculptured capitals of the arcade, or carrying on their silent meditations. The rule of silence was rigidly maintained except for two periods of about half an hour each, one coming in the morning after the chapter was held, and the other after Sext when the monks were allowed to attend to their personal and domestic duties. The form of the cloister was undoubtedly derived from the atriums that stood before the Early Christian basilicas; and, like them, they usually contained a fountain for ceremonial ablutions before entering the church. In the Cluny plan a font, labeled the *lavabo*, can be seen standing before the entrance of the refectory, which was located typically on the south side of the cloister. Since this renowned marble-columned cloister no longer exists, the one of St. Trophime at Arles (Fig. 5:2) will serve as an example. The columns and their outstanding Romanesque capitals date from the year 1100 when the abbey was one of the dependencies of Cluny.

At mealtimes, after washing their hands at the *lavabo*, the brethren entered the refectory where they ate in common. Here the silence was broken only by the lector who read aloud from the lives of the saints and the writings of the Church fathers. The refectory shown in the plan is the one Hugh rebuilt to accommodate the ever-growing population of resident monks which numbered in his time around 200, in contrast with the 70-odd who were there during the abbacy of his predecessor. The refectory measured 112 feet in length and 67 feet in width, with a row of six pillars on either side. Besides the rows of tables for the monks, there were two tables on a raised platform, one for the grand prior of the order and one for the claustral prior. Mural paintings of scenes from the Old and New Testaments decorated its walls, and a large picture of Christ in Majesty as at the Last Judgment was found at one end. Adjacent to the refectory were the kitchens, bakeries, and pantries; and opening out from the monk's kitchen and running along the west side of the cloister were the storerooms for food with cellars below. One of the rooms led into an outside court where alms were distributed to the poor.

Fig. 5:2 (above). Abbey of St. Trophime, *Cloister*, Arles. Fig. 5:3 (below). Abbey of Vézelay, *Chapter Room*. *c*.1170. (Courtesy French Government Tourist Office)

Fig. 5:4. *Abbey of Cluny*, East Side. *c*.1043. Reconstruction by K. J. Conant, showing the Second Abbey Church and other monastic buildings. (Courtesy Mediaeval Academy)

Opening off the east walk of the cloister was the chapter house, where the monks gathered each morning following church services and breakfast. After a prayer and the reading of a chapter from the Rule of St. Benedict, the abbot presided over the meeting from his throne. At this time the monks were given any necessary information, received instruction, and participated in any business that might properly come before them. This might have included anything from the admission of novices into the order to the expulsion of an unworthy monk; matters connected with the sale, purchase, or leasing of property; or the acceptance of gifts. Their most solemn business, however, came at the time when the abbot himself was chosen from among their numbers on the death of his predecessor. The Chapter House at Vézelay (Fig. 5:3) is one of the best-preserved Cluniac rooms of this type. It dates from about 1170, is typically oblong in shape, and is divided by two columns with foliated capitals which support the fine quadripartite ribbed vaults above. It is known to be like that at Cluny in its use of windowlike arcades on either side of the open portal that led to and from the cloister.

Except for the church, cloister, refectory, chapter house, and the quarters for distinguished guests, the other monastic buildings were almost entirely utilitarian in character, as the elevation by Professor Conant (Fig. 5:4) will show. Above the chapter house and the other large rooms adjoining it, was the monks' dormitory. Since services were held during the night as well as by day, it had to be located near one of the entrances to the church. It can be seen in the plan that at Cluny the monks could go downstairs, move along the eastern walk of the cloister, and enter the church through the end of the greater transept. The dormitory itself was a long hall with tall narrow windows between which, on either side of a central aisle, were the beds of the monks. The sanitary conveniences were far above anything comparable in the secular life of the time, as the great latrine adjoining the dormitory will show (Fig. 5:1).

In addition to these main centers of monastic activity, a complete abbey had to make provision for many other functions and contingencies. Beyond the dormitory on the east was the chapel of Notre Dame, which had a small cloister where the aged or infirm monks could worship and meditate. Further on, beyond the monks' cemetery, was the infirmary hall, which had rows of beds in separate cubicles with smaller rooms set aside for the laundry and servants' quarters. Another section, amounting to a small monastery in itself, had to be set aside for the training of novices who were not as yet fully admitted to the order. Complete with its own cloister, it can be found on the extreme southern side. Nearby were workshops for such craftsmen as blacksmiths, carpenters, cobblers, and tailors. Their location near the novices' quarters and outside the inner precincts of the abbey itself indicates that they were primarily intended for lay workers rather than for monks. These people could thus come and go without interfering with the routine of the monastery itself.

Along the western confines were the stables for dairy cattle and other domestic animals with sleeping quarters for lay brethren above. Hospices to house poor pilgrims were also located here, while across the court was the building where distinguished guests were housed. The old guest house, for example, was a spacious room heated by a large ornate fireplace. Above it were separate dormitories for 40 men and 30 women with a common refectory in between. The abbot often entertained hundreds of guests, many of whom were of the princely class who traveled with large retinues. Since donations for the new church and support for the monastery came in part from such visitors, it was imperative that they gained the best possible impression. Surrounding the monastery on all sides were thick walls to protect it from marauders, thieves, and armed bands in time of invasion. Outside the walls lay the gardens, groves, and farmlands under its control, which produced the necessities of life. As on the domain of a feudal lord, the soil was tilled by bound serfs working under the supervision of the lay brothers, and sometimes by free peasants who rented land from the monks on a crop-sharing basis. The buildings in this area included only such necessary structures as barns, granaries, and mills.

The plan of Cluny was thus a coherent system of adjoining quadrangles that embraced courts and cloisters of a size and importance which varied in accordance with the differing activities they were designed to accommodate. Its most direct historical antecedent was the ancient Roman country villa with variations for its functions as a religious shrine, and as a manufacturing and agricultural center as well as the spiritual and intellectual capital of its region. Altogether it is a highly complex and at the same time logical plan for a complete community, taking into account the ideals, aspirations, practices, and everyday activities of a group which gathered together to work physically and spiritually toward a common end.

ARCHITECTURE

Hugh of Semur, the greatest of the Cluniac abbots, succeeded Odilo in the year 1049. Under him Cluny was destined to attain a period of such resplendence that it could be described by an enthusiastic chronicler of the time as "shining on the earth like a second sun." Taking as his model the accepted feudal structure of society, by which smaller and more dependent landowners swore allegiance to the larger and more powerful landlords in return for protection, Hugh became the organizer who brought the traditionally independent Benedictine monasteries into the Cluniac orbit. With the express approval of the popes, Hugh gradually concentrated the power of the whole order into his hands and transformed Cluny into a vast monastic empire over which he ruled benignly for 60 years. In the Church hierarchy he was outranked only by the pope, and in the secular world he was the peer of kings. He figured prominently in most of the historical events of his day, even to the extent of acting as intermediary between an emperor and a pope on the famous occasion at Canossa, when Henry IV had to come on bended knee to beseech Pope Gregory VII for forgiveness. His greatest moment, however, came when Pope Urban II, who had received his training as a monk and prior at Cluny under Hugh's personal guidance, was present to dedicate the high altar of his great new abbey church. Honor after honor was bestowed upon the monastery by this Cluniac Pope, who was also the preacher of the First Crusade. On his deathbed he wrote to Hugh, his former master, saying that he "committed to him the care of his mother the Church, as Christ His mother to the beloved apostle."

In a period when cities were declining in size and prosperity, the influence of bishops and their ability to undertake new buildings decreased proportionately. When kings were constantly moving their courts from one place to another, they had little time or inclination to do any building of importance. However, with the consolidation of monastic life into a centralized system, and with the increasing concentration of wealth into the collective hands of these stable and growing institutions, it is hardly a cause for wonder that the monasteries were the scene of the most significant architectural and artistic developments of the time. Furthermore, the rise of the Cluniac star under the indomitable will of its great organizing genius and builder made Cluny itself the point where the most important and progressive developments of the period took place. As the influence of the mother house gradually permeated the entire order, a characteristic touch becomes discernible; and a Cluniac style emerges, which, in turn, becomes synonymous with the highest development of Romanesque art.

Hugh had started by undertaking many new monastic buildings at Cluny to accommodate the ever-growing number of resident monks. The old second church also proved inadequate for the mother house of a great order, especially when delegations of monks from the priories far and wide assembled there for the chapters general. Records show that on one such occasion in the year 1132, there were over 1200 monks in the processional line. The growing importance of Cluny as a center for pilgrimages also added to the need for greater space in the abbey church. For these practical reasons, as well as his desire to crown his many achievements with a monument that would rival the legendary temple of Solomon, the great new third abbey church was begun. Even with all his power and influence, however, Hugh did not attempt it before the dominant position of Cluny in the scheme of things was completely consolidated, and before he was certain of generous financial support. The far-flung priories of the order, numbering at this time well over 1000 and extending as far as Scotland in the north, Portugal in the west, and Jerusalem in the east, could all be counted on for contributions. In addition, offerings were received from people of all classes from bishops to the humblest of their parishioners and from great lords down to the poorest pilgrims who came to worship at the shrine. Thus in the year 1088, when he was past 65 years of age and in his fortieth year as abbot, Hugh of Semur began the monumental abbey church that in its magnitude and glory eclipsed all other churches in Western Christendom. One of his earliest biographers said that he "began and erected such a church within twenty years that if an emperor had built it within so short a time, it would have been considered marvelous." [2]

The Great Third Abbey Church at Cluny

Hugh's great church was dominated on the exterior by its imposing tower forms, one of which is still to be seen atop its single surviving transept (Fig. 5:5). The ground plan (Fig. 5:1) shows its unusual double transepts, the many apsidal chapels radiating outward from the choir, and its massive proportions. It was normal for large abbey churches to have an impressive lantern tower over the crossing of the nave and the transept. At Cluny its immense size dominated the silhouette of the whole exterior. The twin octagonal towers astride the transept wings, however, were less common. The minor transept also had its central tower, thus making four on the east end, which, added to the two on either side of the narthex entrance, brought the total to six. Unlike later Gothic cathedrals, the exterior was unadorned by sculpture, all such embellishments being concentrated in the interior. Even the western façade was bare, since it was designed for an introspective cloistered community, and thus there was no need to extend sculptured invitations to the world outside as in a city church. Rich façades as entrances to the nave did indeed exist in abbey churches, but they were masked by the narthex and hence essentially a part of the interior.

While the monks on everyday occasions entered the church from the cloister, high holidays, such as Easter, Pentecost, and the Feast of Sts. Peter and Paul to whom the church was dedicated, called for a ceremonial entrance from the west end. Here the double portal between the towers led into a spacious three-aisled narthex, which was called the minor nave. In most churches it was symbolically referred to as the Galilee because the celebrant, usually the abbot, who was at the head of the procession going into the nave, was likened to Jesus leading his disciples into the city of Galilee. At Cluny, however, the monks had their own Galilee portal which can be found in the plan about halfway down the nave. The narthex, besides serving as the place where the grand processions could be marshaled, also took care of the overflow of laymen who could gather there during the pilgrimage season. At Vézelay, for instance, the narthex was actually called the *ecclesia peregrinorum*, or church of the pilgrims. When such an entrance was made at Cluny, it was through three carved portals, the central one of which was 21 feet in height. Over it was an immense tympanum containing a sculptured relief representing Christ in Glory surrounded by a heavenly host, the four symbolic evangelical beasts, and various Apostles and elders.

Upon entering the nave (Fig. 5:6) the mighty proportions of the huge basilica loomed up. From the entrance portal to the end of the apse, it

Fig. 5:5. Third Abbey Church of Cluny, *Surviving Transept*. 1088–1130. (Courtesy French Government Tourist Office)

extended a distance of 415 feet; while the entire horizontal axis from front to back including the narthex reached to an over-all length of 615 feet. The nave itself had 11 bays that stretched forward a distance of 260 feet. Each bay was separated by a group of columns clustered around the supporting piers which, as the architectural counterpart of the monks, marched in solemn procession toward the climax of the building at the high altar. In width the nave spread outward 118 feet and was divided into five aisles. This division was owing in part to the need for providing extra space for altars when it became the custom for priests to say Mass every day. The outside aisles, extending all the way around the church and choir, gave pilgrims access to these numerous altars, and more especially to the smaller chapels in the choir, without disturbing the monastic liturgy while it was in progress. It also provided more room for the grand processionals that distinguished the Cluniac liturgy, and which demanded ever more impressive and spacious settings. It can be seen that a screen reached into the nave and closed off a space set aside for the monks' choir. The great height of the church was such that the unified impression of the whole was not broken by it, and the eye was drawn aloft to the tall columns standing around the high altar and above them, in turn, to the lofty figure of Christ painted in fresco on the interior of the half dome of the apse, which could be seen gazing benignly downward as if in a vision.

Whereas the Early Christian basilicas were largely horizontal in orientation, the Romanesque examples, because of the northern influence, raised the levels of the nave upward vertically. This gradually resulted in more and more accent being placed on the parts above the nave arcade. At Cluny a double row of windows was found, the lower of which was filled in with masonry, while the upper was left open and served as the clearstory. Though it had numerous windows, the church was criticized by the later Gothic builders as being too dark. Its thick walls, and massive proportions generally, allowed little direct sunlight to penetrate into the church itself. However, since so much of the monastic liturgy took place at night, the interior had to depend mostly on candlelight for illumination. But for the later churches, which were designed for city people who assembled by day, the lighting became a much more important architectural problem.

Over the clearstory the nave was spanned by barrel vaulting 32 feet in the clear supported by slightly pointed transverse arches. By rising a full 98 feet above the pavement, the highest vaults up to this time were achieved. The emotional exuberance in attaining such height actually outstripped the engineering knowledge necessary to maintain it, and a part of the vaulting collapsed soon after it was built. This trial-and-error process, however, led to the discovery of the flying buttress. In the rebuilding, a range of rudimentary supports with open round arches were placed outside the aisle roofs, and Cluny achieved the distinction of being the first church to have external flying buttresses supporting its nave vaults. Thus with its pointed arches, high vaulting, and its primitive flying buttresses, many of the necessary conditions of the future Gothic style were combined for the first time in one structure at Cluny.

Fig. 5:6. Third Abbey Church of Cluny. 1088–1130. *Reconstruction of the Nave* by K. J. Conant. Drawing by T. C. Bannister with additions by Conant (Courtesy Mediaeval Academy)

The Romanesque basilica differs little from its Early Christian counterpart except in size, vertical accents, and in development of the transept and the parts beyond it. Monastic churches all gravitated toward the eastern end (Fig. 5:7) where the choir assembled after the procession, and especially toward the high altar where the solemn rites were performed. In a city church, the nave has to be developed to provide space for a congregation. But in a monastic church, the clergy, including the monks, numbered into the hundreds, while there was often no congregation at all. Logically, then, the space around the altar had to be extended so that all the monks who formed the choir could be seated. The enlarged apse and double transepts at Cluny were clearly developed so as to give the monks a sense of surrounding the high altar and to produce a spacious and resonant setting for the almost ceaseless chanting.

The high altar itself was set off from the surrounding ambulatory by eight columns of surpassing slenderness and beauty (Fig. 5:8). Crowning them were the capitals, carved with incomparable skill, which are all that remains of the apse today. That these were as impressive in Romanesque

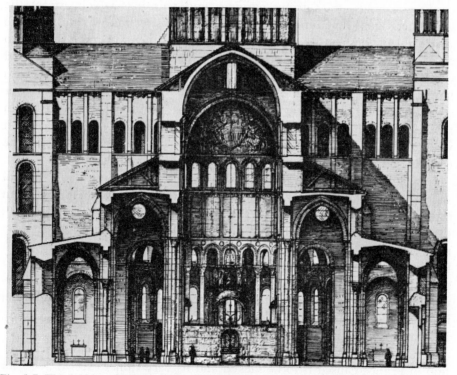

Fig. 5:7. Third Abbey Church of Cluny, *Transverse Section at the Transept.* Drawing by K. J. Conant (Courtesy Mediaeval Academy of America)

times as they are now is attested to by a bishop who saw them on a visit to Cluny. "If it were possible," he wrote, "for those who dwell in heaven to take pleasure in a house made by hands, the ambulatory of Cluny would be a place where angels walked." [3] The decorative plan of the church was carried out on a scale comparable in quality to the grandeur of its spatial dimensions. Over 1200 sculptured capitals surmounted the columns of the structure, while the graceful pointed arches of the nave arcade had carved moldings to outline them. Most of the sculpture was painted in rich colors that gave an added glow to the splendor of the interior. The whole church was also paved with mosaic floors inlaid with images of saints and angels as well as with abstract designs.

All this magnificence did not go unchallenged. The redoubtable opponent of the Cluniac order, St. Bernard, disapproved violently of such extravagances. In doing so in writing, however, he unwittingly left a first-hand account of the glory of Hugh's church soon after it was finished. In a letter to one of the Cluniac abbots he commented on "the vast height of your churches, their immoderate length, their superfluous breadth, the costly polishings, the curious carvings and paintings which attract the worshiper's gaze and hinder his attentions." His feeling was that "at the very sight of these costly yet marvelous vanities men are more kindled to offer gifts than to pray. . . . Hence the church is adorned with gemmed crowns of light—nay, with lustres like cart-wheels, girt all round with lamps, but no less brilliant with precious stones that stud them. Moreover we see candelabra standing like trees of massive bronze, fashioned with marvellous subtlety of art, and glistening no less brightly with gems than with the lights they carry. What, think you, is the purpose of all this? The compunction of penitents, or the admiration of beholders?" [4]

In spite of Bernard's diatribe, the church became a model for all subsequent Cluniac abbey churches and spread the fame of the Burgundian building art, as well as the taste for its pointed arches and other features that eventually were incorporated into Gothic cathedrals. As the most representative of all Romanesque churches, embodying as it did the most highly developed forms of the time, Hugh's church became the greatest single factor in the crystallization of the high Romanesque style. Furthermore, it was destined to remain the largest and most magnificent edifice of its kind for a full five centuries—specifically until the new basilica of St. Peter was undertaken in Rome in the 16th century.

It stood proudly until the year 1798 when a wave of Revolutionary reaction in France caused it to be sacked and its very stones carried away for building materials. Before the romantic interest in the Middle Ages had

Fig. 5:8. Third Abbey Church of Cluny, *Apse Arcade*. Reconstruction by K. J. Conant in the Fogg Museum, Cambridge, Mass. (Courtesy Mediaeval Academy of America)

developed, and before the tourist traffic—that modern counterpart of the medieval pilgrimages—could intervene, Cluny was blown up by dynamite and the rubble sold as common building stone. All that now remains is a single transept with its tower still in place, the capitals of the ambulatory, and a number of odd fragments of its architectural sculptures. And so it is that the other priories of Hugh's time must be cited for clues about its architecture and sculpture. It is therefore fortunate that the influence of Cluny was so extensive. The great increase in the power and prestige of the order was reflected not only in the growth of the mother abbey but in the numbers who were attracted as monks and pilgrims to its priories and dependencies. At the same time that Hugh was engaged in his great building program, abbey churches were in the process of construction in more than a dozen other monasteries in France alone, including those of Moissac, Beaulieu, La-Charité-sur-Loire, and Vézelay. Each in some way reflected directly the influence of Hugh's great basilica.

SCULPTURE

Fragments of the great period of Cluny's sculptural as well as architectural grandeur are today found scattered among its various extant abbeys, priories, and dependencies as well as in museums. Some of the finest Cluniac sculpture still to be seen today is in the abbey church of La Madeleine at Vézelay, the apse of which is seen in Figure 5:9. The nave (Fig. 5:10) and narthex there date from the time Hugh's church at Cluny was in the later stages of its construction, but its Gothic choir is a product of the latter part of the 12th century. The excellent condition of the building at the present time is owed to the intelligent restoration carried out by Viollet-le-Duc around the middle of the 19th century. While its proportions are considerably smaller than the great basilica at Cluny, La Madeleine is now the largest Romanesque abbey church still in existence in France. Rich in historical associations, it derived its principal fame in medieval times because it housed the relics of St. Mary Magdalene. On the eve of her feast in the year 1120, after the completion of the nave, a disastrous fire destroyed the wooden portions of the roof and burning timbers fell on the assembled pilgrims. After the fire the revaulting of the nave was undertaken, and, for the first time in France, the new principle of the groin vault was used. This type of vaulting, also called cross vaulting, can roughly be described as the result of the intersection at right angles of two barrel vaults of an equivalent span and height. The resulting diagonal lines seen from underneath are referred to as the groins. The principle used at Vézelay is illustrated in

Fig. 5:9. Abbey Church of La Madeleine at Vézelay, *Apse. c.*1130–1180 (Courtesy French Government Tourist Office)

Figure 3:12, and it can be contrasted with the simpler type of the half-cylinder barrel vaulting used at Cluny as shown in Figure 5:6. Strong transverse arches span the nave as at Cluny, but the alternation of the lighter pink and the darker grayish-brown stone of those at Vézelay results in an interesting color effect. While photographs tend to exaggerate the contrast, the irregularity of the cut stone voussoirs comes out clearly.

The principal interest at Vézelay, however, is not so much in its architecture as in the seemingly inexhaustible wealth of its sculptured capitals and, above all, by the relief compositions over the three portals leading from the narthex into the nave and side aisles. In Cluniac churches, the tympanums above such portals were elaborately decorated, and the largest and most intricate one was that over the central doorway. Only a few fragments of the great portal tympanum of Cluny are now extant. At Moissac, however, there is a fine example which shows a crowned figure of Christ enclosed by the four symbolic beasts representing the Evangelists, and the 24 elders with their lutes and phials who gaze upward as in the apocalyptical vision of St. John. Its counterpart at Beaulieu is again dominated by the figure of Christ, this time with his hands outstretched as on the Cross and surrounded by the Apostles. He is depicted here as at the Last Judgment, and the dead are called up from their graves by the trumpet blasts of the angels. At La

Fig. 5:10. Abbey Church of La Madeleine at Vézelay. *Nave* looking toward the West Portal from the Triforium Gallery. *c.*1110 (Courtesy French Government Tourist Office)

Charité the composition depicts the transfiguration of Christ who is shown between Moses and Elias.

The splendid tympanum over the central portal at Vézelay (Fig. 5:11) stems from the first quarter of the 12th century. It is by far the most complex in iconography and workmanship of them all, yet the logical division of space keeps the composition from seeming cluttered or confused. Here, as well as in the other places, these transcendental scenes owed their origin to the drawings and miniature paintings that illustrated the texts of the Scriptures in monastic libraries. Such illuminated manuscripts provided convenient models that the monks could show the sculptors who were to carry out the project. The robe of Christ at Vézelay, as well as those of the Apostles, reveals a pattern of clear sharp swirling lines, which point unmistakably to the pen drawings found in some of the manuscripts of the time.

The interpretation most often suggested is that of the commission of the Apostles as found in the last chapter of Luke's Gospel, and the description of the Pentecost scene in the second chapter of the Acts of the Apostles. A more likely source, however, is in the final vision of St. John from the last part of the Book of Revelations. Whether a single scene is intended, or whether there was a subtle Cluniac synthesis of two or even three scenes, is a subject for scholarly speculation. If it is a single scene, the most convincing theory is contained in the first two verses of the 22d Chapter of the Book of Revelations: "And he shewed me a pure river of water of life, clear as crystal, proceeding out of the throne of God and of the Lamb. In the midst of the street of it, and on either side of the river, was there the tree of life, which bare twelve manner of fruits, and yielded her fruit every month: and the leaves of the tree were for the healing of the nations."

Here again the figure of Christ dominates the composition, seated, as St. John says, on "a great white throne," but not so much to judge mankind as to redeem it. While the figure is supremely majestic, Christ is not crowned. The streams emanating from his fingers descend upon the barefooted Apostles, the archetypes of the clergy, who bring spiritual understanding through the books they hold in their hands and physical healing through the divine mercy which they transmit to mankind. On one side of Christ's head the water referred to in the quotation is flowing forth, while on the other the branches of the tree are found. The 12 fruits, one for each month, are found among the 29 medallions in the middle band of the archivolt which frames the composition. A figure trading grapes, for instance, represents September, while October is symbolized by a man gathering acorns for his pigs. The months themselves besides being connected with

Fig. 5:11. Abbey Church of La Madeleine at Vézelay. *Tympanum*. 31′ 4″ wide, 35′ 6″ high. *c.*1130 (Archives Photographiques)

these labors, are also symbolized by the signs of the zodiac, which, in turn, remind man of the limited time he has in which to attain his salvation. A few of the other medallions picture strange exotic beasts taken from the bestiaries, those curious books of the time which recounted the lore about animals actual and fabulous. A survival from antiquity can be noted in the one fourth from the lower right which depicts a centaur.

The inner band of the archivolt is divided into eight irregular compartments that contain figures representing the nations which the leaves of the tree of life are intended to heal. The one on the top left, next to the head of Christ, contains two dog-headed men, called in Isidore's *Etymologies* the Cynocephaloi, who represent a tribe supposed to have inhabited India. The corresponding compartment on the right side shows the crippled and bent figure of a man and that of a blind woman taking a few halting steps as she is led forward. In the others, the lame on crutches are found along with lepers pointing to their sores, all of whom stand in the need of physical healing.

Along the lintel below, a parade of the nations moves from the outer sides toward the center. While the compartments above had pictured those in physical distress, here are found the pagans and heathens of the earth who need spiritual aid. Among these strange peoples who populate the remote regions of the earth are a man and woman in the far right corner with enormous ears and feathered bodies. A race of dwarfs or pygmies is cleverly represented by making the people so small they have to mount a horse by means of a ladder. On the far left, half-naked savages are seen hunting with bows and arrows, while toward the left center some heathens are shown leading a bull to sacrifice. They converge from both sides toward the center where St. John the Baptist stands holding a medallion with the image of the lamb on it. This is doubtless intended to convey the explanation that the "river of the water of life" is none other than baptism, which is the road to salvation that all must take if they want to enter into eternal life. It is a logical symbol with which to adorn the portal leading into the nave of the church, the interior of which with its glowing colors and jeweled decorations was often likened to the heavenly city, the new Jerusalem, which is so eloquently described by St. John: "And the gates of it shall not be shut at all by day: for there shall be no night there. And they shall bring the glory and honour of the nations into it" (Rev. 21:25–26). The open books of the Apostles seated next to St. Peter on the left recall the following verse which states that all who enter it are the ones "which are written in the Lamb's book of life" (Rev. 21:27). Furthermore, in a monastic church especially, the monks would have been conscious of the final reference to these gates: "Blessed are they that do his commandments, that they may have the right to the tree of life, and may enter in through the gates into the city" (Rev. 22:14).

The awakened interest in foreign countries and peoples was doubtless owing to the influence of the early crusades, which were then being preached. Furthermore a specific Cluniac application can be found in the writings of Peter the Venerable, the abbot of Cluny at this time. He was concerned mainly with the refutation of the arguments of the Jews against the divinity of Christ. And before he went to Spain he had the Hebrew literature and the entire Koran translated, so that he could preach more intelligently to both the Jews and Mohammedans.

The imaginative scope displayed in the profusion of sculptured capitals is breath-taking. Biblical scenes, incidents from the lives of the saints, allegorical commentaries, and the play of pure fantasy are found throughout the narthex and the nave. One of the narthex capitals depicts the flight of the Angel Gabriel with his trumpet ready to sound the call to the Last

Abbey Church of La Madeleine at Vézelay. Fig. 5:12 (left). Narthex Capital, *Judgment Angel*. Fig. 5:13 (center). Nave Capital, *Angel of Death Killing the Eldest Son of Pharaoh*. Fig. 5:14 (right). Nave Capital, *Moses and St. Paul Grinding Corn*. *c*.1130 (Archives Photographiques)

Fig. 5:15 (left). Nave Capital, *Demon*. Fig. 5:16 (center). Nave Capital, *Combat between Two Demons*. Fig. 5:17 (right). Nave Capital, *St. Martin and the Woodcutters*. *c*.1130 (Archives Photographiques)

Judgment (Fig. 5:12). Another in the nave shows the angel of death striking down the eldest son of Pharaoh (Fig. 5:13). In still another a bearded figure is shown pouring grain into a handmill which a barefooted man is grinding (Fig. 5:14). But for a chance remark in the writings of Suger, the abbot of St. Denis, the meaning would never have been known. He said, however, that the corn is the old law that is poured into the mystic mill by an ancient Hebrew prophet, probably Moses, and is being ground into the meal of the new law by St. Paul. Frequently depicted are incidents from the lives of the two favorite Cluniac saints, Anthony and Paul, who both lived as hermits in the Egyptian desert. In one of the fearful temptations of St. Anthony, a demon symbolizing Luxury (Fig. 5:15) appears in the guise of a ferocious monster, whose hair leaps upward like sulphurous flames, and whose grimacing mouth opens to reveal his fangs. Other demons are seen combating for the souls of the unwary (Fig. 5:16). One which is especially skillfully executed shows St. Martin of Tours ordering the pagans to chop down a sacred tree (Fig. 5:17).

Unlike the marble and bronze statuary of antiquity, these Romanesque examples were carved in the soft sandstone and limestone that is found in such abundance in France. The purpose of such work was mainly to decorate interiors where it did not have to resist the elements. The soft material, furthermore, was better adapted to the pictorial forms of Romanesque sculpture, and its plasticity responded more quickly to the imaginative demands made on it than a harder stone could have done.

While the examples discussed have been stone carvings, the general category of Romanesque sculpture in this period should be broadened to include works wrought in metal as well. Only a few examples of this kind have survived, owing to the fact that they were made of such precious materials as gold, silver, and copper, adorned with enamel work, and studded with precious gems. Cluny, according to an early inventory, had a golden statue of the Virgin seated on a silver throne and wearing a jeweled crown. Churches also needed such utensils as chalices and pitchers for the sacred services. On important feast days, books with ivory or metal covers encrusted with jewels were used on the high altar. Reliquaries fashioned to contain the relics of saints also reposed there; while candelabras, incense burners, and metal choir screens added their beauty to the sacred precincts.

Romanesque sculpture always remained an integral part of the complete architectonic design and is inseparable from the whole picture. The walls, ceiling, portals, columns, and capitals were not merely mute structural necessities, but the space for the decorative devices that brought to the

structural members a communicative value all their own, which spoke to
monk and pilgrim alike in the eloquent visual language of form, line, and
color.

PAINTING AND OTHER MONASTIC CRAFTS

Miniatures of modest proportions on the parchment pages of books and
monumental murals in the apses of abbey churches were the two extremities
of form the art of painting assumed in the high Romanesque period. The
one craft known definitely to have been consistently practiced by the monks
themselves was the copying, illustrating, and binding of books, activities
which were carried on in a large communal room called the *scriptorium*.
This tradition, which dates from the time of Cassiodorus, was followed by
all Benedictine houses, and those in the Cluniac order fostered it with both
diligence and enthusiasm. The Cluniac copyists were known for the beauty
of their lettering and the accuracy of their texts. A monk skilled in his
craft, however, would certainly not have been content merely to copy
letters all his life. Blank places in the manuscript provided both the space
and the necessary challenge for him to fill them in. At first these were
nothing more than fanciful little pen drawings or an elaborate initial letter
at the beginning of a paragraph. Gradually these drawings grew into
miniature paintings, and the initial letters became highly complex designs.
The luxurious development of this art of illuminating manuscripts seems to
have been one compensation for the austerity of Benedictine life. As the
practice became more widely accepted, specialists in the various phases
began to be designated. A painter of small illuminated scenes, for instance,
was called a *miniator*, while one who did initial letters was known as a
rubricator.

Cluny itself was among the most important centers of the time for the
illumination of manuscripts. The work there was often done with the utmost delicacy. Miniatures were painted in many colors, and the halos of
saints and crowns of kings were made with thin gold leaf. One of the Bibles
produced in Hugh's time was as famous for its illustrations as it was for the
accuracy of its text. While it is now lost, an elaborately illuminated Lec-
tionary survives from this period that conveys at least an idea of the subtlety
of this phase of Cluniac art. One of the many thousands of examples of the
rubricator's art can be seen in the letter *Q* from an 11th-century Evangeliary of the Cluniac abbey at St. Omer (Fig. 5:18). Great imaginative freedom was provided by the medium, and no two illuminated letters were
ever the same.

Fig. 5:18. *Initial Q.* Illuminated Manuscript from an Evangeliary of the Abbey of St. Omer. Early 11th Century. Pierpont Morgan Library, New York

Such flourishes of the pen made by expert copyists on their parchment pages, and the gradual refinement of the painstaking miniature art of illumination had effects on the art of the period far beyond the medium for which they were originally intended. They became the prototypes for the large murals that decorated the walls and apses of the churches, and for the sculpture that embellished the spaces above portals and columns, and later for the designs of the stained glass windows of Gothic cathedrals. The greater freedom provided by the pen and brush on the parchment page had to be developed before the art could be transferred to the more monumental mediums of stone and glass. Thus these miniature examples of the medieval painter's art were far more important than their diminutive size would indicate. Not only do they provide the few surviving examples of pictorial art in Western Europe from the 7th through the 10th centuries, but they were the source which gradually swelled into the flood of monumental sculpture, mural painting, and stained glass.

Contrasting with the diminutive art of illuminating manuscripts were the huge frescoes painted on the surfaces of the barrel-vaulted ceilings, the arches, and the semidomed apses of the churches during the century and a half of the high Romanesque period. Here again the most notable examples were found at Cluny and its satellite monasteries. In the narthex at Vézelay there is still one of these frescoes, showing Christ surrounded by the four evangelical beasts, though it is now so faded as to be barely visible. A monk visiting Cluny in 1063 sang the praises of the wall paintings in the great refectory. The most notable of all, however, was the colossal painting of *Christ in Glory* in the apse of Hugh's great church. From a study of the fragments that have been recovered, authorities have declared it to be as outstanding in its way as the sculpture and architecture of the great building. Its style and technique, as well as its subject, is known to have been similar to that of an excellently preserved apsidal mural in the little chapel at Berzé-la-ville, less than ten miles from Cluny (Fig. 5:19). This small residence and chapel was built between the years 1100 and 1103 as a retreat for Hugh in the last years of his life. So close is the resemblance of the painting there to that in his great church at Cluny, that it may even have been done by the same artist.

In the Berzé-la-ville painting the seated figure of Christ is enclosed in a many-hued mandorla, a form familiar from the relief sculptures over the portals of the churches. Here he is clothed in a robe of white over which is draped a red mantle. While blessing the 16 surrounding Apostles and saints with his right hand, he gives St. Peter a scroll containing the law with his left. The heavenly setting is suggested by the dark blue background of

Fig. 5:19. Cluniac Chapel at Berzé-la-ville, Apse Mural. *Christ in Glory*. Fresco. *c*.13′ high. *c*.1103 (Archives Photographiques)

the mandorla, which is studded with golden stars, and by the hand of God the Father, which hovers above him holding a crown. The term *fresco* is not used in the ordinary sense when it is applied to this style of painting. A true fresco technique involves the mixing of the color pigments with water, then applying them directly to fresh plaster. The lime in the plaster then binds the pigments to the wall by chemical action, and a permanent though somewhat opaque surface is the result. This process seems to have been used only for the red ocher undercoats in the examples at Cluny and Berzé-la-ville. The undersurface was then coated with several layers of tempera and finally glazed with wax overpainting to achieve the brighter and more transparent effect needed for the dark interiors. While the range of colors was not great, those they did develop had an extraordinary intensity well suited to the expressive needs of the style. In the desire for brilliant color and strongly articulated outlines, these murals were undoubtedly influenced to some extent by Byzantine mosaics, especially by those of Ravenna.

Besides the arts of building, stone carving, and painting, many other crafts were practiced in the workshops of Cluny and the other monasteries. These included weaving, ceramics, goldsmithing and other metal crafts, leather work, and the casting of bells. The constant experimentation and research carried on in these centers resulted in a continuous improvement of the methods employed in such activities, such as better ways of manufacturing glass, and the invention of chemical formulas for stained glass. Just how extensively the monks themselves took part in the actual production of such handicrafts at Cluny or elsewhere is not definitely known. There is no evidence, for instance, that a monk ever worked there as a sculptor in stone. The capitals and relief sculpture were executed for the most part by journeymen carvers, who went from place to place in groups wherever building activity was in progress. Similar work in other media was probably also performed by itinerant craftsmen or by lay workers from the region. The iconographic schemes, however, were always done under the direct supervision of the monks, some of whom may have possessed the necessary skills so that they could train the craftsmen who worked under them. The variety and subtle character of the work, therefore, is often as much the monks' as if they had taken the chisel or other tools into their own hands. Wherever names have survived in connection with sculpture, painting, or other work, it is almost invariably that of some monk who is said to have "made" it. This, however, could mean anything from donating the material, suggesting the subject, to the actual supervision of the work in progress or even the carving or painting itself.

The monastic attitude toward decorating a church is well summed up by Theophilus, a writer on the various crafts of this time, who addressed his fellow monks, saying: ". . . you have confidently approached the house of God, have decorated with utmost beauty ceilings or walls with various work, and, showing forth with different colours a likeness of the paradise of God, glowing with various flowers, and verdant with herbs and leaves, and cherishing the lives of the saints with crowns of various merit, you have, after a fashion, shown the beholders everything in creation praising God, its creator, and have caused them to proclaim him admirable in all his works. Nor is the eye of man even able to decide upon which work it may first fix its glance; if it beholds the ceilings, they glow like draperies; if it regards the walls, there is the appearance of paradise; if it marks the abundance of light from the windows, it admires the inestimable beauty of the glass and the variety of the costly work. . . ." [5]

MUSIC

Odo of Cluny, abbot from 927 to 942, brought the monastery its earliest musical distinction through his active fostering of choral music. Documents tell of more than 100 psalms being sung there daily in his time; and on his tours of inspection to other monasteries, he devoted much of his energies to the instruction of choirs. His great success made it necessary for his teaching methods to be written down, and from this fortunate circumstance something about the early status of music at Cluny can be ascertained. [6] His great accomplishments include the arranging of the tones of the scale into an orderly progression from A to G; and by thus assigning to them a system of letters, he was responsible for the earliest effective system of Western musical notation. His method also included the mathematical measurement of spaces on the monochord, which made it possible to determine accurately the pitches and intervals of each of the Gregorian modes. Before Odo's time the chants used in the sacred service had laboriously to be learned by rote; and if any degree of authenticity were to be achieved, they had to be taught by a graduate of the Schola Cantorum established by Gregory the Great in Rome. Now, however, singers could be taught to read notes; and, it is stated in the treatise: "With the passage of not many days they were singing at first sight and extempore and without a fault anything written in music, something which until now ordinary singers had never been able to do, many continuing to practice and study for fifty years without profit." [7]

Further refinements on Odo's method were made in the 11th century by another monk, Guido of Arezzo. His treatise, which was in the library of Cluny, made it clear that he embraced the Cluniac musical reforms. He also freely acknowledged his debt to the work of his great predecessor, the Abbot Odo, "from whose example," he said, "I have departed only in the forms of the notes." [8] This slight departure by Guido was actually the invention of the basis for modern musical notation on a staff of lines. As he explained it: "The sounds, then, are so arranged that each sound, however

often it may be repeated in a melody, is always found in its own row. And
in order that you may better distinguish these rows, lines are drawn close
together, and some rows of sounds occur on the lines themselves, others in
the intervening intervals or spaces. Then the sounds on one line or in one
space all sound alike." [9] Odo's work also led to Guido's system of solmiza-
tion, which assigned certain syllables, derived from the following hymn to
St. John, to each degree of the scale:

> *Ut* queant laxis   *Re*sonare fibris,
> *Mi*ra gestorum   *Fa*muli tuorum,
> *Sol*ve polluti   *La*bii reatum,
>   Sancte Ioannes.

Later, the syllable *si*, which is compounded from the first two letters
of the Latin form of St. John's name (Sancte Ioannes), was added as the
seventh degree of the scale. In France these syllables are still used just as
in Guido's time; in Italy and elsewhere, the first note, *ut*, is replaced by the
vocally more grateful sound of *do*.

The most remarkable fact about both Odo's and Guido's treatises is that
they champion music as an art designed to be performed in the praise of the
Creator and to enhance the beauty and meaning of prayer. Previously,
Boethius, along with most early writers on music, had conceived it as a
branch of mathematics that could reveal the secrets of the universe. Guido,
however, made a point of stating that the writings of Boethius were "useful
to philosophers, but not to singers." [10] Such speculations were intentionally
omitted by both Odo and Guido. Cluny, therefore, emerged as a center of
practical music-making rather than as a place where theoreticians pondered on it as an abstruse science.

In addition to such treatises of instruction, the story of music at Cluny
was told with compelling beauty in a visual record, which survives in two
of the capitals from the apse of Hugh's great church. In the sanctuary,
which was the architectural climax of the whole edifice, there was a series of
capitals grouped in a semicircle around the high altar, which constituted
the apogee of late 11th-century sculptural skill. The highest ideals and
aspirations of the monk's life found expression here in a series of quaternities
presented on the four faces of each capital. On two, for instance, the monk's
moral precepts were symbolized by the four theological and four cardinal
virtues. The cycle and labors of his year were pictured on another by means
of the four seasons; and his hopes for the hereafter were portrayed by the
four rivers and trees of Paradise. Finally his praise for the Creator of all
goodness and beauty was found in a double quaternity, symbolized by the

eight tones of sacred psalmody in which the chants were sung. The inclusion of such a reference to music in the sacred precinct, next to those telling of the highest human virtues and heavenly beauties, was still another sign of the high esteem in which the tonal art was held by the monks of Cluny.

In the Cluny capitals the first panel is inscribed: "This tone is the first in the order of musical intonations (Fig. 5:20)." The figure is that of a young man of sad countenance playing on a stringed instrument resembling a lute. This is probably a reference to the beginning of the Mass, where the celebrant and his attendants sing the words of the fourth verse of the 43d Psalm: "Then I will go unto the altar of God; to God who givest joy to my youth. To thee O God, I will give praise on the harp [cithara]: why art thou sad O my soul? and why dost thou disquiet me?" The symbolism of the stringed instrument is connected with the power of music to drive out evil spirits and to effect the transition from the sadness of the soul to the joy of God, just as David had cast out Saul's evil spirit when he played to him. In the New Testament this is taken as a prophecy of the victory of Christ, the lineal descendant of David, over the devil and over death.

The second tone is represented by the figure of a young woman dancing and beating a small drum, while the inscription reads: "There follows the tone which by number and law is second" (Fig. 5:21). This can be interpreted as referring to the Introit, or processional entry into the church. The monks, observing strict rules of seniority, then began their procession into the church led by the chorus chanting the Psalm appropriate to the day with the acolytes, deacons, and finally the celebrant all moving toward the altar in stately measure. One of the verses of the 68th Psalm, which is prescribed for use on Palm Sunday, seems to point to the figure depicted on the capital: "The singers went before, the players on instruments followed after; among them were damsels playing with timbrels." Since the Introit precedes the Proper of the Mass, the joyous attitude expressed here is not out of place. Such processional chants emphasized movement and progress. The rhythm is therefore more regular and the mood livelier than in the stationary chants, which are quieter so that they will harmonize better with the attitude of prayer. Since such chants were more metrical, it is quite possible that percussion instruments such as the one depicted here were used.

The next inscription goes: "The third strikes, and represents the resurrection of Christ" (Fig. 5:22). The instrument here is of the lyre type with a sounding board added, which is one of the 11th-century forms of the psaltery, the legendary instrument with which David accompanied himself as he sang the psalms. This instrument with its gut strings stretched over

Third Abbey Church of Cluny, Ambulatory Capitals. Fig. 5:20 (above left). *First Tone*. Fig. 5:21 (above right). *Second Tone*. Fig. 5:22 (below left). *Third Tone*. Fig. 5:23 (below right). *Fourth Tone*. 1088–1095. Ochier Museum, Cluny

the wooden frame roughly resembles a cross and was used as a symbolic reference to Christ stretched on the Cross for the redemption of the world. The liturgical connection refers to the point in the Mass where Christ is first mentioned; and where the chorus, now in a stationary position, chants the prayer "*Kyrie eleison* [Lord have mercy], *Christe eleison* [Christ have mercy], *Kyrie eleison.*" Each is repeated three times in honor of the Trinity. The number *three* in the inscription thus alludes to the Trinity as well as to the words of the Creed, which tell of Christ rising from the dead on the third day.

The fourth figure is that of a young man playing a set of chime bells, and the accompanying inscription reads: "The fourth follows representing a lament in song" (Fig. 5:23). The Latin word *planctus* denotes a funeral dirge, and the practice of ringing bells at funerals can be compared with the contemporary representation of the burial procession of Edward the Confessor (Fig. 6:2), where the figures accompanying the bier have small bells in their hands.

The second capital, which depicts the last four tones, is badly damaged. The inscriptions, however, are intact, and it is also possible to get a partial picture of the figures and their instruments. In the second, fourth, fifth, and seventh tones, for instance, the figures are moving or standing, which seems to point to the processional chants; while in the other cases they are seated in a manner appropriate to the stationary chants. In those that have to do with action, the instruments are a small hand drum or cymbals, bells, and a horn of some type; while the seated figures all play stringed instruments. This symbolism apparently points out some of the rhythmic and melodic differences in the two types of chant, the processional and the stationary, which in turn reflect the two aspects of life, the active and contemplative.

The skillful chorus of Cluny was undoubtedly in the musical vanguard of the time, just as the monastery led the field in its architecture and sculpture. Odo's teaching methods clearly indicated that a high degree of vocal culture was expected of his monastic choirs; and, since they sang most of the time, it was obvious that they got plenty of practice. They were thus able to perform chants of considerable complexity, and music was well on its way to becoming a highly developed art. While Gregorian plainsong was a purely melodic style and continued to be practiced as such, during the Romanesque period the choral responses began to show variations in the direction of singing in several parts. The 9th, 10th, and 11th centuries thus saw the tentative beginnings of the polyphonic or many-voiced style, which was to flourish in the Gothic period and in the Renaissance.

The polyphonic practice of the pre-Gothic period is known, unfortunately, only through theoretical treatises. From the rules they give for the addition of voices to the traditional chant, however, some idea of the early forms of polyphony can be determined. As might be expected, the influence of mathematics and Pythagorean number theory was woven into the musical usages of the time. The perfect intervals of the octave, fifth, and fourth were preferred over all others, since their mathematical ratios indicated a closer correspondence with the divine order of the universe. In a treatise dating from the beginning of the 10th century, some years before Odo's time, the type of choral response known as parallel organum is discussed.[11] The original Gregorian melody was maintained intact; and, as a variant in two parts, the principal voice was paralleled by an organal voice at the fifth below, so that there was a strict melodic and rhythmic concordance between the two parts. When sung in three parts, the organum was doubled at the octave above, so that the principal voice was embellished by the movement of parallel voices a fifth below and a fourth above. With the addition of the fourth part, both the principal and organal voices were doubled in octaves, thus making a composite intervalic texture which included the parallel movement of the three perfect intervals, the fourth, fifth, and octave.

Parallel Organum (10th century)   From the *Scholia enchiriadus*

Parallel organum in effect built a mighty fortress of choral sound around the traditional Gregorian line of plainsong. By thus enclosing it within the stark and gaunt but strong perfect intervals, a massive and solid style was achieved which is entirely in keeping with the other Romanesque arts.

The music of this time was yet another expression of the praise of God; and, when seen in relation to the great buildings, the richly carved sculptures, the illuminated manuscripts and painted murals, it fits into the picture as a whole. The important part of the planning of the choir section of a monastic church, for instance, was always to provide a resonant setting for the perpetual chant. Hugh's great church was especially renowned for its acoustics. The curved ceiling vaults and the great variety of angles in the wall surfaces of the broad transepts and cavernous nave gave the chant there a characteristic tone color that can never be reproduced except in a similar setting. The effect of a monastic choir of several hundred voices performing jubilations with all its heart and soul must have been over-whelmingly impressive.

The sculptured capitals depicting the tones of plainsong represent an obvious synthesis of the arts of sculpture, music, and literature all fitting into an appropriate architectural setting. Their aesthetic excellence alone would assure them of timeless admiration, but it is possible to go one step beyond and infer something about the practice of music at this time. In a period dominated by vocal music, the fact that each tone is depicted by a figure playing a musical instrument or dancing is most remarkable. It in-dicates that, contrary to general opinion, the music of this period was not entirely a cappella, or unaccompanied. Instruments such as these may very well have been used to accompany the chant and to give the chorus support in both pitch and rhythm. Furthermore, the highly intense char-acter of these sculptural representations bespeak of both the motion and emotion typical of the high Romanesque style in general. As such they are representative products of a people capable of the long and arduous pil-grimages and the fantastic effort associated with the organization of the First Crusade. These sculptures express something of that indomitable energy, and especially of a vigorous attitude toward the act of worship that must have been channeled into a performance style which was em-phatic in rhythm. They are in fact the embodiment of the spirit expressed by St. Augustine to "Sing with your voices, and with your hearts, and with all your moral convictions, sing the new songs, not only with your tongue but with your life." [12] One of the other capitals suggests the representation of athletes with such figures as a boxer, a swimmer, and a tumbler. The whole Cluniac approach was aptly summed up by a friend of St. Hugh's, St. Peter Damian, who referred to Cluny as a "spiritual gymnasium."

IDEAS

The key to the understanding of the Romanesque as a living and active art lies in a knowledge of the opposing forces that created it. As the Roman Christian influence spread northward it encountered the restless surging energies of the former barbarian tribes. A veneration for tradition, which tended in the direction of a static order, in effect met an urge for action and experimentation, which resulted in the creation of many innovations.

When the horizontal Roman basilica, for instance, was combined with the northern spire, the first step toward Romanesque architecture was taken. The further development of the style was the direct result of this union of southern horizontality and northern verticality, reflecting as it did the broad spirit of the late Roman humanism and the soaring northern aspirations. The musical counterpart is found in the joining together of southern monophony and northern polyphony, which is seen when the Mediterranean tradition of unison melody met the northern custom of singing in parts. The result was the experimentation with primitive forms of counterpoint and harmony that characterized the music of the Romanesque period. This meeting of Roman unity with northern variety, and its slow maturation over the centuries, was thus responsible for the first truly European art style, the Romanesque. The ideas that underlie the monastic aspect of the style are an outgrowth of those that motivated the earlier period in Ravenna. The mysticism of the previous period moved into an other-worldly ascetic phase; and Early Christian authoritarianism resulted in the rigid stratification of society into strict hierarchies. The two basic ideas, then, crystallize as asceticism and hierarchism.

Asceticism

The monastic way of life demanded the seclusion of the country as an escape from the distractions of the world. Since the monk conceived this life as a steppingstone to that beyond, living had to be reduced to the barest essentials. Such rural isolation would ordinarily have been exceedingly barren soil for the growth of an important art movement. But the very absence of all externals made it the more imperative that a rich inner life be developed. Such virtues as poverty, chastity, and humility were essentially moral rather than aesthetic impulses. The very severity of the monastery, however, acted as a stimulus to imaginative experience, and individual self-denial released a flood of communal energies. The attitude of turning away from the world found its architectural expression in the plain exteriors and rich interiors of monastic churches. Thus the net effect of asceticism was to increase the fervor of the spirit and to express it with great intensity. Two of the favorite Cluniac saints, for instance, were the John and Anthony who went the farthest into the forbidding African desert; it was they who had the most fantastic visions and the most horrendous temptations. The diffusion of social centers into widely scattered monastic communities likewise lent a peculiar intensity and a wide variety to the expressive forms of the Romanesque. The arts consequently were not intended to mirror the natural world or to decorate the dwelling place of an earthly ruler but, rather, to conjure up other-worldly visions of divine majesty. Thus all the arts find a common ground in their desire to depict the various aspects of the world beyond.

The monks developed an art of such elaborate symbolism that it could be understood only by those versed in the allegorical interpretations of the Scriptures. Such a symbolic language—whether in architecture, sculpture, painting, or music—could only have been fostered by an abbot like Hugh, whose learning was so universal that he succeeded in adding "philosophy to ornament and a meaning to beauty." [13] By contrast the later Gothic arts were directed toward the humble of the world and the unlettered people beyond the cloister. While the sculpture and stained glass of the Gothic cathedral were destined to become the Bible in stone and glass for the poor, the comparable forms in a monastic church were always aloof and aristocratic, and at times intentionally subtle and enigmatic. This does not mean that the art was overly intellectualized and remote from the experience of those to whom it was addressed. On the contrary, it was very directly related to the intensity of the inner life and the visionary other-worldly focus of the religious communities who developed it.

Greco-Roman sculpture was successful in its way precisely because classical man had conceived his gods in human form, and as such they could be rendered so well in marble. When godhood was conceived as an abstract principle, a realistic representation of it became essentially impossible to make. Rational proportions were of no help to Romanesque man, who considered it impossible to understand God intellectually. He had to be felt rather than known or comprehended. Only through the intuitive eye of faith could His essence be grasped. Hence He had to be portrayed symbolically, since a symbol could stand for something intangible rather than a literal representation. Visible physical substance was secondary, and soul stuff was primary; but the latter could be depicted only in the world of the imagination.

A life so metaphysically oriented and one motivated by such deep religious convictions could never have found its models in the natural world. The fantastic proportions of its architecture, the eccentric treatment and distortions of the human body in its sculpture, the unnecessarily elaborated initials in the manuscript illuminations, and the florid melismas added to the syllables of the chant were all evidence of a rejection of the natural order of things and its replacement by the supernatural. The book of the Bible they most admired was that of Revelations, containing as it did the apocalyptical visions of St. John. The pictorial element in sculpture and painting in both large and small forms reflected their convictions with such intensity that the human figures seem to be consumed by the inner fires of their faith. Calm reason would seek to persuade by placid or serene attitudes, but the animated figures of the Apostles perform dances of the spirit in which their slender forms stretch upward to unnatural lengths, and their gestures are more convulsive than graceful.

Romanesque man thus dwelt in a dream world where the trees which grew in Paradise, the angels who populated the heavens, and the denizens of hell were all more real than anything or anybody he beheld in everyday life. Even though he had never seen any of these creatures, their existence was never doubted. Indeed, the monsters whose fearsome characteristics were described in the bestiaries, and which were represented in the manuscripts and sculptures, had a moral and symbolic function far more real to him than any animals of mere physical existence. All these imaginary creatures existed together in a kind of jungle of the imagination where the abnormal was the normal, and the fabulous became the commonplace.

Hierarchism

A strict hierarchical structure of society prevailed throughout the Romanesque period, which was as rigid in its way inside the monastery as was the feudalism outside the cloistered walls. The thought of the time was based on the assumption of a divinely established order of the universe, and the authority to interpret it was vested in the Church. The majestic figure of Christ in Glory carved over the entrance portals of the Cluniac abbey churches, and echoed in the mural compositions painted on the interior of their half-domed apses, proclaimed this concept to the world at large. Christ was no longer the Good Shepherd of Early Christian times but a mighty king, crowned and enthroned in the midst of his heavenly courtiers, sitting in judgment on the entire world. The keys to his heavenly kingdom, as seen in the Vézelay tympanum and the apse painting at Berzé-la-ville, rest firmly in the grasp of St. Peter, the first of the popes according to the Roman tradition. As if to lend additional emphasis to this doctrine, St. Peter at Berzé-la-ville is seen receiving a scroll containing the divine statutes from the hands of Christ. The papacy in the Middle Ages always found its most powerful support in the order of Cluny, and through its aid succeeded in establishing an all-powerful theocracy based on this mandate from on high.

The authority of the Church is nowhere better expressed than in these monumental sculptural and mural compositions that warned from their place of eminence that those who entered were walking a road either to salvation or damnation. The milestones which marked the path were placed there by the Church, whose clergy alone could interpret them and assure the suppliant that he was on his way to the streets of gold instead of the caldrons of fire. The frequence with which the apocalyptic vision of

St. John is represented, with Apostles and elders surrounding the throne of Christ, is evidence of the veneration of the protective father image in the form of the bearded patriarch. Like the clergy, these are the authorities who show the way by their willingness to offer their crowns to God, to praise Him by means of the musical instruments they hold in their hands, and to petition Him by means of the cups which contain their prayers.

In such a divine order, nothing could be left to chance; and all life had to be brought into an organizational plan that would conform to this cosmic scheme of things. The stream of authority, descending from Christ through St. Peter to his papal successors, flowed out from Rome in three main directions. The Holy Roman Emperor received his crown from the hands of the Roman Pontiff, and in turn all the kings of the Western world owed him homage, and on downward from the great lords to the humblest serf, all of whom had a preordained place in this great plan. Next, the archbishops and bishops received their mitres in Rome, and all the so-called secular clergy from the parish priest to the deacon owed their allegiance to the superiors from whom they received their authority. Finally, the monastic orders under their abbots also owed their allegiance to the pope; and through their loyal support of the papacy, the order of Cluny grew so strong that its abbot was the most powerful churchman in Christendom, with the sole exception of the pope himself.

Beginning as a small independent monastery, Cluny was from the first exempted from tribute to any power save that of the pope alone. But instead of remaining an independent unit like other Benedictine abbeys, Cluny adopted the feudal principle by expanding and absorbing other monastic houses until it dominated the monastic movement. As the head of a monarchical system, the order was the most powerful unifying force of the time, not only in religious and political affairs but in architectural, artistic, and musical thought as well. Through this adherence to the feudal system it became a great landowning institution, and in an economy where the land was the sole source of wealth, the monasteries became the principal commissioners of works of art. In a world where faith triumphed over reason, and where the sole road to salvation was through the Church, the Cluniac order acted as the mainstay of the Roman tradition and helped to spread its authority, its doctrines, and its liturgy all over Christendom.

The ranks of the monks were drawn mainly from the aristocratic class, whose members were among the few who were free to choose their own way of life. All the higher Church offices were held principally by men from noble families, often by the younger sons who were not eligible under the law of primogeniture to inherit the feudal estates. The vow of poverty applied only to individual ownership, and collectively a monastic com-

munity resembled a feudal manor. It was only in later times that the
mendicant orders of monks attempted to interpret the vow of poverty
more literally. Hence Romanesque art was also an aristocratic art, and it
remained so throughout the period with the means of patronage concentrated in the hands of its abbots and bishops.

The Romanesque abbey church is organized according to a rigid hierarchical plan that mirrored the strict order of precedence in the processionals of the liturgy for which it was the setting. By its insistence on visible
proportions, it bespoke of the invisible plan of a divinely ordered world.
The regularity of the monastic buildings that surrounded it were likewise
designed to enclose those who expressed their willingness to conform to
such a cosmic regularity of life, and thus to constitute a human reflection
of the divinely established plan for the salvation of mankind. The very
spaciousness of the abbey church was far in excess of anything that was
needed to accommodate the few hundreds who normally worshiped there.
It was, however, the monument that mirrored the unshakable religious
convictions of Romanesque man; and, as the house of the Lord and Ruler
of the universe, it became a palace surpassing the dreams of glory of any
king on the face of the earth. In the insecurity of the feudalistic world,
Romanesque man built a fortress for his faith and for his God, which was
designed to withstand the onslaughts of heretics and heathens as well as
to survive the more elemental forces of wind, weather and fire. Furthermore, the abbey church was the place where the heavenly monarch held
court, and where his subjects could pay Him their never-ceasing homage
in the divine services which went on day and night, year in and year out.

This hierarchical principle, moreover, applied not only to the social and
ecclesiastical stratifications but to the basic thought processes as well.
Authority for all things rested firmly on the Scriptures and the interpretations of them by the early Church fathers. Rightness and fitness was determined by how ancient the tradition was, and scholarship consisted not
so much in treading new intellectual paths as in the elucidations of the
traditional sources. To the educated this process took the form of learned
commentaries; to the unlettered it was expressed in the cult of relics.
Thousands took to the dusty pilgrimage roads and traveled across France
and Spain in order to touch the legendary tomb of the Apostle James at
Compostela. In the arts this veneration of the past made mandatory the
continuance of such traditional forms as the Early Christian basilica and
the music of the Gregorian chant.

Yet this traditionalism, curiously enough, never led to stagnation or uniformity. In making learned commentaries on the Scriptures, the writers
unconsciously, and sometimes quite consciously, interpreted them in the

light of contemporary views. And as the unlettered traveled about Europe on pilgrimages and later went to the Near East on the crusades, they absorbed new ideas that eventually were to jar them out of the provincialism of feudal times into a more dynamic social structure.

Within the Romanesque period, however, all the arts exhibited an extraordinary inventiveness and such a rich variety as to make it one of the most spontaneous and original periods in history. Romanesque forms never crystallized in the manner of the structural systems of Greek temples, Byzantine churches, and the later Gothic cathedrals. Through constant experimentation the Romanesque architects found the key to new structural principles, such as their vaulting techniques; and, by gradually achieving complete command of their medium, their buildings grew from heavy fortresslike structures into ones of considerable elegance. Meanwhile the decorators groped their way toward the revival of monumental sculpture and mural painting. The need for bigger and better choirs likewise led to the invention of notational systems, and the emotional exuberance in religious worship led to many modifications of the traditional chant that eventually culminated in the art of counterpoint. All in all the creative vitality exhibited in each art medium is a constant source of astonishment.

* Within the formal framework provided by the abbey church, the decorative arts and music all fitted in as parts of the grand architectonic design. From the numerous instances in which the arts were combined, it is apparent that they were all considered as an integral whole rather than as separate entities. The vast nave and transepts of the church were designed as a resonant hall for the chant, just as the tympanum over the entrance portal and the half-domed interior of the apse were the settings for sculptural and painted mural embellishments. The sculptured representations of plainsong on the ambulatory capitals in the abbey church at Cluny show a union of music and sculpture, while their inscriptions add a literary third dimension. All the arts converge into the unified structure of the liturgy, since all were created in the monastic concept for service in the glorification of God.

Thus Cluny in the time of St. Hugh of Semur was the gathering place for the most outstanding artists of the time. Under his benign influence the great builder Hezelo worked out his plans for the abbey church. While it was being erected, the chisels of the anonymous school of Burgundian sculptors were heard resounding through its walls as they carved the capitals that were to crown the columns. Great mural painters were mixing their pigments, while skillful choristers were carrying out the precepts of Odo of Cluny and Guido of Arezzo by adding their voices in broad choral cadences to this paean of Romanesque art at the monastery of Cluny.

CHAPTER

CHRONOLOGY: Feudal Romanesque Period in Normandy, Late 11th Century

800 Charlemagne crowned Holy Roman Emperor in Rome

804 Charlemagne's Chapel at Aix-la-Chapelle (Aachen) built in the style of San Vitale in Ravenna

841 Vikings invaded Northern France and colonized on French territory

911 Dukedom of Normandy ceded by King Charles the Simple of France to the Northmen

c.1000 Leif Eriksen, a Viking navigator, believed to have reached the coast of North America

1000 Minstrels convened during the Lenten season at Fécamp in Normandy

1035 William succeeded his father Robert as Duke of Normandy after the latter's death on a pilgrimage to Jerusalem

1040 Abbey of Jumiège rebuilt in the Norman style

1053 Duke William married Matilda, daughter of the Duke of Flanders

1056 Westminster Abbey (Church of Peter the Apostle) in Norman style, dedicated by Edward the Confessor in London

c.1064 Church of St. Étienne (Abbaye-aux-hommes) begun at Caen under the patronage of William
Church of Ste. Trinité (Abbaye-aux-dames) begun at Caen under the patronage of Matilda

1066 Death of Edward the Confessor, King of England
Coronation of Harold as his successor
Invasion of England by William the Conqueror
Battle of Hastings: English forces defeated; Harold killed
William crowned King of England

1078 Tower of London begun by William the Conqueror

1085 Domesday Survey, a census and land survey of England, ordered by William as a basis for taxation

c.1088 Bayeux Tapestry completed in an English embroidery workshop

c.1237–c.1288 Adam de la Halle, author and composer of *Le Jeu de Robin et Marion* (c. 1280), a pastoral play with music, which contains the only authentic example of a *chanson de geste* melody.

6

||||||||||||||||||||||||||||||||||||||||||||||||||||||||||||||||||||||||||||||||||||||||||||||||||||||||||||||||||||||||||||||||||

THE FEUDAL ROMANESQUE STYLE

THE NORMAN CONQUEST AND THE BAYEUX TAPESTRY

The surviving examples of secular art from the Romanesque period are so rare as to make each one practically unique. The treasures of a monastery or cathedral were always under the guardianship of those whose special duty it was to preserve them, and the religious taboos against raiding church property were usually strong enough to prevent their wanton destruction. Feudal castles, on the other hand, were constantly subject to siege; and the ones that avoided destruction were remodeled so frequently with the changing fortunes of their owners, that their original state is difficult to reconstruct. Even less is known about their scanty decorations —mural paintings, wall-hangings, furniture, and the like. Furthermore, since the poetry and music of these people existed only in oral recitation, it was intended to be heard rather than read, and hence most of it was never written down. History, in this case, is full of accidents, and it is a little ironical that the sole example of large-scale secular pictorial art is preserved because it happened to be designed for a church instead of a castle. The only French epic poem before the crusades also owes its present existence to the hand of a monastic scribe, who happened to write it down either for some minstrel with a poor memory or because it was no longer sung and hence in danger of extinction. The one authentic melody to which such poetry was chanted is extant because it was included as a jest in a 13th-century musical play. Finally, the keep, or tower, that William the Conqueror constructed in London is still intact partly because of its usefulness as a prison and possibly because it housed an important chapel.

One of the most eloquent pictorial documents of this or any other time is the so-called Bayeux Tapestry. It recounts in visual form the story of the conquest of England from the Norman point of view, and in the process it gives a vivid picture of the life and attitudes of feudal man. The term *tapestry*, in this case, is justified only because of its function as a wall hanging. Since the design is applied in woolen yarn on the surface of a coarse linen strip, rather than woven into the cloth itself, it is more accurately described as an embroidery. Such cloth decorations were used to cover the bare walls of castles, but in this case the extraordinary dimensions of slightly less than 20 inches in width and 231 feet in length, plus the fact of its preservation through the centuries in the treasury of the Cathedral of Bayeux, indicate that it was intended to cover the plain strip of masonry between the nave arcade and the triforium gallery of that building. According to the most reliable authorities, it was a product of one of the renowned English embroidery workshops and was apparently completed about 20 years after the great battle it describes.

The central figure in the Tapestry is, of course, William the Conqueror whose powerful personality was indelibly stamped on the northern European scene throughout the latter half of the 11th century. The span of time covered in the narrative is that between the closing months of the reign of Edward the Confessor and that fateful day in the year 1066 when the Conqueror made good his claim to the throne by putting the English forces to rout in the Battle of Hastings. The first part of the work (Panels 1–34) [1] is concerned with William's reception of Harold, an English duke, whose mission to Normandy was ostensibly to bear the news that William was to succeed Edward the Confessor on the throne of England. In one of these scenes William and Harold are seen at Bayeux (Fig. 6:1), *where Harold took an oath to Duke William.* (The italics here and in the section that follows indicate literal translations from the inscriptions which, in their wording, have something of the boldness and directness of the action that they describe.) Placing his hands on the reliquaries which repose on the two altars, Harold apparently swears to uphold William's claim, although the exact nature of the oath is left vague. This is, however, the episode which later becomes the justification for the English campaign—because Harold, false to his sworn word, had had himself crowned king. It is interesting, in this connection, to observe the running commentary on the action in the upper and lower borders, a tradition stemming from manuscript illumination. All through the earlier panels certain fables of Aesop are alluded to by the animal figures that were familiar to the people of the time from bestiaries and sculpture. The choice here of the Fox and the Crow, the Wolf and the Stork, and the Ewe, Goat and Cow in the presence of the Lion, all have to do with violence and treachery, and serve to point out the perfidious character of Harold.

William is seated serenely on his ducal throne foreshadowing his future dignity in the role of king. The scene, furthermore, actually takes place in the Cathedral of Bayeux, the exterior of which is shown in the curious representation in back of the seated William. Its bishop was none other than Odo, William's half brother, who was in all probability the commissioner of the Tapestry. The part he played in the course of events, if this visual evidence is taken literally, was a considerable one. Besides his implied presence on this occasion, Odo invariably turns up in every important scene—he is shown giving William advice on the building of his fleet, blessing the meal after the landing in England, sitting in on the council of war, and exhorting the troops to greater deeds in the thick of battle. As a feudal bishop, this is not at all improbable, since he was not only the master of manors and forests but the liege lord of more than a hundred knights. As if this were not enough, Odo is shown personally riding into battle swinging a huge mace, thus bearing out the medieval saying, "The bloodier the hand, the better the bishop." According to the curious convention of the time, however, his ecclesiastical position forbade his spilling the blood of the enemy with such worldly weapons as the sword and the spear. On this occasion he seemed determined to keep up with Archbishop Turpin in the *Song of Roland*, who delivered in the battle described in this literary epic, "more than one thousand blows." The Tapestry was intended by Odo to be exhibited each year on the anniversary of the conquest, and thus forever to commemorate the glory of that occasion—and, of course, the bravery of the bishop and builder of the church.

The main course of the action moves like the words on a printed page—that is, from left to right. At times, however, it is necessary to represent a pertinent episode apart from the principal course of action. The pictorial narrator in this case simply reversed the usual order and moved his scene from right to left, thus in effect obtaining a kind of visual parenthesis and avoiding thereby any confusion with the flow of the main story. Such a device is employed in the scene depicting the death and burial of the Confessor (Fig. 6:2). In the upper right corner is *King Edward in his bed* as he *addresses his faithful retainers*. On one side of him is a priest; Harold is on the other; while the Queen and her lady-in-waiting are mourning at the foot of the bed. Below, under the words *here he has died*, the body is being pre-

Fig. 6:1. Bayeux Tapestry. *Harold Swearing an Oath.* Cathedral

Fig. 6:2. Bayeux Tapestry. *Death*

Fig. 6:3. Bayeux Tapestry. *Norman Ships Sailing toward the English Coast*

M:FECIT hIC hAROLD:DVX: REVERSVS: ES
CI:

Museum, Bayeux (all photographs from Archives Photographiques)

hIC EADWARDVS:REX
INLECTO:ALLOQVIT:EIDELES:
SIAM:SCI hIC DEDERVNT:hAROLDO:
APLI CORO NA REGIS
ET hIC: DEFVNCTVS
EST

and Burial of Edward the Confessor

hIC CECI DERVN SIMVL:ANGLI ET FRA NCI:INPRELIO:

Fig. 6:4. Bayeux Tapestry. *Climax of the Battle*

pared for the last rites. Moving toward the left, the funeral procession approaches *the church of St. Peter the Apostle*, the Romanesque predecessor of Westminster Abbey, which Edward had built and dedicated but ten years before. The procession includes a group of tonsured monks reading prayers and two acolytes ringing the funeral bells.

When William received word that Harold had been crowned, he immediately determined on the invasion, and the second part of the Tapestry is concerned with the preparations for his revenge up to the eve of the battle (Panels 35–53). After all the necessary preparations were made, he set sail *and crossed the sea* (Fig. 6:3). The ships seen in the Tapestry are similar to those in which William's restless Viking ancestors invaded the French coast two centuries before (and it was in just such ships that Leif Eriksen and his fellow mariners apparently reached the eastern coast of North America earlier in the same century). One of these vessels dating from the 9th century has recently been found almost intact in Norway (Fig. 6:5). Like those in the Tapestry, it was fitted out for sailing with mast and rigging and also with oars for rowing. The elegance of its lines and the rich carving along its bow make these sleek ships things of beauty as well as of utility.

Fig. 6:5. *The Oseberg Ship.* 64′ long, 16½′ at widest point. *c.*850. University Museum, Oslo

After the landing the grand finale begins with the assembling of forces on both sides for the great battle, which is depicted in the third and last part (Panels 54–79). The Norman side has both archers on foot and knights on horseback, while the English fight in a solid phalanx with immense two-handed battle-axes, small spears, and clubs with stone heads. The Tapestry shows the Normans moving in from left to right and the English meeting them from the opposite direction. The climax of the battle is reached in a wild scene at a ravine (Fig. 6:4), where men and horses are tumbling about while the *English and French fall together in battle*. Shortly after this Harold is killed and the fighting concludes with the *English turned in flight*. The lower border spares none of the horrors of warfare, and dismembered limbs are seen strewn about, while scavengers are stripping the bodies of the fallen of their coats of mail and leaving the naked corpses lying on the field.

With no attempt whatever at realism, men are depicted with either blue or green hair, and horses with two blue and two red legs. Much of the detail, such as that of the faces, is merely outlined, though some attempt at portraiture is made in the various representations of King William. Besides three shades of blue, the colors include a light and dark green, a red, a buff yellow, and a gray. All this can, of course, be attributed to artistic license, and it is true that the conventions of the time were more concerned with a colorful design than with realism as such. On other counts, however, there is great accuracy in regard to the details of costume, armor, and the deployment of troops in battle. As such, it is a never-ending source of amazement, and one of the most important historical documents on the manner of life in the 11th century. So much so, in fact, that its historical value is often allowed to overshadow its quality as a work of art. Admittedly crude, and at times quite naïve, the Tapestry does not linger lovingly over details long enough to elaborate them with subtlety and elegance; but, in the manner of so much medieval art, it is frankly a narration, and the sweeping effect of the whole takes precedence over any one of its parts. As Hamlet advised his actors, the play is the thing, not the gesticulation, the declamation, nor the ranting and roaring. It is a work addressed to men of action in a century in which deeds were admired more than pictorial representations of them or words about them.

From the aesthetic viewpoint there is much that commands comment. In the handling of the narration, a slow beginning with frequent digressions and episodes is followed by a rather feverish preparation in the middle part, culminating in the breathless climax of the battle at the end. In both tempo and formal organization this tapestry can stand the test of comparison with the best works in narrative form, whether visual or verbal. The spontaneous inventiveness of detail, whether in the main panels or in the upper or lower borders, serves to enhance the flow of the plot and to add accents, commentary, and embellishment when needed to the over-all mood. In the designs themselves the illustrator shows great ingenuity in the division of his space into parts without prejudicing the unity of the whole. The groups are separated from each other by buildings, most of which are worked into the fabric of the story, and by other devices, such as the stylized trees which have nothing to do with the subject matter. So skillfully are they arranged that the continuity of the whole is never impeded, and the observer is hardly aware of their presence. Between such emotional poles as the solemnity of the Confessor's burial rites, and the turbulent action where men and horses are tumbling into the ravine in the heat of battle, there are many intermediate moods. All in all a successful work of art designed for such a long and narrow space is a feat of visual virtuosity of no small order, and it leaves no doubt about its being the work of a master designer.

SONG OF ROLAND

A *chanson de geste* is literally a song of deeds, or an action story in poetic form, sung by a minstrel to the accompaniment of a viol or lyre. Briefly, the term implies an epic poem on a noble historical theme in the vernacular language rather than in Latin. The *Chanson de Roland*, or *Song of Roland*, is a great medieval epic harking back to the days of Charlemagne. Even though it comes down through an Oxford manuscript dating from the end of the 12th century, it is in both form and spirit a product of the warlike feudalistic 11th century. The action of the poem is direct to the point of abruptness, and the transitions between episodes are sudden and unprepared. A martial atmosphere surrounds all the characters, including the fighting Archbishop Turpin, as well as the images of the Archangels Gabriel and Michael who, like the Valkyries in the German epic *Song of the Nibelungs*, swoop down on the battlefield to bear the souls of the fallen warriors to heaven.

The poem is specifically connected with the battle of Hastings in the records of no less than three important historical sources. Guy of Amiens, one of William and Matilda's courtiers, who died only ten years after the battle, was the author of a Latin poem which mentions a jongleur by the name of Taillefer. This "minstrel whom a very brave heart ennobled," he relates, led William's forces into the battle throwing his sword in the air, catching it again, and singing a Song of Roland. William of Malmesbury, writing about 50 years after the battle, tells that William on that day started the *Song of Roland*, "in order that the warlike example of that hero might stimulate the soldiers." Furthermore, one of the canons of the Bayeux Cathedral was the author of a history of the dukes of Normandy called the *Roman de Rou*, one of the verses of which goes:

> Taillefer who was famed for song,
> Mounted on a charger strong,
> Rode on before the Duke, and sang
> Of Roland and of Charlemagne,
> Oliver and the vassals all
> Who fell in fight at Roncevals.[2]

Taillefer, in the age-old tradition of minstrelsy, was a mime and singer-actor, and his rendition of the epic was undoubtedly accompanied by skillful vocal declamation as well as with appropriate gestures and action.

The *Song of Roland* is thus a direct-action story, set in the time of Charlemagne, and relating some incidents from the campaign in northern Spain in which he had been battling the pagan Saracens for seven long years. Roland, favorite nephew of the Emperor, and the Twelve Peers, flower of French knighthood, were left in charge of the rear guard, while Charles and the main part of his army were crossing the Pyrenees back into France. Betrayed by a false kinsman, strongly paralleling the episode of William and Harold in the Bayeux Tapestry, Roland is attacked near Roncevals by the overwhelming mass of the pagan forces. The rear guard is cut to pieces, and Roland, before dying a hero's death, sounds his ivory horn summoning Charles and his army from a great distance.

The third part of the poem has to do with the vengeance of Charlemagne, just as the corresponding section of the Bayeux Tapestry related that of William. All is action and heroism, with swords flashing, helmets gleaming, drums beating, horns blowing, banners waving, and steeds prancing. The battle unfolds in what amounts to practically a blow-by-blow account, echoing frequently with such phrases as "wondrous and fierce is the battle" (p. 58).[3] First we see the preparations in the camp of Charles. The poet, using a cumulative technique, describes the ten battalions one by one. Knight is added to knight, battle group to battle group, weapon to weapon, in order to build up the full monumentality of the occasion in the listener's mind and imagination. All the forces of Western Christendom are eventually drawn up on Charlemagne's side—the French, Normans, Bavarians, Germans, Bretons, and so on. The virtues of the men are invariably those of bravery, valiance, and hardiness; they have no fear of death; never do they flee the battlefield; and their horses are swift and good.

Then quite suddenly and without any transition we are in the midst of the pagan hordes. Ten Saracen battalions are likewise described, and in order to show how the Christians were outnumbered, still another ten is added. The fearsomeness of the enemy, however, is not due to numbers alone as much as it is to their ferocious character. The only admirable quality allowed them is that of being good fighters; otherwise they are hideous to behold, fierce and cruel, and they love evil. Yet in spite of this they "ride on like goodly warriors" (p. 116). Like the figures on the Vézelay tympanum (Fig. 5:11), the physical appearance of the people from these strange parts is fantastically exaggerated. The men of Milciani, for instance, "have huge heads, and along the spine of their backs grow bristles like those of a wild boar" (p. 115). Of the warriors from the desert of Occiant, it is said that "their skins are hard like iron, wherefore they have no need of hauberks or helms" [coats of mail and helmets] (p. 116). Later on during the battle these same men of Occiant "bray and neigh, and the men of Arguille yelp like dogs" (p. 125). Their religious life is just as much misunderstood as their appearance. The pagans are represented as polytheists who worship as strange an assortment of gods as was ever assembled—Apollo, Tervagant, and Mohamet. When things are not going well from their point of view, they upbraid these gods, take the statue of Apollo and "trod him under their feet" (p. 94); Tervagant is robbed of his carbuncle; and Mohamet is cast "into a ditch, for the dogs and the pigs to worry and gnaw" (p. 94). Later when Marsila, the King of Spain, dies, the listener hears that "eager devils seize upon his soul" (p. 128). All this is not based on the knowledge of the later crusaders, but, like the foreigners depicted on the Vézelay tympanum, falls into the category of naïve wonder and the telling of tall tales.

With the lines of battle thus drawn, the setting is described in a single line: "Vast is the plain and wide the fields." Then as the conflict begins, battalion falls on battalion, hewing and hacking away, Christian knights hurtle against pagan knights the whole day long, until finally the battle boils down to a personal encounter between Charlemagne himself and his opposite number, Baligant the Amiral (admiral). All the formidable fighting qualities of friend and foe are concentrated in these two contestants. Both are described as being older than the hills, and their beards are whiter than snow. The patriarchal image of society is consistently emphasized, just as it is in the representations of the elders of the Apocalypse found so frequently in Romanesque sculpture. Charles is called sometimes "the Emperor with the hoary beard" (p. 95), and at others "Charles the Old."

Since all takes place in the present tense, he is by this time well on into his third century. But his adversary is not to be outdone in this respect, as Baligant is so old that he has actually outlived Vergil and Homer. Charles, of course, is the epitome of Christian virtue, and it is generously allowed that his opponent is wise "according to his law, and in battle he is fierce and mighty" (p. 113). The combat of the centenarians is on, and in their initial clash their spears shiver against one another, their coats of mail are rent, the blows bring them both to the ground, and the battle continues on foot with bare swords. Each tries to convert the other between blows; and just when all seems blackest, with Charlemagne sorely wounded, the Angel Gabriel appears beside him, and his strength miraculously returns. "He smites the Amiral with the sword of France, shatters the helmet which shines with precious stones, carves through the skull that the brains run out, and through the face even to the white beard, that the Amiral falls dead beyond all help" (pp. 127–128). After this, the pagans flee and the day is won.

The lines of the original Old French proceed according to a rhyming scheme of crude assonance in which the final syllables of each line correspond roughly in sound. The last words of each line of one of the strophes will suffice to illustrate this principle of assonance: *magne, Espaigne, altaigne, remaigne, fraindre, muntaigne, m'enaimet, reclaimet,* and *ataignet.* Much of the direct character and rugged strength of the poem is attributable to its rigid avoidance of embellishment. This is observable in such minute details as the forward motion within such single lines as: *So sent Rollanz de tun tens ni ad plus.* Nothing is allowed to impede the progress of these sturdy military monosyllables. So consistently is this carried out all along the line that it even extends to the delineation of the characters themselves. Each is the embodiment of a single ideal and human type: Ganelon is all treachery and hatred; Roland, bravery to the point of rashness; Oliver, reason and caution; and Charles, pre-eminent in his solitary grandeur, represents the majesty of Church and state. Through each one of these devices separately and through all of them cumulatively, the poem as a whole rises to the heights of epic art. Its language, style, and form thus well become the brave deeds of the heroic men with which it is concerned.

THE ART OF MINSTRELSY

"A verse without music is a mill without water," said a troubadour by the name of Folquet of Marseilles who was immortalized by Dante in his *Paradise.* It is very difficult in the present prosaic period, when poetry is so rarely read and even more rarely recited, to recapture the medieval spirit, when it was a popular art form chanted by a *jongleur* to the accompaniment of a viol or lyre. It is just as difficult, in fact, as it is to imagine from the unrelieved gray stones of the interior of an abbey church or cathedral that in medieval times they were gaily painted in many colors. The musical settings of these times went hand in hand with the poetry, both being performed by jongleurs, or minstrels, who were indispensable at all religious and secular festivals where large numbers of people gathered. On these occasions they took a leading part in the entertainment of the crowds by performing sleight-of-hand tricks, playing on instruments, telling tales and fables, and chanting lays, *chansons de geste*, and *romans*, all with instrumental accompaniment.

Records of these jongleurs go back to early times; and it is known that they convened at Fécamp in Normandy in the year 1000. These meets took place regularly during the slack season of Lent, when they were banned by the Church from performing. They took this opportunity to get together, learn one another's tricks and techniques, and increase their repertories with new tales and songs. A lively account of their place in medieval society is contained in a description of a wedding feast in Provence. "Then the *joglars* stood up," the description goes, "each one anxious to make himself heard; then you could hear instruments resounding in many a key. . . . One played the Lay of the Honeysuckle, another that of Tintagel, another that of the Faithful Lovers, another the lay that Ivan made. . . . Everyone performed at his best and the noise of the instrumentalists and the voices of the narrators made a considerable uproar in the hall." [4]

The jongleurs of the 11th century were not of noble birth as were most of the later troubadours and trouvères, but they invariably found a ready welcome in every castle and abbey. Their importance in the creation of a secular literature in the vernacular languages of medieval times can hardly be overestimated. The feudal society of the 11th century was groping its way toward distinctive art forms of its own, and, in so doing, naturally turned to the church models at first. A secular poetic form, however, was evolved in the latter part of the century in the *chanson de geste*. The musical part of these epics was far more primitive than the poetry; but, crude as it was, it marked the beginning of secular art music, separated in style both from the Church models and the lost tradition of the folk music of that time. Under the patronage of the feudal nobility, this music was to bloom later in the 12th and 13th centuries into the full-fledged art of the troubadours, trouvères, and minnesingers.

Since the 11th-century forms were just emerging, the models and prototypes were undoubtedly derived to some extent from the contemporary forms of church music. The music for the *chansons de geste* seems to have evolved from the Litany. The assonated verses and repetitious rhythms of the poetry had much in common with the Litany; though, of course, the subject matter differed radically. It is greatly to be regretted that no single example of the musical setting of the *Song of Roland* has come down to us. While the words were written with care and exactitude, the musical part seems to have been of such an elementary type as not to have taxed the memory of the jongleurs, hence it was thought unnecessary to write it down. It is known, for instance, that the jongleurs wore leather pouches in which manuscripts could be carried, so that from time to time they could refresh their memories on longer epics. However, since no musical portions were included, it is safe to assume that their melodies must have been so simple, and so easily stored in memory, as to obviate the necessity for writing them down.

Evidence exists from a 13th-century source that the music of the *chansons de geste* consisted of a short melody with one note to a syllable, repeated over and over for each verse in the manner of a litany or folk song. At the end of each strophe, or group of lines, there was a melodic appendage, which served as a sort of refrain and functioned like the Alleluias between the verses of psalms or hymns. In the manuscript of the *Chanson de Roland* the enigmatic letters AOI appear between each of the 321 strophes; while in the songs of the troubadours and minnesingers, the letters EUOUAE are sometimes found at the end of verses. The latter is an abbreviation of the last two words of the lesser doxology *saeculorum amen*, thus linking this refrain principle to a Gregorian melody. Variants of this became corrupted into EVOVAE, and in Normandy such forms as *Enne hauvoy* and *Enne ovoi* are found. The AOI in the *Song of Roland* manuscript possibly refers to some such liturgical cadence formula now lost, but its purpose as a refrain seems quite clear. As such it refers either to a repeated vocal cadenza at the end of each strophe, serving as a kind of punctuation mark for the ear and relieving the attention of the audience momentarily from attending the words, as with the "Fa la la's" of the Renaissance madrigals; or it might indicate a place where a short instrumental interlude was performed on the viol or lyre. The focus of attention in these epics was obviously on the words and nuances of the poem itself, and the musical element was clearly subordinate. Here in the closing formula, however, the purely musical flourish could have come to the fore, and the special skill of the jongleur could have found expression at this point in whatever melodic variation or twist he was capable of giving it.

The single authentic example of a *chanson de geste* melody that survives is found in a little pastoral play from the 13th century by Adam de la Halle, where it is quoted humorously by one of the characters.

A *chanson de geste* melody (11th century)   Adam de la Halle
                                                                (After Gennrich)

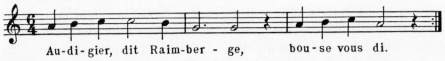

Au-di-gier, dit Raim-ber - ge,   bou-se vous di.

The two halves of this melody are repeated once for each line of the strophe, following which there would have been a short cadenza or refrain for either the voice or an instrument. The operation of this refrain principle is found in a song from *Aucassin et Nicolette*, a French *chante-fable*.

Strophe (or *Laisse*) from *Aucassin et Nicolette* (13th century)   (After Gennrich)

Qui   vau - roit   bons vers   o   -   ir   del   de -
de   deus biax   en - fans   pe   -   tis   Ni   - co -

port du duel cai - tif
1e - te   Au cas - sins...

Written about a century later, it is similar in style to that of the *chanson de geste*. The melody of the first eight measures is sung for each line of the strophe, each time to different words. The refrain in the final three bars is then either sung or played between each of the verses and again at the end.

Thus from the surviving musical examples both sacred and secular, it is possible to reconstruct the musical aspect of the *Chanson de Roland* as based on a short recitativelike tune, repeated over and over as each line of the strophe unfolded; while at the end of each strophe it was punctuated by a short refrain, consisting of a melodic flourish for voice or accompanying instrument. It can readily be seen from the extreme simplicity of the melodies shown in the examples that the musical material would not have held the attention of an audience. The interest was in the content of the epic poetry, and in performance the tale was supplemented by mimicry in which parts of the story would have been acted out with appropriate gestures and vocal nuances. Since the literary form of the *chanson de geste* was in itself somewhat primitive, it is not too surprising to find that the musical setting was even more so, especially when it is considered that these are among the earliest known examples of secular art music in Western culture.

NORMAN ARCHITECTURE

The architectural accomplishments of the Normans were of sufficient stature that their name is synonymous with one entire aspect of the Romanesque style. The building they did in the 11th century in Normandy not only had an effect on that region but reached its logical conclusion in the later keeps, castles, abbeys, and cathedrals they built in England. Since the Romanesque style in England dates from the time of the conquest, it is still generally referred to there as the Norman style. This architecture in its formative stages, together with so many other aspects of Norman culture, was the offspring of the union of the rugged pagan spirit of the Vikings and the Gallic Christian remnants of the disintegrated Carolingian Empire. As a representative product of these peoples, it took on the coloration of their blunt strength and forthright character. Both the Carolingian and Viking societies were nomadic. The royal residences of Charlemagne and his successors, as well as those of the dukes of Normandy down to William's time, were frequently shifted; and the insecurity of the times discouraged building in general. The feudal system in its mature stages tended to make a more settled order of things at least a possibility. Furthermore the unlimited lands acquired by the Norman conquerors brought about a shift in William's policy from the offensive to the defensive. It then remained only to absorb and exploit his vast new domains. While before he had discouraged the construction of castles, and sanctioned only the building of monasteries, it now suited his purposes to impress his new subjects, not only by feats of the sword on the field of battle but also by means of solid and impregnable fortresses.

The so-called Tower of London (Fig. 6:6) was begun by the Conqueror about 1078 and finished under his successor in order to defend and dominate that town. Its form was that of a Norman keep, and as such it was something new to England. It is simply a massive, compact, stone building, divided into four stories which rise 92 feet in height with a turret at each corner. Like other examples of the same type, it is quadrangular in shape, but a glance at ground plan (Fig. 6:7) will show some of its many irregularities. Its four sides, for instance, are unequal in length, and its corners are therefore not right angles; three of its turrets are square, while one is round; the one on the west rises 107 feet, while that on the south is 118 feet high; the walls vary from 11 to 15 feet in thickness; and the interior is divided from top to bottom in two unequal parts by a wall running from north to south.

Fig. 6:6 (above). *Tower of London*. 1078–1090. Air View. Fig. 6:7 (below). *Plan*. (Courtesy British Information Services)

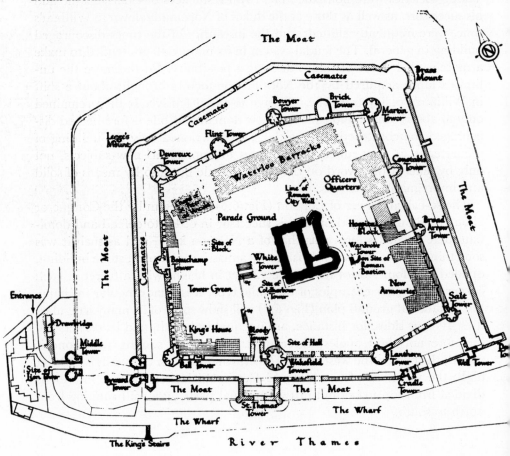

Fig. 6:8. Tower of London. *St. John's Chapel*. 1078–1097. (Courtesy British Information Services)

The barrenness of its exterior was clearly correlated with its function as a fortress; but the austerity of the interior was a commentary on the bleakness and the general lack of physical comforts of life in those times. The Tower was divided into several stories by means of wooden floors, and its darkness was relieved only by the narrow, slitted, glassless windows, whose function as a launching place for arrows against a possible enemy was more important than that of allowing light to enter. After Norman times other buildings were added until the whole became a concentric system of fortifications with the old Norman keep as its heart. The fact that the Tower is in such a fine state of preservation today is a convincing commentary on its continued usefulness throughout the centuries as a fortress, palace, and prison.

From the plan it will be seen that the main floor has three divisions; these were a large council chamber which also doubled as a banqueting hall, a smaller presence chamber, and St. John's Chapel that is still in excellent condition. Like a miniature church, the Chapel (Fig. 6:8) has a nave of four bays, with aisles on either side which command interest because of their early use of cross vaulting. The columns which support the nave arcade are thick and stubby, while their cushion-type capitals have only the most rudimentary scalloped carving by way of decoration. Above is a triforium gallery which was used by the queen and her ladies in attending services. On either side of the barrel-vaulted nave is a rudimentary clearstory whose windows admit very little light.

Two buildings in Normandy from this time also survive. William's marriage to his cousin Matilda, daughter of the Duke of Flanders, while strengthening his claim to the English throne, fell within the forbidden degrees of consanguinity. As a condition for the papal blessing, they promised to found a monastery and a convent in their favorite city of Caen. The Abbaye-aux-hommes, dedicated to the first martyr, St. Stephen, and known in his honor as St. Étienne, was begun under William's personal patronage just prior to the invasion. Matilda's church, the Abbaye-aux-dames, also known as Ste. Trinité, was started at approximately the same time. The interest of William and Matilda in the structures is shown by the fact that the twin abbeys became their respective burial places.

St. Étienne has a well-proportioned façade (Fig. 6:9). Four prominent buttresses divide the section below the towers into three parts, in exact correspondence to its interior plan consisting of a central nave and two side aisles. Vertically the façade rises in three stories with the portals matching the level of the interior nave arcade, while the two rows of windows above are at the triforium and clearstory levels respectively. The windows

Fig. 6:9. *St. Étienne* (*Abbaye-aux-hommes*), Façade. Tower 295′ high. *c.*1064–1135. Caen (Courtesy Clarence Ward)

are mere openings and are in themselves quite undistinguished. The functional honesty, however, in this correspondence of exterior façade design and interior plan was a Norman innovation that eventually was absorbed into later Gothic façades.

The twin towers appear to belong to the original design, but their spires date from a later period. Like the usual Norman church towers they are square and in three stories, thus repeating on a higher level the triple division of the portion of the façade lying below. The first story is of solid masonry; the second consists of alternate blind and open arches, while the third is more open so as to enhance its function as a belfry. These open parts provide a welcome visual contrast to the solidity of the lower portions of the façade, and thus tend to alleviate the general heaviness. Otherwise the austerity and ponderousness of the façade in general is a fitting prelude to the gloomy grandeur of the interior. The church as a whole is as thoroughly rugged and masculine in character as the personality of its founder, and as such it becomes typical of the spirit of the Norman people and their forceful leader.

When the barren façade of St. Étienne is compared to the exterior of the Tower of London, it becomes apparent that the paucity of decorative elements was not due to functional reasons alone. Instead it seems to be a clear case of aesthetic preference. One façade impresses because of its bold outlines, sturdiness, and straightforward honesty, and the other by its sheer strength and bluntness. A definite austerity and restrained absence of refinements is apparent in both cases. The accent the Normans placed on structure rather than on embellishment led, however, to some advances in the art of building. There is little doubt that in its time the Norman keep was a definite improvement in fortress construction, even though it was to be replaced soon after the crusades with new Saracenic models. In their church architecture the Norman builders achieved a greater unity of the interior levels of nave arcade, triforium space, and clearstory by means of tall shafts between the bays, which ran from floor to ceiling, and more adequate lighting by increasing the space and height allotted to the clearstory. Both these features, as well as the harmonious spatial divisions of such a façade as that of St. Étienne, were incorporated later into the Gothic style. In spite of this, however, when the work of the Normans is placed alongside that of their more skillful Burgundian contemporaries, it seems quite crude by comparison. The Normans were as straightforward, blunt, and brash as the Cluniacs were ingenious, resourceful, and subtle. The difference, in short, was that between men of action and men of contemplation.

IDEAS

In attempting to relate such representative examples of the Romanesque style as the Bayeux Tapestry, the poetry and music of the *Song of Roland*, and the architecture of the Tower of London and the Abbey of St. Étienne at Caen, it must be borne in mind that each is a product of the high point of Norman culture, falling between the dates of the Battle of Hastings in 1066 and the gathering of European forces leading to the First Crusade, which began in 1096. The Tapestry was obviously commissioned soon after the battle whose background and subject matter it relates; a direct link between that battle and the *Song of Roland* is seen in the circumstance of its being sung on that occasion; indirect evidence is provided by the similarity in both the form and spirit of these two works; and the building of the Tower and Abbey clearly coincides with the zenith of William's success and prosperity after the conquest. This relationship in time, place, and subject matter comes at the climax of feudalism, and it is under this single all-embracing concept that the separate works find their unity.

Feudalism

In their subject matter, the *Song of Roland* and the Bayeux Tapestry have many points in common. As the song opens: "Charles the King . . . has conquered all the high land down to the sea; not a castle holds out against him, not a wall or city is left unshattered, save Saragossa, which stands on a high mountain. King Marsila holds it, who loves not God, but serves Mahound, and worships Apollon; ill hap must in sooth befall him" (p. 1). If the simple substitution of William for Charles, England for Saragossa in Spain, the barrier of the sea for that of the mountain, and King Harold for Marsila is made, the situation becomes the contemporary one which is so vividly portrayed in the tapestry. Later at the Battle of Roncevals the dominant trio is Roland, Oliver, and the fighting Archbishop Turpin, in whom it is not difficult to recognize their parallels at Hastings in William, and his half brothers Robert of Mortain and the irrepressible Bishop Odo.

In both cases the cause for war was ostensibly religious. In one it was Christianity versus paganism; in the other, the breaking of a Christian tradition in the violation of a sacred oath, and in Harold's being crowned by Stigand, an archbishop appointed under dubious circumstances. In each case the cause was sanctioned by the pope. It is noteworthy also that in both cases the enemy, in the best feudal tradition, was a worthy adversary, noble and brave but religiously misguided. In the *Song of Roland*

Marsila was crafty, but he observed at all times the rules and etiquette of feudal warfare. The glory of Charlemagne's major pagan enemy with his silks from Alexandria, gold of Arabia, carbuncle-studded sword, and bright gonfalons, is glowingly described in poetic language, just as Harold's knightly qualities are repeatedly pictured in visual form. In both cases religious symbols figure prominently. Durendal, Roland's sword, is his most sacred possession, having within it a tooth of St. Peter, blood of St. Basil, hair of St. Denis, and a fragment of the Virgin Mary's garment, all gathered on his pilgrimage to the Holy Land. The importance of such relics at this time was overwhelming. In the Tapestry, Harold's seizure of the kingly power was treacherous principally because of the oath he swore on the reliquaries in the Bayeux Cathedral, which were filled with just such revered remains as these. The importance of an oath so sworn can be seen in the fact that the justification of the invasion rested mainly on Harold's perjury and disregard of an oath sworn under such sacrosanct conditions.

Conviction is forthright and clear in both cases. Such a sweeping statement as "Wrong the pagans, right the Christians are," leaves no room for lingering philosophical or theological doubts on the validity of the cause. In each the importance and glorification of sheer strength and prowess at arms is apparent from the descriptive details of costume, armor, and weapons, which are dwelt upon with obvious pride. Even though the poem is set in the time of Charlemagne, the heraldry, weapons, and modes of combat correspond in both. Whether it is the poem or Tapestry, both are conceived and set in a man's world based on clear-cut loyalties and moral and physical certainties. The chivalry in both instances is based on the ways of fighting men. The code of Roland and Oliver, as well as that of William and Odo, was clearly that of "My soul to God, my life to the king, and honor for myself." It remained for a later period to add: "My heart to the ladies." Roland's dying thoughts, for instance, are occupied with his family and lineage; his king, the great Charles; his country, the fair land of France; and his sword, Durendal. Significantly he makes no mention of the Church, Christianity, or of his betrothed, the Lady Aude. Earlier, the exasperated Oliver had reproached Roland for his rashness in not summoning aid sooner, and at that time he swore: "By this my beard, and I again see my sister, Aude the Fair, never shalt thou lie in her arms" (p. 64). No true or courtly love is this, only the feudal baron bestowing his female relations like his land and goods on those who please him and whose faith and courage he has cause to admire. Later, after Charles returns to France, the poor lady inquires about the fate of her fiancé. The king tells her of his death and as a consolation prize offers her the hand of his son Louis. Where-

upon the lady expires at his feet, and whether she dies of her grief for
Roland or from the indelicacy of Charlemagne's suggestion is left open to
conjecture. Since scarcely more than a dozen of the 4000-odd lines of the
poem are devoted to her, Henry Adams was well justified in his observation: "Never after the first crusade did any great poem rise to such heroism
as to sustain itself without a heroine." [5] Curiously enough on the Saracen
side Marsila's queen is shown taking an important part in the affairs of
state on the incapacitation of her husband, while nowhere is a woman
accorded anything like a similar status on the Christian side.

Likewise in the Tapestry the only case where a woman is even mentioned
by name is in an enigmatic inscription: *Where a cleric and Aelfgyva*. This
apparently is introduced to give a motive for the minor episode describing
an invasion of Brittany. While a few other female figures are found in the
borders and in attendance at the death of the Confessor, none figures with
any degree of prominence. Both works are thus as brash, bold, and direct
as the poetry and art of the Gothic period was delicate, subtle, and allegorical. Roland and his counterparts in the Tapestry fought the good fight for
king and country, while the knightly heroes of the later period entered the
lists for a loving glance from a pair of blue eyes, the fleeting image of a
smile from fair lips, or the faded petals of a rose tossed from a lady's bower.

The formal considerations of both Song and Tapestry stem from the
character of this type of subject matter. The emphasis is everywhere on the
concrete rather than the abstract; content rather than form; and narrative
sequence over structure. However, in spite of this, certain formal factors
are noteworthy, and even in this respect many similarities of approach are
discernible. In the over-all composition of both poem and Tapestry, a
division into three parts is made. The first part in each instance is concerned
with the treachery of a supposed friend who goes over to the enemy: in the
poem it is Ganelon's; in the Tapestry it is Harold's. In both a minor battle
precedes the major event: in the *Chanson* it is the rear-guard skirmish at
Roncevals which results in tragedy; in the embroidery it is the Brittany
campaign which turns out successfully. The final part in each case is a
climactic battle scene with all the reserves thrown in: in the poem it is the
vengeance of Charles; in the Tapestry that of William. The preference for
such a three-part division is shared with many other manifestations of medieval art both sacred and secular. Of importance here is the clear articulation of it in such instances as the *Song of Roland*, the Bayeux Tapestry,
the triple meter of the music, and the tripartite horizontal and vertical
divisions of the façade of St. Étienne.

Just as the main themes and divisions of epic poem and Tapestry correspond, so also do the minor divisions and episodes that support the whole. In the concluding portions of each, for instance, there is a close parallel in narrative form which corresponds, in turn, with the stylized mode of feudal warfare. First, messengers from both sides are received by the royal figure; next, the challenge is accepted and the forces drawn up. These, in turn, are described in detail—verbally in one case and visually in the other. Now the battle is joined and the opposing sides move toward one another in force. A furious combat ensues and its indecisiveness shows how evenly the material forces are matched, thus paving the way for the coming triumph of the spiritual element. In the *Chanson* it comes as a result of the personal combat between Charles and the Amiral with the symbolic crossing of Christian and pagan swords and with the victory awarded by God to the righteous cause. In the Tapestry the indecision of the day's fighting is resolved first by Bishop Odo's exhortation to the troops, and by William's lifting his helmet to address his knights.

The telling of the tale in both cases is almost completely unencumbered with either visual or literary flourishes. Just as deeds take precedence over poetic form in the *Chanson*, the narrative element in the Bayeux Tapestry is more important than the decorative detail. Every part of the Tapestry has some direct bearing on the story, and the action in the poem is so direct that in its 4000-odd lines there is hardly a single figure of speech. In each instance the attributes are fixed. In the tapestry the English always have moustaches and the Normans are clean shaven. In the poem, kings are always mighty no matter what side they may be on; and knights are invariably brave whatever their allegiance may be. Similarly in the sculpture of the period, kings always have crowns on their heads, even if they are in bed; Apostles always have bare feet, and so on. The curiously unrealistic trees in the Tapestry come directly from manuscript drawings rather than from nature; and they function either as an indication that the action is taking place out of doors, or as formal devices to divide one scene from another. In the epic when Roland rests, it is always under a pine tree because he is French; while his enemies pause only under olive trees because they are Saracens.

Symmetry is seldom a major consideration. The lines of the poem, for instance, are rough hewn but heroic pentameters, which group themselves into irregular strophes averaging 14 lines in length, but they may at times be either more or less. Similarly the space given to individual scenes in the Bayeux Tapestry, as well as the size of the compartments in the archivolt of the Vézelay tympanum (Fig. 5:11), and the unequal height of the arches

Fig. 6:10. *Pisa Cathedral.* Begun 1063 (Brogi)

in a Romanesque cathedral, such as Pisa (Fig. 6:10), are all disproportionate and asymmetrical.

Details in the case of Song, Tapestry, Church, and Tower thus remain crude and unpolished. It was an era of forming, building, experimentation, and reaching out toward new modes of expression rather than a time of crystallization, polished expression, and ultimate arrival. In architecture it was the process of building that was more important than that which was built. The emphasis given in the Tapestry to representations of castles, fortifications, and specific buildings, such as Westminster Abbey and Mont-St.-Michel, suggest the image of a builder's world and a century of architectural activity and progress. The forthright and direct narration of deeds in the case of Song and Tapestry finds its architectural counterpart in the functional honesty of the style of the Tower and William's church of St. Étienne. Just as the direct-action story in the poem and Tapestry takes precedence over literary form and decorative flourish, so the structural honesty of the building process, as exemplified in the Tower and Abbaye-aux-hommes, becomes the leading characteristic. The process by which the balladic poetry was lengthened into the epic form of the *chanson de geste* capable of sustaining attention through the long Norman winter evenings, by which a few pictorial panels were extended into the heroic completeness of a tapestry depicting a major historical episode in its entirety, was essentially one and the same with piling up tall towers capable of piercing the gloomy northern skies.

The image of the Norman world as it thus builds up through the various arts is not essentially a complex one. There was little of the mystical about these clear-headed Viking adventurers. They caught on with alacrity to all the progressive developments of the time, whether it was in discarding their rather inflexible mother tongue in favor of the more supple French or in adopting many of the Cluniac moral and architectural reforms. A good instance of their forthrightness is shown by the fact that their pictorial epic was not told, as in the case of the Old French *chanson*, by invoking the ghost of Charlemagne and placing him in a contemporary setting. The Tapestry tells exactly who it was, when, where and why, documenting it with names, dates, and places. Whatever it was they did, they always endowed it with their characteristic determination and energy.

All the separate concepts of their world are contained in the overpowering central idea of feudalism. It was a highly concentric society, in which an individual was essentially an institution without any real place in the scheme of things except in his relations to his peers, superiors, and inferiors. It was a social structure modeled on the principles of an army; and the ethic which bound the whole fabric together was that of fealty, a kind of blind loyalty, in which right and wrong were determined by physical force rather than reason and principle. All was held together by the feudal idea which provided a proper place for all men in a strict hierarchy, with barons holding their power from their overlords, ecclesiastical or secular; the duke holding his realm from his king; and the king, emperor, and pope holding the earth as a fief from God.

Charlemagne and his twelve peers are actually the feudal image and earthly counterpart of Christ and his twelve Apostles, the Apostles being vassals of Christ, and Christ himself a vassal of God the Father. The virtues are those of faith, courage, and blind loyalty to peer and superior; any departure from this code is treachery and must be dealt with by isolation and defeat. Any defection was decided on the field of battle, God awarding the victory to the side He favored. Enemies, however, provided their lineage was in order and their family trees properly pruned and cultivated, were accorded the distinctions of honor and bravery, otherwise it would have been socially impossible to do battle with them. No one in either poem or tapestry figures with any degree of prominence who is below the rank of baron; and, likewise, the abbeys of William and Matilda were intended mainly for persons of rank. By their foundation William expiated his sin, and by thus pledging his feudal oath to God he acknowledged His superior authority and at the same time propitiated Him with a worthy tribute. Thus the rugged man of action in William unites with the military monosyllables of the *Chanson*, the frank, almost comic-strip directness of the Bayeux Tapestry, and the rough-hewn stones of the Tower and Abbey, to make a single structure. All were concerned with forms of action, and whether in picture, word, or stone, the epical spirit is present. Deed on deed, syllable on syllable, stitch on stitch, image on image, stone on stone— all build up into the great personality, heroic epic, impressive Tapestry, and gaunt Tower, and in the process reveal a unified Norman structure of truly monumental proportions.

C H A P T E R

CHRONOLOGY: Ile-de-France, 12th and 13th Centuries

1096 – 1291 The Crusades, in which European Christians fought Moslems and .Saracens and extended Christianity as well as opened up trade routes

1137 Louis VII began reign as King of France and married Eleanor of Aquitaine

1140 Abbey Church of St. Denis, prototype of Gothic cathedrals, begun by Abbot Suger

1142 Abelard, Master of the School of Notre Dame in Paris, died at the Monastery of Cluny

1163 – 1235 Building of the Cathedral of Notre Dame in Paris

1180 Philip Augustus crowned King of France
Enclosed Paris with walls
Promoted Paris as his capital city

1194 Chartres Cathedral begun after fire destroyed the earlier structure
1006 Fulbert appointed Bishop of Chartres
1020–1028 Romanesque Cathedral built by Fulbert
1134 Fulbert's Cathedral destroyed by fire
1145 Romanesque Cathedral again rebuilt
1194 Fire destroyed Romanesque Cathedral with exception of narthex and west portals, two towers, and three stained glass windows

1210 Rheims Cathedral rebuilt
1215 University of Paris incorporated
Magna Charta signed in England

1220 Amiens Cathedral begun
1223 Louis VIII crowned King of France
1225 Beauvais Cathedral begun; Choir finished in 1272

1226 Louis IX became King of France under the regency of his mother, Blanche of Castile

1233 Chartres added to the Crown territory of France

1236 Regency of Blanche of Castile ended

1240 St. Chapelle, the Royal Chapel of French Kings, begun in Paris

1250 University of Paris founded, with Albertus Magnus as one of its teachers

1260 Cathedral of Chartres dedicated in the presence of Louis IX

1274 Height of Scholastic movement in Philosophy
Death of St. Bonaventura and St. Thomas Aquinas

Philosophy
1079 – 1142 Abelard
c.1193 – 1280 Albertus Magnus
1221 – 1274 Bonaventura
c.1225 – 1274 Thomas Aquinas

Music
c.1122 – 1192 Adam of St. Victor, joint author of hymns with St. Bernard of Clairvaux

c.1150 Leonin active at the Cathedral of Notre Dame in Paris

c.1183 Perotin active at the Cathedral of Notre Dame in Paris

c.1237–c.1288 Adam de la Halle, author and composer of *Le Jeu de Robin et Marion*, a pastoral play with music

c.1240 "Sumer is icumen in," oldest surviving piece of secular polyphony, written

c.1260 Franco of Cologne, musical theorist, active

7

THE GOTHIC STYLE

THE ÎLE-DE-FRANCE, LATE 12th AND 13th CENTURIES

By comparison with the shores of the Mediterranean, where such resplendent centers of culture as Athens, Alexandria, Antioch, Constantinople, and Rome had flourished for centuries, northern Europe had never been much more than a rural region with a few Roman provincial outposts and later a scattering of castles, monasteries, and villages. Before the 13th century, in fact, not one center north of the Alps could properly have been described as a city. Toward the end of the 12th century, however, Philip Augustus as King of France was promoting the destiny of Paris as his capital, enclosing it with walls, and paving some of its streets with stone. The work was continued under his successors, notably by Louis IX, and by the end of the 13th century Paris was the capital of a kingdom of growing importance. With its splendid Cathedral of Notre Dame, its university famed for the teaching of Abelard, Albertus Magnus, Thomas Aquinas, and Bonaventura, and with its flourishing mercantile trade capable of supporting its more than 150,000 inhabitants, Paris could well claim the status of a capital city. When it is remembered, however, that Constantinople at the same time was the hub of the rich Eastern Roman Empire, and had been a city of over a million souls ever since Justinian's time, the status of this first transalpine urban center is seen in its proper perspective.

The growth of Paris, while more rapid than other northern centers, was nevertheless far from an isolated instance. For a full century the town as a social unit had been gaining ascendancy over the manorial estate, and the literature of the time began to mention some of these growing centers, associating each with certain attributes. Guillaume le Breton's *Philippide*

253

speaks of Ghent with its turreted houses, Lille and its cloth, Tours and its grain, and how all were carrying on commerce with distant lands. With the exception of these occasional references, however, the life of medieval French towns would have remained a closed book, were it not for the visual record preserved in the castles of their feudal lords, in the monasteries, and, above all, in their cathedrals.

The prototype of the Gothic cathedral has been recognized in the abbey church of St. Denis just outside Paris. This monastery was under the direct patronage of the French kings and was their traditional burial place. Around the middle of the 12th century its abbot was Suger, a man whose talents were as remarkable as his origin was obscure. As the trusted confidant of two kings, he ruled France as regent while Louis VII was away on a crusade. When he undertook the rebuilding of his abbey church, its importance as the royal monastery and his own great personal prestige enabled him to call together the most expert craftsmen from all parts of the kingdom. His church thus became a kind of practical synthesis of all the ideas that had been tried and found successful by the best Romanesque builders. In 1130, for instance, when he had its construction in mind, he made a prolonged visit to Cluny and undoubtedly learned much from first-hand observation of its recently completed church. Posterity has had reason to rejoice because Suger's enthusiasm for his project caused him to write extensively on it; and his book is an invaluable source of information about the architectural thought of the time. His commentary on the iconography of the church windows and sculpture suggests that he took a personal hand in this part of the project, but no mention whatsoever is made of the architect who carried it out. His church was not notable so much for its innovations as it was for its successful synthesis of such late Romanesque devices as the pointed arch, the groin vault, and the flying buttress. Many late Cluniac Romanesque churches used these features in separate instances, but never before as at St. Denis had they been grouped together into a coherent structural system. Suger's position at the French court, as well as the proximity of his church to Paris as the capital city of the Île-de-France, assured the widest possible currency for his ideas. And his church was so widely imitated, that St. Denis became the model for many of the Gothic cathedrals which were built in the region soon after it was finished.

The Île-de-France was thus the setting where the Gothic style originated; and where, over a period extending approximately from 1150 to 1300, it also reached the climax of its development. The name of this rather flexible region referred to the royal domain, or the territory under the direct control of the French king, in contrast to those parts of France that still remained under the dominion of the various feudal lords. By heredity, marriage, conquest, and purchase, the region gradually grew over the years and eventually formed the nucleus of the future French nation. Like a wheel with Paris as its hub at this time, it radiated outward with spokes extending in the direction of Amiens, Rheims, Bourges, and Chartres, all of which were cathedral towns.

Unlike an abbey church, a cathedral must be located in a populated area where it comes under the jurisdiction of a bishop, whose official seat it is. A cathedral cannot rise from a plain like a monastic church; it needs the setting of a town where it can soar above the roofs and gables of the buildings which cluster around it. The barren exterior of an abbey forbids, while the intricate carving on the outside of a cathedral awakens curiosity and invites entrance. As the center of a cloistered life, a monastic church is richest in its dim interior, while the most elaborate decoration of a cathedral points toward the dwellings of the people. The tall towers of a Gothic cathedral demand room from which to spring and space on which to cast their shadows. Their spires beckon the distant traveler to the shrine beneath and direct the weary steps of the toiling peasant homeward. The bells they enclose peal out to regulate not the internal life of a small community of monks but that of a whole town and its surrounding countryside. They not only summon to prayer but tell of weddings and funerals, and of the time for work and rest.

The cathedral was always, of course, primarily a religious center; but in a time when sacred and mundane affairs were so closely interwoven, the line of demarcation was difficult to draw. Its nave was not only the gathering place for religious services but on occasion a town hall where the entire populace could come together for a meeting. The rich decorations that covered the body of the church told not only the story of Christianity but also the history of the town and of the activities of its people. The cathedral was thus a municipal museum on whose walls the living record of the town was carved. The iconography of a cathedral dedicated to Notre Dame was by no means concerned only with religious subjects. Since the Virgin Mary was also the patroness of the liberal arts, it was often a visual encyclopedia whose subjects ranged over the entire field of human knowledge. The pulpit was not only the place from which sermons were preached but also a podium for lectures and instruction. The sanctuary was the theater in which the constantly changing sequence of the religious drama was enacted; but outside, the deep-set portals served as the stage sets for the mystery plays appropriate to the season, and the porches became platforms

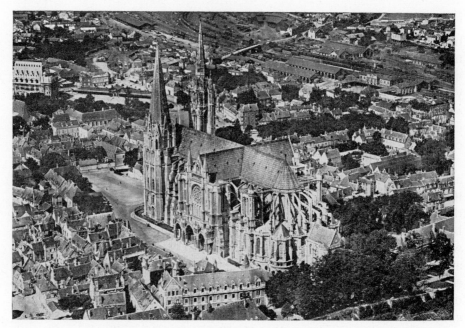

Fig. 7:1. *Chartres Cathedral*, Air View

from which the minstrels and jugglers could entertain their audiences. The stone statues and stained glass were useful not only as illustrations for sermons but as picture galleries to stimulate the imagination as well. The choir was not only the setting for liturgical song but a concert hall or opera house, where intricate polyphonic motets were performed and the music of the religious dramas was chanted.

Chartres (Fig. 7:1), unlike Paris, was never a center of commerce but a small bishopric in the midst of a rural district quite off the beaten track, deriving its greatest distinction from the shrine of the Virgin Mary that was located there. The cathedral here, as elsewhere, was not only the spiritual center of the lives of its townsfolk but the geographical center of the medieval town as well. Its west façade constituted one side of the market place where everyone frequently gathered. Its great shadow fell upon the other church buildings that clustered around it, among which were the bishop's palace, the cathedral school, a cloister, a hospice, and an alms-house. Above them all was the cathedral itself toward which all eyes and steps were drawn. The year at Chartres was dramatized by the usual sequence of Church festivals, but the grand climax came at the Feast of the Virgin, when pilgrims by the thousands congregated from far and wide to honor her in her shrine.

Radiating outward from the square were the narrow streets on which the houses and shops of the townspeople were located. There were those of the butchers, bakers, and candlestick-makers, since all who practiced the same craft lived on the same street. Their associations or guilds contributed their labor and products to the cathedral at the time it was being built. As groups they donated windows and statuary, as the many examples at Chartres will show. They also undertook to maintain certain continuing functions, such as the supply of candles for the altar and the bread for the Communion service. The cathedral itself represented a composite effort of the stone cutters, masons, carpenters, and metal workers, all of whom gave of their time, skill, and treasure to build it. It thus was the greatest single product a town and its craftsmen could produce. As a great civic monument it was the pride of the community, and the ambitions and aspirations of its citizens determined its character and contours. The importance of a town was rated by the size and height of its cathedral as well as by the importance of the religious relics housed there. Civic rivalry was involved when the vaulting of Chartres rose 122 feet above the ground, thus bettering the achievement of Paris by 7 feet. Next came Amiens which rose 147 feet; and finally Beauvais, in order to top them all added 10 more feet, but at the same time went beyond the limits of skill and safety so that the walls collapsed. The growth of town and cathedral at this time were indistinguishable from one another, and in the broader sense the cathedral itself and the buildings and dwellings that grouped themselves around it formed a single unit.

The extraordinary spirit of religious enthusiasm that prompted the undertaking and construction of these immense projects is well brought out in the accounts of several medieval writers. "Who has ever heard tell, in times past," wrote Abbot Haimon of Normandy to his brother monks in Tutbury, England after visiting Chartres, "that powerful princes of the world, that men brought up in honor and wealth, that nobles, men and women, have bent their proud and haughty necks to the harness of carts, and that, like beasts of burden, they have dragged to the abode of Christ these waggons, loaded with wines, grains, oil, stone, wood, and all that is necessary for the wants of life, or for the construction of the church? . . . When they have reached the church, they arrange the waggons about it like a spiritual camp, and during the whole night they celebrate the watch by hymns and canticles. On each waggon they light tapers and lamps; they place there the infirm and sick, and bring them the precious relics of the Saints for their relief." [1]

ARCHITECTURE: THE CATHEDRAL OF CHARTRES

When the harmonious proportions of the west façade of the Cathedral of Notre Dame at Chartres (Fig. 7:2) are first observed, everything seems as right as if it were the revelation of some immutable truth. This always comes as something of a surprise when it is recalled that what seems so certain, so solid, so monumental is actually the end result of fire salvage, a long process of growth, and a goodly amount of improvisation. Four centuries, in fact, separate the earliest parts from the latest, and the interval between saw rapid construction in time of prosperity, lag in time of poverty, work inspired with religious ardor, and cruel destruction by fire.

The triple portal and lancet windows first stood a full 40 feet back of the twin towers, and together they were all that remained of the previous Romanesque church after the conflagration of 1194. In the building of the present structure, they were moved forward flush with the front towers. The large rose window was designed to fill the intervening space, and above it the arcade of kings and a gable were added to mask the apex of the wooden roof which protects the vaulting of the nave.

The stylistic difference between the two unsymmetrical spires is one of the most striking features of the façade. The supporting towers, as a part of the previous church, are approximately contemporary. The upper part and the spire of the one on the right, however, date from the time the later parts of the abbey church at Cluny were being finished; while their counterparts on the left are contemporary with the laying of the foundations for St. Peter's basilica in Rome in the early 16th century. Close scrutiny will reveal such minor flaws as the discrepancy between the proportions of the portals and the scale of the façade as a whole, the rose window being set slightly to one side, and the awkward joining of the gallery and arcade of kings above it with the south tower. In spite of these disparities the façade bears out the initial impression of unity surprisingly well, and its space is so logically divided as to become an external promise of the interior plan. Horizontally the three entrance portals lead into the nave while the flanking towers face the aisles. Vertically the portals correspond to the nave arcade within, the lancets to the triforium gallery, and the rose window to the clearstory level. By this means its composition maintains an admirable integrity of relationship between the inner and outer aspects of the structure.

Rising above the twin towers are the tall tapering spires that seem such a logical and necessary continuation of the vertical lines of the supporting

Fig. 7:2. Chartres Cathedral. *Façade*. 157′ wide, South Tower 344′ high, North Tower 377′ high. West Portals c.1145, South Tower c.1180, North Spire 1507–1513 (Courtesy French Government Tourist Office)

Fig. 7:3. Chartres Cathedral. *Interior of Nave.* c.130′ long, 53′ wide, 122′ high. c.1194–1260
(Houvet)

buttresses below, and that also seem to be such a fitting expression of the Gothic spirit of aspiration generally. The façade of Chartres, however, is almost unique in having a pair of them. In Paris, Rouen, Amiens, and elsewhere such spires were projected for the towers but were never completed; and at Strasbourg one tower has a spire while the other does not. The two at Chartres make for an interesting contrast between the attitudes of the early and late architects. In the older one on the south the builder felt that the junction between the tower and spire should be made as smoothly and effortlessly as possible. This he accomplished by adding a story between the three levels of the tower below and the single shaft of the spire above. Here the eight dormerlike windows are each surmounted by alternating higher and lower miniature spire forms of their own, and, in turn, they overlap the base of the large spire and break the line by adding to the rhythm of the vertical movement. The transition from the square supporting tower to the octagonal form of the spire, and the continuation of the straight upward lines rising from the ground level to the receding sloping ones of the spire which culminate 350 feet above, is thus accomplished with continuity and finesse. The later Gothic architect, whose task was to replace the old wooden spire which had burned, was more concerned with greater intricacy of design and with sending his slimmer and more elegant spire 27 feet higher than its neighbor. While both excel in terms of their separate stylistic frames of reference, it is the old south tower, still sound after seven

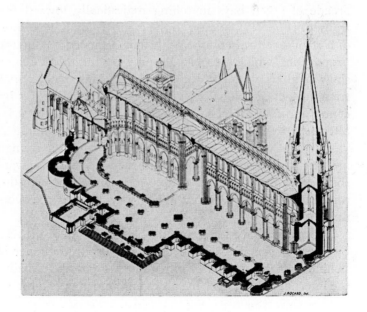

Fig. 7:4. Chartres Cathedral. *Plan*

centuries and almost as many fires, that attracts the greater number of admirers.

On entering Chartres through the central portal, the broad nave (Fig. 7:3) spreads out to a width of 53 feet, making it one of the most spacious of all Gothic naves. On either side are amply proportioned aisles with their stained-glass windows that allow a rich flood of light to enter. A look at the plan (Fig. 7:4) will show that in comparison with the abbey church at Cluny (Fig. 5:1), the Gothic architect has practically dispensed with walls. Instead of running parallel to the nave, the supporting piers are now at right angles to it, and the area between is bridged over with vaults, thus allowing enough open space for glass so that the interior can be lighted at the ground level as well as at the clearstory. Since the eye is naturally drawn to light, the interior gives the impression of being all windows. The walls, therefore, instead of serving to bear the weight of the superstructure, now exist mainly to enclose the interior and as a framework for the glass. Through the language of form and color the wall space can now communicate with the worshipers in the nave by means of representations of religious subjects; and on a sunny day the beams of filtered light transform the floor into a constantly changing mosaic of color. Together with the clearstory windows the shafts of mysterious light serve also to accent the structural system of arches, piers, and vaults in such a way as to contribute to the illusion of infinite size and height.

Returning to the center of the nave, the attention is next drawn to the arcade of seven bays marching majestically toward the crossing of the transept (Fig. 7:5), and on to the choir beyond. The immense piers consist of a strong central column with four attached colonettes of more slender proportions, which are spaced evenly around them. Close examination will show an alternating pattern whereby one has an octagonal center with four round attached colonettes, while the next reverses this by having a round center and four attached octagonal colonettes. Interest is provided by this alternate projection and recession of the core columns as well as by the variation in the light as reflected from a round and angular surface. The architect has here shown still another instance of his awareness of light and shade; and by this rather simple means he has given the nave arcade an unobtrusive variety without in any way marring the over-all impression of unity.

The space above the graceful pointed arches of the nave arcade is filled by a series of smaller open arches which span the space between the bays. Behind them runs the triforium gallery, a passage utilizing the space above the internal roofing over the aisles and under the slanting external roof that

Fig. 7:5. Chartres Cathedral. *Interior. c.*1194–1260 (Clarence Ward)

extends outward from the base of the clearstory. Above the triforium runs the clearstory level, which now fully accomplishes its purpose. Its space is occupied by a minimum of masonry and a maximum of glass in the form of a triple pattern of two lancet windows below and a circular one above, which almost completely fill the allotted space horizontally and vertically.

Covering the span of the nave is the triumph of the Gothic builders, the broad quadripartite vaulting (Fig. 7:6), which here rises at Chartres 122 feet above the ground level. It is this principle of vaulting that underlies all Gothic thinking and, in turn, explains all the supporting facts of shafts, colonnettes, clustered columns, piers, and pointed arches—all of which exist to direct the descending weight of the intersecting ribs of the vaults toward the ground as efficiently as possible. The heavier transverse ribbing is carried past the clearstory and triforium levels by the large central shaft, while the smaller cross ribs are borne by the groups of slender colonnettes that extend downward and cluster around the massive central piers of the nave arcade below. Chartres is about midway in the cumulative trial-and-error process by which the Gothic system was eventually perfected. The central piers of the nave arcade are still somewhat bulky, as though the architect could not entirely trust his own daring. Greater slenderness was achieved at Rheims and Amiens, and the tendency toward slimness and height continued until the limit was passed at Beauvais.

Externally there is an opposite number to each of these interior members (Fig. 7:7). The function of the flying buttress is to carry the thrust of the vaulting at specific points outward over the aisles to the piers that are set at right angles to the length of the nave. The function of flying buttress, pinnacle, and pier are now likewise clarified. From the observer's point of view, just as the eye is drawn irresistibly upward on the interior by the rising vertical lines, so also on the outside it follows the rising vertical piers to the pinnacles, along the rhythmic procession of the flying buttresses toward the gabled roof of the transepts and on to the infinitude of space beyond.

The structural purpose of the pointed arch likewise becomes clear. The Romanesque architects of Burgundy had used it at Cluny and Vézelay mainly as a decorative device to give the feeling of height and elegance. Gothic architects, however, pointed their arches to achieve equality on the levels of the crowns in the intersecting ribs of the arches (Fig. 7:8), and it was for them primarily an element in the construction. By the ever-increasing skill with which they used this device, they were able to achieve a constantly increasing height, which in turn led to loftier vaults and more ethereal effects.

Fig. 7:6 (above). Chartres Cathedral, *Vaulting over Apse.* *c*.1194–1260 (Clarence Ward). Fig. 7:7 (left). *Perspective Cross Section of the Amiens Cathedral.* Drawing by Viollet-le-Duc. Fig. 7:8 (below). *Developed Gothic Vault.* Drawing by W. D. Richmond (Courtesy John Ives Sewall)

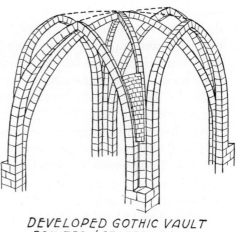

DEVELOPED GOTHIC VAULT
POINTED & STILTED ARCHES
ALMOST LEVEL CROWNS
A SECTION OF THE THIN WEB
SHOWN IN PLACE

By using all these means in conjunction with one another, the Gothic architect was able to effect an activation of dead mass into an equilibrium of weights and balances. Gothic architecture must therefore be considered primarily as a logical system of vaulting that is maintained in a state of equipoise by a complex opposition of thrusts and counterthrusts. As such it is a dynamic force in which every part bears a necessary functional relation to the whole. Each stone, in fact, had to be carefully adjusted according to its weight, and its dynamic tendency had to be calculated in terms of what was above and below it, so that its mass could be successfully transferred along the various levels until it came to rest at the proper point. If any part should give way the entire structure would be in danger. The result becomes all the more remarkable when it is remembered that the Gothic builders used mortar and concrete in the joinings only as reinforcement and as a kind of structural insurance. Even if no mortar were used, the 122-foot arches would still stand simply by the mathematical accuracy of the formula of stone upon stone.

On the other hand, the logic of the interior and exterior supports was not always consistent with the irregularity of the site. Over a period of time the ground might settle or the piers and buttresses might be undermined at certain points by floods, which would place the whole structure in danger Another weakness came from the impossibility of making the vaults at such a high level heavy enough to withstand the wind and weather. At Chartres and elsewhere the thin masonry had to be protected on top by the addition of wooden roofs, which at Chartres actually burned several times without, however, destroying the vaults underneath. The triumph of the builder of Chartres is that his structure has never had to be reinforced, and that it stands today substantially the same as it did seven centuries ago. Its sister church at Rheims has fared equally well by surviving the centuries, two fires, and an artillery bombardment in World War I. The Gothic cathedrals, in fact, bid fair to realize the ardent hopes of the people who built them, as was expressed so aptly by Guillaume le Breton when the walls of Chartres were still rising, "it now need have nothing to fear from fire till the day of judgment." [2]

At Chartres the wings of the transepts each terminate in triple portals (Fig. 7:9) that eclipse in size and magnificence those of the western façade. Since the latter were a survival from the previous church, they resemble the flat Romanesque portals and contrast strongly with the 13th-century style of those of the transepts, which are enframed by row after row of richly sculptured archivolts. A sense of projection by means of light and shadow is achieved by these triple portals; and, in spite of their indentation, the

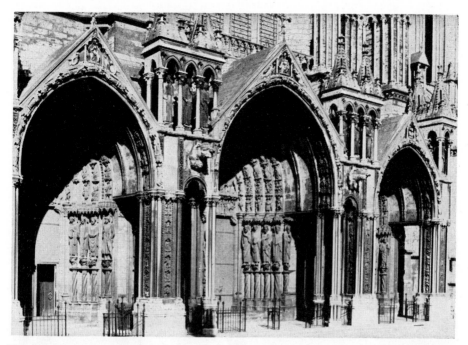

Fig. 7:9. Chartres Cathedral. *South Porch*. 13th Century (Courtesy French Government Tourist Office)

doors actually seem to come forward in a gesture of welcome to those who enter. Another glance at the plan will reveal one more instance of the unwillingness of Gothic builders to be bound too rigidly by the laws of symmetry, since the two porches are of differing size and proportion. The size of such parts was determined by the needs of different times and the tastes of the individual donors. The north transept with its portals and porch and stained glass was the project of the royal family of France, especially of Blanche of Castile and her son St. Louis (Fig. 7:10), while its southern counterpart was donated by their rival in power, the Duke of Brittany. When the cathedral was dedicated in the year 1260, Louis himself was present with such an assembly of bishops, canons, princes, and peasants as had rarely been seen.

Beyond the transepts extend the spacious choir and sanctuary, which are surrounded by the double-aisled ambulatory in order to give easy access to the apse and its crown of radiating chapels. The increasingly ornate Gothic liturgy demanded the participation of more and more clergymen, and the cavernous recesses of the huge structure made an ever-larger number of voices in the choir necessary. The apsidal chapels are also one of the most distinctive features of a developed Gothic plan. The need for them arose during the pilgrimage period from the religious idea of the intercession of

Fig. 7:10. *Blanche of Castile and St. Louis.* Illuminated Manuscript. *c.*1226–1234. Pierpont Morgan Library, New York

the saints, each of whom was thought to specialize in certain sorts of petitions. The godhead centering in the Trinity was much too abstract to fire the popular imagination, and it always remained a subject of speculation mainly for theologians. The saints, however, who were once human, had a special significance at this time, and smaller chapels in which their relics reposed were needed to fulfil the function of the church as a shrine. The most important of all, of course, was the Virgin herself who, according to the thought of the period, was the prime interceder with her Son. The Lady Chapel in Gothic churches therefore almost always is placed in the apse on the main axis of the nave, while the chapels of the lesser saints are grouped on either side. All these considerations were responsible for the expansion of the parts beyond the transepts to quite unprecedented proportions.

As far as the decorative detail is concerned, the Gothic interior needs little more than the vertical lines of its structural members, the variety of representations in its stained glass, and, above all, the flow of light. At Chartres the lighting is so organized as to achieve a gradual crescendo from the low intensity of the dominantly blue lancets and rose window in the west, through the aisle and clearstory windows of the nave, past the rich reds of the transept rose windows, until the climax is reached in the high intensity of the five lancets in the apse, which soar above the altar and capture the essence of the morning sunlight. Early Christian and Romanesque churches had depended mainly on the inner illumination of candlelight. The Gothic church, however, becomes etherealized by making external light into an interior fact through the process of capturing the rays of the sun and transforming them into a myriad of brilliant prismatic colors. The unity of the interior thus depends mainly on the dual means of the uniformity of structural detail and the direction of the flow of light. Both material and immaterial elements thus share in the function of integrating the vast interior into a complete and harmonious whole.

THE SCULPTURE OF CHARTRES CATHEDRAL

As important to the medieval mind as the structure itself was the choice and location of the sculptural and pictorial representations that were to give the church its significance and meaning. In a Romanesque monastic church these were found in the carved tympanums over the portals, on the capitals of the columns throughout the interior, and in wall paintings, especially in the apsidal end. Since such representations were designed for those leading cloistered and contemplative lives, they were found in the interior; and the character of the representations was seldom obvious and frequently enigmatic. In a Gothic building, however, the interior columns rise to such a height that specific pictorial subjects would be out of the normal range of vision. They also would be eclipsed by the complex lines of the vaulting. The interior capitals at Chartres and elsewhere are decorated mainly with foliage and flower forms (Fig. 7:5), and more specific representations were left for the windows. Gothic capitals differed from their Romanesque counterparts in the more naturalistic treatment of the leaves and fruit; and instead of fanciful conceptions, such as the trees of Paradise, they became more and more realistic. Bishop Durand, writing in 1284, seemed hard pressed to find any of the traditional spiritual meanings for them at all and was content in his description with saying that they "represent the fruits of good works that grow from the roots of virtue." To thus dismiss so summarily the several hundred capitals of a Gothic interior makes it abundantly clear that they now conveyed little profundity of meaning.

At Chartres, with the exception of these foliated capitals and an elaborate choir screen that was added in the Renaissance, there is little sculptural interest in the interior. The intention of the medieval builders was quite clearly to concentrate it on the exterior, and the profusion and quality of the sculpture outside is such as to leave no doubt about the high regard in which the art was held at this time. The exterior of Chartres has, in fact, well over 2000 carved figures, which are about evenly distributed between the west façade and the north and south porches of the transepts. The Gothic sculptor remains as anonymous as his Romanesque brother, as in both periods the work was done by schools of traveling craftsmen who congregated wherever the building of churches was in progress. From the enormous number of examples produced in the 13th century alone, the ranks of these craftsmen must have been well populated, and the stroke of the sculptor's chisel on stone must have been one of the more familiar sounds of that time. The Gothic sculptor had the advantage over his predecessors in being able to follow stone models rather than having to translate the lines of an illuminated manuscript into another medium. While the Romanesque sculpture tends to be more linear, as in the drapery of the tympanum figures at Vézelay (Fig. 5:11), the Gothic is more concerned with carving in depth; and the placement of the sculpture out of doors also made the artists more conscious of the play of light and shade on their forms. Most Gothic sculpture also seems to have been finished before being set in place, whereas the opposite was apparently the practice in the Romanesque period. While the technique of the Gothic sculptor was undoubtedly superior, the standardization of the iconography in his time did not allow him quite as much imaginative freedom as his predecessor had enjoyed. Both periods, however, shared the inevitable ups and downs of school sculpture where the skill of some craftsmen far exceeds that of others.

The profusion of sculpture in a Gothic cathedral would lead to considerable confusion were it not for the close relationship its forms have with the architectural framework. The Gothic structure itself was so complete, so overwhelming, that no amount of decorative license would be able to overshadow it; nor, indeed, did the Gothic carvers have any intention of going their separate way, and their work was always conceived and executed in terms of the architectural frame of reference. Even so, the enormous number of examples would be a bit bewildering were it not for some attempt to unify the iconography. Since the cathedral is a people's church, it cannot follow so consistent a system as that of an abbey, which was designed for a small group who followed a common ideal of life. Instead of single unified compositions, therefore, the Gothic went in for greater variety, so as to be sure to provide something for every level of taste. At Chartres, furthermore, where the west portals are a carryover from a previous church, and where every century since the building was begun has contributed something to the grand total, it can be seen that the problem of discerning a unified plan is almost impossible. Since most of the sculpture as well as the structure dates from the first half of the 13th century, it is possible from these examples, from a common tradition, and from the thought of the period, to derive something resembling a general plan.

The iconographical scheme at Chartres was determined first of all by its dedication as a shrine of the Virgin Mary—something that was shared by so many other Notre Dame cathedrals of the time, such as those of Paris, Rheims, Rouen, and Amiens. More than any of these, however, Chartres was more closely associated with her because of a long-standing tradition, the dedication of the former churches which stood on the same spot, and because of its possession of some famous relics. The greatest of these was the legendary veil of the Virgin, which, by tradition, had been presented by the Byzantine Empress Irene to Charlemagne and donated to the cathedral by his grandson Charles the Bald. Next in importance was the skull of the Virgin's mother, St. Anne, which was brought back from the crusades and presented to the church in 1205. This latter relic accounts for the prominence at Chartres of the representations of St. Anne, and the fact that her feast was the occasion of pilgrimages almost as great as those honoring her daughter. At Chartres, then, the iconography was determined principally by the cult of the Virgin, and secondarily as a kind of Christian pantheon. Since the Virgin in 13th-century thought was considered to be the patroness of the arts and sciences as well as the heavenly protectress, mediator, and mother of all humanity, it can be seen that the subject matter was not very rigidly restricted.

The cathedral of Chartres as the court of Mary, the Queen of Heaven, had to surpass in magnificence all the grandeur that surrounded earthly queens. This was the era in which strong-armed military feudalism was being replaced by courtliness, and just as the clergy sang the praises of Notre Dame, so the knights of the castles lauded their ladies in particular and Our Lady as the universal symbol. The high place created for womanhood in secular circles is thus the courtly parallel of the religious cult of the Virgin. In the poetry of the time a knight's lady love appears as the unapproachable paragon of all feminine virtue and charm. To woo and win her, he who aspired to her favor had to storm the fortress of her heart by techniques far more intricate and subtle than those needed to take a castle. When successful he became the vassal of his mistress, and she his liege lady who could command him as she would. The concept of romantic love originated here in the Gothic Middle Ages and came to full flower in the complex code of chivalry. With its exaltation of the position of women and its concern with the defense of the weak against the strong, it established the Western code of manners that is still valid to a degree even today.

The favored reading matter in aristocratic circles ranged from Ovid's *Art of Love* of ancient Roman days to the contemporary *Romance of the Rose*. Included also were such stories as Tristan and Iseult, Aucassin and Nicolette, and the legends of King Arthur's court. Since such works were addressed mainly to the knightly class, they usually began with extended lists of the ancestors of the hero and heroine, and at Chartres their visual counterpart is found in such Biblical genealogies as those showing the kings and queens of Judah as the ancestors of Mary and Christ. A law of precedence as rigid as any courtly etiquette was observed in the order of presentation and the location of these figures. Because the Old Testament prophets, for instance, lived before the Christian era, they were placed in the shadows of the north porch, while the Apostles and personalities of the New Testament are found in the sunlit south porch. Christ and Mary, as King and Queen of Heaven, are found over the central portals, while figures of lesser rank in their court are found in various places with proximity to them determined by their importance.

The iconography of the sculptures at Chartres, like the form of its façade, was partly the result of profound planning, compromises by the clergy with the donors who came from all social classes, some concessions to popular taste, and just plain happenstance. What consistency the scheme has is seen in a beginning on the west façade, a middle on the north porch, and an end on the south. On the west façade the story of Christ from his ancestors to the ascension is told in the 700-odd carved figures of the three tympanums, the archivolts which surround them, the columns below with their bases and capitals, and the gallery above. The central tympanum encloses the figure of Christ in Majesty surrounded by the apocalyptic beasts and the 24 elders, which is called by tradition the Royal Portal (Fig. 7:11).

Fig. 7:11. Chartres Cathedral. West Portal, *Kings and Queens*. 20' 6" high. 1145–1170 (Archives Photographiques)

This is the vision of the eternal Christ as he was in the beginning, is now, and ever shall be. The tympanum over the right portal depicts the beginning of his earthly life with the annunciation and birth, in which the Virgin Mary figures so prominently; while that over the left portal gives the close of his days on earth with his ascension. The composition of the north porch is concerned primarily with the history of Mary, which is traced along Old Testament lines from the creation of man to her death and heavenly coronation. The south porch continues this drama of redemption and takes up the story at the beginning of the New Testament; carries it on through the work of the church and its saints, popes, abbots, and bishops; and closes with a prophetic vision of the final day of the universe at the Last Judgment. It is this latter event that is the culmination and climax of the whole iconographical scheme, and it is stirringly depicted in the central tympanum of the south porch.

Worked in along the way is a complete visual record of the thought of the medieval period. The myriad of statues and relief figures, in combination with the stained glass within, constitutes a kind of visual encyclopedia containing an A to Z account of 13th-century knowledge. As such, the representations constitute a medieval pictorial synthesis similar to the *Summa Theologiae* of St. Thomas Aquinas, in which he assembled in one huge work the arguments and answers to every possible theological problem; or similar to the *Speculum Majus* of Vincent of Beauvais, who departmentalized all knowledge into Mirrors of Nature, Knowledge, and History, and to which another hand added Morality. The Mirror of Nature would be found in the frequent representations of the forms of flora and fauna; Knowledge in those of the liberal arts, signs of the zodiac, and labors of the months; History in the story of humanity from Adam and Eve to the Last Judgment; and Morality in the virtues and vices, and wise and foolish virgins. Both of these works in their way, as well as the cathedral sculptures, were compendiums of all the available knowledge of the time.

In addition to the usual Scriptural scenes and legends from the lives of the saints, there was a place for ancient lore and contemporary history; for prophecy and fact; for the forms of fabulous animals and those of the beasts of burden found on the farms of the district; for old wives' tales and the latest scientific learning as taught in the universities; for portraits of princes and those of tradesmen; for representations of angelic beauty and the shapes of grotesque gargoyles, which served sometimes as water spouts and, more decoratively, as curious forms darting centrifugally outward over the cornices of the roof or lurking in unexpected places; and for the liberal arts and allegories of virtue and vice. The function of these representations

Chartres Cathedral, West Façade. Fig. 7:12 (left). *Tympanum of the Virgin Portal.* 1145–1170. Fig. 7:13 (below). Detail. *Shepherds Led by an Angel* (Houvet)

as the Bible of the poor and the books of the illiterate has been so often pointed out that their equal importance as a kind of theological and secular encyclopedia for the educated has sometimes been overlooked. The iconography of Chartres becomes, then, a kind of visual *Summa*, and the cathedral itself functioning as the center of the town's activities becomes, in turn, a synthesis of the life of its time. It is this element of all-inclusiveness, plus its elasticity and capacity for growth and change, as much as its structure and monumental size that makes the medieval cathedral the great institution that it was. Since the number of representations is so vast that they would take up volumes if described in detail, the discussion will be narrowed down to two typical compositions, that of the 12th-century portal of the Virgin on the west façade, and a part of its 13th-century counterpart on the north transept.

The tympanum of the Virgin Portal of the west façade at Chartres (Fig. 7:12) is a typical early Gothic composition, which set a precedent for all later Notre Dame churches. The story is told in the simplest possible terms in three rising panels. Beginning in the lower left is the Annunciation, with just the figures of the Angel Gabriel and Mary; the next pair shows the Visitation; the Nativity is in the center; and the shepherds in the midst of their sheep (Fig. 7:13) are coming from the right for the Adoration, just as their successors came in from the fields near Chartres to worship at Mary's shrine. The middle band depicts the presentation of the young Jesus in the temple. His position on the altar foreshadows his later sacrifice. Friends approach from both sides bearing gifts. In the space above, the Virgin sits crowned and enthroned, holding her Divine Son and attended by a pair of archangels. She is shown frontally as a queen accepting the homage of the humble, who bow their heads as they enter her court through the portal below.

Of the greatest interest are the figures symbolizing her attributes in the archivolts which frame the tympanum. It is most striking, perhaps, to find Mary associated so prominently with the seven liberal arts; and, like Athena of old, the patroness of the intellectual disciplines. Albertus Magnus in his *Mariale* declared that the Virgin was perfect in the arts; and in his *Summa*, Thomas Aquinas includes among his propositions the question of "Whether the Blessed Virgin Mary possessed perfectly the seven liberal arts"—which, of course, was triumphantly affirmed. These representations are also reminders that this was an age which produced great scholars, and that intellectual understanding as well as faith was now one of the conditions of salvation. The fact that Chartres was the location of one of the great cathedral schools is also brought out; and before the founding of the University of Paris, it shared with Rheims the distinction of being the best-known center of learning in Europe.

The curriculum of the cathedral school was, of course, the seven liberal arts, which were divided into the Trivium, which dealt with the science of words in the three subjects of Grammar, Rhetoric, and Dialectic; and the higher faculty of the Quadrivium, which was concerned with the science of numbers through the study of Arithmetic, Geometry, Astronomy, and Music. They are symbolized abstractly by female figures somewhat akin to the ancient muses, while below them are found their most renowned human exponents. Beginning with the lower left corner of the outside archivolt, Aristotle is seen dipping his pen into the inkwell. Above him is a thoughtful figure representing Dialectic. In one hand she holds a dragon-headed serpent symbolizing subtlety of thought, and in the other the torch of knowledge. Then comes Cicero as the great orator and over him the figure of rhetoric making a characteristic oratorical gesture. The next pair

Chartres Cathedral, West Façade. Tympanum of the Virgin Portal, Details. Fig. 7:14 (above left). *Grammar*. Fig. 7:15 (above right). *Pythagoras*. Fig. 7:16 (right). *Music*. 1145–1170 (Houvet)

are Euclid and Geometry, both of whom are deep in their calculations. In the same band, moving now from the top downward are Arithmetic and probably Boethius. Below them is the star-gazing figure of Astronomy, who holds a bushel basket which signifies the relationship of her science to the calendar, so important in a farming district like Chartres. Ptolemy, to whom the medievalists ascribed the invention of the calendar and clock, is her human representative.

The figures on the lowest level are Grammar and Donatus, the ancient Roman grammarian. Grammar (Fig. 7:14) holds an open book in one hand and the disciplinary switch in the other over the heads of two young pupils, one of whom is laughing and pulling the other's hair. The last pair in the series of seven are adjacent to those in the inner archivolt. Below is Pythagoras (Fig. 7:15) the reputed founder of music theory, who is shown writing in medieval fashion with a desk over his knees, while on the wall behind him is a shelf holding a supply of pens for writing and sponges for erasures. Above him is the figure of Music surrounded by instruments (Fig. 7:16). At her back is a monochord, used to calculate the intervals and for accuracy of pitch; on her lap is a psaltery; on the wall hangs a three-stringed viol; and she is striking the set of three chime bells, which alludes to the Pythagorean discovery of the mathematical ratios of the perfect intervals—the octave, the fifth, and the fourth. Both Gerbert of Rheims and his pupil Bishop Fulbert of Chartres are known to have taken an active interest not only in the theory of music but in its performance as well, and the two figures, showing Pythagoras as the thinker and Music as the performer, symbolize that Chartres was an important center for both the theoretical as well as the practical aspects of music.

A comparison of these figures representing the liberal arts with those on the north porch show how far intellectual curiosity had extended a century later. While the universities had absorbed the humanistic tradition of the arts as taught in the cathedral schools, they also included the study of theology, law, and medicine. There are personifications here of Philosophy, still by Aristotle; of Geometry, now coupled with Architecture and with Archimedes as their exponent; and of Medicine, represented by Hippocrates. In addition, there are some nonuniversity pursuits, such as Painting, personified by Apelles, Metalcrafts by Tubal-cain, and Agriculture by a group made up of Adam, Abel, and Cain.

Far more elaborate in scope and less restrained in decorative detail than the west façade is the incomparable north porch which, with its three portals, stretches out to a width of 120 feet, thus spanning the transept completely. A gift of the royal family of France, its construction and decoration extended from the reign of Louis VIII and the regency of his queen, Blanche of Castile, through that of their son, St. Louis, or roughly the first three quarters of the 13th century. It is dedicated to the Virgin and expands the theme of the Virgin Portal on the west façade to encyclopedic proportions. Her history from the annunciation and nativity through the childhood of Jesus is found on the left portal, while the scenes of her death and assumption are depicted on the lintel over the central door, and that of her enthronement and coronation in the tympanum above. Her attributes

Chartres Cathedral, North Porch. Fig. 7:17 (left). Detail. *Contemplative Life*. Fig. 7:18 (right). Trumeau of Central Portal. *St. Anne with the Virgin*. Middle 13th Century (Houvet)

are revealed in the archivolts through series after series of cyclical representations, such as those of the 14 heavenly beatitudes and 12 feminine personifications of the active and contemplative life, one of the latter of which is seen in Figure 7:17. Especially fine is the single figure of her mother, St. Anne, holding the infant Mary in her arms, which adorns the trumeau of the central doorway (Fig. 7:18). From the harmonious lines of the folds of her drapery to the dignified and matronly face, the work is one of the most satisfying realizations of the mature Gothic sculptural style.

It will be noted from the contours of the south porch (Fig. 7:9) that the arches of the portals are now more highly pointed, and their enclosure by gables further emphasizes their verticality. The deep recession of the porch allows for a much greater play of light and shade in the statuary that is used so lavishly that every available space from the bases of the columns to the peak of the gable is covered. The figures on both the north and south porches in comparison with the earlier ones on the west façade have bodies more naturally proportioned; their postures show greater variety and informality; and there is much more mobility of facial expression. The representations of plants and animals are considerably closer to nature; and in comparison with the impersonality of those on the west front, many of the human figures are so individualized that they seem like portraits of living persons. In the change of style, however, they have in turn forfeited something of the previous monumentality as well as a closer union with the architecture.

THE STAINED GLASS OF CHARTRES

Time has taken its inevitable toll of the exterior sculptures, and only traces of their original polychrome and gilt remain to remind the observer that they constituted at one time a rich and colorful pageant. Only in the flow of carved lines and in the varied play of light and shade that now relieve the present monochrome gray, can their original effect be reconstructed in the imagination. The full color of medieval pageantry, however, still exists in the interior where the stained glass has remained undimmed throughout the centuries. Here, in Chartres, the prodigious wealth of pure color in the 175 surviving glass panels hypnotizes the senses; and through the medium of polychromatic light something of the emotional exaltation that inspired medieval man to create such a temple to the Queen of Heaven can still be felt. Here, as elsewhere, the structural and decorative elements are tied together as closely as possible; and just as with the sculpture, the glass never seems applied but rather to be an integral part of the whole. The designer was always aware of the size, proportion, and placement of his window in relation to its architectural setting. While glass before the 19th and 20th centuries is not usually thought of in the structural sense, it nevertheless had to fill a large architectural void and to take the pressure of wind and weather into account. This was accomplished mainly by dividing the space geometrically into smaller parts by the use of stone tracery as in the mullions, by parallel iron bars across the open expanse, and more minutely by the fine strips of lead which held the small pieces of glass in place. While Chartres must divide its architectural and sculptural honors with its neighboring cities, the town was especially renowned as the center of glassmaking, and the highest achievement of its glaziers, as exemplified in their own cathedral, made it in this respect incomparable.

All the visual arts must come to terms in their separate ways with the problem of light. Architectural exteriors must take sunlight into account; sculpture, whether in relief or in the round, demands an expressive use of light and shade; and painting, whether on a wall or on canvas, must be done with an eye toward the reflection of light. In each case, however, the observer receives his impression by means of refracted light. Only in the case of stained glass is the direct ray the primary concern of the artist. In this medium he transforms his light prismatically through his colored glass and thus achieves a greater brilliance and intensity than is possible in any other medium, a fact which accounts for the immediate appeal of his art to connoisseur and layman alike. The use of stained glass as wall panels allies it to the earlier use of mosaics, fresco paintings, embroidered wall hangings and tapestries. While the glazier's art was developed in Romanesque times, it was not until the earliest Gothic structure was built by Abbot Suger that stained glass received a place in the iconography on a par with that of sculpture and painting. With the virtual disappearance of the walls and the great height of the vaulting in Gothic buildings, mural and ceiling painting was out of the question. Pictorial decoration, however, was needed more than ever before, if the stony logic of the piers and vaults were not entirely to dominate the interior. The window space consequently became the only available surface for such decoration, and much of the expressive impact of Gothic art depended on the effectiveness of these luminous tapestries.

The great variety of jewellike color was achieved chemically by the addition of certain minerals to the glass when it was in a molten state. When cool, the sheets were cut into smaller sections, and the designer could then fit them into his previously prepared outline. Pieces of various sizes were next joined together by lead strips. Details, such as the features in the faces, were then applied in the form of metal oxides and made permanent by firing in a kiln. Finally, the individual panels making up the pattern of the whole window were fastened to the iron bars already imbedded in the masonry. When seen against the light the glass appears translucent, while the lead and iron became opaque black lines that serve to outline the figures as well as to separate the colors and prevent them from becoming blurred when viewed at a distance. Black and white reproductions can convey only the faintest idea of the brilliantly colored originals, and it should be noted especially that the black lines of the iron and lead are overaccented. It is nevertheless possible to observe from photographs the care with which the formal design and the details were executed.

The stained-glass artists shared with mosaicists and manuscript illuminators a distinct preference for two-dimensional designs. The dignified formality of their figures and the abstract patterns of the borders blended their work admirably into the architectural setting. By thus avoiding any hint of naturalistic effects, such as landscape backgrounds and the like, and by concentrating on patterns of pure color and geometrical forms, they helped to promote the illusion of infinite space.

The iconographical plan of the glass at Chartres has little more unity than an encyclopedia; like the exterior sculpture, it is held together mainly by the dedication of the church as a shrine of the Virgin Mary. There is never any doubt on the part of those who enter that they are in the presence of the Queen of Heaven, who sits enthroned in majesty in the central panel of the apse over the high altar. Grouped around her in neighboring panels

Chartres Cathedral. Stained Glass Windows, Details. Fig. 7:19 (above left). *Bakers*. Fig. 7:20 (above right). *Furriers*. Middle 13th Century (Houvet)

Fig. 7:21 (left). *Wheelwright and Barrel-makers*. Middle 13th Century (Houvet)

Fig. 7:22. Chartres Cathedral. *North Rose Window*. Diameter 44′. 1223–1226 (Houvet)

are the archangels, saints, prophets; portraits of the noble donors, and symbols of the craftsmen and tradespeople, almost 4000 figures in all, who honor her and make up her court. Below, on her feast days, were the crowds of living pilgrims who gathered in the nave and chapels at her feet, and who aspired to come into her eternal presence one day as they had come into her shrine on this occasion.

An interesting commentary on the changing social conditions of the 13th century can be read in the records of the donors of the windows. In the lowest part of each one is a "signature" indicating the individual, family, or group who defrayed the great expense of the glass. Only a royal purse was equal to a large rose window; while the lancets of the nave and choir were within the means of members of the aristocracy and the church hierarchy, such as bishops and canons. The status and prosperity of the medieval guilds of craftsmen and merchants, however, was such that the vast majority of the windows was donated by them. While the royal family of France and the Duke of Brittany were content with the wings of the transepts, the most prominent windows of all, the 47-foot-high center lancets of the apse, were given by the guilds; and the one over the high altar toward which all eyes were drawn was the gift of the bakers. Each guild had a patron saint, and most windows under their patronage were concerned with the life and miracles of their special saint. In the case of the nobility, the family coat of arms was sufficient identification; but with the guilds, the "signature" took the form of a craftsman engaged in some typical phase of his work. Some 19 different confraternities are represented in the windows at Chartres, including the bakers (Fig. 7:19), furriers (Fig. 7:20), and wheelwrights and barrel-makers (Fig. 7:21).

The great rose window of the west façade dates from the early 13th century and is thus contemporary with the majority of examples in the rest of the church. The three lancets below it, however, like the portals under them on the exterior, were originally part of the previous church. Besides being the earliest of all the windows, they are, by common agreement of the experts on the subject, also the best. Their origin has been traced to the school which did the windows of Suger's church at St. Denis and which was working at Chartres for the first time on an assignment outside of Paris. The work of the 12th-century designers was on the whole much finer grained and more jewellike, and infinite care was lavished on the geometrical and arabesque patterns in the borders. They are dominated by their vibrant blue backgrounds, while the figures and abstract patterns are done in several shades of red, emerald green, yellow, sapphire, white, and black.

The great rose window of the north transept (Fig. 7:22) repeats the iconography of the sculpture of the north porch below it—the glorification of the Virgin. Together with its five lancets the composition shares with the other glass of the 13th century a preference for red backgrounds instead of the earlier blue; the individual panes are larger, the borders more conventionalized, and its effectiveness rests on large splashes of warm color in contrast to the cool tones of the lancets of the west façade.

The art of stained glass thus replaced the mosaics and mural paintings of the Early Christian and Romanesque churches, and its evolution represents the final stage in the etherealization of interior space. By giving form and meaning to light, the art of the glazier is perhaps better adapted to the expression of transcendental concepts than any other medium. By the transformation of raw sunlight into a spectrum of brilliant prismatic color, the architect gained complete control over his interior lighting, which he could cause to flow in any manner he willed. This material control over an immaterial medium could then be placed at the disposal of the iconographers, who could shape it to their pictorial and expressive needs. Something of the ecstasy felt by medieval man in the contemplation of the precious stones that adorned the altar and the jeweled glass of the windows is expressed in the following passage by Abbot Suger: "When the house of God, many colored as the radiance of precious jewels, called me from the cares of this world, then holy meditation led my mind to thoughts of piety, exalting my soul from the material to the immaterial, and I seemed to find myself, as it were, in some strange part of the universe which was neither wholly of the baseness of the earth, nor wholly of the serenity of heaven, but by the grace of God I seemed lifted in a mystic manner from this lower toward that upper sphere." [3]

GOTHIC MUSIC

Massive and magnificent as the Gothic cathedral is, it can be conceived as the highest achievement of Gothic man only if associated with the various activities it was designed to house. The most important of these is, of course, the liturgy. As the space of the enclosed area increased, the cathedral grew into such a vast auditorium that the spoken word in sermons and the like was intelligible only in the immediate area of the pulpit, which for this reason was placed in the middle of the nave. The acoustics, however, are just right for solo and choral song, which resounds and reverberates most agreeably from the irregular surfaces of the vaults and piers, echoing and re-echoing through the entire resonant space. The music emanating from the choirs of the Chartres or Paris cathedrals was, if anything, even more closely allied with the church service than its sister arts in stone and glass, and without doubt music was just as effective on the contemporary audience in its way and just as worthy of its magnificent setting.

The enormously increased choir space of Gothic churches was designed to provide room for the greater number of clergymen and for the larger choruses who participated in the elaborate liturgy. Since no direct performance tradition links Gothic music with that of our own time, it must be reconstructed from the scanty signs on the manuscript page and from the tantalizingly meager literary descriptions and visual representations of the period. Gothic music, therefore, is today something like a frame without the picture. Its approximate melodic and rhythmic structure are known; but since music comes to life only when performed, the melodic freedom, rhythmic flexibility, dynamic accentuation, as well as the parts known to have been improvised, must remain subjects of conjecture. It must also be taken into consideration that just as a statue or painting loses much of its significance when removed from its original architectural setting to a museum, so also does music suffer when transferred from the resonant spaces of the cathedral to a modern concert hall or recording studio. When heard in such settings, the stark intervals of the fifth and octave seem barren and hollow, and the sharp dissonances somewhat harsh. Those who have heard the same works in a cathedral find them by contrast astonishingly alive and colorful. The long-drawn-out tones reverberate against the irregular surfaces of the vaulting, resound resonantly through the cavernous vertical and horizontal expanses, and awaken the chants into a vibrant life all their own. In this way, then, the music of the period is just as much a part of the indissoluble whole as the Gothic structural system, the sculptural embellishments, and the stained glass.

Just as the Île-de-France had been the source of the most significant developments of the 12th and 13th century in architecture, it was also the scene of the most important musical innovations of the Gothic period. Specifically this was the development of polyphonic, or many-voiced, music in addition to the still universally practiced monophonic, or one-voiced, art of Gregorian chant. Singing in parts was of northern origin in contrast with the prevailing Mediterranean style of singing in unison, and its practice in folk music apparently predates its incorporation into church music by several centuries. Just as the Gothic cathedral was the culminating point in the long process of reconciling the northern urge for verticality with the horizontal southern basilica form, so Gothic music was the union of the two traditions of northern many-voiced and southern one-voiced singing.

The role of Chartres in these developments is obscure. John of Salisbury, the master of the cathedral school when the beautiful figure of Music was done for the west façade (Fig. 7:16), is known to have approved the theoretical study of music as a part of the Quadrivium as heartily as he disapproved of certain innovations in the music performed by the choir there. Scholarly discussions about the mathematical ratios of musical intervals had been going on ever since antiquity, and such abstract problems as how the music of the spheres or how an angelic choir would sound had been on the academic agenda ever since Boethius' time. It is therefore much more probable that the greatest progress was being made at this time in the field of practical music which John so despised. According to William of Malmesbury, who died about 1142, Chartres was celebrated for its "many musical modulations," and one of the greatest 13th-century musical theorists, Franco of Cologne, is supposed to have been educated at Chartres. From actual documents and the surviving manuscripts, however, it is evident that the most progress was being made in the Cathedral School of Paris, known after 1163 as the School of Notre Dame.

The School of Notre Dame in Paris

It has already been noted that in the construction of the first Gothic church the builder of St. Denis brought together many principles that had been developed separately elsewhere and for the first time used them as a systematic whole. This was also the case with music; and Paris, as the growing capital of the French kingdom, was the logical place for it to occur. The contrapuntal forms and textures developed in such monasteries as Cluny, and in such cathedral schools as Rheims and Chartres, as well as the tradition of folk singing in several parts, were for the first time systematically organized in the School of Notre Dame in Paris. Again as in the case of architecture, the man and the time can be fixed with a considerable degree of certainty. Specifically the first great monument of Gothic music was the *Magnus Liber Organi* by Leonin, dating from about 1163, and which, as its name implies, was a great book bringing together a collection of music in two parts, arranged cyclically so as to spread over the entire calendar year.

In the traditional rendering of the Gregorian chant, some parts were sung by a soloist and answered responsorially by a chorus singing in unison. In the Gothic period the choir still chanted in the usual way as it had done for centuries, but the solo parts began to be performed simultaneously by two or more individual singers. The Paris Cathedral, for instance, employed four such singers. The distinction between solo voice and choir was hence replaced by the opposition of a group of individual singers and a massed chorus. With several skilled soloists available, the way was open for an art of much greater complexity than heretofore. Since the music, however, was still intended for church performance, it was mandatory that one of the traditional sacred melodies be used; and a special part called the *tenor*, a term derived from the Latin *tenere*, meaning to hold, was reserved for it. This melody was also known as the *cantus firmus*, or fixed song, implying that it could not be changed. The development of Gothic music was that of taking this *cantus firmus* as an established basis, and adding one by one the voices called in ascending order, the *duplum*, *triplum*, and *quadruplum*. Since these voices were superimposed one above the other, a definite verticality of concept is implied, which contrasted strongly with the horizontal succession of tones characteristic of the older monophonic chant.

The earliest forms of Gothic polyphony are almost as rigid in their way as the old parallel organum of the Romanesque period, but they are based on the new principle of *punctus contra punctum*, literally note against note, or point counter point. *Mira Lege* (below) illustrates one of the strictest appli-

Mira lege (12th-century Discant)   (After Coussemaker)

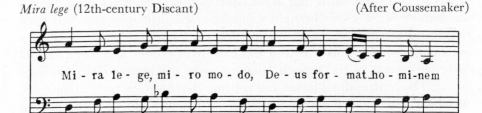

Mi - ra le - ge, mi - ro mo - do, De - us for - mat ho - mi - nem

cations of this idea. The Gregorian melody is in the lower part, while the counterpoint moves as much in opposition to it as possible. While parallel movement is not against the rule, and from time to time does occur, contrary motion is preferred. John Cotton, an English monk, makes this point clear in a treatise written at the beginning of the 12th century in which he states: "If the main voice is ascending, the accompanying part should descend, and vice versa." The name given to this newly created melodic line was the *discantus*, or discant, referring to the practice of singing against the established melody. In various forms and guises, from melodic obbligatos to popular music, this principle has remained a part of religious and secular music ever since.

Leonin's *Magnus Liber* contains numerous examples as strict as *Mira Lege* in which the opposition of note against note is both melodically and rhythmically as exact. In addition to these, however, another type known as *organum duplum* is found. The Gregorian *cantus firmus*, in this case, still remains intact, but unlike the practice in parallel organum, it is transferred to the lower part, and the individual tones are stretched out to extraordinary lengths. The discanting, or duplum voice, moves now in free counterpoints consisting of long florid melismas over what has now become in effect a relatively fixed bass.

Duplum (*c.*1175)   In Leonin's style

The greater melodic and rhythmic freedom that the discant now assumed called for expert solo singers, and much of the discanting of Gothic times is known to have been improvised. The practice of such a freely flowing melodic line over a relatively fixed bass points to a possible origin in one of the old types of folk singing. Survivals are found in the instrumental music of the Scottish bagpipers, where the tune is heard over a droning bass note, and in such songs as "The Campbells Are Coming," where the bass remains relatively constant. In performance the slowly moving tenor, or *cantus firmus*, may have been sung by the choir, while the soloist sang his freely moving duplum part over it; or the tenor may have been played on the organ, as the instrument is known to have been in use at this time. The organ keyboard was a 13th-century Gothic innovation, and the numerous pictures from the period point to the wide usage of organs. The term "organ point," furthermore, is still used to refer to a musical passage in which a bass tone remains static, while the other parts move freely over it.

The next most significant development was the addition of a third part above the other two, which was known as the *triplum*, and from which the

term treble is derived. This step is associated with the name of the first
practicing musician in history to have the attribution of greatness attached
to his name. He was Magister Perotinus Magnus, or Perotin the Great,
active in Paris in the late 12th and probably the early 13th century. In his
revision of the work of his predecessor Leonin, he moved away from polyphonic improvisational practices toward an art based on stricter melodic
control and clearer rhythmic articulation. By thus achieving a surer command of his materials, and evolving a logical technique for manipulating
them, he was able to add the third voice to the original two, and in two
known instances even a fourth. The form of the three-part motet, like its
predecessors, still had its *cantus firmus* in the tenor, which was the lowest
part and held the *mot*, or word, from which the term *motet* is probably
derived. Over it the contrapuntal voices wove a web of two different
strands, singing their independent melodic lines. In the hands of Perotin
the three-part motet became the most favored and characteristic style of
Gothic music, and the form dominating 13th-century musical developments.

Triplum (13th century)   In Perotinus' style
                                                              (After Yvonne Rokseth)

Besides achieving ever greater melodic independence, the two contrapuntal voices even had their own separate texts. A three-part motet thus
had three distinct sets of words—the tenor, with its traditional line, and
usually two contemporary hymnlike verses over and above it—which were
sung simultaneously. Intended as they were for church performance, the
words customarily expressed appropriate religious sentiments. However,
even before the middle of the 13th century, it was not uncommon for one
of the contrapuntal voices to have its verses in French, while the others
were in Latin. With the entrance of the vernacular language came also
popular melodies, so that above the stately tenor, it was possible to have a
hymn to the Virgin in Latin and a secular love song in French all going on
at the same time. By the simple expedient of replacing the sacred melodies
by secular tunes, a fully developed musical art independent of the church

was not only possible but by the end of the 13th century was a widely
practiced reality.

It is not difficult to see that an art of such growing popularity and increasing complexity needed to have a new set of rules, the most important
of which was the development of a notation that would take into account
not only the exact indications of pitch the new art demanded but also a
way in which the rhythmical relationships could be put down. Especially
was this the case when the tenor was in the dignified cadence of Gregorian
chant; the part above it, perhaps a dance melody in 3/4 time; and the
triplum, a French love song in 6/8 time. The concern of the treatises with
rhythmic problems can therefore be readily understood. Indeed, the whole
ars antiqua, as it was called, is often referred to as *musica mensurata*, or measurable music.

Gothic music exists in such close unity with other manifestations of the
style that it can scarcely be understood as a thing apart. The subjects of
the new hymns, especially those with the words of St. Bernard and the
melodies of Adam of St. Victor, were mainly in praise of the Virgin Mary,
just as was the case in the dedications of the cathedrals and the iconography
of the sculpture and stained glass. Instead of a monolithic choir chanting
in unison or in parallel organum, the Gothic listener was now aware of the
emergence of a small group of individual singers. In the case of a three-part
motet he could choose, according to his temperament or mood, to follow
either the solemn traditional tenor melody, the Latin commentary above
it, or the French triplum in his own everyday mode of speech. This allowance for diversity of musical taste is a part of the general shift from the
homogeneity of monastic life in the abbey to the heterogeneity of city life,
of which the cathedral is the expression. The new melodic, rhythmic, and
textual variety implies a congregation made up of people from all walks of
life, just as had been the case with the diversified sculptural and glass
representations.

Since the individual voices were superimposed one above the other, a
definite concept of verticality, similar to the architectural developments, is
discernible in the music. As such, Gothic music presents the strongest possible contrast with the horizontal succession of tones characteristic of the
older monophonic chant. This distinction implies the presence of a fixed
point by which the verticality can be measured. In the *Mira Lege* example
it was that of the intervals of the lower part over which the discant moved
in strict contrary motion. In the case of the *organum duplum*, it was that of a
long sustained tone in the tenor against which the soaring upward and
plunging downward movement of the melody is perceived. In addition to
this linear impulse, all types of counterpoint achieve a sense of rhythmical

progress by having a relatively static point against which the more rapid mobility of the other voices can be measured. Together with the several opposing melodies, the clash of dissonant intervals, the simultaneous declamation of separate texts, as well as the progress of several independent rhythms, Gothic music was able to build up a sense of mounting tension that set it apart as a distinctive new style.

IDEAS

In the round century that marked the interval between the dedication of the great Romanesque abbey church at Cluny and the beginning of the Cathedral of Chartres, a mighty shift in social and political institutions and in basic modes of thought, as well as in artistic styles, had taken place. The resulting changes in ecclesiastical, secular, and artistic affairs divide themselves into two groups of opposing forces, some of which represented smoldering conflicts hitherto held in check by the powerful medieval theocracy, while others were those of new voices clamoring to be heard. Running as an undercurrent through all these varied manifestations of the Gothic mind was the consistent and largely successful attempt to reconcile these oppositions by the application of scholastic rational processes. These dualities were often so extremely opposed to each other that they produced sharp intellectual clashes and violent emotional tensions. The Gothic must therefore be understood as a clashing and dissonant style, in which these opposing elements were maintained temporarily in a state of uneasy equilibrium and one in which the resolutions were only approximate. With the eventual dissolution of the scholastic synthesis in the 14th century, the basic divisions became so irreconcilable that they led in some cases to the battlefield, in others to schisms within the Church, and generally to growing philosophical and artistic tensions.

Gothic Dualism

Politically, the age-old struggle of Church and state, which was evidenced in Romanesque times by the interminable quarrels between the popes and the Holy Roman emperors, was now widened to include the conflict of ecclesiastical authorities and the growing power of a group of northern European kingdoms, especially France and England. Apart from the religious and political overtones, it was also the beginning of a split between the traditional internationalism of the Church and Holy Roman Empire, and a rising nationalistic consciousness, which set the stage for centuries of rivalry between the south and the north for the domination of Europe.

The prevailing monastic and feudal organization of Romanesque times tended to segregate society into the widely scattered units of cloister and manor and thereby kept many of the social strains from breaking out into the open. With the growth of city populations, the disparate elements were brought together to live in common centers where the problems were made much sharper. No longer was it possible to divide humanity on the simple basis of whether they were saved or damned. Tension between the landed aristocrats and the more volatile urban groups mounted on the one hand, while that between the monastic orders and power of the secular clergy in the cities was heightened on the other. In the towns the struggle was brought into close range; and the rivalries of abbot and bishop, lord and burger, clergy and laity, were often bitterly acute. In the lives of individual people there were odd contrasts between the squalor of the hovels in which most of them lived and the magnificence of the palaces of their lords, bishops, and abbots; between the poverty of their daily existence and the glowing promises of heavenly glory in the beyond; and between the strife of their world and the visions of serenity and peace in the next. The arts were likewise torn by an inner contradiction between the expression of the aspirations of this world and the next, and the artist himself between an anonymous status in the service of God and an active competition with his fellows in search of more worldly recognition. In contrast to the comparative unity of artistic patronage in the aristocratically oriented Romanesque period, patronage now was divided between the social groups of the city, with the aristocrats and clergy on one side, and the increasing importance of the bourgeoisie on the other.

In architecture, whether it is the interior or exterior of the Gothic cathedral, there is an awareness of the opposition between the masses and voids, the interplay of thrust and counterthrust, and of the principle of attraction and repulsion which awaken dead weights into dynamic life. In the sculpture the conflict of the particular and universal is seen in the remarkable feeling for human individuality in some of the separate figures and the iconographic necessity of molding them into the dignified impersonality required of a row of prophets and saints. In literature the opposition between Latin and the vernacular languages rapidly became as evident as the growing distinction between the sacred and secular musical styles. Within the province of the tonal art are found such external disparities as the fruitless academic discussions about the hypothetical nature of the music of the spheres and the increasing importance of the actual sounds heard in the choirs of the churches; the abstract study of theoretical acoustics in the universities and the practical art of writing and making

music; as well as the awareness of such internal differences as the singing
of monophonic choruses alternately with a smaller group singing poly-
phonically, the contrast between voices and instruments, the flow of horizontally moving melodic lines versus their simultaneous vertical aspects,
the juxtaposition of consonance and dissonance, the rhythmical opposition
between the independent voices within a polyphonic motet, line against
line, *cantus* versus *discantus*—in short all the inherent oppositions of an art
based on the principle of point counter point.

The Scholastic Synthesis

In the face of all these disparities, it seems only a step short of the miraculous that the Gothic style was able to effect a synthesis at all. Such dualities, however, generated the need for some sort of *modus vivendi*, and that
such was in fact achieved is yet another proof of the remarkable intellectual
ingenuity and creative vitality of this period. The method was that devised
by scholasticism, and the results shaped up in the form of the Gothic monarchy, university, encyclopedia, *summa*, and cathedral to mention but a
few. It will be remembered that the west façade of the Chartres cathedral
had proclaimed by its representations of the arts and sciences that the age
of pure faith was over, and those entering through its portals were put on
notice that faith alone was no longer the sole condition of salvation. Hence-
forward faith had to be justified by forms of reason arrived at through the
discipline of the seven liberal arts. Architecture had to be a kind of logic
in stone, the sculpture and glass encyclopedic in scope, and music a form
of mathematics in sound. All experience, in fact, had to be interpreted
intellectually in contrast to the intuitive and emotional orientation of the
preceding period. God to the scholastic philosophers was a rational being
and the creator of a world based on principles of reason. Hence the key to
the understanding of the universe was in the exercise of man's rational
faculties. Philosophical truth or artistic value was determined by how
logically it fitted into this preconceived and rationally ordered system.

Abelard's *Sic et Non* was a kind of early manifesto of Gothic dualistic
thinking. With unparalleled audacity he posed one pertinent question after
another, then proceeded to cite all the approved authorities of the Church
for and against the proposition. Even though he revealed thereby some
wide cleavages of thought, he made no attempt at reconciliation. In the
work of his immediate successors, arguments raged over whether the source
of ultimate truth was in faith or knowledge; blind acceptance of the hallowed church authorities or in the evidence of the senses; universals or
particulars; ideas or words; thesis or antithesis; determinism or freedom of

the will; irrational mysticism or reasoning power; emotional aspirations or intellectual theorizations. Thomas Aquinas and his fellow scholastics found the answer in the dialectical method; and Aquinas' synthesis, as found in his *Summa Theologiae*, represented a comprehensive attempt to answer some 631 questions ranging over the entire articles of faith. His work was a kind of climax to the scholastic spirit in which the divergent views of the previous 1000 years of speculation were finally organized into one logical system. Abelard's pro-and-con arguments were reconciled by a subtlety of intellect that has never been surpassed; but just as in the case of Gothic vaulting, if one of the premises or syllogisms is taken away, the whole structure falls like an arch deprived of its keystone.

From this highly rationalistic viewpoint followed the scholastic definition of beauty, which, according to Thomas, rested on the criteria of perfection, proportion, and consonance, because, he said, the mind needed order and demanded unity above all other considerations. Mathematical calculation and symbolism therefore played an important part in the thought of the time, though it was more closely allied with the sort of Pythagorean number-magic now associated with numerology than with the purely logical processes of mathematics in the modern sense. The number 3 was especially favored because of its association with the Trinity; 4 to a lesser extent because it signified the material elements of fire, air, earth, and water; 7, as the sum of the two, indicated man, since his dual nature was composed of both spirit and matter; and their product pointed to such groups as the 12 Apostles, 12 lesser prophets, and so on. Since the sacred number was 3, most of the over-all formal divisions fall into this category, with the encyclopedia of Vincent of Beauvais and the *Summa* of Thomas Aquinas each having three divisions; the syllogism its three parts; the façades of cathedrals three portals; their naves a main and two side aisles; vertically they ascend in the triple division of the nave arcade, triforium gallery, and clearstory; in the clearstory each bay at Chartres had two lancets and one rose window, and so on. The triple rhyming plan of the Latin poetry, as in the *Dies Irae* (Ch. 8, p. 322); and in the *terza rima*, a French invention employed later by Dante, will serve as literary examples. In music the favorite Gothic form was the three-part motet; and the prevailing rhythm was ternary, which was called *tempus perfectum* because of its Trinity symbolism, while binary rhythms were ruled out because they were considered too worldly.

In the cathedral schools and later in the universities, music was studied mainly as a branch of mathematics. Bishop Fulbert emphasized theory in the training of singers, saying that without it "the songs are worthless."

His view was generally held throughout the Gothic period. John Cotton, for instance, at the beginning of the 12th century said that a singer who is ignorant of theory is like "a drunkard who, while he is able to find his home, is completely ignorant of the way that took him home." Mathematical considerations, in fact, led composers to emphasize the perfect intervals of the octave, fifth, and fourth for theoretical reasons more than for their agreeableness of sound. The whole tendency was to suppress sensuous beauty of tone and emphasize the mathematical, theoretical, and symbolic aspects of the art.

The rise of the monarchies in France and England and the accompanying centralization of civil authority was an attempt to overcome the diversification of feudal power with its inevitable provinciality. A political resolution between king and nobles, and between nobles and commoners, was made in the English Magna Charta that established the basis for parliamentary government, and in France the establishment of a working relationship between the king and the urban middle classes accomplished approximately the same purpose. Louis IX of France even found a way of maintaining cordial relations with the papacy in so successful a manner as to bring him posthumously the crown of sainthood. The undertaking of the fantastic crusades was found to be a way of uniting many opposing European factions in a cause against a common enemy. The code of chivalry was a definite attempt to reconcile the opposition between idealistic love and the gratification of the senses, and more broadly to establish a standard of behavior between strong and weak, lord and peasant, oppressor and the oppressed. Externally the university was set up as an institution to bring together all the diverse disciplines and controversial personalities, and to fit all the various intellectual activities into a single universal framework. Internally scholasticism was primarily concerned with the development of the dialectical method as a common mode of thought designed to bring about the solution of intellectual problems. In the cities the guild was the answer to the need for standardization of skills and to assure by means of apprenticeships and examinations a certain uniformity of quality and craftsmanship. The structural uniformity of Gothic vaulting and buttressing was, in effect, the Gothic builder's answer to Romanesque experimentalism. Ample allowance for urban heterogeneity was made in the iconography of the individual cathedral and in the differences of cathedrals from town to town, where each had distinctive attributes of its own. Both internally and externally Gothic architecture tried to synthesize the building with the space surrounding it. Externally the eye follows the multiplicity of rising vertical lines to the spires and pinnacles and then to the sky.

Inside, the experience is similar with the vertical lines rising to the window levels and thence through the glass to the space beyond. In contrast to the monastic church that was based on the notion of excluding the outside world, the Gothic cathedral attempted an architectural union of the inner and outer world. The thrust and counterthrust of the interior vaulting was paralleled on the outside by that of pier and flying buttress; the sculptural embellishments of the exterior were repeated in the iconography of the glass in the interior. Through the medium of stained glass, outside light was made the dominating interior fact.

The various European languages and dialects found a place for themselves in secular literature, but Latin was championed by the Church and universities as the universal language of scholarship. In music the Latin and vernacular were reconciled in the polytextual motet; and when one language was used, the same form provided a highly ingenious method by which an authoritative text was declaimed, while at the same time one or more running commentaries upon it were presented. Gothic music also represented a synthesis of theory and practice functioning together as equals. Through all these separate manifestations the Gothic spirit was revealed, whether in the soaring logic of St. Thomas, in the heightened sense of time and movement achieved by the musicians, or the visual aspirations and linear tensions of the builders. In each case it was based as little on actual experience as the universals of the scholastic philosophers and their endless syllogistic concatenations.

No one of these resolutions was in any sense final, and the Gothic style must, in the last analysis, be viewed as a dynamic process rather than an end result. By contrast a Greek temple and even a Romanesque abbey is a completed whole, and the observer's eye in both cases can eventually come to rest. The appeal of the Gothic is in the very restlessness that prevents this sense of completion. The observer is mobilized, so to speak, and swept up in the general stream of movement, and in the process he is given a sense of direction and the impulse to continue it. The completion, however, can only be in the imagination. There were, in fact, no finished cathedrals; each lacked something, from a set of spires in some cases to a nave as at Beauvais. Vincent's encyclopedia and St. Thomas' *Summa* were likewise never finished.

Gothic unity therefore existed only in a method of procedure, as in its dialectics; in a principle of construction, as in its architecture; or in a technique of writing, as in its literature and music. No more effective processes could have been devised to deal with the specific incongruities with which the Gothic mind had to contend. They were, in fact, the only possible ways to make the noble attempts to reconcile the irreconcilable; to achieve the irrational by the most ingenious rational techniques; to strive for the utmost in immateriality through material means. The object of Gothic thought was thus to work out a methodology for comprehending the incomprehensible and for pondering on the imponderables. Gothic art as a whole was designed to bridge over the impossible gap between matter and spirit, mass and void, natural and supernatural, inspiration and aspiration, the finite and the infinite.

PART 3

THE RENAISSANCE

CHAPTER

CHRONOLOGY: Italian Panorama, Late 13th and 14th Centuries

General Events

1140 Guelph and Ghibelline Wars began

1182 – 1226 St. Francis of Assisi
1210 Founded Franciscan Order
1225 Wrote *Canticle of the Sun*
1228 – 29 Thomas of Celano's first *Life of St. Francis*
1247 Thomas of Celano's second *Life of St. Francis*
1261 – 62 St. Bonaventura's *Life of St. Francis*
1322 *Little Flowers of St. Francis*

1198 – 1216 Pontificate of Innocent III Church reaches highest point in its power

1223 Franciscan Order confirmed by Pope Honorius III

1228 St. Francis canonized two years after his death by Pope Gregory IX

1228 – 1253 Building of the Church of St. Francis at Assisi

*c.*1260 Pulpit in the Baptistry at Pisa finished by Niccolo Pisano

1278 – 1283 Campo Santo at Pisa built by Giovanni Pisano

*c.*1296 – 1300 Giotto painted frescoes on the life of St. Francis at Assisi

*c.*1305 – 1309 Giotto painted frescoes on the history of the Virgin at Padua

1309 – 1376 Popes reside at Avignon in southern France

1310 First *Compagnie dei Laudesi* (Society of Laudists) founded in Florence

1314 – 1321 *Divine Comedy* written by Dante Alighieri

1316 *Ars Nova*, a musical treatise, by Philippe de Vitry

*c.*1320 Giotto painted frescoes in the Bardi Chapel of the Church of Santa Croce in Florence

1330 – 1339 Bronze doors of Baptistry at Florence cast by Andrea Pisano

*c.*1334 Andrea Pisano and Giotto collaborate on sculpture for the Campanile at Florence

1348 Black Death swept Europe

1348 – 1352 *Decameron* written by Boccaccio

*c.*1350 *Triumph of Death* painted in the Campo Santo by Francesco Traini

*c.*1354 *Triumph of Death* written by Petrarch

1378 – 1417 Great Schism between rival popes.

Philosophy

*c.*1214 – 1294 Roger Bacon, Franciscan monk and scientist

*c.*1225 – 1274 Thomas Aquinas, scholastic philosopher

*c.*1270 – 1347 William of Occam, Franciscan monk and nominalist philosopher

Painting

1240–*c.*1302 Cimabue, Giotto's Master

1255 – 1319 Duccio, leader of the Siennese School

*c.*1266–*c.*1337 Giotto

*c.*1283 – 1344 Simone Martini of Siena

1305 – 1348 Pietro Lorenzetti active

1323 – 1348 Ambrogio Lorenzetti active

1321 – 1363 Francesco Traini active

Sculpture

*c.*1205 – 1278 Niccolo (d'Apulia) Pisano

*c.*1250–*c.*1317 Giovanni Pisano

*c.*1270 – 1349 Andrea Pisano

Literature

1265 – 1321 Dante Alighieri

1304 – 1374 Petrarch

1312 – 1353 Boccaccio

Music

*c.*1200–*c.*1255 Thomas of Celano

1306 Jacopone da Todi died

1291 – 1361 Philippe de Vitry

1325 – 1397 Francesco Landini, organist-composer at Florence

8

THE EARLY ITALIAN RENAISSANCE STYLE

ITALIAN PANORAMA, 14th CENTURY

Instead of presenting a picture of harmonious unity, the 14th century reveals itself in a kaleidoscope of conflicting diversities. Like a particularly tempestuous April, it was an interval of struggle between the waning medieval winter and the rising life of a Renaissance spring. First one then the other gained ascendency. Italy, as well as the rest of Europe, was swept by the winds of the warring Ghibelline and Guelph factions, the whirlwinds of heresy and dogma, and the gentler breezes of a new humanistic world view. Gothic cathedrals were still being built in the north, while the latent beauty of Roman sculpture was being revived in the south. Thundrous fire-and-brimstone exhortations to repentance were heard from church pulpits alternately with the comforting warmth of Franciscan parables. People were taught to fear a God of vengeance one day and to love a God of mercy the next. A philosophy of tortuous scholastic intellectualism was still being argued in the universities, while peasants were persuaded by the simpler truths they heard from the lips of the followers of St. Francis. Some painters were composing horrendous murals depicting the doom of Judgment Day, while others were presenting happier Biblical stories in visual terms enacted by simple people like themselves. Everywhere people were wondering whether the world they lived in was really a moral trap set by the devil to ensnare the unwary, or whether it was a place a benign Creator meant them to enjoy. The 14th century can thus be described as transitional rather than one with a settled style.

For a drama of such titanic scope, no one capital could serve as the scene. All Europe, in fact, was the theater for this many-sided struggle, in which men and ideas were in such a constant state of creative flux. People were moving from the country to the towns, and the rising power of the city merchants collided with the entrenched might of the landowning aristocrats. The new monastic orders, such as the Dominicans and Franciscans, no longer kept to their cloisters but took to the highways and byways as preachers to all classes wherever people would gather and listen. Internal dissension within the Church was such that even the popes were driven from their hereditary See in Rome to hold court in widely scattered residences, most notably in southern France at Avignon. Writers, such as Dante and Petrarch, became exiles from their native cities, and their words were written during extended sojourns at half a dozen centers; and, like them, the great painters were journeymen, traveling about wherever they could get commissions. Giotto, the leader of the Florentine school, did cycles of frescoes that occupied him several years each in Rome, Ravenna, Assisi, and Padua as well as in his home city. Simone Martini, the leading light of Siena, painted one of the chapels of the church of St. Francis in Assisi and another in the papal palace at Avignon. The great sculptors of Pisa worked in Siena, Florence, Padua, and Arezzo. Musicians likewise sought their fortunes at various courts, and French influences and musical forms dominated the Italian musical scene. Artistic idioms in general showed wide variation with local styles flourishing in such centers as Venice, Pisa, Siena, and Florence, while an international style took shape at Avignon where the best talents from every country were attracted to the papal court.

In this state of flux, such large centers as Rome were less representative than little Assisi, a small hillside town in the Umbrian district of central Italy. Assisi served as a focal point for the gathering of many of the most distinguished talents who reflected the conflicts and tensions of the age. A town of such a small size would have been too insignificant ever to have supported a major art movement of any kind had it not been for the happy accident of the birth there of the greatest of the medieval saints. Even so, no artist could have survived indefinitely in such a provincial location. After the building of the great pilgrimage church there in the 13th century, however, the best painters were attracted as journeymen to decorate its walls.

The town of Assisi was built upon a rocky hill in the midst of a countryside which is more austere than lush. A more mountainous terrain might have nurtured a rugged and rarified spirit capable of bringing down some forceful new commandments from above, but instead, the gentle rolling green hills brought forth the most benign and beloved of Christian saints. A larger city might have produced a great organizer of men, capable of moving the minds of the many with his eloquence and wit, and then of molding them into a new social order. St. Francis, however, instinctively recognized the dangers of bombastic oratory and the transient nature of all forms of social organization, and he accomplished his mission with the sweet persuasion of simple parables and the overwhelming eloquence of his own exemplary life.

While the mature life of St. Francis fell within the 13th century, the collection of tales that made him a living legend, as well as the full development of the Franciscan movement, belongs more properly to the 14th century. The clergy who received their training in the universities and the scholarly orders of monks had never really reached a very wide segment of society. The Franciscans, on the contrary, found a way into the hearts and minds of the multitudes by preaching to them in their own language and in the simplest terms. Their voices, furthermore, were heard at this time more often in village squares than in the pulpits of the churches. The essence of the Franciscan idea is contained in the mystical marriage of the saint to Lady Poverty, which was the subject of one of Giotto's frescoes. When a young man approached Christ and asked what he should do in order to have eternal life, the answer came, " . . . go and sell that thou hast, and give to the poor, and thou shalt have treasure in heaven: and come and follow me" (Matt. 19:21). St. Francis took this commandment quite literally, and in his last will and testament described his early life and that of his first followers. "They contented themselves," he wrote, "with a tunic, patched within and without, with the cord and breeches, and we desired to have nothing more. . . . We loved to live in poor and abandoned churches, and we were ignorant and submissive to all." [1] Then in the same document he asked that "The brothers shall appropriate nothing to themselves, neither a house, nor a place, nor anything; but as pilgrims and strangers in this world, in poverty and humility serving God, they shall confidently go seeking for alms." [2]

THE CHURCH OF ST. FRANCIS AT ASSISI

It can readily be seen that if St. Francis' precept of poverty were followed too closely, no great art movement could have developed. Immediately after his death, however, dissension on this point grew up among those who had been closest to him. Brother Elias, for instance, wanted to build a great

Fig. 8:1 (above). *Franciscan Monastery and the Town of Assisi*, Air View (Alinari). Fig. 8:2 (below). *Church of St. Francis*. 1228–1523 (Courtesy Italian State Tourist Office)

church as a fitting monument to his friend and master, while others thought it more fitting to honor the saint by following his simple life pattern as strictly as possible. Such a monument as Brother Elias had in mind would take vast treasure to erect, and the majority of his fellow friars were shocked when he set up a porphyry vase to collect offerings from the pilgrims who traveled to Assisi to do St. Francis honor. Yet only two years after his death, a great basilica and monastery were begun on the crest of the hill where St. Francis had wished to be buried (Fig. 8:1). Taking advantage of the natural contours of the site, the architects designed the structure so as to include two churches, a large one above for the pilgrims (Fig. 8:2) and a smaller one below for the monks themselves, both of which combine to make the great Basilica di San Francesco. The twin churches seem to grow out of the hillside, and the upper one rests like a crown on its lordly brow. It is more this striking location that gives the structure its particular quality of impressiveness than the distinction or originality of the architecture as such.

In spite of their comparative size, both churches are without side aisles, having only central naves terminating beyond their transepts in polygonal apses. The large interior areas are spanned by spacious quadripartite groin vaults in the Lombard manner, which are partially supported by rows of columns set against the walls. Italian Gothic, contrary to the northern style, did not accent well-lighted interiors in which the walls were practically replaced with stained-glass windows. The southern sun made shade more welcome, and the interiors took on the character of cool retreats from the burning brightness of the world outside. The resulting interior darkness contributed a degree of mystery to the general effect. The absence of aisles, and the small number of stained-glass windows allowed ample wall space for the brightly colored fresco paintings that cover them. Lighted principally by the clearstory, the walls glow in the dim interior with a mild inner light all their own, illuminated as they are by scenes from the life of St. Francis. More than anything else, it is these murals that bring the twin churches their most special distinction, and the names of the artists who worked on them read like a roster of the great painters of the period— Cimabue, Simone Martini, Pietro Lorenzetti, and, above all, the great Giotto, who came here presumably in his early maturity. All the frescoes are fitted so admirably into the architectonic design that each is free to make its individual contribution. The general effect is that of giving the walls, arches, vaulting, and ceiling such a wealth of brilliant colors and such a variety of forms that they can convincingly convey all of the glowing warmth of the human message they are designed to carry.

GIOTTO'S FRESCOES ON THE LIFE OF ST. FRANCIS

On entering the nave of the Upper Church (Fig. 8:3), the observer encounters on its walls the series of frescoes on the life of St. Francis that tradition has ascribed to Giotto. The date generally assigned to the work is the four-year span just before the jubilee year of 1300. Knowing that pilgrims would be traveling to Rome in unprecedented numbers, the artists made every effort to have the bare walls of the new church covered with appropriate decoration. Unlike France, Italy had never been noted for its stained glass, and the architectural design at Assisi makes it clear that this medium was never intended to play a major role. Sculpture in this period was used mainly for such interior embellishments as pulpits, altars, choir screens, and the carving of columns. Mosaic work was still a possibility, but it progressed extremely slowly and its materials were rare and costly. Fresco painting, on the other hand, being both rapid and inexpensive, was the obvious choice for the decorative scheme of St. Francis' basilica.

Giotto, like other master artists of his time, had learned to work in a variety of techniques. In addition to that in the fresco medium, he is known to have executed mosaics and to have painted in the mode favored for altar pieces: tempera on wood. He also was a sculptor, and several years before his death, his renown brought him the distinction of being named the chief architect of the city of Florence. It was in this capacity that he designed the bell tower of the cathedral there (Fig. 9:1), though he lived long enough to see only its lower story completed. Even though the plans were altered after his death, this campanile is still called Giotto's Tower. Some of the sculptured reliefs on the ground-floor level may have been from his hand, and others were presumably carried out from his designs by Andrea Pisano. His greatest present fame, however, rests most securely on the three fresco cycles that survive in Assisi, Padua, and Florence.

The fresco medium calls for the rapid and deft strokes of a sure hand, and for designs that harmonize with the architectural scheme, yet bring to it a certain warmth of expression which awakens the static walls into a vibrant and colorful life of their own. The artist must first make his drawing on the dry plaster of the wall. Then, taking an area he can finish in a single day, he spreads a thin coat of wet plaster over the dry, making it necessary to retrace the lines underneath. Earth pigments are then mixed with water, combined with white of egg as a binder, and applied directly to the fresh plaster—hence the term *fresco*. The pigments and wet plaster combine

Fig. 8:3. Upper Church of St. Francis, *Interior*. Assisi (Alinari)

chemically to produce a surface as permanent as that of any medium in painting. Artists sometimes paint over the surface after it is dry, but this repainting usually flakes off in time. If corrections are necessary, the whole surface must be scraped off and the section redone. Fresco, then, is a medium which does not encourage overly subtle types of expression; and it is best adapted to a certain monumentality of utterance, simplicity of composition, and an emphasis on linear elements rather than on the comparatively limited range of possible colors. All this was recognized by Giotto and incorporated into the style of his cycles, which for emotional depth, communicative value, and masterly execution rank with the highest achievements in world art.

Tradition and the historians are generally agreed that the first two of the series of panels at Assisi are from the hand of Giotto himself. Since, however, he worked with a corps of assistants, it is impossible to be completely certain which of the individual panels were done by him and which belong to his school. On the right, after passing through the entrance portals, the *Miracle of the Spring* (Fig. 8:4) is found, while opposite to it on the left appears the well-known *Sermon to the Birds*. The order of the scenes is psychological rather than chronological, and it seems that Giotto must have placed this pair nearest to the entrance in order to impress the entering pilgrims at the outset with the essence of the Franciscan legend. This would explain the appearance at this point of the representations showing the ministrations of the saint to the poor and humble on one side, and his kinship with all God's creatures, including his brothers the birds, on the other.

Giotto's series is based principally on the biography of St. Francis by St. Bonaventura, though the source for the *Miracle of the Spring* is found in an incident in the travels of the saint in the *Legend of the Three Companions*. In order to get to the monastery at Monte La Verna, St. Francis and two of his companions had to enlist the help of a poor peasant and his donkey. Since the weather was hot and dry and the difficult road led through such barren mountains, the peasant was overcome with thirst. When he could bear it no longer, he cried out that he would surely die if he could not find some water to drink. St. Francis then knelt in prayer and turning to the peasant, he said: "Hasten to that rock and thou shalt find a living water which in pity Christ hath sent thee from the stone to drink." The implication is clear that the thirst was not physical only, and the entering pilgrim was thus reminded that he had at last arrived at a living spring of the spirit where his deeper longings could be satisfied.

Giotto's composition is as simple as it is masterly. The figure of St. Francis, clothed in the habit of his order, is the focal center. Beyond him

Fig. 8:4. Giotto. *Miracle of the Spring*. Fresco. *c*.1296–1300. Upper Church of St. Francis, Assisi (Alinari)

are two rocky peaks; the one behind him is in shadow, and the one before which he raises his arms in prayer is bathed in glowing light. Descending diagonally downward in a series of planes, the light conforms to the contours of the mountain until it reaches its greatest intensity around his head where it unites with his halo. In the shadow of the saint are his two companions and the donkey, who are also in line with the direction of the descending light. The dark figure of the peasant, who is slaking his thirst at the spring on the lower right, is counterbalanced by the shadowy mountainside at the upper left. The implication is that he is still in spiritual darkness, but since St. Francis is also on this diagonal line the way toward enlightenment is suggested.

The picture contains one of Giotto's inimitable mountains, which are also found in so many of his major compositions, such as *Joachim Returning to the Sheepfold*, the *Flight into Egypt*, and the great *Pietà* from the series in the Arena Chapel in Padua. In each case the mountains are not represented so much in their own right but as extensions of human nature in its relationship with the divine. The mountains are always on intimate terms with the figures they support, and in this picture they speak to the spectator and suggest that he ponder on the meaning of the miraculous event, just as the two monks are conversing and looking quizzically at each other. Giotto's proportions are psychologically rather than actually correct. Human figures in keeping with their expressive importance loom large in relation to the mountains; and his scattered trees are likewise placed so as to suggest spaciousness rather than representations of natural trees that would be seen in such a locality. By the jagged contours of the mountains, as well as by the judicious use of light and shade, Giotto is able to bring out the volume and mass that his figures need to bring them to life and make them a tangible reality.

The opposite panel, the *Sermon to the Birds*, is less dramatic and more lyrical. The incident, taken from St. Bonaventura's life of the saint, is the one in which the birds hovered around St. Francis, perched in the bushes and inclined their heads as he addressed them in this wise: "My brothers the birds, much ought ye to praise your Creator, who hath clothed you with feathers and given you wings to fly, and hath made over unto you the pure air and careth for you without your taking thought for yourselves." [3] Again the hand of the master reveals itself in the depth of the expressive meaning and the utter economy of means employed to convey it. Balanced by the massive stylized tree on the right, the two human figures contrast interestingly with each other. While St. Francis himself is intent on the birds and his hands are raised in a gesture of blessing, those of his less-

Fig. 8:5. Giotto. *St. Francis Renouncing His Father*. Fresco. *c.*1296–1300. Upper Church of St. Francis, Assisi (Alinari)

inspired companion are lifted as if to say that the limits of human toleration have been reached, and he appears quite ready to shoo his little feathered brothers right out of the picture. The ravages of time and the work of numerous restorers have taken their toll of Giotto's work; but in spite of all this, the expressive message of the picture comes through with unobstructed clarity.

Of the entire series at Assisi the one which contains the most poignant human drama is that of *St. Francis Renouncing His Father* (Fig. 8:5). The scene described by St. Bonaventura is that in which the young St. Francis has been brought before the bishop of the city by his exasperated father "that he might resign his claims unto his father's inheritance and render up all that had been his." Francis in his haste to abandon the material world has cast off all his garments restoring them to his father and stood up naked before everyone saying: "Until this hour I have called thee my father upon earth; from henceforth, I may say confidently, my Father who art in Heaven, in whose hands I have laid up all my treasure, all my trust, and all my hope." The bishop, continues St. Bonaventura, "seeing this, and marvelling at such exceeding fervour in the man of God, rose forthwith and weeping put his arms around him; then, devout and kindly man as he was, he covered him with the cloak wherewith he was clad, bidding his servants give him something to clothe his limbs." [4]

Such a scene in lesser hands could easily have become melodramatic, maudlin, or downright ridiculous; but Giotto's sense of drama is equal to his task. The father, wishing to resort to physical violence in order to discourage his son, has to be restrained by a bystander. Yet his face still shows the puzzled concern of a fond parent for a wayward son whose ideas and behavior he cannot understand. By portraying him sympathetically Giotto reveals the father's inner conflict in having to renounce his high hopes for his son's worldly success. The figure of this antagonist of the drama is balanced by that of the bishop who symbolically becomes the new father of the saint in the Church. Like all administrators he dislikes such a showdown; and, as he glances around, he betrays his embarrassment, confusion, and sympathy. These parallel figures are reinforced on one side by the house in the background with its flight of steps, and by the crowd of townspeople; while the two monks and the church architecture, symbolic of the house of God, support the other. Between them the figure of the saint is shown now wholly on the side of the Church. As his hand reaches upward in an attitude of prayer, it is answered by the descending hand of God which reaches downward from the top of the picture. Although many have criticized the composition unfavorably, the very twofold division that is

Fig. 8:6. Giotto. *Death of St. Francis*. Fresco. *c.*1320. Bardi Chapel, Church of Santa Croce, Florence (Anderson)

thought to deprive the picture of unity is its greatest dramatic asset. The cleavage of the world of the flesh and that of the spirit, the pursuit of material and spiritual ends, the worship of Mammon and of God, are most forcefully brought out by this very means. The horizontal tensions of the two divided groups below is resolved vertically in the formation of a triangle, based on the two groups below, which moves upward through the gesture of St. Francis and reaches its apex with the hand of God above. Even if the means are a bit naïve, possibly even crude, it is doubtful that the full force of the inner drama could have been externalized in clearer or more direct visual terms.

A notable example of Giotto's late style is found in the *Death of St. Francis* (Fig. 8:6). It is the climax of a series of seven he did 20 years later for the Church of Santa Croce in Florence. In spite of the hands of many restorers, Giotto's conception and design still assure the picture a place among the highest achievements of the Renaissance. The time is the exact moment of death; the place, according to St. Bonaventura, is in the courtyard of the

Franciscan monastery in Assisi. No motion is seen in the recumbent body, and its serene and static form gives the picture its unity. All the curved lines formed by the garments and gestures of the five surrounding groups converge on the head of St. Francis, the focal center of the drama. The architectural framework echoes the grouping of the human figures, and likewise serves to make the picture seem as a legitimate part of the wall that it decorates. The portals surmounted by gables on either side serve as a kind of architectural counterpoint to the side groups. The horizontal lines of the back wall parallel those of the body of the saint, while the upright lines support the standing and kneeling figures. These predominantly horizontal and vertical lines are tempered somewhat by the diagonal of the crucifix, which is held in the hands of the group on the right side. The suggestion of depth is conveyed by means of the color, which unfortunately cannot be seen in the reproduction. The robe of the kneeling nobleman is a rich red, which projects it into the foreground, while the color of the sky over the wall of the courtyard is a receding dark blue. The other figures are clothed in neutral browns and grays, which keeps them rather statically in the middleground. The formal organization in this way is geared closely to the expressive intent, and the emotional element is tied in with the linear rhythm. By such discreet means, Giotto is able to achieve a dignified restraint in keeping with the passing of one of the immortals.

The description of St. Francis' death in St. Bonaventura's biography holds the key to the drama of Giotto's picture. "At length," he wrote, "when all the mysteries had been fulfilled in him, and his most holy spirit was freed from the flesh, and absorbed into the boundless depth of the divine glory, the blessed man fell on sleep in the Lord. One of his brethren and disciples saw that blessed soul, under the likeness of a star exceeding bright borne on a dazzling cloudlet over many waters, mounting in a straight curve unto heaven. . . . " [5] The dramatic tension is thus heightened by means of the serene form terminating in the haloed head below and the transcendent vision full of freedom and movement above. As in St. Bonaventura's account, the observer beholds the vision through the eyes of the disciple in back of the saint's head. His hand carries the eye upward toward the celestial journey, while all the other figures are bowed low by their grief in taking leave of their friend and master. The triangle formed by the glance and gesture of the one who sees the vision on one side, and the line of the crucifix on the other, meeting as they do in the apex of the heavenly journey, complete the linear pattern and bring its expressive aspirations within the limits of Giotto's comprehensible space.

THE BLACK DEATH AND ITS AFTERMATH

All went well in Italy during the first third of the 14th century. The towns-people prospered, life was good, the arts flourished, and few were struck by the pangs of moral recrimination. Beginning in 1340, however, a series of disasters befell the peninsula, starting with local crop failures and continuing with the miseries of famine and pestilence. The climax came in a fearful outbreak of bubonic plague in the catastrophic year of 1348. In this so-called Black Death more than half the populations of such cities as Florence, Siena, and Pisa perished. A chronicler of Siena, after burying five of his children with his own hands, said quite simply: "No one wept for the dead, because everyone expected death himself." [6]

An event so cataclysmic, and one which spread over the entire continent, was bound to have a deep effect upon social and cultural trends. Many survivors found themselves suddenly impoverished or, through unexpected inheritances, vastly enriched. Thousands of residents in the relatively immune countryside flocked into the cities to take the place of those who had died. The psychological effect on the individual lives of the people was to quicken their normal instincts. The "eat, drink, and be merry" philosophy, exemplified so well in Boccaccio's *Decameron*, gained ascendancy on one side; while an intense religious preoccupation and outburst of piety, as seen in the purgatorial vision of the same author's later *Corbaccio*, took place on the other. Driven by fear and a sense of guilt, people took the general viewpoint that something had gone disastrously wrong and the Black Death, like the Biblical plagues of old, must have been sent by an angry God to chastise mankind and turn him from his wicked ways. Both Boccaccio and Petrarch among the literary men took this view, and what was true of literature was true also of painting. It can readily be seen that this image of God was diametrically opposed to that of the loving deity projected in the Franciscan ideal.

The attitude before and after the Black Death is sharply illustrated at Pisa, which was the scene in the late 13th and 14th centuries of some important architectural, sculptural, and pictorial developments. The Cathedral of Pisa and its campanile (Fig. 6:10), the famous leaning tower, both date from Romanesque times. The Baptistry and Campo Santo, which complete the group, are from the late 13th century. The Campo Santo (Fig. 8:7), literally a holy field and functionally a burial place, was designed and built by Giovanni Pisano in the form of a Gothic cloister.

The garth, or open courtyard, derived much fame at the time because its soil was from Mount Calvary, which was brought by the shipload from Palestine.

In addition to his architectural activities, Giovanni and his father, Niccolo, were the two outstanding sculptors of their time. Niccolo Pisano, who is often called Nicola d'Apulia because of his southern Italian origin, designed a handsome pulpit for the Baptistry while his son Giovanni some years later executed one for the Cathedral. Both contain panels depicting scenes from the New Testament. The differing attitudes of their respective generations can be discovered when panels dealing with the same subject are placed side by side; while together, their work as a whole contrasts even more strongly with the period after the Black Death.

Niccolo's panel of the *Annunciation and Nativity* (Fig. 8:8) is clearly influenced by the ancient sarcophagi the sculptor knew from his formative years which were spent near Rome. The Virgin appears as a dignified Roman matron reclining in a characteristic classical pose, while the angel at the left in the Annunciation section is dressed in a Roman toga. Niccolo employs the old simultaneous mode of narration, with the Virgin making three appearances on the same panel; and the relief as a whole is dominated by a monumental calm. Giovanni's work, as evidenced by his *Nativity and Annunciation to the Shepherds* (Fig. 8:9), moved away from his father's classicism into the French Gothic orbit. His figures are smaller in scale and are related more naturally to their spatial environment. Greater animation

Fig. 8:7. *Campo Santo.* 1278–1283. Pisa

Fig. 8:8 (above). Niccolo Pisano. *Annunciation and Nativity*. Marble. *c*.1260. Fig. 8:9 (below). Giovanni Pisano. *Nativity and Annunciation to the Shepherds*. Marble. *c*.1310. Details of Cathedral Pulpit, Pisa (Alinari)

Fig. 8:10. Traini (?). *Triumph of Death*, Left Half. Fresco. *c*.1350. Campo Santo, Pisa (Alinari)

and movement replace the repose of his father's style. The work of both father and son, however, is permeated by a sense of human warmth that relates their panels closely to the spirit of Giotto's frescoes.

After the Black Death of 1348, however, the Campo Santo that Giovanni built was decorated by a series of fresco murals on the theme of the Last Judgment. The *Triumph of Death* (Figs. 8:10–11) took its name from the later poem of Petrarch. While no cause-and-effect relationship between picture and poem can be proved, both were reactions to the plague, both shared certain common attitudes of the time, and both were based on a similar theme. The picture has been attributed to several painters including Pietro Lorenzetti and Orcagna, but it is now believed to have been done about the year 1350 by an artist active in Pisa at that time by the name of Francesco Traini.

Fig. 8:11. Traini (?). *Triumph of Death*, Right Half. Fresco. *c.*1350. Campo Santo, Pisa (Alinari)

The *Triumph of Death* is a grandiose utterance, obviously painted for a large and heterogeneous audience, with so much detail crowded into every square inch of its composition that there was bound to be something in it that would appeal to everybody. Like so many sermons of the time, each part warned of the imminence of death, the terrors of hell if the soul were claimed by the devil, or the relative bliss of being carried off by the angels. The latter process, however, seemed to be anything but peaceful, since the flying devils contend furiously with the hovering angels over the spirits of the dead that are represented as nude forms. The tug of war over the soul of the fat monk on the right side above the scene in the pleasure garden is a typical example. When the demons win, they cast their victims into the flames of the open volcano at the top. What happens to the ones saved by the angels is left to the imagination.

Death is represented in the hideous guise of a blond woman flying on enormous bat's wings and carrying a scythe like Father Time. She passes over the miserable creatures in the lower center who cry out to be relieved of their intolerable sufferings. Instead she is about to swoop down on the group of ten figures in the prime of their lives, who are reading, conversing, and enjoying the delights of the world. Everything dies in her wake, as seen in the piles of corpses beneath her; and the next two victims are being pointed out by the black-winged angels of death who hover above the two on the left of the group. One is a youth holding a falcon and the other a maiden fondling a dog in her lap. In Petrarch's poem, Death is also represented by a feminine form and the description of the scene has some similarity.

> A lady clothed in black, whose stern looks were
> With horror fill'd, and did like hell appear,
> Advanced, as said, "You who are proud to be
> So fair and young, yet have no eyes to see
> How near you are your end; behold, I am
> She whom they fierce and blind and cruel name,
> Who meet untimely deaths; . . ."[7]

The similarity of the group in the pleasure garden to that in Boccaccio's *Decameron* seems too close to be a coincidence. The book has to do with ten well-to-do young Florentines who escape from the plague, which is ravaging the city, to a country villa where they entertain themselves with lively tales, music, and dancing. As in the *Decameron*, the group in the fresco is composed of seven women and three men; all are animated by a vivacious spirit; and, as the description in Boccaccio's introduction goes: "Breakfast done, the tables were removed, and the queen bade fetch instruments of music; for all, ladies and young men alike, knew how to tread a measure, and some of them played and sang with great skill. So, at her command, Dioneo having taken a lute, and Fiametta a viol, they struck up a dance in sweet concert; . . ."[8] The resemblance of the group, even to those on the far right who are playing the musical instruments, points to the fact that the painter must have had the *Decameron* in mind when he designed his fresco.

In the lower left, a group of mounted nobles are equipped for the chase, but instead of the quarry they are pursuing, they find only the prey of death. Inside the three open coffins serpents are consuming the corpses of the onetime great of the earth. As Petrarch asks in his poem: "the Popes, Emperors, nor Kings, no ensigns wore of their past hight but naked show'd and poor. Where be their riches, where their precious gems. Their miters, scepters, robes and diadems?" [9] Hard by is a bearded monk unfolding a prophetic scroll on which is inscribed a warning for them to repent before it is too late. The only relief from this scene of utter horror and desolation is found in the upper left where a few monks are gathered around a chapel busying themselves with the usual monastic occupations. The implication is that only those who live such secluded lives can find respite from the general turmoil; and the terror of death can be avoided only by those who imitate them.

It is noteworthy that the space allotted to the tortures of hell by Giotto in his *Last Judgment* at Padua is held to an irreducible minimum. In Traini's mural and in the others which were done after the Black Plague, the stark horror is relieved only by such occasional tranquil scenes as the monastery chapel. The attitude is quite opposed to the milder, more humanistic spirit of Giotto. Traini's design, furthermore, is as complex and overwhelmed with minute detail as Giotto's are simple. In addition, Traini burdens his mural with an elaborate allegory that reaches out beyond the pictorial medium. The two angels behind the figure of Death, for instance, unfold a written scroll; the miserable ones petition Death in writing as well as in gesture; and the monk warning the hunting party does so with an inscription. These burdensome details weigh the picture down with a heaviness quite foreign to Giotto's buoyant work, and more often they succeed in obscuring than in clarifying the expressive intent.

MUSIC AND LITERATURE

The *Dies Irae* and the *Canticle of the Sun*

The contrast between the dour, threatening medieval church attitude and the benign, joyful Franciscan view is illustrated by two 13th-century hymns. The facts of their composition alone are sufficient to point out the ideational cleavage of the period. The *Dies Irae*, which so admirably reflects the prevailing medieval spirit, was written by the great Latin stylist Thomas of Celano a few years before he met St. Francis. The second, the *Canticle of the Sun*, is by St. Francis himself. Thomas of Celano entered the Franciscan order about the year 1215, enjoyed the friendship of St. Francis for several years, and was entrusted by Pope Gregory IX with the official biography that was written shortly after the saint's death and canonization.

In the triple stanzas and 51 lines of the *Dies Irae*, the medieval Latin poetic style reaches its highest point. Its content invokes the vision of the final dissolution of the universe, the sounding of the angelic trumpets calling the dead forth from their tombs, and the overwhelming majesty of the coming of Christ as king to judge the quick and the dead. The grandeur of its language and the perfection of its poetic form are in every way equal to this solemn and awesome theme. The images and moods run a wide gamut from anger and terror to hope and glimpses of celestial beauty before coming to a close with a final supplication for eternal rest. Sir Walter Scott incorporated a part of the *Dies Irae* in his *Lay of the Last Minstrel*, but since his poem was based on a different metrical and rhyming scheme, he sacrificed the form of the original while preserving its content:

> That day of wrath, that dreadful day,
> When heaven and earth shall pass away,
> What power shall be the sinner's stay?
> How shall he meet that dreadful day?
>
> When, shrivelling like a parched scroll,
> The flaming heavens together roll;
> When louder yet, and yet more dread,
> Swells the high trump that wakes the dead,
>
> Oh! on that day, that wrathful day,
> When man to judgment wakes from clay,
> Be THOU the trembling sinner's stay,
> Though heaven and earth shall pass away.[10]

While the colorful alliterations and verbal rhythms of the Latin original have a music all their own, the *Dies Irae* is inseparable from a melodic setting in the mixed Dorian mode. While the melody cannot with certainty be attributed to Thomas of Celano himself, the close correspondence of tone and word makes it definite that they were at least from the same time.

Dies Irae (Sequence from the early 13th century)   Thomas of Celano

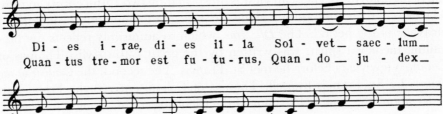

Both the poem and its melody eventually found their way into the liturgy as a sequence, where it is still an indispensable part of the Requiem

Mass for the Dead. Sequences are so named because they follow the Gradual and Alleluia in the part of the Mass between the reading of the Epistle and the Gospel. They attained wide popularity during this period and were usually sung by both the congregation and the choir.

The most characteristic Franciscan contribution to poetry and music is found in a body of informal spontaneous hymns called *laudi spirituali*—that is, songs of praise, or simply lauds. The inception of this form is traceable directly to St. Francis himself and his immediate circle. Since the composers of these lauds were almost exclusively from the ranks of Franciscan monks, it is to all intents and purposes a Franciscan movement. The practice continued from his time onward and was firmly established as the most popular form of religious music in the 14th century. Singing societies known as the *Compagnie dei Laudesi*, literally companies of laudists, have existed mainly in Italy up to the present time. St. Francis learned Provençal French as well as the songs of that region from his mother, who came from an old Provence family. The biography known as the *Legend of the Three Companions* relates how he sang aloud the lauds and canticles while praying, and how during his travels "the holy man sang praises in French with a voice loud and clear."

Since this was the great period of the lyrical poetry of the troubadours, and since many of the best known of these poets visited Italy in his time, it is certain that St. Francis was well acquainted with their lyrics and music. By his knowledge of the forms of these Provençal poets, and by his practice of bursting into rhapsodic verse in his own vernacular Italian dialect, he played a leading role in the new poetic movement. It is also significant that he called himself and his companions who sang the lauds with him, *jongleurs de dieu*, or minstrels of God, thus identifying himself with the performing musicians of the people rather than with the aristocratic writers of amorous verse.

St. Francis, in music as in his religious work, drew the sacred, courtly, and popular traditions closer together. The lauds were thus a kind of poetic bridge between the traditional music of the church, the music of the castle, and the music of the streets. The words always had a religious theme; often they were mere paraphrases of psalms and litanies sung to popular airs. They were, above all, music and poetry that the people could both sing and feel with their hearts. Contrapuntal choral music, whether it was in the form of a church motet or a secular madrigal, was a sophisticated musical medium that needed the voices of skilled musicians. By contrast the lauds were folklike in spirit, simple and direct in their appeal, and sung either as solos or jointly with others in unison. Just as the highly trained monastic choir was characteristic of the Cluniac movement and the contrapuntal chorus the musical counterpart of the northern Gothic spirit, the lauds were the special expression of the Franciscans.

The *Canticle of the Sun*, known definitely to be by St. Francis himself, is at once the most sublime of all the lauds as well as the most original. The legend goes that when St. Francis was recovering from an illness in a hut outside the convent of St. Clare, the nuns heard from his lips this rapturous new song. The informality, even casualness of its composition, its rambling rhythms and rhymes, all make it as simple and unaffected in its form as the Umbrian dialect in which it is written. It is thus characteristically opposed to the canons of scholarly Latin on one hand and to the erotic courtly utterances of the troubadours on the other. Sincerity and deep human feeling dominate its unequal strophes rather than any attempt at learned communication or poetic elegance.

> Altissimu, onnipotente, bon signore, tue so' le laude la gloria
> e l'onore, et onne benedizione a te solu, altissimu, se konfanno
> a nullu homo ene dignu to mentovare!

> O most high, almighty, good Lord God, to Thee belong praise, glory,
> honor, and all blessing!

> Praised be my Lord God with all his creatures, and especially our
> brother the sun, who brings us the day and who brings us the
> light; fair is he and shines with very great splendor; O Lord,
> he signifies to us Thee!

> Praised be my Lord for our sister the moon, and for the stars, the
> which He has set clear and lovely in heaven.

> Praised be my Lord for our sister water, who is very serviceable
> unto us and humble and precious and clean.

> Praised be my Lord for our brother fire, through whom thou givest
> us light in the darkness; and he is bright and pleasant and
> very mighty and strong.

> Praised be my Lord for our mother the earth, the which doth sustain us
> and keep us, and bringeth forth divers fruits and flowers of
> many colors, and grass.[11]

The Assisi manuscript that contains the words of the *Canticle of the Sun* in its purest form also has space provided for musical notation, which is, alas, blank. While the melody seems to have been lost forever, a vast body of lauds does, however, survive, some of which date back to shortly after St. Francis' time. A Franciscan monk by the name of Jacopone da Todi, who died in 1306, was one of the most prolific producers of lauds. His most famous hymn is the *Stabat Mater Dolorosa*, which, along with the *Dies Irae*, was one of the four sequences to be retained in the official liturgy after the reforms of the Council of Trent in the 16th century. In both cases their retention was based not only on their inherent beauty but also on the deep hold they had on the people. This remarkable man, like St. Francis before him, was of Umbrian origin; and, after a succession of diverse careers as a lawyer, a hermit, a Franciscan preacher, he turned poet and composer. His hymns readily found their way into the texts of the early miracle plays, and his music became the foundation of the laudistic tradition. The following example is a part of one of his lauds, which continues in the form of a dialogue. Its emotional intensity, as well as its stylistic character, marks it as typical of the early Franciscan movement.

Lauda (Late 13th century)

Jacopone da Todi
(After F. Liuzzi)

O Chri-sto' ni-po - ten - te, Do - ve sie-te __ in-vi - a - to, Che

si po-ve - ra - men - te ____ Gi - te_pel-le - gri - na-to?

Dante's *Divine Comedy*

In the early years of the 14th century, a synthesis of the divergent intellectual viewpoints and emotional orientations was not only attempted but carried through to triumphant completion. Dante Alighieri in his *Divine Comedy* wrote at one stroke not only the greatest book of the Middle Ages but a work containing also many of the germinal ideas of the future. At one and the same time he also established Italian as a modern literary language and endowed his country with its most enduring literary masterpiece. The *Divine Comedy* is not only a synthesis of scholasticism and the Franciscan viewpoints but of the whole thought of the Middle Ages and of Greco-Roman antiquity as its author knew it. Classical figures, such as Aristotle, Vergil, Ovid, and Cicero, rub shoulders in the course of its pages with Boethius, St. Thomas Aquinas, and St. Francis.

The form of the poem is laden with medieval mathematical symbolism, with the mystical number 3 serving as a kind of motive in honor of the Trinity. His stanzas each have three verses; the rhyming scheme is the beautiful *terza rima;* one time after another, Dante is terrified by three animals; in each case he is saved by the mediation of three holy women; he is in turn piloted on his travels by three guides; the whole poem is divided into three parts, Hell, Purgatory, and Heaven; each section of the poem contains 33 cantos, the number of Christ's years on earth; and finally the introductory canto, when added to the thrice 33 others brings the total to an even 100, that number having as its mystical property the quality of wholeness or completion.

In spite of the heavy burden of number theory and other scholastic baggage—discourses on the laws of planetary motion, civil and canon law, medieval science, dialectical argumentation, and allegorical meanings, such as that of Vergil representing reason and Beatrice inspiration—Dante is far from an orthodox scholastic thinker. If he were, he would have written a treatise in the learned Latin instead of a poem in the vernacular Tuscan Italian. No scholarly discourse ever began with the announcement: "the style is careless and humble, because it is in the vulgar tongue, in which even housewives hold converse." [12] The revolutionary nature of this linguistic departure is almost impossible for the modern reader to understand. But in Dante's time literature was a possession of the learned few who possessed an adequate knowledge of Latin. All those who read any poetry, philosophy, or history in effect had to do so in a foreign language. Even so, Dante's progress through the Inferno, Purgatory, and Paradise is not an easy one to follow, either for him or for the reader. The path is hard and rough, and its obscurity is at least partially owing to the multiple doubts and conflicts of the time. That it was also difficult for those who lived much closer to Dante's time is proved by the fact that lecturers began giving courses on it in the Italian universities soon after the poet was dead.

For all its carefully worked out form, and in spite of the presence of a cross section of all the scientific knowledge of the late Middle Ages, the *Divine Comedy* is neither learned, elegant, nor aristocratic. It is, in fact, obscure, unpolished, and abrupt. It is also so complex that no one key, whether that of theology, metaphysics, philosophy, or politics, will open the door to its understanding. In contrast with the philosophical writings of the time, it mixes its subjects at times to the point of jumbled confusion. References to local politics of the day are found side by side with glimpses into the beauty of Paradise; the names of unknown inhabitants of the places Dante visited are placed beside those of the immortals; crude gossip and old wives' tales are in the company of the scientific knowledge of the period. Hell and heaven, faith and reason, events of the past and present, prophecy and history, paganism and Christianity, and the world of Greece and Rome together with that of the Middle Ages are all present in its pages. The mass of detail is kept from marring the greatness of the poem only by the vast conception of the whole, which tends to throw the multiplicity of its parts into proper perspective. Compensation for this erstwhile confusion is found in the incomparable beauty of its language, so much of which is lost in translation. Dante, like Giotto, possessed the gift of making his characters live by just a few deft strokes. Like St. Francis', his allegories are not mere riddles for the learned doctors but lively tales for the untutored.

Dante also has the expert painter's eye for the minute details of appearances. One instance of the richness of his imagery can be illustrated by his sensitivity to the medium of light. His verses delight the ear with a music of their own, but his images of light are a feast for the inner eye of the imagination. It is primarily a spiritual light which concerns him, but he conjures up its vision in familiar everyday impressions filtered through the mind's eye of a great poet. He sings of sunlight, firelight, starlight; the sparkle of precious stones; the gleaming rays of a lamp in the darkness; the translucent effects of light filtered through water, glass, and jewels; rainbows and the colored reflections from clouds; the ruddy glow of infernal flames and the pure unearthly radiance of Paradise; the light of the human eye and that of the haloes surrounding the heads of the saints; and finally each one of the three sections of the poem closes on the word "stars."

In spite of the preponderance of so many medieval elements, Dante also achieves much that is associated with the Renaissance viewpoint. For all its mathematical structure, the *Divine Comedy* is full of violent human storms, passionate outbursts on the unnecessary wickedness of those in high places of power, and a general reassertion of the role of emotion in human affairs. For all his austerity, remoteness, and unapproachability, Dante does not pronounce a stern and final judgment. The very title would preclude this, because in his conception, "Comedy, indeed, beginneth with some adverse circumstances, but its theme hath a happy termination. . . ." [13] Dante further specifically states that the didactic purpose of his poem is "to remove those living in this life from a state of misery and to guide them to a state of happiness." [14] He uniformly writes with an unbounded faith in humanity, and when he relates the punishments meted out to those who suffer in his Inferno, it is with the practical moral purpose of correcting such worldly evils as simony, usury, and avarice that he saw being practiced in the world as he knew it. It is important to point out that Dante did not write only the Inferno—a general impression derived from the fact that most readers seldom get past the first section and that the romantic 19th-century writers took this part to be the whole. His hell, however, shares its space line for line with that of his Purgatory and Heaven.

Dante's vision was thus not purely of the other world in the medieval sense as much as it was with the course of life as he saw it, beginning as it did in original sin, but having within it the capacity of progressing through the purification of the purgatory of experience, to a knowledge of ineffable goodness as perceived in the beatific vision of Paradise. This dynamic spiritual journey is full of quite unmedieval motions and emotions. After plunging with Dante into the bowels of the earth, the reader makes an upward ascent through the infernal regions on the back of Satan to the mountain of Purgatory, and finally into the metaphysical stratosphere of the various stages of Heaven. Civilization likewise, as Dante saw it, had struggled upward from the pagan world of Greece and Rome to the theocratic foundations of the medieval world, which rested on an all-powerful Church and its secular counterpart, the Holy Roman Empire. It is a vertical and dynamic concept representing the ascent of humanity from the depths to the heights, from darkness into the light.

IDEAS

The opposing forces that the Gothic 13th century had managed to maintain in a state of uneasy equilibrium, by the application of scholastic logic and strict structurality, in the 14th century broke out into open conflict. The result can be seen in the crisis within the Church; in the social struggle between the new cities and the old landed aristocracy; in the incompatibility of Gothic architecture and the sunny landscape of Italy; in the presence of medieval devils and real human types in Giotto's frescoes; in the opposing visions of the Inferno and Paradise in the *Divine Comedy*; in the attitudes expressed in poetry and painting before and after the Black Death; in Petrarch's curious blend of Gothic chivalry and his interest in the literature of ancient Rome; in his indecision whether to write in Latin or in the vernacular Italian; and in his earlier sensuous love sonnets to Laura and his later moralistic dialogue with the ghost of St. Augustine in the *Secret*.

The deep-seated nature of the conflict is found even more dramatically in the struggle raging within the minds and consciences of individual men than in the arguments between consistent champions of opposing points of view. In the course of his own life, for instance, St. Francis combined an other-worldly pattern of self-denial with an obvious this-worldly love of natural beauty. Fire for him was not created so much for the fearful purpose of roasting the souls of sinners in hell as it was to give light in the darkness and warmth on a cold night. He found evidence of God's goodness everywhere—in the radiance of the sun, in the eternal miracle of the growth of grass and flowers in the spring. The synthesis for him was that all these diverse phenomena were revelations of divinity, and his frank pantheism foreshadowed a departure from the extreme medieval dualism based on the rigid opposition of flesh and spirit. After a lifetime of mortification of the body, he renounced his asceticism by humbly begging the pardon of his brother the body. Boccaccio, on the other hand, went so far in the other direction that after 1360 he disavowed his joyous *Decameron* and tried to dispose of his great library because it contained so many pagan books.

The 14th century thus straddles the medieval world on one side and that of the Renaissance on the other. Looking in one direction it seems to be a culmination of certain tendencies present during the late Middle Ages; while looking in the other, it seems to anticipate many of the ideas of the Renaissance. The breakdown of medieval authoritarianism is seen in the growth of naturalism; and the tendency away from an other-worldly focus to a this-worldly approach is apparent in the rise of humanism. It is most important, however, to distinguish between the 14th-century naturalism, which is largely an outgrowth of a late Gothic idea, and its more scientific equivalent in the 15th century; and between Franciscan humanism and its more classically oriented counterpart in the later Renaissance.

Naturalism

The abstractions of the scholastic mind found a new challenge in the concretions of the group of philosophers who called themselves nominalists. Late scholasticism had, in fact, become more and more a strained exercise in logical gymnastics, and its forms all too often took flight from the facts that are so necessary to give substance to thought. The nominalists tried to turn the scholastic processes of thought completely upside down. They insisted that generalities are built up from the plurality of individual objects, whereas scholasticism, by beginning with a hypothetical proposition or eternal Platonic idea, had derived the facts of the phenomenal world from it. To use the language of the schoolmen themselves, the scholastics reasoned *a priori*, while the nominalists did so *a posteriori;* one started from premises *ante rem* and the other from propositions *in re;* or, to put it more simply, one reasoned *before* and the other *after* the fact. These systems of thought approximate the difference between deductive and inductive logic, the latter being the basis of the empirical method of modern science. This nominalist viewpoint, as it gained momentum, actually meant the breakdown of medieval authoritarianism, in which the word of Aristotle and the church fathers was accepted without question, and the beginning of the modern practice of getting facts from first-hand observation. The result of this new mental orientation was a renewed interest in a tangible reality that was to have quite as important consequences in the world of art as it did in the realm of scientific inquiry. In the next century it led to the formation of the mathematical laws of linear perspective, to the representation of the human body according to anatomical observations and mathematical measurements, and to the establishment of the modern harmonic basis of music.

This formidable philosophical feud went hand in hand with the rise of the new Franciscan world view. The decline of authoritarianism was partially owing to St. Francis' conception of religion as a voluntary, spontaneous relationship between God and man which was based on love rather than fear; and in the search for a common bond between man and his fellowmen. It was essentially a shift from the vertical organization of society, in which men in the hierarchical sense were related by ever-higher degrees of authority, to a system of horizontally oriented ethical relationships that bound every man to his fellowmen. The joy St. Francis took in the tangible evidences of the love of God for man, seen in such things as the fruits and flowers of the earth, were to have great consequences on the course of art. The birds St. Francis preached to, for instance, were the kind that were heard chirping and singing every day, not the mystical dove of the Holy Ghost or the apocalyptical eagle of St. John. While this tendency was already noticeable in the 13th-century sculpture of Chartres and elsewhere, it did not gain wide acceptance until the 14th century. As the natural world gained ascendancy over the supernatural, based as it was on concrete observation rather than metaphysical abstractions, it released the visual arts from one of their most perplexing problems. This love of St. Francis for his fellowmen and for such simple things as grass and trees, which could so readily be represented, opened up new vistas for artists to explore.

St. Francis' message was taught in parables and simple pictures of life that all could understand, and Giotto was able to translate them into living pictorial form. It is all but impossible for the modern literate mind fully to comprehend the importance of visual and auditory imagery in this period. While St. Francis could read and write, he pursued a way of life diametrically opposed to that of a scholar, even to the extent of priding himself on his ignorance. Since the majority of the people he preached to could not read, he had to make use of the more primary forms of visual and auditory images rather than secondary verbal ones. When St. Catherine of Siena or St. Joan of Arc, neither of whom could read, told of having visions or hearing voices, they were in fact relating the realities of their mental and spiritual lives. Even Dante's poem was put in the form of a vision, and it bore the subtitle, "The Vision of Dante Alighieri." In similar fashion, the images of artists and musicians as presented in paint, stone, glass, as well as in the spoken and sung word, had an immediate and direct communicative value to the people of this time far transcending the effect of such works on the modern mind.

More than anything else, it was this favorable climate that helped Giotto find his balance between the abstract and the concrete, between divine essence and human reality. By refraining from placing his accent on abstract symbolism, he succeeded in moving away from the mystical medieval atmosphere and in endowing his pictures with understandable human situations. To him the saints were not so much remote transcendental beings as they were eminently human people, who felt all the usual human emotions from joy to despair just as did the people in the Italian towns he knew so well. Now that he no longer had to be concerned mainly with allegories but could reproduce the world of objects and actions as he saw them, a new pathway was opened. Even his contemporaries could see that he was pouring new wine into the old Byzantine and medieval wineskins. When they extolled him for his faithfulness to nature, it must be measured by the art that preceded his time rather than by 15th-century or later standards. While he undoubtedly showed a love of nature as such, he never accented it to the point where it might weaken his primary human values. His interest was less in nature for its own sake than in its contribution to the reality and life of his figures.

In viewing a Giotto picture it is better to begin with his people and be only secondarily concerned with their natural surroundings, because his pictures are in psychological rather than linear perspective. His subjects seem to create their environment by their expressive attitudes and dramatic situations. While his work shows an increasing preoccupation with problems of natural space, it remains subordinate to his expressive intentions, and his use of color and shading gives his human figures the sense of depth and volume that awaken them to life. In this way both human nature and nature as such attain an intimate identity in his pictorial conceptions.

Franciscan Humanism

Long before, Cluny had made a fundamental change in monasticism by its union with feudalism, and the new orientation of the Franciscan movement was no less revolutionary. St. Francis did not enclose his monks in cloisters but sent them forth as fishers of men. The idea of evangelical poverty, humility, and love for mankind expressed through living and working with simple people resulted in a union with, rather than a withdrawal from, society. The Franciscans did not so much shun the world as they did worldly pursuits. This change of attitude is aptly described in the perceptive words of G. K. Chesterton to the effect that what St. Benedict had stored, St. Francis scattered. The Cluniacs were, in the proper sense of the word, an order—that is, a strict hierarchical organization. The Franciscans by contrast were, in every sense of the word, a movement.

The grip of the icy intellectualism of the medieval universities was bound to thaw in the wake of this warm flood of Franciscan emotionalism. Asceticism as such held little appeal for an increasingly prosperous urban middle class. The mathematical elegance of Gothic structurality began to yield little by little to more informal types of buildings. The logical linear patterns of the surviving Byzantine pictorial style were displaced by the expressive warmth of Giotto's figures. The vacuous stylized faces of Byzantine saints paled in comparison with the human tenderness found in a smiling mouth or a tearful eye in a Giotto picture. His men and women reveal a gamut of emotion from hope to despair through such facial expressions and bodily postures. The formal architectural sculpture and abstract patterns of the stained glass of the Romanesque and Gothic gave way to the colorful informality of mural painting in fresco. St. Francis in his music as in his religious work drew the sacred and popular traditions closer together; and in the lauds he encouraged people to sing, he gave them a music which they could feel with their hearts without having to understand with their brains.

St. Francis, coming as he did from a middle-class mercantile family, was not an aristocratic saint. Although his company was sought out by popes, bishops, and even St. Louis, the King of France, he was concerned primarily with the poor and humble of town and country alike. A series of frescoes in the church of St. Francis at Assisi by Simone Martini of Siena shows an extreme concern with social stratification. Unlike St. Francis and Giotto, this painter was a member of the knightly class and moved in aristocratic circles. His painting, however, harks back to the courtly Gothic, while the work in the same church by Giotto, a commoner, appears by comparison strikingly modern. His art was frankly oriented toward the new middle class. Above all, however, his figures were neither aristocrats nor commoners; they are simply human beings in all their warmth, frailty, and dignity. In this way his work attains something of St. Francis' universal spirit of humanity. The music favored by St. Francis and his successors was the simple folklike songs of the jongleurs rather than either those of the more aristocratic troubadours or the more formal style of Gothic counterpoint. Since his mission was that of preaching to the common people as they paused from their labors in the market places or in the fields, the musical forms he promoted exhibited an appropriate degree of directness and a corresponding lack of sophistication.

When Dante declared that Giotto's fame outshone that of his master Cimabue, and Boccaccio proclaimed that Giotto revived painting after it had "been in the grave" for centuries, it is apparent that his contemporaries recognized in his art the presence of a new spirit and style. This is also felt in the *Decameron*, where the ten city dwellers mercilessly satirize the manners and foibles of knights, abbots, and monks as well as the outmoded feudal ideal to which they clung. In France Philippe de Vitry published a musical treatise about 1316 with the title of *Ars Nova*, or new art, which he opposed to the *ars antiqua*, or old art, of the Gothic 13th century. The new movement of which he was the spokesman, especially in its ardent championship of the new secular rhythms, was deemed sufficiently important to become a subject of censure in a vigorous bull issued by Pope John XXII at Avignon in 1325.

There was a new spirit of freedom in the air, a freedom from tradition. St. Francis had struck out earlier in a new direction, and Giotto by translating his life into pictures could avoid the traditional Biblical subjects and their stylized treatment altogether. He was actually working on an almost-contemporary subject as well as rendering it in a new manner. The biographies of the saint allowed him ample freedom to improvise his designs as he saw fit and to achieve thereby something quite unprecedented. In his cycle at Padua on the history of the Virgin, such subjects as *Joachim Returning to the Sheepfold* and the *Meeting at the Golden Gate*, for instance, had no previous existence in the iconographical tradition. In the same series, the *Lamentation over the Body of Christ*, or *Pietà*, was treated far more dramatically than the traditional Crucifixion. In general, his figures moved about in the space he created for them with a new suppleness. His world was marked by a new and intelligible relationship between man and his fellowmen, between man and nature, and between man and God.

Representations of Christ as an infant in arms began to replace his mature image and that of his coming in divine majesty. The legend of Mary became more and more prominent along with the growing interest in the cycle of Christ's infancy. The emotional element in the Passion was largely conveyed through the empathic feeling for the Virgin Mary as the mother of sorrows. This was as true for Giotto's cycle in Padua as it was for Jacopone da Todi's *Stabat Mater Dolorosa*. The adoption of the vernacular tongue in literature, the informal medium of fresco painting, and the folklike spirit in the music all make it apparent that the works of art were being addressed to a new group of patrons. One of Giotto's recorded sayings, furthermore, reveals a new attitude in the conception of the artist of himself. Each man, he stated, "should save his soul as best he can. As for me, I intend to serve painting in my own way and only so far as it serves me, for the sake of the lovely moments it gives at the price of an agreeable fatigue." Even the plague had some beneficial effects for the artists after Giotto's time, since the younger masters could assert their independence and develop new ideas and techniques with less restrictions from their conservative guilds.

What appears to be a renewed interest in classical antiquity began to be seen, heard, and read in the works of the artists and writers of the 14th century. The panels of Niccolo Pisano's pulpit show unmistakably the classical Roman influence of such narrative reliefs as Trajan's Column (Fig. 3:22). His son Giovanni, in spite of the Gothic orientation of his own work, placed ancient Roman sarcophagi alongside contemporary examples in the arcade of the Campo Santo in Pisa. The Roman poet Vergil appears prominently in Dante's *Divine Comedy*. All these phenomena can be explained, however, much more logically as the continuation of a tradition that had, in fact, never really died out. If Niccolo's sculpture is placed chronologically after a group of French Gothic examples, it certainly seems to be closer to the art of ancient Rome. But since Roman sculpture was present everywhere in Italy, any Italian sculptor with his eyes open could hardly have been unaware of it. Simple as it may seem, the explanation is probably more geographical than chronological or psychological, since central Italy is closer to Rome than northern France is. The references in Dante to Vergil likewise are hardly a novelty. Since he was writing an epic poem, the obvious antecedent was the *Aeneid*, a work that had never ceased to be read. While a growing consciousness of the classical in Dante and his younger contemporaries is not to be overlooked, it must be seen from the 14th-century point of view more as a continuation of an ancient cultural tradition than as a rebirth as such. The influence of classic authors and classical art had never been quite so neglected or dead as many historians have supposed. Vergil and Cicero as well as certain works of Aristotle were quite as widely read in the Middle Ages as they were in the 14th and 15th centuries.

This is not to overlook the fact that there was a new spirit of curiosity present in the search through the monastic libraries instituted by Petrarch and Boccaccio for the manuscripts of Greek and Roman authors other than those which bore the hallowed approval of Church tradition. This also went hand in hand with the discovery of some buried antique sculpture in Rome and with the study of Roman building methods. Even though Petrarch was crowned with much classical fanfare in Rome with the laurel wreath, the ancient token of immortal fame, and wrote his cycle of Triumphs with the Roman triumphal arch form in mind, it is doubtful if he, Dante, or Boccaccio did much toward bringing the ancient world very much closer to their own time. There was certainly no admiration for pagan antiquity for its own sake in their case as there was in 15th-century Florence. And while St. Francis' pantheism bears an astonishing resemblance in some respects to the animistic phase of primitive Greek thought, it cannot be claimed that he arrived at his position through a knowledge of ancient civilization. Even though Giotto spent some time in Rome, the joyous humanistic spirit that permeates his work is much closer to the new Franciscan point of view and the continuous tradition of Roman relief sculpture and fresco painting than to any conscious reappraisal of classical culture as such. It becomes of great importance, then, to disassociate the spontaneous 14th-century Franciscan phase of humanism from the more self-conscious revival of antiquity that characterized the developments in 15th-century Florence and early 16th-century Rome.

Thus, from our vantage point, all this may seem as a conflict of opposing ideas and a mixture of forward and backward trends, but any period that contains the magic names of St. Francis, Dante, and Giotto, and one which exhibits such a high degree of originality and creativity, is best understood as one with a style of its own rather than as a postlude or prelude to another.

CHAPTER

General Events

1401   Competition for the bronze north doors of Baptistry

1403–1424   Ghiberti worked on the Baptistry north doors

1406   Pisa came under Florentine rule

1421   Giovanni de' Medici elected *gonfaloniere* of justice

1425–1452   Ghiberti worked on the Baptistry east doors

c.1429   Pazzi Chapel begun by Brunelleschi

1434   Pope Eugene IV began sojourn in Florence after revolt in Rome

Pro-Medici Signory elected Cosimo de' Medici (1389–1464) began rule of Florence

1436   Cathedral of Florence dedicated by Pope Eugene IV Begun in 1298 Dome by Brunelleschi

1439–1442   Council of Florence Nominal union of Eastern and Western churches

1444–1459   Medici-Riccardi Palace built by Michelozzo

1447   Parentucelli, a Florentine humanist, elected Pope Nicholas V

1464–1469   Piero de' Medici ruled Florence after Cosimo's death

1469–1492   Lorenzo de' Medici ruled Florence after Piero's death

1478   Pazzi family led unsuccessful revolt against Medicis Giuliano de' Medici, assassinated Lorenzo consolidated power

c.1480   Heinrich Isaac succeeded Squarcialupi as organist at the Cathedral; court composer to Lorenzo

1482   Marsilio Ficino's translations of Plato's dialogues began appearing in print

c.1485   Alberti's treatise *On Architecture* printed 1436 his book *On Painting* circulated in ms. form 1464 his book *On Sculpture* circulated in ms. form

1486   Savonarola began preaching his moral reform

1489   Michelangelo apprenticed to Ghirlandaio

c.1490   Aldine Press founded in Venice by Aldus Manutius

1492   Death of Lorenzo de' Medici

1494   Medicis exiled from Florence Signory dominated by Savonarola

1495–1498   Five volumes of Aristotle published by Aldine Press

1497   Burning of books, pictures, costumes, and "vanities"

1498   Savonarola (1452–1498) burned at stake

Architecture

1377–1446   Brunelleschi
1391–1473   Michelozzo
1404–1472   Alberti

Painting

1387–1455   Fra Angelico
1397–1475   Paolo Ucello
1401–1428   Masaccio
c.1406–1469   Filippo Lippi
c.1416–1492   Piero della Francesca
1420–1497   Benozzo Gozzoli
c.1429–1498   Antonio Pollaiuolo
1444–1510   Botticelli
1449–1494   Ghirlandaio
1452–1519   Leonardo da Vinci

Sculpture

1371–1438   Jacopo della Quercia
1378–1455   Ghiberti
1386–1466   Donatello
1400–1482   Luca della Robbia
c.1429–1498   Antonio Pollaiuolo
1435–1488   Verrocchio
1475–1564   Michelangelo

Music

1325–1397   Landini
1400–1474   Dufay
1430–1495   Ockeghem
1436–1475   Squarcialupi
c.1450–1517   Heinrich Isaac
1450–1505   Jacob Obrecht
c.1460–1521   Josquin des Prez

Literature and Philosophy

1304–1374   Petrarch
1313–1375   Boccaccio
1433–1499   Marsilio Ficino
1454–1494   Angelo Poliziano (Politian)
1469–1527   Machiavelli
1478–1529   Baldassare Castiglione

9

THE FLORENTINE RENAISSANCE STYLE

FLORENCE, 15th CENTURY

Seldom has the muse of history gazed upon such a gathering of dignitaries, artists, men of letters, and musicians as that which assembled in Florence during the last week of March in the year 1436 for the dedication of the Cathedral (Fig. 9:1). It was Filippo Brunelleschi whose architectural skill had added the crowning glory of a mighty dome to the structure that had been begun in the late 13th century. Ghiberti had finished the handsome bronze north doors of the Baptistry and was well along on the east doors, which Michelangelo was later to hail as worthy of being the Gates of Paradise. Helping him at various times in his bronze foundry with the casting were the architect Michelozzo, the sculptor Donatello, and the painters Paolo Ucello and Benozzo Gozzoli. Donatello had just been paid for the series of statues that occupied niches in both the Cathedral building and in the Campanile, affectionately known as Giotto's Tower.

Present to officiate at the ceremonies was Pope Eugene IV, who had taken up temporary residence in Florence after the revolt in Rome of 1434. This enforced sojourn brought him and his advisers under the influence of the group of Florentine humanists, resulting in a meeting of minds that was destined to have far-reaching intellectual and artistic consequences. In his entourage was the brilliant scholar Leone Battista Alberti, who had just finished and dedicated his treatise *On Painting* to Brunelleschi. His later book *On Architecture* was to become one of the most influential works of its kind on the thought of his own and subsequent times. On hand to provide the music was the papal choir, whose ranks included the foremost musician of his generation, Guillaume Dufay, who composed the special commemorative motet for the occasion.

Lining the streets for the grand procession and crowding their way into the vast nave of the Cathedral were the colorfully costumed citizens of this prosperous Tuscan town. In contrast with northern countries, in this region city life had by this time come of age. At a time when many feudal aristocrats still inhabited their dank fortresslike castles, the Florentine patrician families lived in a style that could well have been the envy of kings. The working members of the population belonged to the various guilds and trade organizations, the most important of which were those dealing with the carding, weaving, and dyeing of wool and silk for the famous Florentine textile industry. Metal crafts and stonework followed in importance, and so on down to the butchers and bakers. The masters of the principal guilds were the influential citizens from whose ranks the members of the Signory were chosen, and from which the wealthy merchant and banking families emerged.

The most renowned of these was the Medici family, whose head at this time was Cosimo. By a combination of political sagacity and the shrewd manipulation of his large fortune, he dominated the government of the city. Knowing the passion of his fellow townsmen for equality, he never assumed a title or other outward signs of authority. Instead he was the benign political boss, ruling behind the scenes with the support of the guilds, who knew that a stable government and peaceful relations with their neighbors were the best safeguards of their prosperity. The Medicis were also the papal bankers who received church funds from England, France, and Flanders on deposit; and from their branch offices in London, Lyon, and Antwerp, they lent the money at fantastic rates of interest to foreign heads of state. With the papal revenues they also bought English wool, shipped it to Florence where it was woven into fine fabrics, and exported it again at a handsome profit.

In addition to making the florin the soundest unit of currency in Europe, Cosimo's list of accomplishments was unusual for a Renaissance merchant capitalist. As a diligent student of Plato, for instance, he became the founder of the Neo-Platonic Academy, an institution that had enormous intellectual influence. He commissioned works of art from all the parts of Europe where his fortune extended, while at home he gathered a library of rare manuscripts for his scholars to study and translate. Through his generosity, a group of Dominican monks had just moved into the monastery of San Marco, which was being rebuilt for them by his personal architect Michelozzo. Among them was Fra Angelico whom Cosimo encouraged to undertake the decoration of its walls with his famous frescoes. Though one of the century's most original painters, Masaccio, had been dead for six

Fig. 9:1. *Florence Cathedral, "Giotto's" Tower, and Baptistry.* 1296–1462. Cathedral 508′ long, Dome 367′ high. (Courtesy Italian State Tourist Office)

years, such others as Filippo Lippi, the future teacher of Botticelli, were active and looking in Cosimo's direction for commissions. Cosimo took Donatello's advice, collected antique statuary, and placed it in the cloister gardens of San Marco. By encouraging young sculptors to work there, he founded the first art academy since antiquity. Small wonder, then, that after his death in 1464, the Signory voted him the posthumous title *pater patriae*, father of his country.

The eyes and thoughts of all Florence that March day were on the great new dome which dominated their city and gave it its characteristic profile. It had been undertaken some 16 years before by Brunelleschi after he had returned from studying the Pantheon and other monuments of ancient Rome. He had built it over a gaping octagonal space almost 140 feet in diameter, starting at a point 180 feet above the ground. The construction had to be as light as possible, since heavy scaffolding in such a location was out of the question. With extraordinary daring he threw eight ribs from the angles of the supporting octagon almost 100 feet upward into space where they converged at the base of the lantern. Concealed from external view, he added two more minor radial ribs between each major one, making 24 in all. Reinforced by wooden beams and iron clasps at key points, this system constituted the necessary support for the brick work and stone masonry used for the inner and outer shells of the dome respectively. As it stands, the structure is in effect an eight-sided Gothic vault. The concealment of the functional elements and the concentration on the formal design of the exterior, however, belong to the Renaissance. Brunelleschi was thus able to combine medieval structural principles and yet maintain the outward appearance of classical repose.

The pontifical ceremony for the consecration of the Cathedral began the Sunday before when the Pope had blessed a golden rose, wrought no doubt by one of the expert Florentine goldsmiths. Such emblems were traditionally presented to sovereign heads of state. In this instance it was offered to the Virgin Mary in her capacity as Queen of Heaven; and, as the dedication implies, to Santa Maria del Fiore, or Mary of the Flower. The allusion in this case is particularly appropriate, since the name of the city, whose Cathedral it was, is also derived from *flora*, making it nominally the "city of flowers." The actual consecration took place on Passion Sunday, March 25, 1436, a day which had been chosen by the pope because it coincided with the feast day of the Annunciation to the Blessed Virgin. Especially impressive was the music that was written for the ceremony. Antonio Squarcialupi, the regular organist of the Cathedral and private music master in the Medici household, is thought to have composed the Solemn High Mass; while Dufay, a member of the papal choir, is known to have written the dedicatory motet. According to Gianozzo Manetti, an eye witness, the magnificent pontifical procession was preceded by a great band of wind and string players, "each carrying his instrument in his hand, and arrayed in gorgeous cloth of gold garments." After them came the combined choirs which, as Manetti reports, "sang at times with such mighty harmonies that the songs seemed to the listeners to be coming from the angels themselves."

For such solemn ceremonies as coronations and royal marriages, it was the custom to perform a motet especially written for the occasion. Dufay, a musician educated in the Burgundian French tradition, had been a member of the papal choir since 1428 and had composed such an occasional motet for the ceremonies at the conclusion of peace between Pope Eugene and the Emperor Sigismund in 1433. The motet, coming as it does outside the normal liturgical music of the Mass, lent itself well to the purposes of an occasional piece that could be composed for a specific ceremony to a text which contained topical allusions. The words in this case begin: *Nuper rosarum flores ex dono pontificis*—Flower of roses, gift of the pontiff. The Cathedral is referred to as this "most spacious temple," and Brunelleschi's dome is praised as a "mighty artifice," or a "marvel of art." The text appropriately concludes with a supplication to the Virgin Mary on behalf of the people of Florence: "O Virgin, the glory of virgins, thy devoted people of Florence beseech thee that he who prays . . . may deserve to receive thy gracious benefits. . . . " Since such motets were composed for official occasions, their style tended toward traditional practices rather than experimentation. Dufay therefore built his formal structure on the severe isorhythmic principles developed by the 14th-century French composers. Such a method is governed by certain rules of musical logic, and the forms are compounded of sections that are unified by an identity of rhythmic relationships but not necessarily of melodic patterns. Such music was never intended primarily to please the ear or stir the emotions, but rather to mirror the hidden harmonies of the universe and thus to constitute a worthy offering to its Creator. In Dufay's conception, however, the universe is no longer mere structure but is populated with shapely melodies, warm harmonic colors, and a variety of rhythmic forms.

The motet *Nuper Rosarum* [1] is written in four parts with its two tenor lines most probably played by the organ, reinforced by the trombones. Together they sounded the awesome tones of the Gregorian chant traditional for the dedication of churches. Over this ground structure the two upper choral parts weave an airy lacy pattern based on melodic motives that recur constantly throughout in various guises and disguises. In performance the string orchestra doubled these two choral lines, and our eye-and-ear witness speaks especially of the delightful and sweet instrumental sounds "when the customary pauses in the singing occurred." At these points it seems likely that the trumpets must have joined the ensemble. With the solemn organ and trombones, the festive trumpets, the sonorous strings, and the massive choruses all filling the Cathedral with magnificent sounds, the effect must have been impressive indeed. Our observer, never one to be at a loss for superlatives, found as usual the glowing words to describe it. "All our more exalted feelings [were aroused]," he wrote, "partly by hearing the sweetest songs and most pleasant sounds, partly by smelling the most redolent odors, and partly by beholding all kinds of wonderful ornaments." At the climax of the service, he reports, "all parts of the basilica resounded with such symphonies of harmony, and with such mighty sounds from the various instruments, that it seemed to be descending from Heaven itself. . . . "

This dedicatory scene of the Cathedral has often been cited, both by those who witnessed it and by later historians, as the beginning of a new era. There was, of course, a new spirit in the air, but at the same time it was never clearer that no sharp break with the medieval past was being made. The Cathedral itself was late Gothic in style; Brunelleschi's dome was constructed by Gothic vaulting methods; and Dufay's isorhythmic motet was a late Gothic musical form. The Italian Gothic, however, had never had either the dynamic verticality or the aspiring force of its northern counterpart. Brunelleschi's dome was, to be sure, the first of such magnitude to be constructed since antiquity. Smaller domes over the crossing were, however, not unusual in Tuscany, as a glance at the Cathedral of nearby Pisa (Fig. 6:10) will show. But while the construction of Brunelleschi's dome fell within the scope of the Gothic, the new emphasis was on smoother lines and the shapeliness of the external silhouette. Dufay's motet, for its part, showed an increasing secular feeling in church music, since the composer was apparently much less concerned with making a pious setting of his text than he was with making his mathematical proportions fit smoothly into his musical structure. While such mental gymnastics were late Gothic in conception, the Italian sense of melodic contour, the increased emphasis on secular duple time, the softening of the dissonant passing tones, and the pliancy of the contrapuntal texture, all point in the direction of the Renaissance. Dufay's special contribution was in clothing the austere skeletal structure of such a composition with skillful voice leading and a fluency of sound that made it a joy to the ear as well as to the mind.

THE PAZZI CHAPEL AND THE MEDICI-RICCARDI PALACE

The new architectural spirit is more readily grasped in Brunelleschi's smaller Pazzi Chapel (Fig. 9:2) than in the immense cupola of the Cathedral. In a building of diminutive proportions the architect could give his full attention to design without being absorbed in complex construction problems. The fruits of Brunelleschi's studies of ancient Roman buildings are here very much more in evidence; and, with the exception of the vaulting of the portico and interior, the break with the Gothic tradition is practically complete. The harmonious spacing of the columns of the portico, the novel treatment of the walls as flat surfaces, and the just balance of horizontal and vertical elements make Brunelleschi's design the proto-

Fig. 9:2 (above). Brunelleschi.
*Pazzi Chapel. c.*1429–1451. 59′ 9″
× 35′ 8″. Cloister of Santa Croce,
Florence (Alinari)

Fig. 9:3 (right). *Detail of Façade*
(Alinari)

type of the Renaissance architectural style. The entablature (Fig. 9:3) gives still further evidence of the classical influence. The curved pattern above comes directly from ancient Roman sarcophagi; otherwise the treatment of the Roman detail is quite free. The elegant carving of the Corinthian capitals, the Composite pilasters, and other details of the design reveal Brunelleschi's early training as a silversmith.

The interior (Fig. 9:4) fully bears out the initial promise of the façade, and shows a Roman classical concern with the molding of interior space. Without a trace of Gothic gloom the pilastered walls give a cool, crisp impression. Frames of colored stone divide the surfaces into compartments easily apprehended by the eye. Mystery and infinity have yielded to the clarity of geometrical form. Overhead the rectangular room is covered by transverse barrel vaults, with a low dome on pendentives rising in the center over their point of intersection. Somewhat hesitantly to be sure, this interior indicates a new concept of space without, however, realizing its full implications. The clarity and simplicity of its design made the Pazzi Chapel highly influential throughout the Renaissance, and the unity of organization under the dome became the point of departure for the centralized church plans of Alberti, Bramante, and Michelangelo.

Fig. 9:4. Brunelleschi. Pazzi Chapel. *Interior*. *c*.1429–1451. Florence (Alinari)

When Cosimo de' Medici decided to build himself a new house, he is said to have rejected a palatial plan submitted by Brunelleschi, with the observation that envy was a plant that should not be watered. For the Medici-Riccardi Palace (Fig. 9:5) he chose instead a less ostentatious design submitted by Brunelleschi's disciple Michelozzo. (The hyphenated name comes from the fact that the Riccardi family acquired the palace from the Medicis in the middle of the 17th century.) As the design materialized, the building turned out to be an appropriately solid structure, eminently suited to the taste of a man of such considerable substance as Cosimo. Such buildings as a type were actually a continuation, rather than a revival, of the multistoried Roman city apartment house, such as the House of Diana at Ostia (Fig. 3:18). The dominance here of solid mass over the space allotted to the windows, plus the heavily rusticated masonry of the first story, however, still have something of the forbidding aspect of a medieval fortress. As the eye moves upward, however, the second and third floors present an increasingly urbane appearance. The accent on horizontal lines, seen in the molding strips which separate the several stories and in the boldly projecting cornice at the roof level, are quite unmedieval. An allusion to the classical tradition can be seen in the semicircular arches that frame the windows (the pediments over those on the lower story are a somewhat later addition). Details, such as the colonettes of the windows on the second and third floors as well as the egg-and-tongue pattern and the dentil range that appear in the cornice frieze, are definitely Renaissance in style.

In the courtyard (Fig. 9:7) the classical interest is even more apparent. The various rooms are grouped around it as in a Pompeiian peristylar court, and courtyard as well as staircase connect the various parts of the house as in a Roman atrium. An interesting detail is found in the use of the Medici coat of arms in the frieze, which is also observable in a corner of the exterior (Fig. 9:6). These are the *palle*, or red balls on a field of gold. Some say they were derived originally from the form of apothecary's pills, going all the way back to the time when *medico* meant that the family profession was that of the physician. In the 15th century, however, they were interpreted with an appropriately classical flourish as the golden apples of the Hesperides. More realistically they were the symbol of the Medici banking firm. In slightly modified form, they have since evolved into the international emblem of pawnbrokers.

Cosimo's sense of austerity was limited to the exterior, and once inside the portals everything was carried out on a princely scale. With the fresco murals of Benozzo Gozzoli (Fig. 9:20) and Filippo Lippi decorating its second-floor chapel, antique and contemporary bronze statues standing in

Fig. 9:5 (above). Michelozzo. *Medici-Riccardi Palace*. 1444–1449. *c.*225′ long, 80′ high. Florence (Anderson). Fig. 9:6 (left). *Detail*

Fig. 9:7. Michelozzo. Medici-Riccardi Palace, *Court* (Barsotti)

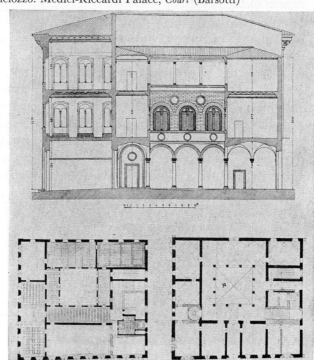

Fig. 9:8 (right). *Plan* (From Stegmann and Geymüller *Architecture of the Renaissance in Tuscany*)

the courtyards and gardens, tapestries and paintings hanging on its walls, collections of ancient and medieval carved gems and coins in its cabinets, and precious metal vessels and figurines standing on its tables, the Medici-Riccardi Palace was, in fact, one of the first and richest museums in Europe.

SCULPTURE

In the year 1401 the Signory of Florence together with the Guild of Merchants held a competition to determine who should be awarded the contract for the projected north doors of the Baptistry. Like the earlier set by Andrea Pisano, the medium was to be bronze; the individual panels had to be enclosed in the traditional quatrefoil pattern; and the subject, for the purpose of the contest, was to be the Sacrifice of Isaac. Six noted sculptors were invited to submit models, among them Brunelleschi (Fig. 9:9) and Lorenzo Ghiberti (Fig. 9:10). Both were contemporaries; both were skilled workers in metal and members in good standing of the Goldsmith's Guild. A comparison of their panels, however, reveals many significant differences of technique and viewpoint. Brunelleschi's is cast in several pieces, while Ghiberti's is in a single mold. Brunelleschi is interested in the inherent drama of the situation, while Ghiberti sacrifices dramatic intensity for the sake of decorative beauty. Brunelleschi is less interested in space and allows his high-relief figures to spill out of their frames, while Ghiberti wanted a more unified focus of interest. Isaac's body, as seen by Brunelleschi, is still somewhat angular and medieval in concept, while its counterpart in Ghiberti's composition has all the impersonal grace of a Hellenistic statue. In Ghiberti's memoirs is an account of the discovery of an ancient statue near Florence, and in this instance the body of Isaac is known to have been modeled on a classical torso Ghiberti had in his possession at the time. The decision in Ghiberti's favor was an early prognosis of the way the aesthetic winds were blowing. Ghiberti then set to work on the 20 panels of the north doors, which were to occupy the major part of his time for the next 24 years; while sculpture's loss in Brunelleschi's case was architecture's gain.

Ghiberti's doors were no sooner in place than he was forthwith commissioned, this time without competition, to execute still another set. As a further commentary on the aesthetic thought of the century as it unfolded, the famous east doors (Fig. 9:11) on which he worked from 1425 to 1452 tell their own tale. The Gothic quatrefoil frames were now a thing of the past. The earlier doors were still conceived in terms of their architectural function, while now they serve as a convenient framework for decoration.

Fig. 9:9. Brunelleschi. *Sacrifice of Isaac*, Competition Panel. Bronze. 18″ high. 1401. National Museum, Florence (Alinari)

Fig. 9:10. Ghiberti. *Sacrifice of Isaac*, Competition Panel. Bronze. 18″ high. 1401. National Museum, Florence (Alinari)

Fig. 9:11. Ghiberti. *East Doors of the Baptistry at Florence*. Bronze. 18′ 6″ high. 1425–1452 (Brogi)

Instead of sculpture in relief, Ghiberti now paints pictures in bronze. In the Adam and Eve panel (Fig. 9:12) he attempts daring perspective effects far in advance of the painting of the period. The foreground figures are done in high relief to project them forward; the angelic cloud in the background is in such low relief that it seems to be dissolving into thin air, while such details as the springlike Garden of Eden in the middleground are done in half relief.

On either side of the pictorial panels appears a series of full-length figurines that alternate with heads which recall Roman portrait busts. Hebrew prophets are seen next to the pagan sibyl who were supposed to have foretold the coming of Christ. Even when a representation of Samson is intended, such as that on the right of the Abraham panel, he is por-

Fig. 9:12. Ghiberti. East Doors of the Baptistry at Florence, Detail. *Story of Adam and Eve.* 1425–1452 (Brogi)

trayed with the stance and full musculature of a Hellenistic Hercules. Ghiberti mentions in his *Commentaries* how he tried to imitate nature in emulation of the ancient Greeks when molding the flora and fauna of the door frames. The care he lavished on the delicacy of detail in the metal medium makes these doors a culmination of the goldsmith's art. Since all the important Florentine sculptors were members of the Goldsmith's Guild, this tradition permeated the art of the century. Evidence of this influence is to be seen everywhere, not only in such door moldings, but in pulpits, wall panels, window brackets, columns, pilasters, cornices, all of which were done with a wealth of finely wrought detail lovingly dwelt upon.

Donatello's career presents a strong contrast to that of his older contemporary Ghiberti. He surveyed all possible fields of sculpture and executed notable examples in each, while Ghiberti for the most part remained a specialist. Donatello's work does not have one style but many; he was at home in the bronze, wood, and marble mediums; and he produced colossal figures in the round with the same facility that he made bronze and marble reliefs. While Ghiberti knew classical statuary only from the local examples and the writings of Vitruvius and others, Donatello had gone down to Rome with Brunelleschi to see things for himself. As a man of fiery temperament and bold imagination, he scorned the fussy details that were the goldsmith's trademark; and his work, consequently, took on an aspect of rugged grandeur which makes that of Ghiberti appear precious by comparison. His power of epical expression, enormous energies, vehemence, and impetuosity make him the artistic ancestor of Michelangelo.

Lo Zuccone, or *Baldpate* (Fig. 9:13), was one of a series of marble statues for the Cathedral and Campanile that he was commissioned to do in 1424. Designed for a third-story niche of the Campanile, it was intended to be seen about 55 feet above the ground level. The deep-cut drapery and lines of the face were made with this lighting and angle of vision in mind. By the boniness of the huge frame, the powerful musculature of the arms, the convulsive gesture of the right wrist, the tension of the sinews of the neck, and the intensity of the face, Donatello sought to produce a powerfully expressive rather than a beautiful figure. While the exact identification is not known, the figure is intended either as a Habakkuk or a Jeremiah. At any rate it is one of a Hebrew prophet full of inner fire, imbued with the fear of the Lord, capable of fasting in the desert, dwelling alone on a mountaintop, or haranguing an unheeding multitude from his niche and exhorting them to penitence. The classical influence is discernible in the drapery, which is an adaptation of the toga; and in the rugged features and

Fig. 9:13. Donatello. *Lo Zuccone* (Baldpate). Marble. *c.*6′ 8″ high. *c.*1430. Cathedral Museum, Florence. Courtesy H. W. Janson (Brogi)

Fig. 9:14. Donatello. *David*. Bronze. 5'1½" high. *c*.1430. National Museum, Florence. Courtesy H. W. Janson (Brogi)

Fig. 9:15. Antonio Pollaiuolo. *Hercules Strangling Antaeus*. Bronze. 17¾" high. *c*.1460. National Museum, Florence (Alinari)

baldness, which recall the realistic approach of Roman portraiture. With *Lo Zuccone*, Donatello created a unique human being of strong individuality rather than one of the traditional iconographical types; and the nickname, which was given to the statue by the Florentines, is proof that it was accepted as such.

In his bronze *David* (Fig. 9:14), Donatello works in a more lyrical vein. Although it dates from approximately the same time as *Lo Zuccone*, the circumstances of the commission are not known. Later in the century, however, it stood in a courtyard of the Medici Palace. The early date stamps it as a revival of the classical male nude; and, as a figure meant to be seen from all angles, it is definitely a departure from the Gothic tradition of sculpture in niches and as architectural embellishment. David stands alone in the confident attitude of the victor over the vanquished, a sword in his right hand, a stone in his left. The serenity of the classical profile and the stance and modeling of the youthful body point to Hellenistic models. Touches of realism, however, are seen in the Tuscan shepherd's hat, which throws the face into strong shadow thus accenting the lines of the body, which, in turn, betrays something of the awkwardness of adolescence.

Donatello's *Gattamelata* (Fig. 9:16), an equestrian statue of Erasmo da Narni, a condottiere of the Venetian Republic, was the first bronze monument of such proportions to be executed since the days of the Roman Empire. It stands in Padua where the sculptor worked during the decade 1443–1453. The portrait was undoubtedly inspired by that of the Emperor Marcus Aurelius (Fig. 3:9) which Donatello had observed in Rome; and the horse was possibly modeled after those above the portals of St. Mark's in nearby Venice, which date from the time of Nero. Other classical touches are found in the short-skirted Roman armor worn by the rider and the general poise of the composition. The anatomy of the horse is well observed, and the contrasting textures of the horseflesh, leather saddle, and metal armor are handled with assurance and telling effect.

Quite another attitude is revealed in the sculpture of the succeeding generation, of which Antonio Pollaiuolo and Verrocchio are the leading representatives. The work of Pollaiuolo is dominated by scientific curiosity, especially in regard to human anatomy. He is known to have dissected cadavers in order to study the muscle and bone structure at first hand. Trained along with his brothers in his father's goldsmith shop, he is best known for his small figures in bronze, such as the group of *Hercules Strangling Antaeus* (Fig. 9:15). The legends of the strong man of antiquity were well adapted to bring out the musculature of the male figure in action. In this instance, Hercules overcomes his adversary, the Lybian giant, by raising

Fig. 9:16 (above). Donatello. *Gattamelata*. Bronze. 10′ 6″ high. 1443–1453. Piazzo del Santo, Padua. Courtesy H. W. Janson (Brogi). Fig. 9:17 (below). Verrocchio. *Monument to Bartolommeo Colleoni*. Bronze. Heroic size. 1481. Venice (Alinari)

him off the ground, the source of his strength being the earth. Antaeus is seen desperately struggling to release himself from the stranglehold Hercules has upon him. The sinews in Hercules' legs as they bear the weight of both bodies should be noted. Pollaiuolo also painted a series of pictures on the tasks of Hercules. Like his work in bronze they are studies of muscular tension, full of athletic energy and quite unrelieved by gracefulness.

Verrocchio, a younger contemporary of Pollaiuolo's, was the official sculptor of the Medici family. For them he designed everything from tournament trophies and parade paraphernalia to the tomb of Cosimo. Like Donatello, he occasionally worked outside Florence; and at the time of his death in 1481, he was just completing the monument to Bartolommeo Colleoni (Fig. 9:17), a condottiere, who left his entire fortune to the Venetian Republic in return for such an equestrian statue which would stand in the city he had served so long. Verrocchio portrays him as the stern 15th-century man of action he was. With arrogant mien he dominates his mount, just as he seems to domineer the troops under his command. Donatello's *Gattamelata* appears to have won his battles with brains, while Verrocchio's general depended more on brute force and brawn. Donatello's rider and mount are generalized, while Verrocchio's are more individually and literally treated. Bartolommeo's steed, a warhorse capable of bearing the fully armored figure on his back, stands with one foot unsupported, impatient to be off. Details of the saddle and armor definitely belong to the 15th century and are richly wrought with all of Verrocchio's silversmith's skill.

Both Pollaiuolo and Verrocchio were also painters at a time when sculpture led the field in experiments with perspective, anatomy, and light and shadow. When they painted, however, the sharp outlines and hard contours of their figures reveal them primarily as workers in metal, especially bronze. Unlike the classical orientation of Ghiberti and Donatello, Pollaiuolo and Verrocchio were primarily scientifically minded, and it was in Verrocchio's workshop that Leonardo da Vinci got his training. It was Leonardo who carried on the unquenchable scientific curiosity of his master, while it remained for Michelangelo, under the stimulus of Donatello's art, to carry on the humanistic ideal into the next century.

PAINTING

Along with Brunelleschi and Donatello, the third member of the triumvirate of early 15th-century innovators and the only one to be born within the century, was Masaccio. The importance of his series of frescoes in the Brancacci Chapel can hardly be overestimated. In the *Expulsion from the*

Fig. 9:18 (left). Masaccio. *Expulsion from the Garden*. Fresco. 6′ 6″ × 2′ 9″. *c.*1426. Brancacci Chapel, Church of Santa Maria del Carmine, Florence (Alinari)

Fig. 9:19 (below). Fra Angelico. *Annunciation*. Fresco. 7′ 6″ × 10′ 5″. *c.*1440. San Marco, Florence (Anderson)

Garden (Fig. 9:18) he chose one of the few subjects in the iconographical tradition in which the nude human body could be portrayed in churches without raising ecclesiastical eyebrows at the time. By visualizing the source of light as coming from the right and having Adam and Eve approach it diagonally, Masaccio could have their figures cast natural shadows. The contours of their bodies are thus modeled by means of light and shade, so that they appear as if seen in the round and with all the weight and volume of living forms. Masaccio, however, was also fully aware of the drama of the situation. The full force of man's first moral crisis is expressed by the human body alone with almost no reliance on secondary elements. Eve, aware of her nakedness, cries aloud; while Adam, ashamed to face the light, expresses his remorse by covering his face. Even the avenging angel who drives them out reflects the tragedy of the fall of man by an expression of human concern and solicitude. Adam's right leg was apparently drawn so as to show the motion of the expulsion; but the proportions of his arms, and the drawing of Eve's lower hand, are definitely incorrect. Such flaws, however, are minor in comparison with the momentous step that shows man in an entirely new relationship to his spatial environment. Masaccio's premature death at the early age of 27 prevented a more complete realization of his vision, and it remained for Leonardo da Vinci and Michelangelo to work out its full implications.

Fra Angelico, by way of contrast, was spiritually still a late-Gothic figure, who never painted anything but religious subjects. While he dwelt lovingly on the older forms, however, he often treated them within the new frame of reference. The *Annunciation* (Fig. 9:19), which was painted for the upper corridor of his own cloister of San Marco, is a remarkable blend of these old and new elements. A mystic by temperament, angels to Fra Angelico were as real as his fellow human beings, and the Madonna was his favorite subject, just as she had been in the previous two centuries. But while he always paints with the deepest religious sentiment, his figures in this case appear within the new conception of space. The perspective and architectural setting are skillfully handled, and the loggia could well represent one of Michelozzo's latest designs, such as that of the Medici-Riccardi Palace courtyard (Fig. 9:7). Furthermore, the native Tuscan flowers seen in the garden are well enough observed to satisfy a botanical expert. The lighting, however, is far from the natural illumination of Masaccio; Fra Angelico manages it so that the figure of Gabriel, and the ineffable purity of Mary are beheld as if in a vision.

Unlike the eyes of Fra Angelico, those of his pupil Benozzo Gozzoli were focused entirely on this world. While the subject of his series of murals, which cover three walls of the Medici Chapel, was ostensibly the *Journey of the Magi*, the religious content is in name only. Though painted some 20 years later, the event commemorated one of Cosimo's diplomatic triumphs, the convening of the Council of Florence in 1439 to discuss the union of the Oriental and Occidental churches. Benozzo appropriately depicts it as a pageantlike procession of the Three Wise Men from the east. The heads of the Eastern delegation, Emperor John Paleologos and the Patriarch of Constantinople, attended by their retinue of theologians, philosophers, and scholars, appear as two of the kings. In a detail (Fig. 9:20) the third king and leader of the train is none other than the youthful Lorenzo de' Medici, magnificently attired and sitting astride a splendid white horse. Behind him ride the rest of the Medici clan and a host of their retainers, with the elderly Cosimo, who housed and feted the entire delegation, riding a gray mule with a blackamoor groom at his side. Around him are other members of the family. Of special interest is the face in the rear ranks between two heavily bearded men, which is that of the artist himself who signed his picture in the letters around the band of his cap which read *"Opus Benotii."*

The temporary union of the Eastern and Western churches that resulted from the deliberations was in reality a desperate appeal for Western aid in the face of the growing Turkish menace. The intellectual influence of the scholars, many of whom stayed on at Cosimo's invitation, proved more lasting and profound. After the fall of Constantinople in 1453 more philosophers followed, bringing with them priceless libraries of ancient manuscripts. With the founding of the Neo-Platonic Academy and the interest in the study of ancient Greek, translations of the dialogues of Plato, many of which were unknown in the West since Roman times, were made.

Benozzo's picture is painted against an eroded mountainside south of Florence, stylized to some extent but otherwise quite recognizable. While the composition is heavily overloaded with detail, the horizontal masses of rock and the vertical trunks of the trees show that some attempt at pictorial balance was made. Benozzo, however, remains essentially a decorator; and, as such, the lively tapestrylike mural with its bright color and documentary interest, admirably captures something of the Florentine love of pageantry.

The Medici family appear again in Botticelli's *Adoration of the Magi* (Fig. 9:21), where the festive spirit is also present. This time, however, it is under the firm control of a master of pictorial organization. Two of the admirably arranged figures have been identified beyond scholarly doubt— that of Cosimo, kneeling at the feet of the Christ child, and the self-portrait of the painter, standing in the extreme right foreground. Vasari is the authority for the identification of the other two kneeling figures as Cosimo's

Fig. 9:20 (above). Benozzo Gozzoli. *Journey of the Magi*, Detail. Fresco. *c.*1459–1463. Medici Chapel, Medici-Riccardi Palace, Florence (Anderson). Fig. 9:21 (below). Botticelli. *Adoration of the Magi*. Tempera on wood. 43½″ × 52¾″. *c.*1475. Uffizi, Florence (Anderson)

sons, Piero and Giovanni. The standing figure clothed in rich black velvet is probably Giuliano, the handsome younger brother of Lorenzo the Magnificent, while the young man standing with his hands on his sword may be Lorenzo himself. The bright and beautiful coloring is based on a complicated but harmonious scheme varying from the cool azure of the Virgin's robe and the dark green and gold embroidery of Cosimo's costume, to the ermine-lined crimson cloak of the kneeling Piero and the bright orange of Botticelli's mantle. Attention should also be called to the classical touch provided by the ancient Roman ruin in the left background.

Botticelli, however, was not a popular painter of pageants like Benozzo and his contemporary Ghirlandaio but a member of the sophisticated group of humanists who gathered around his patron, Lorenzo. In this circle, which included the poet Angelo Poliziano and the philosophers Marsilio Ficino and Pico della Mirandola, classical myths were constantly discussed and interpreted. The dialogues of Plato, the *Enneads* of Plotinus, and Greek musical theory were all thoroughly explored. With the Florentine interest in the pictorial arts, the ancient references to sculpture and painting were not neglected. This neo-pagan atmosphere is reflected directly in many of Botticelli's paintings.

In his *Venus and Mars* (Fig. 9:22) Botticelli is concerned with the intellectual phases of Florentine life. It is an allegory relating to the tournament given by Giuliano de' Medici in honor of Simonetta Vespucci on January 28, 1475. Simonetta Cattaneo was the wife of Marco Vespucci and hence a cousin by marriage of Amerigo Vespucci, the Florentine geographer who modestly gave his name to the new world that Columbus discovered. The blonde Simonetta was celebrated for her beauty as well as her docile disposition; and, as a member of the exclusive Florentine Neo-Platonic set, she could not have been entirely devoid of intellectual accomplishments. Known as the *gentilissima*, she was not only the object of Giuliano's most ardent affections but the subject of sonnets by Lorenzo the Magnificent, verses by Poliziano, and the pictures of Botticelli. To each, though in a different way, she represented the ideal Platonic type of beauty and goodness and was enshrined by them in a poetic niche much as Beatrice was by Dante and Laura by Petrarch. In spite of the presence of the playful young satyrs, the picture is tinged with a certain melancholy, since Simonetta was destined for an early death, and Giuliano was killed in the Pazzi conspiracy on the same day two years later. Both events apparently occurred before the picture was finished, which is a possible explanation of the shape of the wooden panel on which it is painted recalling that of a sarcophagus. Giuliano won the tournament that day in 1475 and received the trophy of

Fig. 9:22. Botticelli. *Venus and Mars*. Oil on wood. National Gallery, London (Anderson)

victory from the hands of Simonetta. He is depicted here as Mars dreaming after the battle of the ideal beauty of Venus who appears to him in the form of the fair Simonetta.

The *Birth of Venus* (Fig. 9:23) is likewise filled with the mythological and allegorical allusions of the Neo-Platonic circle. In Poliziano's poem *La Giostra*—The Joust or Tournament—the birth of the goddess of love is vividly described as she floats across the sea on a pink shell gently blown by the Zephyrs. On the shore waiting to clothe her in a flowery mantle is one of the Horae, or Hours. In one verse there is an allusion to the ancient picture of Venus Anadyomene by Apelles, painter to Alexander the Great, which was known only through literary references and some relief sculptures it was thought to have inspired. The legendary place where Venus is supposed to have landed on Italian shores is named Portovenere, which, by coincidence, was also the birthplace of Simonetta. The head of the goddess accordingly bears the features of Simonetta, while the pose of the body is that of the *Venus de Medici*, an antique marble statue belonging to that family and now in the Uffizi Gallery. The coloring of the picture is as cool as called for by such a classical subject. The fluttering drapery of the side figures imparts a sense of lightness and movement and leads the eye toward the head of Venus, which is surrounded by an aura of golden bronze hair. The features of the face have an individuality notably lacking in the more impersonal antique statuary, while the incisiveness of outline recalls the technique of relief sculpture. The chief expressive interest, however, is in the balletlike choreography of dancing lines and the skillful pattern of the richly varied linear rhythms.

Botticelli's penchant for intellectualized interpretations of antiquity reaches record proportions in his later picture called *Calumny* (Fig. 9:24).

Fig. 9:23 (above). Botticelli. *Birth of Venus*. Tempera on canvas. 8′ 11″ × 5′ 3¼″. 1486–1487. Uffizi, Florence (Alinari). Fig. 9:24 (below). Botticelli. *Calumny*. Oil on wood. 24″ × 35⅜″. *c*.1490. Uffizi, Florence (Anderson)

This is yet another attempt to reconstruct a lost painting by Apelles. A literary description by the Roman author Lucian was known to Botticelli in a translation by Alberti, and the subject was undoubtedly discussed at length by the group of scholars around Lorenzo. Moving from right to left in this elaborate allegory on justice, the observer notes that the seat of judgment is occupied by a wicked prince. On either side of him are his advisers, Ignorance and Superstition, who whisper their evil counsel into his long donkeylike ears. Before him in tattered clothing stands the plaintiff, Envy, who is leading Calumny, the holder of the flaming torch, before the judge. She, in turn, is dragging by the hair the innocent victim, who raises his hands in a gesture of supplication. Treachery and Deceit, personified by two feminine figures, are entwining Calumny's hair with precious ornaments. The dark-hooded figure in mourning garments to their left is Remorse, whose hands point to the accused and whose face is turned toward the naked Truth, who, in turn, raises her hand to high heaven.

In spite of the heavy allegorical burden it has to carry, the picture is a success. The painting has a smooth surface finish, and the colors, even after the passage of more than 450 years, are still of enamellike clarity and brilliance. The placement of the figures in relation to the architectural setting makes pictorial as well as allegorical sense. The movement of the draperies expresses extreme agitation, but the turbulence of the human drama is kept within bounds by Botticelli's mastery of composition. The finely proportioned and spacious building, though it was intended to represent a Roman basilica, is completely in the Florentine Renaissance style. Even the relief sculptures and statuary in niches, in spite of their classical intentions, are far more Florentine in feeling than they are antique.

With Lorenzo's death in 1492, just about the time *Calumny* was finished, Botticelli's career and the arts generally underwent a period of eclipse. Under the influence of the monk Savonarola, a fiery preacher and prophet of doom, all sorts of apocalyptical visions were conjured up. His maledictions and deprecations gathered all the anti-Medici factions around him and succeeded in driving the ruling family out of Florence only two years after the death of the Magnificent. Botticelli, always an introspective personality, repented of his paganism, reputedly burned as many of his pictures of nude subjects as he could lay his hands on, and then became a follower of Savonarola. His late work reflects this religious preoccupation. The beautiful pagan dream of Lorenzo's time, however, had burst like a bubble, and with it Botticelli's inspiration which he never succeeded in recapturing.

POETRY AND MUSIC

Lorenzo de' Medici's title *Il Magnifico* seems in the retrospective view of history to rest on his activities as a poet, humanist, philosopher, discoverer of genius, patron of the arts and sciences, and adviser to writers, sculptors, painters, and musicians. From the terracotta bust out of Verrocchio's workshop (Fig. 9:25), it is apparent that his contemporaries saw another side of his nature, that of the bold and forceful statesman, the victor over the Pazzi family conspiracy, the averter of war with Naples, the holder of the political balance of power in Italy, the sponsor of lavish civic celebrations—in short, the Machiavellian prince. There is little in Verrocchio's portrait to suggest that behind this mask, which shows his subject's will to power so well, there was also the soul of a poet; that in addition to the man of action, there was the contemplative mind of a philosopher; that behind the impassive face of the shrewd professional diplomat, there lurked that of a man capable of the warmest human understanding. For a portrait of the other side of this complex personality, it is necessary to turn to his creative interests that led the historian Guicciardini to conclude in 1530 that Florence could not have had a better or more delightful tyrant.

Under the wise guidance of his grandfather Cosimo *Pater Patriae*, Lorenzo had been educated by Latin and Greek scholars of the highest repute to be the type of philosopher-ruler that Plato had expounded upon in his *Republic*. Social conditions, however, had changed considerably since Cosimo's time. While his grandfather had been a banker with intellectual and artistic tastes, Lorenzo became a prince whose power rested on philosophical prestige and leadership in matters of taste, as well as on his banking fortune. Lorenzo maintained ambassadors at all the principal courts to which he made loans. The King of France was pleased to address him as cousin; and the nearer the time for meeting the interest payments approached, the more flowery the language became. While Lorenzo was always willing to finance foreign conflicts, provided he saw a substantial profit for himself, he preferred to fight his own wars with words. By having the services of the greatest humanists under his command, he never ran out of ammunition in the form of elegantly turned phrases, apt epithets, veiled threats, invectives, fulminations, or diatribes. Changes in the status of the arts had also come about as the century progressed. In the early decades Ghiberti had been employed by the Signory, and his work was intended for public view. Later the major commissions came from a few families; and under Lorenzo the Magnificent the arts took on more of a courtly character, while the audiences grew correspondingly more restricted. Some painters,

Ghirlandaio for instance, were able to remain outside the charmed circle and made careers painting social scenes of births and marriages for an upper middle-class clientele. Botticelli's pictures, however, were done almost entirely for the group of humanistic connoisseurs.

Lorenzo himself, though the leader of this exclusive group, had the instincts of a popular ruler which prompted him not to neglect the common touch. His special delight was participating in the brilliant and colorful Florentine festivals, which took place during the carnival season and after Lent, from May Day to the feast of the city's patron saint John the Baptist in June. Such occasions were celebrated with mummery, masquerading, dancing, and singing in the streets. Before he took an active interest, the level of poetry and music at these affairs was, on the whole, rather low. By composing new verses to the traditional folk tunes, by encouraging others in his circle to do the same, and by holding competitions among composers for better musical settings of the songs, Lorenzo began a movement for the revival of a popular literature in the native Tuscan tongue. While Dante, Petrarch, and Boccaccio in the previous century had written in Italian, this aspect of their work had been neglected by the Latin and Greek scholars who succeeded them; and, except for a few favorite Petrarchian sonnets, they were all but forgotten by the people.

In a commentary on four of his own sonnets, Lorenzo went to considerable lengths to defend the expressive possibilities of the Tuscan Italian; and, after comparing it with Hebrew, Greek, and Latin, he found that its harmoniousness and sweetness outdid all the others. While Lorenzo continued to write subtle sonnets calling for scholarly commentaries, he also wrote popular verses that have, in addition to their beauty and literary polish, all the spontaneous freshness, humor, and charm of folk poetry. In some of his pastoral poetry, the rustic dialogue of real country folk appears in European literature almost for the first time. Few poets could rival the

Fig. 9:25. Verrocchio. *Lorenzo de' Medici*. Painted terra cotta. 25⅞" high. *c.*1480. National Gallery, Washington, D. C.

lyricism of his *canti carnascialeschi*, or carnival songs, which contain such oft-quoted lines on the beauty and fleeting nature of youth as those which open his *Bacchus and Ariadne*:

Quanto è bella giovinezza,	Fair is youth and free of sorrow,
Che si fugge tuttavia!	Yet how soon its joys we bury!
Chi vuol esser lieto, sia:	Let who would be, now be merry:
Di doman non c' è certezza.	Sure is no one of tomorrow.[2]

In order to flourish properly such popular poetry needed appropriate musical settings. Here again Lorenzo was ambitious, though he well knew that musical composition was not among his many talents. As a young man of 18, he was already searching for a composer to set his lyrics. From a letter of 1467, for instance, it is known that he did not look to one of the Florentine musicians. Instead he requested the music master in his household, Antonio Squarcialupi, to get in touch with the "venerable Gugliemo Dufay," who by this time was approaching his 70th year. The setting was made but, unfortunately, it has been lost.

Music in Florence was far from a languishing art. Squarcialupi enjoyed a high reputation for his skill on the organ and lute; but, as a composer, he was a minor figure in comparison with his great northern colleagues. In addition to the more formal church music practiced in the Cathedral and the Church of San Lorenzo, the popular religious music known as lauds were sung in Advent, Lent, and especially in Holy Week. This form was a carry-over from the previous century, and the lauds were performed in unison or in four-part choral settings, with and without instrumental accompaniment. Both Lorenzo and his mother, Lucrezia Tournabuoni, composed lauds. Secular choral music, like the light-hearted ballads known as *frottole* and the *canzone a ballo*, songs that were danced as well as sung, were enthusiastically cultivated and highly popular. Leone Battista Alberti, the architect, man of letters, poet, philosopher, and historian, was also a musician. When the Duke of Milan wanted an expert lute player, he wrote to Lorenzo, who sent him no less a personage than Leonardo da Vinci. It was thus his skill as a musician rather than his painting that first called Leonardo forth from Florence. Since so little of this music was ever written down, it is apparent that it was largely an art of improvisation and performance rather than of composition. The plain fact is that there were no great native Italian masters of composition at this time, while the tonal art in all its forms flourished in Flanders, Burgundy, and the Netherlands. The rich rewards that were to be reaped at the Italian courts, however, drew most of the outstanding representatives of the northern school southward. It must also be kept in mind that nationalism, as far as music was concerned, simply did not exist; and that most of the major musicians of the century, such as Dufay, Ockeghem, Obrecht, Agricola, Isaac, and even the great Josquin des Prez, were active in Florence at one time or another.

When the time came to appoint a successor to Squarcialupi after his death in 1475, Lorenzo's choice fell to Heinrich Isaac, a native of Flanders and a rapid and prolific composer. Florence immediately became a second home to this truly cosmopolitan figure; and the native Italian idioms were combined with those of his own background and training. His duties included those of organist and choirmaster at the Cathedral as well as at the Medici Palace, where Lorenzo is known to have had no less than five organs. Together with the poet Angelo Poliziano, he was also the teacher of Lorenzo's sons, one of whom was destined to be the future music and art-loving pope, Leo X. Most important of all, however, was his collaboration with Lorenzo on the songs written for the popular festivals. He thus became co-creator of one of the popular genres of secular choral music, which eventually led to the madrigal.

During the festive season, there were gaily costumed torchlight processions and parades with floats sponsored by the city's guild and trade organizations. These floats, or cars, which moved through the streets, were designed by such men as Verrocchio and Ghirlandaio, who lavished as much artistry on them as they did on a statue or painting. On or around them were grouped the masked mummers who sang and danced. From descriptions and the surviving poetic and musical examples they fell into two types. First there were the floats with representations of myths or legends, such as the triumph of Bacchus and Ariadne sponsored by the proud Merchant's Guild. For this type Lorenzo wrote the poem, the opening lines of which were quoted on page 368. Then there were the floats of the craftsmen, vendors, and even the beggars, for which the "Song of the Pastry Cooks" and the "Song of the Oil Pressers" were composed. While the poems survive in all three cases, only the latter still has a musical setting, not by Isaac but by Agricola.

If the effect of Savonarola's burning of the "vanities" in 1497 was unfortunate for the visual arts, its effect on secular music was all but catastrophic. Before printed scores were available the loss of the few manuscript copies of such songs meant that the unique record of the popular music of the great Florentine 15th century went up in flames. Enough of this side of Isaac's work remains, fortunately, to show both the style and technique he used. A thematic example which can be documented is part of a choral setting of one of the so-called *Calendimaggio* songs, written for the post-Lenten festival in May. At various points he introduced parts of a popular Florentine melody: [3]

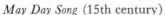

May Day Song (15th century)   Florentine Folk Song

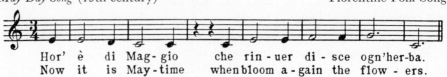

Hor' è di Mag- gio che rin - uer di - sce ogn'her-ba.
Now it is May - time when bloom a - gain the flow - ers.

In *Un dì lieto giamai*, one of Isaac's more sophisticated settings of a poem by Lorenzo survives in complete form. Its homophonic texture is in the style of the carnival songs as well as that of the Florentine *frottola*. Its lilting rhythm, which shifts its meter from time to time, is in the character of the songs which were both sung and danced.[4]

Un dì lieto giamai non hebbi   Words by Lorenzo de' Medici
                                                   Music by Heinrich Isaac

A-mor a tal fol-li - a M'in - dus-se al-lor_ ch'-i' rup-pi

As the setting stands, it could be performed for three-part chorus; as a solo song with the two lower parts taken by the lute or two viols; or as a vocal duet with the soprano and any one of the two other voices. The collaboration of Lorenzo and Isaac thus resulted both in a meeting of minds and a merging of poetic and musical forms. Lorenzo's verses were a union of the courtly *ballata* and popular poetry; while Isaac succeeded in Italianizing the Burgundian *chanson*, or song. Italianizing in this case means simplifying, omitting all artificiality, and enlivening a rather stiff form with the graceful Florentine folk melodies and rhythms. It can be seen that such a movement worked both ways by raising the level of popular poetry on the one hand, and at the same time rejuvenating the more sophisticated poetic and musical forms by contact with popular idioms.

IDEAS

The dominating ideas of the Florentine 15th century cluster around three central concepts—classical humanism, scientific naturalism, and Renaissance individualism. In their broadest meaning humanism, naturalism, and individualism are far from new to the 15th century. Humanism in the Franciscan sense was a carry-over from the two previous centuries; naturalism stems out of late-Gothic times; and individualism as such has probably never been absent from any human society or historical period. The term *Renaissance*, implying as it does a rebirth, is also a source of some confusion. First found in the 16th century in Vasari's *Lives of the Most Eminent Painters, Sculptors and Architects*, the birth certificate of this new movement has never been properly authenticated, and just what was re-born has never been quite satisfactorily explained. Furthermore, if all the principal ideas were present in the two preceding centuries, it might be wiser to speak of a maturation of certain tendencies present in the late Middle Ages. Nevertheless there was a specific color and drive that gave an extraordinary impetus to the creative life and thought of this small Tuscan city-state in the 15th century. Therefore it is important to discover just what it was, and what it was not, that gave Florence its special flavor.

It is often asserted, for instance, that the Renaissance meant a secularization of life as opposed to the predominantly religious outlook of the Middle Ages. The secular spirit may indeed have been stronger, but in medieval times there was a secular tradition in the architecture of castles, guild halls, and market buildings; pictorial works, such as the Bayeux Tapestry; epics, such as the *Chanson de Roland;* the Goliardic folk verse; the aristocratic poetry of the troubadours; and the music of the minstrels. The fact that so much of it has not survived has led too often to the conclusion that it did not exist. A look at the record of the 15th century, however, will reveal that more than 90 per cent of the statuary, paintings, and music were religious works intended for placement or performance in churches. Such works as Pollaiuolo's Hercules series, the mythological pictures of Botticelli, and the carnival songs of Isaac and Lorenzo are seen in the light of history to be outstanding; but in their own time they were conspicuous exceptions rather than the rule. On the other hand, Dufay's dedicatory motet *Nuper Rosarum* and Benozzo Gozzoli's *Journey of the Magi*, though nominally religious, are actually records of contemporary events. Lorenzo's sacred drama *San Giovanni e Paolo* with music by Isaac was a family affair performed at the Medici Palace, and Botticelli's *Adoration of the Magi* was in reality a family portrait. While the piety of a Fra Angelico was becoming increasingly rare, there is no reason to assume that the period was antireligious or even ir-religious. Religious motivation was still a powerful force, as the career of Savonarola proves, but its expression simply assumed another form.

Though Florentine humanism evolved from the Franciscan spirit, it took on a consciously classical coloration. Here again, however, a word of caution is necessary when speaking of a "rebirth" of the spirit of antiquity. In Italy, much more than in northern Europe, the classical tradition had been more-or-less continuous. Roman remains were everywhere in evidence. Many arches, aqueducts, bridges, and roads were still in use, while fragments of ancient buildings, such as columns, were used and reused over and over again as building materials. In the late 13th century, Niccolo Pisano's sculptural models were the Roman fragments he saw all around him, and the same influence is seen in the work of Ghiberti. Aristotle was still the official philosopher of the Church, and ancient musical theory was still studied. What was new to Florence was the study of the Greek language, the setting up of Ciceronian rather than medieval Latin as a standard, and a passionate interest in Plato. In spite of a certain antiquarianism, however, the net result was less a revival of things past than a step forward. It was—as such movements usually are—a search for past precedents in order to justify present practices.

Much has been said also about the pagan aspect of this interest in antiquity. Here again it was less anti-Christian than appears on the surface. Florentine Neo-Platonism was certainly antischolastic, but it was mainly a substitution of the authority of Plato for that of Aristotle. Marsilio Ficino, as the high priest of the movement, in his interpretation of the *Republic* and *Laws*, speaks of Plato as the Attic "Moses." He is also known to have added "Saint" Socrates to the litany and to have burned a candle before the bust of Plato. In this light his thought appears more as a reinterpretation of Christianity in Platonic terms than paganism as such. There was also a certain amount of anticlericalism in Florence, just as there was in other places at this time. Lorenzo, however, as the papal banker and as a father who chose the Church for his son Giovanni's career, was not so much a religious skeptic as he was a political realist. It is also important to remember in this regard that the Florentine humanists were a small band of learned men, whose Platonic disputations have made much more noise in history books than they did in their own time. Actually they never had, nor even sought, a large audience. In the first quarter of the following century, however, the humanists had the international forum of Rome. The artistic expression of Neo-Platonism came to its climax in the works of Michelangelo, and the full discussion of the movement will therefore be deferred until the next chapter.

Naturalism in the sense of fidelity to nature appears in a developed form both in the northern Gothic sculpture and in the poetry of St. Francis who died as early as 1226. By the 14th century, representations of man and nature alike had pretty well lost their value as other-worldly symbols. Rather than remaining a generalized interest in this world, however, the naturalism of the Florentine 15th century took a noticeable scientific turn. Careful observation of natural phenomena and the will to reproduce objects as the eye sees them is evidence of an empirical attitude; dissection of cadavers in order to see the structure of the human body reveals a spirit of free inquiry; and the study of mathematics so as to put objects into proper perspective involves a new concept of space. Thus, while Fra Angelico's religious and Botticelli's pagan dreams are ample evidence that the visionary element is still present, it is also clear that a new scientific spirit has entered the picture.

While individualism as such is practically universal, the distinctive feature of its Florentine expression was that in this small city-state conditions were almost ideal for the artists to come into immediate and fruitful contact with their patrons and audience. Competition was keen; desire for personal fame was intense; and a high regard for personality is seen in the portraiture, biographies, and autobiographies.

It should therefore be clear that the Florentine Renaissance was characterized by no sharp cleavage with the past, and that the special savor of the period in question lies in the quality of its humanism, in the tendency of its naturalism, and in its particular regard for individualism.

Scientific Naturalism

The two basic directions taken by the naturalism of the period had to do with a new experimental attitude and a new concept of space. The spirit of free inquiry was by no means confined to the arts alone. It permeated all the progressive aspects of the life of the time from a re-examination of the forms of secular government to Machiavelli's observations on how men behave in a certain given set of political circumstances. This searching curiosity reached its full fruition in the early years of the next century in Machiavelli's political handbook *The Prince*; in the same author's attempt to apply the Thucydidean method of rational historical analysis in his *History of Florence*; and in the scientific observations in Leonardo's notebooks, which cover everything from hydraulics to astronomy. Well within the 15th century, however, the same spirit manifested itself. Ghiberti's *Commentaries* took up the mathematical proportions of the human body as the basis of its beauty, and he wrote the first treatise in Italian on optics. Brunelleschi, as a diligent student of Vitruvius, was concerned with the mathematical proportions of his buildings. Alberti, in his books on painting, sculpture, and architecture, supplied a codification of the principles and theories of art, together with the study of mathematics as their underlying force.

The sculptors and painters who followed the leadership of Antonio Pollaiuolo and Verrocchio were animated by the desire to express the structural forms of the body beneath its external appearance. Their studies of anatomy opened the way to the modeling of the movements and gestures of the human body, varying from Verrocchio's realization of incipient muscular movements to Pollaiuolo's energetic athleticism. In painting, naturalism meant a more faithful representation of the world of appearances and one based on detailed and accurate observation. Even Fra Angelico showed an interest in the exact reproduction of Tuscan botanical specimens in the garden of his *Annunciation;* and Botticelli, under the influence of Pollaiuolo and Verrocchio, combined objective techniques with his highly imaginative subject matter. The culmination of this line of thought was reached in Verrocchio's pupil Leonardo da Vinci, who considered painting a science and sculpture a mechanical art. In music there was a continued interest in Greek theory, coupled, however, with attempts to experiment with acoustical problems. The compositions of Dufay and others of the northern school were characterized by extreme erudition; and mathematical laws were strictly applied to such aspects of composition as rhythmical progressions, formal proportions, and the development of elaborate technical devices.

Most dramatic of all, however, was the 15th-century conquest of space, whether in the form of the navigational discoveries of a certain Genoese adventurer named Columbus, in the raising of Brunelleschi's cupola almost 400 feet into the air, in the development of linear perspective by Ghiberti, atmospheric perspective by Masaccio, or the new organizations of tonal space in music. By applying the principles of Euclidean geometry to the optical aspects of drawing, space could be made to conform to objective mathematical laws, and the result was the discovery of linear perspective. Through this means pictorial composition was more truthful to nature as represented from a particular vantage point. In the bronze reliefs of Ghiberti, in the paintings of Masaccio and Ucello, objects were arranged in planes as seen by the eye, and their size was in relation to distance or proximity rather than to absolute or psychological importance.

Since the subjects of most medieval artists were drawn from the other world, they were outside the scope of naturalistic representation and had to be rendered symbolically. The Renaissance approach, by contrast, became a new departure. In view of its novelty in the context of the time, the fact that it was universally adopted is all the more remarkable. Once the idea was worked out, artists showed no hesitancy in employing it, and their patrons and audiences apparently had no hesitancy in accepting it. In a more subtle way it even affected music, and the fertile mind of Alberti is found making analogies between the spatial dimensions of line, plane, and volume and the musical elements of melody, interval, and chord. The increasing of the range of musical instruments in order to broaden the scope of tonal space, the development of homophonic textures, such as those of Isaac, so as to enhance the perception of harmonic space, and the acoustical experiments of the time are all related phenomena. The arts of painting and sculpture, however, were firmly wed to geometrical and mathematical laws, a union which lasted with relatively few extramarital deviations up to the 20th century. The 15th-century Florentine artists literally reveled in their perspective, optical, anatomical, and acoustical discoveries. By the 16th century, however, the novelty had worn off, so that artists, such as Leonardo, Michelangelo, and Raphael were free to explore their expressive possibilities and implications more fully.

Renaissance Individualism

Whether one considers the reasons why Renaissance patrons commissioned artists, the forms and techniques employed in the various arts, the regard for human personality seen in the portraiture, the desire for personal prestige through art, or the social status of the artist, there is evidence everywhere of a special attitude of Renaissance man toward himself, his fellow men, and his place in the world. The religious nature of the vast majority of the works of art has already been pointed out. Brunelleschi, however, built the Pazzi Chapel, Masolino and Masaccio decorated the Brancacci Chapel, and Benozzo Gozzoli and Filippo Lippi did the murals for the Medici Chapel for private donors as memorials to themselves and their families. Fra Angelico decorated the corridors of the monastery of San Marco, which was under the protection of the Medici family; and Squarcialupi and Isaac, who played the organs in the Cathedral and other churches, were on the payroll of the Medicis and played in their palace as well. Piousness and the desire for spiritual salvation, therefore, were not the only motives for such munificence. A knowledge that the donor's present and posthumous fame depended on the building of monuments and his choice of the artists to decorate them also entered the picture.

In addition to the circumstances of patronage, there were certain technical considerations within the arts themselves that point in the same individualistic direction. The development of perspective drawing, for instance, implied that the subject in the picture—whether a Madonna, a saint, or an angel—was definitely placed in this world rather than symbolically in the next and hence was more on a par with the observer. The unification of space by having all the lines converge at one point on the horizon is also an enhancement of the status of the individual spectator. By such clear organization of lines and planes, central perspective presupposes that everything is seen from a single optical vantage point. While it is actually that of the artist, he makes it seem as if it were also that of the observer. By closing his form, the artist further implies that nothing of importance lies outside, and the whole of the picture can then be taken in at a glance. Since nothing, then, is beyond the grasp of the viewer, and all can be comprehended with relatively little effort, the eye and mind of the viewer are both reassured and flattered. The preference by Alberti, Bramante, and later by Michelangelo and Palladio for central type churches, in which the space is unified under a dome, is the architectural expression of the same idea. The Gothic cathedral purposely led the eye and imagination outward into the transcendental beyond, while the central type plan revolves around man himself. Standing under the cupola, the observer is aware that the axis of the building is not objectively outside or transcendentally beyond, but subjectively in himself. He is, for the moment at least, the center of the architectural space; and the center of the universe is not therefore at some remote point beyond the horizon but within man himself.

Human figures, whether intended as prophets or portraits, tended to become more personal and individual. Each statue of Donatello, whether it happens to be *Lo Zuccone*, the *David*, or the *Gattamelata*, is a human individuality who makes a powerful and unique impression. Even Fra Angelico's Madonna is a personality more than an abstraction, and the figure of the Angel Gabriel possesses genuine human dignity. Whether the medium is marble, terra cotta, paint, words or tones, there is evidence of the new value placed on human individuality. Whether the picture is a family group, disguised as in Botticelli's *Adoration of the Magi*, or a personal portrait, as in Verrocchio's bust of Lorenzo, the figures are authentic personages rather than stylized abstractions; even though Lorenzo was the most powerful political figure of Florence, Verrocchio sees him as a man, not as an institution.

The self-awareness of the artist as an individual is seen in the inclusion of obvious self-portraits in paintings, such as that of Benozzo Gozzoli in his *Journey of the Magi* and the extremely prominent position Botticelli accords himself in his *Adoration of the Magi*. In architecture Brunelleschi becomes the subject of a biography; Ghiberti's personal reminiscences in his *Commentaries* are probably the first autobiography of an artist in history; his inclusion of the lives and legends of his famous 14th-century predecessors are also the first biographies of individual artists of this kind; the signatures of artists on their own works become the rule not the exception; and the culmination comes when Michelangelo realizes he is so renowned, and that his works have such a unique quality all their own, that he does not have to sign them. The desire for personal fame grows to such an extent that such an artist as Benvenuto Cellini is no longer content to let his works speak for him, but takes up the pen and writes a voluminous autobiography filled with the utmost egotism. Vasari's lives of the artists he knew personally and by reputation are so far from the pious medieval lives of the saints, that they begin to take on the gossipy quality of a society column. Such works as Pico della Mirandola's essay on the *Dignity of Man*, Machiavelli's *The Prince*, and Castiglione's *The Courtier* were all written with the idea of enhancing the intellectual, political, and social status of man.

One who possessed the quality of *virtù* was admired above all others. The word comes closer to the modern meaning of *virtuoso* than *virtuous*, though it was then used in a broader sense. The man with *virtù* had a certain boundless vitality and extraordinary ability that led to the distinguished achievements of a Lorenzo the Magnificent, or the kind of breathtaking conceptions of a Michelangelo. The one striking exception to modern thought is the Renaissance artist's attitude toward specialization. It goes back to the workshop principle where an apprentice was trained to grind pigments, carve wooden chests, make engravings, and prepare the wall surface for frescoes, as well as to carve marble reliefs and paint pictures. When this breadth of technical background is sublimated into the theoretical and intellectual atmosphere of the period and combined with a notable degree of individual genius, the emergence of the *uomo universale*, or universal man, is seen. Brunelleschi was a goldsmith, sculptor, engineer, mathematician, and student of ancient languages as well as one of the leading lights of Renaissance architecture. Alberti was an athlete, horseman, brilliant conversationalist, Latin stylist, mathematician, architect, musician, and playwright as well as the founder of the Renaissance theory of art. In Leonardo da Vinci's case it is more difficult to find a field in which he was not proficient than those in which he excelled.

It was thus not enough for an artist to create works of art. He had to be a great human being as well. In late medieval and early Renaissance times, the artist was content with his relatively modest status as a craftsman in his studio. Giotto, the Pisani, Ghiberti, the della Robbias, and Donatello—all had workshops in which they employed apprentices and assistants, and where manual dexterity was the highest accomplishment. During Lorenzo's time, however, the theory of art assumed ever greater importance. Alberti was a scholar-architect who wrote books on the subject, designed buildings on paper, and left the actual construction to a master-mason. Botticelli associated with men of letters and worked elaborate allegorical meanings into his pictures. Leonardo realized the ideal of Renaissance man in his knowledge of science and engineering as well as in his practice of painting, sculpture, and music. Bramante and Raphael were artist-scholars as well as architects and painters. Michelangelo hated the workshop, even though the realization of his grandiose designs depended on such collaboration. In this respect he is the modern individualistic artist, consciously an intellectual, dealing with popes and princes as equals, insisting that he paints with his brains not with his hands, rejecting all offers of noble titles, and when people began calling him "the divine," the cycle is complete.

CHAPTER

CHRONOLOGY: Rome, 16th Century

General Events

1471–1484 Sixtus IV (della Rovere), Pope
1473 Sistine Chapel built
c.1481 Botticelli and others commissioned to decorate walls of Sistine Chapel
1484–1492 Innocent VIII (Cibò), Pope
1486–1494 Josquin des Prez served in the Sistine Chapel Choir
1492–1503 Alexander VI (Borgia), Pope
Mural decorations of ancient Rome uncovered
Apollo Belvedere found
1496–1501 Michelangelo in Rome
1503–1513 Julius II (della Rovere), Pope
1505 Michelangelo commissioned to do the tomb of Julius II
1506 Destruction of Old St. Peter's begun by Bramante
Foundation stone of new basilica of St. Peter laid
Laocoön statue discovered
1508–1512 Michelangelo painted the Sistine Chapel ceiling
1508 Raphael summoned to Rome
1512 Cappella Giulia Choir founded by Julius II
1513–1521 Leo X (de' Medici), Pope
1513–1516 Leonardo da Vinci in Rome
1515 Orlando Furioso (Madness of Roland) written by Ariosto
1517 Protestant Reformation began in Germany
1519 Charles V became Holy Roman Emperor
1520 Leo X issued papal bull condemning Martin Luther's theological position
1521 Luther declared a heretic and is excommunicated
1523–1534 Clement VII (de' Medici), Pope
1527 Rome sacked by the imperial troops of Charles V
Clement VII held prisoner in the Castle of St. Angelo
1528 Book of the Courtier published by Castiglione
1532 The Prince by Machiavelli published posthumously
1534–1549 Paul III (Farnese), Pope
1534 Church of England separated from Rome

1534 Michelangelo became permanent resident of Rome
Counter-Reformation begun
1534–1541 Michelangelo painted Last Judgment in Sistine Chapel
1538 Ignatius Loyola in Rome
1540 Society of Jesus (Jesuit Order) founded by Loyola
1542 Congregation of the Inquisition established
1543 Copernicus published De Revolutionibus Orbium Coelestorum
Censorship of printed matter begun
1545–1563 Council of Trent sat in Rome
1547 Michelangelo made architect of St. Peter's
1550 Lives of the Most Eminent Painters, Sculptors and Architects published by Vasari
c.1550 Philippe de Monte in Rome. Published his first book of madrigals in 1554
1551 Orlando Lassus in Rome
1564 Death of Michelangelo

Architects

c.1444–1514 Bramante
1475–1564 Michelangelo
1556–1629 Carlo Maderna
1598–1680 Lorenzo Bernini

Sculptors

1460–1529 Andrea Sansovino
1475–1564 Michelangelo
1500–1571 Benvenuto Cellini
c.1524–1608 Giovanni da Bologna

Painters

1452–1519 Leonardo da Vinci
1454–1513 Pinturicchio
1475–1564 Michelangelo
1483–1520 Raphael Sanzio

Writers

1474–1533 Ludovico Ariosto
1478–1529 Baldassare Castiglione
1483–1531 Martin Luther
1511–1574 Vasari
1544–1595 Torquato Tasso
1548–1600 Giordano Bruno

Musicians

c.1445–1521 Josquin des Prez
c.1521–1603 Philippe de Monte
1525–1594 Giovanni da Palestrina
c.1532–1594 Orlando Lassus

10

THE ROMAN RENAISSANCE STYLE

ROME, EARLY 16th CENTURY

On April 18, 1506, when the foundation stone of the new basilica of St. Peter (Fig. 10:18) was laid, Rome was well on its way toward becoming the undisputed artistic and intellectual capital of the Western world. Pope Julius II was gathering about him the foremost living artists in all fields, and together they began the transformation of the Eternal City from a medieval stronghold into the splendor of the Rome of today. Donato Bramante was the architect at work on the plans for the central church of Christendom. Michelangelo Buonarroti was collecting the marble for a monumental papal tomb and was about to begin the painting of the Sistine Chapel ceiling. Raffaelo Sanzio was soon to be summoned from Florence to decorate the walls of the Vatican Palace. Andrea Sansovino was carving a cardinal's tomb in one of Julius II's favorite Roman churches, Santa Maria del Popolo, while Pinturicchio was covering its choir vaults with a series of murals in fresco. One of the exceptions to the rule was the restless Leonardo da Vinci, who had already been in Rome and was continuing his peregrinations elsewhere. Another was the singer-composer Josquin des Prez, who had been a member of the papal choir for eight years and had left to become choirmaster to the King of France.

The flight of the Medicis from Florence was accompanied by a general exodus of artists as well. Many were attracted to temporary havens in the ducal courts of Italy, but the most magnetic attraction of all was that of the papal court. The cultural capital therefore shifted from Florence to Rome during the days of the two great Renaissance popes, Julius II (della Rovere) and Leo X (de' Medici). Since Leonardo, Andrea Sansovino,

Fig. 10:1 (left). Raphael. *Portrait of Julius II*. Oil on wood. 39″ × 32″. 1512. Pitti Palace, Florence

Fig. 10:2 (right). Raphael. *Portrait of Leo X with Two Cardinals*. Oil on wood. 50″ × 47″. *c*.1518. Pitti Palace, Florence (Alinari)

Michelangelo, and Pope Leo were from Florence, and since Bramante and Raphael had absorbed the Florentine style and ideas in extended sojourns there, the cultural continuity remained unbroken. It was, in fact, like a smooth transplantation from the confines of a nursery to that of an open field. For some it simply meant a change of residences and patrons; for all it was an opportunity to branch out from their local styles into the universal air of Rome. Such projects as the building of the world's largest church, the construction of Julius II's tomb, the painting of the Sistine ceiling, and the murals for the Vatican Palace, could only be found in Rome. In no other place were monuments of such proportions or commissions of such magnitude possible. In addition there were the cardinals in residence there, who maintained palaces and princely retinues of their own that reflected on a smaller scale the brilliance of the papal court.

The Eternal City, though it was the artistic heir of all the ages, curiously enough lacked an indigenous Renaissance style of its own. There were, in fact, no native artists of any stature; and during the 15th century, architects, sculptors, painters, and musicians were imported from various European centers. When their projects were completed, they departed. The plans of the 16th-century popes, however, were on such a colossal scale that they were able to absorb the major creative energies of the giants of their age. They were, furthermore, determined to regenerate the authority and glory of the Holy See—as well as to insure their own immortality—through their patronage of the arts. While Lorenzo, for instance, had remained more or less a local Florentine figure, his son Leo X became a *magnifico* on an international scale that made his pontificate a golden age for the arts.

The interest in antiquity had animated many other Italian Renaissance centers; but when the movement got underway in Rome, it was, so to speak, on its home soil. When antique statues were excavated elsewhere, they caused a considerable stir. In Rome, however, many of the ancient monuments were still standing, and when the archeological shovels were applied in the proper places, a veritable treasure trove was waiting for them. One by one the *Apollo Belvedere*, the *Venus of the Vatican*, and the *Laocoön* (Fig. 2:15) came to light and gave a new impetus to the work of Michelangelo and other sculptors. The frescoes from Nero's Domus Aureus and the Baths of Titus provided the first important specimens of ancient painting. While the art of working in tempera on fresh plaster had never actually died out, these ancient Roman fragments gave fresco painting a new respectability in the Renaissance vocabulary. But for their powerful challenge, Michelangelo might otherwise never have been persuaded to try his hand at the art.

Julius II had received most of his training in diplomacy and statecraft from his uncle, Pope Sixtus IV. A passionate love of the arts fortunately was included in this heritage. It was Sixtus who had built the chapel that has subsequently borne his name, and who had installed the group of papal singers there which has ever since been called the *Cappella Sixtina*, or the Sistine Chapel Choir. It remained for Julius to provide still another chorus to perform in St. Peter's, which is known after him as the *Cappella Giulia*, or Julian Choir. This latter group corresponded to the ancient Schola Cantorum and prepared the singers for the Sistine Choir. Both have always received strong pontifical support, and both are still flourishing institutions.

Julius II was essentially a man of action, and an expert wielder of the sword as well as the crozier. He met his age on its own terms, and the spectacle of *il papa terribile*, or the extraordinary pope, riding a fiery steed into the smoke of battle had a remarkably demoralizing effect on his enemies. As one of the principal architects of the modern papacy, he also saw the need of a setting in keeping with the magnificence of the Church and made it a matter of policy to command artists as well as soldiers. At the end of his career, his volcanic energies spent, Julius II became the subject of one of Raphael's most penetrating portraits (Fig. 10:1).

When Leo X ascended the papal throne, one of the eulogies ran: "Venus has had her day, and Mars his, now comes the turn of Minerva." Venus symbolized the reign of the Borgia pope, Alexander VI; Mars, of course, referred to Julius II; and it was the son of Lorenzo the Magnificent who set the official seal of Florence, as the latter-day Athens, on the papacy. Michelangelo, whom he had known since his childhood at the Medici palace, was unfortunately bound by the terms of his contract to serve the heirs of Pope Julius. The suave and worldly Raphael, however, was available and more congenial to the personal taste of Pope Leo than the gruff titan. Here again Raphael served as papal portraitist in the unusually fine study of *Pope Leo X with Two Cardinals* (Fig. 10:2). Ludovico Ariosto, a friend of Leo's from his university days, came to Rome. His *Horatian Epistles* are still the best and most accurate picture of the Rome of this time, and his *Orlando Furioso*, or *Madness of Roland*, is one of the great Italian epic poems. From contemporary accounts it is known that one of Ariosto's poetic comedies, *Suppositi*, was presented before Leo with a solo singer, a chorus, and with orchestral intermezzos in which fifes, viols, two cornets, bagpipes, a lute, and a small organ took part. The latter was apparently the rare instrument, "so varied of voice," with an alabaster case which was made for Leo by a Neapolitan organ builder, and which is mentioned in Castiglione's *The Courtier*. Leo's old music teacher, Heinrich Isaac, wrote the six-part motet that commemorated his accession, and Isaac's pupil became one of the most liberal of all Renaissance patrons of music. All the other princes in Europe had difficulty in keeping their musicians, since the pope's love of the tonal art was so well known. He collected lute and viol players, organists, and the finest singers. Chamber music was avidly cultivated at the pontifical palace, and a wind ensemble performed at the papal meals. Leo's encouragement of music to the point of putting it on a par with literary pursuits caused considerable murmuring among men of letters. As a competent composer in his own right, Leo knew the art from the inside as few patrons have ever known it. As a philosopher, writer, connoisseur, and collector, his patronage, like that of his father before him, was accompanied by an active participation in many of the pursuits that he sponsored.

As one of the leading representatives of the Florentine humanistic point of view, Leo X brought a lofty intellectual tone to Rome, which raised the prestige of the papacy and made his reign a heyday of humanism. He was, in fact, the personification of a Platonic philosopher-king. His conception of the papacy was that of a great civilizing force; and under him the visual arts, letters, music, and the theater entered a period of rare florescence. Other aspects of his pontificate appeared somewhat less lustrous. There were ominous rumblings of a religious schism coming from across the Alps, and the papal treasury was approaching bankruptcy. Athena, however, had rarely been served so well, and his reign might indeed be called a carnival of culture. Burckhardt spoke well when he said that Rome "possessed in the unique court of Leo X a society to which the history of the world offers no parallel." [1]

SCULPTURE

In spite of Michelangelo's many masterpieces in other media, in his own mind he was always first and foremost a sculptor. Other projects were undertaken with reluctance, and in the case of the painting of the Sistine Chapel ceiling, he ostentatiously signed the contract, Michelangelo *Scultore* —Michelangelo the Sculptor—as a protest. His earliest visit to Rome coincided with the discovery of some ancient statuary, including the *Apollo Belvedere*, that proved a powerful stimulus to his own productivity. The most important works of this early period are a *Bacchus* and a *Pietà*, which illustrate the dualism of the pagan and Christian ideals that were to affect his aesthetic thought throughout his long creative career.

The *Pietà* (Fig. 10:3), now in the Crucifixion Chapel of St. Peter's, was commissioned in 1498 by Cardinal Villiers, the French ambassador to the Holy See. Its beauty of execution, delicacy of detail, and poignancy of expression reveal that Michelangelo was still under the spell of the Florentine Renaissance. The pyramidal composition was a type worked out by Leonardo da Vinci as exemplified in his drawing for *Madonna and Child with St. Anne* (Fig. 10:4). Michelangelo modifies it somewhat by using the voluminous folds of the Madonna's drapery as the base of the pyramid and the head of the Virgin as its apex. The figure of Christ is cast in the perfect form of a Greek god, while the Madonna, though overwhelmed with grief,

Fig. 10:3. Michelangelo. *Pietà*. Marble. 69″ high. 1498–1499. St. Peter's, Rome (Alinari)

Fig. 10:4. Leonardo da Vinci. *Study for the painting Madonna and Child with St. Anne.* Drawing in black and white chalk. 54¾″ × 39¾″. Between 1482 and 1500. Royal Academy of Arts, Burlington House, London

maintains a classical composure. No tears, no outcry, no external gesture mars this conception of Mary as the matronly mother of sorrows. Yet Michelangelo allows himself many liberties with the proportions of his figures in order to heighten their expressive effect and enhance the harmony of his design. The excessive amount of drapery can exist only to provide a multiplication of folds and sweeping lines. The body of Christ is far smaller in proportion to that of the Madonna in the interest of making the composition more compact. The triangular shape, as a self-sufficient form, tends to hold the attention within the composition itself and to obviate the necessity for such external considerations as a niche or architectural background. As such it is a kind of sculptural declaration of independence, and it bears the unique distinction of being the only work Michelangelo ever signed.

After finishing the *Pietà*, Michelangelo was once more in his home territory of Florence where he worked on the *Bruges Madonna* and the *David*. In 1505, however, he was summoned to Rome by the imperious Pope Julius II to discuss a project for a colossal tomb. In the inception of this gigantic composition, the artist's imagination for once met its match in his patron's ambitions. The monument was to be quadrangular in shape and was intended to be seen from all sides. The entire marble quarries of Carrara had to be placed at Michelangelo's disposal, since the tomb was to include well over 40 statues. It was to be placed in Old St. Peter's, but as its proportions grew, even the largest church in Christendom seemed too small to contain it, a fact which made Julius all the more determined to tear down St. Peter's and replace it with a larger and more imposing structure. Like all such challenges to the gods, human will power proved no match for fate. Floods on the Tiber prevented the marble from reaching Rome; wars and rumors of wars distracted the attention of the pontiff; and the monumental dream soon turned into a nightmare. In exasperation Michelangelo defied papal authority and fled from the Eternal City. "If I were to remain in Rome," he wrote to a friend, "my own tomb would be prepared before that of the Pope. This is the reason for my sudden departure." [2]

When Julius died in 1513, only a few parts of the project were finished and a new contract with the Pope's heirs had to be negotiated. Further revisions were made later, each time reducing the proportions of the project and eliminating some of the unfinished statues. In its final form of 1545, it had shrunk to the relatively modest wall tomb now to be seen in the aisle of the Church of San Pietro in Vincoli. Thus it is that his biographers have referred to this unfinished chapter in Michelangelo's life as the

Tragedy of the Tomb. Like all true tragedies, however, its towering implications always take precedence over its realization, and its original conception transcends all later compromises.

Tombs of the popes, like the triple tiaras with which they are crowned, were traditionally in three rising zones, symbolizing earthly existence, death, and salvation. For the original project Michelangelo translated these divisions into Neo-Platonic terms representing the successive stages of the liberation of the soul from its bodily prison. For the final project, the monument lapsed back into the more traditional stratifications. In the original scheme the lowest level was to have figures of slaves alternating with victories, symbolizing those who are crushed by the burden of life and those who rise above the bonds of matter. This idea was retained in some of the later revisions, and there are six slaves and one victory in various stages of completion.

On the second level of the original project, heroic figures of the leaders of mankind were to be placed. These were the individuals who pointed the way toward the divine goal of humanity in its effort to effect a reunion with God. Moses and St. Paul were to represent the old and the new law, while Rachel and Leah were to personify the active and contemplative aspects of life. Of these, only the Moses was finished by Michelangelo. Figures of Rachel and Leah were begun by the master and finished by assistants. They stand on either side of Moses in the finished tomb, though whether they are in the form intended for the initial project is questionable. The third and highest sphere was to represent the gates of heaven with angels waiting to receive the soul of Pope Julius. Of these none was completed by Michelangelo himself, nor apparently ever begun.

The three figures which date from the years 1513 to 1516, when Leo X was pope, are the two slaves now in the Louvre and the *Moses*. The *Bound Slave* (Fig. 10:5) is the most nearly finished of the two, and seems to represent a sleeping adolescent tormented by a dream rather than a "dying captive" as it is usually called. The imprisoned soul, tortured by the memory of its divine origin, has found momentary respite in sleep. The cloth bands by which the figure is bound are only symbolic, since Michelangelo is not concerned with the external aspect of captivity but rather with the internal torment. Its companion piece, the so-called *Rebellious Slave*, represents the violent though vain struggle of a wide-awake, enormously muscular figure. The implied power of the strong bodies in both cases only emphasizes their ineffectiveness and makes their attempts at escape seem all the more futile. In both there is the same grappling with fate; in both the battle is hopeless. It is the tragedy of man, limited by time

Fig. 10:5. Michelangelo. *Bound Slave*. Marble. 90½″ high. 1514–1516. Louvre, Paris (Alinari)

Fig. 10:6 (left). Michelangelo. "*Boboli Captive.*" Marble. 90½″ high. *c.*1530–1534. Academy of Fine Arts, Florence (Brogi)

Fig. 10:7 (right). Michelangelo. "*Boboli Captive.*" Marble. 90½″ high. *c.*1530–1534. Academy of Fine Arts, Florence (Brogi)

but troubled by the knowledge of eternity; mortal but with a vision of immortality; bound by the weight of his own body yet dreaming of a boundless freedom. This tragedy of the tomb was understood only too well by Michelangelo himself, who had the conception of his great project in mind but was doomed to see only a few fragments of his dream completed. Figures, such as the slaves and victory that Michelangelo envisaged, were associated with the triumphal arches as well as with the mausoleums and sarcophagi of ancient Rome. Models for the *Bound Slave* can be traced to the Hellenistic Marsyas figures, though the similarity between this Slave and the younger son in the *Laocoön* group (Fig. 2:15) has aptly been pointed out.

Still another aspect of this same idea is found in the so-called *Boboli Captives*, two of which are seen in Figs. 10:6 and 10:7. They are thought to have been designed as caryatids for the corners of the base of the revised project of 1532, but they were eventually given by Michelangelo to Duke Cosimo de' Medici, who placed them in a grotto of the Boboli Gardens in Florence. Here the imprisonment by matter is all but complete. Locked inextricably in their blocks of stone, unconscious as yet, even their human status is indeterminate. In their effort to be born they struggle and writhe against their material medium but are as yet undifferentiated from it. Their unfinished state gives an interesting glimpse into Michelangelo's methods, which were similar to that of relief sculpture. In one of his sonnets Michelangelo addressed his friend Vittoria Colonna: "Lady, it is the taking off that puts into the rough hard stone a living figure, grown most great just where the stone has grown most small." [3] The statue, therefore, to Michelangelo was a potential form hidden in the block of marble awaiting the hand of the master sculptor to be born. The Neo-Platonic implication is that the soul of man is still entombed in the body and can only be perfected into pure being by the hand of a higher creative power.

Moses (Fig. 10:8) was the only statue completed entirely by Michelangelo's hand to find its place in the completed tomb. Both Julius II and Michelangelo himself possessed the quality of *terribilità* that is incarnated in this figure. Julius was known as *il papa terribile*, meaning the forceful or powerful pope, imbued with the fear of the Lord. Michelangelo conceives his *Moses* as the personification of a powerful will, and partially as an idealized portrait of the indomitable Julius who, as the codifier of canon law, had something in common with the ancient Hebrew lawgiver. Moses is further portrayed as the personification of the elemental forces—the human volcano about to erupt with righteous wrath, the calm before a storm of moral indignation, the dead center of a hurricane of emotional

Fig. 10:8. Michelangelo. *Moses*. Marble. 100½" high. 1513–1516. San Pietro in Vincoli, Rome
(Anderson)

fury, the author of those thunderous Thou-shalt-nots of the Ten Commandments, the man capable of ascending Mount Sinai and discoursing with God, and coming back down again to review all humanity from the seat of judgment.

Medieval rather than classical precedents are to be cited here, with Moses' immediate ancestor found in Donatello's seated *St. John the Evangelist*. Details such as the stone tablets of the law and the long beard are in keeping with the iconographical tradition. The horns, symbolizing rays of light, are also traditional, stemming from a mistranslation of the Hebrew word for light in the Latin Vulgate version of the Bible. Rodin once made the observation that the statue could be rolled down a hill without any essential part being broken off. This compactness reinforces its expressive power by holding it in check. The smoldering agitation revealed through the drapery, the powerful musculature of the arms, the dominating intellectuality of the face, and the fiery mood are all Michelangelo's own. An interesting detail is seen in his carving of the eye, which he also did with the *David*, in order to express a look of fixed determination. When he wanted the quality of gentleness and resignation, as with the Madonnas, he left the eye untouched.

From 1521 to 1534 Michelangelo worked on various sculptural projects in Florence again, the most outstanding of these being the Medici tombs. Thereafter he went once more to Rome where he was occupied with fresco painting and architectural projects. Only in the spare moments of the last 30 years of his long life, and without specific commissions, did he have the time or inclination to work on two *Pietàs*. One of them at long last was intended for his own tomb; but, like all the others, it too remained unfinished at his death.

Michelangelo's work coincided with a time when many of the most outstanding examples of antique statuary were being unearthed and admired. Inevitably this led to critical comparisons. Michelangelo, like the Greco-Roman artists, saw man as the lord of creation, but nature itself was always a matter of indifference to him. His early art especially was an affirmation of man's supreme place in the universal scheme of things. That world was populated by godlike beings at the peak of their physical power, full of vitality, creatively active, and buoyantly self-confident. As his art matured, his men and women were beset with quite unclassical tensions, problems, and conflicts. Unlike the statues of antiquity, his figures, when they come to grips with fate, are armed with mental and moral powers that imply the hope of ultimate victory. Having thus excelled the art of the ancients as well as that of his own time, not only by his technical mastery but by his expressive power, he came to be regarded by his contemporaries with awe. Vasari, for instance, wrote: "The man who bears the palm of all ages, transcending and eclipsing all the rest, is the divine M. Buonarroti, who is supreme not in one art only but in all three at once." [4] History has had no reason to reverse this judgment.

THE CEILING OF THE SISTINE CHAPEL

When Michelangelo fled from Rome because of the accumulated frustrations in connection with the plans for Julius II's tomb, the Pope resorted to every means from force to diplomacy to get him to return. Knowing he had a genius on his hands, he conceived two interim projects to keep Michelangelo busy until all the problems with his tomb were solved. The first was a colossal bronze statue of himself, sword in hand, for the newly conquered city of Bologna; the statue was destroyed after the pontifical power was overthrown a few years later. The second was the painting of the ceiling of the Sistine Chapel. The building itself, the roof of which can be seen paralleling the nave of St. Peter's in Figure 10:18, was built and named after Julius' uncle, Sixtus IV, as the private chapel of the popes. The interior consists of a single rectangular room 44 by 132 feet. Around the walls were frescoes painted by the foremost 15th-century artists, including the Florentines Ghirlandaio, who was one of Michelangelo's teachers, and Botticelli. Above them were six windows high up on either side and a barrel-vaulted ceiling 68 feet above the floor with 700 square yards of surface stretching before Michelangelo.

All Julius apparently had in mind was a series showing the Twelve Apostles, but, according to a letter of 1523, Michelangelo was given a free hand. "Then he [Pope Julius]," wrote the sculptor, "gave me a new commission to make what I wanted, whatever pleased me." [5] The design and details of the iconography evolved slowly from the mind of the artist as he worked. As the time for this "interim project" dragged on from months into years, the pope's impatience increased correspondingly. On his periodic visits of inspection the scenes mounted in violence with threats being hurled from below and above the scaffolding. Julius knew Michelangelo's temperament as only one volcano can know another, and his eruptions alternated with periods of quiescence and generosity, with the result that the job finally got done—though it took four years to do it.

The entire Sistine ceiling (Fig. 10:9) was conceived as an organic composition motivated by a single unifying philosophical as well as artistic design, as has so convincingly been pointed out by Charles de Tolnay in

Fig. 10:9. Michelangelo. *Sistine Chapel Ceiling*. Frescoes. 45' x 128'. 1508–1512. Vatican, Rome (Anderson)

the second volume of his monumental monographs on Michelangelo.[6] As with the initial project for the Julius tomb and in the later Medici tombs, the iconography is a fusion of the traditional Hebrew-Christian theology and the Neo-Platonic philosophy that Michelangelo knew from his days in the Medici household, where he came into daily conversation with Lorenzo de' Medici, Poliziano, Marsilio Ficino, and Pico della Mirandola. His space is divided into geometrical forms, such as the triangle, circle, and square, which were regarded in Plato's philosophy as the eternal forms that furnish clues to the true nature of the universe. Next there is a three-way division into zones in which the intensity of the lighting plays a part. The lowest and darkest comprises that of the eight triangular spandrels and the four corner pendentive-shaped spandrels. The second is the intermediate zone that includes all the space outside the spandrels except that allotted to the nine center panels, which in turn constitute the third and highest zone.

Symbolically these divisions correspond to the three Platonic stages of the world of matter, the world of becoming, and the world of being. Analogies to such triple divisions run as an undercurrent through all aspects of Plato's thought. He divided society, for instance, into three classes: workers, free men, and philosophers, which he symbolized by the metals brass, silver, and gold. Each stratum had its characteristic goal: the love of gain, the development of ambition, and the pursuit of truth. Learning was likewise broken down into the stages of ignorance, opinion, and knowledge. His theory of the human soul was also tripartite in nature, consisting of the appetitive, emotional, and rational faculties, located in the abdomen, breast, and head, respectively. Of these only the rational or intellective part could aspire to immortality. Man, by reason of his intellect, said Plato at the end of his *Timaeus*, "is like a tree with its root not in the earth but in the sky." It is then the rational element of the soul which "raises us from earth to our kindred who are in heaven." [7]

Michelangelo therefore places uninspired man on the lower level of the spandrels. In the intermediate area are the Old Testament prophets and pagan sibyls who, by reason of their higher mental faculties, mediate between man and God. In the central sphere are the panels that tell the story of man in his direct relationship to God, and they are seen through the architectural divisions as if taking place above on a higher and more cosmic level. In Michelangelo's time the chapel was separated into two parts by a screen with the section near the altar reserved for the clergy and the other for laymen. The central space of the ceiling is divided lengthwise into nine panels, with the part over the lay section telling the story of man and that over the altar, the story of God. Instead of starting at the beginning and proceeding chronologically as in the Book of Genesis, Michelangelo conceives it in reverse order, or as the Platonic ascent of man from his lowest estate back to his divine origin. In this return to God, the soul from its bodily imprisonment gradually becomes aware of God and moves from finiteness to infinity, and from material bondage to spiritual freedom. Immortality in this sense is not the reward for a passive and blameless existence but the ultimate achievement of a tremendous effort of the soul as it struggles out of the darkness of ignorance into the blinding light of truth.

One of the eight spandrels (Fig. 10:11) will show the dreary aspect of humanity without vision. "And Ezekias begat Manasses; and Manasses begat Amon; and Amon begat Josias," so reads the genealogy of the ancestors of Christ at the beginning of St. Matthew's Gospel. Endless generations of humdrum humanity, whose sole purpose is to reproduce themselves and hand the spark of life down to their children; as St. Luke says, they "sit in darkness and in the shadow of death," awaiting the light that will come when the Savior is born. In Gothic iconography the ancestors were the kings of Judah starting with Jesse, David, and Solomon. Here in this spandrel, the child is the future King Josias, but Michelangelo represents him and all the others as a succession of common people dwelling in darkness. The mixture of good and evil is implied by the beauty of the mother on the child's right, and the unenlightened form of his father Amon, who adored idols, on his left. The families huddled within these triangular prisons are but dimly aware of the words of the prophets above them and are quite unconscious of the divine happenings in the ideal region. In the four corner spandrels are the heroic men and women whose active deeds secured temporal deliverance for their people. David's slaying of Goliath, Judith's decapitation of Holophernes, and Haman's punishment through Esther, all have to do with the victory of the weak over the strong with the aid of God. A note of prophecy and ultimate hope is sounded by the episode of Moses and the brazen serpent, an incident in the delivery of the children of Israel from their Egyptian bondage. The allusion comes from the Gospel of St. John: "And as Moses lifted up the serpent in the wilderness, even so must the Son of man be lifted up: that whosoever believeth in him should not perish, but have eternal life" (3:14–15).

This serves as an introduction to the representations of the seven Hebrew prophets, who alternate with the five pagan sibyls like a chorus prophesying salvation. These are the inspired men and women who, through the exercise

Michelangelo. Sistine Ceiling, Details. Fig. 10:10 (top). *Delphic Sibyl*. Fig. 10:11 (lower).
Ancestor of Christ (Josias). 1509 (Anderson)

of the higher faculties of the mind and imagination, become the mediators between the human and divine spheres. They are consequently placed outside the confines of the dark spandrels and in a zone where the lighting approaches that of the central panels.

The *Delphic Sibyl* (Fig. 10:10) is the first of the series. In the Greek tradition and in Plato, she was the priestess of Apollo at Delphi. In Vergil's *Aeneid*, Book VI, she is described as a young woman possessed by the spirit of prophecy. In the grip of the *furor divinus*, or divine fury, she turns her head toward the voice of her inspiration. Though clothed in Greek garments, her beauty is similar to that of Michelangelo's early Madonna types. On either side of her throne are pairs of caryatidlike figures which are a part of the painted architectural pattern. In the shadow below the tablet, the head of a figure which symbolizes her corporeal nature can be seen. Diagonally behind her are a pair of nude figures which symbolize her inspiration. According to Plato, the soul when concerned with the truth is borne aloft by two wings. Ficino interprets these as the mind and will, and Landino as the contemplative and active aspects of life. Above them enframing the central panels are the *ignudi*, or nude youths, which can best be seen in Figure 10:16. These representations in the Christian tradition would have to be angels, but in the Platonic theory they personify the intellective or rational faculties of the souls of the sibyls and prophets, by which they rise to the contemplation of the divine truth, and by which they are able to bridge the gap between the physical and spiritual, or earthly and heavenly regions. Thus, with the single figure below, the paired group on the same level as the prophet or sibyl, and the nude figures above them, the body, spirit, and souls of the seers are symbolized. These correspond, of course, to the tripartite Platonic levels of the appetitive, the emotional, and the intellective. Each of these figures also plays an aesthetic part in the softening of the harsh contours of the architectural design. The nude adolescents function ostensibly as the bearers of the garland that runs around the central panels and from which the painted bronze medallions are suspended. By covering the corners of the frames, and by their postures, they contribute a needed diagonal accent and bring a welcome variety to the design as a whole.

The first of the histories in the central group is the *Drunkenness of Noah* (Fig. 10:12). As in the slave figures of the Julius monument, the picture of Noah shows man in his most abysmal condition as the victim of his own bodily appetites. His servitude is symbolized at the left, where he is seen tilling the parched soil. Though still strong physically, his spirit is overwhelmed by the flesh. His sons, young adolescents in their physical prime, do not seem to be discovering their father's nakedness as related in the Bible, but the tragic fate of man himself, who must work, grow old, and die. Noah's reclining posture recalls that of the ancient Roman river gods, and in this case the head has sunk forward on his chest in what seems to be a premonition of death. Beyond this picture of Noah as the prisoner of his own baser nature, the next panel pictures the Deluge, which shows the plight of man when beset by the elemental forces of nature beyond his control. In the third panel, *Noah's Sacrifice*, man's dependence on God is first implied.

Fall of Man and Expulsion from Paradise (Fig. 10:13) follows next. Temptation here is no mere passive affair but a willful act of man. Adam eagerly reaches out for the fruit—again the victim of his appetites but with the power of making decisions. Eve, contrary to the Biblical story, is seen as the more passive of the two. Adam's hulking body is almost subhuman, while that of Eve is soft and sensuous. The motive of her uplifted arm is repeated by the branch springing out of the tree trunk in the background. The serpent with the torso of a woman recalls that of the ancient sirens or maenads. The dualism of the serpent and the avenging angel of the expulsion side probably implies that sin and retribution, like cause and effect, are the twin aspects of evil. Masaccio's fresco in the Brancacci Chapel (Fig. 9:18) was clearly the model for Michelangelo's Adam and Eve on this side. Adam's body, however, has undergone a significant change from the temptation side, and he now appears morally aware of his action, while Eve cringes and attempts to hide in his shadow. On one side the concern was with blind desire; on the other it is a matter of knowledge and remorse.

The last five panels are concerned with the various aspects of God's nature. In the *Creation of Eve*, He appears as a patriarchal figure closed within the folds of His mantle, His head bent forward as if in deep thought. As in the Gospel according to St. John: "In the beginning was the Word, and the Word was with God, and the Word was God." The implication in Michelangelo's Neo-Platonic conception is that the creative process is a rational one. In the *Creation of Adam* (Fig. 10:14), God reveals His heavenly affinity and appears in the midst of a celestial cloud moving toward the earth and the inert body of Adam. The creative force is here the divine fire that flashes like lightning from the cloud to the earth. Adam's body is one with the rock on which he lies, recalling the unfinished slaves designed for the Julius tomb. In keeping with the Platonic idea of the burden of life, Adam awakens reluctantly rather than eagerly.

In the *Creation of the Sun and the Moon* (Fig. 10:15), the representation of God becomes a personification of the creative principle. Like one of the

Michelangelo. Sistine Ceiling, Details. Fig. 10:12 (above). *Drunkenness of Noah*. 1508–1509 (Anderson). Fig. 10:13 (below). *Fall of Man and the Expulsion from Paradise*. 1509–1510 (Alinari)

Michelangelo. Sistine Chapel, Details. Fig. 10:14 (above). *Creation of Adam*. 1511. Fig. 10:15 (below). *Creation of the Sun and the Moon*. 1511 (Anderson)

Fig. 10:16. Michelangelo. Sistine Chapel, Detail. *God Dividing the Light from the Darkness*. 1511 (Anderson)

celestial bodies, He moves in an orbit throwing off stars and planets, which continue in the courses He sets for them. This flight through the firmament implies the omnipresent aspect of God. The progressive minimizing of the subject matter in these acts of God clearly shows that Michelangelo's idea was to portray His creative nature rather than depict the things which He created.

In *God Dividing the Light from Darkness* (Fig. 10:16), the final panel of the series, the climax and the realm of pure being are attained. This is clarity coming out of chaos, order from the void, existence from nothingness, the idea from unconsciousness. You shall know the truth and the truth shall make you free, according to the Scriptures; or know thyself, as the Delphic oracle told Socrates. The conception of God has progressed from the anthropomorphic figure of the *Creation of Eve*, to that of a cosmic spirit in the intervening panels, and now He is seen as a swirling abstraction in the realm of pure being. The Neo-Platonic objective of the union of the soul with God has been achieved by the gradual progress from the bondage of the spandrels, through the prophetic visions of the seers, and, finally, by ascending the ladder of the histories into the pure light of knowledge, reaching the point of dissolution into the freedom of infinity.

The surface Michelangelo covered was approximately 10,000 square feet, and the composition includes over 300 figures. The method of work commands considerable interest. The cartoon of the whole was first drawn on paper, next cut up into sections of a size corresponding to each day's work, then transferred to the ceiling surface. A section of moistened lime wash of the same proportions was prepared, and the painting was then done in the technique known as fresco-buono. The departures Michelangelo made from the cartoons show that there was an element of improvisation as he went along. The colors are limited by the medium, and as the work progressed his preference was more and more in the direction of shades of gray, which accented the three-dimensional, sculpturesque quality of the figures. Such large projects are almost always school jobs, but from the internal evidence of the frescoes, as well as from documentary sources, Michelangelo appears to have done all the painting himself, with assistants doing the preparatory work only.

Owing to the extremely awkward nature of ceiling painting, Michelangelo had to lie on his back most of the time—a fact which gave rise to one of his most eloquent sonnets, that goes in part: "My beard turns up to heaven; my nape falls in, Fixed on my spine: my breast-bone visibly Grows like a harp: a rich embroidery Bedews my face from brush-drops thick and thin." [8] Though he later returned to the Sistine Chapel to paint the *Last*

Fig. 10:17. Raphael. *School of Athens*. Fresco. *c*.26′ × 18′. 1508–1513. Stanza della Segnatura, Vatican, Rome (Alinari)

Judgment and worked on still another group for the Pauline Chapel in the Vatican, the buoyant optimism and creative force of the earlier series was never recaptured. The impact of the Sistine Chapel ceiling today, as it was on Michelangelo's contemporaries, is like a revelation of one of the eternal verities. Coming as this stupendous work did at the height of the artist's creative powers, the composition as a whole is among the highest peaks in the mountain range of Western art.

At the same time that Michelangelo was painting the Sistine ceiling, Raphael, his younger contemporary, was hard at work on the murals of the Vatican Palace. In the *School of Athens* (Fig. 10:17), Raphael presents such a complete visual philosophy that it places him, along with Michelangelo, in the rarified ranks of artist-scholars. This picture is a work that should be treated either at considerable length or else quite briefly. In the present instance, unfortunately, the latter is the choice that must be made. Space, however, is sufficient to point out a few of its most striking features. The setting itself is generally believed to be the original plan for the new basilica of St. Peter as projected by his friend and adviser Bramante. While Michelangelo goes all the way down the line for Neo-Platonism, the more diplomatic Raphael steers a middle course between the two great philosophies by placing both Plato and Aristotle on either side of the central axis of his picture with the vanishing point squarely between them. The book Plato holds in his hand is his *Timaeus*, and he points skyward to indicate his idealistic world view, while Aristotle carries a copy of his *Ethics* and indicates by his earthward gesture his greater concern with the real and practical world. This division of the central figures equates the entire picture, with the metaphysical philosophers all ranked on Plato's side and the physical scientists pursuing their various researches on Aristotle's. The distribution of the figures into smaller groups on either side corresponds to the divergent schools of thought within the two major divisions. In this way Raphael conceives and carries out his pictorial space so that it synthesizes both his subject matter as well as his grouping of the figures. The picture thus sums up the state of Renaissance humanism through the eyes of still another profound artist.

THE DOME OF ST. PETER'S

In 1545, during the latter years of the pontificate of his friend Pope Paul III (Farnese), Michelangelo had completed the series of frescoes on the martyrdom of Sts. Peter and Paul in the Pauline Chapel of the Vatican. In his 70th year, the religious and intellectual atmosphere of Rome was a far cry from what it had been in the days of Julius II and Leo X. The Protestant Reformation was already an established fact in many European countries, and the Council of Trent was beginning deliberations that set the forces of the Counter-Reformation in motion. Ignatius Loyola had already been in Rome, and the Society of Jesus had received papal approval. The Congregation of the Inquisition and the censorship of printed matter promised restrictions on the expression of ideas. Artists were no longer given more or less a free hand with their pictures but had to accept the advice of ecclesiastical authorities. Even Michelangelo himself was under attack for the nudes and pagan elements of his *Last Judgment* mural in the Sistine Chapel. Such considerations must have weighed heavily in Michelangelo's

Fig. 10:18. *St. Peter's Basilica and the Vatican*, Rome. Apse and Dome by Michelangelo, 1547–1564; Dome completed by Giacomo della Porta, 1588–1592; Nave and Façade by Carlo Maderna, 1606–1626; Colonnades by Bernini, 1656–1663 (Alinari)

mind and influenced to a certain extent his decision to devote himself mainly to architecture during the remainder of his life. At any rate his papal patron first persuaded him to finish the Farnese Palace in 1546, and then to become the chief architect of St. Peter's (Fig. 10:18) the following year, a project that was to absorb most of the energies of his final years.

While the foundations of St. Peter's had been laid as early as 1506, comparatively little progress on the basilica had been made in the tempestuous years that followed, in spite of the succession of brilliant architects. Michelangelo favored the centralized church plans of Brunelleschi and Alberti just as his predecessor Bramante had done. The latter's design, however, was to have culminated in a low dome, modeled on that of the Pantheon but with a peristyle base and a lantern on top. Michelangelo accepted Bramante's Greek-cross ground plan with a few alterations of his own (Fig. 10:19), but he envisaged a loftier canopy rising over the legendary site of St. Peter's tomb. This dome was to be of such monumental proportions that it would unify not only the interior spaces and exterior masses of the building itself but would serve also as the climax of the liturgical, religious, and artistic forces of the Catholic world in the capacity of a symbol at the center of Christendom.

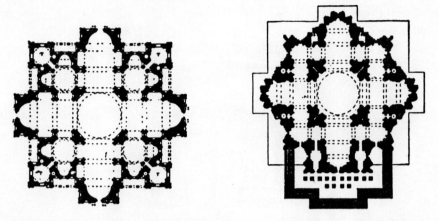

Fig. 10:19 (above). Bramante and Michelangelo. *Plans for St. Peter's*, Rome. Fig. 10:20 (below). St. Peter's, Rome. *Present Plan* (University Prints)

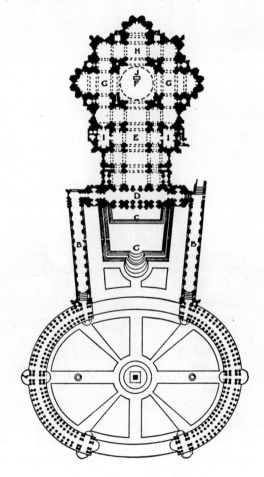

Fig. 10:21. Michelangelo and Maderna. St. Peter's, *Interior beneath Dome* (Alinari)

Fig. 10:22. Michelangelo. St. Peter's, *Apse*. Begun 1546. Rome (Alinari)

His first task was an engineering problem—that of seeing whether the masonry was strong enough to support such a dome. He had to reinforce the four main piers until they were a massive 60 feet square. Pendentives became the means by which the square was circled, and the drum was then ready to rise. Meanwhile he was at work on a large model of the dome itself, so that it could be built by others if necessary. All the preparatory work was thus completed, and Michelangelo lived just long enough to see the drum finished. The dome itself was carried through to completion after his death by two of his associates without substantial alterations. But for the aftermath of the Council of Trent and the Counter-Reformation, Michelangelo's centralized church might also have been finished. The new spirit of orthodoxy, however, frowned on anything that might be considered a pagan form, and a reactionary wave was started in favor of a return to the traditional Latin-cross plan. In the early 17th century, Carlo Maderna undertook the lengthening of the nave (Fig. 10:20). Liturgically it provided more space for the grandiose processions; practically it provided room for larger congregations; historically it absorbed all the area formerly occupied by Constantine's basilica, which had been demolished to make way for the new structure; but aesthetically the proportions suffered, and the climactic effect of the great dome was greatly impaired. The scale of the interior (Fig. 10:21), however, was already set by Michelangelo's huge piers beneath the dome, and Maderna had to continue it in the same proportions. The vaulting thus rises a little over 150 feet above the pavement, a height equivalent to that of the early skyscrapers; while the enormous interior covers more than 25,000 square yards in area.

The church Michelangelo planned can best be seen beneath the dome where it appears as the compact unified structure he wanted. From the apse of the completed church (Fig. 10:22), where the lengthened nave does not detract, the effect is still substantially as Michelangelo intended it to be. From this vantage point the building itself appears as a great podium for the support of the vast superstructure; and, from the ground level to the base of the dome there is a rise of about 250 feet. The cupola then continues upward to the top of the lantern, where an ultimate height of 452 feet above the ground level is attained. Until the advent of the Eiffel Tower and the 20th-century skyscrapers, St. Peter's was at once the world's tallest as well as the largest building. Coming as it did at the climax of the Renaissance, the great dome had an influence on subsequent developments in architecture that was incalculable. It was in no way, however, disproportionate to the significance and beauty of Michelangelo's achievement.

JOSQUIN DES PREZ AND THE SISTINE CHAPEL CHOIR

"I am well aware that in his day Ockeghem was as it were the first to re-discover music, then as good as dead, just as Donatello discovered sculpture in his; and that of Josquin, Ockeghem's pupil, one might say that he was a natural prodigy in music, just as our own Michelangelo Buonarroti has been in architecture, painting, and sculpture; for just as Josquin has still to be surpassed in his compositions, so Michelangelo stands alone and without a peer among all who have practiced his arts; and the one and the other have opened the eyes of all who delight in these arts, now and in the future." [9] So wrote a Florentine literary historian in a book on Dante published in Venice in 1567. Josquin des Prez, to whom he referred, was thus still regarded almost half a century after his death as a figure comparable to that of Michelangelo. A Florentine could bestow no higher praise. The same opinion, moreover, was held by musicians as well. The distinguished theorist Glareanus, for instance, wrote that the work of Josquin was "the perfect art to which nothing can be added, after which nothing but decline can be expected." [10]

The so-called *ars perfecta*, or perfect art, rested on the typical Renaissance historical assumption of the great development of the arts in antiquity, which had been lost in the Middle Ages and subsequently rediscovered in the then-modern times. The above quotations are a critical application of this doctrine of perfection regained to the art of music. Italians, whether at home or abroad, took the greatest pride in the achievements of their own architects, sculptors, and painters, but universally they acknowledged the supremacy of the northern composers. The spread of this polyphonic art dated from the time the popes had become acquainted with it during their Avignon period. Later this led to the establishment of the *Cappella Sixtina* in 1473, which was dominated by Flemish, Burgundian, and French musicians, whose influence from there spread over the entire Christian world. From this time forward their mastery of contrapuntal writing became the standard of perfection.

Under Pope Sixtus IV church music had moved from its status as the modest handmaiden of the liturgy to a position of major importance in the religious experience. The grandeur of the Roman liturgical displays called for music of comparable magnificence. Owing to the prevailing taste of the time, musicians from the great singing centers of Antwerp, Liège, and Cambrai flocked to Rome to seek their fortunes. The highest honor of all was an appointment to the Sistine Choir, whose privilege it was to perform on the occasions at which the pope himself officiated. Membership was highly selective, since the usual quota ran from 16 to 24 singers except during the time of the musical Leo X when it was increased to 36. They were divided into four parts, consisting of boy sopranos, male altos, tenors, and basses; normally they sang *a cappella*—that is, without instrumental accompaniment—a practice which was exceptional rather than usual at the time. The quality of the choir can be deduced from the roster of distinguished men who made their reputations in its ranks. Dufay, the first composer to view the Mass as an organic work of art, entered the choir in 1428. In its archives are numerous masses, motets, and psalm settings by Josquin des Prez, who served from 1486 to 1494. Palestrina, who learned his fluency from Josquin, first became a member in 1551 and brought the organization to a pinnacle of technical perfection.

Josquin's attitude on the dignity of the art of composition is most revealing. When the Duke of Ferrara needed a composer, he hesitated between Isaac and Josquin. He was advised in an extant letter from a friend who knew them both to choose Isaac, "because he is able to get along with his colleagues and composes new pieces quicker. It is true, Josquin composes better, but he does it only when it suits him and not when he is requested. More than this Josquin asks 200 ducats while Isaac is pleased with 120." [11] Like Michelangelo, then, Josquin behaved very much as the modern independent artist with high standards of proficiency, rather than as a craftsman who produced works on order regardless of quality.

In Josquin's compositions the stark barren intervals of Gothic polyphony, and all traces of harshness in the voice leading are eliminated. He allows dissonances to occur only on weak beats or as suspensions on the stronger ones. His rhythms and forms are based on strict symmetry and mathematically regular proportions. His writing is characterized by the usual northern fondness for canonic imitations and other complicated contrapuntal constructions. Such devices, however, are managed with complete mastery, and his tremendous technique in composition never intrudes upon his expressive design. He was at home in all Renaissance musical forms, excelling perhaps in his motets and in his solo and choral chansons. In Rome where his unique abilities were combined with the warmth and fluidity of Italian lyricism, his art mellowed into a style of incomparable beauty, formal clarity, and the purest expressivity.

Josquin's four-part motet *Ave Maria* will serve as an admirable illustration of his art. Like Michelangelo's *Pietà* it is in a perfectly self-contained form, emotionally restrained, and full of luxuriantly flowing lines. Even

Ave Maria (4-Part Motet)   Josquin des Prez

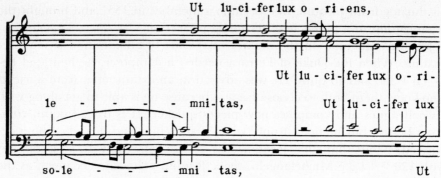

such a short excerpt as this shows his penchant for canonic imitation between the voices, and the smoothness of contour which comes with stepwise
melodic motion. He treats all four voices with balanced impartiality but
prefers to group them, as in this instance, in pairs in order to achieve a
transparency of texture and an ineffable purity of sound. Darker sides of
Josquin's emotional spectrum can be found in his Requiem Masses and in
his setting of the psalm De Profundis.

Later periods saw in Michelangelo both a summing up of the Renaissance and the beginning of the Baroque style. Josquin's place was more
limited; and while he was universally acknowledged as the greatest musical
mind of the early 16th century, the very perfection of his art implied that
it was on the verge of becoming archaic. His mantle was inherited by a
number of composers in the succeeding generation, who carried his art to
its logical conclusion. Palestrina's music has been held to be better adapted
to religious purposes, though he remains Josquin's inferior in invention,
inspiration, and depth of expression. Victoria carried the style to Spain,
William Byrd to England; and through Philippe de Monte and Orlando

Lassus, it spread throughout France and Germany. In the 17th century, though the art was still studied, it became known as the "antique style" in contrast to the Baroque music, which was called the "modern style." Within its limitations the art has never been surpassed. Even today it is considered the ideal for church music, and no conservatory curriculum is complete without a course in 16th-century counterpoint.

HUMANISM AND THE REACTION

The Italian Renaissance presents a curiously conflicting picture of bold humanistic thinking and timid reaction; Neo-Platonism and Aristotelian scholasticism; promises of a liberal religious attitude and the reversion to a narrow orthodoxy; establishment of scientific facts then the recanting of them; a reveling in sensuous beauty followed by bitter self-reproach and penitence; the spark of genuine creativity and a scholarly antiquarianism; a love of pagan antiquity, coupled with reminders of the Hebraic-Christian tradition; classical discoveries and the medieval heritage; Platonic disputations and Savonarolic fulminations; gaiety and gloom; Botticelli's Venuses and Virgins; Michelangelo's Bacchus and Christ figures; the organic form of his Sistine Ceiling and the calculated shapelessness of his *Last Judgment*; secular versus sacred elements in music; Palestrina's madrigals and Masses; Reformation and Counter-Reformation.

Florentine humanism and its Roman aftermath were motivated by a reappraisal of the values of Greco-Roman antiquity, by an attempt to reconcile pagan forms with Christian practices, and by a desire to substitute the philosophy of Plato for that of Aristotle. The Renaissance humanist was not primarily religious- or scientific-minded. He tended to substitute the authority of respected classical writers for that of the Bible and Church dogma. In looking forward he found more convenient and convincing precedents in the civilizations of Greece and Rome than in the immediate medieval past. Lorenzo, for instance, found a new orientation for secular government in Plato's *Republic*, Machiavelli, a new method for writing history in Thucydides.

The humanists preferred purer versions of classical art forms over the adaptations that had been made in the 1000-year period between the fall of Rome and their own time. The members of the Florentine humanistic circle learned to read and speak ancient Greek under native tutors. Ficino translated the dialogues of Plato, while Poliziano translated Homer from the original Greek into Italian and wrote treatises in Latin on Greek poetic and musical theory. Other scholars catalogued and edited books for the Medici library, while Squarcialupi compiled the musical compositions of the preceding century. The interest in cataloguing, editing, translating, and commenting was pursued with such enthusiasm that it all but blotted out the production of live literature. Their Latin was Ciceronian rather than the medieval Latin which they considered corrupt. The architects read Vitruvius and preferred central type churches modeled on the Pantheon to the basilica form that the Church had evolved over the centuries. They revived the classical orders and architectural proportions in a more authentic form. Decorative motives were derived directly from ancient sarcophagi, reliefs, and carved gems. Sculptors reaffirmed the importance of the nude human body, and with Michelangelo it became the chief expressive element of his art. Painters, lacking such tangible survivals, used mythological subjects and the literary descriptions of ancient masterpieces.

Musicians reinterpreted Greek musical theory, and there were concrete attempts to put some of the problems posed by Euclid's musical treatise into practice. The Greek assertion that art imitates nature was universally adopted, but in architecture and music it had to be applied in the general sense of nature as an orderly and regular system conforming to mathematical proportions and laws. Josquin des Prez was hailed as a modern Orpheus who had regained the lost perfect art of the ancients, though the Greeks would have been bewildered by his musical style. Josquin's less-enthusiastic admirers did not hesitate to point out that the trees and stones still showed some reluctance in following him as they had not in the case of Orpheus. His art, however, like that of Michelangelo, was thought by the humanists to be a path back to a lost classical paradise.

Two specific and conscious applications of Neo-Platonism are found in the works of Botticelli and Michelangelo. The literary ancestry of Botticelli's *Allegory of Spring, Birth of Venus* (Fig. 9:23), and *Venus and Mars* (Fig. 9:22) has been traced back to the Roman poets Lucretius and Horace through the poetry of his own contemporary, Poliziano. Its philosophical forebear, however, is the Plato of the *Symposium*, which has to do with the nature of love and beauty. Man, according to this theory, has drunk of the waters of oblivion and forgotten his divine origin. Falling in love with a beautiful woman reminds him of his natural affinity for beauty. From physical attraction and ephemeral loveliness he is led to thoughts of the lasting beauty of truth, and finally to the contemplation of the eternal verities of absolute beauty, truth, and goodness. Venus was, of course, the image of this transcendent beauty, and the way toward it is through love. The eternal feminine, as Goethe put it in the closing lines of his *Faust*, draws us ever onward. When Botticelli came under the influence of the fiery Savonarola, he repented of his paganism and turned exclusively to religious pictures. Botticelli never tried to combine his paganism and Christianity as Michelangelo did. For him they remained in separate compartments, and on an either-or basis.

The two great determining forces in Michelangelo's thought also were the Florentine Neo-Platonism and the resurgence of medievalism in Savonarola's sermons. His Plato, however, was that of the *Timaeus*, which discourses on the creation of the world by the Demiurge, the metaphysical nature of the human soul, and the return to God. Unlike Botticelli's fragile dream of beauty, Michelangelo was obsessed by a virile vision of the creative process itself. The voice of Savonarola also spoke loudly in his ear; and in his rugged mind, he was destined to wrestle with these two essentially irreconcilable philosophies throughout his life. He had, moreover, the mind to assimilate such Platonic abstractions, the overwhelming emotional urge to express his ideas, and the technical equipment to translate them into dramatic visual form.

To Michelangelo a work of art always had to participate in the world of ideas, and all his works are philosophical as well as aesthetic creations. In his early *Bacchus* he wholeheartedly embraced paganism, a fact which made the *Pietà* that followed it no less a sincere declaration of religious faith. Then came the synthesis of the Sistine Ceiling, in which pagan sibyls sit side by side with Hebrew prophets, and the Platonic theory of the return to God is made to coincide with the Christian doctrine of salvation. Even in the apocalyptical fury of the *Last Judgment*, mythological characters are juxtaposed with those from the Old and New Testaments. In his late years he entered a passionate religious phase, but his sonnets at that time reveal him still true to the Platonic ideas of his youth. His Madonnas reveal the unity between bodily beauty and eternal beauty; his *Moses* links human moral power and eternal goodness; and his organic compositions connect temporal with eternal truth. His triple divisions symbolizing the stages of the soul as it progresses from its bodily tomb to its reunion with God are a constantly recurring preoccupation. Even in his abstract architectural forms, the columns are the "slaves" imprisoned by the weight of the material burden they must carry, while overhead hovers the lofty dome in the geometrical perfection of the circular form, symbolic of the heaven from which man has fallen and to which he must somehow find his way back. The whole building is thus conceived as an organic system of pressures and tensions leading upward and culminating in a cupola that soars aloft and finally dissolves into infinity.

The Reaction

Even before the Council of Trent, there were voices that pointed out the antitheses between the tenets of humanism and the articles of Christian faith. The humanistic popes, however, had pursued a policy of letting sleeping dogmas lie and tried to avoid begging the inevitable questions. When the test came, Plato yielded to the established authority of Aristotle, and humanism was eclipsed by a cloud of intolerance and reaction. Before Michelangelo's death, Pope Paul IV ordered drapery painted on some of the "offending" nude figures in the *Last Judgment*. Some sections were later removed, and the whole mural barely escaped destruction. The Counter-Reformation seems to have diverted Michelangelo from sculpture and painting into the less-controversial forms of architecture. The projects of other artists were supervised by clergymen who worked out the iconographical schemes for them. The principal poet of the late 16th century, Torquato Tasso, was haunted by the fear that his writings might in some way be considered heretical. His *Jerusalem Delivered* was set in the time of the First Crusade in an effort to rekindle the spark of medieval fervor. It was later revised, and pretty well ruined, lest certain passages be construed as anti-Catholic, and in general the poem is a literary reflection of the chastened attitude of Roman Catholic thought after the Council of Trent.

Palestrina was banished from the Sistine Choir because he was married and refused to give up his wife. When he was reinstated by a later pope, he expressed his regret for the indiscretion of having composed some secular madrigals many years before. He was then entrusted with the revision of church music along the lines laid down by the Council of Trent. "The Antiphoners, Graduals, and Psalters," read the papal brief of 1577 authorizing him to undertake the work, "have been filled to overflowing with barbarisms, obscurities, contrarieties, and superfluities as a result of the clumsiness or negligence or even wickedness of the composers, scribes and printers: in order that these books may agree with the aforesaid Breviary and Missal, as is appropriate and fitting, and may at the same time be so ordered, their superfluities having been shorn away and their barbarisms and obscurities removed, that through their agency God's name may be reverently, distinctly, and devoutly praised." [12]

While much of the liberal attitude of the Renaissance was thus swept away, humanism survived in secular art forms, in scholarship, and in education, where the "humanities" still constitute a major division of the liberal arts that emancipate the mind.

PART 4

THE BAROQUE
PERIOD

CHRONOLOGY: Venice, 16th Century

General Events

1453 Fall of Constantinople to the Turks initiated the challenge of the Ottoman Empire to the commercial power of Venice

1492 Voyages and geographical discoveries for Spain and Portugal by Columbus, Vasco da Gama, Ferdinand Magellan, and others weakened Venetian maritime supremacy

1495 – 1515 Aldine Press published inexpensive editions of Greek and Roman classics

1496 Gentile Bellini painted *Procession in St. Mark's Square*

1501 *Odhecaton,* an anthology of vocal and instrumental compositions by recognized masters, such as Josquin des Prez, Obrecht, and Isaac, printed in Venice by Petrucci

1517 Protestant Reformation began in Germany

1527 Willaert appointed choirmaster of St. Mark's

1536 Library of St. Mark built by J. Sansovino to house the valuable collection of manuscripts left to Venice by Petrarch and Cardinal Bessarion

1545 – 1563 Council of Trent, sitting in Rome, initiated the Counter-Reformation movement

1570 Palladio published his *Four Books of Architecture*

1571 Battle of Lepanto, in which Venice joined with the Papal forces and Spain, defeated the Turks. Victory was short-lived, and Venice continued to lose her island possessions

1573 Veronese summoned before the Inquisition to account for his picture, *Feast in the House of Levi*

1576 Palladio's Church of the Redeemer (Il Redentore) dedicated during the plague; finished in 1592 after Palladio's death.

1585 Giovanni Gabrieli appointed organist of St. Mark's

1589 Olympic Theater at Vicenza finished after Palladio's death from his designs, dedicated with a performance of Sophocles' *Oedipus* with incidental choruses by Gabrieli

Architects

1477 – 1570	Jacopo Sansovino
1518 – 1580	Andrea Palladio
1552 – 1616	Vincenzo Scamozzi
1604 – 1675	Baldassare Longhena

Painters

*c.*1429 – 1507	Gentile Bellini
*c.*1450–*c.*1522	Carpaccio
1477 – 1576	Titian
1478 – 1510	Giorgione
1518 – 1594	Tintoretto
1528 – 1588	Veronese

Musicians

*c.*1480 – 1562	Adrian Willaert
1510 – 1586	Andrea Gabrieli
1516 – 1565	Cipriano de Rore
1517 – 1590	Gioseffe Zarlino
1557 – 1612	Giovanni Gabrieli
1567 – 1643	Claudio Monteverdi

11

THE VENETIAN BAROQUE STYLE

VENICE, 16th CENTURY

Through the eyes of the painter Gentile Bellini, it is possible to catch a glimpse of Venice at the threshold of the 16th century. Although Gentile belongs to the earlier period, his accurate reporting provides an insight into the life of his beloved city with such faithfulness that no written records, chronicles, or evidence in any other medium can rival it for directness and truth. Apart from its purely artistic interest, the *Procession in St. Mark's Square* (Fig. 11:1) painted in 1496, is a veritable history of the city. Using it as documentary evidence, archaeologists have been able to study the mosaics, sculptural details, and other ornaments of the Church of St. Mark's as they were before the later restorations. Through its aid architectural historians can make reconstructions of buildings that have since been removed to make way for newer structures. In the histories of costume and liturgy, it is important source material; and, as will be seen later, it is an invaluable document in the history of musical performance. However, beyond the historical interest, the artist has captured here the spirit of a solemn and festive occasion, endowed it with both form and substance, and, in short, created a significant work of art.

In many respects the particular quality of such a work as this can be traced to the unique environmental circumstances that underlie its origin. The position of Venice, and the many institutions which flourished under its enlightened protection, is due in part to the security afforded by both the geography and history that shaped its development. Located literally in the sea, and built on a series of island lagoons at the head of the Adriatic,

Fig. 11:1. Gentile Bellini. *Procession in St. Mark's Square.* 10′ high. 1496. Academy, Venice (Anderson)

Venice was truly what the Florentine poet Francesco Sacchetti saw: "A city in the water without walls." Secure by location from attack by any army on land, and on the sea by the possession in the 14th and 15th centuries of a navy larger and more powerful than any on earth, with a trade between Orient and Occident building up for its citizens a manner of life unrivaled in its time for sumptuousness and opulence, the island city-state well deserved its chosen title of *La Serenissima*, or Most Serene Republic. Lacking the ups and downs of other medieval and Renaissance Italian cities, such as Pisa and Siena with their comparatively brief periods of florescence, Venice developed slowly and consistently from the early glow of its Byzantine dawn to the magnificence of its florid Baroque sunset. Here there were no literary giants such as Dante, no Magnificos with the vision and personality of Lorenzo, no subtle political philosophers of the caliber of Machiavelli, no soul-searching revelations of Michelangelo, no terrifying religious reformers like Savonarola. In fact, without a great man of letters, without outstanding individual art patrons, without personal political geniuses, without a great sculptor, without an inspired religious leader—in short, without experiencing the heights and depths of the human spirit known in Florence or Rome—Venice nevertheless built up in its architecture, painting, and music a visual and musical culture that is without parallel.

Because Venice was governed by an oligarchy with distributed responsibility under the titular headship of the doge, an elected rather than a hereditary ruler, the distinguishing feature of its government was the subordination of the church to the secular authority. The resulting religious and liturgical freedom, unknown elsewhere in Europe, exerted a profound influence on developments in the arts. While religious devotion permeated all Venetian institutions, it was always kept well in hand. The principal setting of this joint secular and religious life was the Church of St. Mark's, the chapel of the doges, in conjunction with the piazza outside. The façade, as seen in Bellini's picture, confirms that aspect of Venetian life as the meeting place between Orient and Occident. Begun in its present form in the 11th century, it is a product of hundreds of years of community effort. An early law of the Republic made it mandatory for every voyage to bring back material for the construction and decoration of the church, and fragments of buildings of every Mediterranean country make up its whole. Since this process continued for centuries, the building itself is not only a confluence of East and West but of many architectural styles, principally Byzantine and Gothic, while the sculptural embellishments extend from

Fig. 11:2. *St. Mark's Square and the Doge's Palace*, Air View (Courtesy Italian State Tourist Office)

the ancient Roman colossal bronze horses over the main portal to the 19th-century additions and alterations. It is thus today, a veritable museum of the long history of the city and its foreign relations.

In Bellini's picture, three of the five domes of St. Mark's can be seen, while all of them are visible in the aerial photograph (Fig. 11:2). The plan is that of a Greek cross, with a dome covering each of the four arms plus a large central dome some 42 feet in diameter. A narthex has been added in front, the top of which forms the wide gallery on which, in Bellini's picture, several figures can be seen standing. Above this gallery, stretching the width of the façade, are seen five 13th-century Gothic ogee gables. On the crest of the large middle one can be seen a winged lion, one of the four evangelical beasts representing St. Mark and the symbol of Venice. Four of these ogee gables frame the upper tier of mosaics, which unite with those above the five portals to constitute one of the glories of that art. Unfortunately they now exist intact only in Bellini's picture, as all but one of those seen today are "improvements" made in the 17th and 18th centuries. More than on its structure, the beauty of St. Mark's depends on the wealth of color produced by the fiery glow of these mosaics; on the blend of polished bronze, Alexandrian marble columns, and transparent alabaster; and, above all, on its setting under the light of the eternally variable Venetian sky mirrored in the shimmering blue Adriatic waters.

The most striking feature of the architectural setting as a whole is the multiplicity of styles. As in the history of the city itself, the Eastern tradition and influences are found blending with the Western in the style of St. Mark's. To the right the Doge and his guests are seated in the second-story arcade of the ducal palace, a bizarre 13th-century variation of the Gothic style, with two stories of pointed arches surmounted by a walled third story notable for its diamond-shaped design in marble. On the extreme left is the library from which many spectators are observing the activities in the square below. The style of this building has some features of the Renaissance palace design, but the castellated roof and the large number of odd-shaped chimney pots give it a highly individual character defying exact classification. More remarkable than its architecture is the institution of the library itself. In lieu of outstanding native literary figures, Venice treasured its great collection of books left to her by such donors as the poet Petrarch and the Greek scholar Cardinal Bessarion. These collections became the basis of the great Library of San Marco, the first public library in Europe. In addition the Library housed all the specimens of the city's elegant printing and book-making industry, which included the fine inexpensive editions of the classics published here for the first time by the

Aldine Press, and which were such an impelling force in the spread of learning throughout the educated world. In the 16th century these collections were all transferred to the building designed by Sansovino (Fig. 11:3).

A sense of open public life and a dignified freedom of social movement are to be found in the prosperous and elegantly clad bystanders Bellini has painted in St. Mark's Square. This spacious piazza, large enough for most of the populace to move about in with ease, was the center of the city's life to an even greater extent than was, for instance, a forum in ancient Rome. Here the smell of incense accompanying a religious festival combined with that of baking bread, just as the colorful costumes of the nobles and burghers mingled with the drab ones of the commoners. The unique quality of Venetian life found its logical setting in this vast marble-paved area that served also as a large public atrium before the church honoring St. Mark. These spectators seem to manifest only casual interest in the grand procession, thus revealing by their attitude that such festivities were frequent occurrences. Indeed, this was but one of many such annual processions, each under the patronage of one of the *scuole*.

A *scuola*, literally a school, was a social institution basic to Venetian life with no exact equivalent in that of other cities. To compare one with our own institutions, a *scuola* combined in one confraternity many of the functions of a lodge, secret order, service club, trade union or professional society, church auxiliary, insurance company, and patron of the arts. In fact about the only function it did not perform was that of a school in the educational sense. Nobles and commoners, men and women, priests and laymen—all in all about two thirds of the population—were members of the 200-odd *scuole*. Of these about two dozen were of major importance and annually celebrated the day of their patron saint with all the considerable pomp and ceremony at their command. In their processions each craft was dignified by appropriate robes. A master sailor wore a costume spangled with vermillion stars, symbolic of his knowledge of navigation; a weaver wore cloth of gold decorated with pearls, exhibiting one of the highest achievements of his craft; a goldsmith was resplendent with jewels and heavy necklaces of gold chain to designate his art; and ermine robes revealed the estate of their noble wearers. Moving in a prescribed ritual, they carried a relic of their patron saint housed in a bejeweled reliquary, attended by candle bearers, incense, and choral chanting. Since such days were also civic holidays, the saints were not conceived as dour medieval martyrs, but as gay spirits receiving their just reward on these festive occasions, thus reflecting the general hedonism of the Venetian temperament.

Such was the *Gran Scuola di San Giovanni Evangelista*, or Great School of St. John the Evangelist, which commissioned Bellini to do this picture as a mural decoration for their chapterhouse. This love of large monumental paintings had a direct influence on the character of Venetian art and was particularly congenial to the abilities and temperaments of such painters as Carpaccio, Titian, Tintoretto, and Veronese.

The picture narrates an event in the history of the school, whose members, all individually portrayed, are represented on Corpus Christi Day, the occasion of their annual procession. Their distinction was the possession of a priceless relic with miracle-working powers that were never doubted in those times. It was a fragment of the true Cross, contained in the golden reliquary seen in the foreground under the canopy just as it is passing in front of the main portal of St. Mark's. Choristers precede it, with candle bearers flanking the canopy on either side of the white robed priests who are entrusted with the custody of the sacred relic. The length of the procession is impressive as it stretches from the passageway between the Church and the Doge's Palace in the right background, past the campanile and other buildings, all the way around the square to the opposite side where the groups are assembling. The narrative element of the picture is severely subordinated to the pageantry. One has to search closely between the two canopy bearers back of the reliquary and the foremost of the candle bearers bringing up the rear, to discover the kneeling figure of one Jacopo di Salis, a citizen of Brescia, who has prostrated himself near the relic, imploring aid for his crippled son. Later he hears that the son was restored to health at that very moment. It can readily be seen that while Gentile is painting the story of this miracle, he is less concerned with the dramatic human consequences than with the scene as a whole.

When Gentile was commissioned to do this study of the miracle in St. Mark's Square, his theory of art demanded that he literally and conscientiously paint the whole Square with all the exactness of detail at his command, all in skillful perspective, and with all his patrons in the *Scuola* represented. This latter consideration is important in all corporation pictures and is a necessary condition of this type of patronage. Then after all this has been done with impartiality and objectivity, he finds a place for his story, which is incidental rather than dominating. This is already symptomatic of the later breaking away from the tyranny of subject matter that leads the art of Giorgione and Titian into abstract moods and themes. However, granting the narration, one has only to imagine the dramatic and turbulent treatment such a story would have received if Titian or Tintoretto had undertaken it. Yet such is Bellini's art that in spite of the wealth of detail the picture is spacious and uncluttered. The division of the people into formal groups blends well with the formality of the architectural setting, while the suffused light from the clouded sky softens the harsh contours; and thus in spite of the overwhelming amount of variety, the unity of the whole is preserved.

ARCHITECTURE

As in all the arts Venetian architecture reaches out toward new forms. Although begun as early as 1536 and hence still within the Renaissance tradition, the Library of Venice (Fig. 11:3) by Jacopo Sansovino already has enough new ideas to make it transitional to the coming Baroque style. Here standing out boldly and almost independently from the façade of the building itself are the rich decorative details the Venetians loved. The contours of its projecting planes depart from the flatness of the prevailing Renaissance façades and make for fine and effective use of light and shade. This is an element that had traditionally been associated more with the art of sculpture than with architecture, and it is a fact of no small significance that the origin of the Baroque architectural style can be traced to the designs of Michelangelo, Jacopo Sansovino, and Palladio, all of whom were first trained in the field of sculpture. This carrying-over of sculptural thinking into the domain of architecture is largely responsible for the ascendancy of decorative embellishment over architectural function that is such a distinctive trait of the Baroque. But, in this Library, Sansovino's design is notable for its restraint in regard to ornamentation and can hardly be described as florid. The austere Doric arcade of the lower story is an open gallery and serves as a base for the increasingly rich adornment of the upper parts. The deeply arched windows of the second floor are punctuated by the rhythm of the Ionic columns between them, and above runs a frieze elaborately decorated with small windows, between which cherubs in high relief are holding festoons of floral garlands. Over this is surmounted a balustrade going all the way around the roof and supporting a row of statues silhouetted against the skyline. The proportion of the upper entablature is noteworthy in that it is over one third the height of the supporting order itself.

Sansovino's designs exerted a notable influence on Andrea Palladio, the greatest architect associated with the Venetian style. As the author of the highly influential *Four Books of Architecture*, first published in Venice in 1570, Palladio has left a detailed exposition of his philosophy of architecture. In the Preface he pays eloquent tribute to his ancient Roman mentor Vitru-

Fig. 11:3. Jacopo Sansovino. *Library. c.*290′ long, 60′ high. 1536–1553. Venice

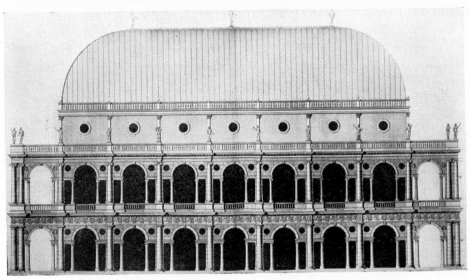

Fig. 11:4. Palladio. *Basilica. c.*1550. Architectural drawing. Vicenza

vius. Through the extant writings of this classical architect he was stimulated to make a detailed study of the remaining ruins. "Finding that they deserved a much more diligent Observation than I thought at first Sight," he noted, "I began with the utmost Accuracy to measure every minutest part by itself." Palladio's ideas are thus based on a thorough grounding in traditional design. He likewise pays tribute to his immediate predecessor Sansovino, whose Library is praised as "perhaps the most sumptuous and the most beautiful Edifice that has been erected since the time of the Ancients." [1]

While Venice can claim some of the surviving Palladian buildings, his native Vicenza is much richer in this respect. The winged lion of St. Mark is as prominently featured in the Piazza dei Signori in Vicenza as it is in the corresponding main square in Venice some 42 miles away, since the city was once a part of the extensive area on the mainland of Italy that was included in the Venetian Republic. The most imposing building facing the Piazza in Vicenza is the Basilica (Fig. 11:4), which Palladio refashioned out of a late-Gothic building. He explained his intentions in Book III, where he states: "As the Ancients made their *Basilicas* after such a manner, that in the Spring and Summer People might come together there, to treat of their affairs, and to carry on their Law-suits; so in our times every City, both in *Italy* and out of it, do erect certain spacious publick Halls, which may deservedly be term'd *Basilicas*." For this basilica he claims that "the porticos around it are my own invention: and that I make no doubt, but that this Edifice may be compar'd to the ancient Fabricks, and be reckon'd among the noblest and most beautiful Buildings erected since the time of the ancients; as well on account of its largeness and ornaments, as of its matter, which is all hewn Stone, extremely hard, join'd and bound together with utmost care." [2]

Dating from about 1550, Palladio's Basilica is thus a conscious carrying on of the tradition of the old Roman public building. As in Sansovino's Library, he uses the Doric order on the ground floor and above it the Ionic. In each case the stories are separated by balustrades, just as in each case another is found above outlining the roof and supporting a row of statues. In Palladio's building, however, the exterior arcades of both floors are open galleries (Fig. 11:5). Palladio further intensifies the Baroque sense of space by hollowing the piers and puncturing the spandrels, thus achieving a greater sense of depth and more surface play of light and shade.

Just outside the city is found the Villa Rotonda (Fig. 11:6), which Palladio built for his own retirement and where he spent the last few years of his life. It is a country villa in the grand style and the prototype of many

Fig. 11:5. Palladio. Basilica. *Detail of Façade. c.*1550. Vicenza (Courtesy Italian State Tourist Office)

later buildings. Occupying a hill which dominates the surrounding country side, it is well adapted to its site. Facing the four point of the compass, grand flights of steps lead up to porticos that project forward some 14 feet and that are faced with Ionic columns spreading 40 feet outward. The pediments are in the manner of a classical temple and are embellished with statues on either side and in the middle. The porticos provide the entrance passage to one of the most imposing rooms in the world. This is the round reception room that gives the villa the name *rotonda*. It is as high as the house itself and culminates with the cupola above. Alcoves left over from the parts between the round central hall and the square sides of the building provide space for four winding staircases. From the exterior it would seem to have only a single hall, but in reality no less than 32 rooms are found in the adjoining corners, all excellently lighted both from the outside and from the eight round windows at the base of the cupola. At the corners of the main floor there are four large reception rooms, each 20 by 30 feet, and four smaller ones—eight in all on this floor alone. In addition there are store rooms, servant's quarters, and the kitchen in the basement. Palladio's achievement here is a house that is spacious without being ponderous, designed on a grand scale but simple and reasonable in plan. The architect's conception of the noble purpose and the formal living style of his aristocratic clients that he associated with this type of building are set forth in his book. When an architect "builds for Persons of Quality, and more especially for those that are in publick Employment," wrote Palladio, "he must build their Palaces with Portico's, Galleries, and large stately Halls richly adorn'd: that those who come for business, or to pay their respects to the Owner, may be received commodiously, and delighted and amused whilst they wait for him." [3]

When advancing years curtailed Sansovino's activities, Palladio was called to Venice to undertake the construction of several buildings. The two principal surviving examples are the churches of San Giorgio Maggiore and Il Redentore (Fig. 11:8), both of which were finished from his models after his death. Although these churches have many similarities, the former has the advantage of the ideal location on the isolation of a small island facing the Doge's Palace across the lagoon. Palladio's problem was to adapt the classical temple to the prescribed design of a Roman Catholic church, which had to be in the form of a Latin cross, with a high central nave and two lower aisles on either side. Since a Greco-Roman temple is of uniform height, the originality of his solution is highly interesting. In the façades of both buildings he has the portico of a classical temple, complete with columns and pediment, across the center corresponding to the high portion

Fig. 11:6 (above). Palladio. *Villa Rotonda*. 80' x 80', Dome 70' high. 1552–1553. Near Vicenza.

Fig. 11:7. Palladio (below). *Olympic Theater*. Begun 1580. Vicenza (Courtesy Italian State Tourist Office)

Fig. 11:8. Palladio. *Church of Il Redentore* (*The Redeemer*). 1576–1592. Venice (Alinari)

of the nave. This is superimposed on a second pediment broken into two halves facing the two lower side aisles, and is decorated with flat pilasters in contrast to the rounded columns of the first to give the illusion of recession. Through Palladio's ingenuity we have what amounts to two interpenetrating temple façades at different depths, the one with the greater height placed in front of the lower. The broken-pediment idea associated with the latter became practically a symbol of the Baroque style. The last building Palladio undertook was the Olympic Theater in his native Vicenza (Fig. 11:7). It was begun the year of his death and finished later from his designs by Scamozzi. Clearly inspired by ancient Roman models, it has in turn been the inspiration for many later theaters, such as the Palladium in London.

Palladio's expressed preference for the greater capaciousness of churches built after a round plan (which he undoubtedly derived from the Roman Pantheon) was realized later in his successor Longhena's Santa Maria della Salute (Fig. 11:9), which was begun in 1631. It is the logical outcome of his thoughtful restraint when combined with the exuberance of the Venetian temperament. In its octagonal shape, with all sides faced with classical pediments, one has an excellent example in the best early-Baroque style. The fine big dome is buttressed by large ornamental scrolls that mediate between it and the broader mass below. The elaborately decorated exterior is held together by the good composition of the design as a whole. This building was far more to the taste of the Venetians than the two rather austere examples described above.

A notable contrast in the work of Sansovino and Palladio that deserves mention is found in their respective use of materials. Sansovino by doing large public edifices had his choice of rare marbles and the finest stone; but Palladio, because of the greater frequency of his work on private dwellings and other buildings in the more provincial and less wealthy Vicenza, had to content himself for the most part with brick, stucco, and terra cotta. He comments many times on the greater importance of design over materials, and his achievement of richness and monumentality with the restriction of baser materials proves that architectural grandeur lies more in the conception of form that in content. Reasoned proportion of the whole and the logical disposition of the parts are two of the leading characteristics of his art. His love of symmetry and his adherence to the highly rational division of the five architectural orders into the Tuscan, Doric, Ionic, Corinthian, and Composite were transmitted to the succeeding age. His skillful use of the principle of dualism and opposition—both in the winged organization of his palace façades and in the reflection of façades in the water as at San

Fig. 11:9. Longhena. *Church of Santa Maria della Salute.* 1631–1656. Venice (Courtesy Italian State Tourist Office)

Giorgio Maggiore and other Venetian buildings—also became earmarks of the Baroque. In other countries buildings lacking the rippling motion of the water of a Venetian canal had to rely on an artificial pool before the façade constructed for this purpose.* After Palladio and throughout the succeeding century the classical temple façade is accepted as a norm for Roman Catholic church buildings, but with later architects it becomes structurally weaker and increasingly the basis for the elaborate ornamentation characteristic of the florid Baroque.† To counteract this tendency Palladio's academicism is also carried over into the new style, and his objectivity and exactness operated as a balance to the more exuberant tendencies of the new style. One of his remarks that must have been frequently pondered by later generations was: "But as for what concerns the ornaments, that is, the Bases, Columns, Capitels, Cornishes, and such like things, I have intermix'd nothing of my own; but they were measur'd by me with the utmost care and exactness, from divers fragments found in the very places where stood the Temples themselves." [4] And finally his thought as expressed in his *Four Books of Architecture* with their sketches and drawings had an even wider influence in France, England, Ireland, and America than did his buildings. The English translation, published with notes by his disciple Inigo Jones, did much to establish the Georgian tradition both in England and in America, where it was carried on by Thomas Jefferson. The latter's staunch Palladianism led him to propose that the White House in Washington, D. C., be built as a replica of the Villa Rotonda (Fig. 11:6), and only at the last moment was Jefferson overruled. However, even in its present form the White House still has Palladio's winged design on either side of a classical temple portico.

PAINTING

The principal characteristics of the Venetian visual world can readily be found in some of the outstanding examples of the art of Giorgione, Titian, Veronese, and Tintoretto.

The *Pastoral Concert* (Fig. 11:10) by Giorgione—or as it is called in France, *Concert Champêtre*—is notable for its spaciousness and the distribution of interest. The eye first focuses on the four figures in the foreground, then moves toward the point in the middle where a shepherd is tending his flock, and finally comes to rest where the sunlit water is gleaming in the background. The picture holds interest both as a composition in depth and as a study in opposing elements. The contrast between the clothed

* See Figures 12:2 and 13:4.   † See Figures 12:5, 16:4, and 16:5.

Fig. 11:10. Giorgione. *Pastoral Concert.* 3′ 7¼″ high. *c.*1510. Louvre, Paris (Alinari)

male figures and feminine nudes is at once apparent. So also is the division of the group into the urbane sophisticated pair at the left and the rusticity of the shepherd and shepherdess at the right. The courtly costume and polished manner of the lute player opposes the peasant garb and relative awkwardness of his rural counterpart. The same contrast exists between the graceful form of the figure pouring water into the fountain and the more earthy qualities of her feminine opposite. The contrast is further emphasized in the attitude of the two women, the one turning away from her lover, while the other, intent upon her shepherd, is awaiting a pause in the conversation so that she can delight him with the sounds of her flute. The contrast between loving and being loved is likewise present, with the ardor of the courtier matching that of the shepherdess, and the casual attitude of the shepherd finding a parallel in the inconstancy of the urbane lady as she turns away. A literary element is present with the lute as prince of instruments symbolizing lyric poetry, opposing the flute as the rustic pipe of Pan symbolic of the pastoral idyl. A further contrast is found in the musical pairing of the three figures in the center with those on the outside where on the extreme right the shepherd in the distance is playing the bag-pipes, while the stately lady on the left listens to the sound of the water splashing into the fountain from her crystal pitcher, recalling Leonardo da Vinci's comment on "the music of water falling into its vessel." [5] Other than this it is impossible to establish any more concrete meaning. Giorgione's pictures move completely away from the traditional narrative content of religious subjects and classical myths. After a visit to Venice, Vasari said that he could never understand what the meaning of them was, and was equally unsuccessful in finding anyone who could explain them to him. It is thus comforting to know that they were as baffling to his contemporaries as they seem to us.

A similar play of opposites with less pictorial unity is found in Titian's *Venus and the Organ Player* (Fig. 11:11), one of the many versions of this theme that the artist did in his later years. The young man at the organ is torn between the sacred pursuits symbolized by that instrument and the sensual pleasures implied by the undraped figure of Venus. In addition to this major contrast, there are numerous minor ones, such as the foreground interior against the exterior landscape in the background; the clothed figure of the young man and the unclothed Venus; the immature Cupid beside the mature Venus; and the tactile value of the nude flesh against that of the velvet couch cover. These opposites find a certain harmony here principally in the unified sensuousness and warmth of coloring with which the artist brings them together as a whole.

A far more complex and subtle handling of this dualistic idea is contained in Titian's *Sacred and Profane Love* (Fig. 11:12). This name for the picture is only a convenience and one of the many modern titles which have been brought forward to solve the riddle of its interpretation. It will be sufficient here to point out some of the abstract elements in the composition. To begin with, the facial resemblance of the contrasting clothed and unclothed figures is close enough to make them alter egos. The setting is in a secluded spot in the quiet hour of dawn, and is far enough away to be undisturbed by the awakening of new life on all sides as evidenced by the rabbits and butterflies, the shepherd tending his flock, and the hunters going forth to the chase. The attitudes of the two women set a contemplative mood, while between them a playful Cupid swishing the water of the fountain, seems sufficient to establish that the subject of their thoughts is love. This is reinforced by the clear resemblance of the nude figure to the goddess of Love in so many of Titian's other pictures. The first rays of the sun come from Venus's side and have just touched the high tower on the left. A clear duality is exemplified in the light-bathed open landscape stretching behind Venus to the horizon and the sea, and the shadowy confined space between the clothed figure and the castled hill behind her. The warmth of the right

Fig. 11:11. Titian. *Venus and the Organ Player*. 4′ 6″ x 7′ 6″. *c*.1547. Prado, Madrid (Anderson)

Fig. 11:12. Titian. *Sacred and Profane Love*. 8′ 7″ x 3′ 6″. *c*.1514. Borghese Gallery, Rome (Anderson)

Fig. 11:13. Titian. *Assumption of the Virgin*. 22′ 6″ x 11′ 8″. 1516–1518. Frari, Venice (Anderson)

side is further supported by the red-colored drape of Venus and the burning
lamp she holds in her hand, against the cool steel-gray dress of the reserved
figure on the left. The dimension of time is introduced with the wreath of
flowers in her hand and by the strewn petals and leaves of the rose on the
edge of the fountain, which are doomed like her beauty to fade. Under her
arm is a brazier, filled with the dying embers of coals, which Venetian
ladies customarily carried around with them for warmth. On the other side
we have the timeless beauty of the goddess holding in her hand the brightly
burning lamp that points to the sky. For dramatic continuity the eye is
quietly led from the darkness at the lower left by the lines of the drapery
and the inclining attitude of the clothed figure past the playful Cupid
diagonally to the nude figure and upward by her extended arm to the
eternal sea and sky at the right. This quiet and dignified action fits well
with the Platonic theory of earthly love as the means by which the thoughts
of time-bound mortals are led to the contemplation of the immutable and
eternal aspect of things, or from physical beauty to the ideal form of divine
beauty. The Platonic concept of time is also present in the contrast of the
changing ephemeral world of appearances, and the eternal and unchange-
able world of forms beyond. These were frequently the subjects for the Neo-
Platonic dialogues of the Renaissance and seem to fit the intent of this
picture better than any of the other interpretations.

An entirely different mode of composition is found in Titian's *Assumption
of the Virgin* (Fig. 11:13), which was painted in 1516–1518 as an altarpiece
for the Church of the Frari. The space is divided into three vertical planes
united by a strong dynamic ascending motion. In this dramatic composition
the forces of heaven and earth converge momentarily with the Madonna
as mediator, who, by her suffering, has transcended all earthly things. The
focus is on God the Father surrounded in heaven by His seraphs, with the
rising movement carried upward from below, first by the lifted arms of
the Apostles, then by those of the heavenly host, and finally by the extending arms of the Virgin herself. The skillful use of chiaroscuro ac-
centuates this movement, with the dark tones of the lower group blending
with the intermediate ones in the center up to the dazzling brightness at
the top. The flight of the Madonna emphasizes the transcendence of
spiritual laws over those of mere gravitation. Titian has created here a new
pictorial type that was to have profound influence on El Greco, Bernini,
and the whole Counter-Reformation phase of the Baroque period.

Of all possible subjects the one most congenial to Veronese and his art
was that of festivity. It is also the one most typical of an important phase
of Venetian art and life: the love of sumptuous surroundings, the urbanity

Fig. 11:14 (above). Veronese. *Marriage at Cana*. 21′ 10″ x 32′ 5″. 1563. Louvre, Paris. Fig. 11:15 (below). *Details* (Alinari)

of large social gatherings, and decorative schemes rich with fruit, flowers, animals, furniture, draperies, jesters in bizarre costumes—all painted with the primary object of delighting the eye. He seems never to have refused a commission to do a feast, and a note on the back of one of his drawings, believed to be in his own handwriting, shows him still ambitious to do another. "If I ever have time," he says, "I want to represent a sumptuous banquet in a superb hall, at which will be present the Virgin, the Saviour, and St. Joseph. They will be served by the most brilliant retinue of angels which one can imagine, busied in offering them the daintiest viands and an abundance of splendid fruit in dishes of silver and gold. Other angels will hand them precious wines in transparent crystal glasses and gilded goblets, in order to show with what zeal blessed spirits serve the Lord." [6] It is in this consummate realization of the world of appearances that Veronese most completely realizes himself, and in so doing, despite the foreign origin implied in his name, he succeeds in being more Venetian than the Venetians. Even the cosmopolitan Titian, with all his sense of the dramatic and his deep human insights, never realizes this festive spirit so completely as did Veronese.

In his *Marriage at Cana* (Fig. 11:14) the scene, except for the recognizable central figures of Jesus and the Virgin Mary, is that of a rich wedding feast in Venice which the artist has taken from his own observation and imagination. The black-bearded groom, dressed in purple and gold and seated at the extreme left, is Alfonso d'Avalos, a contemporary Spanish grandee. Seated next to him as the bride is Eleanor of Austria, sister of Charles V, and the wife in real life not of Alfonso but of Francis I, King of France. Other royal portraits appear on the left and include Francis I, Charles V, the Sultan of Turkey Suleiman I, and Queen Mary of England. The remainder are portraits of monks, cardinals, and the artist's personal friends. The major interest in portraiture is concentrated in the center foreground where the orchestra is made up of the principal Venetian painters of the time (Fig. 11:15). Just left of center, the striking bald, black-bearded figure in the yellow cloak playing the large viol is Veronese himself. Opposite him in a red damask robe the elderly Titian is represented playing the bass viol. Holding another viol and whispering in Veronese's ear is Tintoretto. The flutist next to Tintoretto is Jacopo Bassano. The standing figure at the right holding the cup in his left hand is the artist's brother Benedetto Cagliari, who is known to have collaborated with him principally in putting in the architectural backgrounds of some of his large paintings. Surrounding these figures in all directions are a host of minor ones. Over Christ's head behind the balustrade, a butcher is chopping meat with a cleaver, while bustling servants preparing the food rush to and fro as they serve it on smoking gold and silver platters.

In its composition the picture relies for unity principally on the horizontal and vertical linear patterns beginning with the table, back through the balustrade and the rich Corinthian columns on either side, to the Sansovinian-Palladian architecture against the bright sky. The rigidity of such a plan is softened by the series of intricate curves that carry the eye to the head of Christ. A fine balance is contained in the opposition of the crowded scene below to the serene architectural order and the spaciousness of the open sky above.

The last and most mature of these colossal canvases depicting the feasts attended by Jesus and his disciples, the *Feast at the House of Levi* (Fig. 11:16), was done for the monks of SS. Giovanni e Paolo in 1573 about ten years after he did the *Marriage at Cana*. The appropriateness of its huge size and spacious design cannot be questioned when its original setting is taken into account, and one must imagine it at the end of such a long room to comprehend its significance. Here the contours of its architectural background and the open sky through the three arches combined to give to the cloistered monks the illusion of the out of doors. Though it is somewhat smaller than the *Marriage at Cana* and contains approximately 50 life-sized figures, it seems less crowded.

The appropriateness of its content, however, is quite another matter. A Last Supper was the traditional scene to decorate such monastic refectories. This example was done to replace an earlier picture on that subject by Titian which had been destroyed by fire, and Veronese's departure from tradition and historical exactitude brought him before the Inquisition. In one of the most remarkable documents in the history of painting, a summary of the painter's actual testimony reveals a great deal not only about this picture in particular but about Veronese's conception of art in general. The inquisitors were disturbed by the presence of a dog which Veronese had painted in the foreground, and the omission of the traditional figure of Mary Magdalene. Even more disquieting, however, were the German soldiers sitting on the staircase at the extreme right, especially at the very time when the Church was having such trouble in that country with the Lutheran Reformation.

Question. Did anyone commission you to paint Germans, buffoons, and similar things in that picture?
Answer. No, milords, but I received the commission to decorate the picture as I saw fit. It is large and, it seemed to me, it could hold many figures.

Fig. 11:16. Veronese. *Feast at the House of Levi*. 19' 8" x 46'. 1573. Academy, Venice (Alinari)

Q. Are not the decorations which you painters are accustomed to add to paintings or pictures supposed to be suitable and proper to the subject and the principal figures or are they just for pleasure—simply what comes to your imagination without any discretion or judiciousness?

A. I paint pictures as I see fit and as well as my talent permits.

Q. Does it seem fitting at the Last Supper of the Lord to paint buffoons, drunkards, Germans, dwarfs and similar vulgarities?

A. No, milords.

Q. Do you not know that in Germany and in other places infected with heresy it is customary with various pictures full of scurrilousness and similar inventions to mock, vituperate, and scorn the things of the Holy Catholic Church in order to teach bad doctrines to foolish and ignorant people?

A. Yes, that is wrong; but I return to what I have said, that I am obliged to follow what my superiors have done.

Q. What have your superiors done? Have they perhaps done similar things?

A. Michelangelo in Rome in the Pontifical Chapel painted Our Lord, Jesus Christ, His Mother, St. John, St. Peter, and the Heavenly Host. These are all represented in the nude—even the Virgin Mary—and in poses with little reverence.[7]

By the judgment which was rendered, Veronese was required to make certain changes in the picture. His solution, however, was worthy of his genius. He simply changed the title from that of *Last Supper* to *Feast in the House of Levi*, a subject which was outside the iconographical tradition. So that no further misunderstandings might arise, he took the unusual step of painting the title on the molding at the top of the left staircase, while the corresponding place at the right of the picture cites the fifth chapter of St. Luke's Gospel. This passage (5:29–31) reads in part: "And Levi made him a great feast in his own house: and there was a great company of publicans and of others that sat down with them. But their scribes and Pharisees murmured against his disciples, saying, Why do ye eat and drink with publicans and sinners? And Jesus answering said unto them, They that are whole need not a physician; but they that are sick." Thus there would here be a place even for the German halberdiers! Most important of all, however, through Veronese's defense of his artistic code, the picture is a symbol of the emancipation of aesthetic and formal considerations over the narrow religious subject-matter tradition, and that the laws of space, color, composition, and the like rank higher than any other kind of truth.

This transcendence over historical tradition is reflected also in the unusual method of handling even the technical details. A comparison with Leonardo's *Last Supper* will quickly reveal that all the lines of his architectural setting focus on the head of Christ, who by this means becomes the center of the composition. With Veronese only the lines of the tiled floor converge on the figure of Christ, while the far more important diagonal lines of the staircase railings meet in the sky above, thus leading the eye to the figure of Veronese himself on the left as the host and, for balance, to that of the steward occupying the corresponding position on the other side. This balance is further accented by the upright lines of the two large Corinthian columns before which these two figures are placed.

At the center of the damask-covered table are seated those whom Veronese identifies as Christ and the Twelve Apostles. Only the one at the right of Jesus is specifically identified by the artist. This is St. Peter, who is in robes of rose and gray and, according to the painter, is "carving the lamb in order to pass it to the other end of the table." Jesus is turning to his left to speak to the Apostle who is traditionally St. John. When questioned about the others, Veronese is significantly evasive, pleading that he cannot recall them as he had "painted the picture some time ago." Since this lapse of time was only a matter of ten months, his memory proves a convenient way of avoiding an explanation of the portrait of Titian seated at the table in the prominent place at the extreme left, and Michelangelo who occupies the equivalent position at the right. The two soldiers seated on the right stairway eating and drinking were the ones who particularly infuriated the Inquisition because their uniforms were those of German mercenaries. They nevertheless remained in the picture, as did the offending buffoon seated below the host, a dwarf with a parrot on his wrist being teased by a young Negro. In addition, the lively scene contains bustling servants, some drinking wine from goblets intended for the guests, and the dog intently eyeing a cat under the table. The extreme informality of one of the guests sitting at the table with a slouch hat on his head, and that of the figure picking his teeth and peering out at Veronese between the two columns, seems to be introduced by the artist to counteract the formality of the academic and almost frigidly symmetrical architectural setting. It is indeed in this sense of balance and in the power to handle crowds without clutter and disorder that Veronese's mastery of composition reveals itself. As he somewhat naïvely says, after the inquisitors have brought out the fact that only Christ and his Twelve Apostles were present at the Last Supper, "If in a picture there is some space to spare I enrich it with figures. . . ." The balance between open and filled space, between architectural formality and human informality, between strict convention and imaginative freedom, between the decorum of the central group and the greater conviviality of those on the two sides, is one of the distinctions of this picture. This applies also to the architecture itself, where there is a balance maintained between the decorative figures in the spandrels and the formal Corinthian columns between the three arches. And it is further extended to the domain of color, where the rich warmth of the gala costumes of the guests and others in the foreground contrast strongly with the gleaming white marble and the cool sky of the projected Venetian architecture in the background.

When one moves from this particular example to its classification in the broader category of style, it seems quite beyond dispute that many elements place it within the sphere of the early Baroque. One certainly is the conscious departure from central perspective in the many different converging points of its lines. Another is the disregard for diminution in the indication of distance. The arches of the portico are in central perspective while the floor tiles tend slightly toward the oblique. This distortion makes for Baroque action rather than Renaissance repose, and leads to the illusionistic. In still another aspect of Veronese's art this illusionism is much more in evidence, namely, in the ceiling paintings done for the Church of San Sebastiano and those painted for the Senate Chamber of the Doge's Palace. On these horizontal surfaces his use of overhead foreshortening and daring perspective effects later led to a great demand for this type of decoration. Additional Baroque aspects are the grandiose size of this picture and the importance given to the diagonal lines of its composition. It is also significant that, while the subject matter is handled with extreme freedom, there is a distinct academicism in the Palladian architecture of its organization. It is thus amply clear that this is one of the early land-

Fig. 11:17. Tintoretto. *Marriage at Cana.* 16' x 21'. 1561. Santa Maria della Salute, Venice (Alinari)

marks of the style that is to dominate the pictorial art for more than a century to come.

With Tintoretto's *Marriage at Cana* (Fig. 11:17) the transition is complete. "The drawing of Michelangelo and the color of Titian," so read the motto which Tintoretto is traditionally supposed to have written on the walls of his studio. It might indeed have continued—"and the monumental grandeur of Veronese," since all these qualities were united in the art of this unusual painter. The *Marriage at Cana* is quite typical of his expressive aims. The lines formed by the receding table, the walls, and the timbered ceiling lead the eye into an indefinite halolike area surrounding the head of Christ. From this linear climax, the dramatic element of light and shadow takes over and moves diagonally forward along the row of feminine figures toward the center foreground where the servants are filling the flagons with the "water that was made wine." The off-center accent formed by the lines that converge in the deep left background, the diagonal direction of the table, and the opposing diagonal of the light which streams in from the windows—all make for a highly complex construction of pictorial space. By these and other means at his command, the painter sets his stage for the contrasting interplay of natural and supernatural elements, earthly and unearthly light, human and divine figures. Thus is Tintoretto able to create a plausible atmosphere for the miraculous occurrence.

Throughout all these paintings the recurrence of certain ideas is clearly apparent. The Venetian preference for ample and mature feminine forms, both clothed and in the nude, is noteworthy. Practically no painter shows the slightest interest in the lithe undeveloped adolescent form so much in favor during the Florentine Renaissance. An atmosphere of festivity and a rich sensuous treatment of decorative forms underlies it all. Likewise there is particularly sensitive handling of tactile values, as well as marked preference for depicting musical subjects. That the two arts are close allies in Venetian thinking is made quite clear in Veronese's representation of the painters themselves as musicians in the *Marriage at Cana*. The predilection for large dimensions both in murals as well as in paintings on canvas is evident throughout the 16th century. This love of spaciousness, size, and light reaches a culmination in Tintoretto's *Paradise*, a mural done for the Council Chamber of the Doge's Palace, which is 30 by 74 feet, the world's largest example in oil by a major painter. This picture, while on a flat horizontal surface, is nevertheless built up on the principle of a series of concentric circular zones, such as might be found in the interior of a cupola. Containing as it does more than half a thousand figures, including an entire orchestra and angelic choir, it was apparently inspired by the celestial vision Dante beheld in the third part of his *Divine Comedy*.

Several compositional forms are used often enough to establish themselves as typical. The first is the equal winged balance of opposites found in the *Pastoral Concert* (Fig. 11:10), *Venus and the Organ Player* (Fig. 11:11), and *Sacred and Profane Love* (Fig. 11:12). The counterpart of this is the balance of forward and backward movement of compositions in depth as exemplified in the latter two of these paintings. Secondly there are the spacious architectural settings found in the early example by Bellini and in the later academicism of Veronese's feasts. Thirdly, there is the tendency toward a linear accent on the diagonal, as found in *Sacred and Profane Love*, in Titian's *Rape of Europa*, *Presentation in the Temple*, and *Bacchus and Ariadne*, as well as in Veronese's *Feast in the House of Levi*. And, finally, the building up of a picture in vertical ascending planes as found in Titian's *Assumption* and the rising concentric zones of Tintoretto's *Paradise*. Combined with the many experiments in perspective and illusionism, these factors all link together to locate the work of this place and time well within the broad style classification of the Venetian Baroque.

MUSIC

The frequency of the representation of musical subjects in Venetian painting from the 14th century onward is in itself indicative of the important
role this art played in the life of the city. While it is true that in other
schools of painting musical subjects also occur, nowhere do they appear
with greater frequency and with more emphasis. Angelic choirs with
complex orchestrations appear regularly in 14th-century scenes honoring
the Virgin. One of these, for example, a Madonna by Lorenzo, painted in
1359, has a group of angels forming an orchestra consisting of two viols,
two harps, four clarionets, a single trumpet, one zither, a lute, and two
portable organs, with a tambourine as the percussion section. In later
paintings the frequency with which keyboard instruments occur is especially notable. Particularly is this so in the 16th century when the organists
of St. Mark's were among the leading musicians in Europe, commanding
the respect and admiration of the entire civilized world. This tradition
continued throughout the history of Venetian painting, and the examples
included here will bear this out. It is also of some importance that musical
terminology has been widely used in art criticism, particularly in application to the works of the Venetian school. Marco Boschini, a 17th-century
art critic, used such terms as *orchestrale* and *concertare* when referring to the
composition of a picture, and this has continued up to the present time
when we find historians still speaking of Giorgione's "plastic orchestration." This seems to be an unnecessarily fanciful analogy leading principally to confusion, and the term *orchestration* had better be confined only to
pictures in which an orchestra is actually represented. Far more significant
is the fact that Giorgione, Titian, Tintoretto, and Veronese all actually
played musical instruments, took a lively interest in the developments in
the city's musical life, and frequently employed small house orchestras to
play for them while they were painting. A literary friend of Titian's,
Pietro Aretino, describes in a letter, dated April 7, 1540, how he arranged
an exchange of services between the painter and the famed organ builder
Alessandro degli Organi. [8] In this deal Titian agreed to paint Alessandro's
portrait, while the latter constructed a specially built organ for Titian's
house as his part of the bargain. It is quite possible that this is the instrument depicted in Titian's several versions of *Venus and the Organ Player*.

One can see in Venice's unique island situation some possibilities that
would predispose the city to musical developments. Since there were no
suburbs as in the ordinary city, the people would tend to come together

more frequently for their recreation than to scatter, and music-making is always an important group activity in such circumstances. The Italian love of song was greatly enhanced by the natural sounding board of the waters of the canals. Everyone who knows the added resonance connected with singing in the bath can see that the Venetian canals formed a kind of gigantic community choral bathtub. Without trees and hills to break up the sound waves, the sonority of voices and church bells is greatly enhanced by floating over the water. The rhythmic lapping of the waves and the regular splash of the oars of the gondoliers added the rhythmical element to this natural acoustical environment. It is indeed hardly an accident that the romantic serenade sung by a lover under a fair lady's balcony to the accompaniment of a lute, mandolin, or guitar was a Venetian invention. When all these factors are united with a distinguished musical tradition as well as the splendor of Venetian life, it can readily be seen that the stage was set for a high point in the development of the musical art.

The Renaissance had reached its highest peak of musical development with the crystallization of the polyphonic style in the writing of the Netherland composers. The general admiration for this art at the beginning of the 16th century is reflected in the remark of one Vincenzo Quirini, Venetian ambassador to the court of Burgundy, to the effect that "there were three things of the highest excellence: first, the finest, most exquisite linen of Holland; second, the tapestries of Brabant, most beautiful in design; and third, the music, which certainly can be said to be perfect." [9]

With such sentiments and admiration being expressed in official circles, it is not surprising to find that a Netherlander, Adrian Willaert, was appointed in the year 1527 to the highest musical position in Venice, that of choirmaster of St. Mark's. This adoption of the northern musical ideal is still another instance of the cosmopolitanism of the Venetians, and Willaert, as a leading representative of this art, together with his successors, established Venice as a center of musical progress while Rome remained the bastion of tradition. Supporting this progressive aspect of Venetian music was the relatively greater degree of religious freedom that the city enjoyed. Both the clergy and the musicians of St. Mark's were directly responsible to the Council of Ten and the Doge, rather than primarily to ecclesiastical authorities. This greater independence gave the Venetian composers chances for experimentation denied to those in more traditional centers. A host of new forms and modifications of older ones was the result. Among the vocal forms were the invention of the madrigal, the modification of the church motet, and the highly significant development of the polychoral style which made simultaneous use of two, three, and even four choirs.

A new idiom of independent instrumental music is found in the organ *intonazione*, *ricercar*, and *toccata* for keyboard solo, and in the *sinfonia*, and early *concertato* and *concerto* forms for orchestra. Here the Venetian school spoke with a new voice and in tones of a highly individual character, modifying the old style and establishing the new. During the 16th century as the *ars perfecta* gradually lost favor, it became known as the *stile antico* in contrast to the *stile moderno*, which was so definitely associated with Giovanni Gabrieli in Venice, Vincenzo Galilei in Florence, Frescobaldi within the Roman orbit, and Claudio Monteverdi in Mantua and Venice.

The culmination of the musical development that had begun earlier in the century with Willaert was reached in the work of Giovanni Gabrieli, who held the position of first organist at St. Mark's from the year 1585 until his death. His principal works were published under the title of *Symphoniae Sacrae*, Book I of which appeared in 1597, while Book II containing his later work was published posthumously in 1615. The architectural plan of St. Mark's predisposed the choir toward developments distinct from those associated with the usual church plan. When a choir is concentrated in the relatively smaller space at the end of a long nave, it tends to be more unified than in a church built on the pattern of a Greek cross with equal arms. In St. Mark's the choir was placed on both sides of the transept in two distinct groups, and each was supported by its own organ. The acoustical possibilities of such a placement were realized as early as Willaert's time and after much experimentation formed the basis of Gabrieli's art. This polychoral style dissolved the unified choruses of the Netherland tradition and heralded a new development in the choral art. These *chori spezzati*—literally broken choruses—as they were called, added the element of spatial contrast to Venetian music and new color effects were made possible by them. These included the echo nuance, so important in the entire Baroque tradition; the alternation of two contrasting bodies of sound, such as chorus against chorus, a single choral line over a full choir, solo voice opposing full choir, instruments versus voices, and contrasting instrumental groups; the alternation of high and low voices; a soft dynamic range juxtaposed with a loud one; the fragmentary versus the continuous; massive chords on one side with contrapuntal weaving together of many melodies on the other; and numerous contrasts of musical textures. The resultant principle of duality is the basis for the *concertato* or concerting style, both words being derived from *concertare*, meaning to compete with or to strive against. The word appears in the title of some works Giovanni published jointly with his uncle Andrea Gabrieli in 1587: *Concerti . . . per voci et stromenti* (Concertos . . . for voices and instruments). The term later came to be widely used, with such titles as *Concerti Ecclesiastici* appearing frequently. Giovanni Gabrieli was one of the first to develop a distinction between a vocal and instrumental style of writing, and the precise directions given in his later works as to instrumentation make it quite clear that he was thinking in terms of the color of the various instruments at his command. This is in contrast to the custom of his predecessors who specified principally the range of the instrumental parts only, leaving the choice up to the performer. When Gabrieli called for such combinations as violins, bass viols, cornetti (trumpets of wood), trombones, and bassoons, it is possible to begin to speak of a specific orchestration, and his work thus lays the foundation for the modern orchestra.

The motet *In Ecclesiis* (page 454) from the second part of the *Symphoniae Sacrae* is an example of Gabrieli's most mature style. It is a nonliturgical motet in the sense that it was not intended for use in the regular part of the service, such as the Mass or Canonical Hours. In such occasional pieces as this the composer was able to relax the strong though unwritten rules of tradition in favor of a greater freedom. An astonishing instance of the liturgical independence of Venice happened just about the time this motet was written. Under the guidance of the English Ambassador, Sir Henry Wotton, Venice adopted the Anglican ritual in the year 1604, some eight years before Gabrieli's death. The fury of Rome was contained in Pope Paul's subsequent threat of excommunication. Though the specific occasion for which this music was intended is unknown, this type of motet was the appropriate music to supply the needs for such ceremonies as that depicted in Bellini's picture. Since the setting was in the piazza rather than inside the church, all the Venetian love of civic pomp and splendor was here in evidence, and Gabrieli's music was in every respect able to fulfill such demands. His art is as perfect an expression of the spirit of the time and place as was that of his colleagues in the other arts—Titian, Veronese, Sansovino, and Palladio.

The text of the work is as follows: [10]

1. In ecclesiis benedicite Domino,
   Alleluia, alleluia, alleluia.

2. In omni loco dominationis benedic,
   anima mea, Dominum.
   Alleluia, alleluia, alleluia.

3. In Deo, salutari meo et gloria mea.
   Deus auxilium meum et spes mea
   in Deo est.
   Alleluia, alleluia, alleluia.

1. Praise the Lord in the congregation,
   Alleluia, alleluia, alleluia.

2. In every place of worship praise the
   Lord, O my soul.
   Alleluia, alleluia, alleluia.

3. In God, who is my salvation and
   glory, my help, and my hope
   is in God.
   Alleluia, alleluia, alleluia.

Gentile Bellini. *Procession in St. Mark's Square*. Fig. 11:18 and Fig. 11:19. Details. 1496. Academy, Venice

4. Deus, te invocamus, te adoramus,
Libera nos, salva nos, vivifica nos.
Alleluia, alleluia, alleluia.

4. O God, we invoke thee, we adore
thee,
Deliver us, save us, enliven us.
Alleluia, alleluia, alleluia.

5. Deus, Deus, adjutor noster aeternam.
Alleluia, alleluia, alleluia.

5. O God, my God, our eternal judge.
Alleluia, alleluia, alleluia.

It will be noted that the text itself emphasizes the spatial element in the words *congregation* and *in every place of worship*, and that its external rather than inward orientation is hardly intended to plumb the depths of the human spirit. Hence the large and spacious tonal mural that Gabrieli makes of it is extremely appropriate. The structure of this work is based on the recurrence of the word *Alleluia*. This functions as a refrain and is set apart from the rest of the composition, both by the joyful mood implied by the word itself and by the triple rhythm of its setting, which is in contrast to the prevailing quadruple measure of the principal sections. This notable rhythmic emphasis brought about by the contrast of the marchlike measure and the *tripla* section is a possible clue to its function as a processional. The rhythm of four suggests the progress of the secular march step, and the calm religious triple meter of the refrain suggests a pause in that progress. The sectional form punctuated by the rondolike recurrence of the Alleluia part would also lend itself to the deployment of groups in a procession, leading to the finale where all forces are gathered together and united in one massive block of sound.

While Bellini's processional picture (Fig. 11:1) was painted a century before the splendor of Gabrieli's music came into being, there is evidence that the composer was carrying on a well-established tradition. It will be noted that a brass choir is playing in the group on the extreme right of the picture (Fig. 11:18), and that a group of choristers in the lower left (Fig. 11:19) is singing from scores they are carrying in their hands. Finally the gathering of the whole procession is taking place in front of the library building at the extreme left, paralleling the gathering of all groups in the final part of Gabrieli's motet. While the musical forces depicted in the painting are meager in comparison to those available to Gabrieli, this is entirely in keeping with the general growth of musical resources in the century that intervened between the two works. The separation of groups within the motet, together with the cumulative effect brought about as they gradually build up in volume, is both logical and appropriate for this type of occasion. In a reconstruction of the scene of Gabrieli's motet, the four-part first chorus with the solo voices would be in the lead. Supporting it would be a portable organ of proportions similar to the one in Titian's *Venus and the Organ Player* (Fig. 11:11). They would be followed by the

In ecclesiis (Processional Motet)   Giovanni Gabrieli

instrumental group consisting of three cornetti, one viola, and two trombones. The fact that the procession is taking place out of doors with the placement of the groups at some distance apart calls for the use of brass instruments whose outdoor carrying power is greater than either the voices or organ. Finally comes the large second chorus with at least four sopranos, four altos, four tenors, and four basses, supported by its own portable organ. Only Chorus I is broken by the separation of its voices, Chorus II always functions as a unit.

The motet [11] opens with the sopranos of Chorus I singing the first verse to the accompaniment of the organ. The first Alleluia refrain (measures 6 through 12) is taken by the sopranos of Chorus I, all of Chorus II and the organ. The tenors of Chorus I then do the second verse with organ accompaniment (measures 13–31), while the Alleluia following this verse is the same as at first. Now come the blazing chords of the instrumental Sinfonia (32–43) with their strange almost barbaric dissonances. The third verse is done in two-part counterpoint by the altos and tenors of Chorus I supported now by the six part instrumental group without organ. The Alleluia after this verse (93–99) is taken by the same two voices of Chorus I with the full Chorus II and organ without the brass ensemble. Verse 4 with its Alleluia is sometimes omitted in performance, and the fifth verse is done for full double chorus, instrumental ensemble, and organ, making a total of 14 independent parts. The cumulative climax is brought about by the final grandiose union of all vocal and instrumental forces ending in a massive cadence radiating with glowing color and producing the huge sonority necessary to bring such a work to its close. The brassy magnificence of these massive sounds seems determined to fill the out of doors, just as they had filled the vast interior of St. Mark's.

The skillful and gradual building up of volume should be noted in the concerted effect of the alternation of sopranos and full chorus, tenors and full chorus, the instrumental Sinfonia first alone, then in combination with tenors and altos, the instrumental texture against the choral supported by organ, and finally the union of all. The frequent doubling of a line in octaves serves as a means of projecting it out of the ensemble into the foreground and is one of the distinctive traits of Gabrieli's style. An example of this is found in measure 176, where the ascending figure in eighth notes in the soprano line of Chorus II is doubled an octave higher by the first trumpet part, and in the following measure the contrapuntal imitation of this appears in the tenor part of Chorus II doubled an octave lower by the first trombone. This doubling process, particularly in relation to the outside parts, is a means by which the composer achieves spaciousness. This is particularly noticeable, for example, in such a place as measures 7, 9, 10, and 12, and in the similar place in each succeeding Alleluia, where the notes of the high sopranos of Chorus I are doubled by the basses of Chorus II. The great elaboration of the instrumental parts as in the swooping sixteenth-note figure of measures 43–47 point to a system of ornamentation specifically associated with instrumental virtuosity. Toward the end in measures 165–167 the four top parts clearly indicate a vocal line written for highly trained soloists, which reveals a *concertato* between four solo voices and the full chorus. Finally it should be pointed out that the recurrence of the seven-measure Alleluia refrain holds the structure of the composition together in a tightly knit rondolike form that has the effect of preventing the intervening episodes, the diversified broken choral lines, and the vocal and instrumental color effects from disrupting the unity of the whole.

The identification of Gabrieli's music with the early Baroque style is contained in his union of opposites and his emphasis of the new law of duality. This is found in such instances as his opposition of soprano and bass; the echoing of his double choirs; the color of voices and instruments; solo and chorus; the rivalry in virtuosity of two organs or instrumental ensembles; the harmonic and contrapuntal textures; the interplay of high and low extremes of pitch; piano and forte dynamics; diatonic and chromatic harmony; the forward movement of the march rhythm against the more static triple meter; the progressive ideal embodied in the changing episodic sections of the motets versus the retrogressive tendency inherent in the idea of repetition; and the sacred liturgical manner of writing contrasted with the free occasional style associated with civic ceremonials. All these oppositions merge together in the Baroque union of antitheses, the resolution of which into a significant unity of opposites becomes one of the principal distinguishing features of the new style.

IDEAS

While Venice reached the climax of her cultural hegemony in the 16th and early 17th centuries, a long history of general eminence extended back into the early Byzantine period and was to project forward in decline to comparatively recent times. The fact that it was not one of those brief meteoric florescences tended to secure far greater influence in the spread of the ideas that developed there. The lavishness of its style of living, for instance, was the envy of the civilized world, and the commercial relations with both Orient and Occident paved the way for the eventual currency of its artistic and musical ideals. In all directions and in all the arts the influence of Venice was facilitated by the highly developed printing industry that flourished there. The writings of Palladio and others found their way by this means into libraries all over Europe and eventually to America. The printing of musical scores assured Venetian composers of general fame and prominence in other countries, just as the printing there of the works of the composers of other countries kept them abreast of developments else-where. Venetian diplomacy successfully steered a middle course between the Scylla of Reformation and the Charybdis of Counter-Reformation. As a consequence Venetian innovations in the arts of architecture and painting were eagerly adopted in the Church and court circles of Spain and France, two of the staunchest supporters of the Roman hierarchy. Both the clergy and the aristocracy needed the impressive splendor of the arts in building and maintaining their exalted positions in the society of those times. The more monumental the buildings, the more lavish their decorations, the more grandiose and more costly their musical entertainments, the more the arts served their purpose. Hence their patronage eagerly sought out the representatives of the richest expression of this ideal, which was found at that time in the work of the Venetian artists and craftsmen. In the Counter-Reformation countries church music remained more constant to the Roman tradition, and Venetian musical invention found acceptance principally in secular circles. However, to the Reformation countries, such as Holland, Scandinavia, and particularly northern Germany, Venice became a veritable musical Mecca. Sweelinck (1562–1621), foremost composer of the Netherlands in the late 16th and early 17th centuries, was a pupil of Andrea Gabrieli and a colleague and admirer of his nephew Giovanni. Heinrich Schütz (1585–1672), most illustrious German composer of the 17th century, brought the Venetian musical ideals to his country from long sojourns there as a pupil and colleague of Giovanni Gabrieli. The greater liturgical freedom found in Venetian musical forms promoted their accept-ance in the religious observances of the new Protestant faith precisely be-cause of their deviation from orthodox Roman models. This artistic tradi-tion was thus established in Germany through Schütz and his successors and was transmitted intact to J. S. Bach (1685–1750), becoming one of the foundations of his great art. Thus the principal ideas found in the arts here are not confined by any means to the Venetian city limits, and by their wide currency they actually became the basic vocabulary of the new language of the Baroque style. These ideas in the several arts converge in four principal tendencies that lift the Venetian arts over the Renaissance threshold into the Baroque style: a new dynamic and progressive concept of space, a frankly hedonistic enjoyment of life, the restraining force of academicism, and a ruling principle based on the dramatic union of opposites.

Dynamic Space

The merging of religious and secular elements embracing all the arts as exemplified in the festivals of the *scuole* and, in particular, the one shown in Bellini's painting is evidence of a new attitude toward life and a distinctive form of civic gathering. The coming and going of great crowds, comprising at times almost the entire populace of the city, within the ample dimensions of St. Mark's Square also points to a certain freedom of social movement. It was natural, therefore, for the Venetians to think in terms of spaciousness. The friendly open quality of Sansovino's Library building, and that of the Basilica by Palladio at Vicenza, is an architectural expression of this idea. The Venetian concept of space is never inert but always dynamic in the sense that it forms a setting for progressive movement in well-defined directions. The progress of Bellini's *Procession in St. Mark's Square* is clearly indicated in the movement in the picture from the right background, passing in front of the observer, and ending in the left background. The dramatic content of Titian's *Sacred and Profane Love* is felt in the diagonal movement from lower left to upper right. The same painter's *Assumption* moves in planes from the bottom to the top of the picture. Forward and backward movement is present in such compositions in depth as Giorgione's *Pastoral Concert*, and Titian's *Venus and the Organ Player*, while Veronese's feasts teem with movement in all directions. The architectural designs of Sansovino and Palladio take this freedom of motion into account and provide for the accessibility of all parts of a building to the whole, such as in the Villa Rotonda. This is equally true of the cumulative effect produced by Gabrieli's broken choirs as they merge into ever larger volumes of sound climaxed by the union of them all. The tossing back and forth of sound masses, and the frequent cadences and use of refrain also reinforce the sense of movement in Gabrieli's music. The visual reflection of the façade of a building in the water of a canal, the use of mirrors in interiors to increase the perception of light and space, the shifting of foreground and background interest in a painting composed on the principle of composition in depth, and the spatial exploitation of acoustics in the echo dynamic in music are all translations of a common basic idea worked out in the separate technical possibilities of the various arts.

Just as the visual arts reveled in illusions, such as the broken pediments of Palladio's interpenetrating temple façades (as in that of Il Redentore) and

Veronese's exaggerated spatial effects, so also does the Venetian music make spatial and acoustical experiments a part of its style. The increased dimensions in all the various arts is also quite evident. Palladio's interiors are designed for large gatherings and also to impress visitors by their very spaciousness so necessary to the grand manner of living to which his clients aspired. His preference for central plans for such private dwellings as the Villa Rotonda as well as for church buildings is, as he says, because "none is more capacious than the round." The growth in size of paintings with Titian, Tintoretto, and Veronese is a remarkable phenomenon in itself. The dimensions alone predispose them to the monumental. The grandeur of sound and the vast musical resources employed in Gabrieli's polychoral motets also exceeded anything before their time. The Venetian concept of the human figure is likewise large and ample. Even womanhood, draped and undraped, approaches the monumentality of the spacious façades of the buildings, the large dimensions of the canvases, and the huge vocal and instrumental sonorities of the motets. All these things point in the direction of the grandiose; and in this dynamic concept of space, one aspect of the life and arts of Venice finds its unity.

Hedonism

The inevitable accompaniment of this idea of spaciousness was the desire to fill it with an appropriately lavish style of living. The essential hedonism of the Venetian merchant found expression both in his religious as well as in his secular life. The frequence with which representations of the Bacchus and Ariadne myth occur in the paintings, in poetic allusions, and as a subject for drama and opera leave little doubt about the popularity there of the Greco-Roman god of wine, feasting, and revelry. Veronese's love of crowds is reflected in his painting of feasts as well as in his disarming remark to the Inquisition when he says that if a large picture has some room left over, he fills it up with figures. The multichoral musical style with the large number of participants is the musical equivalent of this love of crowds and festivity. The love of ornamentation runs also as a cross current through the architectural embellishments of such buildings as the Loggietta at the base of the Campanile by Sansovino, the elaborate details of Veronese's feasts, and the trills and other melodic adornments of the vocal and instrumental lines of Gabrieli's music. This hedonistic delight in the senses—whether for the eye, the ear, the palate, or the mind—denotes a joyous pursuit of pleasure for its own sake. Here again a common idea pervades each of the arts.

Academicism

The idea of academicism stands in contrast with both the foregoing tendencies. It runs counter to lavishness and overdecoration by promoting the continuity of the Renaissance love for the austere structures of Greco-Roman antiquity. When compared to the dynamic forward-looking and progressive developments of Venetian space, the academic idea acts as a balance to spatial excesses by leaning in the opposite direction backward toward a more static ideal. This academicism is clearly evident in the architectural designs of Sansovino and Palladio, both of whom made consistent attempts to adapt classical architectural forms to fulfill contemporary needs. Veronese also exemplifies the same academicism in his compositional structure. His predilection for symmetry, closed form, and the unifying function of architectural backgrounds are all earmarks of the academic approach. This also is a Venetian pictorial adaptation of a Renaissance painting principle that ran as an undercurrent through the work of artists from Giotto to Leonardo da Vinci. Lastly Gabrieli's continuation of the Renaissance contrapuntal technique is a musical counterpart of the above. With all his innovations, Gabrieli really continued the Netherlands tradition that was established by Willaert. It remained for his great Venetian successor Claudio Monteverdi to make the full break. By transmitting the Renaissance contrapuntal tradition to the northern composers of the 17th century, he saved them from the monodic extremes associated with the Florentine composers Galilei, Peri, Caccini, and their followers. Hence the idea of academicism finds its place in each of the expressive facets of the Venetian style.

Dramatic Union of Opposites

While simple contrast is found in all art styles, the Venetian artists consistently employed opposing elements in their designs to promote a feeling of dramatic tension. Their style transcends simple duality by pairing off carefully chosen opposites, by emphasizing the interplay of positive and negative forces, and by stressing dissonance. This dramatic aspect of the several arts has already been pointed out in the sections that treated each separately. It remains only to point out the extent to which this contrast of opposites is present in all. In architecture it is found in such instances as the opposition between the structural elements of a building and the individual units of ornamentation, and between two interpenetrating temple pediments, one complete and one broken, as in Palladio's church façades. It is also found in the contrast of the predominantly rectangular designs of such temple façades and the circular forms of the rotunda and cupola in Palladian buildings. In painting it is manifest in such compositions as Titian's *Sacred and Profane Love* with its closed and open backgrounds and opposing interests on either side, in the filled and open spaces of Veronese's festive pictures, and in many others. It is contained in the very essence of the concerting idea in the music of Gabrieli with the continuous counterplay of a rich variety of vocal and instrumental sonorities and the opposition of homophonic and polyphonic textures. The recurrence of contrasting textures in each of the arts is still another instance of the same idea. In architecture it is the opposition of smooth and rough materials; in painting, the clothed and unclothed figures, the smooth flesh and rich textiles; in music, the voices versus instruments, large and small ensembles. In finding unity in such a rich surface play of contrast and colors, the arts of Venice truly achieved a miracle that compares favorably with that which took place in Bellini's *Procession in St. Mark's Square.*

CHAPTER

CHRONOLOGY: Spain, Late 16th and Early 17th Century

General Events

1474–1516	Reign of Ferdinand of Aragon and Isabella of Castile over the united Spanish kingdom
1492	Discovery of the West Indies by Columbus (c.1446–1506)
	Fall of Granada
	Expulsion of the Moors and Jews from Spain
1497	Title of Catholic Sovereigns conferred by the pope on Ferdinand and Isabella
1498	Discovery of the North American continent by Columbus
1516–1556	Reign of Charles I as King of Spain
1519	Charles I became Charles V of the Holy Roman Empire
1534	Counter-Reformation began
1540	Jesuit Order founded by St. Ignatius Loyola (1491–1556)
1545–1563	Council of Trent
1556–1598	Reign of Philip II as King of Spain
	Spanish kingdom and empire reached their greatest extent and power
1557	France defeated by Spain in the Battle of St. Quentin
1561	Madrid chosen as his capital city by Philip II
1562	St. Theresa of Avila (1515–1582), famous mystic writer, reformed Carmelite Order
1563–1584	Building of the Escorial Palace

1571	Spain victorious in the naval battle of Lepanto
	Turkish power temporarily checked
1580	Portugal annexed by Spain
1588	Spanish Armada defeated by the English navy
1598–1621	Reign of Philip III as King of Spain
	Spanish power began to decline
1604	Cervantes' *Don Quixote*, Part I, published in Madrid
1615	Cervantes' *Don Quixote*, Part II, published in Madrid
1621–1665	Reign of Philip IV as King of Spain
1623	Velásquez appointed court painter to Philip IV
1648	Treaty of Westphalia, Spanish power in Europe checked

Architecture

? –1567	Juan Bautista de Toledo
1530–1597	Juan de Herrera
c.1580–1648	Juan Gomez de Mora
1650–1723	Jose de Churriguera

Music

c.1500–1553	Morales
c.1500–1566	Antonio de Cabezón
c.1548–1611	Victoria
c.1562–1596	Philipp Rogier

Painting

c.1541–1614	El Greco
1599–1660	Velásquez
1617–1682	Murillo

Literature

1547–1616	Cervantes
1562–1635	Lope da Vega
1600–1681	Calderon

12

THE COUNTER-REFORMA-TION BAROQUE STYLE

SPAIN, LATE 16th CENTURY

Through the venerable institutions of conquest, matrimony, and patri-
mony, Spain in the latter part of the 16th century had become the most
powerful country in the world. The voyages of Columbus and the exploits of
the conquistadores who followed in his wake brought most of North,
Central, and South America under the Spanish crown. By a combination of
marriage, heredity, and high finance, Charles I of Spain became ruler of
Austria, the Low Countries, most of Germany, and Charles V of the Holy
Roman Empire. Thereafter he continued to add to his dominions by seizing
many of the islands of the Mediterranean and large parts of Italy. When he
finally abdicated to spend his declining years in monastic seclusion, it could
be stated with conviction that he had been the most powerful European
ruler since the days of ancient Rome. His vast realm fell to his younger
brother Ferdinand and his son Philip. As king of Spain, Philip II was still
the lord of the Low Countries and most of the Western Hemisphere. By
annexing Portugal, together with its Asiatic and African possessions as well
as its islands scattered over the seven seas, he could claim in truth that he
was the ruler of an empire on which the sun never set. The monopoly of the
spice trade of the Orient and the gold and silver mines of the New World
were pouring such fabulous riches into the Spanish treasury that Philip had
the wherewithal at his disposal to become one of the greatest art patrons the
world has ever known. His youthful environment at his father's cosmopolitan court, where he was in daily contact with Titian and other leading
European artists, further paved the way for his lifelong interest in the arts.

463

Spain had always been a land of contrasts, with its verdant subtropical regions and its desolate barren plateaus, its legendary heroes and its quixotic knights, wealthy grandees and landless peons, saints such as Ignatius Loyola and sinners such as Don Juan, visionary mystics and unyielding heretics, sincere piety and fanatical religiosity; love of life and center of the cruel Inquisition. If these contrasts seem somewhat sharper in the second half of the 16th century than at other times, it is probably because the world's spotlight was beamed more intensely on Spain during the period of her greatness, and because the conflicts brought about by the forces of the Counter-Reformation, colonial expansion, and the struggle for European hegemony were centered at this time in the Iberian peninsula. Many of these contrasts were reflected in the personality of Philip himself, who was perpetually torn between the desire for religious devotion and the necessity for worldly activity, between austerity and grandeur, frugality and magnificence. While his personal tastes were simple to the point of severity, he nevertheless surrounded his royal office with all the rigors of the Spanish ceremonial, the most circumscribed courtly etiquette known in Europe. It had the effect of isolating the monarch himself and of imposing an almost intolerable loneliness that served only to intensify his interest in religious and artistic expression.

Philip was always acutely aware of the responsibility that went with the title of His Catholic Majesty, and during his reign Spain became the secular center of the Counter-Reformation. Pious to the point of fanaticism, he would have preferred the life of a monk, yet it was mandatory that the Spanish court be maintained on an appropriately lavish level. Politically he was an exponent of monarchical absolutism and the centralized state; and he saw that the best way of promoting the unity of his kingdom was to draw all the feudal nobles to his court where he could keep a watchful eye on their activities. He personally selected the obscure but centrally located town of Madrid for his capital, though at the time it was not even important enough to be the see of a bishop. An enormous building program consequently had to be undertaken in order to house the court and provide city palaces for the aristocracy. With the riches of the Old World and the unlimited resources of the New at his command, he tried to attract the leading artists of Europe to help him build and embellish his chosen capital. His ambassadors were all under instructions to report the availability of any masterpiece of painting or sculpture, and to comb Italy for artists who would be willing to go to Spain and attach themselves to his entourage.

While remaining in their native cities, Titian and other Italian artists continued to paint for Philip. The Spanish architect Juan Bautista de Toledo was persuaded to leave Italy and journey to Madrid. Domenicos

Theotocopoulos, a young Greek painter who had studied in Venice and Rome, was attracted to Spain where he was to become known as the foreigner El Greco (the Greek). The Spanish composer Victoria, though he was fully established in Rome, dedicated a book of Masses to Philip in the hope of receiving a court commission. From all parts of Europe, artists known and unknown, attracted by the glitter of Spanish gold, flocked to Madrid in search of fame and fortune. While the 16th century thus saw the rise of Spain to a pinnacle of power and prestige, the following century was to witness its diminution and decline. The precedent that Charles V and Philip II established as patrons of the arts, however, had sufficient momentum to continue undiminished through the reigns of Philip III and Philip IV, and thus to round out a full century of brilliant artistic activity.

ARCHITECTURE

Bound by the terms of his father's will to build him a tomb, bound by his own solemn oath to found a monastery dedicated to the Spanish martyr St. Lawrence, on whose day he gained his great military victory over the French, and bound also by his intense religious fervor and his consciousness of his royal prerogatives, Philip II envisioned a vast architectural project that would coordinate all these diverse objectives as well as resolve some of his own inner conflicts. As the plan matured in his mind, this monument was to be at once a temple to God, a mausoleum for his ancestors and descendants, a national archive of arts and letters, a dwelling place for the Hieronomite monks, a college and seminary, a place of pilgrimage with a hospice for the reception of strangers, a royal residence, and in general a symbol of the magnificence of the Spanish monarchy.

The Escorial

A site in the barren foothills of the Guadarrama Mountains about 30 miles from Madrid was chosen. The small nearby village, which was named Escorial from the *scoriae*, or refuse, of the ancient iron mines of the region, gave the royal retreat its name; while the adjacent stone quarries provided the unending supply of yellowish-gray granite blocks with which the structure was built. The original plans were drawn up by Juan Bautista de Toledo who had studied with Jacopo Sansovino and Palladio and worked on St. Peter's in Rome under the direction of Michelangelo. Philip, however, had a hand in the planning and was continuously making suggestions and alterations. Juan Bautista died soon after the project was begun, and by the time his disciple and collaborator Juan de Herrera took over, Philip's ideas had grown so that the plans had to be completely revised.

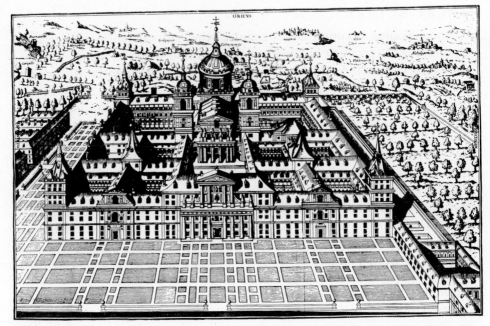

Fig. 12:1 (above). Herrera. *The Escorial*. 675′ x 685′, Towers 200′ high, Dome 312′ high. 1563–1584. Engraving by Pedro Peret after an elevation by Herrera. Fig. 12:2 (below). *Side View* (Anderson)

According to Philip's instructions, the monument had to embody the ideals of "nobility without arrogance, majesty without ostentation." Both Philip and his father, as pillars of the Church and as international rulers, were conscious of the reincarnation of Roman power in their empire and kingdoms. The Roman classical style, as formulated by Palladio and others, seemed best to symbolize their international position and prestige. The simplicity of the Escorial and its generally severe character were therefore in keeping with Philip's personal taste; and the hard unyielding stone itself exercised a still further restraining influence on the architects and decorators. As it stands, the monument is a vast quadrangle of almost 500,000 square feet, which is subdivided into a symmetrical system of courts and cloisters (Fig. 12:1). The form symbolically refers to the gridiron of St. Lawrence on which he met his martyrdom. The corner towers can be said to represent the legs of the iron grill, while the palace, which projects from the east end, forms its handle. Elsewhere in the building the grill idea is widely used as a decorative motive.

The sides (Fig. 12:2) present a long expanse of wall, entirely devoid of decoration, their monotony broken only by the endless rows of seriated windows. The principal entrance, found on the west front (Fig. 12:1), is carried out in the strict Doric order with only the royal coat of arms and a colossal statue of St. Lawrence holding his gridiron to relieve the general austerity. The portal leads into the Patio of the Kings, which is named from the statues of David, Solomon, and the other kings of Israel that stand over the entrance to the imposing church, which is located on the central axis. Herrera adapted the plan as well as many of the interior and exterior details of the basilica from Michelangelo's original design for St. Peter's (Fig. 10:19). It is a centralized structure, following the form of a Greek cross and culminating in a dome that rises more than 300 feet over the floor. The main body of the basilica is conceived in the strong and dignified Doric style, relieved by a series of chapels, numerous altars with painted altar pieces, and the ornate organ lofts. The choir is carried out in the Corinthian order and is divided into two sections, each wing having a separate organ loft with balconies of brass gilt enclosing the instruments themselves. Since Philip frequently participated in the devotions of the monks, he had his own stall in the choir near a door through which messages could be handed to him. Still another door communicated with his private apartment so that it was possible for him to attend services from there as well. Below the high altar is the burial crypt known as the Royal Chapel of the Pantheon, which was finished later during the reign of Philip IV. In it the kings and queens of Spain repose in Baroque coffins arranged in strict hierarchical order.

Fig. 12:3. Herrera. Escorial. *Court of the Evangelists.* 210′ x 207′. 1563–1584 (Courtesy Spanish State Tourist Office)

Much of the Escorial's area is devoted to the monastery and seminary of the order of St. Jerome. The heart of their section is the handsomely designed double-decked cloister known as the Patio de los Evangelistas (Fig. 12:3). It faces one wing of the church, and the enclosed walk below is again in the Doric order with its severe frieze punctuated by the rhythmical triglyphs. Still more space for monastic meditations is provided by the Ionic gallery, which, in turn, is surmounted above by a balustrade in the Palladian manner. In the center of the garth is a small structure of polychrome marble that functions as an echo of the great dome of the church which soars above it. Statues by Monegro of each of the four Evangelists look outward from their niches toward their respective pools, which are watered from spouts in the forms of the symbolic evangelical beasts.

In the palace section are found the reception halls, the impressive galleries, and the state dining rooms that go with the grandeur of the proud Spanish monarchy. The only departure from the prevailing air of pomp and splendor is the monastic severity of Philip's own apartment. Elsewhere there are the quarters of the major-domos, the secretaries of state, the lords of the bedchamber, lodgings for ambassadors, and apartments for members of the royal family. Some galleries have mural and ceiling decorations devoted to the great battles of Spanish history; others are hung with rich Flemish tapestries depicting Biblical, mythological, and literary subjects. The picture galleries contain a vast number of the paintings that were purchased so liberally over the centuries by the Spanish kings. The Escorial still houses many of Philip's own collection of the Venetian masters he so much admired. Other Italian schools as well as Flemish and native Spanish artists are also represented with outstanding examples. Of interest also is the library, a barrel-vaulted structure with its east and west windows arranged according to the maxims of Vitruvius. A drawing for its decoration (Fig. 12:4) with detailed notes of instruction to the artists shows that Herrera kept a firm hand on every aspect of the design of his building. Many rare medieval manuscripts and codices are housed in this library as well as the royal collection of medals, coins, and bronzes. Among its treasures are the manuscripts of the books of St. Theresa of Avila, that pillar of the Counter-Reformation who was once a guest of King Philip at the Escorial. Works of the great Arabic and Jewish authors are placed in a special enclosure where they can be seen but not read or touched.

So vast is the Escorial as a whole that it has been estimated it would be necessary to walk ten miles in order to go through every room. On it Philip lavished the energies of nearly 40 years of his leisure, and it was his fondest wish to see it completed during his lifetime. Most of the work actually was done before his demise, but the Pantheon and many details of the

Fig. 12:4. Herrera. *Design for the Decoration of the Escorial Library.* Drawing. 11¾″ x 19″. British Museum, London

complex structure remained for his successors to carry through to completion. The fact that the building was conceived and built mainly under one patron in less than half a century gives it a closer unity than palaces such as the Vatican and the Louvre, which evolved over many centuries and constantly were changing with the varying tastes and fortunes of their proprietors. For this reason too, the Escorial appears to be dominated by the restless melancholy spirit of its founder, which seems to have crystallized here into the rigidity and majesty of death. The Escorial nevertheless remains unique among the buildings of the world, combining as it does in a single structure the functions of a royal residence, military fortress, colossal church, national art gallery, state archives and library, monastery, theological college, pantheon of Spanish kings, and sepulchre of princes.

The Florid Baroque

Exercising the prerogatives of an absolute monarch, Philip insisted on the right to pass on the suitability and style of every public building that was undertaken during his reign. Herrera, as the court architect, was commissioned to inspect the plans of all such structures and as a consequence became an artistic dictator who enforced the conservative, restricted preferences of his royal master on the nation. Not until after Philip's death was Spain free to develop the florid Baroque style that is now such a prominent

Fig. 12:5. Gomez de Mora. *La Clérica*, Façade. 1617. *Casa de las Conchas* (House of the Shells). 1514. Salamanca (Courtesy Spanish State Tourist Office)

feature of the face of its large cities. Some of its emotional exuberance and excesses as well came about as a direct reaction to the austere formalism of Philip's time. Daring designs, fantastic forms, curved lines, the spiral twist of corkscrew columns rapidly replaced the severe façades and traditional classical orders enforced by Herrera.

Two buildings in Salamanca (Fig. 12:5) dating about a century apart will serve as illustrations. The Casa de las Conchas, or House of the Shells, is a Renaissance structure built in 1514, well before Philip's time. It nevertheless shows the tendency toward applied decoration that was popularly known as the plateresque style, a name derived from the Spanish word *platero*, or silversmith. Across the street is the church of the Jesuit College of La Clérica, which was begun after the period of Philip and Herrera. The lower part dates from the early 17th century and was designed by Juan Gomez de Mora. Even though it still adheres nominally to the classical orders, the decorative urge is clearly active in the attached composite columns and in the Baroque triglyphs above them, as well as in many of the other details. The towers and gable belong to the latter part of the century and were executed by Churriguera, whose name is associated with the more florid aspects of the Spanish Baroque.

PAINTING

When El Greco left Italy for Spain, he carried with him recommendations to the Church authorities but not to the court. The logical destination therefore was Toledo, the religious center where he first established himself; but the activities at Madrid naturally enough exerted a magnetic attraction for the young artist. It was not until 1580, however, that he received a commission from Philip II which resulted in his early masterpiece, *The Martyrdom of St. Maurice* (Fig. 12:6). It was intended as an altarpiece for the chapel dedicated to that saint in the large church at the Escorial where his relics are preserved. The subject is one typical of the Counter-Reformation in that it has to do with the dilemma of the individual who is caught between conflicting loyalties. St. Maurice, the figure in the right foreground, was the commander of the Theban Legion, a unit of Christians serving in the Roman imperial army. An order has come through commanding them to acknowledge the orthodox Roman deities or be put to death. As he consults with his staff officers, their positions in the argument are revealed by the expressive gestures of their hands. Christ, it is true, had sanctioned by his own example the rendering unto Caesar the material things that are Caesar's, but the worship of false idols was another matter. The line was

Fig. 12:6. El Greco. *Martyrdom of St. Maurice and the Theban Legion.* 174″ x 118″. 1581–1584. Prado, Madrid (Anderson)

Fig. 12:7. El Greco. *Assumption of the Virgin.* 13′ 2″ x 7′ 6″. *c.*1577. Art Institute, Chicago

thus clearly drawn, and a choice had to be made between duty to the state and Church, between the city of man and the city of God. For St. Maurice there is only one possible decision, and his hand therefore points upward.

El Greco's spiral composition is well adapted to convey the tension between the material and spiritual realms, the earthly and unearthly, the natural and supernatural, the terrestrial and celestial. It is felt in the twitching muscles, the flamelike fingers, the taut faces, and in the swirling upward motion of the composition itself. In serpentine fashion it winds around to the left middleground where St. Maurice is seen again, this time giving comfort to the men as they await their turn for decapitation. The tempo is accelerated toward the background where the nude figures of the army seem already to have parted company with corporeality and are drawn into the spiritual vortex that bears them aloft on a Dantesque whirlwind. The eye is led inexorably upward by the constantly increasing color movement and light intensity from the darker hues below to the vaporous pink and white clouds above. There one beholds a visionary vista in the heavens, where some of the floating angelic figures are hovering and holding crowns for those who suffer and die below, while still others are producing the strains of celestial harmony.

In spite of the grimness of the subject, the light transparent color palette El Greco uses gives the work an almost festive air, with the rose-colored banners and steel blue and yellow costumes set against a background of silvery gray. The originality of the work, with its daring color dissonances and the lavish use of costly ultramarine blue, forfeited for El Greco the favor of King Philip, whose tastes ran to the more conservative Italian style. Only one further attempt to interest the royal patron was made with a study for a picture later called the *Dream of Philip II*. The commission for its execution on a large scale, however, was never forthcoming.

When the artist found that the doors of the Escorial were closed to him, he knew that the gates of Toledo, the religious capital of Spain and see of the archbishop primate, were always open. His reputation there had been securely established by the series of paintings he had done for the Church of Santo Domingo el Antiguo. The most renowned of these was the work for the high altar, the *Assumption of the Virgin* (Fig. 12:7). There are many similarities as well as some significant differences between this picture and the one on the same subject (Fig. 11:13) that Titian had painted some 60 years before. By dividing his composition into three vertical planes, together with his use of light and color, Titian had achieved an irresistible upward motion. In El Greco's work there is much less movement and far greater serenity. The open sarcophagus defines a horizontal depth and diagonal plane that are not to be found in Titian's composition. He then divides the groups below so that they form the base of a pyramid while the Virgin above forms its apex. With El Greco the two groups of Apostles betray neither surprise nor sorrow at the parting; instead there is an atmosphere of calm contemplation as if the event were the fulfillment of a prophecy for which they had been waiting. The coloring is brilliant, the modeling well handled, and the conception highly imaginative but convincing.

The *Expulsion from the Temple* (Fig. 12:8) was a religious subject hitherto outside the iconographical tradition. The fact that El Greco painted no less than six versions of it shows that the theme had become an important one in the Counter-Reformation period. The driving out of the money changers from the temple is the only incident in the Gospels where Christ is seen in an attitude of righteous anger, and the only time he resorted to physical action and corporal punishment. The Church, after the Council of Trent, was in the throes of a rigid self-purification process, and the image of Christ as a reformer was therefore foremost in their minds. Since this was the period of the church militant as well as that of the Inquisition, it is likely that the churches which ordered the pictures intended to revive the incident as a justification of their course of action.

Christ appears here in the role of the refining fire as prophesied by Isaiah, and his mood of fiery anger is reflected in El Greco's clashing colors of crimson red, pink, orange, and greenish yellow. While his gesture bespeaks violence, his face is serene in the knowledge that what he does is for the good of those whom he chastises. The atmosphere recalls that of a Last Judgment with the figure of Christ separating the two groups. The side toward which his lash is directed is full of turbulence and confusion as the traders cringe under the accusing eye, yet try to save their wares. On the other side all is calm, and the figures who probably represent Disciples seem to ponder on the meaning of the event. The contrast is also carried out in the reliefs painted between the columns in the upper part of the picture. The one over the left side shows Adam and Eve being driven from the garden by the sword of the avenging angel, while that on the other depicts the messenger of the Lord staying the sword of Abraham as he is about to sacrifice his son Isaac.

In his penetrating portrait of Cardinal Don Fernando Niño de Guevara (Fig. 12:9), El Greco has produced a personification of the spirit of the Counter-Reformation. At the time it was painted, the Cardinal was about to leave his post as Archbishop of Toledo to assume the office of Grand Inquisi-

Fig. 12:8. El Greco (above). *Expulsion from the Temple.* 16½″ × 20⅝″. *c.*1577. Copyright The Frick Collection, New York

Fig. 12:9 (right). El Greco. *Cardinal de Guevara.* 67¼″ × 42½″. *c.*1600. Metropolitan Museum, New York

tor at Seville, a position which gave him the leadership of the dread Inquisition. His bearded face betrays an attitude of uncompromising righteousness. The piercing eyes, magnified by thick lenses, bespeak a feverish intelligence and a religious fanaticism accompanied by pitiless logic. The pose of the body is that of a prosecutor and the practitioner of a rigid spiritual discipline. The generally austere impression is relieved only by the obvious delight El Greco took in the brilliant carmine red and the contrasting white lace of the Cardinal's robes, which are sumptuously painted.

In the attempt to understand the various aspects of El Greco's style, it is possible to offer some rationalistic arguments. His use of bright colors, for instance, undoubtedly had something to do with the dark Spanish churches for which his pictures were painted. The conventional lengthening of the bodies as well as the hands and heads of his figures might be explained by the artist's Byzantine background; or they might have been distorted as an expressive device to promote the illusion that the figures were on a higher level, somewhat like statues seen from a kneeling position. Such factors, however, contribute little to a true understanding of El Greco's art. The Counter-Reformation, of which he was the greatest pictorial interpreter, saw in the growing scientific point of view a threat to the traditional acceptance of miracles. El Greco was concerned with the translation of such miracles into convincing visual terms, reinforced by a heightened emotionalism and an exploration of mystical experience. Within this frame of reference naturalistic and logical explanations simply do not apply; but his inner world does not for this reason lack either coherence or consistency. When El Greco is accepted on his own terms, his world responds to its own laws, and its forms then become communicable patterns of the utmost expressivity.

Less than a decade after El Greco's death, King Philip IV appointed Velásquez as his court painter. In contrast to El Greco, Velásquez was a visual realist who was concerned more with the experience of the eye than with the inner world of the spirit. While El Greco concerned himself almost exclusively with religious subjects, Velásquez gave himself up almost entirely to scenes of courtly life. His work is admirably summed up in his masterpiece *Las Meninas*, or the *Maids of Honor* (Fig. 12:10). In it the painter combines the formality of a group portrait with the informality of a genre scene in his studio. The attention is about evenly distributed between the various groups. In the foreground the Infanta Margarita dressed in a gown of white satin is seen standing in the center. On the left a maid of honor is offering her a drink of water from a red cup on a gold tray. At the right is a group made up of a second maid of honor and two of the court

Fig. 12:10. Velásquez. *Las Meninas* (*Maids of Honor*). 10′ 5¼″ x 9′ ¾″. 1656. Prado, Madrid (Anderson)

dwarfs, one of whom is teasing the sleepy mastiff with his foot. In the middleground on the left is Velásquez himself wearing the cross of the Order of Santiago, which was conferred on him by his friend and patron, the king. He stands before a canvas which, by reason of its large dimensions, seems to be *Las Meninas* itself. He is looking at King Philip IV and Queen Mariana whose faces are reflected in the mirror at the back of the room. As a balance for his own figure, Velásquez paints the conversing lady-in-waiting and courtier in the right middleground. In the rear of the room a court attendant stands in the open doorway pulling back a curtain, possibly to adjust the light for the painter.

Velásquez is a virtuoso in the handling of space and light. With the utmost precision he has organized the room into a series of receding planes and by so doing gives the figures their spatial relationships. The first plane is in front of the picture itself where the King and Queen, and by inference, the observer are standing. Next comes that in which the principal group stands in the light of the window at the right, which again is outside the picture but which provides the most intense illumination that falls on the blonde hair of the princess. The light here is balanced by that from the door at the rear, which defines the plane in the background. In between is the intermediate plane with the figures of Velásquez and the attendants, who are shown in more subdued light. Otherwise the space is broken up geometrically into a pattern of rectangles, such as the floor, ceiling, the easel, the pictures hanging on the wall, the mirror, and the door at the back.

In such a precise analytical study of space and light, which lacks either the spiritual mysticism of El Greco or the worldly grandiosity of the Venetian painters, the Baroque qualities are not immediately apparent. Velásquez, however, is a virtuoso of external rather than internal vision, and his Baroque qualities are therefore found in such things as the intricate play of light and shadow, in the complex spatial arrangements, in the fact that much lies outside the picture space itself, and in the subtle relationships of the subjects to each other. The proof of the latter is evidenced by the fact that Velásquez experts still cannot agree on what is actually going on. Is Velásquez painting the King and Queen, and is it the Infanta and her ladies who have wandered in to look around? Or is Velásquez looking into a mirror as he paints the Infanta, and is it the King and Queen who have dropped in to watch the proceedings?

Just as Spanish architecture showed a reaction when the restraints of the earlier period were lifted, Spanish painting also moved away from the austerity and intensity of the previous century. No painter could sustain the spiritual insight and emotional power of El Greco. The relaxation into sentimentality is clearly seen in Murillo's *Immaculate Conception* (Fig. 12:11). The subject was one in particular favor with the Spanish Church, and Murillo and his workshop are known to have turned out some 20 versions of it. According to the ecclesiastical formula, the Virgin should be shown in all the beauty of her late girlhood, and, like the vision in the 12th chapter of Revelations, clothed with the sun and with the moon under her feet, and borne aloft by a cherubic choir. In this instance the cherubs hold the lily, olive branch, and palm leaf—symbols of purity, peace, and martyrdom.

Fig. 12:11. Murillo Workshop. *Immaculate Conception*. 78″ x 53″. Institute of Arts, Detroit

MUSIC

The music at the court of Philip II, like the architecture, painting, and sculpture, was religiously oriented; and the records of the period, as well as the design of the church at the Escorial, testify to the important place accorded the tonal art there. The choir at the Escorial was established even before the whole building was completed, and in 1586 numbered in its ranks 150 monks. The choir section of the church is divided into two parts, since Philip's musical preferences were for the Venetian double choral style he had heard in his youth. Besides the two organs in the choir, there are two others on either side of the nave, which are large double-manual concert instruments of Flemish manufacture, 50 feet wide and 40 feet high. The same maker also built three portable organs for processions, which were placed in the galleries, thus making it possible on high feast days to hear seven organs pealing forth. Antonio de Cabezón served Philip as organist and clavecinist, and his compositions include works in the Venetian concerting style written for two, three, and four organs. Toward the end of Philip's reign, the choirmaster was the Flemish musician, Philipp Rogier, among whose compositions is a motet for three choirs accompanied by two organs and harp.

The greatest Spanish musician of Philip's reign, as with the foremost painter, was found just outside the immediate court circle. Owing to the close connection between Spain and the Holy See, the real center of Spanish religious music was to be found in Rome. Tomás Luis de Victoria followed in the footsteps of his great Spanish predecessor Cristobal Morales, a contemporary of Charles V, and went to Rome by means of a grant from Philip II. The following year he was established as a singer and priest in the German College, which had been founded there by his fellow Spaniard Ignatius Loyola. When Victoria published his second book of Masses in 1583, he inscribed it with a long and florid dedication to Philip II, obviously in the hope of obtaining a court appointment. Records of the period are obscure, and some authorities claim that Victoria was appointed vice-choirmaster of the Escorial under Rogier. His appointment as chaplain and choirmaster to the Dowager Empress Maria, daughter of Charles V and sister of Philip II, seems more certain. Since the Empress returned to Spain it is quite possible that he held both positions. The book of Masses that Victoria published in 1600 are in the massive Venetian choral style with an accompanying organ part in the tradition of the Spanish royal chapel. The vocal demands are of such complexity as to warrant the assumption that they were composed for the skilled chorus of the Escorial.

Victoria's art, like that of Herrera and El Greco, grew out of the late Renaissance tradition. In this case it was the choral style of the Flemish masters known as the *ars perfecta*, or perfected art. In his Roman period Victoria's style shows the same fluidity and purity of texture as that of his older contemporary Palestrina. He deviates from it only in the direction of darker emotional coloration and a deeper insight into the dramatic meaning of his texts. Certain motives recur often enough to give tangible clues to his expressive purposes, such as the characteristic descent on the line of the minor triad and the use of the interval of the minor second to symbolize sorrow and pain. His *Offices for Holy Week* were traditionally performed in the Sistine Chapel for more than 300 years. One of these is the four-part motet *O Vos Omnes*, the text of which comes from Jeremiah and the mood is one of lamentation. The passage, which is quoted below, shows the characteristic grief motive in the descending tenor voice in measure 4, as well as the dissonance created by the dip of the minor second by the same voice in the 5th measure, both of which intensify the meaning of the word *dolor*, or sorrow.

O vos omnes (4-Part Motet)   Victoria

Si est do - lor   do -   lor   si - mi-lis

Victoria's music is so exclusively religious and so thoroughly imbued with the spirit, that he never wrote a single note of secular music. As he stated in one of his dedications, he was led by some secret impulse to devote himself solely to church music. In his motets and Masses, he even avoided the secular *cantus firmus* themes that were customarily employed by his contemporaries. Instead, he chose his motives and melodies from his own religious works or from the traditional plainsong. In his later compositions after his return to Spain, his work takes on an even greater fervor and passionate intensity. With its ascetic quality, religious ardor, and devotional spirit, his music rises in its way to the same heights of mystical grandeur as the writings of St. Theresa of Avila, the architecture of Herrera, and the pictures of El Greco.

IDEAS

Militant Mysticism

With the Counter-Reformation, the Roman Catholic countries experienced a vigorous reassertion and reaffirmation of the mystical world view. In keeping with the spirit of the times, however, it was more a mysticism of this world than that of the next, as in the Middle Ages; it was social in character, as it had to do with the Church as the mystical body of Christ. It was not, therefore, expressed by a monastic retreat behind convent walls; it was rather a mysticism of men of action rather than of contemplation; it was a call to arms for all loyal Roman Catholics to stand up and be counted; it set up a selective-service system to draft all those willing to fight for their faith in a war to the finish against heresy; in short, it was a military mysticism of a church militant on the march. An entirely new type of saint enlisted for the duration in the vanguard of this new ecclesiastical army. There was the band of spiritual social workers, such as Philip Neri and Carlo Borromeo, who were in contact with all classes of people, and there was the soldier and man of action, Ignatius Loyola, who mobilized the Jesuits for missionary duty in his priestly army of occupation. Then there was the *Mistica Doctora*, St. Theresa, who, as a woman of action, made sure that the celestial communication system was in working order day and night, and who put her Carmelite nuns on a wartime footing, so that their prayers could become effective instruments of psychological warfare.

It was the papacy that sounded the declaration of war, while the Council of Trent issued the series of white papers that established the legal case for the Roman Catholic Church. Its members were principally concerned with the adaptation of church doctrine to modern conditions, and with making as few radical changes in its traditional position as possible. During the sessions of the Council, the Church underwent 18 years of basic training to reduce its excess fat, prune away the overgrowth around its camp, counteract the effects of luxurious living, and reaffirm the neglected vows and obligations of its clergy. It was a reformation movement too, but one that went on within its own ranks. After its deliberations were concluded, the Church emerged from its process of self-purification, stripped for action and ready for its self-appointed task. With a formidable will it went forth to reassert its supremacy and to do battle with its enemies any place on earth.

The most typical division of this army of the church militant was the Society of Jesus, which adopted the principles of political and moral realism, had its Director General, divided the whole world into Jesuitic provinces, used the navy of commercial vessels as troop transports, moved in behind the conquistadores as a spiritual army of occupation, and vigorously prosecuted the war by every Machiavellian means at their disposal. The military police force was the Congregation of the Inquisition, which was

Fig. 12:12. Bernini. *St. Theresa in Ecstasy*. Life size. Marble. 1646. Coronaro Chapel, Santa Maria della Vittoria, Rome (Alinari)

constantly on guard for any espionage agents of heresy who might be lurking in the dark places of the territories under its command. No side in this war, however, had a monopoly on cruelty, intolerance, or fanaticism. Calvin used physical torture in Geneva; Spinoza was banned from the synagogue in Amsterdam and narrowly escaped assassination in the process; and, of course, they hanged witches in New England. A system of thought control was enforced by the *Index Expurgatorius*, which exercised rigid censorship of reading matter, lest any form of spiritual subversion be forthcoming from this source. The strong secular army of the movement was that of the monarchy of Philip II with its headquarters in Spain. This staunch Defender of the Faith pledged all his heavy artillery, backed by the resources of two continents, to the cause. In his zeal he turned his country into a mighty fortress in which priests became prosecuting attorneys, and the dramatists Lope da Vega and Calderon, as well as the musicians Morales and Victoria, became priests. When he built his Escorial Palace, he cast it in the image of a martyr's instrument of torture, and incorporated a church, a monastery, a seminary, and a mausoleum into the plan.

The ranks of the enemy were made up of the various Protestant movements that the Church regarded as heretical; the materialistic world view, which often accompanied the Protestant manifestations; and above all, the forces of rampant rationalism that were unleashed by free scientific inquiry. The Counter-Reformation was just as much a reassertion of spiritual and moral values in the face of the growing scientific materialism as it was an anti-Protestant movement. The Church plainly saw that such rationalism, if followed to its logical conclusion, would threaten the belief in miracles, destroy the notion of divine intervention in worldly affairs, eliminate the supernatural from the universe, and eventually drain all the mystery out of the cosmos.

This war also had a secret weapon in its chief instrument of popular propaganda—art. Through aesthetic appeal, miracles could be made to seem real to the senses; and through architectural, sculptural, pictorial, literary, and musical illusions, obscure transcendental ideas could be made into concrete realities. The building of St. Peter's in Rome, the grandest and most magnificent ecclesiastical edifice on earth, was calculated as an overwhelming visual proof of the spiritual might of Roman Catholicism. Its semisecular echo, the Palace of the Escorial, was designed to show the worldly power of His Catholic Majesty. The fervent flames of El Greco's pictures were a means of rekindling the fires of faith in the souls of those who beheld his pictorial miracles. The marble angelic figures of saints in the sculpture, which defied the laws of gravity, served the same end. St. Theresa was advised to make written records of the ecstatic visions she beheld, and her sparkling Spanish prose turned them into the best sellers of the Counter-Reformation. Victoria brought all the unique power of his moving melodic lines to illuminate the texts of the hymns of the liturgical year, so as to make them glow with new mystic meaning. Nothing seemed too fantastic, too illogical, or impossible to the creative mind of the Counter-Reformation artist.

The Jesuits banished the last vestiges of medieval gloom from their churches and enlisted all the Baroque artists in the service of religion. Baroque churches became theaters where a concert of the arts played a prelude in an optimistic tonality to the delights and heavenly beauties of the life to come. The artists had, of course, to conform to the official interpretations of church dogma, but otherwise their imaginative flights could soar without limitation. By their adoption of the artistic vocabulary of the time, the Jesuits not only brought Baroque art down from the exclusive aristocratic level but carried the new idioms with them wherever they went, thus converting the Baroque into an international style. Counter-Reformation Baroque churches are thus found as far afield as Mexico, South America, and the Philippines. The extraordinary vigor of the church militant succeeded in tapping new spiritual sources and invigorating Catholicism to such an extent that it emerged once more as a popular religious movement.

CHAPTER

||||||||||||||||||||||||||||||||||||||||||||||||||||||||||||||||||||||||||||||||||||||||||||||||||||||||||||||||||||||||||||||||

CHRONOLOGY: France in the Time of Louis XIV

General Events

1598–1610	Henry IV reigned as King of France
1610–1643	Louis XIII reigned as King of France with his mother Maria de' Medici (1573–1642) acting as Regent during his minority
1615–1624	Luxembourg Palace built for Queen Mother by Salomon de Brosse
1621	Rubens commissioned to paint ceiling murals in the Luxembourg Palace
1624–1642	Cardinal Richelieu (1585–1642) Prime Minister under Louis XIII
1635	French Academy of Language and Literature established
1636	*Traité de l'Harmonie Universelle* (*Treatise on Universal Harmony*) published by Mersenne
1640	Poussin returned from Rome to decorate the Louvre Palace
1643–1715	Louis XIV reigned as King of France
1643–1661	Cardinal Mazarin (1602–1661) Prime Minister under Louis XIV
1648	Treaty of Westphalia concluded Thirty Years' War Spain and Austria defeated; France became dominant European nation
1661–1715	Louis XIV ruled without a Prime Minister
1661–1688	Versailles Palace built for Louis XIV by Louis Levau and J. Hardouin Mansart Chapel added 1699–1708
1665–1683	Colbert (1619–1683) Minister of Finance under Louis XIV
1665	Bernini in Paris to rebuild the Louvre Palace French Academy in Rome established
1666	Academy of Sciences established

1667–1674	East Façade of the Louvre Palace built by Perrault
1669	Paris Opera established by Lully
1671	Academy of Architecture established
1674	Alceste, lyrical tragedy by Quinault and Lully performed at Versailles *L'Art Poétique* (*Art of Poetry*) published by Boileau
1682	Government and ministries of France installed at Versailles

Architecture

1552–1626	Salomon de Brosse
1612–1670	Louis Levau
1613–1688	Claude Perrault
1613–1700	André Le Nôtre
1646–1708	J. Hardouin Mansart

Painting

1577–1640	Peter Paul Rubens
1594–1665	Nicolas Poussin
1600–1682	Claude Lorrain (Claude Gellée)
1619–1690	Charles Lebrun
1659–1743	Hyacinthe Rigaud

Literature and Philosophy

1596–1650	Descartes
1606–1684	Corneille
1621–1695	La Fontaine
1622–1673	Molière
1623–1662	Pascal
1635–1688	Quinault
1636–1711	Boileau
1639–1699	Racine

Sculpture

1598–1680	Lorenzo Bernini
1622–1694	Pierre Puget
1640–1720	Coysevox

Music

1602–1676	Cavalli, Venetian opera composer
c.1602–1672	Chambonnières, organist and clavecinist
1632–1687	Jean Baptiste Lully
1668–1733	Couperin le Grand, clavecinist

13

THE ARISTOCRATIC BAROQUE STYLE

FRANCE IN THE TIME OF LOUIS XIV

Everything about Louis XIV was designed to suggest grandeur. His concept of kingship assured him of the designation of *le grand roi;* his code of etiquette created the grand manner; he was in every sense of the word the *grand seigneur;* and his reign gave his century the name of *le grand siècle.* At the time his portrait (Fig. 13:1) was painted by Hyacinthe Rigaud in 1701, he had been king in name for well over half a century and a king in fact for a full 40 of those years. Dressed in his courtly ermine-lined coronation robes, with the collar of the Grand Master of the Order of the Holy Ghost draped about his regal neck, he might actually be uttering the very words for which he was so famous: *L'état c'est moi*—I am the state. Since he was in fact the personification of France, his portrait, appropriately enough, was that of an institution; and his figure was as much a pillar holding up the state as that of the imposing column which supports the building in the background. Pompous and theatrical though the portrait is, it was part and parcel of the illusionism of a period that strove to make such transcendental abstractions as the divine right of kings seem real to the senses.

Absolute monarchy, accompanied by the cult of majesty, did not lack a rational basis. Louis' favorite image was provided, possibly, by the astronomer Copernicus, who proclaimed in his famous treatise that "the sun, as if sitting on a royal throne, governs the family of stars which move around it." Louis was indeed the center of a solar system that included among its satellites innumerable ministers and mistresses as well as a slightly more select company of poets and artists. Descartes, furthermore, built his

489

Fig. 13:1. Rigaud. *Louis XIV*. 9′ 1½″ x 6′ 2⅝″. 1701. Louvre, Paris (Alinari)

philosophy on the premise that the universe was an orderly system, whose parts were derived from the whole and where all the forces emanated from a single center. The philosopher believed that the things he clearly and distinctly perceived were true, and in this connection often cited the image of sunlight. Political theorists hastened to point out that since the sun was the center of the solar system and the source of light, the king was the logical center of the state, the apex of the social pyramid, the head of the civil service, the army, the police, and so on. In this frame of reference Louis' exalted place in the scheme of things was not quite so arbitrary as it appears today, and it would certainly have been impossible even in his own time had it not enjoyed the support of the most astute French politicians of the century, Henry IV, Richelieu, Mazarin, and Colbert.

The success of this system of centralization is seen in the list of positive accomplishments of a reign in which the feudal power of the provincial nobles was broken; the Church became a part of the state instead of the state a part of the Church; Paris became the intellectual and artistic capital of the world; and France attained the dominant position among European nations. In the arts the alliance with absolutism meant that they were of value as instruments of propaganda; factors in the assertion of national power and prestige; and the means of enhancing the glory of the court, impressing visiting dignitaries, and stimulating export trade. All this led, of course, toward the concept of art as an adjunct to the cult of majesty and as the perpetuator of the myth. With the king as principal patron, art inevitably became a department of the government, and Louis was surrounded with a system of cultural satellites each of whom was supreme in his own field. The foundation of the Academy of Language and Literature in 1635, the Royal Academy of Painting and Sculpture in 1648, and the others which followed later, made it possible for Boileau to dominate the field of letters, Lebrun that of the visual arts, and Lully the art of music. Absolutism in this sense meant standardization, since no artist could receive a commission or even employment except through official channels. Louis, however, was quite aware of what he was doing, and in an address to the Academy he once remarked: "Gentlemen, I entrust to you the most precious thing on earth, my fame." Knowing this, he defended his writers and artists, supported them generously, and above all exercised that most noble attribute any patron can possess—good taste.

The outward and visible sign of this absolutism was to be seen in the dramatization of the personal and social life of this *roi du soleil*, or Sun King. The adoption of the sun as his symbol was natural enough, and such motives as the sunburst were widely used in the decor of his palaces. As patron of the arts Louis could identify himself freely with Apollo, the sun god, who was also the Olympian protector of the muses. In the morning, when it was time for the Sun King to rise and shine, the *lever du roi* was as dazzling in its way as a second sunrise. This special dawn was accompanied by a cloud of attendants who flocked into the royal bedchamber precisely at 8 A. M. in order to hand the king the various parts of his royal apparel. A similarly colorful ceremony accompanied the *coucher du roi*, when the Sun King in a golden glow of candlelight finally set at 10 P. M. Louis' life was one continuous pageant in which each hour had its appropriate activity, costume, cast, and audience. Less frequent events, such as a christening, a wedding, or a coronation, all had their special ceremonies. Even the royal births called for an audience so as to assure the country of the legitimacy of any future sovereign. In our day of prosaic cabinet officers and drab parliamentary bodies, it is difficult to imagine the overwhelming effect of the formal pomp and circumstance surrounding an absolute monarch's court. If his peers and subjects beheld a sufficiently majestic spectacle or grandiose procession, a ruler apparently could get by with anything.

Throughout a reign of 72 years Louis XIV played the leading role in this incessant court drama with all the effortless technique and consummate self-discipline of an accomplished actor. His play was a success from the opening night, his press notices invariably extravagant, and the ambition of every aristocrat in the world was to get into the act if possible—or at the very least to receive a ticket to the performance. Such a great actor needed, of course, a great audience; and such a dramatic spectacle demanded an appropriate stage setting. The architects were therefore called upon to plan the endless series of communicating salons as impressive backdrops for the triumphal entries; the landscape designers to fashion the grand avenues for the open air processions; the painters to decorate the ceilings with pink clouds so that the monarch could descend the long flights of stairs as if from the sky; and the musicians to sound the ruffles and flourishes that accompanied the grand entrances. It was therefore no accident that the Louvre and Versailles Palaces resembled vast theaters, that the paintings and tapestries of Lebrun seemed like curtains and backdrops, that Bernini's, Puget's and Coysevox' sculptural adornments took on the aspect of stage props, that the most important literary expression should be the tragedies of Racine and the comedies of Molière, and that the characteristic musical forms should be Lully's court ballets and operas.

ARCHITECTURE

In 1665 at the insistence of his minister Colbert, Louis XIV requested the pope to permit his principal architect Lorenzo Bernini to come to Paris to supervise the rebuilding of the Louvre Palace. When he arrived on French soil, Bernini was received with all the honor due him as the ranking artist of his day. The design he made for the Louvre was radical in many ways. It would have necessitated the replacement of the existing parts of the building by a grandiose Baroque city palace of the Italian type, and it completely neglected to take certain particular qualities of French life into account. His plan got as far as the laying of the cornerstone. Then after a round of festivities he returned to Rome; his plan was scrapped; and a French architect, Claude Perrault, was appointed to finish the job. This little episode in cultural history marked the weakening of Italian artistic

Fig. 13:2. Perrault. *Louvre*, East Front. 600′ long. 1667–1674. Paris (Courtesy French Government Tourist Office)

influence in France, and it further indicated that Louis XIV had certain plans of his own.

Perrault's façade (Fig. 13:2) incorporated some parts of Bernini's project, such as the flat roof concealed behind a Palladian balustrade, and the long straight front with the wings extending laterally instead of projecting forward to enclose a court in the traditional French manner. Perrault's own contributions can be seen in the solid ground floor, which is relieved only by the seriated windows. This story functions as a platform for the support of the classically proportioned Corinthian colonnade, with its rhythmic row of paired columns marching majestically across the broad expanse of the façade. Their projection in depth as well as that of the ends and center parts allows for the rich play of light and shadow that was so much a part of the Baroque ideal. The frieze of garlands adds a florid touch, while the central pediment as well as the classical orders of the columns and pilasters act as a restraining influence. Both combine harmoniously with the other details to complete this highly successful design.

Even before Bernini came to Paris and long before the Louvre was completed, Louis XIV had conceived the idea of a royal residence outside Paris where he could get away from the restrictions of the city, take nature into partnership, and design a new way of life. Colbert, who felt that a king's place was in his capital, advised against it, and Louis allowed the Louvre to be completed as a concession to Paris, while his real capital was destined to be Versailles (Fig. 13:3). This project was sufficiently breath-taking in scope and awe-inspiring enough to serve as a symbol of the su-premacy of the young absolute monarch as he asserted his power over rival nations, the landed aristocracy of his own country, the parliament, the provincial governments, the town councils, and the middle-class merchants. Away from Paris there would be a minimum of distraction and a maximum of concentration on his own person. In a wooded site almost half the size of Paris, which belonged entirely to the crown, everything could be planned from the beginning, an entirely new way of life could be organized, and nothing need be left to chance.

In a schematic arrangement laid out with mathematical accuracy, the grand axis of Versailles actually runs from the Louvre in Paris along the Champs Elysées 12 miles to the southwest where it enters the palace grounds (Fig. 13:3, lower left). On either side of the avenue are the bar-racks, coach houses, stables, kennels, and the orangery. The latter building caused an ambassador from a foreign country to remark that Louis XIV must indeed be the most magnificent of beings since he had a palace for his orange trees more beautiful than the residences of many kings. The axis sweeps on through the middle of the parade grounds to the palace buildings where the attention is drawn by a progressive narrowing process toward the marble court of honor (Fig. 13:5), above which on the exact axial center is the heart of the plan, the state bedroom of Louis XIV (Fig. 13:6). On the garden side the axis continues onward via a broad avenue to the mile-long grand canal (Fig. 13:3, upper part), thence it sweeps onward to the horizon where it trails off into infinity. The whole grand design is so logical, so symmetrical, that it becomes a study in absolute space composition and makes Versailles an all-embracing universal structure which encompasses a vast segment of external as well as internal space. No one building or any part of it is a law unto itself, and together they are inconceivable outside their natural environment. The gardens, parks, avenues, and radiating pathways are just as much an integral part of the whole as the halls, salons, and communicating corridors of the palace itself.

As the king's power expanded, the palace grew like a living organism capable of adapting itself to changing conditions. With the victories over Spain and Franche-Compté, the palace sprouted new wings as if to sym-bolize the triumph. For well over a quarter of a century the place hummed with the activities of architects, sculptors, painters, decorators, wood-carvers, masons, and carpenters. Altogether it has been estimated that more than 30,000 men, including practically all the trained artists and craftsmen in the country, were employed at one time or another in the various build-

Fig. 13:3. Mansart. *Versailles Palace*, Air View. Palace 1935' wide (Courtesy French Government Tourist Office)

Fig. 13:4 (above). Mansart. *Versailles Palace*, Garden Façade, Detail (Courtesy French Government Tourist Office). Fig. 13:5 (below). Levau. *Marble Court at Versailles during a Performance of Lully's Opera "Alceste."* Engraving by LePautre. 1674. Metropolitan Museum, New York

Mansart. Versailles Palace.
Fig. 13:6 (above). *Louis XIV's State Bedchamber.*

Fig. 13:7 (*right*). *State Bedchamber of the Queen.* (Courtesy French Government Tourist Office)

ing activities. Finally in 1683 the palace was proclaimed Louis' official residence, and all the ministries of France were eventually installed in the new wing that was designed for them. Versailles thus became a royal residence housing the king and his family, the court with all its attendant social activities, and the administrative center of the French government. The roofed area of the palace covered 17 acres and housed a population of around 10,000 people, including the royal family, the lords and ladies of the court, the priests and clergy, and the military guard of honor, plus the armies of servants, gardeners, and grooms.

Jules Hardouin Mansart was the architect of the two wings that extended the main building to a width of over a quarter of a mile. His design is noteworthy for the horizontal accent attained by the uniform level of the roof line, broken only by that of the chapel, which was added in the early 18th century. The simplicity and elegance of these long straight lines, in contrast to the irregular profile of a medieval building, proclaims a new feeling for space. From every room vistas of the garden are a part of the interior design and tell of a new awareness of nature. A detail of the garden façade (Fig. 13:4) reveals how freely Mansart treated the classical orders, and how the levels become increasingly ornate from the podiumlike base below to the attic and balustrade with the silhouetted statuary above. As a whole the building is a commanding example of Baroque exuberance tempered by Palladian restraint.

Some of the interior rooms have been preserved or restored in the style of Louis XIV. All the heavy ornateness of the period can be seen in Louis' state bedroom (Fig. 13:6). Above the bed is a gilded stucco relief depicting France between two figures representing Fame. Elsewhere tapestries, paintings, carved wood, and mirrors cover every available inch of space. On the mantlepiece is a marble bust of the Duchess of Bourgogne by Coysevox. Since comfort was considered a purely private matter, it seems to have been given hardly a thought. In one of the rooms of the queen's apartments (Fig. 13:7), the Baroque interior style is again seen in the heavily decorated ceiling, with its painted murals, caryatids perched on the fanciful scroll frames; the large Gobelin tapestries on the walls; and the furnishings of carved wood, bronze, polychrome marble, and rich fabrics.

The grandest room of the palace, however, was the famous Hall of Mirrors stretching across the main axis of the building and looking out toward the spacious gardens. Designed by Mansart and decorated by Lebrun, it was the scene of the most important state ceremonies and a kind of apotheosis of the absolute monarchy. Corinthian pilasters of green marble support the ornate vault that is covered with paintings by Lebrun and inscriptions by Boileau and Racine—all to the greater glorification of the Sun King. The room was originally decorated sumptuously with brocaded damask curtains, chairs of enameled silver, orange trees reposing in silver urns, mirrors framed with chased copper, and chandeliers of crystal and gold. Clear geometrical divisions prevented the elaborate details from getting out of hand yet allowed full scope for the general magnificent effect of the composition.

The gardens, which were laid out by André Le Nôtre, are not just a frame for the buildings but are incorporated into the whole spatial design. Their formality and high degree of geometrical organization symbolized the dominance of man over nature, but with the idea of embracing it rather than keeping it at arm's length. The square pools across the garden side, so liberally populated with goldfish and swans, reflected the contours of the building like an external echo of the mirrored halls within. The statues of river gods and nymphs, which are found at the angles, were executed from sketches by Lebrun and personify the rivers and streams of France. The gardens and park form a logical system of terraces, broad avenues, and pathways radiating outward from clearings. They are liberally embellished by fountains, pools, canals, pavilions, and grottos, all of which are richly decorated with statuary. More than 1200 fountains were installed by skilled engineers of waterworks, and with their jets spouting water into the air in many different patterns, they were marvels of their craft. Each had its name, and each was adorned with an appropriate sculptural group.

The great fetes which took place at Versailles served the purpose of distracting the unemployed nobility and compensating them for the loss of their power. Since royal favors were obtainable only at court and since the entertainment there was on such a lavish scale, the proud nobles were inevitably drawn into Louis' orbit, thus relinquishing their local privileges in exchange for an opportunity to participate in the festivities. This shift of the aristocrats from their country castles to the ultraurbane surroundings of Versailles sometimes necessitated a hasty and hectic education in the social graces for many of the courtiers. Lessons in courtly deportment, dancing, and the elegant use of language were obligatory in a place where one of the worst disasters that could befall a man was to make a *faux pas*, literally a false step, in the minuet. It might even necessitate his withdrawal from courtly life for an indefinite period. The gardens, parks, and canals provided endless opportunities for strolling, picnicking, love-making, hunting, fireworks displays, boating, and water pageants. The various salons in the palace provided the setting for card games, gambling, masquerade balls, theatrical entertainments, concerts, ballets, and opera performances.

The Versailles Palace, therefore, was not so much a monument to the vanity of Louis XIV as it was a symbol of the absolute monarchy and the outstanding example of aristocratic Baroque architecture. It represented a movement away from a feudal decentralized government toward a modern centralized state. As a vast advertising project it was a highly influential factor in the international diplomacy of the time. By urbanizing the country aristocracy and promoting court activities, a larger and more discriminating audience was built up for the arts. It assured the shift of the artistic center of gravity from Italy to France. The court also functioned as a center of style and dress; and, as a school for the training of skilled craftsmen, it virtually assured the status of France as a continuous center of elegant workmanship and fashion to this day. By combining all the activities of a court in a single structure, Versailles pointed the way toward the concept of architecture as a means of creating a new pattern of life. At Versailles a large housing development the size of a town was constructed so as to encompass rather than escape from nature. Details of Le Nôtre's garden plan, such as the radiating pathways, were the acknowledged basis for the laying out of new sections of Paris; and the city plan of Washington, D. C., for instance, was a direct descendant of the parks of Versailles. Modern city planners and housing developers have hailed Versailles as the prototype of the contemporary ideal of placing large residential units in close contact with nature. Finally, by starting with a grand design, Versailles pointed the way to the planning of whole cities from the start without having to go through all the usual vicissitudes of haphazard growth and change. In this light Versailles is seen as one of the earliest examples of modern urbanism and city planning on a large scale.

SCULPTURE

While Lorenzo Bernini was working on the Louvre, he was besieged by requests from would-be patrons to design everything from fountains for their gardens to tombs for their ancestors. The king as usual came first in such matters, and Bernini received a commission from Louis XIV for a portrait bust (Fig. 13:8). This minor by-product of the artist's Paris sojourn ultimately turned out to be far more successful than his major mission. The recorded conversations of the artist and the accounts of his contemporaries make this portrait one of the most amply documented works in art history.[1]

Fig. 13:8. Bernini. *Bust of Louis XIV*. Marble. 33⅛″ high. 1665 (Alinari)

Fig. 13:9. Bernini. *Apollo and Daphne*. Marble. Life size. 1622–1625. Borghese Gallery, Rome (Alinari)

Dispensing with the usual formal sittings, Bernini made rapid pencil sketches while the king was playing tennis and presiding at cabinet meetings, so that he could observe his subject in action. He was convinced that movement was the medium that best defined the personality and brought out the unique characteristics of his subjects. The informal sketches were made, as he said, "to steep myself in, and imbue myself with, the king's features." After he had captured the individuality he was to portray, the next step was to decide on the general ideas—nobility, majesty, and the optimistic pride of youth. Here all the accessories, such as the costume, drapery, position of the head, and so on, would play their part. After the preliminaries were over, and the particular as well as the general aspects were settled, the king sat 13 times, while Bernini, working directly on the marble now, put on the finishing touches.

Bernini's expressed intention was to paint in marble, but the problem was always that of transferring the impression of color to the white material. He said that if a man's hair and face were completely whitened, "even those who see him daily would have difficulty in recognizing him." His solution was in the use of shadow for the features, even if it meant altering them somewhat, and elsewhere making strong contrasts in the textures, such as those of the soft hair, starched lace collar, metallic armor, and silken drapery. To liven the static medium, Bernini's thought was that "the best moment to choose is when the model is about to speak, and I have tried to catch that moment." It will be seen that the lips are slightly parted as if about to give a command. The eyes were of great importance to Bernini, who at the sittings marked in the irises with black chalk. Only after many changes was he ready to use the chisel, and the proper look of determination was thus achieved. The complex folds of the deep-cut drapery were done with great care so that they would appear as if blown by the wind and so bring a spontaneous moment into the otherwise static form.

Like all the works of the period, the bust had its allegorical allusions. Bernini noted in his conversations the resemblance of the king to Alexander the Great, whose countenance was familiar to him from ancient coins. Courtly flattery was partially responsible, of course; but according to the conventions of the time, if the king were to appear as a military hero, it would be as a Roman emperor on horseback; or, if he were to be the *roi soleil*, it would be in the guise of Apollo. Since Bernini's intention here was to convey grandeur and majesty, Alexander, as the personification of kingly character, was the logical choice.

After his return to Rome, Bernini did one more sculptural work for

Versailles—this time an equestrian statue of Louis XIV in marble. It was so fiery and turbulent and met with so much disfavor that the king ordered its removal to a remote part of the garden where the features were altered, and it was renamed for the ancient Roman hero Martius Curtius.

In addition to such portraits, Bernini's fame as a sculptor rested more broadly on religious statues, such as his *St. Theresa in Ecstasy* (Fig. 12:12), on the many fountains he designed for Rome, and on mythological groups to embellish aristocratic residences, such as his *Apollo and Daphne* (Fig. 13:9). This youthful work of the artist is full of breathless motion and tense excitement. According to the myth, Apollo as the patron of the muses, was eternally in pursuit of ideal beauty, symbolized here by the nymph Daphne. The sculptor chose to make permanent the pregnant moment from which the previous and forthcoming action may be inferred. As Daphne flees from Apollo's ardent embrace, she cries aloud to the gods who hear her plea and change her into a laurel tree. Though she is root-bound and the bark is already enclosing her limbs, she still seems to be in quivering motion. The diagonal line from Apollo's hand to Daphne's leafy fingers leads the eye upward and outward. The complex surfaces are handled so as to give maximum play to light and shadow. The sculptor has carefully delineated the various textures, such as the smooth flesh, flowing drapery, floating hair, and the leaves and branches, in keeping with his objective of painting in marble. But above all Bernini has realized his express intention, which was to achieve emotion and movement at all costs and to make marble seem to float in space.

The Versailles gardens provided French sculptors with an inexhaustible outlet for their wares. Many went to Italy to copy such admired antiques as the *Laocoön* (Fig. 2:15), the *Farnese Hercules*, and the *Slave Sharpening Knife* (Fig. 2:13). These replicas were then sent back and placed on pedestals along the various walks at Versailles. Others like Giraudon made variants of Bernini's fountains and incorporated the movement of the water into their designs as he had done. Most of the statuary at Versailles, how-ever, is effective mainly as part of the general setting, and only in a few instances have the works survived the test of time and emerged as individual masterpieces. Puget's *Perseus Delivering Andromeda* and his well-known *Milo of Crotona* originally stood along the Royal Walk but are now to be found in the Louvre. Coysevox, who lived and worked at Versailles, likewise was influenced by Bernini. Such examples as his oval relief in the Hall of War and his numerous portrait busts were instrumental in establishing the tradition of French academic sculpture.

Fig. 13:10. Rubens. *Self-portrait.* 43⅛″ x 33½″. *c.*1638–1640. Kunsthistorisches Museum, Vienna

PAINTING

Peter Paul Rubens (Fig. 13:10), as the ranking painter of his day, had been summoned to Paris by Louis XIII a generation earlier in a way closely paralleling Bernini's later visit to the court of his son. At that time the Luxembourg Palace was being completed as the residence of the Queen Mother Maria de' Medici, and her expressed desire was for a painter who could decorate the ceiling of its Festival Gallery in a manner matching the Italian Baroque style of its architecture. Maria's career as Henry IV's queen and as Louis XIII's regent was as lacking in luster as her own mediocre endowments could possibly have made it. Nevertheless, as the direct descendant of Lorenzo the Magnificent, she well knew that the posthumous reputations of princes often depended more on their choice of poets and painters than on their skill in statecraft. The famous Flemish artist was brought to her attention by her sister, the Duchess of Mantua, at whose court Rubens had spent eight of his youthful years. Since then he had achieved a formidable reputation for his accomplishments as a courtier and diplomat as well as for his pictures, which were eagerly sought after by popes, kings, and cardinals.

Rubens' cycle of 21 murals gave the needed imaginary apotheosis to Maria's highly unimaginative life, and the triumph belonged more truly to the man who painted it than to the lady who lived it. The remarkable thing was how Rubens could exercise so much individual freedom within the confines of courtly officialdom and succeed so well in pleasing both himself and his royal mistress. In his grandiose conception, the ancient gods had deserted the rarified regions of Mount Olympus and taken up their abode in the vastly more exhilarating atmosphere of Paris. Even before Maria's birth, Juno and Jupiter had cajoled the three Fates into spinning a brilliant web of destiny for her. The governess who taught her to read was none other than Minerva, while her music teacher was Apollo himself. Her mythical eloquence came from the lips of Mercury, and every possible feminine fascination was imparted to her by the three Graces. When this paragon of brilliance and virtue reached the apex of her grace and beauty, the Capitoline Triad themselves presided over the scene where *Henry IV Receives the Portrait of Maria de' Medici* (Fig. 13:11). Minerva, as goddess of Peace and War, whispers words of wisdom into the king's ear, while a whimsical touch is provided by the cupids who playfully try to lift the heavy helmet and shield of the king's armor. The celestial scene above assures everyone concerned that marriages are indeed made in heaven, where Jupiter with his eagle and Juno with her peacocks are seen bestowing their Olympian blessing.

When the royal marriage was solemnized in Florence, the accompanying festivities included the performance of Peri's *Eurydice*, the earliest extant opera. This great event, however, was much too incidental for inclusion in such a cosmic conception, and the observer is next privileged to witness the *Disembarkation of Maria de' Medici at Marseilles* (Fig. 13:12). As she steps ashore, a personification of France falls on her knees to welcome her, while figures representing Fame sound the triumphal trumpets to announce the arrival. The denizens of the sea are overjoyed at the safe conclusion of

Fig. 13:11. Rubens. *Henry IV Receiving the Portrait of Maria de' Medici.* 13′ × 9′8″. 1622–1625. Louvre, Paris (Alinari)

Fig. 13:12. Rubens. *Disembarkation of Maria de' Medici at Marseilles.* 13′ × 9′8″. 1622–1625. Louvre, Paris (Alinari)

Fig. 13:13. Rubens. *Garden of Love.* 6' 5⅞" x 9' 3⅜". 1632–1634. Prado, Madrid (Anderson)

the voyage, and Neptune himself issues the commands to moor the galley, while Tritons and sea nymphs disport themselves in the rippling rhythms of the water and playfully tug at the ropes. From the accentuated lighting and undulating movement, it is obvious that the painter was most concerned with this part of his picture. Authorities have also established that the voluptuous water nymphs were done by Rubens' own hand. All his love of the robust female form is present in these opulent figures. He was painting large surfaces, in this instance the picture is 13 by almost 10 feet, and his concept of space demanded feminine forms capable of filling both the canvas and the eye.

The demand for Rubens' work was such that he employed about 200 apprentices and assistants. This series was executed in his studio in Antwerp beginning in 1622. As was his custom in such a project, Rubens sketched out the composition of each picture, then delegated the preparatory work to one assistant, an architectural background to another, landscape and animal figures to specialists in those departments, and for himself reserved certain choice parts. When the pictures were installed at the Luxembourg Palace in 1625, Rubens was on hand to put the finishing touches on them, while Queen Maria watched him at work and from reports took pleasure in his conversation.

The free Baroque ideal of richness and lavishness is seen once again in a picture from Rubens' later years, the *Garden of Love* (Fig. 13:13). The setting for this allegory was the garden of his palatial home at Antwerp, and the ornate doorway in the background still exists. The bacchanalian theme unfolds in a diagonal line beginning with the chubby cherub in the lower left. Rubens himself is seen urging his second wife Helena Fourment, who appeared in so many of his later pictures, to join the others in the garden of love. The rest of the picture unfolds in a series of spirals mounting upward toward the figure of Venus who presides over the festivities as a part of the fountain. The use of large areas of strong primary colors—reds, blues, yellows—enlivens the scene and enhances the pictorial structure.

Rubens succeeded in combining the rich color of Titian and the dramatic tension of Tintoretto with an unbounded energy and physical exuberance of his own. His conceptions have something of the heroic sweep of Michelangelo, though they lack the latter's introspection and restraint. His complex organization of space and freedom of movement recall El Greco, but his figures are as broad and robust as the latter's were long and emaciated. His success in religious pictures, hunting scenes, and landscapes, as well as the mythological paintings that suited his temperament so well, shows the enormous sweep of his pictorial powers. For sheer imaginative invention and bravura with a brush he has rarely been equalled.

An obscure French painter named Nicolas Poussin was working on some minor decorations for the Luxembourg Palace at the same time that Rubens was executing his murals for the Festival Hall. Finding the official atmosphere too confining, he went to Rome where he could paint with greater independence. The solid reputation he built there soon came to the attention of Cardinal Richelieu, who bought many of his pictures and was determined to bring him back to Paris. In 1640 Poussin returned to decorate the grand gallery of the Louvre, and Louis XIII showered him with favors and gave him the coveted title of First Painter to the King. The inevitable courtly intrigues that followed such marked attention made Poussin so miserable that after two years he returned to Rome where he spent the rest of his life. There he acted as the artistic ambassador of France and supervised the French painters who were sent to Rome under government subsidies to study and copy Italian masterpieces for the decoration of the Louvre. There, too, Poussin had the freedom to pursue his classical studies, the independence to work out his own principles and ideals, and the time to paint a series of pictures ranging from mythological and religious subjects to historical canvases and architectural landscapes.

The *Rape of the Sabine Women* (Fig. 13:14) shows how Poussin, in his effort to recreate the classical past, turned to the Roman historians Livy and Plutarch for his subject, to the Roman museums for the models of many of his figures, and to Vitruvius for his architectural setting. In the incident he depicts, Romulus, the legendary founder of Rome, has been unsuccessful in negotiating marriages for his warriors. A religious celebration with games and festivities has therefore been arranged as a stratagem to attract the people from the neighboring towns including Sabina to the Roman Forum. From his position of prominence on the portico of the temple at the left, Romulus gives the signal by unfolding his mantle, whereupon, as previously arranged, every Roman seizes a Sabine girl and makes off with her. Though his subject is one of passion and violence, Poussin manages to temper his picture by a judicious juxtaposition of opposites. The anger of the outraged victims contrasts with the impassive calm of Romulus and his attendants. As a ruler, he knows that the future of his city rests on the foundation of families, and that in this case the end justifies the means. The turbulent human action is counterbalanced also by the ordered repose of the architectural and landscape background. The contours of the figures are as clearly defined as if they had been chiseled out of stone. The smooth marblelike flesh of the women contrasts with the bulging musculature beneath the bronzed skins of the Romans. A comparison of the group in the right foreground with the Hellenistic group of the *Gaul and his Wife* (Fig. 2:4) will quickly reveal the source of Poussin's inspiration. While such

Fig. 13:14 (above). Poussin. *Rape of the Sabine Women.* $60\frac{1}{8}''$ x $81\frac{1}{8}''$. *c.*1635. Metropolitan Museum, New York. Fig. 13:15 (below). Poussin. *Et in Arcadia Ego* (*Shepherds in Arcadia*). 33" x 47". 1638–1639. Louvre, Paris (Alinari)

direct derivations are comparatively rare, it is indicative of the close study
the artist made of the antique statuary in the Roman museums. The building at the right, a reconstruction Poussin made from a description of a
Roman basilica by Vitruvius, is still another instance of Poussin's desire for
accuracy of detail.

Et in Arcadia Ego (Fig. 13:15) shows Poussin in a quieter and more lyrical
mood. The rustic figures of the shepherds might well have stepped out of
one of Vergil's pastoral poems, while that of the shepherdess could be the
tragic muse in one of Corneille's dramas. As they trace out the letters of
the Latin inscription on the sarcophagus, "I Too Once Dwelled in Arcadia," their mood becomes pensive. The thought that the shepherd in the
tomb once lived and loved as they, casts a spell of gentle melancholy over
the group. In this meditative study in spatial composition, the feminine
figure parallels the trunk of the tree to define the vertical axis, while the
arm of the shepherd on the left rests on the sarcophagus to supply the
horizontal balance. Each gesture, each line, follows inevitably from this
initial premise with all the cool logic of a geometrical theorem. The subject
is obviously a sympathetic one to Poussin, as he had found his own Arcadia
in Italy and took a lifelong delight in the monuments of antiquity and the
voices from the past that spoke through just such inscriptions. Like the
ancients he tried to conduct his own search for truth and beauty in a
dignified tempo and with a graceful gesture. Like them, too, he sought for
the permanent in the transient, the type in the individual, the universal in
the particular, and the one in the many.

Claude Lorrain, like his countryman Poussin, also preferred life in Italy
to that in his native country. His lifelong interest was landscape, but the
convention of the time demanded human beings as well as titles with pictures. He solved the problem by painting his landscapes, letting his assistants put in a few incidental figures, and giving the pictures obscure names,
such as *Embarkation of the Queen of Sheba*, *Landing of Cleopatra*, *Expulsion of
Hagar*, or *David at the Cave of Adullam*. With tongue in cheek, he once remarked that he sold his figures and gave away his landscapes. Scenes like
the *Harbor at Sunset* (Fig. 13:16) were his special delight. In them he could
concentrate on limitless space and the soft atmospheric effect of sunlight on misty air. His usual procedure was to balance his compositions
on either side of the foreground with buildings or trees, which are treated
in considerable detail. Then the eye is drawn deeper into the intervening
space with long vistas over land or sea toward the indefinite horizon. Formal values dominate and nothing arbitrary or accidental intrudes to mar
their stately quality.

Fig. 13:16. Claude Lorrain. *Harbor at Sunset*. 45″ x 41″. Courtesy of Frick Art Reference Library

Charles Lebrun was one of the painters who came under Poussin's influence when he was in Rome. Though a friend and ardent admirer of Poussin, he preferred the fuss and feathers of life at Versailles to the more tranquil tempo of Italy. An opportunist of the first magnitude, he ingratiated himself there by designing the costumes for Louis XIV's pageants, fountains for the parks, and tapestries for the salons. His facile painting technique and his talent for courtly flattery aided him in his rapid rise to the position of leader of the Academy, first painter to the king, head of the royal tapestry and furniture studios, and artistic arbiter of the reign. His *Alexander the Great Entering Babylon* (Fig. 13:17), like most of his other pictures, was one of a series of huge canvases designed for the pompous interiors of the Versailles Palace. Since Louis XIV spent much of his time and energy cultivating the art of Mars, and since his courtiers invariably hailed the returning victor as a second Alexander, the significance of the central figure was not likely to be overlooked by anyone. Lebrun left the victorious army discreetly outside his picture, so that Alexander could dominate the scene in lonely triumph from his elephant-drawn chariot. While he thought he was carrying out Poussin's theories, Lebrun's pictures illustrate what happens to an artist when he allows the letter to crowd out the spirit. In all fairness, however, it must be said that Lebrun was a better decorator than he was a painter; and, as a consequence, his pictures usually make better sense in the context of their original surroundings than as separate entities.

The acquisition of paintings by the crown was begun under Colbert on a massive scale. The purchases reveal the gradual veering away from an international toward a national viewpoint. Rubens and the Italian artists were liberally represented, but, on Lebrun's advice, the systematic buying of Poussin's pictures and those by French artists exhibiting in the annual salons was begun. By 1709 the collection of Louis XIV numbered over 2400 pictures including 29 Poussins. While their primary purpose was to decorate the royal galleries, they were available for study to French painters

Fig. 13:17. Lebrun. *Alexander the Great Entering Babylon.* 14' 9" x 23'. *c.*1666. Louvre, Paris (Alinari)

and were the subjects of discussion at sessions of the Academy. The polarity of styles in the Rubens and Poussin pictures became the basis for heated arguments. Both painters were well versed in the classics, both reflected the spirit of the Counter-Reformation, and both in their way represented the aristocratic tradition. While Rubens' impetuosity knew no bounds, Poussin remained aloof and reserved; while Rubens cast restraint to the winds and filled his pictures with violent movement, Poussin was austerely pursuing his formal values; while Rubens' figures are soft and fleshy, Poussin's are hard and statuesque; while Rubens sweeps up his spectators in the tidal wave of his volcanic energy, Poussin's pictures are more conducive to quiet meditation. It is little wonder that the Academy's championship of Poussin divided the painters of the latter half of the 17th century into two opposing camps who called themselves Rubenists and Poussinists.

MUSIC

The musical and dramatic productions at the court of Louis XIV were maintained on as lavish a scale as the other arts. The musicians were organized into three branches. First came the *chambre* group, which included the famous *Vingt-quatre Violons*, or Twenty-four Viols, the first permanent orchestra in Europe. This was the string ensemble that played for balls, dinners, concerts, and the opera. Lutenists and clavecinists were also found in this category. Next came the *chapelle*, the chorus that sang for religious services, and the organists. The *Grand Écurie* formed the third group, which consisted mainly of the wind ensemble that was available for military processions, outdoor fetes, and hunting parties.

The favored form of entertainment during the early years of Louis XIV's reign was the *ballet de cour*, an elaborate form of the ballet that began with an instrumental overture and included a sequence of sung recitatives, choruses, and songs as well as instrumental interludes in addition to the dancing. Louis XIV himself, who was an excellent dancer, took an active interest in these court ballets and frequently appeared at the climactic moment in the role of Apollo, the sun god. He was serious enough about his acting to rehearse diligently under the supervision of Lully and Molière.

The popularity of the court ballet had been challenged during the years of Louis' minority by the attempts of Cardinal Mazarin to replace it by the "spectacle of princes," Italian opera. Cavalli, who had brought the Venetian lyric drama to the high point of its development, was invited to Paris to write and produce an opera in 1660. It met with a mixed reception, but two years later Cavalli was again on hand to write still another, this time for Louis XIV's wedding celebration. Another challenge to the court ballet came from Molière, who united the elements of comedy, music, and the dance into a form he called the *comédie-ballet*. The best known of these is the perennially popular *Le Bourgeois Gentilhomme—The Burgher as Gentleman* —which was first performed at the court in 1670. A full decade of these brilliant performances was brought to a close by the death of the great dramatist.

The ever-resourceful Jean Baptiste Lully, however, was biding his time on the sidelines until he could spring some surprises of his own. A Florentine by birth and French by education, he was fiddling away at the early age of 17 as a violinist in the Vingt-quatre Violons. When Cavalli produced his two operas, it was Lully who wrote the ballet sequences that, incidentally, proved more popular than the operas themselves. It was Lully again who collaborated with Molière by supplying the musical portions of the *comédie-ballets*. And when the propitious moment arrived, it was Lully who came up with a French form of the opera which he called *tragédie lyrique*, or lyrical tragedy. One of the earliest of these was the performance of *Alceste* in the Marble Court at Versailles July 4, 1674 (Fig. 13:5). With a genius for organization, Lully used the Vingt-quatre Violons as the nucleus of his orchestra, supplementing them with wind instruments from the Grand Écurie for fanfares as well as for the hunting, battle, and climactic transformation scenes. The chapel choir was also drafted into the operatic service, and the generous dance sequences he included assured the ballet group plenty of activity. Lully could have had the collaboration of the great dramatist Racine for the texts; but he deliberately chose Quinault, a poet of some distinction, who would be more pliable to his demands and who could be counted upon not to claim too much of the credit.

The form of these lyrical tragedies crystallized early and changed relatively little in the following years. They began with an instrumental overture of a type that still bears Lully's name, though he did not invent it. The first part is a ponderous dignified march with dotted notes, massive sonorities, and chains of resolving dissonances as in the Ritornello, page 516. The second half is livelier in tempo and more contrapuntal in texture. Next came the prologue, and that of *Alceste* is quite typical. The setting is in the garden of the Tuileries, still the official royal residence at this time, where the Nymph of the Seine is discovered. Declaiming her lines in recitative style, she makes some topical allusions to the current war, couched, of course, in flowery mythological terms. Glory now enters to the tune of a triumphal march, and a duet and solo air ensue. The two are joined eventually by a chorus of naiads and pastoral divinities, whose songs and dances give assurance that France will be ever-victorious under the leadership of a great hero, whose identity is never for a moment in doubt. After this the overture was repeated, and the five acts of a classical tragedy followed with much the same formal pattern as that of the prologue.

Two excerpts from Act III, Scene V of *Alceste* will serve to illustrate Lully's style. After the death of Alceste, a long instrumental ritornello provides the pompous elegiac strains for the entrance of the mourning chorus. One of the grief-stricken women comes forward, indicating her sorrow by her gestures and facial expressions.

Air from *Alceste*, Act III, Scene 5   Lully

Her Air (above) is in the recitative style which J. J. Rousseau considered Lully's chief "title to glory." The composer always insisted that the music as well as the other elements of the opera were the servants of drama and poetry, and he always counseled his singers to emulate the noble and expansive intonations of the actors trained by Racine. A Lully air consequently is never so set as an Italian aria, but follows instead the elastic speech rhythms and the natural declamation of French Baroque poetry and prose. The mourning chorus takes up where the Air leaves off with a variant of the opening ritornello, and the scene closes with a long cadential passage alternately for orchestra and chorus based on a continuation of the ritornello.

Ritornello from *Alceste*, Act III, Scene 5   Lully

Since the hero was so closely identified with the monarch, a tragic ending was quite impossible. A *deus ex machina*, therefore, invariably appeared in the fourth act, just when all seemed darkest, and the fifth act always brought the lyrical tragedy to a triumphant and glorious conclusion.

By exploiting the success of his operas and through clever diplomatic strategy, Lully became by royal warrant the founder and head of the *Academie Royale de Musique*. With the substitution of the word *Nationale* for *Royale*, this is still the official title of the Paris grand opera company. With incredible energy, this musical monopolist of the regime produced an opera every year; and in addition to writing the score, he conducted the orchestra, trained the choir, coached the singers and dancers in their parts, and directed the staging. He ruled his musical and dramatic forces with the iron hand of an absolutist, allowing nothing arbitrary or capricious to creep in anywhere. As a consequence he developed the best-disciplined group of singers, dancers, and instrumentalists in Europe. Their fame spread far and wide, and from contemporary accounts, his orchestra was especially noted for the purity of its intonation, and uniform bowing of the strings, the accuracy of tempo and measure, and the elegance of its trills and melodic ornaments that were compared to the "sparkling of precious stones."

Practically singlehanded, Lully unified the ballet and founded French opera. His standardization of the sequence of dances became known as the French suite; his form of the overture, the French overture; and his organization of the opera became standard practice for almost two centuries. Even though Quinault wrote the texts, Lully's operas may be considered the musical reflection of Racine's tragedies. In them is found the same almost slavish observance of classical proprieties, the same dignified declamation, the same polished correctness. Their limitations were the inevitable outgrowth of the circumstances of their creation. By being addressed so exclusively to a single social group, they neglected to provide the more resonant human sounding board needed for survival in the repertory. Like Poussin they remained aloof, restrained, and aristocratic. Opera, however, by its combination of grandiloquent language, emotional appeal, sonorous splendor, majestic movement, and visual elegance emerges as one of the most magnificent creations of the Baroque era.

IDEAS

The many manifestations of the aristocratic Baroque style crystallize mainly around two distinct but interrelated ideas—absolutism and academicism.

Absolutism

The concept of the modern unified state, which first emerged in the Spain of Philip II, was adapted to French political purposes by Cardinal Richelieu and ultimately reached its triumphant consummation under Louis XIV. "It is the respect which absolute power demands, that none should question when a king commands," was the way Corneille stated the doctrine in 1637 in his heroic drama *The Cid*. As the principal exponent of monarchical absolutism and the centralized state, Louis XIV as the Sun King assumed the authority to replace natural and human disorderliness with a reasonable facsimile of cosmic law and order. All human and social activities came under his protectorship, and by taking the arts under his paternal wing, he saw that they served as useful adjuncts to the cult of majesty. Versailles thus became the symbol of his absolutism, the seat of the absolute monarchy, and the personal apotheosis of the king.

Just as political absolutism meant the unification of all social and governmental institutions under one head, its aesthetic counterpart implied the bringing together of all the separate arts into a single rational plan. While the period produced some buildings, statuary, paintings, literature, and music that command attention in their own right, they spoke out most impressively in their combined forms. It is impossible to think of Versailles except as a combination of all art forms woven together into a unified pattern and as a reflection of the life and institutions of the absolute monarchy. The parks, gardens, fountains, statuary, buildings, courtyards, halls, murals, tapestries, furnishings, and recreational activities are all united into a single coordinated design. As such Versailles accomplished the daring feat of unifying all visible space and all units of time into a spatio-temporal setting for the aristocratic way of life. Indoor and outdoor space are inseparable, even music and the theater went outdoors at Versailles. Sculpture was an embellishment of the landscape; painting became the handmaiden of interior design; comedy was allied with the ballet; and tragedy was absorbed into the opera. All the arts, in fact, were mirrored in the operatic form with its literary lyricism, orchestral rhetoric, dramatic declamation, instrumental interludes, statuesque dancing, architectural stage settings, mechanical marvels, and picturesque posturings. In Lully's hands it became a kind of microcosm of court life, an absolute art form in which all the separate parts existed in the closest possible relation to the whole. None was allowed to dominate, nothing was disproportionate. The spirit of absolutism was also directly revealed in the drama surrounding the life of the monarch. All the arts took the cue, became theatrical, and sought to surprise and astonish. The purely human element was buried under an avalanche of palatial scenery, pompous wigs, props, and protocol. Only in Molière's satires, La Fontaine's fables, and the secret memoirs of the period is it possible to catch glimpses of a more truthful version of the actualities behind the scenes of courtly life. Otherwise the architecture of Versailles, the statuary of Bernini and Coysevox, the triumphal murals of Lebrun, the tragedies of Racine, and the operas of Lully were all designed to promote the illusion that Louis XIV and his courtiers were beings of heroic stature, powerful will, and grandiose utterance.

Academicism

While the academic movement began formally with the foundation of the first French Academy during the reign of Louis XIII, it was not until later in the century that its implications were completely realized and its force fully mobilized. Both Louis XIV and his minister Colbert believed that art was much too important to be left exclusively in the hands of artists. The various academies, therefore, became branches of the government and the means by which the arts were drafted into the civil service. Boileau as the head of the Academy of Language and Literature, Lebrun of the Academy of Painting and Sculpture, Mansart of the Academy of Architecture, and Lully of the Academy of Music were subject directly to the king; and, in turn, they were absolute dictators in their respective fields. As such they were the principal advisers to the king and his ministers; and, in turn, they were responsible for carrying out the royal will. Complete control of patronage was centered in their hands; theirs was the final word in determining those who would receive commissions, appointments, titles, licenses, degrees, pensions, prizes, entrance to art schools, and the privilege of exhibiting in the annual salons.

The academies were thus the means of transmitting the absolute idea into the aesthetic sphere. Academicism invariably implied a patriarchal principle whereby regularly constituted arbiters of taste placed their stamp of approval on the products in the various art media. As such they were the interpreters of the official point of view that inevitably tended to become highly conservative. Aristocratic art was the superpersonal expression of a class whose code of behavior was based on etiquette, politeness, and good taste. All intimate personal feeling, capriciousness, and eccentricity had to yield to self-discipline, urbanity, correctness, and accepted standards of good form. The academies were therefore charged with the making of aesthetic definitions, artistic codes, and technical formulas valid for their respective fields. They functioned as a kind of board of directors who decided what was best for the stockholders. Their official status, moreover, gave them the power to enforce their principles, a system that at best could establish and maintain a high level of creative quality. Moving downward in varying degrees from standardization and uniformity, it could also degenerate into conventionalism and downright regimentation. What the artists stood to gain in official recognition, they were liable to lose in a corresponding degree of artistic freedom.

One of the policies of the Academy of Painting and Sculpture can be cited as an example of the way the system worked. Under Lebrun the restrained style of Poussin was favored over the passionate exuberance of Rubens. It thereby set up an academic subdivision of the Baroque style as opposed to a type of free Baroque expression. Many reasons for the choice can, of course, be advanced. Poussin's pictorialism, for instance, can more readily and demonstrably be reduced to a system of formal values based on geometrical principles, while Rubens' style was so personal, impetuous, voluptuous, and violently emotional that it always remained a bit beyond the grasp. Academicism in this case was trying to tame Baroque exuberance and reduce it to formulas and rules. Nothing eccentric, nothing unpredictable, was allowed to creep in and destroy the general impression of orderliness. The Academy always remained somewhat skeptical of emotion just as it was of color, since neither was subject to scientific laws. The pictorial standards of the Academy were therefore based on formal purity, demonstrable mathematical relationships, logical definition and rational analysis. These were the qualities that brought academic art the designation of classic, a term which was defined at the time as belonging to the highest class and hence approved as a model. Since similar standards were generally to be found in Roman antiquity, the two inevitably became associated with each other. The interpretation of such models in the 17th century, however, were quite in the spirit of the time, and hence must not be confused with the archeological exactitude that was set up as the standard of the late 18th century and the Napoleonic period.

French academicism was from the start an unqualified practical success. Under the system, the artistic hegemony of Europe passed from Italy to France where it has effectively remained up to the present time. The hundreds of skilled artists and artisans who were trained on the vast projects of Louis XIV became the teachers and founders of a tradition of high technical excellence. French painting alone, to use the most obvious example, has continued its unbroken supremacy from the foundation of the Academy to the present day. In Spain the only successor to El Greco, Velásquez, and Murillo was the lonely figure of Goya; in Flanders there were no outstanding followers of Rubens and Van Dyck, except Watteau who to all intents and purposes was French; in Holland there was no one to take up where Rembrandt and Vermeer had left off. In France, however, painting continued on a high level throughout the 18th and 19th centuries; and, by setting high technical standards, it was a determining force even in non-academic circles. The work of Perrault and Mansart in architecture, Boileau in criticism, Molière in comedy, Racine in tragedy, Lully in opera was also absorbed directly into a tradition that succeeded in setting up measuring sticks of symmetry, order, regularity, dignity, reserve, and clarity, which to this day still have a certain validity even if only as a point of departure.

CHAPTER

CHRONOLOGY: Amsterdam, 17th Century

General Events

1517 Protestant Reformation began in Germany

1535 *Institution of Christian Religion* published by John Calvin (1509–1564)

Dutch Reformed Church established later along Calvinistic lines

1566 Revolt of the Netherlands against Spain began

1575 University of Leyden, first of the Dutch Universities, founded by William the Silent, Prince of Orange

1602 Dutch East India Company organized

1609 Low Countries given virtual independence in truce with Spain

1618–1648 Thirty Years' War

1621 Dutch West India Company founded

1629–1648 René Descartes resided in Holland

1630–1687 Limited public art patronage dispensed through Constantijn Huygens

1631 Rembrandt settled in Amsterdam

1637 *Discourse of Method* first published in Leyden by Descartes

1644 *Principles of Philosophy* first published by Descartes in Amsterdam

1648 Independence of the Netherlands recognized by Treaty of Westphalia

1652–1674 Anglo-Dutch commercial wars

1670 Spinoza published *Tractatus theologica-politicus*

Painting

*c.*1580–1666 Frans Hals
1609–1669 Rembrandt van Rijn
1617–1681 Gerhardt Terborch
1628–1682 Jakob van Ruisdael
1629–1683 Pieter de Hooch
1632–1675 Jan Vermeer van Delft

Philosophy and Science

1583–1645 Hugo Grotius, founder of international law
1596–1650 Descartes
1629–1695 Christian Huygens
1632–1677 Baruch Spinoza

Literature

1587–1679 Joost van den Vondel, Dutch dramatist and author of *Lucifer*, a poem similar to Milton's *Paradise Lost*

1596–1687 Constantijn Huygens, poet, humanist, diplomat

Music

1562–1621 Jan Pieterszoon Sweelinck
English School
*c.*1542–1623 William Byrd
*c.*1562–1628 John Bull, organist of the Cathedral of Antwerp (1617–1628), friend of Sweelinck

*c.*1562–1638 Francis Pilkington
*c.*1576–1643 Henry Peacham, author of *Compleat Gentleman*, teacher and composer

1583–1625 Orlando Gibbons
German School
1587–1654 Samuel Scheidt, pupil of Sweelinck
1596–1663 Heinrich Scheidemann, pupil of Sweelinck
1623–1722 J. A. Reinken, successor of Scheidemann as organist at Hamburg, and influencer of J. S. Bach
1685–1750 Johann Sebastian Bach
1685–1756 Georg Friedrich Handel

14

THE BOURGEOIS BAROQUE STYLE

AMSTERDAM, 17th CENTURY

If a visitor to 17th-century Amsterdam—or any of the other sturdy Dutch towns for that matter—looked about for triumphal arches, pretentious palaces, or military monuments, he was doomed to disappointment. In fact, if there was anything grand at all about life in the Low Countries, it was in its complete commonplaceness. After they had achieved their cherished independence by wresting their country town by town and province by province from the grasp of the Spanish despots, the people organized it with a minimum of unity and a maximum of diversity. The Netherlanders had no intention whatsoever of substituting one brand of tyranny for another, much less a domestic variety; and so the land became the United Provinces under a *stadtholder*, or governor. Let their English rivals call them the "united bogs" if they would. Even if their muddy swamps and marshlands were poor things, at least they were their own. Their wars of independence, geographical isolation, constant struggle against the encroachments of the sea, dour climate, seafaring economy, Calvinistic Protestantism, and individualistic temperaments conspired with all the other circumstances of Dutch life to focus the center of interest in the home. A Dutchman's home was not even his castle; it was just his solid, comfortable, plain, brick house. Instead of the cult of majesty, his was the cult of the home.

When Jakob van Ruisdael painted the *Quay at Amsterdam* (Fig. 14:1), he was painting more than just a view of the old fish market at the end of the broad canal known as the Damrak. He was in fact picturing the bourgeois way of life in a scene where thrifty housewives were going about gathering up good things for their dinner tables; where a part of the fishing fleet that gave the Dutch a monopoly of the herring industry was moored; where lying at anchor in the distance were some of the merchant vessels that helped the Dutch create modern commerce by plying the seven seas, trading their clay pipes, glazed tiles, Delft pottery, and cured herrings for Russian furs, West Indian sugar, tobacco, and other raw materials; where the spice trade of the Indies had led to the formation of corporations whose shares were traded on a modern stock exchange—complete with booms, like that in the stock of the Dutch West India Company in 1628 after it had declared a 50-per-cent dividend, and busts, like that of the tulip crash a decade later when more bulbs had been sold than could be delivered. In short, Ruisdael was painting the scene of the active mercantilism that spread the base of prosperity so widely that every industrious citizen could aspire to have at least some share of the good things of life for his home.

In such a scheme of things, some families inevitably accumulated more than others; and by means of the wealth that was concentrated in their hands, they became a ruling oligarchy. These so-called regent families were the ones from whose ranks the members of the town councils and mayors were selected. They were, however, an upper-middle-class group rather than an aristocracy, and there was safety in their numbers. Their power, together with that of the professional and mercantile societies known as guilds, depended upon the retention of a maximum of local authority. Such decentralization favored the growth of universities—such as those at Leyden and Utrecht, which became the most distinguished in Europe—and promoted the careers of such eminent native humanists as Constantijn Huygens, friend and patron of Rembrandt, and Hugo Grotius, founder of the new discipline of international law. The freedom to think and work attracted such men as the French philosopher René Descartes, who resided in Holland for almost 20 years, and the parents of Baruch Spinoza—one of the profoundest human intellects of all time—who found refuge in Amsterdam after the persecution of the Jews had made life intolerable in their native Portugal.

The architectural expression of this bourgeois way of life is found in the various town halls, of which that of Amsterdam is a good example; in such mercantile structures as warehouses, counting houses, and the market building, seen on the extreme right of Ruisdael's painting; and, above all, in the long rows of gabled brick houses, such as those seen on either side of the canal in the same picture. Dating from former times were such ecclesiastical buildings as the Oudekerk, or Old Church, whose tower is

Fig. 14:1. Ruisdael. *Quay at Amsterdam.* 20¾″ x 26″. *c.*1669. Copyright The Frick Collection, New York

silhouetted against the sky in the right background, originally Roman Catholic but taken over by the Dutch Reformed Church after the Reformation. As organized under the precepts of John Calvin, the Reformed Church held that religious truth was not the monopoly of any individual or any group, and that the word of God was available to all without the mediation of priestly authority. Through the development of the printing press, every family could have its own Bible, and by means of the high degree of literacy which prevailed, almost everyone could read it. As in the case of their government, the Dutch people were wary of authority; and as confirmed Protestants, they took rather literally the words of Christ to go into their closets and pray. Thus through family devotions, hymn singing, and Bible reading, much of the important religious activity took place in the home. According to the teaching of Calvin, the reason for going to church was to hear a sermon and sing the praises of the Lord. This, of course, discouraged anything that might distract from these primary activities, such as architectural embellishments, statuary, paintings, and professional choirs or orchestras. Since commissions were no longer forthcoming from church sources, the artist had to conceive his work more and more in terms of the home.

The prosperous Dutch families fortunately felt the need of an art that would reflect their healthy materialism and that would reveal their outlook, their institutions, and their country without flattery or frivolousness but in a solid matter-of-fact way—just as they were. In this happy state of affairs patronage was spread on a broad-enough basis so that every home had at least a small collection of pictures. Above all, the Dutch burgher wanted to have family portraits for his living room; commemorative pictures of such family festivals as christenings and weddings; paintings of quiet interiors with women like his wife or daughter dutifully doing some household chore, or if one of them showed special talent, then perhaps playing a musical instrument; a genre scene, if it were proper and not likely to put peculiar notions into his children's heads; a still life with some flowers or fruit, if there was no nonsense about it, and if things looked like what they were; or a neat landscape, perhaps, if it were not too large to hang comfortably on his parlor wall. If he were a man of affairs, he wanted to be portrayed at his work surrounded by the distinctions of his worldly position; or if he were a man of responsibility, he would chip in with his fellow trustees or board members for a group portrait to hang in the halls of his institution so that posterity would be properly impressed with his importance. In short, Dutch painting was one vast family album.

Under Calvinistic austerity, the only professional musicians to survive were the church organists; the hired groups of singers and instrumentalists who performed for such occasions as weddings, banquets, and parades; and the band of music teachers who taught the younger members of the family to sing, and play the lute, viola da gamba, and keyboard instruments, such as the virginals and spinet. Music, therefore, like all the other aspects of Dutch life, was centered in the home. During the Renaissance, the Low Countries had dominated European music with the polyphonic glories of their distinguished composers. Owing to the fact, however, that the artistic and material rewards were so much greater elsewhere, a lively export trade in musicians developed that eventually left the home ranks depleted. Only one last musical genius of universal stature was left in the Amsterdam of the early 17th century, Jan Pieterszoon Sweelinck, whose career brought the radiant chapter of Netherlands music to a brilliant close.

All the arts were thus centered in the home. The simple and unpretentious Dutch domestic architecture with its polished tiled floors, tidy interiors, and window boxes for the tulips was the modest framework for this bourgeois way of life. Unless ceramics are included there was little sculpture except for a few figurines on the mantlepiece and an occasional statuette, such as that over the doorway in Figure 14:7. Their primary aesthetic indulgences were their pictures and domestic music-making. Such things as their Delft pottery jugs, tablecloths, laces, and draperies also enriched their world of qualities. The reality of daily life was made up of the routine of the business establishment, the market place, and the household. It was a reality of simple truths in which nothing was too small to be overlooked. All things, even the most insignificant, were considered to be gifts of God; and, as such, they were studied in the Dutch art of the 17th century in the minutest detail.

PAINTING

Towering above all other Dutch painters, because of the breadth of his vision, the power of his characterizations, and the uncompromising integrity of his ideals, stands the figure of Rembrandt van Rijn in lonely eminence. Like his contemporaries he was interested in portraits, genre scenes, mythological and Biblical stories, and landscapes, but unlike them he refused to specialize and succeeded in doing them all. Furthermore, he brought a new psychological profundity to his portraiture, an unaccustomed animation to his genre scenes, a greater dramatic intensity to his religious pictures, and a broader sweep to his landscapes than had been achieved before in the northern tradition. His discoveries of the power of light, in all its varying degrees, to illuminate character both from without and from within, to define space by the interpenetration of light, and to animate that space by the flowing movement of shadows, identify him as one of the prime movers in the establishment of the northern Baroque pictorial style. His art as a whole reveals a consistent growth from his early to his late years in the power to penetrate the world of appearances so as to lay bare the quickening spiritual forces that lie beneath.

Soon after he settled in Amsterdam, the 26-year-old painter received his first important assignment from the local Guild of Surgeons. The result was *Dr. Tulp's Anatomy Lesson* (Fig. 14:2), a typical corporation picture, which went far toward establishing Rembrandt's reputation. The subjects of the group portrait were the heads of the Guild, and their names are duly recorded on the sheet of paper in the hand of the figure next to that of Dr. Tulp. Less typical is Rembrandt's unusual grouping, which imparts a certain freedom and informality to the composition yet allows each of the almost life-sized figures to be seen impartially. By the use of light, he

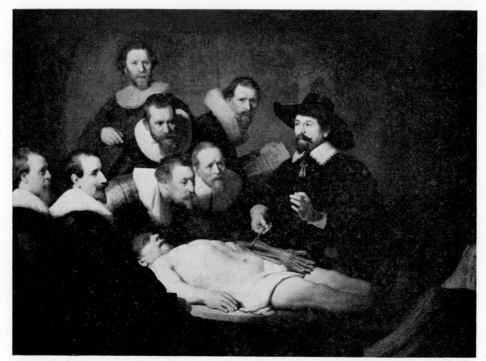

Fig. 14:2 (above). Rembrandt. *Dr. Tulp's Anatomy Lesson.* 5′ 5″ x 7′ 2½″. 1632. Mauritshuis Museum, The Hague. Fig. 14:3 (below). Rembrandt. *Sortie of Captain Banning Cocq's Company of the Civic Guard.* 11′ 9″ x 14′ 3¼″. 1642. Rijksmuseum, Amsterdam (Courtesy Netherlands Information Bureau)

develops the inherent drama of the situation and brings out the expression of each of the faces, which vary from intentness to casual indifference. The fullest light falls on the cadaver, the body of a newly executed criminal, and on the hands and face of Dr. Nicolaes Tulp, the Professor of Anatomy. The large folio volume at the feet of the corpse is most probably the 1555 edition of Vesalius' *Anatomy* opened to the page that shows the structure of the arm which the lecturer is demonstrating. The subject is an admirable illustration of the scientific spirit of the time, and Rembrandt's objective statement in this case is well suited to the intellectual atmosphere. What some historians have referred to as Rembrandt's indecisive treatment of space has had to be revised in this instance, because a thorough recent cleaning sharpened up the architectural background and revealed clearly the vaulted contours of the Anatomical Hall of the Amsterdam Athenaeum in which such lectures were held. The somber yellowish and dark brown tints also yielded in the process to a wider color range than was apparent before.

Exactly a decade elapsed between the *Anatomy Lesson* and Rembrandt's masterpiece in this genre, the *Sortie of Captain Banning Cocq's Company* (Fig. 14:3). Such group portraits of military units who fought against the Spaniards were common enough at the time to have the special designation of "musketeer pictures." After their original purpose in the struggle for independence was over, many of the organizations were continued as parts of the civic guard and as officers' clubs, who were available as the occasion warranted for anything from an emergency to a parade. Most members were by now prosperous shopkeepers who hugely enjoyed dressing up now and then in their dashing uniforms, polishing up their shooting irons, and posing as warriors in processions and civic celebrations. In such pictures they were usually shown in convivial situations, such as a gathering around the banquet table, but in order to get some life and movement into this rather stilted form, Rembrandt chose to show them in action as if responding to a call to arms. They are therefore seen moving out of the city gate before falling into formation.

For generations the picture has been popularly known as the *Night Watch*. An expert cleaning job in 1946–1947, however, revealed to a startled world that it was actually daylight, and that Rembrandt's varnish, which had thickened in the course of time, was responsible for the general gloom. Now the free flow of light can be seen moving rhythmically throughout the whole composition, pervading every corner of it with dynamic gradations varying from dark to bright. It is most intense in the center, where the captain is explaining the plans to his lieutenant. The shadow of his hand, which falls across the lieutenant's uniform, helps to define the direction of the light, which in turn relates all the other figures to the central pair by the degree of illumination that falls upon them. Such virtuosity in the handling of light and shadow for dramatic purposes was one of Rembrandt's most unique achievements and stamps him as being far ahead of his colleagues. Contrary to popular legend, the picture was not a failure, and it was proudly hung in the company's hall.

The etching, *Christ Healing the Sick* (Fig. 14:4), popularly known as the "Hundred Guilder Print," is one of Rembrandt's several hundred examples in this new medium. The relatively modest price of an etching assured a wider distribution of Rembrandt's work at the times when many of his paintings were piling up unsold in his studio. The price in this instance, however, was a record rather than a rule. Technically the medium gave him the opportunity to explore the qualities of light by means of simple line patterns independent of pigments and colors. By scratching a wax-covered metal plate with a stylus, a linear pattern is formed that is etched or bitten into the metal upon immersion in an acid solution. When transferred to paper, the range runs from such inky blackness as that behind the figure of Christ to the whiteness of the untouched paper as that of the rock in the extreme left.

Rembrandt's true artistic stature is revealed in the way he is able to scale the heights of moral grandeur within such severe limitations. The expressive power of *Christ Healing the Sick* is as great as the material medium is small. Rembrandt was brought up in a family of Anabaptists who tried to live according to strict Biblical precepts. His religious subjects are seen from a Protestant point of view and as such show an intimate personal knowledge of the Scriptures. Since he was not painting for churches, and thus was under no compulsion to conform to the usual iconographical tradition of Madonnas and Child, Crucifixions, and so on, he was free to develop new themes and new points of view. Much of the intimacy and effectiveness of this type of work are due to the fact that they were not conceived as public showpieces. Rembrandt also loved to explore the Amsterdam ghetto and found stimulation as well as many of the types for his religious pictures among the descendants of the people who created the Old Testament.

No painter ever did more portraits of himself than Rembrandt. The motivation, however, came more from a deep introspective tendency than from personal vanity. In a late *Self-portrait* (Fig. 14:5), done when he was 52, the artist is seen seated in an armchair, tired to the point of exhaustion. With no attempt at self-flattery, he shows himself clad in a shabby yellow smock with his head enframed by an old black velvet hat with an upturned

Fig. 14:4 (above). Rembrandt. *Christ Healing the Sick*, the "Hundred Guilder Print." Etching. *c.*1650. Metropolitan Museum, New York

Fig. 14:5 (right). Rembrandt. *Self-portrait.* 51⅝″ x 40¼″. 1658. Copyright The Frick Collection, New York

Fig. 14:6 (left). Hals. *Merry Lute Player.* 35½" x 29½". *c.*1627. Oscar B. Cintas Collection

Fig. 14:7 (below). De Hooch. *The Linen Cupboard.* 28¾" x 30¼". 1663. Rijksmuseum, Amsterdam (Courtesy Netherlands Information Bureau)

brim. Most striking are the luminous dark eyes, whose searching glance seems to be studying the spectator but which are actually focused on himself as he peers into the mirror next to his easel. As an example of his late psychological portraiture, it reveals the artist as one who has endured all the slings and arrows of outrageous fortune, but who has been mellowed and ennobled by the experience and emerged with all his human dignity unimpaired. The penetrating gaze, glowing with an internal light, looks into the depths of his own character and seems to be asking, Whither now? From this point onward Rembrandt realized more and more that his mission was to explore the world of the imagination and leave the world of appearances to others. Consequently his countenance bespeaks the serenity of a man who has chosen his course, and who knows that there is now no turning back.

Between the polar extremes of the introspective Rembrandt and the objective Vermeer, three pictures will serve to illustrate the emotional range of their contemporaries—the infectious gaiety of Frans Hals in the *Merry Lute Player* (Fig. 14:6), the quiet domesticity of de Hooch's *Linen Cupboard* (Fig. 14:7), and the brooding melancholy of Ruisdael's *The Cemetery* (Fig. 14:8). The *Merry Lute Player* is typical of Frans Hals' most brilliant period. With his tousled hair and black cap cocked at a jaunty angle, the subject might be an entertainer at a public tavern. The way he holds up the glass of sparkling wine defines the source of light, which falls most strongly on one side of his face and on the varnished wooden surface of his instrument. In Hals' pictures the people of his native Haarlem—quarreling fishwives, carousing officers, and tipsy merrymakers—live again with all their animal vitality and capacity for life. Hals found his inspiration in the lighter moments of his slightly disreputable fellow townspeople who were without the moral restraints of the more sober Bible-reading burghers. In his earlier work he was interested more in appearances than essences. Later when he came under the shadow of Rembrandt, he gave up his vivid colors and light touch for more somber subjects.

Pieter de Hooch's *Linen Cupboard* (Fig. 14:7) is a quiet study of domestic life in a proper household. Like his fellow painters de Hooch knew that light was the magnet which attracted the eye, and that its vibrations give such an interior its share of life and movement. But de Hooch works with a subdued light that matches the tranquillity of his subject matter. The highest intensity is reflected from the canal and sunlit wall of the house, which are visible through the open door in the background. The painter shows interest in delineating the contrasting textures of the tiled floor, the carved wood of the walls and oaken cupboard, and the qualities of the linen

Fig. 14:8. Ruisdael. *The Cemetery*. 56″ x 74½″. *c*.1655. Institute of Arts, Detroit (Courtesy Netherlands Information Bureau)

cloth and the costumes of the mistress, maid, and child. In contrast with Vermeer, de Hooch is more concerned with what his figures are doing, while Vermeer is more interested in what they are. The looseness of de Hooch's pictorial organization is also noticeably different from Vermeer's tight-knit interiors.

Jakob van Ruisdael's somber study, *The Cemetery* (Fig. 14:8), comes in the category of the landscapes that meant so much to the Dutch people who fought for their country so persistently against the Spanish oppressors. Ruisdael, however, seems to be searching in this instance for deeper values than the usual quiet country scene. The abandoned ruins of the old castle and the skeletonlike trunks of the two trees unite with the white stone slabs of the tombs to permeate the picture with thoughts of death. The inscriptions on the headstones—several of which are still there—remind the viewer that the religious toleration of the Netherlands made the country the haven for the refugees from the Spanish and Portuguese inquisitions. Under one of them a Dr. Montalto, physician to King Henry IV of France, was buried in 1615. Another grave contains the remains of Chaicham Usiel, head rabbi of Amsterdam, who was a native of Fez in Morocco. Ruisdael projects a depth of feeling as well as of space into this landscape. With the waterfall and threatening sky he hints at the force and sublimity of nature that sweeps both man and all his works before it. His eye for the picturesque anticipates in a remarkable way certain aspects of 19th-century romanticism.

In his *View of Delft* (Fig. 14:9), Jan Vermeer paints a typical Dutch town sandwiched cozily between the elements of water and sky. From the canal opposite the town, where some people are gathering in the lower left foreground, the artist draws the attention along the profile of the mercantile buildings and houses behind the city wall on the left, past the stone bridge in the center with the steeple of the church rising in the background, and toward the moored boats and drawbridge on the extreme right. His feeling for space is revealed in this horizontal sweep and in the fact that he makes little attempt to treat it as a study in deep perspective. Missing in the photograph, but most important to the effectiveness of the picture, is the subtle treatment of color. As the sunlight filters through the broken clouds, the static light falls unevenly over the landscape, leaving the brick houses in the shadowy foreground a dull red that contrasts with the flame-red and orange tones of those in the sunny background. More than half the area of the picture is allotted to the sky, where patches of blue alternate with the silvery and leaden grays of the clouds that are mirrored below in the placid water.

A Street in Delft (Fig. 14:10) again uses the warm red color of brick, tempered by the cool gray tints of a cloudy Dutch sky. A touch of contrast is provided by the brown pavement, the green shutters, and the yellows and blues of the women's dresses. More important than the color this time, however, is the meticulous geometrical organization in which each part is related to the whole. The picture can be broken down into a system of rectangular surfaces, such as those of the pavement, open doorways, the shuttered and unshuttered windows, and the stepped gables of the houses. Highly selective rather than literal, Vermeer has eliminated everything that is not germane to his picture. Nothing extraneous is allowed to clutter up the tidiness of the composition, and each element of texture and surface is worked out to the minutest detail.

The same meticulousness and economy of means apply to such interior scenes as the *Officer and Laughing Girl* (Fig. 14:11). The logical organization of rectangles and intersecting surfaces is somewhat softened here by the prominence given to the conversing figures. The daring cameralike perspective projects the figure of the officer forward and gives greater size to his large slouch hat and head than to that of the girl. His red coat and

Fig. 14:11. Vermeer. *Officer and Laughing Girl*. 20″ x 18″. *c*.1656. Copyright The Frick Collection, New York

Fig. 14:9 (left, above). Vermeer. *View of Delft*. 38¾″ x 46″. *c*.1658. Mauritshuis Museum, The Hague. Fig. 14:10 (left, below). Vermeer. *A Street in Delft*. 21¼″ x 17¼″. *c*.1658. Rijksmuseum, Amsterdam (Courtesy Netherlands Information Bureau)

sash also contrast noticeably with the cooler colors of the girl's white cap, black and yellow bodice, and blue apron that allow her figure to recede. The map on the wall is painted with the greatest care in relation to the light and angle of the wall. Its Latin title is quite clear, and reads: "New and Accurate Map of all Holland and West Friesland." The warm, rich, natural light that streams in from the open casement window gives both unity and life to the severe division of planes. It bathes every object and pervades every corner of the room, starting with the maximum intensity of the area adjacent to the source and tapering off by degrees into the cool bluish tones of the shadows in the lower right.

The contrast between Rembrandt's restless searching spirit and Vermeer's sober objective detachment is fully as great as that between El Greco and Velásquez, or Rubens and Poussin. Rembrandt's light is the glow of the burning human spirit, Vermeer's that from the open casement window. Rembrandt tries to penetrate the world of appearances, Vermeer is content with the visual image. With his warm personal quality, Rembrandt embraces humanity as completely as Vermeer's cool impersonality encompasses space. Rembrandt is concerned at all times with moral beauty, Vermeer with physical perfection. Rembrandt's inner dramas need only the crescendo of a single color from deep brown to golden yellow or in an etching from black to white, while Vermeer's absence of drama consumes the entire chromatic spectrum. Like a philosopher, Rembrandt lays the soul bare in his moving characterizations, while Vermeer, like a jeweler, delights the eye with his unique perception of the quality and texture of things. Thus, in both Spain and France as well as Holland, the 17th century, like a stormy March, had been swept in on the leonine gusts of Baroque flamboyance and had gone out on a gentle lamblike academic breeze.

MUSIC

The one great musician of 17th-century Holland was Jan Pieterszoon Sweelinck, who succeeded his father and was, in turn, succeeded by his son as organist at the Oudekerk, so that the family rounded out a century of music-making there. Under the strict tenets of Calvinism, church music consisted mainly of the congregational singing of psalms and hymns, preferably unaccompanied. As such the development of music as an art would have been ruled out except for the fact that the Dutch tradition favored the organ and the organist was allowed to play preludes and postludes on sacred themes before and after the service. On special occasions choral settings of the psalms with some degree of elaboration were performed. Sweelinck's viewpoint, like that of the other Dutch composers of the century, was international in scope. He had studied in Venice with Zarlino and Andrea Gabrieli and was a colleague of the famous Giovanni Gabrieli. He had also visited England and was thoroughly familiar with the English keyboard school and choral-composing tradition. His official title was Organist of Amsterdam, and as such his duties included the giving of public concerts. The church, according to contemporary accounts, was always crowded on these occasions, and large audiences consistently took delight in his improvisations and variations on sacred and secular themes; the Baroque flourishes of his Venetian toccatas; his fantasies "in the manner of an echo," a keyboard adaptation of the Venetian double choral style; and the choral preludes and fugues that he built on Protestant hymn tunes.

The other public music was of the occasional type, given by choral groups and instrumental ensembles that for a modest price would furnish anything from the madrigals which were sung at weddings to the dances played at receptions. All available evidence points to the fact that the center of the major part of the musical life of the time was in the home. Most of the extant compositions from this period are found in the numerous manuscript copies that were made for home use. Printed scores, however, were obtainable from Venice and London, and early in the century music printing began to flourish in Antwerp, Leyden, and Amsterdam. Holland also became noted as a center for the manufacture of musical instruments. The musical practices of the time can be vividly reconstructed by combining the surviving scores and musical instruments with the rich visual evidence available in the paintings of the period. Vermeer's *The Concert* (Fig. 14:12), for instance, shows a typical musical situation in the home. The trio is made up of the young woman, who reads her song part from the score she holds in her hand; the seated man, who supplies the harmonic background on his theorbo, a species of the lute; and the girl at the spinet, the winged version of the virginals, who plays the keyboard part. A viola da gamba, which corresponds to the modern 'cello, is seen on the floor; and, ordinarily, if a player were available, it would be used to duplicate the bass line of the keyboard part in the instrumental combination known as the *continuo*.

The widespread custom of domestic music-making resulted in a large body of literature that was designed for home rather than public performance. Since such music was always on a friendly, sociable basis, it was mainly for two or more participants. Even the solo pieces, however, were

Fig. 14:12. Vermeer. *The Concert*. 28″ x 24¾″. *c.*1660. Isabella Stewart Gardner Museum, Boston

written for amateurs and purposely avoided any complexities that might imply showing off. The attitude is well summed up in *The Compleat Gentleman*, published in London in 1622 by the English schoolmaster Henry Peacham. "I desire no more in you," he said, "than to sing your part at first sight; withal to play the same upon your Viol, or the exercise of the Lute, privately to yourself." [1]

An example of the type of music Mr. Peacham's gentlemen or Vermeer's ladies were prepared to perform is found in Francis Pilkington's "Now Peep, Boe Peep," a number from that composer's *First Booke of Ayres*, published in 1605. The score was arranged and printed so that the participants could be seated comfortably around a table (Fig. 14:13). On the left side the words and melody of the Canto, in this case the soprano part, appear above the lute tablature. Next to them is seated the tenor, the alto is placed on the opposite side, while the bass sits at the end of the table. A transcription of the beginning of the piece is given here.[2]

Now Peep, Boe Peep (1605)   Francis Pilkington

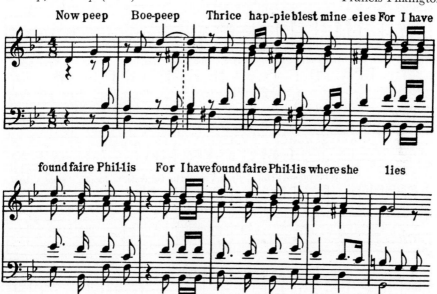

One of the interesting things about the piece is the great number of ways it can be performed. In its complete form it is a vocal quartet with a lute accompaniment that duplicates the three lower parts. It can also be performed as a soprano solo with lute accompaniment, as given on the left half of the page; a cappella—that is, for four voices without the lute; as a duet for soprano and any one of the other voices; as a lute solo; as an instrumental piece with viols instead of voices; as a combination of voices and viols; as an instrumental ensemble with doublings of the parts, or with wind instruments substituting for the voices and viols, and so on practically ad infinitum. Such music had to be adaptable to the size and skill of any group that might gather together for an evening of musical pleasure in the home.

The music of the Netherlands at this time was much more international in its scope and character than the painting. While Italian and French influences were far from negligible in the visual arts, such painters as Frans Hals, Rembrandt, Vermeer, and their contemporaries were identified with a distinct national style. English influences were strong, especially in

Ow peep, boe peep, thrife happie bleft mine eies, For I haue found faire Phillis, for I haue found faire *Phillis* where fhe lies, Vpon her bed, with armes vnfpred, all faft a fleepe, Vnmaskt her face, thrife happie grace, fare-well, fare-well my Sheepe, Looke to your felues, new charge I muft ap-proue, *Phillis* doth fleepe, *Phillis* doth fleepe, And I muft guard my Loue. Looke.

2 Now peep boe peep, mine eyes to fee your bliffe,
Phillis clofd eyes atrackts you, hers to kiffe :
Oh may I now performe my vow, loues ioy t'impart,
Affay the while, how to be-guile, farewell faint hart.
Taken fhe is, new ioyes I muft approue,
Phillis doth fleep, and I will kiffe my Loue.

3 Now peep, boe peep, be not too bould my hand,
Wake not thy *Phillis*, feare fhee doe with-ftand :
Shee ftirs alas, alas, alas I faint in fpright,
Shee opes her eie, vnhappie I, farewell delight.
Awakt fhee is, new woes I muft approue,
Phillis awakes, and I muft leaue my Loue.

Fig. 14:13. *The First Booke of Songs or Ayres of 4 Parts: With Tablature for the Lute or Orpherian, with the violl de gamba.* Newly composed by Francis Pilkington, . . . London, 1605 (Courtesy Huntington Library, San Marino, California)

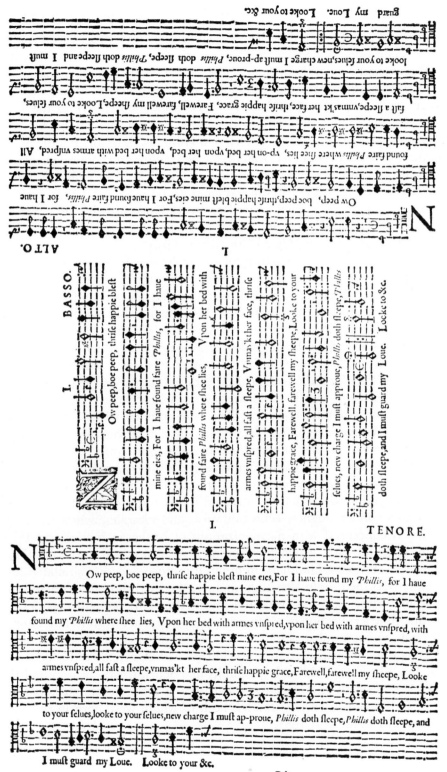

the case of the keyboard style; and, as the century progressed, Italian influences gradually became dominant in the Netherlands just as they did in France and England. In the decade before 1650 the Dutch composers were publishing instrumental ensemble pieces for from two- to five-stringed instruments called Symphoniae, which corresponded closely to the Fantasies for the same combinations that were written in England by such composers as William Byrd and Orlando Gibbons. After the middle of the century, however, Italian trio sonatas for two violins and continuo began to be heard. Eventually this became the standard form of chamber music here as elsewhere. Such trio sonatas came to be written by French, German, and Dutch composers as well as by Italians, but the form was essentially international in style.

The style that did develop a distinctively northern character was that of the keyboard literature, whether for organ, virginals, spinet, clavichord, or harpsichord. Sweelinck had absorbed both the Venetian and English traditions, and his organ playing attracted to Amsterdam students from all over northern Europe. Through them his influence was widely extended, especially over the Protestant parts of Germany. His most noted pupil here was Samuel Scheidt of Halle, whose *Tablatura Nova*, which he published in 1624, did much to crystallize the German Protestant organ and choral style. In this book all the technical procedures he had learned from Sweelinck were brought together and worked out with characteristic Germanic thoroughness. Happily, however, they were coupled with a considerable degree of creative imagination as well as technical invention. In its pages are found compositions intended for home performance, mainly in the form of variations. French and Flemish secular songs as well as dances, like the *allemande, paduan, courant*, and *gaillard*, appear with variants which are full of the complexities that so intrigued the Baroque mind. The first two parts also contain fugues, echo fantasies, and chorales, while the third section is concerned with harmonizations of Lutheran hymns and Protestant chorales with ornamental commentaries in the form of variations. The work became a landmark in organ literature since it assimilated and systematized the ornate Venetian manner, the English keyboard variation style, and Sweelinck's contrapuntal inventiveness. It brought together for the first time a collection of pieces admirably adapted for Protestant church purposes, and a number of musical models for other composers to emulate. A direct line thus extended from Sweelinck, who coordinated the Venetian and English schools, through his pupils like Scheidt, who transmitted the tradition to northern Germany, down to the time of Johann Sebastian Bach and Georg Friedrich Handel, both of whom were born in this part of Germany in the year 1685.

IDEAS

Domesticity

The various aspects of the bourgeois Baroque style find a common under-current in the idea of domesticity. Many related ideas, such as mercantil-ism, Protestantism, anti-authoritarianism, nationalism, and individualism, together with the championship of individual rights and liberties all im-pinge on this central concept, but the unity lies in the cult of the home. Bourgeois house comforts, for instance, were never so highly cultivated in the warmer friendlier south where so much recreational activity can take place in the open air. The northern climate, however, was conducive to the concentration of communal pleasures in the home.

The spirit of commerce led to navigational adventure on the high seas and to the exploration of distant lands. The Dutch conquests, however, were mainly those of the businessman; their empire was based on corporate enterprise; and their multiple monarchies were those of the banking houses and holding companies, which were often under the dynastic control of a single family. All was undertaken with the thought of ultimately enriching and enlivening their many different homes. The success of Calvinistic Protestantism was owing in no small part to the fact that it sanctioned business activity and actually regarded success as a sign of divine favor. The Calvinist could charge interest with good conscience and without the fear of bringing down priestly maledictions on the practice of usury. Hard work and industriousness coupled with frugality led to a widespread ac-cumulation of wealth in the hands of the middle class. No riotous living or public displays of luxury were possible when the church sanctioned no lavish decoration whatsoever even for its own buildings. While both the Anglican and Lutheran reform movements preserved much of the beauty of the traditional liturgy in a modified form, the Calvinistic movement was marked by its extreme austerity. A strict interpretation of Calvinism would lead directly to a gloomy form of asceticism, but the innate good sense and honest enjoyment of material pleasures saved the Dutch from the bleaker aspects of this doctrine. But the only possible outlet for their prosperity and desire for aesthetic enjoyment was in their homes.

The wealthy burgher, however, did not build a palace—though he certainly had the means to do so. He was content with a comfortable house that was functionally suited to his needs. Fighting the Spanish crown for their independence, and resisting the growing menace of Louis XIV's absolute state, made the Dutch look with disfavor on any form of courtly pomp and ostentatiousness. The Protestant movement also fortified their hostility to authority and awakened a latent nationalistic consciousness. The middle-class merchant particularly resented the draining off of the wealth of his province toward Rome, and the resentment was equally strong against the secular arm of the Catholic Church in the form of the Holy Roman Empire. Calvinistic Protestantism thus took root and became synonymous in the Dutch mind with patriotism. The protection of their national and provincial rights, together with their individual freedoms, further focused their attention on their homes where they were their own lords and masters.

Philosophy, philology, social theory, and the natural sciences flourished in the universities. Such intellectual pursuits speculated on the existence of an ordered and regulated universe in which everything could be measured and understood. The solid citizen instinctively distrusted the physical and emotional forces that could render his world chaotic and unpredictable. Hence such an ideal universe had considerable appeal for a bourgeoisie whose security and comforts would thus be assured. Descartes' rationalistic cosmology and psychology, and Spinoza's mathematically demonstrable ethical system led to the concept of art as a form of reasoned depiction, though it took a Rembrandt to achieve an emotional spectrum capable of infusing it with the warmth of life.

The circumstances of the Dutch state of mind and material prosperity led to the placement of artistic patronage in the hands of a well-to-do middle class. Outside such necessary public buildings as the town halls, churches, and mercantile structures, Dutch architecture was for all intents and purposes domestic architecture. Since the houses were about the same size as middle-class homes today, there was no place in the scheme of things for monumental sculpture. The major domestic aesthetic expressions, therefore, were painting and music, together with all the minor decorative arts that added to the comfort and beauty of the home. The interest in pictures was such that the ranks of painters multiplied until literally hundreds were kept busy keeping up with the demand. Dutch thrift, however, saw to it that paintings were bought at rock-bottom prices and that no painter ever got rich at his trade. Such numbers led inevitably to pictorial specialization. In portraiture there were the painters of the decorous *pater familias* types, of the wine bibbers in public taverns, and of corporation pictures. There were landscapists, seascapists, skyscapists, and even those whose specialty was cows. The social levels were also stratified with Frans Hals finding his subjects among the fishwives and fruit pedlars, de Hooch and Vermeer in the proper middle class, and Terborch among the most prosperous group.

The character of music was likewise molded by bourgeois patronage. In free cities the organist and other municipal musicians were chosen by committees of the town councils, who supervised the musical life of the community as diligently as any of its other aspects. Auditions were held and competition encouraged. Public employment from the musician's point of view meant freedom from the arbitrary whims of a single aristocratic patron, and it was generally preferred because of the security it implied. When the tastes of the many had to be taken into consideration, however, it often tended to inhibit experimentation and promote standardization. This was balanced to a considerable extent by the vast opportunities for private music-making in the home, where musical expression took on a distinct domestic coloration.

The home was thus the factor that determined the art forms and imparted to them such an intimate character and quality. Dutch domestic architecture, painting, and music were all designed to be lived with and enjoyed by a middle-class group who frankly took delight in their physical comforts and the arts that enriched their home life. Large canvases designed for altar pieces or to cover palace ceilings, colossal choral compositions for cathedrals or operatic performances for palaces were productive of grandiose oratorical utterances but had no place in the home. The more modest dimensions of a painting or an etching designed for a living-room wall, a chamber sonata or solo keyboard piece meant to be played in such a room were conducive to a more intimate and personal form of communication. The expressive range is analogous to a composer's choice of the modern symphony orchestra for his epical pronouncements and a chamber music group or a piano sonata for his more confidential statements. The home was the dominant architectural form as well as the place where the pictures were hung, the books read, and the music played. In Holland and the northern countries generally, the Baroque style was thus adapted both to Protestantism and to the tastes of the middle class. The bourgeois aspect of Baroque art thus finds its unity in the cult of the home, and domesticity is the key to the understanding of the style.

CHAPTER

15

THE BAROQUE, LIMITED

LONDON DURING THE RESTORATION

That day in the year of our Lord 1661, as Charles II made his triumphal progress to Westminster Abbey for his coronation, the sounds of Mr. Matthew Locke's march music for the sackbuts and cornets mingled with the cordial cheers of his subjects. They were the cheers of a people wearied by a generation of civil strife and the effort of conforming to the rigors of puritanical idealism. They were the cheers of a people who hoped and prayed that the Restoration would bring them peace and normalcy. They were the cheers of a people who did not know that their numbers would be decimated a few years hence by an outbreak of the dreaded bubonic plague; that their city would be leveled by the Great Fire of London; and that the Restoration, which was supposed to be bringing back the old order, was actually the force that was ushering in the new.

The picture of a period embellished by a merry monarch, libertine lords, licentious ladies, and amorous adventurers has been painted all too often. That of a time which vibrated to the thunder of John Milton's poetry, spoke with the polished rhetoric of John Dryden, wondered at the mathematical ingenuity of Isaac Newton's equations, marveled at the majesty of Christopher Wren's architecture, and heard the harmonies of Henry Purcell's music has received much less attention. The merry monarch even had a serious side, which was developed through the trials and tribulations of a troubled youth during which his father's stormy reign had led to Charles I losing his head, and throughout the following period of exile in France where he spent his most formative and impressionable years. Charles II was an amateur astronomer, whose enthusiasm led to the founding of the Greenwich Observatory; a patron of the theater, whose interest played an important role in the development of the Restoration drama; a connois-

549

Fig. 15:1. Van Dyck. *Charles I of England*. 8′ 11″ x 6′ 11″. *c.*1635. Louvre, Paris (Archives Photographiques)

seur of the arts, whose support of Christopher Wren led to an architectural rebirth in his country; and a music lover, who took pride now and then in lifting his voice in song in what has politely been described as a "plump bass." His years at Louis XIV's court were, in fact, about to pay off handsomely, because in addition to some questionable absolutistic political ideas and some doubtful French courtly morals, he had brought back with him a goodly measure of Continental enthusiasm for the arts. During his reign, London was to become as much a cultural suburb of Versailles as the common sense of his subjects would bear.

London had caught a brief glimpse of Continental elegance under his father Charles I, who had appointed Anthony Van Dyck, a pupil of Rubens, to paint the family portraits (Figs. 15:1 and 15:2), and when Inigo Jones built the Banqueting House at Whitehall as the first unit of a projected royal palace. This faithful follower of Palladio might have done much more had not other and more pressing matters intervened. The gates now, however, were to be flung wide open. Nicholas Laniere was dispatched to Italy to purchase pictures for the royal collection. William Davenant, who had been a guest in Paris of Charles and his mother and had closely observed Lully's musical methods, was summoned to become England's first opera manager. When the French opera composer Robert

Fig. 15:2. Van Dyck. *Children of Charles I.* 5' 4½" x 6' 6½". 1637. Replica of the original at Windsor Castle. Metropolitan Museum, New York

Cambert was outmaneuvered by the wily Lully, he found a ready welcome at the English court. Pelham Humfrey, a promising young composer of 17 and later the teacher of Purcell, was sent to Paris by Charles to see how Lully managed his orchestra and ballet. Since Louis XIV had his *Vingt-quatre Violons*, Charles would have his Four-and-twenty Fiddles. When he was looking around for a poet laureate, the choice fell to Dryden who was most familiar with Boileau and the French Baroque drama. When Charles heard that King Louis and Colbert were getting ready to remodel the Louvre, he saw that Wren was on the spot to see the plans and to meet Bernini and Perrault.

The stage on which the Restoration scene was to be played, however, had a distinctive character of its own. The City of London was a mercantile center that was not under the domination of either a church or a monarchy. To this day the London County Council does not have jurisdiction over the City of London, and the British sovereign must—theoretically at least—request the permission of the Lord Mayor to enter its territorial limits. In the 17th century the City of London, with its population of about 500,000, was London. The aristocracy maintained their country houses elsewhere, leaving London to the merchants and clerks who worked in their shops and counting houses and lived upstairs. To change anything in this conservative middle-class stronghold took one of those decisive events that are defined legally as acts of God. In 1666 it came in the form of the fire which, according to the diary of Samuel Pepys, destroyed 13,000 houses, 400 streets, and 90 churches, including much of Old St. Paul's Cathedral dating from shortly after the Norman conquest. Before the charred ruins had stopped smoking, Christopher Wren was sketching out a plan for the rebuilding of the entire city. The fire gave him the greatest opportunity ever afforded an English architect; and even though his plan was not to be carried out completely, enough of it was realized to determine the architectural course of late 17th-century London and to give that city its superb skyline.

The collision between this staunch middle-class citizenry and their foreign-bred king brought about still another tangible proof of the English genius for compromise. The Stuarts from the beginning had tried to impose the Continental concept of absolutism on their reluctant subjects. The extremes of Charles I and his failure to come to terms with the middle-class merchants and their official body, the House of Commons, had brought about the Cromwellian Commonwealth. The uncompromising Oliver Cromwell on his side had alienated the still-powerful aristocracy. Charles II had some success in trying to find a middle ground. His successor James II, however, again overstepped his prerogatives, and it took still another revolution—this time a bloodless and Glorious one—to bring about the alliance between the sovereign and the middle class under the compromise formula known as the limited monarchy.

Much the same struggle is mirrored in the arts. The French aristocratic Baroque, just like the absolute monarchy, was a little too rich for the English diet. When it came time to build a new cathedral, for instance, Charles and his Principal Architect, Sir Christopher, thought in terms of the richly embellished classical orders, the splendor and spaciousness of the Louvre and Versailles, and the centralized church plans of Palladio and Michelangelo. The clergy and their lay advisors, however, still thought of a cathedral as a tall, imposing Gothic structure. Wren wanted it to be crowned with a dome; the churchmen thought it should have a spire. So Wren built his dome and put a high lantern tower on top of it. Charles wanted Lullian opera, but the theater-goers showed remarkable resistance toward sung recitative. So they got a hybrid form of spoken dialogue, interspersed with some songs and punctuated with instrumental interludes.

With political authority divided between the monarchy and parliament, literary precedents between the classical and Elizabethan traditions, architectural ideas between the French Baroque and English Gothic, and musical expression between the latest Continental developments and native preferences, the English succeeded in working out a compromise that is symbolized by the word *limited*. In government it was a limited monarchy, and in finance the corporation with limited liability. Through the efforts and genius of three men—Wren in architecture, Dryden in literature, and Purcell in music—the Continental influences were absorbed, adapted, mingled with native traditions, and finally merged into a distinctive Restoration style. In the arts, therefore, it was the Baroque, Limited.

ARCHITECTURE

In the crypt beneath St. Paul's Cathedral in London an inscription on a stone slab reads: "Beneath is laid the builder of this church and city, Christopher Wren, who lived more than ninety years, not for himself but for the good of the state. If you seek a monument, look around you." As the observer begins to look around one thing becomes immediately apparent, namely that St. Paul's (Fig. 15:3) has the unique distinction of being the only major cathedral in Europe built during the 35 years of the episcopate of one bishop, by one architect, and one master mason. By way of comparison, it took more than a century, 20 popes, and 13 architects to build St. Peter's in Rome (Fig. 10:18). It is this fortunate circumstance that gives St. Paul's the unity that it enjoys. The last stone on the lantern tower above the dome was put in place by one of Wren's sons in 1710 in the presence of the 78-year-old builder. For another eight years Wren continued to supervise the completion of the decorative details that were then still in progress.

Even before the Great Fire, Wren was a member of a commission charged with the remodeling of the old building. The plan had to be scrapped when a survey after the fire showed the building to be beyond repair. It was this which gave Wren his great opportunity. Like Bramante and Michelangelo before him, Wren envisaged a centralized area of great spaciousness surrounded radially by subsidiary spatial units. Like his predecessors he also wanted to get away from a ground plan laid out in the lengthened form of the Latin cross in favor of a centralized structure based on the more compact Greek cross. In this way a building of such monumental proportions could have both its exterior mass and interior space dominated by the all-embracing unifying force of a dome. From a practical point of view he was also aware that he was designing a Protestant cathedral, which should permit as many people as possible to be within earshot of the pulpit so as to hear the sermon-centered service of the Anglican church of his day.

The conservative members of the clergy, with thoughts of the ancient Catholic processional liturgy in mind, still wanted a long nave with aisles on either side. Wren, therefore, without sacrificing the heart of his plan, lengthened it by adding an apse in the east and a domed vestibule with an extended porch in the west. His model (Fig. 15:5), however, brought further objections on the part of the clergy which made still further revisions necessary. All Wren's tactical skill, his versatility, his ingenuity, and above all his patience were called into play in order to effect a workable compromise that would satisfy his difficult clients and yet save the essence of his cherished conception. He therefore gave the clergy their aisled nave and transepts and their deep choir, but he grouped them around the central plan of his original design. In this way he could still concentrate as much space under the dome as possible. Wren thus was actually building two churches, the clergy's and his own, a procedure that was bound to produce some architectural dissonances but for which he was able to find a satisfactory if somewhat uneasy resolution in the building that was finally completed.

After the diplomatic problems were disposed of, Wren was confronted with many practical difficulties for which his knowledge of science and inventive turn of mind stood him in good stead. First of all, he was handi-

Fig. 15:3 (right). Wren. *St. Paul's Cathedral*, Façade. 1675–1710. London (Courtesy British Travel Association)

Fig. 15:4 (below). *Apse and Choir*, View from the East (Courtesy British Information Services)

Fig. 15:5 (above). Wren. St. Paul's Cathedral, *Perspective View* of the Great Model Design. Engraving by Soane. 1726. Fig. 15:6 (below). *Rotunda*. Aquatint by Thomas Malton. 1798

capped by a difficult site where solid ground was buried beneath 40 feet of clay and sand; and in addition, his funds were severely limited. In order to avoid excessive weight he had to lighten the vaulting of the choir, nave, and transepts by constructing them with the thinner masonry demanded of a series of Byzantine saucer domes resting on pendentives. Even so, their outward thrust had to be counteracted by a row of flying buttresses. Such Gothic details were, however, in his opinion, crude and unsightly, so he concealed them from below by extending the outside walls upward high enough to hide them.

Wren hoped to clear the way for an axial approach to his façade (Fig. 15:3) up Ludgate Hill on which the cathedral rests so that the view would be unimpeded. The property, however, could not be cleared, and even before his building was completed it was cluttered up with the surrounding houses. It actually took the German air force in World War II to clear the land around the sides and choir so that the building could cast a decent shadow (Fig. 15:4). His façade originally called for columns of great height as seen in Figure 15:5. No quarry, however, could supply stone of the necessary dimensions, so the design had to be separated into two stories of the Corinthian and Composite order, the lower of which is barely discernible in Figure 15:3. The use of paired columns recalls that of Perrault's colonnade on the east front of the Louvre (Fig. 13:2). The side turrets were designed after 1700, and it is interesting to take passing note of the fact that one of them was left hollow except for a circular staircase, so that Wren and his fellow astronomers could use it temporarily for an observatory.

Externally the proportions needed a massive dome, while internally one of lesser size would suffice. With the foundations demanding as little weight as possible, Wren's solution was a double dome with a smaller inner shell of brick ingeniously supporting the outer sheath of timber coated with lead, which rises over 275 feet above the ground below. The colonnade around the outer part of the drum functions practically to absorb the lateral thrust of the masonry and decoratively to complete the rhythm of the classical orders that mount upward from below. The clergy still longed for a lofty spire which would dominate the city's skyline as that of Old St. Paul's had done. Wren therefore added a tall lantern tower that soared upward a full 90 feet above the top of his dome.

The effect of Wren's preferred plan is felt most strongly in the rotunda beneath the dome (Fig. 15:6). Geometrically the space is bounded by a gigantic octagon, punctuated at the angles by the eight piers on which the cupola rests. These are bridged over by a ring of contiguous Roman triumphal arches, which, in turn, are crowned by the great dome, the culmination of the entire composition. From this central area the arches open outward into eight spatial subdivisions that give the interior such constant variety and interest. It is this central accent, together with the Roman detail, the complex interplay of spatial volumes, the freedom of the design, and their unification into an integral whole by means of the lofty dome, which combine to place Wren's design within the scope of the Baroque. The restraining influences of the conservative clergy, the lack of unlimited funds, and Wren's rationalistic viewpoint that kept his design from following some of the Continental extravagances of the style and keeping it within what has been defined as the boundaries of the Baroque, Limited.

Wren's plan for the rebuilding of London met with even stiffer resistance than his project for St. Paul's. It included the laying out of a series of new streets that radiated outward starlike from central squares and that took the main traffic routes into consideration. Certain public buildings were to be oriented on an axis involving the new Cathedral and the Royal Exchange. The spires of the various parish churches were to punctuate the silhouette at certain points and by degrees lead up to the grand climax of St. Paul's dome. The plan, if it had been carried out, would have gone far beyond Versailles. But Wren's king was not an absolute monarch with the power to condemn property and the money to buy it. Time also ran against Wren as the shopkeepers were in a hurry to rebuild and start their business concerns again. About all he was able to rescue this time were the steeples of the parish churches he was called upon to design.

As Principal Architect, Wren was commissioned to build more than 50 of these new parish churches. Consultations with the churchwardens on the problems and needs of each church had to be held. Owing to the limited funds at his disposal the churches themselves had of necessity to be rather modest affairs. Wren, in keeping with the spirit of the time, wanted to build them in the restrained Baroque style based on the classical orders. His clients and the Gothic tradition still demanded the spires that not only had the force of symbols but the practical purpose of housing the bell tower, which was still a functional unit of a church. Wren's problem, therefore, was to balance the vertical tendency of the steeple with the horizontality of his classical temple façades. The focal point of the problem was, once more, the reconciliation of the northern and southern building traditions. Wren's solution, which can be counted among his minor miracles, can only be understood in the way he actually handles one of them.

The steeple of St. Mary-le-Bow (Fig. 15:7), where the famous Bow Bells once rang out, shows the mathematician's obvious delight in a free play of geometrical forms. From a solid square base it moves through several

Fig. 15:7 (left). Wren. *St. Mary-le-Bow*, Steeple. 216′ 1″ high. 1671–1680. London (Courtesy British Information Services). Fig. 15:8 (right). Gibbs. *St. Martin-in-the-Fields*. 1722. London (Courtesy British Travel Association)

circular phases and terminates finally in an octagonal pyramid. By the judicious use of Baroque scrolls and twists at various points, this is achieved without a hint of abruptness. Knowing that the churches themselves were bound to be hidden by the proximity of the surrounding buildings, Wren lavished most of his skill on their spires. The continuation of the Wren tradition into the next century is seen in James Gibbs' church of St. Martin-in-the-Fields (Fig. 15:8). Wren had always planted his steeples firmly in the ground, so to speak, so that they seemed to grow in an organic relation to the whole composition. Gibbs' spire, by contrast, appears to sprout unexpectedly out of the roof. The memory of these churches and their steeples was carried all the way to the American colonies by the founding fathers; and when they came to build their own churches in the new cities of Boston and Philadelphia, it was to the designs of Wren and Gibbs that they turned for their models.

Among all his other responsibilities, Wren also found the time to design some commodious houses for well-to-do middle-class clients. During the reign of William and Mary, he was also commissioned to build a new wing for the Hampton Court palace. His patron, William of Orange, remembered the good red brick of his native Holland, while Wren recalled the grandeur of the Louvre and Versailles palaces. Another of Wren's famous compromises was effected in his design for the Fountain Court and the garden façade at Hampton Court (Fig. 15:9).

Fig. 15:9. Wren. *Hampton Court Palace*, Garden Façade. Near London (Courtesy British Travel Association)

Thus it was that the professor of astronomy at London and Oxford left off probing the mysteries of the heavens with his telescope and equations to become, instead, the engineer and architect who penetrated only that segment of the sky above London with the majestic spires and domes that gave the city its characteristic profile and skyline.

DRAMA AND MUSIC

On the gala occasion of the formal opening of the King's Theatre in 1674, His Majesty and London's most distinguished audience gathered there for the evening's entertainment. John Dryden, that cold, aristocratic but brilliant author, took advantage of the situation afforded by the Prologue to express his sentiments in some well-chosen words, which went in part:

> 'Twere folly now a stately pile to raise,
> To build a playhouse while you throw down plays;
> Whilst scenes, machines and empty Operas reign,
> And for the Pencil you the Pen disdain;
> While Troops of famished Frenchmen hither drive,
> And laugh at those upon whose Alms they live:
> Our English Authors vanish, and give place
> To these new Conquerors of the Norman race.[1]

Dryden was thus making the valiant effort of an exasperated man of letters to stem the tide toward the foreign forms of opera which, in his opinion, threatened to engulf reason with rhyme. The course of events, however, was flowing far too strongly; and, to keep from being inundated, he found himself before very long collaborating with one of those fashionable Frenchmen and writing some very fancy "scenes and machines" himself.

With all the adaptability of a thoroughly equipped professional writer, he honestly tried to squeeze some content into those "empty Operas." To help acclimate this exotic form to its new surroundings, he fell back on the tradition of the English court masque, a native equivalent of the French *ballet de cour*, which had set the precedent for the development of opera at the court of Louis XIV. The masque was a hybrid form that included poems, songs, dances, dialogue, and scenic spectacle. During the days of James I, it was none other than Inigo Jones, the famous architect, who had designed the costumes and scenery for these lavish entertainments—and all too often his machines stole the show. Milton's *Comus*, a masque with music by Henry Lawes, had some less-distinguished machines for competition, and lyric poetry was thus able to enjoy a brief triumph.

When Dryden came to write his *Albion and Albianus*, he had to summon all his tactical skill to balance these opposing elements and try to keep them in proper proportion. In his Preface he was more than a little apologetic about having to write so as "to please the hearing rather than gratify the understanding"; and, he continued, "it appears, indeed, preposterous at first sight, that rhyme, on any consideration, should take the place of reason." His solution was to use spoken dialogue for the ordinary mortals in the play, but to include what he called a "songish part" for such super-natural characters as gods, goddesses, and heroes. Their behavior, he observed, "being extended beyond the limits of human nature, admits of that sort of marvelous and surprising conduct, which is rejected in other plays." [2]

This opera of Dryden contains many remarkable scenes and machines. In one, "Mercury descends in a chariot drawn by ravens"; in another, "the clouds divide, and Juno appears in a Machine drawn by Peacocks; while a Symphony is playing"; in yet another, Venus and Albianus rise out of the sea in a great scallop-shell drawn by dolphins to a symphony of "flutes-doux." The stage directions for the final scene read: "Whilst a Symphony is playing, a very large, and very glorious Machine descends; the figure of it oval, all the clouds shining with gold, abundance of Angels and Cherubins flying about them, and playing in them; in the midst of it sits Apollo on a throne of gold; he comes from the machine to Albion." [3]

Dryden's attempt in this instance, in spite of the gaudy machines, was a failure, possibly because it was not sufficiently distinguished from the court masque to be a true opera, but more probably because the music provided by Monsieur Grabu was too mediocre. Though Henry Purcell was already 26 years old, England had to wait almost a decade before it was to have the collaboration of a poet and musician comparable in stature to Molière and Lully in France.

While awaiting the invitation from Dryden to collaborate on *King Arthur*, England's greatest composer had to content himself with writing incidental music to dozens of undistinguished plays. The best of them were Shakespearean adaptations, such as *The Tempest* and *The Fairy Queen* (from *A Midsummer Night's Dream*), which bear only a remote resemblance to the originals. For his one great opportunity in the operatic field, *Dido and Aeneas*, he had to get along with a book by Nahum Tate, whose stature in English letters is several notches below that of his French counterpart Quinault, who was Lully's chief librettist. But there is not a shred of evidence to show that Purcell was unhappy about the situation. The picture of his career is simply that of a professional composer, diligently active at all times, and technically capable of fulfilling any commission which came his way, whether from church, court, or independent sources.

It was through Josias Priest, a dancing master in one of the London theaters, that Purcell received the invitation to write a short opera to be performed at his boarding school for young gentlewomen at Chelsea. Thus it was that sometime between 1688 and 1690, Purcell came to write his little operatic masterpiece for a group of schoolgirls. As such it is a true chamber opera, designed for a limited space and restricted to a limited cast of characters. Though it is small in scale, it is large in its emotional scope; and while it falls within the province of amateur performance, it is filled with the utmost musical sophistication. Its immediate antecedent was *Venus and Adonis*, a three-act chamber opera written about four years before by his teacher John Blow. This charming intimate work had been performed for the entertainment of Charles II and his court circle shortly before the monarch's death. It was one of the few existing through-composed operas in English; otherwise there was only the masque tradition and the Dryden-Grabu experiments to guide him. Purcell, however, was conversant with the latest Continental developments in the operatic field, and it is the piquant blend of these native and foreign elements that give his work its characteristic color and variety.

Dido and Aeneas [4] opens with a dignified overture in the Lully style, marked by the halting rhythms and harmonic suspensions of its slow beginning, and the fugal imitations of its lively conclusion. All the orchestral sections seem to have been scored only for strings with the usual keyboard support. For his recitatives and airs he turns to the models developed by Monteverdi and his successor at the Venetian opera, Cavalli. He makes particularly bold use of the so-called "representative style," a type of word-painting, by which the descriptive imagery of the text is reflected in the shape and turn of the melodic line. This can be illustrated by the first word in the opera, "Shake" (a), and the menacing movement of the line for "storms" (b). When speaking of Aeneas' parentage, the valor of his father

Recitative excerpts from *Dido and Aeneas*   Purcell

Anchises is characterized by a martial rhythm (c); while immediately afterward a modulation to the minor mode and a caressing chromaticism express the voluptuousness of Venus' charms (d); and when Aeneas' entrance is announced, Belinda's words take on the shape of a trumpet fanfare (e).

The airs show a considerable variety as to type. Dido's opening and closing songs are built over a short repeated bass pattern as in the Italian *ostinato aria*. The melody of "Oft She Visits" is written over a continuously flowing bass line in the manner of an Italian *continuo aria;* while the three-part melodic form of "Pursue Thy Conquest, Love," in which the final section is a repetition of the beginning, identifies it as a *da capo aria*.

The emphasis on the choruses and dances is in the English court masque tradition, but they are handled with a highly ingenious blend of native and Continental elements. In the palace scenes, the courtiers function as a true Greek chorus by making solemn comments in unison on the action. The final number, "With Drooping Wings," is a typical French mourning chorus straight out of Lullian opera. The witches, however, sing in the English madrigal style with the amusing substitution of some malicious "Ho, ho, ho's" for the jollier "Fa la la's," so as to signify their sinister purposes. Highly interesting is Purcell's introduction of a Venetian echo chorus in these solemn surroundings. While the witches sing "In Our Deep Vaulted Cell," an off-stage chorus softly echoes "-ed cell." By thus increasing the perception of space, Purcell is able to add the necessary uncanny touch he needs as the witches start to prepare their mysterious charms. The spell is further carried out in the *Echo Dance of Furies*, in which an off-stage instrumental ensemble echoes the principal orchestra with telling effect. The dances show much of the same stylistic mixture as the choruses. Scene I concludes with the courtiers doing a *Triumphing Dance*, which is a vigorous version of a Lully *chaconne* treated as a set of instrumental variations over a ground bass. During Act III, when Aeneas is preparing to sail away from Carthage, Purcell paints a typical English seaport scene in which the swinging sailors' dances mingle with the salty comments of a chorus of common people. The angularity of such native dance rhythms is a distinct contrast to the more formal *courantes* and *chaconnes* that are danced by the courtiers.

Purcell's logic and fine dramatic perception does not permit him to soften his opera toward the end by allowing a *deus ex machina* to bring it to a happy ending in the manner of the French court style of Lully. The human will when contending with the gods is always doomed, and the plot must move inexorably onward. The tragedy is therefore carried through to its predestined conclusion with growing eloquence and mounting emotion. As a consequence, "Dido's Farewell" (below) becomes one of the most moving moments in all music, combining as it does the most passionate feeling with the dignified restraint demanded of a tragic heroine out of Vergil's *Aeneid*. It is cast in the form of an *ostinato aria* with an obstinately repetitive bass figure, which descends chromatically to the rhythm of the stately *passacaglia*. Her inner struggle is expressed by the tension between the free obbligato melodic line that she sings and the inflexible bass, and she contends with this fixed force as with her tragic fate. Vainly she tries to bend it to her will, as seen in some of the assymetrical diagonal shifts of her phrases off their center, but in the end she must resign herself to it while the orchestra carries the aria onward to its tragic conclusion.

Air, "When I am laid in earth," from *Dido and Aeneas*   Purcell

my fate, Re-mem-ber me, but ah!____ for-get my_fate!

Within the limitations of this short opera, which takes but little more than an hour to perform, Purcell produced a major work of art. Though it is his only through-composed piece for the lyric stage, it reveals the sure touch of one who knows every aspect of his dramatic business. The extensive emotional range and the variety of technical devices are all the more astonishing in view of the meager resources he had at his disposal. Purcell possesses, first of all, the rare power to delineate and create believable human characters by musical means, a gift he shares with Gluck and Mozart. He is also one of the few composers who know how to convert the dry academic techniques of counterpoint into lively dramatic devices, a quality he shares with Bach and Handel. This is apparent, for instance, in Dido's first air, "Ah, Belinda." Her melody is like a series of descending sighs over a ground bass that, like destiny, is relentless and unyielding. At the words "Peace and I are strangers grown," the parting of the ways is depicted by a canon at the octave; and on the word "strangers," the predominant four-bar pattern begins to wander and is stretched out into five bars. Again, after Aeneas declares he will defy destiny itself in order to remain with Dido, the chorus makes contrapuntal comments that graphically give expression to their disturbed and conflicting emotions. When Purcell wants to depict the hustle and bustle around the departing ships in the scene at the dockside in Act III, the independent lines of the fugal introduction, with their imitative thematic entries and exits, humorously describe the coming and going of the people. When such skillful means as these are combined with his fanciful orchestration, colorful use of chromaticism, and deep poetic feeling, they are sure to lead to significant ends— as indeed, in this case, they did.

One more chance presented itself to Purcell when Dryden, the literary arbiter of Restoration drama, invited him to collaborate on *King Arthur* in 1691. Dryden in this case was trying to breathe something of the grandiloquence of the French Baroque theater into a patriotic English drama. His Preface shows that he was still groping for a formula to adapt music and poetry to the English lyric stage. His sincere misgivings are apparent when he complains: "I have been obliged to cramp my Verses, and make them rugged to the Reader, that they may be harmonious to the Hearer." Like a good rationalist, he was also worried about writing a play "principally designed for the Ear and Eye," rather than for the mind. He still felt that the human characters should speak and that only the superhuman ones should sing. In this parenthetical way the music could be made to sound more plausible and thus not seem like an intrusion into the course of the dramatic sequence. Fortunately for Purcell there were so many superhuman characters that his score assumed very ample proportions. *King Arthur* was a truly distinguished attempt to solve the problem of English opera; and, in its way, it was still another typically English compromise, since it was neither an opera nor a play but a compound of elements drawn from both. If this collaboration had continued, it might eventually have led to a distinctive English form of the music drama. As it stands, it remains a noble but somewhat inconclusive experiment.

In spite of Purcell's sparing but convincing use of the sung recitative, and his efforts to extract the essence out of Monteverdi's representative style by removing some of the Italian bombast in order to render it palatable to London audiences, recitative simply did not take root, and the through-composed opera remained an exotic plant on English soil. As the *Gentlemen's Journal* of January 1692 put it, "Experience hath taught us that our English genius will not rellish that perpetual singing."

A judicious comparison between the three great figures of the Restoration style—Wren, Dryden, and Purcell—can be highly illuminating. Each in his way was trying to bring his country up to date on the latest Continental developments, just as each was trying to inject something of the grandeur of the Baroque style into English art forms. In order to do it, each was willing to make the necessary compromises so as not to part company with English audiences. When Wren was designing his preferred models on his drawing board, when Dryden was writing solely for his readers, and when Purcell was composing experimentally for amateurs, each could be as free as he chose. But when it came to building a cathedral, mounting a play, and composing music for the theater, many subtle and even drastic adjustments had to be made. Each had sufficient mastery in his field and each was sufficiently versatile and inventive to make those adjustments. Each preferred and developed an aristocratic style but never neglected the common touch. Each in his turn had an effect on posterity that lasted well into the next century. Wren's buildings became the backbone of the Georgian style; Dryden's works, the background for 18th-century classicism in English letters; and the fact that many of Purcell's works have until recently been thought to be by Bach and Handel is proof enough that they were absorbed directly into the sacred and secular music of the succeeding generation.

IDEAS

Baroque Rationalism

Stimulated by the explorations of the navigators of the globe, the scanning of the skies by the astronomers, and the ingenuity of the inventors, Baroque man came to have a new concept of himself and his place in the universe. Galileo's telescope confirmed and popularized Copernicus' theory of a solar system in which the earth revolved around the sun rather than vice versa. The concept of the static Aristotelean universe thus had to yield to one which was full of whirling motion. Since the earth was no longer considered as a fixed point located at the nerve center of the cosmos, man could hardly be regarded any longer as the sole purpose of creation. It was some consolation, however, to know that this strange new moving universe was at least subject to mechanical and mathematical laws, and therefore to a considerable extent predictable. Copernicus and Kepler as well as the other scientists were convinced of its unity, proportion, and harmony; and the fact that man had the privilege of probing into the secrets of nature, if his intellect proved equal to the task, was a highly exhilarating thought. The rationalism of the 17th century, then, was based on the view that the universe could at last be understood in logical, mathematical, and mechanical terms. As a philosophy and semireligion, this viewpoint had far-reaching consequences by preparing the pathway for the theories of positivism and materialism, the doctrines of deism and atheism, and the mechanical and industrial revolutions.

While Greek rationalism had been based on the perception and measurement of a static world, Baroque rationalism had to come to terms with a dynamic universe. Scientific thought was concerned with movement in space and time. The need for a mathematics capable of comprehending a world of matter in motion led Descartes to his analytical geometry, Pascal to a study of cycloid curves, and both Leibniz and Newton to the simultaneous discovery of integral and differential calculus. Baroque invention led to refinements in navigation, improvements in the telescope and microscope for the exploration of distant and minute regions of space, the barometer for the measurement of air pressure, the thermometer for the recording of temperature changes, and the anemometer for the calculation of the force of winds. Astronomers were occupied with the study of planetary motion; William Harvey discovered the circulation of the blood in the human body; and physicists were making speculations in the field of thermodynamics and gravitation.

Newton's preoccupation with mass, force, and momentum, his speculations on the principles of attraction and repulsion, and his calculations on terrestrial and celestial mechanics led him to a monumental synthesis that he presented to the British Royal Society in 1686 and published in London a year later. Newton's *Principia* embraced a complete and systematic view of an orderly world based on mechanical principles, capable of mathematical proof, and demonstrable by accurate prediction. His work was, in fact, a scientific *summa* that established the intellectual architecture of the new view of the universe.

Such a changed world view was bound to have important consequences on the arts, which responded in this case with a ringing reassertion of man's supremacy and a joyous acceptance of this new understanding of the universe. The application of rationalistic principles to aesthetic expression is by no means accidental or casual. Before he became an architect, Christopher Wren was a mechanical inventor, an experimental scientist, and a professor of astronomy at London and Oxford. As one of the founders of the Royal Society, he was in close communication with such men as Robert Boyle and Isaac Newton. The fellows of the Royal Society appointed John Dryden to a committee whose purpose was to study the English language with a view toward linguistic reforms. They recommended that English prose should have both purity and brevity, so that verbal communication could be brought as close to mathematical plainness and precision as possible. Dryden's embarrassment in writing an opera that was designed to please the ear rather than gratify the understanding was therefore quite understandable. Purcell's music likewise was based on a system of intricate contrapuntal principles and tonal logic in which certain given premises, as in a sequence for instance, are followed by predictable conclusions. His music, moreover, is characterized by intellectual discipline, symmetry, clarity, and a sure sense of direction. His forms are models of brevity in which each part has its proper place, no loose ends are left dangling around, and his cadences bring everything to a positive conclusion. Together with Wren's architecture and Dryden's poetic drama, Purcell's music reflects a buoyant self-confidence, an inventive spirit that gave birth to new forms, an exploration of novel optical and acoustical ideas, and a conviction that a work of art should in its way be a reflection of an orderly and lawful universe.

CONCLUSION

While the Baroque period generally falls within the 17th century, its extreme temporal limits extend all the way from Michelangelo to Johann Sebastian Bach. During this time the concept of the world had moved from a terracentric to a heliocentric universe; philosophical speculation turned from a supernatural to a natural world view; the fundamental processes of thought shifted from the acceptance of authority on faith to scientific experimentation; the unity of Christianity symbolized by one universal Church dissolved into a number of Protestant sects; and the theoretical political unity of the Holy Roman Empire gave way to the practical fact of a balance of power distributed among a family of nations. The Baroque period was one in which irresistible modern forces met immovable traditional objects. Out of the resulting theological disputations, philosophical discussions, scientific arguments, social tensions, political strife, and warring nations, both the Baroque style and the modern age were born.

The Baroque world was one in which irreconcilable oppositions had to find a way of coexistence. The rise of rationalism was accompanied by the march of militant mysticism; the aristocratic cult of majesty was echoed by the bourgeois cult of domesticity; the international viewpoint of Roman Catholicism was in conflict with the nationalism of the Protestant sects; religious orthodoxy had to contend with freedom of thought; the Jesuits brought all the arts into their churches, while Calvin did his utmost to exclude them; Philip II built a palatial mausoleum and monastery, while Louis XIV erected a pleasure palace and theater; Charles I tried to force an absolute monarchy on England, and Cromwell's answer was a republican commonwealth; the printing press made books available, while suppression by censorship took them away; the boldest scientific speculation took place alongside a reassertion of the belief in miracles and a renewal of religious fundamentalism; Newton's *Principia* and the final part of Bunyan's *Pilgrim's Progress* appeared in London within two years of each other. In Spain the emotional involvement of El Greco was succeeded by the optical detachment of Velásquez; in France the spontaneity of Rubens was followed by the academic formalism of Poussin; in Holland the freedom of Rembrandt led to the restraint of Vermeer.

Such oppositions could hardly be expected to resolve themselves into a single uniform style. At best they could achieve a state of uneasy equilibrium and a fusion of forms such as that found in a Counter-Reformation church, the Versailles Palace, Rembrandt's visual dramatization of the Bible, or Purcell's operatic synthesis. In them forceful striving and restless motion are more characteristic than serenity and repose. Baroque art thus emerges from this struggle and speaks in eloquent accents of the expanding range of human activities, grandiose achievements, and a ceaseless search for new and more powerful means of expression.

All this took place within the framework of a tremendously enlarged sense of space. The astronomers told of remote regions populated by an infinite number of stars. Pascal speculated on the mathematical implications of infinity. The gardens and avenues of Versailles were laid out in keeping with this vastly extended conception of space. The vistas led the eye toward the horizon and invited the imagination to continue beyond. The unification of the vast buildings and gardens there placed Baroque man wholly within the scope of nature and declared him to be a part of the new measurable universe. Wren's attempt to bring his cathedral, parish churches, and public buildings into one all-embracing scheme was also in keeping with this image of the comprehensive Baroque universe. Painters likewise delighted in leading the eye outside their pictures and attempted to convey the impression of infinity through the bold use of light and exaggerated perspective effects. The Dutch landscapists tried to capture atmospheric perspective, and Rembrandt was concerned with the infinite gradations of light. Through use of illusionistic effects ceilings of Counter-Reformation churches tried to promote the feeling of a world without end.

In music there was a corresponding expansion of tonal space. The organs and other keyboard instruments were built to encompass a wider range from bass to soprano. Both the wind as well as the stringed instruments were constructed in families, ranging all the way from what Orlando Gibbons called the "Great Dooble Base" to the high soprano register of the violin. Louis XIV and Charles II incorporated this string family into ensembles of twenty-four viols, thus increasing both the resonance and volume of sound through the doubling process. The coming into use of chromatic harmony with all the half-tone divisions of the octave was the internal extension of the same idea. Purcell's opposition between his ground basses and soprano melodies emphasized the Baroque love of a spacious distribution of sonorities. His adoption of the Venetian double chorus and his dramatic use of the echo effect in *Dido and Aeneas* was still further evidence of the desire to increase the perception of space through sound and to use it for expressive purposes.

Above all, the Baroque universe was in ceaseless movement. Whether a rationalist thought of it in terms of whirling particles or a mystic as full of swirling spirits, both saw their world as a vortex of spheres and spirals describing infinitely complex patterns of motion. Kepler's planets revolved in elliptical orbits; Counter-Reformation churches were built over undulating floor plans; their walls rippled like stage curtains; the decorative profusion of their façades further activated the static masses and increased their rhythmic pulsation; under their domes terra-cotta angels flew in parabolas; the unyielding stone of the statuary finally rose off the ground and melted into a myriad of fluid forms; paintings escaped from their flat wall spaces up to the more congenial concave surfaces of the ceilings, where they could soar skyward and where more daring perspective effects were possible. Baroque music also mirrored this moving universe. Its restless forms took on the color of this dynamic age, and its sound patterns floated freely through their tonal spaces unencumbered by gravitational laws. No longer in bondage to religious ritual, to the dance, or to poetry, its emancipation was now complete. Of such ideas and materials was the image of this brave new Baroque world constructed.

C H A P T E R

CHRONOLOGY: 18th-century Panorama

General Events

1715   Death of Louis XIV
1715–1774   Reign of Louis XV
1726   *Gulliver's Travels* published by Jonathan Swift
1728   *The Beggar's Opera* by John Gay (1685–1732) performed in London
1740–1780   Reign of Empress Maria Theresa of Austria
1740–1786   Reign of King Frederick the Great of Prussia
1744   Building of the Schönbrunn Palace in Vienna resumed after having been begun in 1696 by Fischer von Erlach
1748   *Spirit of Laws* published
     Excavations at Pompeii begun
1751–1772   *Encyclopedia,* or *A Classified Dictionary of Sciences, Arts and Trades* published serially by Diderot
1752   *Guerre des Bouffons,* the war in Paris over serious versus comic opera
1759   *Candide* published by Voltaire
1762   *Social Contract* published by J. J. Rousseau
     Gluck's *Orpheus* performed in Vienna
1762–1796   Reign of Empress Catherine the Great of Russia
1774–1792   Reign of Louis XVI
1774   Gluck's *Orpheus* and *Iphigenia in Aulis* performed in Paris
1775   Beaumarchais' play *Barber of Seville* presented in Paris
1776   American Declaration of Independence
     Sturm und Drang (Storm and Stress), a play by Maximilian von Klinger (1752–1831), which gave its name to the art movement, written
1780–1790   Reign of Emperor Joseph II of Austria
1781   Mozart settled in Vienna
     Critique of Pure Reason published by Kant
1784   Beaumarchais' play *Marriage of Figaro* presented

1786   *Marriage of Figaro* by Mozart performed in Vienna
1787   *Don Giovanni* by Mozart performed in Prague, in Vienna the next year
1789   French Revolution begun
1790   *Faust, A Fragment* published by Goethe in Leipzig
1794   *Progress of the Human Spirit* published by Condorcet
1797   *Sense and Sensibility* written by Jane Austen (1775–1817); published in 1811

Architecture

1599–1667   Francesco Borromini
1650–1723   Fischer von Erlach
c.1660–1726   Jakob Prandtauer
1668–1745   Lukas von Hildebrandt

Painting

1684–1721   Watteau
1697–1764   Hogarth
1699–1779   Chardin
1703–1770   Boucher
1725–1805   Greuze
1732–1806   Fragonard

Sculpture

1716–1791   Falconet
1738–1814   Clodion
1741–1828   Houdon

Music

1683–1764   Rameau
1685–1750   J. S. Bach
1685–1756   G. F. Handel
1688–1733   Couperin (Le Grand)
1714–1787   C. W. Gluck
1714–1788   C. P. E. Bach
1732–1809   Joseph Haydn
1756–1791   W. A. Mozart

Literature and Philosophy

1667–1745   Swift
1689–1761   Richardson
1694–1778   Voltaire
1698–1782   Metastasio
1707–1754   Fielding
1712–1778   J. J. Rousseau
1713–1784   Diderot
1724–1804   Kant
1728–1774   Goldsmith
1729–1781   Lessing
1732–1799   Beaumarchais
1744–1803   Herder
1749–1832   Goethe
1749–1838   Da Ponte
1759–1805   Schiller

16

THE 18th-CENTURY STYLES

THE 18th-CENTURY PANORAMA

The momentum of the Baroque style had sufficient force to propel it well into the 18th century. New social dynamics, new constellations of ideas, new aesthetic currents came together to bring about a confluence of the main Baroque streams in some cases and the formation of new ones in others. With the death of Louis XIV in 1715 the aristocratic Baroque style moved into its final Rococo phase. The regent for his young successor closed the majestic Versailles Palace and re-established the royal residence in Paris. Artistic patronage was no longer the monopoly of the court but spread to the fashionable society of Paris, which included the upper bourgeoisie as well as the urban aristocracy. The painter Watteau, who arrived in Paris the same year the Sun King died, had to look for his patrons among a broad group drawn from the ranks of both the nobility and the middle class. Throughout the century the operas of Rameau, Gluck, and Mozart were composed for public opera houses where aristocrats rubbed shoulders with the bourgeoisie. The arts in effect moved out of the marble halls into the elegant salons where finesse and charm were considered higher aesthetic virtues than impressiveness and grandeur.

This latter-day manifestation of the aristocratic style was by no means confined to Paris. All European courts assumed in some degree the character of cultural suburbs of Versailles. French fashions in architecture, painting, furniture, costume, and manners were echoed in such far-off corners as the courts of Catherine the Great of Russia and Maria Theresa in Vienna. Whether a prince ruled a province in Poland or a duchy in Denmark, French was spoken in his household more naturally than the language of his native country. In Prussia Frederick the Great built a Rococo palace at Potsdam and called it *Sans-souci*, the king of Saxony com-

573

missioned the jewellike Zwinger Palace in Dresden, and the Prince-Bishop erected a handsome residence in Würzburg. French authors, such as Voltaire and Jean Jacques Rousseau, found an international reading public; French dances dominated the balls; and French plays the theaters. In southern Germany and Austria, however, Italian influence was still strong. At the court of Vienna an Italian architect finished the Schönbrunn Palace for Maria Theresa; Italian paintings decorated its walls; Metastasio was the poet laureate and opera librettist; and only plays and operas in Italian could be performed in the royal theaters. The missionary zeal of the Jesuits working outward from Rome spread and popularized the ecclesiastical counterpart of the aristocratic style wherever the Counter-Reformation could gain a footing.

Baroque rationalism had remained restricted to a relatively few eminent minds. In the 18th century, however, as the scientific knowledge of Newton and the social theories of John Locke became the common property of the educated classes, rationalism broadened into the movement known as the *Enlightenment,* a term—like the *Rococo*—generally referring to the period between 1715 and 1789. Here the streams of rationalism and academicism converged, and the most characteristic expression of the Enlightenment is the *Encyclopédie,* which was edited by Denis Diderot. In this *Classified Dictionary of the Sciences, Arts, and Trades,* the outstanding intellects of the time collected and made available in clear language all the knowledge that had heretofore existed only in difficult scientific tracts. Trade secrets that for centuries had been the closely guarded property of the guilds and a few master craftsmen now appeared in print. Knowledge that had in the 17th century remained for the most part in the realm of pure science began to be applied to the solution of practical problems. Middle-class manufacturers saw the commercial usefulness of Baroque inventiveness and turned it toward the production of wealth.

The fruits of rationalism became the common property of the middle class, but in the vocabulary of the 18th century, reason by no means implied only cold intellectuality. It was thought of as a faculty shared by all who chose to cultivate it. Among its implications were common sense, exercise of good judgment, and the development of taste, all of which were accompanied by a healthy involvement in active human pursuits. As applied to the arts, reason meant the search for expressive forms and sentiments of sufficient universality and validity to be accepted by all who subscribed to the principles of good taste and judgment. With the broadening of the bases of wealth and education, the middle class was able to rise and challenge the ancient authority and prerogatives of the aristocracy. Through the power of knowledge released by the Enlightenment, the age-old shackles of superstition, intolerance, and fear began to be thrown off. The ideals of freedom it engendered were eventually written into the American Declaration of Independence and Bill of Rights and became the moving force behind the French Revolution. More and more it was now the middle class who wrote and read the books, who built and lived in the buildings, who painted and bought the pictures, and who composed and listened to the music.

The philosophy of the Enlightenment did not, however, go unchallenged, as is evidenced by the trend toward irrationalism found in a number of scattered movements which presaged 19th-century Romanticism. Just as the more emotional approaches to religion emphasized revelation, in literature and the other arts intuition came to be considered a higher human faculty than reason. In England such novelists as Fielding told their tales in the first person, a device designed to promote greater subjectivity of feeling on the part of their readers and a break with the Enlightenment ideal of viewing events with objective detachment. A similar opposition is implied in the title and the two principal characters of Jane Austen's novel, *Sense and Sensibility*. In France it was Rousseau who gave the movement its emotional tone. Here it was expressed in the admiration for *sensibilité*, which meant a free exercise of the sympathetic nerves even if it led in directions quite contrary to reason. In its literature the poor were always nature's noblemen in proud possession of a few paternal acres, living by the honest sweat of their brows, constantly having their peace of mind disturbed by the intrusion of material progress, which usually appeared in the guise of an elegant city slicker. In Germany it burst out in the more violent form of the so-called Storm-and-Stress movement. This group made a rather personal interpretation of Rousseau's initial statement in his *Social Contract:* "Man is born free, and everywhere he is in chains." Goethe's characterizations of Faust and Prometheus and Mozart's Don Giovanni were independent human beings, who defied the gods of convention and demanded a gamut of inner and outer experience, even if they had to pay the penalty of eternal torment. The truth they sought was one of feeling rather than logic, and their curiosity was insatiable. By bursting the bonds of civilized restraints they were in full rebellion against middle-class morality as well as ancient privilege and prerogative. Their freedom was far from that of the age of reason; it was in fact an anti-rationalistic, anti-universal, powerfully pro-individualistic freedom that bordered on destructiveness and anarchy.

The 18th century as a whole was marked by a quickening of the pulse in human affairs. The flood of material from the printing presses alone made it all but impossible to keep up with the pace set in philosophy, literature, and music. The spread of wealth led to the development of urban centers and widespread building projects. Writers, painters, and musicians no longer aimed their output exclusively at one social group. While it is usually called the Age of Reason, the 18th century gave birth to some of the most bizarre and irrational beings, real or imaginary, ever to populate the planet or the mind. While the passionate disputes begun in the 17th century were continued, the divisions on the surface at least did not appear to be so sharp. The irreconcilable oppositions of the Baroque were softened into sarcastic satires, gentle ironies, witty repartee, and wistful melancholies. What appeared as a period of comparative quiescence, however, was but the calm before the storm, the prelude to a social explosion that brought the aristocratic Rococo to a violent revolutionary end, but which catapulted the forces of reason and emotion it had generated into the next century.

LES JARDINS DE BACHUS

Fig. 16:1. Watteau. *Drawing*, after an engraving by Huquier. 10¼″ x 15″. Cooper Union Museum, New York

Fig. 16:2. Erlach and Paccassi. *Schönbrunn Palace*, Salon. 1760–1780. Vienna (Courtesy Austrian Information Service, New York)

THE ROCOCO

The name *Rococo* apparently was a pun on *Barocco*, the Italian word for Baroque, alluding to the *rocailles* and *coquilles*, or rocks and shells, which were so widely used as decorative motives in the style. As such it must be considered as a modification or variation of the Baroque rather than in opposition to it. Its effect is more that of a domesticated Baroque, better suited to fashionable town houses than palace halls, though it was used in both. It was mainly an interior style adapted to the small salons where intimate groups could gather tête a tête and match their wits in the subtle art of conversation. The Rococo was not confined to the major arts but could apply to any interior feature from the graceful curves of a table leg to the gilded scroll tracery of a ceiling design. Quite typical of the time is a drawing by Watteau (Fig. 16:1) that makes prominent use of the shell motive. It is seen here as an engraving, but the design could be used for the paneling of a room, a wall paper, a terra-cotta relief finished in white and gold, a piece of tapestry, a mantlepiece, a needlepoint piece for the back of a chair, and so on. When a Rococo interior like that in the Schönbrunn Palace in Vienna (Fig. 16:2) is compared with one from the time of Louis XIV (Fig. 13:7), the difference becomes at once apparent. Where the Baroque was ponderous, massive, and overwhelming, the Rococo is delicate, light, and charming. Monumentality is succeeded by finesse, stateliness by elegance, the pompous purples and golds by modulated pastel shades.

In the Belvedere Palace in Vienna (Fig. 16:3) the decorative impulse can be seen as it bursts out of doors into a lavish exterior design. Details that the French architects had for the most part confined to interiors are here found on the garden façade of a summer palace built in 1713 by Lukas von Hildebrandt for Prince Eugene of Savoy. Palladian restraint has been cast to the four winds. On either side of the second-story windows some highly ornate Composite pilasters can be found, and over the portal some grotesque caryatid figures are grouped in a balletlike formation. Otherwise the architectural orders as points of reference have all but disappeared. The angular repose of the temple pediments and window brackets of the academic style has dissolved into a flowing pattern of undulating curves and broken rhythms.

Fig. 16:3. Hildebrandt. *Belvedere Palace*, South Front. 1713. Vienna (Courtesy Austrian Information Service, New York)

Much the same evolution took place in the Austrian Counter-Reformation churches. Fischer von Erlach, who studied in Rome with Bernini, exercised considerable restraint in his design for the Karlskirche in Vienna (Fig. 16:4). Not only was it dedicated to the same saint, Carlo Borromeo, as the Baroque church of San Carlo alle Quattro Fontane in Rome (Fig. 16:5), which was finished in 1667, but Borromini's masterpiece had a direct influence on Erlach's thinking. His façade shows the same tendency to break up a flat surface so as to allow for a sculpturesque play of light and shadow varying with the time of day, and it is in full motion. From side to side there is a swelling of the convex and concave masses—forward and backward from the Corinthian portico to the depth of the elongated oval dome, and upward and downward with the spiral lines of the twin bell towers in the form of Trajanesque columns.

The Counter-Reformation fusion of the arts in order to produce mystical-emotional excitement is well exemplified in the Abbey Church at Melk in Lower Austria (Fig. 16:6). In its colorful interior, designed by a Viennese theater architect, red marble columns writhe upward in serpentine spirals. All the other decorative details combine to carry out this sense of heightened motion. A climax is reached in the choir loft and ceiling (Fig. 16:7), where the tones of the organ mingle with the concealed chorus and float upward past the terra-cotta angels perching precariously on carved clouds, to a point where the eye is lost in the vast atmospheric perspective of the ceiling mural.

The Rococo painter par excellence was Antoine Watteau. A quick comparison of *The Music Party* (Fig. 16:8), an example of his *fêtes galantes* style, with a bombastic Lebrun canvas (Fig. 13:17), or the sensuous *Garden of Love*, by Rubens (Fig. 13:13) will reveal the earmarks of the new idiom. The dimensions of the pictures alone tell their story, since Watteau was painting for the drawing room rather than the grand gallery. Watteau was both a fellow countryman of Rubens and an ardent admirer of his art. In his pictures, however, Rubens' massive figures are reduced to lithe and slender proportions. They are animated with movement, but Rubens' bacchanalian furies now dance the graceful minuet. With Watteau the effect is capricious rather than monumental, and the spirit vivacious rather than voluptuous.

In *The Music Party* (Fig. 16:8) a group has gathered on a terrace for a pleasant afternoon of musical instruction. The 'cello has been laid aside, the score is still open, and the lady who has just had her lesson lets her elbow rest on her guitar. The music master is tuning his theorbo before beginning to play, and a gentle melancholy mood settles over the company

Fig. 16:4 (above). Erlach. *Karlskirche*, Façade. 1715–1737. Vienna (Courtesy Austrian State Tourist Department)

Fig. 16:5 (left). Borromini. *San Carlo alle Quattro Fontane*, Façade. 1662–1667. Rome (Alinari)

Fig. 16:6 (above). Prandtauer. *Abbey Church*. 1702–1736. Melk, Austria. Fig. 16:7 (below).
Interior, showing Choir Loft and Organ (Courtesy Austrian Information Service, New York)

in anticipation. The music teacher was an established character in 18th-century life. Bazile in Beaumarchais' *Barber of Seville* was helpful to the young ladies in carrying on their amorous intrigues and always stood by considerately to console them with sweet music when things turned out badly. Misty languorous landscapes are very important in conveying Watteau's elusive moods. As in the pastoral novels of the time, elegant ladies and their equally elegant lovers stroll at their leisure through lush gardens in fancied emulation of the life of Arcadian shepherds. Watteau handles such scenes with a characteristic lightness of touch, jewellike color, and a delicacy of nuance that set the tone for the later development of the Rococo style.

Fig. 16:8. Watteau. *The Music Party.* 25½″ x 36¼″. Wallace Collection, London

Boucher, the favorite painter of Mme. Pompadour, worked in a gayer vein than Watteau. The *Toilet of Venus* (Fig. 16:9) shows the 18th-century boudoir ideal of feminine charm in all its artificiality. Love is no longer the robust passion it was with Rubens but a sophisticated flirtation. Voluptuous womanhood is replaced by slender girlish forms. Fragonard was Boucher's successor as the leading exponent of the French Rococo. *The Swing* (Fig. 16:10), which was done for a young aristocrat, reveals the pleasure-seeking preoccupation of his class. The artist's fine feeling for color and the masterly draftsmanship with which he handles his diagonal composition saves it from the twin perils of preciousness and triviality. Much the same spirit animates the sculpture of Clodion. The possibility of quick modeling in clay made the terra-cotta medium well suited for capturing the fleeting rhythms of a Bacchic dance. The relief on a monumental urn (Fig. 16:11) and terra-cotta figurines, such as the *Nymph and Satyr* (Fig. 16:12), were much franker in their eroticism than the paintings of the period.

Fig. 16:9. Boucher. *The Toilet of Venus.* 42⅝" x 33½". 1746. Metropolitan Museum, New York

Fig. 16:10. Fragonard. *The Swing*. 32″ x 25½″. *c*.1766–1769. Wallace Collection, London

Fig. 16:11. Clodion. *Monumental Urn*, Detail. Marble. 52⅛″ high x 38″ wide. 1782. National Gallery, Washington, D. C.

Fig. 16:12. Clodion. *Nymph and Satyr*. Terra cotta. 23¼″ high. Metropolitan Museum, New York

THE BOURGEOIS INFLUENCE

While the aristocrats were still powerful as leaders of fashion and arbiters of taste, their influence was on the wane, and the word of the middle class began to carry more weight. Their wealth not only put the means of patronage in their pockets, but through education they were speaking more and more in the accents of a cultured class. In France many of Watteau's pictures were painted for their walls, and in England the clientele for Hogarth's drawings and engravings came mostly from their ranks. The vast majority of Voltaire's and Rousseau's readers were members of the middle class, while the novels of Richardson, Fielding, and Goldsmith were aimed at this growing reading public. Lessing's *Miss Sara Sampson* (1755) and Diderot's *The Natural Son* (1757) established the German and French bourgeois drama. The collective patronage of the concert hall replaced that of the restricted court circle. Instead of aiming to please one patron, the composer and virtuoso now tried to win the favor of the many. Mozart, for instance, felt strong enough to break with his tyrannical archbishop and set up shop as an independent composer; and it is far from an accident that his great opera *Don Giovanni* was commissioned for the municipality of Prague rather than the royal capital of Vienna.

One of Watteau's most significant pictures was painted for M. Gersaint, a Paris art dealer. During a period of inactivity his sponsor suggested that he do a signboard for his shop (Fig. 16:13). Watteau idealized his friend to the extent of showing him as the proprietor of a gallerylike showroom filled with the fashionable élite of Parisian society, though such was not the case at the time. Sometime after the middle of the century the picture was cut in half. On the right Gersaint is extolling the virtues of a Watteaulike painting to a lady and gentleman who view it through their lorgnettes. On the left the packing of pictures after the sale is in progress. The same middle-class spirit can be found in the virtuous and sober subjects chosen by Chardin; and the titles, *Innocence, Reading the Bible, The Village Wedding,* reveal the substance of the pictures of Greuze. Such family scenes had more sentimental than artistic value, but they satisfied Diderot's injunction that art should praise virtue and condemn vice. This earnestness of Greuze is carried even further in *The Father's Curse* and the *Return of the Prodigal Son,* where the borderline area of moral uplift ends and that of hypocrisy begins.

As might be expected, bourgeois sculptural expression was primarily in the domain of portraiture. Houdon's fine feeling for individuality assured him of pre-eminence in this field, and any number of famous 18th-century personalities sat for him including George Washington, Benjamin Franklin,

Fig. 16:13. Watteau. *Gersaint's Signboard.* Left half, 5′ 3⅞″ x 4′ 10⅞″; right half, 5′ 3⅞″ x 5′ ½″. 1720–1721. Charlottenburg Palace, Berlin (Archives Photographiques)

Fig. 16:14. Houdon. *Bust of Voltaire*. Marble. 20″ high. 1781. Victoria and Albert Museum, London

Thomas Jefferson, John Paul Jones, and Robert Fulton. His bust of Voltaire (Fig. 16:14) is one of several portraits he did of the famous French philosopher and dramatist. By the tilt of the head and the humorous gleam of the eye, he captures the bemused look of the philosopher as he ponders and discourses on the foibles and follies of his fellow mortals. To chisel a glance of amiable skepticism in marble is no small feat. By leaving a rough edge in the outline of the pupil of the eye a special glint is produced which gives just the desired effect. By such means he achieves a speaking likeness in which, during a fleeting moment of animated conversation, the philosopher might just have coined one of his famous epigrams.

The English painter William Hogarth must be reckoned among the distinguished company of 18th-century social satirists. His series of six pictures entitled *Marriage à-la-Mode*, like Swift's *Gulliver's Travels*, John Gay's *Beggar's Opera*, and Voltaire's *Candide*, was a merciless exposé of the conditions and customs of his time, tempered by the saving grace of a brilliant wit. As Dickens and Zola, Goya and Daumier were to do in the less-humorous 19th century, Hogarth dramatized the conditions he saw and issued a challenge to society to do something about it. In this case it is the evil of putting human beings on the auction block of marriage. *The Marriage Contract* (Fig. 16:15) introduces the characters as in the first scene of a play. The gouty nobleman points with pride to the family pedigree as he is about to sell his social standing in the person of his son to pay off the mortgage on his ancestral estate. The merchant, who is marrying off his daughter, scrutinizes the settlement through his spectacles just as he would any other hard-driven bargain. The pawns in this game—the future bride and groom—sit with their backs to each other while the lawyer flatters the future Lady Squanderfield and her fiancé consoles himself with a pinch of snuff.

The other five scenes show the unhappy consequences of this loveless union as it progresses from boredom and frivolity to infidelities, a duel, and death. In *The Countess' Dressing Room* (Fig. 16:16), Lady Squanderfield entertains some of her fine-feathered friends while making her morning toilet. Counselor Silvertongue, her lover, reads his latest amorous verses, while an Italian barber dresses her hair, a servant passes cups of chocolate, a fencing master snores, a little Moorish slave points gleefully to the horns on his doll, and a grotesquely fat singer and his lean flute-playing accompanist add to the general din. The singer is considered to be Carestini, the famous castrato, who sang the feminine leads in Handel's Italian operas.

This and such other series as the *Harlot's Progress* and the *Rake's Progress* were first painted, then issued by subscription in the form of copper engravings. The prints were widely sold, and this type of group patronage made them financially successful. Horace Walpole likened them to Molière's plays, and Charles Lamb said: "other pictures we see, Hogarth's we read." The series was indeed managed in the manner of chapters in a novel; and, since they were done for a public whose primary responses were literary, Hogarth knew that his audience expected a picture to have narrative content. Based as they are on an intimate knowledge of London, the stories are told with a zest for life which saves them from cynicism. Every detail in his crowded rooms is both a commentary on the action,

Fig. 16:15 (above). Hogarth. *The Marriage Contract*. 27″ x 35″. Fig. 16:16 (below). Hogarth. *The Countess' Dressing Room*. 27″ x 35″. Scene I and Scene IV from *Marriage à-la-Mode*. 1744. Tate Gallery, London (Courtesy British Information Services)

and on the taste of his time. In addition to their biting satire, Hogarth's draftsmanship and sense of composition give his pictures substance in their own right.

THE MOZARTIAN SYNTHESIS

Mozart's most mature music was written during the last decade of his life as a resident of Vienna. While he continued to compose chamber music for aristocratic salons, an occasional chamber opera for the Schönbrunn Palace, and German *Singspiele* (comic operas) for the popular musical theater, his art attains its most universal expression in the works he created for the public opera houses and concert halls where noblemen and commoners gathered together for their mutual recreation. It was here that his musical cosmopolitanism found its widest scope; here that he could explore the endless variety of tragic and comic situations that give his operas their boundless humanity; and here that his dramatic power could make its greatest impact. It is also these qualities that were carried over into the less direct and more abstract form of his symphonies and concertos and that give them their particular dramatic intensity.

As a highly impressionable child, guided by a wise father, Mozart had been piloted around the important musical centers, met the most eminent composers, and absorbed all the current ideas. In London he came under the sway of Christian Bach, one of the sons of the prolific Johann Sebastian. His generation had reacted to that of J. S. Bach and Handel much as the French painters had done to Rubens and Lebrun, and their music spoke in the gentler accents of the *gallant style* rather than in the more muscular rhythms and massive sonorities of the Baroque. In Paris he was introduced to the Rococo keyboard style, that art of the elegant trifle expressed in tinkling bon-bons for the ear. He also made his first contact there with the operas of Gluck, from which he learned his deep regard for dramatic truth and to eliminate everything except that which was germane to the unfolding of the plot. In Italy he came to know the full beauty of the human voice and the all-persuasive quality of Latin lyricism. In Mannheim he heard the finest orchestra in Europe and was struck by the lightning of its dynamic crescendos and diminuendos as well as the brilliance of its wind instruments. In Vienna he learned from Joseph Haydn how to divine the soul of the orchestra and to explore the full expressive possibilities of the symphonic form. From first-hand contact he had discovered the idioms of the Neapolitan *opera seria*, Pergolesi's *opera buffa*, Rousseau's pastoral opera, and the German *Singspiel*. The spirit of the Enlightenment can be seen in the logical clarity and constructive unity of his forms; his letters show his enthusiasm for Rousseauian naturalness; and from his knowledge of literature, the explosive energy of the Storm-and-Stress movement finds its way into his music. Everything in his epoch was assayed in the laboratory of his brilliant mind, sifted through his creative consciousness and eventually refined into pure musical gold. In opera, however, he found the form in which he could combine all these ideas, idioms, and styles into one grand kaleidoscopic pattern, and for him the musical theater was always his most natural medium of expression.

Mozart's power of characterization is akin to that of Shakespeare, though his dramas are constructed out of musical materials. As the supreme musical dramatist he can awaken a character to life by a phrase or a rhythmical pattern, carry him through living situations by the direction of a melodic line, and develop the most complex interactions with the others in a scene by harmonic modulations and contrapuntal intricacies. His emotional range is enormous. Within but a short span of time he can be both gay and profound, serene and agitated, cheerful and serious, calm and turbulent, ethical and diabolical, yet all takes place within an ordered framework and nothing ever gets out of hand. His *Marriage of Figaro*, an adaptation of Beaumarchais' play, is one vast human panorama in which all the characters, whether master or servant, nobleman or knave, appear as equal partners in the dance of life. Every possible amorous situation is explored with objectivity, deep psychological insight, good humor, and warm understanding. From Cherubino's adolescent awakening to the fascinations of the opposite sex and the mature love of Figaro and Susanna, he moves on to the Count and Countess as the philandering husband and neglected wife, and finally to a pair of scheming blackmailers. The situations meanwhile run a gamut from intrigue, coquetry, and lust to infidelity, forgiveness, and tender reconciliation. Much of Beaumarchais' political satire is missing, but every ounce of human juice is extracted and exploited to the utmost. By contrast, when he had to perform the duties of a court composer and write an opera on a stilted Metastasio libretto in connection with the emperor's coronation, the work was a failure. When, however, the invitation to write a new opera came from the provincial but highly musical city of Prague, Mozart had both the ideas and the audience he needed, and the result was the operatic masterpiece *Don Giovanni*.

Don Giovanni

For *Don Giovanni* Mozart was fortunate in having the collaboration of Lorenzo da Ponte, a skillful writer and facile adapter with a real theatrical and histrionic flair. On hand at the final rehearsals of this saga of the world's greatest lover, and helping put a few finishing touches on the text,

was none other than Giacomo Casanova, a man who had done enough research on the subject to qualify him as an authority. The play itself was
far from a novelty, and Don Juan, like Faust, was a familiar character who
went all the way back to the medieval morality drama. In literature the
earliest known version is by a Spanish playwright, and in Italy it was
frequently played in Jesuit churches under the title of *Atheisto Fulminato*,
or the *Blaspheming Atheist*. Molière made a prose comedy out of it, in which
for the first time the satirical element replaced the moralizing tone. Many
passages and phrases from Molière's play found their way into Da
Ponte's libretto. Donna Elvira, a lady whom Don Juan has kidnaped from
a convent and later deserted, as well as the pastoral pair, Zerlina and
Masetto, also stem from Molière. An English version called *The Libertine*
by Thomas Shadwell, with incidental music by Purcell, was mounted in
London in 1676; and as late as 1817 a play called *Don Giovanni, or A Spectre
on Horseback*, inspired Byron's poem on the subject. The direct ancestor of
Da Ponte's book, however, was an Italian libretto by Bertati, though elements from all the known Italian, French, and German plays made their
contribution.

Both the subject matter and Mozart's marvelous music led to the adop-
tion and deification of *Don Giovanni* by the following generation, who saw
in it the prototype of the Romantic opera. In one of his late conversations,
Goethe remarked rather wistfully that Mozart should have composed
Faust. What the venerable poet overlooked was that Mozart had already
done so, since the Faustian concept completely permeates the character of
Don Giovanni, who was a Mephistopheles and Faust rolled up in one.
Stylistically the opera incorporates the spirit of the Storm-and-Stress drama
and led directly to Spohr's opera *Faust*, E. T. A. Hoffmann's *Undine*,
and Weber's *Freischütz*. The Romantics unfortunately burdened it with all
kinds of interpretations. To the partisans of the French Revolution, Don
Giovanni was the dissolute nobleman bent like an arch-criminal on bringing about the destruction of the moral law. If so, he was certainly the most-
beloved villain in all melodrama, with the sympathies of the audience enlisted for once on the opposite side of law and order. The philosopher
Kierkegaard regarded him as the incarnation of Desire, which by its very
nature can never admit of satisfaction. He thus became a Nietzschean
superman, or personification of the Dionysian life force. How then is it
that in the opera each love affair either ends in frustration or leaves him in
some ridiculous situation? To the classical enthusiasts he was the mortal
who dared to defy the very gods themselves and by so doing brought about
his own destruction. He then became a towering tragic hero who, like
Faust, was the victim of his own insatiable lusts. To others he was the un-

compromising idealist always in pursuit of perfect beauty, and so on. To find its real meaning one must blow off the accumulation of 19th-century moral and philosophical dust and appraise it anew. Is it a tragedy or a comedy? Even today performances tend to emphasize one aspect or the other. Mozart's subtitle *dramma giocosa* suggests a combination of both. In the thematic catalogue of his own works he also refers to it as an "opera buffa in two acts." Bearing in mind that Mozart was entirely capable of leaving it as a subtle enigma, that his inspired music raises it to the status of a unique masterpiece, and that it was originally composed for a small theater, one may decide that the best approach to it is as a high-spirited 18th-century comedy of manners, in which Molièrian satire is mixed with some Storm-and-Stress demonic elements.

The pace of the opera is breathtaking. In the first scene alone there is an attempted rape, a challenge and duel, the dying gasps of an outraged father, blasphemy, the escape of the culprits, and oaths of vengeance. In all this the absolute dramatic center is Don Giovanni himself, who bursts the bonds of civilized restraint, defies all social conventions, sweeps aside any barriers in his way, and stands alone against the world. In the *Marriage of Figaro* all the characters interacted with each other; but here the figures, like the spokes of a wheel, exist only in their relation to the hub, Don Giovanni. Opposite him are the three feminine leads, each of equal importance. Chronologically Donna Elvira comes first, since she has been seduced and deserted before the curtain rises. Hers is the fury of a woman scorned, joined with the desire to forgive and forget and to save Don Giovanni from perdition. Her character is most clearly revealed in Aria No. 8, "*In qual eccessi*," [1] where she advises the lightheaded young Zerlina of the pitfalls of life with the gay Don. Mozart writes it as a typical Handelian Baroque rage aria. By so doing he implies that Elvira's moral preachments are somewhat archaic, and the dignified form makes it an effective contrast to the prevailing frivolity. The emotional life of Donna Anna, whose screams are heard at the beginning of the opera, is no less complicated. Full of righteous wrath, tempered with filial affection for her murdered father, she swears vengeance on his assassin. She is joined in this resolve by her fiancé, Don Ottavio, and together they constitute the serious couple usual in Italian opera buffa. Since Don Ottavio is the lonely champion of lawful love versus licentiousness, he is bound to appear somewhat pale in these highly charged surroundings. His two tenor arias, "*Dalla sua pace*" and "*Il mio tesoro*" (Nos. 10B and 21), contain lovely lyricism but are parenthetical rather than part of the main action. Donna Anna, on the contrary, rises to truly tragic stature in "*Or sai chi l'onore*," Aria No. 10; where, outraged yet attracted, hatred is intermingled with passion. Third in this list is the naïve but flirtatious Zerlina, torn between loyalty to her rustic bridegroom and the flattering attentions of the dashing Don. The duet "*La ci darem la mano*" (No. 7) is a subtle piece of musical characterization in which the division of the melody between the voices and the minute melodic variants point up their respective attitudes. The Don is tender, yet always the imperious aristocrat accustomed to having his own way; while Zerlina is very feminine, hesitant, doubtful of his good intentions, but thoroughly enjoying every moment of it. Later in a reconciliation scene with her young peasant husband, the aria "*Vedrai carino*" (No. 18) brings out all her maternal impulses toward him.

On the male side Don Giovanni has no romantic competition, only a very substantial shadow in the form of Leporello, the comic manservant who plays Sancho Panza to his Don Quixote. Leporello is a stock opera-buffa character who expresses his rather earthy cynicism in some chattering patter songs based on a running series of rapidly repeated syllables and notes. He introduces himself in the first aria of the opera; and in the famous Catalogue Aria (No. 4), he enumerates the list of his master's amorous conquests in what must surely be the most hilarious set of statistics in history.

The two scenes in which all the characters are on stage are the Finales to Acts 1 and 2. In the first, Don Giovanni is entertaining a lively peasant wedding party in the hopes of winning the bride, Zerlina, for himself. Fine dramatic contrast is provided in Don Giovanni's gay drinking song (No. 11) that sparkles like the wine he is ordering, and the sullen resentment of Masetto when he senses that his bride's head is being turned by the glamorous member of the privileged class. The scene reaches its brilliant climax when the dance music strikes up. There are no less than three ensembles on stage in addition to the main orchestra in the pit. Everyone at the time would have recognized this as a typical Viennese public ballroom scene for which Mozart frequently composed music. So that there would be dances that appealed to everybody, minuets were customarily played in one room, waltzes in another, and so on. Here the three groups also play different dances. The first, consisting of two oboes, two horns, and strings, plays the best known of all minuets. On the repetition of the last part, the second stage orchestra, made up of violins and a bass, does a type of square dance known as a contre-danse; while a third band, also of stringed instruments, plays an old-fashioned German waltz. An obvious stratification of social levels is implied, with the masked figures of Donna Anna and Don Ottavio doing the aristocratic minuet; the peasants stamping out the vigorous, laendlerlike meter of the waltz, with strong accentuation on the beats of three and one; and Don Giovanni and Zerlina meeting on the middle-class ground of the bourgeois contre-danse. Each social group is thus expressed through a characteristic rhythm. With the stage bands playing against the main orchestra below, all the plots and subplots boiling merrily away, and all the characters conversing and commenting on the action, the resulting rhythmic complexity and dramatic tension make this scene one of the major miracles of musical literature.

Ballroom Scene from *Don Giovanni*   Mozart

In the cemetery scene, which precedes the Finale to the second act, Don Giovanni as a fugitive from justice is confronted with the equestrian statue of the Commendatore whom he has murdered at the beginning of the opera. The stentorian tones of the voice from the tomb reproach him for his wickedness; and Don Giovanni, always the courteous host, responds by inviting the statue to a midnight meal. The final scene opens with the preparations for the banquet, while the trumpets and drums sound the proper note of aristocratic hospitality. Like all noblemen of his time, Don Giovanni has his own liveried house orchestra standing by to play dinner music. This wind ensemble plays snatches from two popular Italian operas by Mozart's rivals; and a delightful bit of humor is introduced when they quote the "*Non più andrai*" from his own *Marriage of Figaro*, which happened to be a hit tune of that season, not a classic as now.

Donna Elvira, ever the kill-joy, now enters to play her trump card, which is the announcement that she is returning to her convent where life under the veil will presumably be more peaceful. As she reaches the door her shriek heralds the arrival of the statue. With ominously heavy footsteps the monument sings a long melodic line as rigid in its way as rigor mortis itself, reinforced by the sepulchral sounds of the trombones, instruments which were then associated with solemn church festivals and funerals. The contrast between the quick and the dead is brought out by the static pedal point of the statue's melody, around which the other characters react in ways varying from farce to tragedy. When Don Giovanni takes the hand of his marble guest, the horror music which had been foreshadowed in the overture is heard once more. Strings play spine-tingling scale figures upward and downward alternately soft and loud. Claps of thunder are heard, a chorus of demons shouts from below, flames mount upward; and Don Giovanni, unrepentant to the last, goes to his predestined doom singing the descending scale of D major. Breathlessly the other characters arrive too late for the excitement, but in the nick of time to sing a quintet to the following words before the curtain falls:

> Sinner, pause, and ponder well,
> Mark the end of Don Juan!
> Are you going to Heaven or Hell?

IDEAS

The ideational spectrum of the 18th century is colored by the shift of the audience from a declining aristocracy to a rising bourgeoisie. The final phase of the aristocratic style is reflected in the Rococo; the continuation of the rational viewpoint is found in the Enlightenment; voices of a classical revival begin to be heard; and new emotional outbursts are felt in the emphasis on sensibility, and the Storm-and-Stress movement. With the discussion of Neo-classicism deferred to Chapter 17, the ideas that weave the arts of the 18th century into a coherent pattern are Rococo, Enlightenment, and the emotional reaction to them known as Storm-and-Stress.

Rococo

The Rococo is the last Western style that can lay claim to universality, and that adhered strictly to the canons of beauty. This comes about because the aristocracy was the last international social group of sufficient force to control artistic patronage. After the French Revolution and the Napoleonic wars, the power of nationalism grew so strong that the arts appeared more and more in local frames of reference. The Renaissance cult of the beautiful likewise finds its terminal point in the Rococo, where it comes perilously close to mere prettiness and overrefinement. Fischer von Erlach, Lukas von Hildebrandt, Watteau, Boucher, Fragonard, and Clodion never overstep the restraints of beauty. Mozart, in spite of his extraordinary emotional power, makes his aesthetic views on this point quite clear in a letter to his father: "Passions, whether violent or not," he writes, "must never be expressed in such a way as to excite disgust, and as music, even in the most terrible situations, must never offend the ear, but please the hearer, or in other words must never cease to be *music*." [2] Examples of the Rococo style are found in all countries where the aristocracy possessed the means to follow the fashionable style, and where the Counter-Reformation movement undertook the building of churches. The earmarks of the style are found in the details of the interiors of salons; the paintings of Watteau, Boucher, and Fragonard; the sculptures of Clodion; and in such moments in Mozart as the exquisite Serenade from *Don Giovanni* (Aria No. 16) with its fragile mandolin obbligato.

The Enlightenment

The Enlightenment is a blanket term under which it is possible to group such tendencies as the inventive spirit, scientific inquiry, the encyclopedic movement, the optimistic world view, and the belief in progress. The impetus that the Enlightenment gave to scientific invention was applied by middle-class manufacturers and businessmen to the production of wealth. Pure science and nature in this case were less important than technology and artifact. Its consequences were felt most directly in the shift of artistic patronage in the direction of the middle-class audience. For the first time it is possible to speak of the bourgeois novel and drama. Watteau painted one of his most important pictures for an art dealer; Chardin, Greuze, and Hogarth found their clientele among this social segment; and making the Count the villain and the servant the hero in Beaumarchais' and Mozart's *Marriage of Figaro* was certainly not calculated to flatter the aristocracy.

The Enlightenment spirit of free scientific inquiry, which grew out of 17th-century rationalism, was so violently anticlerical that it almost developed into a substitute religion. To the deists, God was a kind of cosmic clockmaker who created a mechanical universe, wound it up for all eternity, and let it go. The experimental method of science became the liturgy of this pseudo religion, the encyclopedia its bible, nature its church, and all men of reason the congregation. One of the most productive impulses of this aspect of the Enlightenment resulted in the encyclopedic movement.

All the important intellects made their contributions to Diderot's *Encyclopédie* with Voltaire writing the historical parts, Rousseau the sections on music, and so on. The same intellectual spirit, though in different religious circumstances, is observable in the comprehensive musical output of J. S. Bach. In *The Art of the Fugue* he applied the scientific method to musical composition. By keeping his themes constant, he carefully controlled the variables of form and thus systematized all possible fugal types. His extant cantatas add up to four for each Sunday of the year. His keyboard compositions are conceived encyclopedically and comprise examples in all possible forms. His 48 preludes and fugues, known as the *Well Tempered Clavier*, are written as a double cycle, two for each possible tonality; and his Brandenburg concertos explore every conceivable instrumental combination. His entire works thus emerge as a comprehensive design consciously planned to survey and sum up all the musical possibilities known to him.

The Enlightenment image of the cool man of reason inhabiting a world governed by purely rational principles was the object of Voltaire's satirical pen in the novel *Candide*. While maintaining his staunch belief that he lived in the Leibnizian "best of all possible worlds," the hero experiences every disaster known on the planet including the great earthquake of Lisbon in 1745. The use of satire as a social weapon takes visual form in Hogarth's *Marriage à-la-Mode*. A certain amount of Voltairean skepticism can also be found in the character of Don Giovanni who fears neither the supernatural nor the hereafter. When the statue talks in the cemetery scene, the unenlightened Leporello cowers with superstitious fear; but Don Giovanni assumes the role of an art critic, sees that the statue is really nothing more than a typical cemetery monument, and addresses it: "*O vecchio buffonissimo*"—ridiculous old gentleman. The Enlightenment spirit finds an even clearer statement and takes a more constructive form in Mozart's last opera, *The Magic Flute*, an allegory of Freemasonry in which the forces of reason are lined up squarely against those of superstition and fear.

Still another tendency is seen in the spirit of optimism the Enlightenment engendered, together with the related notions of progress and the perfectibility of man. Theologically the Hebraic and Christian viewpoints were based on the fall of man and the doctrine of original sin dating from the expulsion of Adam and Eve from the Garden of Eden. Philosophically Plato's theory of knowledge was also founded on a doctrine of prenatal perfection and the subsequent acquisition of knowledge by the process of remembrance. Humanists, such as Gibbon, believed in the intellectual and artistic paradise of ancient Greece and Rome and as a consequence wrote their declines and falls. Without denying the greatness of Greece, the exponents of the Enlightenment were well aware that they had gone far beyond classical science and believed that, if the rational processes could be properly applied, all fields could eventually surpass the ancients. Kant, for instance, enthusiastically hailed Rousseau as the Newton of the moral world, and Condorcet in his *Progress of the Human Spirit* enumerated the ten stages by which man had raised himself from savagery to the threshold of perfection. Material progress was certainly an observable fact; and, they thought, since nature held all the secrets that a man needed to know, and reason could unlock them, eventually he could control his environment. If man therefore would only use his mental and moral powers to their fullest extent, the argument ran, there was only one direction he could go, onward and upward. The full force of this optimism is felt in the American and French revolutions, and in the painting of David and the music of Beethoven, which will be discussed in the next chapter.

"Storm and Stress"

Various irrational tendencies were apparent in the latter half of the 18th century, which came about as a reaction both to the Rococo cult of the beautiful and the Enlightenment's emphasis on reason. As early as 1756 Burke's *Essay on the Sublime and the Beautiful* insisted that in literature and art there is an element more important than beauty. This was the Sublime, which transcends mere beauty and can even admit of the ugly. "Whatever is fitted in any sort to excite the ideas of pain and danger," he said, "whatever is in any sort terrible, or conversant about terrible objects, is the source of the Sublime." The free exercise of the emotions and the imagination, even if it meant the painful, the astonishing, the horrible, was therefore legitimate territory for art to explore. This movement led to a renewed interest in Shakespeare; reveled in Rousseau's descriptions of alpine scenery, accompanied as they were by avalanches and storms; and delighted in the Rousseauian revolt against the restraints of civilization. This line of thought also constituted the background of the Storm-and-Stress movement in Germany. While the Enlightenment was trying to tame nature and bring it under man's control, the *Sturm und Drang* authors were reveling in how nature imposed her obscure and unfathomable will on man. In Goethe's early drama, Faust was the rebel against all accepted forms of wisdom, especially those arrived at through mathematical or scientific formulas. Both Faust and Don Giovanni were engaged in a quest for emotional truth and succeeded in unleashing the infernal forces that eventually consumed them.

Such, in brief, were the social, ideational, and emotional impulses that defined the horizon before which the panorama of the 18th-century arts unfolded.

PART 5

THE REVOLUTIONARY
PERIOD

CHAPTER

CHRONOLOGY: Paris, Early 19th Century

General Events

1748	Excavations begun at Pompeii and Herculaneum
1762	*Antiquities of Athens* published by Stuart and Revett
1764	*History of Ancient Art* published by Winckelmann (1717–1768)
1766	*Laocoön* published by Lessing (1729–1781)
1785–1820	Period of the Federal Style in America
1788–1791	Brandenburg Gate in Berlin built by Langhans
1789	French Revolution began
1792–1794	First French Republic
1796	Napoleon's first Italian campaign
1798	Napoleon's campaign in Egypt Battle of the Pyramids
1799	Napoleon became First Consul
1802	Napoleon made Consul for life
1803	Napoleonic Code of Laws issued
	Beethoven finished his *Eroica* Symphony
1804	Napoleon crowned Emperor
1806	Temple of Glory (afterward La Madeleine) begun by Vignon
	Arc du Carrousel begun by Percier and Fontaine
	Arc du Triomphe de l'Étoile begun by Chalgrin
1814	Napoleon abdicated. Bourbons restored to French throne
1814–1821	Reign of Louis XVIII
1815	Napoleon defeated in Battle of Waterloo
	Elgin Marbles exhibited in London
1816	Elgin Marbles purchased by Parliament and placed in British Museum
1821	Death of Napoleon
1824–1830	Reign of Charles X
1830	July Revolution
1830–1848	Reign of Louis Philippe as constitutional monarch

Painting

1746–1828	Goya
1748–1825	David
1771–1835	Gros
1780–1867	Ingres
1791–1824	Géricault

Sculpture

1757–1822	Canova
1770–1844	Thorwaldsen

Architecture

1739–1811	Chalgrin
1762–1820	Vignon
1762–1853	Fontaine
1764–1838	Percier

Music

1714–1787	Gluck
1741–1813	Grétry
1741–1816	Paisiello
1760–1837	Lesueur
1760–1842	Cherubini
1770–1827	Beethoven
1774–1851	Spontini

17

THE EARLY 19th CENTURY

PARIS, EARLY 19th CENTURY

Some books, some archeological discoveries, and some social upheavals brought about many radical changes in the intellectual orientation, styles in art, and forms of government in Paris during the latter part of the 18th and early part of the 19th century. Stuart and Revett, two Englishmen who had visited Greece, had published in 1762 a volume called *Antiquities of Athens*, which made a clear differentiation between Greek and Roman architecture. It was followed two years later by the equivalent of a bestseller, Winckelmann's *History of Ancient Art*, which stressed the same point in reference to sculpture. "The principal and universal characteristic of the masterpieces of Greek art is a noble simplicity and quiet grandeur," he declared. "As the depths of the sea remain always at rest, however the surface may be agitated, so the expression in the figures of the Greeks reveals in the midst of passion a great and steadfast soul." These words provided the critics of the courtly Rococo style with the needed aesthetic ammunition, and Diderot fired verbal volleys at Boucher and Fragonard because of the frivolous content in their paintings, and insisted that the function of art was to make "virtue adorable and vice repugnant."

The wave of enthusiasm for antiquity that swept France at this time made that country into a kind of classical Phoenix rising from the volcanic ashes of Pompeii and Herculaneum. The news of the discovery and excavation of these ancient cities was eagerly followed by the French. It unfolded before their eyes the image of a high standard of living that was widely spread among the inhabitants of these Roman resort towns. It came as something of a revelation to a middle class that had previously associated such luxury with a decadent aristocracy. Classicism, which had hitherto meant temples, forums, and great monuments, could now be associated with an unpretentious but luxurious domestic architecture with ideals of comfort that people like themselves could live with and understand. Since the French Revolution, for all its fury, was essentially a bourgeois movement in which the rights of property remained unquestioned, the discovery of these ancient ruins gave the people something worth striving for precisely at a time when they were able to do something about it.

Ancient Rome became a symbol for the Revolutionary protest. In politics, Rome at first meant a republican instead of a monarchical form of government. In religion it was associated with a tolerant paganism as opposed to a dogmatic form of Christianity. For a brief time, in fact, the Cathedral of Notre Dame in Paris was rededicated to the goddess of Reason. The Revolutionary spirit was embodied in heroism and the spirit of self-sacrifice, in rugged resolve and spartanical simplicity. The reflection of these qualities was readily found in Roman literature and art; and when Oscar Wilde gave his witty twist to the old Greek aesthetic doctrine by saying that nature, especially human nature, imitates art, he must surely have had this period in mind.

The political writings of Cicero and Seneca were widely read and quoted to confirm the principle that sovereignty resided in the people, and that government should be based on a voluntary agreement among citizens. Political pamphlets of the time were studded with quotations from Tacitus, Sallust, and Horace, and the oratory of the period was modeled on that of Cicero. The convention hall where the legislators met was lined with laurel-crowned statues of Camillus, Solon, and other Roman senators. The painter David even designed a costume for these representatives of the people, which combined the ancient tunic with a togalike cape draped over the shoulders. In their debates the speakers always relied on an apt phrase from Cicero to clinch an important point. They always referred to their partisans as Brutuses and Catos and to their opponents as Catalines. Their postures and gestures were studied imitations of Roman statues, and their oaths were sworn on the head of Brutus, or by the immortal gods.

Everyone was biography-conscious and spoke like living characters out of Plutarch's *Parallel Lives*. Never before, in fact, had public personalities seemed so obviously to have walked straight out of a book. The day she murdered Marat, for instance, Charlotte Corday had spent most of her time reading Plutarch. Many of the Revolutionary symbols were borrowed directly from the ancients. The cap of liberty was, in fact, the headgear of the liberated Roman slaves. The symbol of power was once more the *fasces*, or combined sticks or swords tied together with a common bond, as seen in David's *Oath of the Horatii*. The calendar was reorganized, and even the months of the year were renamed. The rainy month became Pluviose; planting time, Germinal; the month of blossoms, Floreal; midsummer, Thermidor; and harvest time, Fructidor. Façades of houses featured classical columns; rooms were furnished with Roman couches, lighted by bronze lamps, and decorated with replicas of ancient statuary.

Napoleon Bonaparte shared this popular enthusiasm, and his chosen models were Alexander and Julius Caesar, especially the latter since their careers had so many parallels. While Caesar had crossed the Rubicon and come to power by means of his Gallic wars, Napoleon had crossed the Alps into Italy and the Mediterranean into Egypt to achieve substantially the same result. Napoleon was first a Consul; then after a plebiscite, the Senate through the Tribunate had voted him the title of Emperor. Such a manipulation of the forms and images of ancient glory had a vast appeal to a man of his modest birth. Coming to power so soon after the demise of an unpopular monarchy, however, made it necessary to emphasize that many of the Roman emperors had come from equally plebian backgrounds, and that the imperial toga had not always been hereditary. Napoleon's hold on the people was, however, indisputable, and his elevation was made with full popular consent. His mission was to bring order to what had been Revolutionary chaos, and to consolidate the social gains that had been made. His meteoric career was the success story of the 19th century, embodying as it did the ideal of the emancipated individual rising to leadership through his own efforts rather than by an accident of birth. In it the members of the parvenu society of his time could find substance for their fondest materialistic daydreams. The truth was that now they held the reins of power in their hands, they did not know quite what to do with it. Napoleon did.

The achievement of these ancient prerogatives of power, however, was not made with antiquated methods. The highly modern means that were employed forms a fascinating study in contrasts. It could not have been done without the forging of a mighty war machine, which was possible only through the application of all the latest technological and scientific knowledge to industry and agriculture. By being the first modern ruler to employ universal conscription to populate his armies and by his undoubted administrative ability, Napoleon was able to regiment all the various parts of his state into efficient cogs in his wheel of victory. He had inherited, however, the popular classical vocabulary, and he proceeded to capitalize on it. A set of symbols that served his state by upholding the ideals of heroism and self-sacrifice and by awakening latent national ambitions was as useful as it was decorative. Napoleon therefore cast himself at various times in the role of Hannibal, when he was crossing the Alps; Alexander, when on far-off battlefields; and Caesar, when burdened with administrative affairs at home. Those around him also had their assigned roles. When David requested a sitting for a portrait, Napoleon dismissed the thought with a wave of his hand, instructing the astonished artist to paint his genius not his likeness, and asking rhetorically if Alexander had ever posed for Apelles.

Napoleon's Empire, like its Roman prototype, was international in scope, and its intellectual and artistic life transcended national boundary lines. What Greece had been to Rome, Italy was now to France. Napoleon brought the Italian sculptor Canova to Paris for various commissions, and his musical preferences were for such composers as Paisiello and Spontini. His proclamation to the Italian people on the eve of his invasion of their country is an interesting commentary on this point. "We are the friends of all nations," he protested, perhaps too much, "especially the descendants of Brutus, the Scipios, and of the great men we have chosen for our own model." He took frequent pains to point out that he was embarking on a cultural as well as military mission. Here was no barbarian Attila knocking on the gates of Rome, but a conqueror who came to sack it in the company of a group of art experts who were well aware of the value of everything they took. A petition, in fact, had been sent to the Directory in 1796 signed by all the important French artists, which pointed out how the Romans had become civilized by confiscating the art of ancient Greece and how France would likewise flourish by bringing original works to Paris to serve as models. While this returning Caesar brought back with him no human captives, his victory celebration was livened by the presence of such distinguished prisoners of war as the *Apollo Belvedere*, the *Discobolus*, the *Venus de Medici*, the paintings of Raphael, and other rare treasures he had pilfered from the Vatican and other Italian museums.

As an Italian himself, Napoleon knew the value of such pomp and circumstance, and his life was consciously conditioned by these visions of ancient splendor. Inevitably, however, the tables were turned, and he sometimes found that his critics could also find apt parallels from the past with which to plague him. When things began to go from bad to worse, for instance, Chateaubriand, his ambassador in Rome, compared him with Nero. But even when Napoleon found that his cause was hopelessly lost, he summoned one last bit of Plutarchian grandeur to adorn his letter of surrender. "I throw myself," he said, "like Themistocles upon the mercy of the British people."

ARCHITECTURE

With the reorganization of the government, the remaking of the constitution, and the recodification of the laws on the model of his reincarnated
Roman Empire, Napoleon was equally determined that Paris should be
replanned so that his capital city would present an appearance as close to
a new Rome as possible. He therefore undertook the ordering and com-
missioning of buildings with the same incredible vigor that marked his
activities in other fields. The heart of the new city was still to be a spacious
center designed around the old Place Louis XV, which under the Directory
had been renamed the Place de la Concorde (Fig. 17:1). Its axis began on
the left bank of the Seine with the old Palais Bourbon, now the Chamber of
Deputies, which was to have its face lifted by a Corinthian colonnade. It
was then to continue across the river by the bridge, which had been begun
in early Revolutionary days, to the center of the Place, where some statuary
was to cover the spot where the guillotine had done its grim work. Its
termination point was to be the unfinished church of La Madeleine at the
end of the Rue Royale, which was to be rebuilt in the form of a Roman
temple and dedicated to the glory of the Grande Armée by a grateful
Emperor. Finally Percier and Fontaine, his favored architects, were commissioned to redesign the Rue de Rivoli that intersected the axis at right
angles and ran parallel to the river. Elsewhere throughout the city there
were to be triumphal arches and monumental columns proclaiming to the
world the presence of a new Caesar and Trajan.

Fig. 17:1. *Place de la Concorde*, Paris (Courtesy French Government Tourist Office)

Napoleon showed his interest in these projects by frequently conferring with his architects and engineers, by visiting the sites where construction activity was in progress, and by dreaming up new ideas while on distant battlefields. It was at Posen, in fact, that he signed the decree for the building of his Temple of Glory (La Madeleine, Fig. 17:2). According to his express wish, the unfinished church was to be transformed and bear a dedicatory inscription: "From the Emperor to the soldiers of the Grande Armée." The building was not to look like a church but like such a temple as one would find in Athens or Rome. The interior was to contain marble tablets that were to be inscribed with the names of all the troops who had participated in the battles of Ulm, Austerlitz, and Jena; silver panels that would list their names again according to the Departments of France which had sent their sons to the grand army; and gold plaques, which would bear the names of those who had fallen on the field of battle. Around the room were to be bas reliefs of the regiments with their insignia; statues of the marshals were to occupy niches; and elsewhere trophies, regalia, banners, and drums were to be displayed. Each year on the anniversaries of the above battles the temple was to be illuminated and a grand concert given. Preceding the music there were to be odes and eulogies stressing the virtues necessary for a soldier's life; and in a magnanimous mood of self-renunciation, the Emperor expressly forbade any mention of himself in these commemorative poems and orations. The grand council of the Legion of Honor was to be entrusted with the annual ceremonies, choosing the best poetry and music from the works submitted and rewarding the authors with gold medals. The minister of the interior, who was commissioned to carry out the order, promptly issued an artistic call to arms, summoning all the architects, sculptors, and painters to submit designs of a grand and noble character. Napoleon personally selected an architectural plan by Vignon, because it fulfilled his conditions by looking sufficiently ancient and pagan.

The building is indeed a pagan Corinthian temple, and, except for the sculptural details, it was completed according to Vignon's plan. In the Roman manner it stands on a platform 23 feet high and is approached by a flight of steps in the front. Running completely around the building is a series of Corinthian columns about 63 feet in height, 18 on each side, 8 on each end, and an additional row of 6 in the front which support the cornice. The pediment of this pagan temple of glory, after its rededication for religious purposes, now has a large sculptural group by Lemaire representing the Last Judgment. In the center stands a figure of Christ 17 feet high with the repentant Mary Magdalene at his feet. To his left are allegorical figures representing the sins of Envy, Hypocrisy, and Avarice,

Fig. 17:2 (above). Vignon. *Church of La Madeleine*, Façade. 1804–1842. Paris (Courtesy French Government Tourist Office). Fig. 17:3 (below). Interior (Archives Photographiques)

while on his right are found an angel of mercy and personifications of the virtues of Faith, Hope, Charity, and Innocence.

The interior cella of an ancient temple was never intended as a gathering place and always remained dark and mysterious. Hence Vignon had of necessity to depart from precedent and come up with something new. The surprise that awaits the visitor as he passes through the massive bronze doors is complete, for the interior and exterior actually amount to two different buildings. The aisleless nave (Fig. 17:3) is divided into three long bays and a choir, which are not roofed in timber as in a Greek temple nor vaulted in the Roman manner but covered with saucer domes on pendentives in the Byzantine style. The nave terminates in a semicircular apse that is roofed over by a semidome. Chapels are located in the recesses created by the buttresses that support the domes, and two classical orders— the Corinthian and Ionic—form the basis of the decorative scheme. Rich use is made of marble paneling and the domes are coffered in the manner of the Roman Pantheon. What little light there is in this windowless interior comes from skylights at the tops of the domes, an idea derived from the oculus of the Roman Pantheon. The best that can be said about this method is that it keeps the exterior roofline intact. The exterior, as a study in classical design, has a certain dignity in its archeological faithfulness to such older models as the Maison Carrée (Fig. 3:15), though it excels its prototypes only in its larger proportions. The interior, however, can be said to have a certain originality as an early example of the 19th-century eclectic style.

The checkered history of the building ran a varied course from its letters of foundation in 1757 to its final dedication as a parish church in 1845. When Louis XV laid the cornerstone in 1764, he proclaimed it a monument to the piety of the French royal family. Work on it ceased during the Revolution, and it served during the days of the Terror as a morgue for the headless victims of the guillotine. The old unfinished pile was cleared off under Napoleon to become a temple to his cult of military glory. The word *glory*, however, began to have a hollow ring even before the end of the Empire, and after Waterloo the building reverted once more to its status as a church of the Magdalene. Under the Bourbon restoration it was declared to be an expiatory monument to atone for the execution of Louis XVI and his family. This was again changed after the Revolution of 1830; and, after its completion in 1842, it was finally dedicated by Louis Philippe, somewhat anticlimactically, as a simple parish church.

In 1806 after winning his military victories in Germany and Austria, Napoleon entrusted the building of a triumphal arch to his architects

Fig. 17:4 (above). Percier and Fontaine. *Arc de Triomphe du Carrousel*. 1806. Paris (Courtesy French Government Tourist Office)

Fig. 17:5 (left). *Vendôme Column*. 1810. Place Vendôme, Paris (Courtesy French Government Tourist Office)

Percier and Fontaine. Now known as the Arc du Carrousel (Fig. 17:4), it was designed as a gate of honor to the Tuileries. It turned out to be a rather slavish imitation of the Arch of Septimus Severus in Rome, though of more modest proportions. Standing on the platform above it was one of Napoleon's proudest battle trophies, the group of four bronze horses taken from St. Mark's in Venice. Owing to the shifting fortunes of war, however, that city got them back as a result of the peace treaty, and a triumphal chariot drawn by some horses of a considerably later vintage were installed in their place to celebrate, rather ironically, the restoration of Louis XVIII. The face of the arch is decorated with some rather undistinguished bas reliefs depicting scenes, such as the Battle of Austerlitz, the surrender of Ulm, the peace of Tilsit, and Napoleon's triumphal entries into Munich and Vienna.

When finished, the result was too meager to measure up to Napoleon's imperial ambitions, and so another and still grander arch was commissioned for the Place de l'Étoile. This familiar Paris landmark was also Roman in inspiration, but Chalgrin, its architect, achieved some life and elasticity in its form by departing from all known models. For his monumental effect he relied on bold proportions and a grand scale. Conspicuously omitting the classical orders, he relieves the severity of the general outline by the skillful use of high relief sculpture (Figs. 18:8 and 18:9) on a scale comparable to the immense size of the arch itself.

Still not content, Napoleon ordered a monumental Doric column to be erected in the Place Vendôme (Fig. 17:5). In its size and style of ornamentation, it was a conscious copy of Trajan's column in Rome (Fig. 3:22), the main difference being that the spiral reliefs in this instance are done in a strip of bronze cast from the guns and cannons that were captured from the defeated Prussian and Austrian armies. The sculpture recounts the story of the campaign of 1805 in scenes, such as the address of Napoleon to his troops, the capture of Ulm, the meeting of the three emperors, and the conquest of Istria and Dalmatia. On its base are inscribed the words: "This monument was erected to the glory of the Grande Armée by Napoleon the Great, begun in 1806 and finished in 1810." The statue at the top was originally to have been one of Charlemagne, but Napoleon yielded to flattery and allowed himself to be portrayed in the manner of a Roman emperor, crowned with the laurel wreath and holding a globe surmounted by winged victory. This statue was taken off to England by the British army of occupation that entered Paris in 1814. Louis XVIII replaced it with one of Henry IV, but Louis Philippe again put Napoleon back on top, this time as Citizen Bonaparte! In 1865 Napoleon III thought this was an affront to his uncle and predecessor, and so Napoleon once again came down and went up again in the imperial toga. In 1871 under the Commune, the whole column was pulled down with ropes and pulleys by a group which included the painter Courbet; but under the Third Republic it was once more reassembled and stands today substantially as it was in the time of Napoleon III.

This wave of enthusiasm for classical architecture was by no means confined to Paris. While, in general, the Roman Revival was strongest in the countries that were more closely identified with the revival of the Empire under Napoleon, the nations of the anti-Napoleonic coalition, notably England and Germany, accented the Greek phase. In England there were the country houses built by Robert and James Adams and such public buildings as the British Museum that were all strongly Greek in character. In Germany an early example is provided by the Brandenburg Gate in Berlin, modeled after the Athenian Propylaea; two later buildings in Munich were based on the same model; while a Hall of Fame near Regensburg, called, of all things, Walhalla, is an archeologically exact reproduction of the Parthenon. In the United States the period corresponded generally to the Federal style, which ran its course from about 1775 to 1820. Buildings that show the Roman influence are the Virginia state capitol, which Thomas Jefferson designed after the Maison Carrée (Fig. 3:15); the University of Virginia campus, which was planned after the rambling style of a large Roman country villa; and the library of the same institution, which was modeled after the Pantheon (Fig. 3:19).

PAINTING

Into this stern world of Revolutionary fervor and ancient Roman heroism stepped a young painter whose temperament and technique were ideally suited to the spirit of the times. Jacques Louis David was a reformer by nature and a classical enthusiast by nurture. The austerity of his pictures was a conscious reaction to the Rococo extravagances exemplified in the work of his grand uncle, Boucher; and by virtue of his studies in Rome, he had absorbed all that was necessary for the exploitation of the classical enthusiasms of the readers of Plutarch's *Parallel Lives* and Winckelmann's *History of Ancient Art*. It was inevitable that the high moral purposes of the Revolution would be reflected in some kind of didactic art, and David's immediate success can be attributed to the fact that his style extolled the same stalwart ideas that the Revolutionists espoused. Bourgeois by birth and upbringing, David frankly addressed his art to the newly established middle-class social order.

Fig. 17:6 (above). David. *Lictors Bringing Back to Brutus the Bodies of His Sons.* 36″ x 27″. 1789. Atheneum, Hartford, Conn. Fig. 17:7 (below). David. *Battle of the Romans and Sabines.* 12′ 8″ x 17′. 1799. Louvre, Paris (Archives Photographiques)

Apart from his work as a painter and the intrinsic value of his painting, David also played the role of a power politician in the field of art that had far-reaching effects not only on his own time but throughout the rest of the century. In a period when it was something of a triumph for a man to keep his head on his shoulders, David showed a political shrewdness and sense of timing that would have done credit to a prime minister. After accepting many commissions from Louis XVI and election to the Academy of Painting and Sculpture, established under Louis XIV, he went over to the side of the Revolution at the opportune moment. As a member of the Convention he not only voted for the execution of his former patron but succeeded in abolishing the Academy and establishing in its stead the École des Beaux Arts, which he reoriented from the traditional Baroque and Rococo styles toward the study of Roman antiquity. He then blandly hitched his wagon to Napoleon's rising star and became by title the First Painter of the Empire, a commanding position, which he proceeded to exploit to the fullest. His activities now included the organization of official ceremonies, coordination of the system of state museums, and the granting of licenses to the artists who wished to show their works in the annual public exhibitions. More academic than the former academicians, he succeeded in laying the foundations of official art that endured for the rest of the century. While his theories and subject matter are still a matter of controversy, his craftsmanship was on a par with any of the master painters of the past; and many distinguished painters of the present have not overlooked his style and manner of execution. The technique of Salvador Dali and the 20th-century Neo-classicism of Picasso, for instance, owe much to the cool objective draftsmanship of their 19th-century predecessor.

David's picture of the *Lictors Bringing Back to Brutus the Bodies of His Sons* (Fig. 17:6) bears the date of the fateful year of 1789. It is both a reminder that his career had its inception during the latter days of the monarchy and that he was attempting to continue the subject and substance of his spectacular early success with the *Oath of the Horatii*. In it one finds the same stern spirit of self-sacrifice; the same severity of style that had appealed so much to the eyes that were weary of the fussy Rococo, the same somber type of setting, which had interested those who were reading about the archeological discoveries at Pompeii and Herculaneum. With remarkable boldness David was able to flaunt the dour, do-or-die virtues of Roman republicanism right under the noses of his aristocratic patrons. These two pictures were not only the manifesto of a new style in art but of a new image of society as well, and their unparalleled success was due in no small measure to the fact that they appeared at precisely the right moment.

Fig. 17:8. David. *Madame Recamier*. 68″ x 95¾″. 1800. Louvre, Paris (Alinari)

Fig. 17:9 (below). David. *Bonaparte on Mount St. Bernard*. 107½″ x 91½″. 1800. Versailles (Archives Photographiques)

For his subject David chose an incident from the days soon after the founding of the ancient Roman Republic. Lucius Junius Brutus, one of the first two Consuls, had discovered that his own sons were involved in a plot to restore the recently overthrown monarchy. After ordering their execution for treason, his isolated figure is discovered in the statuesque shadow of the goddess Roma. Behind him are the lictors bearing the bodies of his sons, while a third group is formed by his wife and daughters who are crying out in their grief. Many who lived through the trying times of the Revolution could see something of themselves in that figure of stoical resolution, torn between his public duty to the state and his private paternal grief.

Equally melodramatic but with more of the violent action of the Revolution was the picture that followed it a decade later, the *Battle of the Romans and Sabines* (Fig. 17:7). Romulus and Remus, the legendary founders of Rome, had organized a group of warriors and taken the daughters of the Sabine tribe by violence as pictured by Poussin (Fig. 13:14). Here David depicts the sequel when the Sabine fathers and brothers had come to avenge the rape of their womenfolk. By this time, however, the women had become Roman wives and mothers and are shown rushing outward from the city gates with their children and throwing themselves between the combatants in order to stop the bloodshed. Again the subject was one of conflicting loyalties that is brought out by the principal protagonists in the foreground. Romulus is about to throw his spear at the King of the Sabines, while Hersilia, the wife of Romulus, rushes between them begging them to desist. In keeping with his aesthetic theory of placing principles above reality, David idealizes his figures and minimizes the detail by showing the men almost nude and the horses without harness. For all its sound and fury, however, the composition as a whole tends to become almost as cold and hard as the carved stone relief that inspired it.

In his portraiture David reveals himself as an expert appraiser of personality, and his viewers find in this genre a certain relief from his more heroic efforts. A sensitive instance is seen in the portrait of *Madame Recamier* (Fig. 17:8), one of the most fascinating and intelligent women of the period. In her, David found a congenial subject who furnished her salon in the fashionable Pompeiian style he had done so much to popularize. Here she reclines in the classical manner on an Empire chaise longue just as she might have done on the days she received her guests. Her white gown is draped in a manner that is self-consciously reminiscent of antique statuary. The only other pieces of furniture are the footstool and bronze lamp, which were drawn from Pompeiian originals. The clarity with which David handles the outlines of the figure and the silhouette of the head combine with the austere setting to give a general effect of orderliness and elegance.

David did many portraits of Napoleon, mostly in official attitudes, but in his *Bonaparte on Mount St. Bernard* (Fig. 17:9) he captures something of the essence of Napoleon the conqueror. Shortly after the conclusion of the successful Italian campaign, the artist told the First Consul that he wanted to paint him sword in hand on the field of battle. Napoleon is reported to have replied: "No, it is not with the sword that battles are won—paint me calm and serene on a fiery steed." Lest one be swept away by this disarming touch of honesty and realism on Napoleon's part, it is only necessary to recall that the actual crossing was made on the back of a surefooted mule. In addition to the use of such poetic license, David makes doubly sure that no one will miss the point by providing the observer with a history lesson. Written on the rocks in the foreground are the names of the great former transalpine conquerors, Hannibal and Charlemagne, beside that of Napoleon.

In 1804 to commemorate his assumption of the imperial dignity, Napoleon commissioned his court painter, David, to execute four grandiose pictures. Since the Empire was destined to last but a decade, there was time for only two of them to be completed, the *Coronation* (Fig. 17:10) and the *Distribution of the Eagles*, the ancient standards of the Roman imperial legions that had been adopted by Napoleon as his own. Both were historical canvases in the grand tradition of Poussin and Lebrun, but David extended that genre here to include contemporary events. The actual coronation scene also differed from past precedents in that previous ceremonials of the sort were designed principally to impress other aristocrats, while Napoleon, as a popular ruler, was concerned more with impressing the populace at large. By such a spectacle he let them savor the taste of glory and quickened their pulses with a sense of destiny. The event took place in the choir of the Cathedral of Notre Dame in Paris where his decorators, Percier and Fontaine, had designed a special setting for the occasion. The ancient Gothic arches were camouflaged with the imitation marble pilasters seen in the picture, and boxes and galleries for distinguished guests were placed between them. Out of the picture and facing the high altar stood the throne under a triumphal arch festooned with curtains of imperial purple.

David originally proposed to paint the moment after the Pope had blessed the crown, when Napoleon took it from the altar and placed it on his own head. But the Emperor, always a man of action, preferred the more gallant pose of putting it on the brow of the kneeling Empress. Aside

Fig. 17:10. David. *Coronation* (*Le Sacre*). 20' x 30' 6½". 1805–1808. Louvre, Paris (Alinari)

from this bit of incidental activity, the picture amounts to a stately group portrait on a grand scale. As a piece of official art, the placement and attitude of every personage had to be passed on by the master of protocol and ratified by the Emperor himself, even to the inclusion of his mother who happened not to have been present that day. David, however, had been there and made sketches on the spot; but when he drew the Pope with his hands resting on his knees as he had actually observed him, Napoleon told his court painter that the successor of St. Peter had not come so far to do nothing. So David had to revise his drawings to show Pius VII with his arms extended in benediction. In such circumstances it is a minor miracle that David was able to get as much elasticity into the composition as he did. His achievement is all the more remarkable if one reflects on how easily the whole thing could have become little more than a fancy dress ball with Napoleon, as the middle-class messiah, standing in the midst of the members of his family whom he had made kings, princes, cardinals, and so on. By masterly grouping, commanding postures, and the spacious solemn setting, David saves the scene from becoming a masquerade and endows it with a dignity all its own. Thus the versatile David was able to adapt his art to Napoleon's dreams of imperial Roman grandeur.

The immense 20- by 30-foot canvas contains some 150 life-size portraits. It took several years, in fact, for each of the individuals concerned to visit the church where David had set up his studio so that they could sit for him. The assemblage is mostly made up of the beplumed marshals of the imperial army, maids of honor to the Empress, court chamberlains, and members of the diplomatic corps. The United States ambassador is included, but the English delegation is conspicuous by its absence. In the center box is Napoleon's mother and other members of his family, while in the gallery above is a group of artists and intellectuals including the composer Grétry. As a signature, David paints himself standing at an easel, and with him are his wife and daughters, his favorite pupils, as well as his teacher Vien.

The symbolism provides an interesting commentary on the problem of holding a coronation without evoking memories of the hated hereditary aristocracy, yet at the same time giving it an aura of legitimacy. It meant striking a balance between the luxury and elegance of the old regime and the spartanical simplicity of the Revolutionary days. In the form of the government this had been managed by moving the clock of history forward a notch from the image of the austere days of the Roman Republic to those of the more prosperous Empire. The ceremonies here provided the pomp and circumstance that confirmed this evolution. The crimson coronation robes of the imperial pair are embroidered all over with golden bees, Napoleon's chosen symbol for the integrated state in which all members had their appointed place and worked for the good of the hive in order to produce the honey of prosperity. Elsewhere there were sheaves of wheat and cornucopias, symbols of imperial plenty, as well as palm branches and figures of victory, symbols of triumph. Significant, too, is the fact that Napoleon's crown is the laurel wreath, ancient symbol of literary immortality. The papal coat of arms below the canopy at the left gives the necessary touch of historical continuity so much needed by his regime. The supreme symbol of the occasion, however, was the spectacle of Napoleon crowning himself and his Empress, signifying the break with past tradition and the derivation of his authority from the people by means of a plebescite. By this dramatic touch he also proclaimed the existence of the free individual who recognized no authority superior to himself and that his power was not derived from above but through his own efforts and those of his people. Such a scene provided the painter of classical austerity with a chance to exploit the element of color, and David made rich but not lavish use of the medium. His handling of the wealth of detail is such that it preserves the uncluttered spaciousness of the setting and the proportion of the whole.

No presentation of this revival of the Roman Empire would be complete that showed only the histrionic attitudes of the conqueror. The sufferings of a subjugated people, which invariably follow in the wake of an invading army, find vivid expression in the scenes painted by Goya after the French campaign in Spain of 1808. One of these (Fig. 17:11), an execution scene which Goya finished some years later, accents the obverse side of the Napoleonic coin. Goya saw nothing of the heroic aspect of warfare, only the desolation of his country and its accompanying bloodshed and carnage. In this picture both the technique as well as the subject matter are quite the opposite of the correct and pompous presentations of David.

After David, the leading arbiter of the art world was his pupil Ingres. Like his teacher, Ingres realized the importance of championing the arts in official circles; eventually he became a senator of France. The Academy had been re-established after Napoleon's downfall, and the idea of placing the official stamp of approval on writers and painters finds full expression in *The Apotheosis of Homer* (Fig. 17:12). Commissioned as a ceiling mural in the newly established Charles X Museum in the Louvre, the subject is well adapted to its museum setting for it is impressive in content as well as in its large proportions. Ingres treats his subject as if it were some supreme session of an academy of arts and letters for the immortals. In their midst sits the enthroned Homer, the greatest of them all. Behind him is the façade

Fig. 17:11. Goya. *Executions of May Third, 1808.* 8′ 8″ x 11′ 4″. Prado Museum, Madrid

Fig. 17:12. Ingres. *Apotheosis of Homer.* 12′ 8″ x 16′ 10¾″. Louvre, Paris (Archives Photographiques)

of an Ionic temple; winged victory holds the laurel wreath above his brow; at his feet are the personifications of his brain children, the *Iliad* and the *Odyssey;* and about him are his successors who have carried the torch for poetry and art throughout the ages. In this exclusive society Aeschylus is seen unfolding a scroll listing his tragedies; the poet Pindar is holding up his lyre in tribute; Vergil and Dante are present as epic poets; Longinus is standing up for philosophy, Boileau for criticism; at the lower right Racine and Molière, in the courtly wigs of the time of Louis XIV, make an offering of tragic and comic masks; and Raphael, the profiled figure on the upper left, represents the pictorial arts. Conspicuously missing are Shakespeare and Goethe, both of whom were deemed insufficiently classical because of the indiscretions they committed in writing *Macbeth* and *Faust*, respectively.

Ingres' source seems to have been a Hellenistic relief now in the British Museum showing a simplified version of the same subject with allegorical representations of the *Iliad* and *Odyssey* as well as personifications of Time and the muses of History, Poetry, Drama, and Mythology. Ingres' virtuosity in drawing is seen in the sharply delineated figures. Like his contemporaries, he accepted the Greek aesthetic of art as a representation of nature, with the reservation that it was the artist's function to endow it with orderliness through the process of rearrangement and editorial excision. In this case he builds his composition by means of line, which he then organizes into a series of receding planes. Color for him, as it was for David, was always a secondary element.

SCULPTURE

The sculptor Canova, who enjoyed a reputation in his day second to none, was summoned from Rome to Paris by Napoleon to execute statues of himself and his family. Through his Neo-classical spectacles, the Italian artist saw Napoleon's mother as the matronly Agrippina of old, his sister Pauline, not without some justification, as Venus Victorious, and Napoleon himself, most obligingly, as a Roman emperor (Fig. 17:13). Canova was attended on this trip by his brother who recorded some of the conversations between the artist and his patron. From this source we learn that the Emperor had a few qualms about being portrayed, as the saying goes, in the "heroic altogether," and suggested some appropriate costume. To this Canova indignantly replied: "We, like the poets, have our own language. If a poet introduced into a tragedy phrases and idioms used habitually by the lower classes in the public streets, he would rightly be reprimanded by everybody. In like manner, we sculptors cannot clothe our statues in modern costumes without deserving a similar reproach." [1] The sculptor's argument ultimately prevailed, and except for the suggestion of a toga draped over his shoulders, Napoleon stands there in all his bronze glory, holding an orb surmounted by winged victory in his right hand and a staff in lieu of a scepter in his left. The head is idealized but recognizable, while the body points directly to Praxitelean models from the shifting of the weight toward one side down to the inevitable Hellenistic tree trunk below.

Fig. 17:13. Canova. *Napoleon*. Bronze. *c*.11½′ high. 1808. Brera Palace, Milan (Alinari)

Fig. 17:14. Canova. *Pauline Bonaparte as Venus*. Marble. Life size. 1808. Borghese Gallery, Rome (Anderson)

The reclining statue of *Pauline Bonaparte as Venus* (Fig. 17:14) is still another instance of the use of a Hellenistic prototype, since Canova, like David, had come under the sway of Winckelmann. While it is almost an exact sculptural counterpart of David's *Madame Recamier* (Fig. 17:8), it conveys much less of the individuality of its subject than the painting does. Both of the Canova statues show how much more a sculptor was restricted in his expression during this wave of classical enthusiasm than painters, simply because of the wealth of antique material available for study. While practically nothing of ancient painting was known to David, there were whole museums full of well-preserved ancient statues for Canova to study. While the way was clear for one to create a new style, the other had to conform quite closely to existing models. Like a good academician, Canova advised his students on a "scrupulous adherence to rules" in order to guard against "arbitrary and capricious errors." Judicious deviation from them was, however, possible when it could be justified on rational grounds. In Canova's aesthetics everything was defined by classical canons, hence when he did a portrait of a contemporary figure, the body, its pose, and the drapery were taken directly from antique models, and the head of his subject was idealized sufficiently to fit the case. In theory he accepted the Greek idea of art as an imitation of nature, but in practice his art became an imitation of art. For his observations of human nature he looked about the Vatican collections instead of going out on the highways and byways. Furthermore his constant self-conscious striving to create objects of art too often led to artificial results. It is possible that this aesthetic could have produced more significant products in the mind and hands of a greater artist, but in Canova's case it had a definitely stultifying effect.

Because of the great demand for his work, Canova employed a large number of assistants in his studio. His large output, plus the use of some modern devices and methods that were unknown to Praxiteles, gave his workshop something of the aspect of a factory. These included the chemical solutions he employed to achieve the extraordinary smoothness of his surface textures, and the use of a pointing machine to make exact copies of ancient models. In spite of some murmurings from less-successful sculptors, nothing in his lifetime diminished his glowing fame. The many young Americans who were attracted to Rome by Canova's glittering reputation returned from their studies to do things like Horatio Greenough's colossal statue of George Washington as Zeus, which outgrew its intended setting in the Capitol and now stands in the Smithsonian Institution. Even the British Parliament invited Canova to London to pass on the value of the Parthenon sculptures before purchasing them from Lord Elgin. One would have thought after feeling the full force of these originals, the sculptor would have realized their superiority to his previous models. He did show good judgment in refusing to attempt a restoration job and in making some observations on the differences between the real Greek sculpture and the work that was designed for the Roman market. In general, however, he smugly found in them the justification of his own life's work, and seized the opportunity to point out how wrong his critics had been.

MUSIC

"Among all the fine arts, music is the one which exercises the greatest influence upon the passions and is the one which the legislator should most encourage." So wrote Napoleon to the Inspector of the Conservatory soon after he became a Consul. His interest in music, or in any of the arts for that matter, was always conditioned by the effect it would have on the people at large and its function in the service of the state. His personal band, for instance, always stood in readiness for a parade or a public celebration; and the popular side of the art, especially where military music was concerned, was never neglected. The welfare of composers, opera singers, and orchestra musicians was also a matter of much concern to all the post-revolutionary governments. Since the aristocrats had fled the country, patronage had to come from another source. Napoleon, therefore, interested himself in the affairs of the Opera, insisting that all budgetary matters and commissions for new works be submitted to him even when he was away on his military campaigns. He regularly attended public performances whenever possible and took special pleasure in the popular demonstrations his appearances usually provoked. The beneficial effects of this interest, however, must be equated with a control over all aspects of each stage production that amounted to a strict form of state censorship.

Napoleon's attempts to win over the French artists and those of the conquered countries extended into the field of music. His personal preferences leaned rather strongly to the Italian vocal style, especially that of Paisiello, whose gentle lyricism was congenial to his taste. It was he who received the commission to compose the *Te Deum* for the national celebration on the occasion of the Concordat with the Vatican, and the appointment as first conductor of the Imperial Chapel Orchestra. Second in charge was the French composer Lesueur, who had written the music for the coronation ceremonies and a successful opera on MacPherson's *Ossian*, one of Napoleon's favorite books. The production that most closely caught the spirit of the new Empire, however, was that of Spontini's opera *La Vestale*. Appearing as it did in 1807 at the height of Napoleon's military successes, it had the necessary pomp and pageantry to whip public enthusiasm to a pitch of frenzy. It had the requisite Roman setting, and the spectacle of a vestal virgin's struggle between her desire for personal happiness and her vows of service to the state was sufficient to insure more than 100 performances in its first season in Paris. The libretto stressed the gaining of glory on the battlefield, and Spontini supplied the necessary triumphal marches. His music is full of the sounding brass and the trumpet's blare, singing in the grand style, and the declamation of massive choruses. One of his contemporaries wrote: "his *forte* was a hurricane, his *piano* a breath, his *sforzando* enough to wake the dead." It was none other than Berlioz who attributed to him the invention of the "colossal crescendo."

Unknown to Napoleon, however, the essence of the heroic ideal had been distilled in musical form by a musician in one of the conquered countries. Beethoven's *Third Symphony*, which he himself called the *Eroica*, or Heroic, was never heard by the man whose career had suggested it; nor was it even played in Paris until 1828, a quarter of a century after it was composed. Yet a French writer of later times, Romain Rolland, could declare with the full weight of history on his side: "Here is an Austerlitz of music, the conquest of an empire. And Beethoven's has endured longer than Napoleon's." The inception of this mighty work apparently took place in 1798 when General Bernadotte, as an emissary from France, visited Vienna. In his suite was the French violinist Rodolphe Kreutzer, and through the General's interest in music, Beethoven soon came to his attention. He is credited with the suggestion that Beethoven write a work honoring Consul Bonaparte, and it is probable that he had little more than a dedication in mind. For four years the thought was with Beethoven, and the *Eroica* eventually bore the desired dedication. The year of its completion, however, coincided with that in which Napoleon accepted the imperial address. Beethoven, feeling that the erstwhile apostle of liberty had become both a traitor and a new tyrant, erased the name from the title page and inscribed it instead "to the memory of a great man." This memory indeed had stirred Beethoven deeply, and from the days of his youth he had been a lifelong partisan of the ideals of liberty, equality, and fraternity. It was Napoleon's espousal of these principles, his implacable opposition to hereditary privilege, his will and ability to translate these ideals into action, that had moved Beethoven profoundly as it had so many other artists and writers of the time. The symphony is not, and never was, narrowly Napoleonic, but more generally an elaboration of the heroism of one who, for a time at least, rallied the progressive and freedom-loving people of all nations around his standard.

The music Beethoven wrote for the theater was invariably based on themes involving the quest for individual liberty and the cause of popular freedom. His *Prometheus* ballet, for instance, was about two statues that were brought to life by the divine fire of knowledge and human creativity. The overtures and incidental music he wrote for plays had to do with an inner struggle for freedom in the case of Collin's *Coriolanus;* and the liberating of an oppressed people in Goethe's *Egmont,* as well as Kotzebue's *Ruins of Athens* and *King Stephen.* While he admired the music of Mozart's *Marriage of Figaro* and *Don Giovanni,* he was shocked by the immorality of the plots and some of the characters. In his only opera, therefore, Beethoven insisted on a libretto that would reflect high moral purpose and steadfast resolve.

In his instrumental compositions these self-same ideals of liberty, equality, and fraternity attained in his fluid forms their most abstract and universal expression. Beethoven used the power of his art to convey the spirit of these great human declarations; and, by so doing, he illuminated the path of man as he works toward his ultimate destiny of progress and perfectibility. His achievement was all the greater because he was able to do it without programmatic dilutions, thereby strengthening rather than weakening his art. Through the *Eroica*, he was giving tangible shape to the aspirations of a large segment of mankind during those stirring times. In it he mirrored the titanic struggle between the opposing attitudes of submission and assertion, between passivity and activity, and between acceptance and challenge. Through it he gave flesh to the word of the victory of spirit over matter, will over negation, and the victorious human drive against the forces of suppression. Though the length of the symphony is unprecedented and his orchestra somewhat expanded, Beethoven never fell into the trap that many of the French composers of the Revolutionary period did. While they wrote their choruses for 1000 voices, accompanied by cannons and three or four combined orchestras, Beethoven added but one more horn to his brass section. He clothed his ideas in rich folds of lustrous sound that grow out of the poetic idea itself. Furthermore by raising the level of musical content and making it commensurate with his instrumental forces, he succeeded in producing an organic work of art where the others failed. While the symphony as a whole can be criticized on formal grounds and because of a certain lack of unity in the four separate movements, the fiery spirit of creation in which Beethoven is at the height of his mature creative powers has never been surpassed. It was as much a revolution in the musical field as the French Revolution was in that of political thought and action.

Each of the four movements is in its way precedent-shattering. The first is distinguished by its restless surging character and its expansion of the first-movement form to encompass a development section of 245 bars. The mobilization of such forces as well as the transformation of the coda into a terminal development 140 measures in length caused Romain Rolland to call it a "Grand Army of the soul, that will not stop until it has trampled on the whole earth." [2] A cogent formal analysis of this opening movement by Tovey can be found in the *Encyclopædia Britannica*, 14th Edition, under "Sonata Forms." A Funeral March as the second movement of a symphony was another innovation, though Beethoven had included one in his earlier *Sonata for Piano* Op. 26 which bears the inscription "on the death of a hero." Its heroic proportions here, as well as its poetic conception as an apotheosis of the hero, link it with the first movement. While such an apotheosis is a fairly common idea for a painting, statue, poem, play, or opera, its incorporation here into the more abstract symphonic form is unique. The effect is one of a glowing elegy for the heroic among mankind who give up life itself so that the ideals for which they fought may live. It is in this case a collective rather than an individualized expression, though it emphasizes that every great advance of mankind is accompanied by personal tragedy. The stately measured rhythms and muffled sonorities also reminded the listener of Beethoven's time that contemporary heroes, as well as such ancient ones as Socrates and Jesus, often suffered martyrdom at the hands of an uncomprehending society. The title Scherzo over the third movement also appears for the first time in a formal symphony, though again it had been used earlier in piano sonatas and chamber music. Beethoven again reveals himself a man of the Revolutionary period by the substitution of this robust humor for the traditional minuet, but in such a grand design he hardly had any other alternative. Berlioz has referred to its energetic rhythms as a kind of play, "recalling that which the warriors of the *Iliad* celebrated round the tombs of their chiefs."

For his finale Beethoven writes such a monumental set of variations that it becomes a veritable musical arch of triumph through which the image of a liberated humanity joyfully passes in review. To comprehend its full meaning, it is necessary to look both backward and forward to other landmarks in Beethoven's work. The theme itself is taken from the last dance of his ballet music for *Prometheus.* Its frequent appearance in his notebooks, and its existence in two other versions—a set of piano variations and a simple country dance—show that it figured prominently in his musical thought for several years. For him the theme had definite Promethean associations and a certain buoyant optimism. For Beethoven, as for Shelley, the figure of Prometheus represented "the type of the highest perfection of moral and intellectual nature impelled by the purest and truest motives to the best and noblest of ends." [3] It was Prometheus who first defied the gods themselves in order to bring the divine fire of the arts and sciences from the Olympian hearth so as to animate the spirits of men and release them from the bondage of ignorance. He thus became a symbol of creative power through which Beethoven was able to convey his conviction of the ultimate perfectibility of mankind. The fiery and precipitous descent of the opening bars had also been heard in the ballet music in a more literal sense. Here it serves as a mighty preparation for the emergence of the skeleton theme.

What is heard at first is simply a structural outline derived from the bass of the Promethean dance, which defines a tonal center together with the upper and lower dominant limits of the tonality. This harmonic vacuum is gradually populated by the addition of a second, third, and fourth voice, while the rhythmic divisions are simultaneously quickened by similar subdivisions. Not until the 76th bar is the Promethean melody joined to its previously heard skeletal bass.

Symphony No. 3. Finale: Allegro Molto (Bars 76–83)   Beethoven

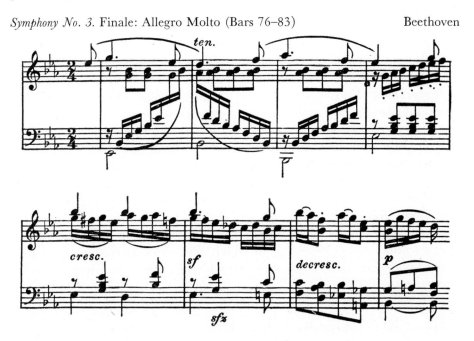

The form thus enfolds in the cyclic manner of a set of variations unequal in length and strongly contrasted in style. What had before been but a pleasant little dance tune now assumes the imposing shape of a triumphant melody, which Beethoven, by the extension of this additive process, is able to build into the cumulative image he needs for his victory finale. Here in one stroke the great idea sprang full-grown and full-armed from the brain of its creator. For all its lofty intentions, however, the *Eroica* finale is not yet completely achieved as a work of art, and its ultimate significance can be understood only when it is placed in the company of the finales of the later *Fifth* and *Ninth Symphonies*.

These finales, which envision the emergence of a strong and free humanity, all begin with quasi-popular themes. In the *Eroica* it is a modest little country dance; in the *Fifth*, a simple marching tune; and in the *Ninth* an unpretentious hymn. One and all, they are built up to epical proportions. By the use of an immense variety of styles, episodic deviations, a wide range of keys, and shifting orchestral color, they become collective rather than individual expressions. Instead of being restricted to one side of life, they embrace a cross section of musical levels and reach out to encompass the entire human panorama. Some variations are aristocratic in sound, while others are rough and ready. Compare, for instance, the elegant sonorities of bars 175–197 in the *Eroica* finale with the boisterous band music heard in bars 211–255. Another such open-air episode as the latter occurs in the finale of the *Ninth* where the composer inserts a popular "Turkish" march, scored in a bizarre manner for bassoons, horns, trombones, cymbals, triangle, and drums. A similar pair of opposites can be heard in the fugal episodes (bars 117–174, and 266–348), which employ sophisticated contrapuntal devices, such as the inversion of the skeleton theme (277–280) and the rather stolid German chorale (249–364) that begins at the point where the tempo is slackened to a Poco Andante. All this vast variety of forms— dances, songs, fugues, chorales—are arranged sequentially in the manner of a procession that eventually leads up to the rousing triumphant climax heard in bars 381 to 395. At this point Beethoven throws in all his orchestral forces, including the brasses and drums, to bring about the image of ultimate achievement of the heroic idea. Afterward there remains only the quieter anticlimax (396–430), in which the whole awesome spectacle is contemplated retrospectively, and the whirlwind *presto* that terminates the movement.

THE ARCHEOLOGICAL IDEA

The picture of the Napoleonic period is one of a paradoxical mixture of progressive and retrogressive tendencies. At the very time, for instance, when the social aspirations of the Revolutionary period were about to crystallize into new forms, the people were confronted with a militant revival of Roman autocracy. The individualism of the 18th century that had given birth to the Revolution was now engulfed in a 19th-century form of regimentation under the guise of an effort to preserve the gains that were made. The ideals of the Revolution contrasted with the actualities of Napoleon's regime; the desire for freedom collided with the necessity for order; the rights of man were in conflict with the might of man; and his spiritual well-being was pitted against his material welfare.

How, for instance, could the use of new scientific and technological ideas be accepted and widely used in a time that devoted so much of its thought and energies to the revival of ancient Roman grandeur? Napoleon boasted of a new culture, yet clothed it in an ancient costume. He employed the latest technological modes of warfare, yet acted out the part of a Roman imperator. In such a building as the Madeleine, the inside was an example of the new eclectic style, while the outside was a calculated archeological study, making it in fact two different buildings. In his portrait sculpture Canova had something of a similar problem in matching the modern heads of his subjects with the bodies he copied after antique statues. In painting the search for the means of expressing new ideas came up against the strength of the inherited academic tradition. The paradox is also reflected in David's rationalism and insistence on rules at a time when widespread emotionalism was rampant. This cleavage between thinking and feeling can only be viewed as a reaction to the excessive passion of the times. Just as Napoleon had introduced a new authoritarianism in the field of governmental and social institutions, so David felt the same necessity in the field of the pictorial arts. In the 18th century Voltaire had said that the voice of the people was the voice of God. Mengs had expressed the same thought in the field of aesthetics when he declared in his *Thoughts on Beauty and Taste* (1765) that the beautiful was that which appealed to the majority. Yet David and other academicians with strong governmental support felt compelled to tell the majority what they should enjoy.

The resolutions of these tensions found their way into the arts in a multiplicity of ways. Deferring the consideration of the progressive directions of thought and the continuation of the Revolutionary principles until the end of the next chapter, the discussion at this point will be limited to the archeological idea and how the new scientific knowledge of Greco-Roman antiquity was applied to the art forms of the time.

There is, after all, nothing unique about a revival of the past. In some form or another a resurrection of Roman ideas and motives is present in all subsequent periods of Western art. The question is more what form the revival takes, the choices that are made from the 1000-year span of the Greco-Roman civilization, and the extent of a period's knowledge and understanding of ancient civilization. In the forms of government, for instance, practically all choices are open—city-state, kingdom, republic, empire. Were the dramas and operas set in Athens, Sparta, the Alexandrian Empire, the Roman Republic, or the Roman Empire? Were the characters to be lofty Olympian deities or rugged Roman historical figures? Were the models for the dramas those of Seneca, as was the case with Quinault and Racine in the Baroque period? Or Aeschylus and Euripides, as with Shelley and Goethe? Were the architects expected to build modern palaces with a few Roman motives, or were they to construct exact copies of Greek or Roman temples?

The humanistic conception of antiquity as found in the Florentine Renaissance was rooted in an antischolastic philosophical view and to some extent an anticlerical religious attitude. The movement was limited largely to a few intellectuals and artists and endured a relatively short time. That of the Napoleonic period, by contrast, was mirrored in the forms of government; it was the basis of an officially approved art; and it rested on a broad social basis. Baroque classicism was the reflection of an aristocratic image of man. The court circle of Louis XIV enjoyed identifying themselves with the gods of Mount Olympus, and the interpretation of their divine activities was in accordance with the standard of morality of a highly privileged class. Napoleonic classicism, by contrast, was oriented toward a middle-class group, which found a congenial hedonistic image in the comfortable life of the cities of Pompeii and Herculaneum. It was thus brought down to the bourgeois level and coupled at first with the austere moral standards of a newly founded republic. In relation to the 18th-century Rococo style that immediately preceded it, the new interest in classical architecture, sculpture, and painting was a conscious bourgeois criticism of the artificiality and extravagances of courtly life. Otherwise the choice of these conservative art forms would have been extremely odd for such a radical Revolutionary period.

The principal difference between the work of the early 19th-century artists and their predecessors was a desire for exact reproductions of antique models. Archeological correctness was made possible by a greater and more detailed knowledge of the past than had been enjoyed by the previous periods. Winckelmann and his generation had made classical archeology a science, and the excavations at Pompeii and Herculaneum had provided the material as well as the stimulus for the desire for authenticity. To be successful, a building had to be archeologically accurate. The Vendôme Column, for instance, was planned as an exact replica of Trajan's Column; the Arc du Carrousel preserved the proportions of the Arch of Septimus Severus while reducing it in size. Where variations were possible, as with the Arc de Triomphe de l'Étoile and the Madeleine, the results were more reassuring. The former instances resemble a pair of competent academic theses, while the latter approximate the lively style of a couple of good historical novels. Archeological correctness meant lifting an ancient building, which was designed for an antiquated purpose, out of its period and century and putting it down bodily into another where it had no reason for being. This was something that never would have occurred to the rational Enlightenment period. While Palladio, Mansart, and Wren had been concerned with adapting classical principles to the needs of their period, Vignon, Percier, and Fontaine were occupied with the problem of how the activities of their time could be made to fit into ancient molds. Using a

Roman portico over the doorway of a contemporary building in the Baroque period was one thing, but Napoleon's invention of a cult of glory as an excuse to build a Roman temple was quite another. If such antiquarianism were carried to its logical conclusion and architecture were to become the handmaid of archeology, a city would eventually be turned into a museum. However, while people occasionally visit museums they do not necessarily want to live in one—and fortunately the Napoleonic period was not that logical.

A successful statue in these times likewise had to be accurate. And since such a profusion of antique models existed, the sculptors were more limited in their creative freedom than other artists. Their desire for exactitude often led them to the point of absurdity. They omitted carving the irises and pupils of the eyes, and left them blank, because they did not know that the Greeks had painted in such details on their statues. The prevailing whiteness made their works resemble mortuary monuments, since they overlooked the fact that the ancients had not designed their friezes for museums but for the strong light and shadow of the open air. The sculptures of Canova and Thorwaldsen always manage to convey the feeling that somehow flesh has been turned to stone instead of breathing the breath of life into marble as the Greeks and Michelangelo had done.

Enthusiasm for antiquity sometimes led David into similar practices, though there were fewer examples of ancient painting for him to imitate. In his early pictures, however, he used ancient Roman portrait busts for the heads of his figures instead of live models. In the Baroque period when Poussin and Claude Lorrain painted Rome, it was usually in terms of picturesque ruins, while David and Ingres painted archeological reconstructions. Madame Recamier was a 19th-century Parisian socialite, but David made her into a fancy-dress reincarnation of a Pompeiian matron. The *Battle of the Romans and Sabines* was inspired by the reproduction of an ancient relief David had come across as an illustration in a book. In this instance, however, he did use living models, but he said that his desire was to paint the ancient walls and drape his figures with such exactness that if an ancient Roman were to view his pictures, he would find himself right at home. David's adherence to lines and planes was often so strict that the effect of his paintings was almost as severe as that of relief sculpture. From his preoccupation with the pallid world of museums and Winckelmann's books, David, like Canova, also gained the impression that the Greeks and Romans had lived in a gray-and-white world. As a result, he neglected the element of color. David was saved, however, from the major pitfalls of his architectural and sculptural colleagues because so few examples of ancient painting were known at the time; and, as a consequence, he was forced to divert his considerable talent as a painter in the direction of a new style.

In poetry a similar motivation is seen in the reforms of André Chénier, which were based on his studies of the Latin and Greek originals. For the forms of his odes and elegies, his pastoral idylls and epics, he drew directly on Homer, Pindar, Vergil, and Horace. "Let us upon new thoughts write antique verses," he had declared; and to a considerable degree his enthusiasm helped him to carry out his announced objective. In this archeological era, however, the musicians fared the best of all because there were no known examples surviving from antiquity for them to emulate. An opera, to be sure, could get some authenticity into its plot, decor, and costumes; and such productions of 1807 as Persuis' and Lesueur's *Triomphe de Trajan*, their *L'Inauguration du Temple de la Victoire*, and Spontini's *La Vestale* tried to make the grade in this respect. All this, however, was on the surface and could hardly compare with the type of authenticity represented by the Vendôme Column or the Napoleonic arches of triumph.

Since the musicians of the period had to evolve their own style, the vitality of their music has overshadowed and outlasted in its general appeal the art of their contemporaries. Just as the fussy Rococo had brought about a countermovement in the prerevolutionary classicism, so in music there had been a similar reform movement carried out under Gluck. By reducing the number of characters in his operas, omitting complicated subplots, strengthening the role of the chorus, transferring much of the lyrical expression to the orchestra, writing simple unadorned melodies, and avoiding Italianate coloratura cadenzas, he had brought about a musical revolution similar to David's in painting and paved the way for a new style. His ideas were based partially on a reinterpretation of Aristotle's *Poetics*. In his Preface to *Alceste* (1767), for instance, he had stated that his music was designed to allow the drama to proceed "without interrupting the action or stifling it with a useless superfluity of ornaments." [4] Echoing Winckelmann, he added that the great principles of beauty were "simplicity, truth and naturalness."

This objective found its ultimate fruition in the sinewy music of Beethoven who, by impatiently brushing aside ancient precedents, achieved an expression of the time that was not merely histrionic but genuinely heroic in stature. Of all the artists of his time, Beethoven emerges as the most truly representative figure; and his art for this reason was and remains the most outstanding expressive accomplishment of the period. It is possible to point to the fact that his idealism had classical overtones; that his devotion to the cause of freedom echoed the creative genius of ancient Greece;

that the dithyrambic finale of the *Eroica* breathes a Promethean spirit; that the elegiac quality of the Funeral March is akin to the Greek tragic form; that by thus paying tribute to past glory, he associates himself with the revival idea; that by taking an individual such as Napoleon and raising his image to an archetype of heroism, he is in harmony with Greek aesthetics; and that the clarity of his forms, the economy of his means, and the simplification of his materials are akin to classical methods. If this is so, it is only in the general sense that Shelley spoke of in his Preface to *Hellas:* "We are all Greeks. Our laws, our literature, our religion, our arts, have their roots in Greece."

C H A P T E R

CHRONOLOGY: Paris, Middle 19th Century

General Events

1814	Fall of Napoleon
	Restoration of the Bourbon monarchy under Louis XVIII
1821	Death of Napoleon
1824	Death of Louis XVIII, succession of Charles X
1830	July Revolution overthrew old line of Bourbons
	Louis Philippe began reign as limited monarch
1837	Commission for the Preservation of Historical Monuments founded by Louis Philippe
1840	Guizot (1787–1874), French historian and statesman, became Prime Minister
1848	February Revolution overthrew Louis Philippe's government
	Second Republic proclaimed
	Louis Napoleon, nephew of Napoleon I, elected president
1852	Louis Napoleon elected emperor, reigns under title of Napoleon III
1870	Napoleon III abdicated after unsuccessful conclusion of the Franco-Prussian War
	Third Republic proclaimed

Architects

1752–1835	John Nash
1790–1853	François Christian Gau
1795–1860	Charles Barry
1814–1879	Viollet-le-Duc

Sculptors

1784–1855	François Rude
1787–1843	Jean Pierre Cortot
1796–1875	Antoine Louis Barye

Painters

1776–1837	John Constable
1780–1867	Jean Auguste Ingres
1791–1824	Théodore Géricault
1796–1875	Camille Corot
1798–1863	Eugène Delacroix
1808–1879	Honoré Daumier
1814–1875	François Millet

Writers

1717–1797	Horace Walpole
1749–1832	Johann Wolfgang Goethe
1771–1832	Walter Scott
1774–1843	Robert Southey
1788–1824	Lord Byron
1788–1860	Arthur Schopenhauer
1792–1822	Percy B. Shelley
1795–1821	John Keats
1797–1856	Heinrich Heine
1799–1850	Honoré Balzac
1802–1870	Alexandre Dumas
1802–1885	Victor Hugo
1803–1870	Prosper Mérimée
1804–1876	George Sand
1811–1872	Théophile Gautier

Musicians

1782–1871	Daniel Auber
1782–1840	Niccolo Paganini
1786–1826	Carl Maria von Weber
1803–1869	Hector Berlioz
1809–1849	Frederic Chopin
1809–1847	Felix Mendelssohn
1810–1856	Robert Schumann
1811–1886	Franz Liszt
1813–1901	Giuseppe Verdi
1813–1883	Richard Wagner
1818–1893	Charles Gounod
1833–1897	Johannes Brahms
1838–1875	Georges Bizet

18

THE MIDDLE 19th CENTURY

PARIS, 1830

During the days before the July Revolution new ideas were stirring in the minds and imaginations of the intellectuals and artists of Paris. In the year 1827, for instance, when the cumulative momentum of the new movement was well under way, Victor Hugo published his *Cromwell*, a drama with a preface that served as a manifesto of Romanticism. Guizot was lecturing at the Sorbonne on the early history of France. François Rude, destined to be the principal sculptor of the period, returned from his Belgian exile. Delacroix, the painter, tells in his journal how in September of that year, when he went to the Odéon Theater to see Shakespeare's *Hamlet*, he met such writers as Alfred de Vigny, Alexander Dumas, and Hugo. The Ophelia in that production was played by Harriet Smithson, later to become the wife of Hector Berlioz. Gérard de Nerval's translation of Goethe's *Faust* had appeared that autumn and had inspired the composition of Berlioz' *Eight Scenes from Faust*, later to reach popularity under the revision called the *Damnation of Faust*. Delacroix, who had just exhibited his *Death of Sardanapalus* in the Salon, was already at work on his famous lithographs for *Faust*, which were to illustrate an edition to be published the following year. All in all it was an inspiring time, and when Théophile Gautier later came to write his history of Romanticism, he looked back on his youthful participation in these events with genuine nostalgia. "What a marvelous time," he wrote, "Walter Scott was then in the flower of his success; one was initiated into the mysteries of Goethe's *Faust*, which as Madame de Staël said, contained everything. One discovered Shakespeare, and the poems of Lord Byron: the *Corsair; Lara; The Giaour; Manfred; Beppo;* and *Don Juan* took us to the orient, which was not banal then as now.

All was young, new, exotically colored, intoxicating, and strongly flavored. It turned our heads; it was as if we had entered into a strange new world." [1]

The new movement in France was swept in on a wave of political unrest culminating in the July Revolution of 1830. Nowhere is there to be found a better example of the mating of an artistic genius and the spirit of his time than that of Eugène Delacroix and the events in Paris of that year. The glorious July days were brought to incandescent expression in his picture *Liberty Leading the People* (Fig. 18:1), in which he captured the distilled essence of that revolution. The canvas is dominated by the fiery allegorical figure of Liberty, here seen as the spirit of the French people whom she leads onward to triumph. No relaxed Mediterranean goddess here, instead a virile, energetic reincarnation of the spirit of 1789. Her muscular arms are strong enough to hold with ease both a bayoneted rifle and the tricolored banner of the Republic. Though bare-breasted she betrays no sign of softness or sensuality, and her powerful limbs stride over the street barricades as she leads her followers forward through the oncoming barrage. Though an allegorical figure, she is treated by the artist as a living personality, clothed in the garments of a daughter of the French people. Only the Phrygian cap (modeled after that worn by liberated slaves in Rome and adopted as a symbol of liberty by the first French Republic) and the almost classic profile, serene in the face of danger, indicate her symbolic significance. She does not hover over the action on wings as so many other artists depicted her; instead, with her feet on the ground, she is in the midst of action. Her motley followers include both impetuous students and battle-scarred soldiers who have heeded her call rather than that of their reactionary king. The boy on the right is recruited from the Paris streets. Too young to understand the significance of the events, he is there, a pistol in each hand, joining in the general excitement for all the world a prototype of the youthful imitators of western cowboys today. In the background are the remnants of the old guard from Revolutionary days still carrying on the struggle. Two main social classes are represented. The man in the shadows on the extreme left and armed with a saber is an obviously proletarian figure, while the more prominent one in front of him toward the center is a bourgeois gentleman in the modish frock coat, top hat, and sideburns, who has grabbed his musket and joined in the general confusion. It was his class that controlled the fighting and derived the benefits from it by stamping their image on the new monarchy represented in the person of Louis Philippe, the Citizen King. Though it was essentially a palace revolution, going no farther than to replace a reactionary Bourbon with his cousin from a more liberal branch of the family, no aristocrats are

Fig. 18:1. Delacroix. *Liberty Leading the People, 1830.* 102″ x 128″. Louvre, Paris (Archives Photographiques)

represented as taking part. In the shadows below, the wounded and dying are strewn about on the loose cobblestones looking toward Liberty as they die, as she is both their inspiration and their reason for being. Through smoke at the right the towers of the cathedral of Notre Dame are discernible.

Because of the contemporary frame of reference in which one recognizes the familiar shirts, blouses, trousers, as well as rifles, pistols, and other 19th-century paraphernalia, the picture has been called realistic. Since the spirit of the work transcends the event itself, and since the artist has clearly rendered the feeling about it more than the actuality, this is surely a misunderstanding. By infusing the reality with the charge of an electrical emotional attitude, he raises it to the level of an idealized, though highly personal, expression, so that all who see it seem to be experiencing the event for themselves. More eloquent than any page in a history book it has captured the feeling as well as the facts that make up the incident. It is as if all the noise had awakened the artist from his dreams of the past, and now suddenly wide awake, he has applied his expressive techniques consciously to one of the stirring happenings of his own time.

As always with Delacroix, color plays an important part in the communication of the mood. A striking instance of its use is seen here in the way he takes the red, white, and blue colors of the banner (the symbol of the patriotic element) and merges them into the picture as a whole. The white central strip, signifying truth and purity, blends with the purifying smoke of the battle; the blue, denoting freedom, matches the parts of the sky visible in the top corners through the smoke; while the red in the flag high above symbolically balances the color of the blood of those below who have fallen for the ideal of liberty. Thus the symbolism of the banner blends into the color scheme and both merge with the dramatic lighting to define the emotional range. All these, in turn, combine to expand an all-pervading patriotic theme into a formal pictorial unity of concentrated intensity. With the purchase of this picture in the name of the state by the new bourgeois king himself at the time it was shown in the Salon of 1831, there was no doubt that the seal of official approval had been put on the aesthetics of the new movement.

PAINTING

It was characteristic of the painting of this period that Delacroix, its leading representative, should look more to the fantasy of the literary world for the sources of his pictorial visions than to that of the world of appearances. His choice of subjects as well as his treatment of them make this immediately apparent. The *Death of Sardanapalus*, *Mazeppa*, *Giaour and the Pasha*, and the *Shipwreck of Don Juan* all point to their inception from the poetry of Byron. His interest in Shakespeare is shown in his drawings of scenes from *Hamlet*, and the witches' scene from *Macbeth* (Fig. 18:2). His *Abduction of Rebecca* steps directly out of Chapter 31 of Scott's *Ivanhoe;* and his illustrations for Goethe's *Faust* (Figs. 18:3–6) won the complete admiration of the author himself, who felt that for clarity and depth of insight they could not be surpassed. Delacroix' imagination was haunted by this drama from the time of his first contact with it in London. He wrote to a friend back in Paris commenting particularly on the diabolical element in it. The lithographs that eventually resulted show his mastery of the illustration medium and prove him as adept in works of smaller dimensions as he was in his epical pictures. In spite of his close kinship with Byron and Goethe, Delacroix was not always in sympathy with the work of his Parisian contemporaries. In his diary he spoke of Meyerbeer's opera *Le Prophète* as being "frightful," and referred to Berlioz and Hugo as those "so-called reformers." "The noise he makes is distracting," he wrote about Berlioz'

Delacroix. Fig. 18:2 (right). *Witches' Scene*. Illustration for *Macbeth*, Act IV, Scene 1. Lithograph. Fig. 18:3 (below left). *Mephistopheles in the Air*. Fig. 18:4 (below right). *Witches' Kitchen*. Fig. 18:5 (bottom left). *Margaret in Church*. Fig. 18:6 (bottom right). *Faust and Mephistopheles Galloping*. Illustrations for Goethe's *Faust*, Part I, lines 1709–19, 2078–89, 3449–3482, and 4095–4124, respectively. Lithographs. 1828. Metropolitan Museum, New York

music, "it is an heroic mess." Of all musicians he admired Mozart the most, and Chopin alone among his contemporaries had the requisite polish and craftsmanship to measure up to his standards. While his own art abounded in subjects of horror and violence, he always managed to keep it within the boundaries of restraint and disapproved of similar tendencies in the work of others.

The technique of his own art was designed as a means toward conveying a highly turbulent and emotional subject matter. Color was dominant over design, and he consciously sought to avoid the grays and browns of his predecessors. "Gray is the enemy of all painting," he wrote, "let us banish from our palette all earth colors . . . the greater the opposition in color, the greater the brilliance." His admitted models in painting were the heroic canvases of Rubens and the dramatic pictures of Rembrandt with their emphasis on the dynamics of light. His art is built on an aesthetic of color, light and emotion rather than on line, drawing and form. This is nowhere better illustrated than in his early masterpiece, *Dante and Vergil in Hell* (Fig. 18:7), the first of his pictures to attract wide attention when it was exhibited in the Salon of the year 1822.

Stemming out of the predilection for the medieval and macabre, the interest in Dante was one of the main facets of the Gothic Revival. What Homer had been to the classical enthusiasts, the Tuscan poet was to the new movement. Shelley and the Pre-Raphaelites were making England Dante-conscious; and while Schlegel and Schelling were translating and interpreting him for the Germans, Chateaubriand and Sainte-Beuve were doing the same for the French. To realize the extent of the *Divine Comedy*'s influence, one needs only to recall such works as Hugo's poem *Après une lecture de Dante* (*After Reading Dante*), which Franz Liszt used as a programme for a piano fantasy, and his *Dante Symphony*.

In his picture Delacroix enters the realm of pure pathos. The central figure is that of Vergil in the robe of a Florentine crowned with the laurel wreath, standing with impassive monumentality as a symbol of classic calm. On his left is Dante with a red hood on his head, expressively human in contrast to the serenity of his immortal companion and emotionally involved with his grotesque and gruesome surroundings. He looks with terror on the damned who swirl about him in the water below. The wake of the boat is livid with the writhing forms of the condemned, who hope eternally to reach the opposite shore by trying to attach themselves to the bark. One attempts to clamber aboard, the gnashing teeth of another bites into the edge of the boat, but in vain as they are plunged again into the dark waters. Distress and despair are everywhere. On the right is Phlegyas,

Fig. 18:7. Delacroix. *Dante and Vergil in Hell*. 74″ x 94⅞″. 1822. Louvre, Paris (Alinari)

the sepulchral boatman, seen from the rear as he strains at the rudder to guide the boat across the river Styx to the flaming shores of the city of Dis, seen in the distant background between the clouds of sulphurous fumes. The lurid coloration serves to create the illusion that the picture has been painted in blood, phosphorus, and flame.

When Delacroix was at work on it he had a young friend read the poem to him, and, as he says in his journal: "The best head in my Dante picture was swept in with the greatest speed and spirit while Pierret was reading me a canto from Dante which I knew already but to which he lent, by his accent, an energy that electrified me. That head is the one of the man behind the boat, facing you and trying to climb aboard, after throwing his arm over the gunwale." [2] The particular passage that inflamed the artist's imagination and on which he built the picture is from the eighth book of the Inferno.

When first exhibited, the picture brought storms of protest and vituperation on Delacroix' head, which helped immeasurably to bring the young artist of 23 to critical attention. One defender of the academic tradition of David called it a "splattering of color," and another thought he had "combined all the parts of the work in view of one emotion." While its expressive intensity was novel for its time, the work now easily falls into place as·a part of the macabre aspect of the Romantic movement. Its contribution to the development of painting consists of a shift from the shadow effects used over and over again from the time of Leonardo da Vinci, to light as a dominant medium of expression but used more in the manner of patterns of color than as tangible forms and shapes. Even the nude figures, as muscular as some by Michelangelo and Rubens, function here pictorially more in terms of masses of color. Such is the contribution Delacroix made to his art with this and later pictures that were destined to have a profound influence on modern painting.

SCULPTURE

Dominant among the sculptural works of the period is the *Departure of the Volunteers* (Fig. 18:9) by François Rude. This is explained both by its vehement expression and sustained heroic mood as well as by its prominent location on one side of the Arc de Triomphe in Paris, which assured it the largest possible audience. Sculptured in the boldest high relief, the dimensions of the composition alone—rising to a height of almost 42 feet and spreading laterally 26 feet—make it of truly colossal proportions. Its conception and commission date from the wave of patriotic emotion associated with the July Revolution of 1830 and the memories it stirred of earlier struggles for freedom. It took Delacroix but a year to get his painting before the public, but the execution of a sculptural work of these proportions delayed its unveiling for six years. The scene depicted is that of a band of volunteers rallying to the defense of the newly established French Republic when it was threatened by foreign invasion in 1792. The five resolute figures in the foreground are coming together to meet the common danger and are receiving mutual inspiration from the figure of Bellona, the Roman goddess of war, who hovers above them, inciting them onward with the singing of *La Marseillaise*. A fine rhythmical mood is established by the compact grouping of the figures, reinforced by the repeated motive of the legs that combine with the arm of the soldier stooping to tie his sandal. This serves to weld the composition together as a whole in the manner of a lively yet majestic march. These representatives of the humanity so recently liberated by the French Revolution are self-motivated protectors of their newly won liberty, equality, and fraternity. The full manhood of four of the volunteers is balanced by the potential strength of the finely realized figure of the impetuous youth and the waning ability of the old man behind him who can only point out the direction to them and wave

Fig. 18:8 (above left). Cortot. *Apotheosis of Napoleon.* 1836. Fig. 18:9 (above right). Rude. *Departure of the Volunteers.* 41′ 8″ high x 26′ wide. 1836. Left and right reliefs on the *Arc de Triomphe*, Paris (Archives Photographiques)

Fig. 18:10 (left). Rude. *Joan of Arc Listening to the Voices.* 1845. Louvre, Paris (Archives Photographiques)

them on. The surging power, directed by the common ideals, impels them onward with irresistible force and momentum.

Because Rude designed the *Departure* for a Napoleonic arch of triumph, his motives are of Roman derivation. The soldiers are outfitted with Roman helmets and shields, though the coats of mail and weapons in the background recall those of the Middle Ages. The avoidance of any contemporary reference in the costumes and symbols in the representation of an event that had taken place less than half a century before links the composition with the tendency to draw on the past for inspiration. Popularly, and quite properly, called "the *Marseillaise* in stone," it represents a most ingenious sculptural use of a musical motive in suggesting the great Revolutionary song, which serves here both in unifying the spirit of the group and in reinforcing the patriotic symbolism. The anthem was originally composed by a young lieutenant in the Revolutionary army, Rouget de Lisle, and was practically forgotten during the days of Napoleon's empire. Under the Bourbon restoration it was, of course, officially banned. Credit for its rediscovery and revival goes to Hector Berlioz. Stirred into a patriotic frenzy by the events of July 1830, though avoiding direct participation, this erratic genius contented himself with scoring this song for double chorus and orchestra, characteristically asking "all who have voices, a heart, and blood in their veins" to join in. The final stanza begins dramatically with three unaccompanied voices; then he gradually marshals his vocal and orchestral forces in a big crescendo leading up to the refrain: "To arms, O citizens." This version received many performances, the most notable being a large benefit with the proceeds going to the families of the victims of the July Revolution. Later it was officially adopted as the French national anthem, though not with Berlioz' orchestration, and it has become one of the world's best-known tunes. It is most probably this revival that was Rude's inspiration for the group.

The treatment of the subject, the momentum of the composition, and the impassioned facial expressions of the figures make Rude's work an odd contrast with its companion piece, Cortot's *Apotheosis of Napoleon* (Fig. 18:8), executed at the same time. A complete design for the decoration of the whole arch was made by Rude, but only the *Departure of the Volunteers* was finally commissioned and carried out. Public taste and official circles still leaned somewhat toward the classical revival, and with Cortot's group we have a typical academic approach. While the classical idea continued throughout the century, the vitality it had through the stimulus of the heroic days of Napoleon was now definitely on the wane. With Rude all is passion and movement, and his composition literally bursts its bonds in its dynamic forward tendency. With Cortot all is balanced and rigidly poised in a static equilibrium centering on the standing figure of Napoleon. Clothed in the toga of a Roman emperor, he is being crowned by a semi-nude personification of the spirit of France, who looks as if the Venus de Milo, with her arms happily restored for the occasion, had walked over from the Louvre Museum. Other allegorical figures, including one representing History, make up the rest of the group. The best that can be said about it is that it has a certain stateliness and gives no offense through blatance or pomposity. However these two examples standing opposite each other on the same monument show the difference between the continuation of the stilted academic tradition and a vigorous new treatment where all is movement, action, and emotion.

In a later work, *Joan of Arc Listening to the Voices* (Fig. 18:10), Rude combines this emotional treatment with Gothic Revival subject matter. Executed originally in 1845 for the gardens of the Luxembourg Palace, it has now found its way into the Louvre. Both the *Departure of the Volunteers* and *Joan of Arc* show how closely the two revivals were intertwined and how the attitude of the artist and his treatment of his material were really far more important than whether his subject was drawn from ancient Rome or medieval France. He represents the maid of Orleans in peasant costume with a suit of armor at her side. The dual aspects of her nature are thus suggested and her inner tension is shown as she strains to hear the supernatural voices that direct her activities. By trying to capture the intangible sounds of these heavenly voices as she listens quiveringly with upraised head, Rude strains his marble medium to its expressive limits.

Rude, who had grown up during the days of the Revolution, was always thoroughly in sympathy with the spirit of his time. He accepted exile in Belgium in 1815 rather than live under a Bourbon ruler. Action was his aesthetic watchword. "The great thing for an artist," he once said, "is to *do*." Some find his *Departure of the Volunteers* overcrowded, overloaded, and unbalanced. Others feel that this is justified by the subject of a concerted uprising of the masses and that it finds unity in the direction of its movement. There is clearly no will toward classical repose in it, and its sheer energy makes a clean break with the academic tradition. By thus liberating sculpture from many outworn idioms and clichés, Rude should be given more credit than has heretofore been accorded him. In retrospect he emerges more and more as the most important French sculptor of the period between 1830 and 1848.

Fig. 18:11 (above). Wyatt. *Fonthill Abbey*. Tower 280′ high. 1796–1814. Wiltshire, England

Fig. 18:12 (left). Wyatt. Fonthill Abbey, *Interior*. 245′ long x 35′ wide

ARCHITECTURE

The primary stimulus to the Gothic Revival movement in architecture is found in the literary genre of the Gothic novel in England. One has but to review some of the titles of the novels and plays of the second half of the 18th century there to realize what was afoot: *The Haunted Priory*; *The Horrid Mysteries*; *Banditti, or Love in a Labyrinth*; *Raymond and Agnes, or The Bleeding Nun of Lindenberg*; and Horace Walpole's novel *The Castle of Otranto*, subtitled *A Gothic Tale*, which appeared in 1764 and proved to be highly influential. These stories were laid in settings consisting of large baronial halls and decayed abbeys, equipped liberally with mysterious trapdoors, sliding panels, creaking postern gates, animated suits of armor, and sepulchral voices emanating from ancient tombs. Such scenes served as backdrops for the injured innocence of fragile and helpless heroines and the intrepid, if somewhat reckless, courage of dashing heroes. These tales played their part in the redefinition of the word *Gothic*—which Voltaire had called a fantastic compound of rudeness and filigree—into something more redolent of the mystical, tinged with weirdness, and bordering on the fantastic. These imaginary castles of the novels first took on concrete form in England as the architectural whims of wealthy eccentrics. Walpole, the well-to-do son of a powerful prime minister, indulged his fancy in a residence that gave its name to one aspect of this style, "Strawberry Hill Gothick." Another wealthy individual, William Beckford, had the architect James Wyatt construct him a residence he called Fonthill Abbey (Fig. 18:11). Its huge central tower rose over a spacious interior hall that was approached by a massive staircase (Fig. 18:12). The rest of the interior was a labyrinth of drafty corridors that provided the wall space for the proprietor's collections of pictures and tapestries as well as a suitable setting for his melancholy musings. In his frenzy to have it completed, he drove the workers day and night to the point where, in their haste, they neglected to provide an adequate foundation for the tower; and, like the dream castle it was, it fell to the ground in 1823. However, since ruins at the time were greatly in demand as residences, this catastrophe served only to enhance its value and make it the more desirable.

The movement steadily gained in momentum until by the end of the 18th century Jane Austen was satirizing it deliciously in her novel *Northanger Abbey*. All this laid the foundation for the huge success of Sir Walter Scott's novels, which, when translated into French beginning in 1816, in turn prepared the way for the popularity of the romances of Hugo and Dumas.

Fig. 18:13. Barry. *Houses of Parliament.* 940' long. 1840–1860. London (Courtesy British Information Services)

Among the surviving English architectural counterparts of this literary phase are the Houses of Parliament (Fig. 18:13), begun by Sir Charles Barry in 1839, and the New Law Courts by Street, both of which are familiar landmarks in the London of today. Significantly too, the Gothic Revival style is found in New York, where the spires of Trinity Church (1839–1846), designed by Upjohn, are overshadowed now by the more materialistic aspirations of Broadway's skyscrapers. Two churches by Renwick furnish further examples—Grace Church in the Bowery of 1845, and the well-known St. Patrick's Cathedral on Fifth Avenue, which was begun in 1850. The movement widens on the American scene with the many cottages, castle residences, and railroad stations; later even some college campuses succumbed to the lure of the Gothic in their desire to be identified with ancient and honorable causes.

On the other side of the Rhine, the young poet Goethe, under the guidance of his university mentor Gottfried Herder, was writing in praise of the builder of the Strasbourg Cathedral, Erwin von Steinbach, as early as 1772. The book was significantly entitled, *Von deutscher Baukunst* (*Of German Architecture*). Later he placed his version of the medieval Faust legend in thoroughly Gothic surroundings. In both England and Germany, this new interest in the Gothic had distinctly nationalistic overtones. Both countries claimed the style as their own invention, and to them it was a conscious departure in their cultural orientation from the Greco-Roman world of antiquity as well as some of the more recent phases of the Mediterranean tradition. In England it was closely bound up with the wave of prosperity caused by a great industrial expansion, a glowing national pride, and a reaction against the Napoleonic dreams of an empire that had threatened their own. A reassertion of the separation of the Church of England from Rome took shape in the Oxford movement, which demanded veering away from Greco-Roman architectural forms as essentially pagan, and restoration of medieval liturgies that, in turn, needed appropriate Gothic settings.

In Germany it took the form of a vision of past national glory associated with that country's entrance upon the European scene under Charlemagne, whom the Germans adopted as a national hero under the name of Karl der Grosse. The relative security and eminence under the rule of the Holy Roman Empire continued intermittently up to the reign in the 16th century of the Habsburg Charles V, the last of the powerful emperors. The past thus played an important role in the 19th-century revival of German power, based as it was on the remembrance of an empire dominated from the north. Stung into action by its abolition under Napoleon, German nationalism fermented during the 19th century until it matured into the rather heady wine of Bismarck's statesmanship, the aroma of which reminded Teutonic connoisseurs of the heroic bouquet of such ancient vintages as those of Attila, Alaric, and Barbarossa.

From the Renaissance on through the Aristocratic Baroque tradition and the 18th century, French art was closely bound to the traditional Greco-Roman forms. During the Revolution of 1789 and its aftermath, a wave of anticlericalism led to the actual destruction of some medieval buildings as symbols of the old church domination and the new freedom. The Roman Revival under the First Empire continued it through the early years of the 19th century, and, though weakened under the Bourbon restoration, it had at least official approval right up to the July Revolution. Underneath the political surface, however, the destruction of medieval monuments had indirectly stimulated certain groups to preserve some parts of these works in museums. When the glories of their own medieval past were brought to the attention of some Frenchmen, at a time when the popular wave of Neo-medieval enthusiasm was gathering such momentum in England and Germany, it was bound to lead to some form of expression in their country.

In France, contrary to the prevailing religious climate of England and Germany, there was little anti-Roman Protestantism. Even Napoleon found it politically expedient to make a concordat with the Vatican and to be crowned in the sacred Gothic precincts of Notre Dame in Paris in the presence of the Roman Pontiff. Since the power of the French state was such that it was able to withstand foreign pressure even at the time of the Revolution and later to embark on the conquest of the continent under Napoleon, there was no national inferiority complex to be taken into account. Very significantly it was not until French national power had been thoroughly subdued under the coalition that defeated Napoleon, and not until the last of the ancient branch of the Bourbons had been swept from the tottering throne of his ancestors, that the Gothic Revival took a firm hold on the French mind and imagination. Even then it endured officially less than a generation—that is, between the Revolutions of 1830 and 1848.

Not being confronted with the populational stresses that characterized England at this time, France had little need of new churches. The Jesuits had diligently seen to the construction of many churches in the 17th and 18th centuries, and neither an enlargement of the population nor any new wave of religious enthusiasm created the need for more. Instead, the principal energy associated with the movement was expended in the preservation of the many fine existing examples, and the precise scholarship of the French academic minds found ready outlet in the establishment of the new science of medieval archeology, which led to the reconstruction of such buildings as the Cathedral of Notre Dame and Ste.-Chapelle in Paris and the Carcassonne castle on the southern border near the Pyrenees. The leader among this new group was Viollet-le-Duc whose skilled restorations, and the collection of essays he published in the form of a dictionary, raised him to prominence.[3] In this work he brought to attention the engineering logic of the medieval builders and demonstrated that in the organic quality of Gothic architecture in its prime every stone had a functional purpose, and in its period of florescence even the decorative details served in the structural aspect of the building. That everything was necessary and nothing used only for effect, not only revised 19th-century thought but even laid one of the bases for the 20th-century return to functional building. The popular enthusiasm for these projects was fanned to flame by Victor Hugo's romance *Notre Dame de Paris* in which the cathedral itself is the real hero of the book. It appeared in France in 1831 and is known to the English-speaking world as the *Hunchback of Notre Dame*. Support in official circles was forthcoming from Guizot, the historian turned prime minister under Louis Philippe. It was he who founded the *Commission pour la Conservation des Monuments Historiques* in the year 1837. Here again the Gothic movement was associated with the revival of patriotic and nationalistic sentiment. It had arrived at last on its true home soil, channeling the national energies into new flights of imagination and providing the French mind with an escape from its recent dreams of Roman imperial glory followed by the rude awakening of the Napoleonic defeat.

As comparatively latecomers on the Gothic Revival scene, the French architects were still in no hurry to leave their reconstructions and design new buildings. The advantage was theirs when they did so, however,

Fig. 18:14. Gau and Ballu. *Church of Ste.-Clotilde.* 1846–1857. Paris

since they could review all the previous experiments and avoid the follies associated with some of the excesses that characterized the movement elsewhere. Though planned long before, it was not until two decades after the early activities of Victor Hugo, Delacroix, and Berlioz that Paris ground was broken in 1846 for the Church of Ste.-Clotilde (Fig. 18:14). Designed by François Christian Gau, a native of Cologne but a naturalized Frenchman, the project was completed after his death by Théodore Ballu. The dedication took place in 1857 and the building was completed two years later. Although Ste.-Clotilde was built principally of white stone, the distinctive technical innovation was in the use of cast-iron girders in the vaulting to assure strength and durability. To be sure, they were disguised by stone blocks, but the fact that a building of medieval design used materials developed by the 19th-century Industrial Revolution was sufficient to arouse much interest on the part of contemporary architects.

Based on Gothic models of the 14th century, the ground plan consists typically of a nave some 111 feet in length, with vaulting rising 85 feet over it; two side aisles; a transept 121 feet in width; a choir 65 feet long; an ambulatory; two sacristies; and five apsidal chapels. The space of the richly ornamented façade is divided by four buttresses into three parts, each with an entrance portal. Those on the sides have tympanums showing the martyrdom of St. Valery and the baptism of Clovis in sculptured relief. The approaches to the portal have niches containing standing figures of the Merovingian saints who were associated with the earliest history of French nationhood. These include saints Césaire, Maurice, Martial, Remi, Benoît, Radegonde, Sigismond, and Ste. Geneviève, patroness of Paris. The tympanum over the central portal contains a figure of Christ on the cross with female figures on either side personifying Gospel and Synagogue, together with the traditional representations of the Virgin and St. John. Immediately above in the triangular gable is a large relief of the risen Christ showing his wounds, with angels on either side bearing the insignia of the passion. Still higher and above the rose window is another gable between the spires that is topped by a statue of Ste. Clotilde herself. These twin octagonally shaped stone spires are perforated in the manner of those at Strasbourg, Burgos, and Cologne and rise to a height of some 235 feet.

The interior is lighted by a clearstory with as many as 60 stained glass windows, which carry out the iconographical scheme promised by the sculptures of the façade. The representations tell the legendary stories of Ste. Clotilde and some of her contemporaries, St. Valery, St. Martin of Tours, St. Remi, and two of her children who were canonized, St. Cloud and Ste. Bathilde. The choir is the setting for a large three-manual organ with an elaborately carved case in the Gothic manner. It was here that the distinguished composer César Franck presided from the year 1872 until his death, and here that he made his famous improvisations.

The dedication of a church to a Merovingian saint connected with the early history of Paris was entirely in the spirit of that part of the Gothic Revival movement which appealed so strongly to nationalistic sentiment. While the source of Clotilde's life is to be found in the writings of Gregory of Tours and other medieval chronicles, it was known to the Paris of this time through Guizot's widely read *History of France*, a book based on his lectures of 1827–1830 at the Sorbonne, which told of the country's evolution from the 5th century A. D. With the growing knowledge of the 19th-century historians, the beginnings of French nationhood could be traced to the early conquests of Clovis, who gathered the remnants of the Roman Empire in Gaul about him and united them into one kingdom. Furthermore, the local civic pride of the Parisians was touched by the fact that Clovis and Clotilde considered their city even at this early date as their royal seat. The dedication of an important new church to Ste. Clotilde, and that of the Sorbonne library to Ste. Geneviève, and the awakening interest in St. Joan of Arc—all point to a growing consciousness of the medieval glory of France's national past. The choice of so many female saints is linked with the revival of the spirit of chivalry, which had its medieval precedent in the numerous Lady churches, such as the Notre Dames of Paris, Chartres, and Rheims. When the Church of Ste.-Clotilde is compared with such original Gothic monuments as these, however, it seems studied, overly symmetrical, and academically frigid. But when it is viewed in the context of its times and combined with the reflections of the medieval fervor of Victor Hugo, the moving craftsmanship of Rude, the lively chromaticism of Delacroix' painting, and the fantastic imagery of Berlioz' music, it catches some rays of their glowing warmth and becomes at once both their worthy architectural companion and an important incident in the unfolding of the whole Gothic Revival movement in Paris.

POETRY

Of the three great literary figures who influenced the writings of Victor Hugo at this time, Dante and Shakespeare were out of the past, and only his elder contemporary Goethe came from his own time. All three were for him the sources of the grotesque elements that he professed to find everywhere, "in the air, water, earth, fire those myriads of intermediate creatures which we find alive in the popular traditions of the middle ages; it is the grotesque which impels the ghastly antics of the witches revels, which gives Satan his horns, his cloven feet and his bat's wings. It is the grotesque, still the grotesque, which now casts into the Christian hell the frightful faces which the severe genius of Dante and Milton will evoke. . . ." [4] Needless to say his understanding of his great predecessors involved a high degree of selectivity. It was the Inferno section that he extracted out of Dante's *Divine Comedy*. A poem he wrote in 1837 closely parallels the Dante picture of Delacroix: "When the poet paints the image of hell," he wrote, "he paints that of his own life." The substance of the poem continues. "Beset by shades and specters, the poet must grope blindly through mysterious forests as weird forms bestrue his dark voyage. Lost amidst indecisive fogs, with each step he hears lamentations and the faint sounds of the grinding of white teeth in the black night. All the vices such as vengeance, famine, ambition, pride and avarice darken the scene still more. Farther on, the souls of those who have tasted the poison of cowardice, fear and treason are mingled with the grimacing masks of those whom hatred has consumed. The only light amidst this general gloom is the voice of the eternal artist, Vergil, who calls, 'Continue onward.' " [5]

In Petrarch it was the triumph of Death that Hugo admired; in Boccaccio, the vivid descriptions of the black plague; in Shakespeare, the macabre scenes from *Hamlet*, and the boiling and bubbling of the witches' caldron in *Macbeth;* and in Goethe's *Faust*, the descriptions of the Walpurgis-Night. Collectively they constitute a veritable carnival of the macabre, the horrible, and visions of doom. The transition to this new psychology is apparent as early as 1826 when he brought out a new edition of his *Odes* to which he added 15 *Ballades*, No. 14 of which was entitled "Witches' Sabbath." This new orientation Hugo explains in his introduction. The odes, he wrote, included his purely religious inspirations and personal expressions, which were cast in classical meters. Those bearing the title of ballad have the character of caprice, and include pictorial fantasies, dreams, and legends of superstition. He tells of the latter coming to him under the inspiration of the medieval troubadours, especially those Christian rhapsodies of epical nature that were chanted by the minstrels to the accompaniment of their harps as they wandered from one castle to another.

The poem begins with a description of a Gothic church at midnight; the clock in the belfry tolls out 12, and the witching hour begins. Strange lights flash, the holy water begins to boil in the fonts, shrieks and howls are heard, and from all directions come those who answer Satan's call—specters, dragons, vampires, ghouls, monsters, and the souls of the damned from their fresh-emptied tombs. While Satan sings a Black Mass, an imp reads the Gospel, and the whole fantastic congregation performs a wild dance.

> All in unison moving with swift-circling feet
> While satan keeps time with his crozier's beat,
> And their steps shake the arches colossal and high,
> Disturbing the dead in their tombs close by.

The last two lines serve as a refrain and are repeated after each of the ten verses, two of which will suffice as samples.

> Come, he-goats profane,
> Come, lizards and snails,
> Come, serpents with scales,
> So fragile and frail.
> Burst into the fane!
> Let discord take wing,
> With melodious swing,
> Come, enter the ring,
> And repeat the refrain.

> And their steps shake the arches colossal and high,
> Disturbing the dead in their tombs close by.

From his tomb with sad moans
Each false monk to his stall
Glides, concealed in his pall,
That robe fatal to all,
Which burns into his bones.
Now a black priest draws nigh,
With a flame he doth fly
On the altar on high
He the curst fire enthrones.

. . .

The dawn whitens the arches colossal and gray,
And drives all the devilish revellers away;
The dead monks retire to their graves 'neath the halls,
And veil their cold faces behind their dark palls.[6]

For his introduction and refrain Hugo uses a dual rhyming scheme, aa, bb, cc, and so on. That of the intervening verses, however, is based on a variant of an old medieval triple-rhyming pattern recalling that of the 13th-century *Dies Irae* (p. 322), which is still an important part of the Requiem Mass. The first, fifth, and ninth lines rhyme, while two groups of triple rhyme are placed between them to make a pattern of a, bbb, a, ccc, a. The *Dies Irae* had made an earlier appearance in the church scene of Goethe's *Faust*, where Margaret, aware of her forthcoming doom, hears the chorus intone the awesome lines (Fig. 18:5). Both the technique and imagery of Hugo's ballad are related to the fantastic sections of *Faust*, while each in turn have a common ancestor in the witches' scene from Shakespeare's *Macbeth*. The similarity of metrical plan and black-magic imagery is unmistakable. Especially in the Walpurgis-Night scene from *Faust*, one finds the same lilting language that is designed to charm the ear and stimulate the imagination rather than make logical sense. The scene is filled with witches riding he-goats and giant owls, the earth crawls with salamanders and coiling snakes, while bats fly around and glittering fireflies provide the illumination. As Mephistopheles describes the ghostly dance:

They crowd and jostle, whirl, and flutter!
They whisper, babble, twirl, and splutter!
They glimmer, sparkle, stink, and flare—
A true witch-element! Beware![7]

The sources of Hugo's inspiration are thus clear, and while he must be counted among the masters of language and the outstanding literary figures, he was never a prime mover or noted for his originality. Highly skilled as a manipulator of symbols and a master of poetic forms, he was able to give articulate expression to the changing voices of his time. In spite of all this verbal virtuosity and the uniform high quality of his output, he never succeeded in producing a poetic masterpiece that stood out above all others. In his work all the ideas of his time are mirrored in his unparalleled rhetoric, and his voice is as typical as any within the framework of this period. The brief but pungent reply of a modern critic pretty well sums it up. When asked whom he considered the greatest French poet of the 19th century, he answered, "Unfortunately, Victor Hugo."

MUSIC

The salons of Paris during these days were populated with poets, playwrights, journalists, critics, architects, painters, sculptors, musicians, and utopian political reformers without number. Heinrich Heine, poet and journalist from north Germany, Chopin from Poland, Liszt from Hungary —all mixed freely with the homegrown artists and intellectuals, such as Hugo, Théophile Gautier, Lamartine, Chateaubriand, de Musset, Dumas, George Sand, and others. Social philosophers, such as Lamennais, Proudhon, Auguste Compte, and Saint-Simon, gave a political tinge to the heated aesthetic debates. To this supercharged world Hector Berlioz must have appeared as an authentic apparition embodying in the flesh their wildest dreams and nightmares. One contemporary described him as a young man trembling with passion, whose large umbrella of hair projected like a movable awning over the beak of a bird of prey. The German composer Robert Schumann saw him as a "shaggy monster with ravenous eyes"; his personality as that of a "raging bacchant"; and spoke of his effect on the society of his times as being "the terror of the Philistines." The suave and polished Felix Mendelssohn on the other hand found his French colleague completely exasperating; and he continually reproached Berlioz because, with all his strenuous efforts to go stark raving mad, he never once really succeeded.

Berlioz combined in one striking personality qualities that made him a great composer, the ranking orchestral conductor of his day, and a brilliant journalist and autobiographer. As a conductor he was the embodiment of the mad musician of popular imagination. His emotional fever chart looked like a psychiatrist's nightmare. At the first performance of one of his overtures, when the orchestra failed to give him the effect he demanded, he burst into tears, tore his hair, and fell sobbing on the kettledrums. His *Memoirs* are stylistically a literary achievement of the first magnitude and rank with the top few autobiographies of world literature. From this lively source one gathers that his development proceeded in a series of emotional shocks that he received from his first contacts with the literature and music of his time. The fires of his explosive imagination were ignited one after the other by Goethe's *Faust*, which resulted in his oratorio the *Damnation of Faust;* the poetry of Byron, which became the symphony for viola and orchestra, *Harold in Italy;* and Dante's *Divine Comedy*, which was sublimated into his great *Requiem*. In music it was first Gluck, then Weber, and he said that he had scarcely recovered from these when he "beheld Beethoven's giant form looming over the horizon. The shock was almost as great as that I had received from Shakespeare, and a new world of music was revealed to me by the musician, just as a new universe of poetry had been opened to me by the poet." [8] It was, of course, the Beethoven of the *Eroica, Pastoral*, and *Ninth* symphonies. To a milder extent the literary figures of Vergil, Walter Scott, and Victor Hugo made up the more distant claps of thunder in his creative brainstorms.

He even insisted on actually living out his enthusiasms to an alarmingly realistic degree. He fell violently in love with the Irish actress who was playing the feminine leads in the Shakespearean troupe that was so successful in the Paris season of 1827. After a desperate romance leading both to the brink of suicide, he finally married the one whom he thought of as Juliet and Ophelia all wrapped up in one beautiful feminine package. When his wife turned out to be merely the actress Miss Harriet Smithson, now Mme. H. Berlioz, he wrote with acute anguish to a friend: "She's an ordinary woman." The cold dawn of disillusionment brought years of personal misery, compensated for by some happier results on the musical side. For all his external flightiness, his literary, musical, and human loves were completely enduring; and he carried them with him to the end of his life. There we find him still musing on the "mild, affable, and accessible" figure of Vergil; on Shakespeare, "that mighty indifferent man, impassable as a mirror"; on Beethoven, "contemptuous and uncouth, yet gifted with such profound sensibility"; and on Gluck, "the superb."

Berlioz' autobiographical *Fantastic Symphony*, first performed in the year 1830, contains a complex of many ideas he gathered from the musical and literary atmosphere that surrounded him. In the detailed programmatic notes he wrote for it, it is clear that he took the idea of poisoning by opium in the first movement from De Quincey's *Confessions of an English Opium Eater*, which had appeared shortly before in a French translation by Alfred de Musset. The musical form of this movement with its *Largo* introduction and the *Allegro agitato e appassionato assai* continuation is in the Beethovenian symphonic tradition. Its principal claim to technical originality is in the use of an *idée fixe*, or fixed idea (below), by which Berlioz conveys the idea of his beloved who is everywhere present and colors his every thought.

Fixed Idea, or Leading Melody, from *Fantastic Symphony*   Berlioz

The metamorphosis of the theme on its appearance in each of the movements fulfills a dual purpose—that of providing a semblance of unity in the sequence of genre pieces, and, by its mutations, of expressing the necessary dramatic progress. It is varied in each of its reappearances and provides the listener with the necessary continuity to build up the image of a dramatic character through the associative process. All evidence, however, points to the fact that this specific programme was written later than most of the music, which was apparently conceived for quite another purpose.

Gérard de Nerval's prose translation of Goethe's *Faust* had appeared late in the year 1827 and was the direct inspiration for Berlioz' *Eight Scenes from Faust*. Since most of the movements of the *Fantastic Symphony* were being written at the same time, this alone would indicate a connection in the creative process. Berlioz was among the earliest to attempt a realization of Goethe's great drama in music. An opera by Spohr had appeared in 1816, but the well-known one by Gounod was many years later. A secular oratorio by Schumann, a *Faust Symphony* by Liszt, and a *Faust Overture* by Wagner are but a few of the many subsequent works on this theme. The subject of Faust was in the wind, and the stages of London, Paris, and other Continental cities rang with the echoes of the many versions of this subject in dramatic and ballet form. The Paris opera alone had accepted no less than three librettos that were waiting to be commissioned. It is known that Berlioz was angling for one of these, and this fact further fortifies the case for the common source of inspiration for the *Damnation of Faust* and the *Fantastic Symphony*. Since the desired commission was not forthcoming, those parts projected for a Faust ballet became instead the movements of the *Fantastic Symphony*.

The reveries and passions of the first movement are certainly Faustian in a general, if not specific, sense. Every Faust ballet of the time contained a gay dance sequence for the Auerbach Cellar scene, and the second movement of the *Symphony*, called the Scene at the Ball, was probably first written for Auerbach's Cellar. The external and internal storms of the third movement, the Scene in the Country, bring out the benign as well as the malignant aspects of the Faustian conception of nature. The closest correspondence, however, comes in the climactic final movements where the relationship is quite unmistakable. The fourth, the grim March to the Scaffold, was probably composed first as the execution scene where Margaret pays the penalty for the dual crimes of matricide and infanticide. In the symphony it becomes a musical nightmare of the first order in which the hero, autobiographically Berlioz himself, marches in grotesque rhythms to his own doom. As other writers have pointed out, this scene may well have been suggested to Berlioz by the unfortunate execution of the gifted young poet André Chénier, who met his death on the guillotine under Robespierre and thus became the martyred poet of the Revolution. In the final bars of this movement the fixed melodic idea is sounded in the high piercing register of the clarinet. It is suddenly cut off to suggest the fall of the blade and the decapitation of the hero. After a dull thud and a roll of the drums, the grimacing crowds roar their bloodthirsty approval of the execution.

The last movements of both the early *Eight Scenes from Faust* and the *Fantastic Symphony* have to do with the triumph of the exultant diabolical forces as they claim the souls of their victims. The endings to Berlioz' early works are often the most wild and dissonant parts. No anticlimactic calms after the storms, no carefully planned resolutions, no safe havens after the shipwrecks. This symphony ends with a diabolical Witches' Sabbath, just as *Harold in Italy* does with an Orgy of the Brigands. The grisly scene here is both the climax and the unresolved end, and the movement that most fully justifies the title "fantastic." It is divided into three distinct sections. The first is introductory and begins with wild shrieks for the piccolo, flute, and oboe, accompanied by the ominous roll of the kettledrums in bars 7 and 8, which is echoed softly by the muted horns in bars 9 and 10 to suggest distance. After a repetition the tempo changes from Larghetto to Allegro and the *idée fixe* is heard (21–28). The ghostly appearance of the fixed melodic idea associated with his beloved in this final movement was undoubtedly derived from the witches' kitchen scene of Goethe's drama where Faust has gone to have his form changed from that of old age back to young and lusty manhood, and where the conjuring up of the image of Margaret is a part of the process (Fig. 18:4). It is also related to the Walpurgis-Night scene where Margaret again puts in a brief appearance. Surely it is a novel notion that the winsome heroine, exemplified in previous

mutations as the embodiment of desirability, should now appear at the
witches' sabbath. Was she a witch all along and disguised only in his
imagination in desirable human form? Or is this merely another manifestation of her "bewitching" power? The entrance at this point of his beloved
on her broomstick, accompanied by a pandemonium of sulfurous sounds,
is therefore somewhat unexpected. The hero, obviously Berlioz himself,
gives a shriek of horror (29–39) as he witnesses her modulation from the
previously chaste C major to the more lurid key of E flat. Her instrumental
coloration, while still that of the pale clarinet, descends now in pitch to a
new low and more sensuous register. After this shocking revelation she
executes a few capers and subsides for the time being as the introduction
concludes with bar 101.

The second section is labeled Lontano ("in the distance") and begins
with the tolling of the chimes recalling the opening lines of Hugo's ballad.
After this signal for the unleashing of the infernal forces, the foreboding
Dies Irae is solemnly intoned, first by the brass instruments in unison octaves. In bars 127–146 it is in dotted half notes; next in bars 147–157 the
rhythm is quickened into dotted quarters, then it becomes syncopated in
triplet eighths (157–162) and ends with an abrupt upward swish of the C
scale. With the appearance here in syncopation and in such surroundings
of this ancient and honorable Gothic liturgical melody, a solemn part of
every Roman Catholic Requiem Mass, Berlioz fulfills the promise of his
programme that he will make a "burlesque parody" on the Dies Irae. Besides serving Berlioz as a symbol conjuring up all the fire and brimstone
aspects of medieval Christianity, it also introduces at this point a form of
macabre humor. This parody of a sacred melody caused considerable comment at the time. Schumann attributed it to Romantic irony, one of the
few forms of humor tolerated in a style practiced by artists who took life
and themselves with deadly seriousness. Another explanation, however,
seems more logical and is to be found by applying a remark that Hugo
made in his Preface to Cromwell. "When Dante had finished his terrible
Inferno," he wrote, "and naught remained save to give his work a name,
the unerring instinct of his genius showed him that multiform poem was
an emanation of the drama, not of the epic; and on the front of that gigantic
monument, he wrote with his pen of bronze: Divina Commedia." [9] Thus
if Dante was justified in conceiving his Inferno as a comedy, albeit a divine
one, then Berlioz could include the Dies Irae in this context. Even the devil
is conceded to be a clever theologian, and in Goethe's drama he is found
in the sacred precincts of the church, whispering in Margaret's ear as she
listens to the choir chant the Dies Irae. This scene was also one of those

Delacroix chose for the subject of a lithograph (Fig. 18:5); and the image of satan saying Mass at midnight in the Gothic setting of Hugo's poem, relate all these works to the same idea.

The title of the final section, which begins with bar 241, is *Ronde du Sabbat*, the same as that of Hugo's poem, again showing the connection with that ballad. A dance fragment hinted at previously now becomes the "Rondo of the Sabbath" theme and a four-bar phrase forming a fugue subject. The first entrance is for the cellos and double basses (241–244); this is followed by the violas (248–251); next for the first violins fortified by the bassoons (255–258); and the final entrance is scored for the wood-wind section and horns. These successive entries, each with a different in-strumental combination, mark Berlioz' departure from the academic tra-dition of the linear fugue. Here he introduces the element of instrumental coloration into the usually austere fugal exposition. Other color combina-tions follow with melodic and chromatic variants of the subject in a fugal development that has won the composer wide admiration. It must be noted that when Berlioz is writing his wildest images, his mind is always in com-mand; and at the climax of such a work as this, he writes a fugue without violating either the rules or sacrificing his expressive intentions. After the fugue on the dance theme has come to its climax with the entire string section playing an extension of the subject (407–413), the *Dies Irae* makes a reappearance, and the two themes are woven together with great skill from bar 414 to the end. Some of Berlioz' enthusiastic admirers have called this contrapuntal section a double fugue. There is only one fugue, however, with the *Dies Irae* running along parallel to it. With the final blood-curdling shrieks and flying images, a composer, perhaps for the first time in music history, has written a fugue that fulfills its literal meaning—that is, a flight.

The use of the *Dies Irae* became after this symphony a symbol of the macabre, and it has been used countless times since. Liszt's *Totentanz* for piano and orchestra is a set of variations on it, while it appears again in Gustav Mahler's symphonies and in one of Rachmaninoff's variations on a theme of Paganini. With this movement Berlioz also established a style that brought the demonic element—and a chain of harmonic and psychological dissonances—into music to stay. Both Moussorgsky's *Night on Bald Mountain* and Saint-Saens' *Danse Macabre* are cut from the same cloth. One writer has even called this movement of Berlioz' the first piece of Russian music. Some of Stravinsky's wilder moments in the *Fire Bird* and the *Rites of Spring* would certainly seem to bear this out. Anyone, in fact, who knows this movement well can hardly be shocked by the dissonances of modern music.

As a composer Berlioz was one of the first to build up his musical forms by the use of tone color. The only way to understand his music is to hear it in all the full richness of its instrumental sound. His scores can never be transcribed successfully for piano or any other medium. In addition to the incomparable richness of his orchestral palette, the sheer quantitative weight he added to the ensembles of his day is nothing short of spectacular. Since he seldom composed in any but the largest forms, and delighted in the use of orchestral and choral combinations of extraordinary complexity, his works have received from his time to ours all too few performances. Even today it is difficult to assemble all the necessary forces, and the demands his works make on the time and effort of the performers are considerable. In his gigantic *Requiem*, for instance, he employs an immense principal orchestra, a chorus of 500, a tenor soloist, and four huge brass bands. The latter were placed facing the four points of the compass, so as to suggest vast space and to enhance their acoustical effect when they sound the call for Judgment Day. All this, plus such additional effects as a battery of 16 kettledrums, caused the newspapers to comment the day following the first performance, that Paris had not heard such a volume of sound since the fall of the Bastille.

There is always something of the conqueror about Berlioz as he marshaled his orchestral forces in such a composition as this. Each orchestra had its own conductor and the choruses were signaled by commanders of lesser rank, with all of them taking their cues from the generalissimo himself, who appeared in the role of a musical Napoleon storming over the battlefield. Berlioz was the first of the great orchestra conductors and the prototype of the great maestros of our day. No wonder his contemporaries did not know how to take him and found both his personality and his compositions somewhat difficult to absorb. He always reminded them of something monstrous, and it remained for Heinrich Heine to find the most apt way of putting this into words. "Here is the wingbeat that reveals no ordinary songbird," he wrote, "it is that of a colossal nightingale, a lark the size of an eagle, such as must have existed in the primeval world."

IDEAS: FORWARD AND BACKWARD TENDENCIES

The constellation of ideas that formed in the skies over the first half of the 19th century was made up of many more stars than just the Roman and Gothic Revivals. Together with the digging of still other styles out of the past, they constituted but one aspect of a highly complex and interrelated pattern. If these two revivals have been dwelt upon at greater length in these pages, it was because of their acceptance in official circles; because they were more sharply focused and less diffused in time and place than some of the others; and because the method of concentration employed may shed light when beamed at the other tendencies of the time. Limitation of space forbids going into all the forces and counterforces that run concurrently with these revivals, and which are also important if the entire panorama is to be seen. In temporal terms their seeds can be traced back to the middle of the 18th century, while the decaying fragrance of their fruit still lingers on well into our own time. They are present throughout this 200-year span, though they are not always championed with equal enthusiasm. Some of the ideas have had a vigorous growth and a productive maturity, and some have been dropped altogether; others have developed spasmodically, while still others have shown a pattern of endurance sufficient to insure their survival until the present time. The soil from which they sprang and which was the cause of their growth was the social decay of an aristocratic class that had grown increasingly indifferent to its responsibilities. The hereditary control of public institutions and the privileged position of this class was challenged by a vigorous and rising middle class.

The effect of this shift of ruling classes was a change in the patrons for whom the buildings were built, the statues carved, the pictures painted, and the music composed. The arts were no longer produced mainly for a small but intelligent group of aristocrats; instead they were for a larger and more inchoate bourgeoisie. Finesse, subtlety, and intellectual grasp of complex forms could no longer be anticipated by the artist in his audience. He had now to exhort, astonish, charm, and astound. Under the new system an architect could no longer count on one patron for a single large project but had to cater to the many with smaller buildings involving many different styles and tastes. Painters and sculptors began to work in a variety of genre forms, while poets and musicians likewise revealed the fragmentation of their world view by writing shorter works and generally showing their unwillingness to conceive or present their world as a systematic whole. Even when such composers as Berlioz did write symphonies, the results were no longer all-embracing universal structures like Beethoven's but collections of genre pieces strung together by a programme or some recurrent motive to give them at least a semblance of unity.

The attitudes that affect the arts both directly and indirectly are grouped in the tendencies toward acceptance of the realities of the Revolutionary Period on one hand, and the various escapes from reality into fanciful flights of the imagination on the other. The former embraces the progressive social and economic gains that were the consequences of the political and industrial revolutions, the increased freedom of individual expression, the growth of self-government, and the rise of nationalism. The obverse side of this coin of sociological and technological advancement is seen in the many escape mechanisms, such as the revivals of past periods, the back-to-nature movement, the cult of local color, and exoticism. In order to touch even briefly on the principal ones, they are reduced for the sake of convenience to the ideas of progress, Romantic individualism, and nationalism on one side; and the revivals of the past, back to nature, and exoticism on the other.

Progress

The intensity of the force of social progress can be measured by the rapid rise and overthrow of the various forms of government in France during the 60-year period from 1789 to 1848. Between an absolute monarchy and a commune, Paris experienced a Revolutionary reign of terror, a republic, an empire, a royal restoration, and a constitutional monarchy. While these social upheavals were making the headlines, an even more powerful and radical change was making itself felt by means of the Industrial Revolution. The growth of factories employing the new machine methods of production meant the shift from an agrarian to an urban economy and the migration of large numbers of people from the farms to the cities. While the 18th-century worker had been able to weigh the tangible produce of his farm or take satisfaction in the completion of a pair of handmade shoes, his 19th-century counterpart sold the intangible element of his time in return for a more precarious and fragmentary state of living.

The application of the new scientific knowledge to industrial progress opened up many new possibilities in the arts. New materials, such as cast iron, facilitated the rapid construction of buildings as well as furnished the means by which complicated decorative devices, hitherto made laboriously by hand, could be reproduced cheaply to satisfy the demand for the picturesque. Painters were likewise indebted to science for the development of chemical pigments. Synthetic products began to replace the old ground minerals and often resulted in greater brilliancy and intensity than the genuine product. New low-cost pictorial processes, such as lithography and the print, made it possible for such artists as Delacroix to find a new public and a wider distribution for their pictures. The new facilities provided by the mechanical printing press brought about the mass distribution of newspapers, novels, and sheet music. Cast-iron frames instead of wooden ones for pianos meant that pianists could have larger and more durable instruments as well as ones that stayed in tune over longer periods of time. The invention of new valve mechanisms for brass instruments and the comparative standardization of their manufacture made it possible

Fig. 18:15. Daumier. *Legislative Body*. Lithograph. 1834. Art Institute, Chicago

for such composers as Berlioz to demand certain instrumental effects in their orchestrations with a reasonable insurance of getting them. In this respect the artists showed themselves perfectly willing to use the new technological processes for the distribution of their pictures, poetry, novels, and musical compositions in order to reach as wide an audience as possible.

In addition to the acceptance and exploitation of these technical aids, there were other instances when the artists were also willing to incorporate the events and spirit of the time in their work. Shortly after the French Revolution, David painted several pictures treating contemporary events in an epical manner—the *Oath in the Tennis Court*, the *Assassination of Marat*, and the *Death of Joseph Bara*, a young flag bearer in the Revolutionary army. Under Napoleon this had continued with his *Bonaparte on Mount St. Bernard* (Fig. 17:9), *Coronation* (*Le Sacre*) (Fig. 17:10), and the *Distribution of the Eagles*. Napoleon was also accompanied on his campaigns by Baron Gros who sketched and painted many battle scenes on the spot. This style was continued with Géricault's *Raft of the Medusa* (1819), a picture based on the story of a shipwreck reported in the Paris press; Delacroix' *Massacre at Scio* (1824), an event in the Greek struggle for independence against the Turks; and, of course, his *Liberty Leading the People* (Fig. 18:1), an incident in the Revolution of 1830. In the days of the July monarchy, Daumier ruthlessly exposed the foibles of the new ruling middle class in such lithographs as the *Legislative Body* (Fig. 18:15). Like Hogarth before him, Daumier faced the reality of the printing press and drew pictures for the daily journals of Paris, which are the prototypes of the newspaper cartoons of today. There was also a whole genre of "call-to-arms" pictures, of which Rude's *Departure of the Volunteers* (Fig. 18:9) on the Arc de Triomphe is a sculptural example. This kind of artistic journalism also finds its way into music with such pieces as Louis Jadin's *Battle of Austerlitz*, and Beethoven's *Battle of Vittoria*, written in celebration of Wellington's victory over Napoleon. There is also no reason to exclude the latter's *Eroica Symphony* from this contemporary frame of reference.

Among the other innovations of the time was a noticeable tendency toward the development of color in the various artistic media, both for its own sake and for its capacity to convey symbolic meaning. For the architects and the sculptors, this tendency assumed the form of the picturesque and the use of local color. Poetry, however, began to depend on the sounds of words and their appeal to the senses more than to the mind. Hugo's "Witches' Sabbath" with its patterns of repeated sounds and colors would be practically meaningless if this literary tone color were omitted. To Delacroix, more than line or composition, color was the dimension on which he depended for his intensity of expression. The only way to understand Berlioz is to hear the realization of his musical ideas in the original instrumentation. He is a composer who defies transcription. If the English horn solo in the Scene in the Country, the third movement of the *Fantastic Symphony*, were to be played by a clarinet or any other instrument in the same range, his expressive intention would instantly vanish. Such an example reveals the extent to which Berlioz relied on the color of particular instruments; and in his hands instrumentation becomes a musical dimension in itself, capable of carrying its own expressive weight independent of melody and rhythm. Both Delacroix and Berlioz base their styles principally on color. It was fortunate for the visual arts that Delacroix rejected the aesthetics of David and the academy, and that Berlioz devoted so much energy to the exploitation of the new instrumental colors that were available. The important new element here, one which was to have interesting consequences on later developments in the arts, was the use of color and sonority for their own sake, and as a means of building up an elaborate and eloquent symbolic language.

New also was the idea that an artistic opus was not a self-contained whole but shared many relationships internally as well as externally with other works of art. This began with the attempts by certain individual artists to overcome many of the arbitrary limitations and technical rules of their separate crafts. The literature of the period was filled with musical allusions, and musicians for their part were drawing on literature with full force for their programme pieces. The architects were called upon to build dream castles out of the novels of Walpole, Scott, and Hugo; and it is difficult to think of Delacroix' painting or Berlioz' music without Vergil, Dante, Shakespeare, Goethe, and Byron coming to mind. The effect on music was a host of new and hybrid forms, such as the programme symphony and the symphonic poem. The tonal art had been associated from its beginnings with words, and programme music was by no means an invention of the 19th century. No other period, however, built an entire style on this mixture. There is also a considerable distinction between the setting of words to music as in a song or the musical dramatization of a play as in an opera, and basing a purely instrumental form on the spirit of a poem or the sequential arrangements of episodes taken from a novel. Overtures were now written not only to operas, but Berlioz began writing them to such novels as Scott's *Waverly* and *Rob Roy*. Mendelssohn wrote *Songs Without Words* for the piano leaving the imagination to supply the text. Berlioz' *Fantastic Symphony* and *Harold in Italy* are practically operas without words. In such later works as the dramatic symphony *Romeo and Juliet* and the *Damnation of Faust*, which are scored for soloists and chorus as well as orchestra, he invents the concert opera in which the costumes and scenery are left to the listener's imagination. This tendency continued until it reached a climax in Richard Wagner's music dramas, which he conceived as *Gesamtkunstwerke*, or complete works of art.

Romantic Individualism and Nationalism

This was also the age of the emancipation of the individual, and the era of the great man who climbed to the heights through his own efforts. Napoleon had stamped his image on the period with his pre-eminence in the realm of military glory and statecraft, thus giving rise to the idea of similar dominating figures in the smaller worlds of letters, painting, sculpture, architecture, and music. Artists vied with each other in virtuosity and technical mastery for the top rung of the ladder in their respective fields. For sheer virtuosity in letters it would be difficult to exceed that of Victor Hugo, who could write with mastery in any style. So also could Viollet-le-Duc and other architects duplicate any building in the history of architecture; and the names of such performers as Paganini and Liszt as violin and piano virtuosos, respectively, are legendary. All this was perhaps a positive assertion of the diminishing self in the face of growing social collectivization. Each work of art had a personal quality by being sifted through the imagination of distinctive individuals. It was no longer enough for an artist to be a craftsman, no matter how high the degree of his skill; he had also to be a great man, a prophet, a leader. It was consequently an age of autobiography, confessions, memoirs, portraiture, and showmanship. The will to biography, the necessity of living a "life," sometimes took so much time it was actually a handicap to artistic production. More than in any other period there was an obligation for the artist to be a personality in the worldly sense in addition to his artistic activities. The place of the artist in society was a matter of vital concern to such men as David and Beethoven, who combined the moralistic fervor of the Revolutionary thought with the feeling of social responsibility. David's championship of the cause of art in the French legislature, and Beethoven's behavior toward his patrons as their social equal, reveal them both as modern artists who placed the aristocracy of genius on a higher plane than that of birth.

The development of nationalism on the part of artists can be seen as an extension of this phenomenon of individualism. Napoleon had tried to ride the wave of a social revolution toward the shores of a new international empire. But that Revolution had liberated too many individuals who were all clamoring for expression, and his ship was wrecked on the rocks of nationalism. The immediate cause of the Gothic Revival in England and Germany was the distrust of the French Revolution and their opposition to Napoleon's dream of a new Roman Empire. The struggle against Napoleon thus became a vicarious re-enactment of the battles of the northern tribes against the encroachments of the ancient Roman Empire, which was reasserting itself once more in disguised political, religious, and aesthetic forms. The great individual could not exist in a social or political vacuum. Byron, Delacroix, and others lent their energies and talents to the cause of liberating an oppressed people from the tyrant's yoke. Whether an artist conceived of himself in classical terms as a Prometheus, or in the medieval vocabulary as a knightly champion of the weak against the strong, was not too important. He simply needed a geographical sounding board, local color, and a linguistic medium suited to his creative needs. One could find it in folk tales and ballads of a particular locale; another in collections and variations of Spanish epics, Scottish ballads, German fairy tales; still others in the writing of Italian symphonies, Hungarian rhapsodies, and Polish mazurkas. In this light, nationalism, like the medieval revival, was a northern declaration of cultural independence from the Mediterranean tradition, tied up in the immediate sense in England and Germany with the opposition to Napoleon's new Roman Empire. Berlioz' nationalism is expressed in a more subtle way, but his operas without words, concert operas, and music dramas were as distinct a departure from the prevailing Italian operatic tradition as were those of Weber in Germany.

While these positive forces and contemporary aspects were highly important, they by no means account for all or even a substantial part of the artistic output of the period. There was, in fact, a growing gulf between

Fig. 18:16. Constable. *Salisbury Cathedral from the Bishop's Garden.* 34¼" x 43⅝". 1826. Copyright The Frick Collection, New York

the realities of the early industrial age and the expressive tendencies in the arts. In recognition of the new technologies an École Polytechnique had been established in 1794 by the Revolutionary government. Napoleon, however, yielded to the advice of David and others and allowed the establishment of a separate École des Beaux Arts in 1806. By thus educating engineers in one school and architects in another, the construction techniques of building tended to be divorced from the stylistic aspects of architecture. When the architects did begin to use cast iron, it was to build dream castles and Neo-medieval cathedrals; and when the musicians began to use the improved horns and trombones, it was to sound the call of Judgment Day and introduce a rain of Neo-medieval fire and brimstone into their symphonies. In general, then, the full significance of the new era remained for a later age to exploit.

Other causes are to be found in the social attitudes of the time. After the glowing initial hopes for the ultimate freedom of man had been fanned to a fever pitch by the flames of the American and French Revolutions, a certain impatient reaction bordering on pessimism had set in, when the results failed to measure up to expectation. After the Revolution of 1830 and the last of the old line of Bourbons was overthrown, the French middle class were finally confronted with a king cast in their own image. When they saw him in his frock coat, umbrella in hand, walking down the boulevard in the direction of the Bourse, they were somewhat dismayed to find that their bourgeois monarch was—like themselves—stouter of figure than of heart, and again—like themselves—engaged in the pursuit of causes more materialistic than ideal. A bit appalled at what they saw, is it any wonder that they sought psychological compensation in the dreams of the more dashing royal personalities of the past, whose recklessness consisted of more hazardous adventures than that of buying and selling shares on the stock exchange? How could King Louis Philippe, living in a palace replete with the bourgeois comforts of modern plumbing, compare in popular fancy with Joan of Arc's dashing dauphin, living dangerously while being pursued by his remorseless enemies from one dank and drafty castle to another?

The activities of Darwin's earthworms, for instance, were infinitely more useful than the sublime spectacle of one of Delacroix' lions in mortal combat with a stallion. But how could the worms of the former capture the popular imagination as the lions of the latter did? A highly productive factory or an ingenious city sewer system made infinitely duller pictures and poetry than the interiors of Oriental harems and the palm-lined shores of the River Ganges. While willing to use the fruits of the Industrial Revolution as aids in the production and dissemination of their artistic wares, the artists of the time were quite convinced that the new technologies were not making their world more beautiful. Thus the conflict between usefulness and beauty began to be deeper and wider. Refusing to reconcile themselves to reality, the artists sought ever more fanciful ways and means of avoiding the issue. This is certainly not to be attributed to the fact that the artists were unaware of what was going on. As intellectuals they were better educated and informed than similar groups in other times had ever been. When employing their various escape mechanisms, they were perfectly aware of what it was they were escaping from. The cry for artists as well as their audiences became "Any time but now and any place but here"— provided, of course, that this applied only to the books they read, the pictures they saw, and the music they heard.

The Revivals

At the end of the previous chapter the foundation of the science of classical archeology was discussed in some detail. It was to be expected in the circumstances that the revival idea should have begun with the Roman phase largely because so much more material for investigation was available. Through the efforts of Winckelmann, the spotlight had been turned on Hellenistic Greece. Then through the writings of Stuart and Revett and Lord Elgin's passion for collecting, the Athens of the 5th century B. C.

began to come to light. Egyptian archeology brought a still more ancient civilization to notice, and so the search continued. The Gothic Revival had brought about further scientific study of the Middle Ages, and as the medieval archeologists extended their studies, the glories of the Romanesque and Byzantine styles were rediscovered. The list, however, does not stop here. Architects, writers, historical painters, and opera composers began to find congenial subject matter in the periods between the Middle Ages and their own time. In Paris the Library of St. Genevieve (Fig. 19:13), and in Boston the Public Library were on the exterior at least revivals of the Renaissance; and, shades of the French Revolution, the Paris opera house, which was begun in 1861, revived the style of Louis XIV. Wagner composed an opera called *Rienzi* after a novel of Bulwer-Lytton on a figure out of the Roman Renaissance, and Mendelssohn discovered the greatness of the oratorios of Bach and performed the *St. Matthew Passion* in 1829 for the first time since the composer's death.

In retrospect the old controversy between classicism and the Romantic interest in the Middle Ages seems rather quaint. Both were aspects of the same revival idea, and the artists who lived through the Napoleonic and post-Napoleonic generations employed both as subject matter with equal facility. John Nash, for instance, built himself a classical town house in London and a Gothic castle in the country; Rude made statues of Roman nymphs and of Joan of Arc; Ingres painted the *Apotheosis of Homer* and later a picture of the Maid of Orleans; Keats wrote his "Ode on a Grecian Urn" and also "St. Agnes' Eve"; Hugo included classical odes in the same volume as his medieval ballads; Berlioz admired Vergil quite as intensely as he did Dante, and wrote the *Trojans at Carthage*, an opera based on the *Aeneid*, as well as his *Requiem* based on the *Dies Irae*. Together with all the other revivals, the end result was simply a broad eclecticism whereby a virtuoso architect could build in any style, a painter could do a portrait or a historical canvas à *la* Titian or Rubens, a poet could duplicate with facility any form or metrical organization, and a composer could pull out a Renaissance or a Baroque stop on his organ at will.

Back to Nature

Rousseau had sounded the clarion call of "back to nature" in the latter part of the 18th century. By so doing he challenged the urbane, civilized, aristocratic image of man with his projection of the noble savage whose rustic charm was achieved by shunning society altogether and communing with a nature unspoiled by human hands. For his own part Rousseau was perfectly willing to be received in courtly circles, and an unsophisticated little opera he wrote was performed for Louis XVI at Versailles with great

Fig. 18:17. Nash. *Royal Pavilion*. 1818–1821. Brighton, England. Courtesy Metropolitan Museum, New York

success. His ideas were partly responsible for the rustic cottage, complete with a dairy and mill, which Marie Antoinette had built for herself there amid the formal gardens of the palace.

The back-to-nature idea took root and became one of the more popular 19th-century escape mechanisms, particularly with that segment of the population who lived in the cities and dreamed of an idyllic country life they had no intention of living. They delighted, however, in reading poetry full of nature imagery as well as folk ballads and fairy tales. They hung pictures on the walls of their apartments and town houses that were painted by the English landscapists and the French painters of the Barbizon Forest. Constable's *Salisbury Cathedral from the Bishop's Garden* (Fig. 18:16) will serve as an example, and the many peasant scenes by Millet are all too familiar. Beethoven's *Pastoral Symphony* and Wagner's *Forest Murmurs*, as well as dozens of piano pieces and songs, sounded the proper bucolic note in music. Weber's opera *Der Freischütz*, which had been the success of the 1826 season in Paris, brought out some of the darker aspects of nature. In it much is made of the sinister powers of the night, and the forces over which it rules are effectively presented in the eerie Wolf's Glen scene. Nature, here, as well as in Goethe's *Faust* was much more than idyllic, since it included all the terrifying elemental forces as well as the magical and fantastic.

Fig. 18:18. Nash. Royal Pavilion, *Interior*. 1818–1821. Brighton, England. Courtesy Metropolitan Museum, New York

Exoticism

The rich perfumes of Oriental life found their way into the nostrils and thence to the thoughts of the intellectuals and artists beginning with the mid-18th century. While shrewd businessmen were opening up new markets and tapping new sources of wealth, and religious missionaries were going forth from Europe to try to bridge the Christian and pagan worlds, the artists were busy capturing the popular imagination with scenes of exotic mysteries associated with far-off lands and peoples. In England, drawing rooms were hung with wallpapers depicting scenes of mandarin China, and fashionable hostesses were pouring tea at Chinese Chippendale tables. The Prince Regent commissioned his architect in 1815 to start building him an Oriental pavilion at his favorite seaside resort of Brighton. John Nash, who had previously built an exotic country house for a gentleman who had lived in India, came up with an Oriental fantasy in a style that was referred to at the time as "Indian Gothic." The exterior (Fig. 18:17) featured a multitude of minaret towers and several bulbous cupolas constructed over cast-iron frames. Under the large central dome was a spacious dining hall (Fig. 18:18), where each detail of the decorative scheme carried out the extravaganza, right up to the chandelier in the middle with its gaily painted cast-iron dragons holding lotus lamps in their mouths.

Schopenhauer's *World as Will and Idea*, based on the Oriental philosophy of the negation of the will, saw the light of day in 1819. Byron wrote his poetic drama *Sardanapalus* (1821), which he based on Alexander the Great's conquest of the east; Delacroix used one of the scenes for his picture, the *Death of Sardanapalus* (1827); while Berlioz took the last part for a cantata (1830). Hugo published a group of poems called *Les Orientales* in 1829; Louis Philippe established the French Foreign Legion in 1831; and Barye was modeling wild animal figures, such as his *Tiger Devouring a Crocodile* (Fig. 18:19). The next year Delacroix returned from a visit to North Africa, where he had made many sketches, and set to work painting scenes, such as his *Algerian Women in Their Harem*, shown in the Salon of 1834.

The colorful Japanese prints that found their way to Europe after Admiral Perry's voyage of 1852–1854 had an important effect on painting. Gautier published a book called *L'Orient* in 1860, which was based on his travels, and the following year an opera by Auber called *La Circassienne* was performed. At this same time Delacroix was painting one of his last pictures, *The Lion Hunt*, which vividly portrayed the violent struggle of men and horses against the unbridled ferocity of wild animals. Gounod's opera, *The Queen of Sheba*, was produced in 1862 at about the same time Ingres was finishing his picture *The Turkish Bath* (Fig. 18:20). The search for exotic settings eventually culminated in two of the greatest works in the lyrical repertory—Verdi's *Aïda*, written in 1871 for the Cairo opera at the time of the opening of the Suez Canal, and Bizet's *Carmen*

Fig. 18:19. Barye. *Tiger Devouring a Crocodile*. Bronze. Modeled in 1831. Metropolitan Museum, New York

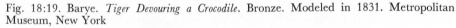

Fig. 18:20. Ingres. *The Turkish Bath.* 42½″ diameter. 1859–1863. Louvre, Paris (Archives Photographiques)

based on a short story of Mérimée, which was first performed in 1875. Toward the end of the century, when the realistic Zola was referring sarcastically to Gautier because "he needed a camel and four dirty Bedouins to tickle his brains into creative activity," Gauguin was off in Tahiti painting exotic scenes on the spot—*Mahana No Atua* (*Day of the God*) (Fig. 19:5).

Thus, just as the political scene had witnessed the dynamics of revolution and counter-revolution, the arts likewise were motivated by positive forces, such as the new machine methods of distribution, freedom of expression, individualism and nationalism; and counterforces such as the various escape mechanisms—the revivals, back to nature, and exoticism. Together all these ideas merge to make up the fuller vocabulary of the time, which was incorporated into the language of the writers, the forms of the sculptors, the canvases of the painters, and the scores of the composers of the period.

CHAPTER

CHRONOLOGY: Paris, Late 19th Century

General Events

1830–1848	Louis Philippe reigned as constitutional monarch
1837–1901	Reign of Queen Victoria
1839	Daguerre and Niepce published findings on photographic images, which resulted in the Daguerreotype process
1843–1850	Library of St. Geneviève built by Labrouste
1848	February Revolution. Monarchy of Louis Philippe overthrown
	Second Republic established
	Communist Manifesto issued by Marx and Engels
1851	Great Exhibition of All the Nations held in London
	Crystal Palace built by Paxton to house the exhibition
	Louis Napoleon, President of the Second Republic, made a successful *coup d'etat* and became dictator
1852–1870	Louis Napoleon's reign as Emperor Napoleon III
1853	Admiral Perry opened Japan
1858–1868	Bibliothèque Nationale built by Labrouste
1859	*Origin of Species* published by Charles Darwin
1863	*On the Sensation of Tone as a Physiological Basis for the Theory of Music* published by Helmholz (1821–1894)
	Life of Jesus by Renan
1870–1871	Franco-Prussian War
	Third Republic established
	Germany became an empire
1871	*Descent of Man* published by Charles Darwin
1874	First impressionist exhibit held
1889	*La Grande Exposition Universelle* held in Paris with the Eiffel Tower as one of its buildings
1892	*Pelléas et Mélisande* by Maeterlinck presented in Paris
1896	*Matter and Memory* published by Henri Bergson
1902	Debussy's opera on Maeterlinck's *Pelléas et Mélisande* produced in Paris

Painting

1808–1879	Daumier
1819–1877	Courbet
1832–1883	Manet
1834–1903	Whistler
1834–1917	Degas
1839–1906	Cézanne
1840–1926	Monet
1841–1919	Renoir
1848–1903	Gauguin
1853–1890	Van Gogh
1859–1891	Seurat
1864–1901	Toulouse-Lautrec

Sculpture

1827–1875	Carpeaux
1840–1917	Rodin

Architecture

1801–1865	Joseph Paxton
1801–1875	Henri Labrouste
1809–1891	Georges-Eugène Haussmann
1832–1923	Gustave Eiffel

Music

1813–1883	Wagner
1822–1890	Franck
1835–1921	Saint-Saens
1838–1875	Bizet
1842–1912	Massenet
1845–1924	Fauré
1860–1956	Charpentier
1862–1918	Debussy
1875–1937	Ravel

Literature and Philosophy

1798–1857	Auguste Comte
1799–1850	Honoré de Balzac
1812–1870	Charles Dickens
1820–1903	Herbert Spencer
1821–1867	Charles Baudelaire
1821–1880	Gustave Flaubert
1828–1906	Henrik Ibsen
1840–1902	Emile Zola
1842–1898	Stéphane Mallarmé
1844–1900	Friedrich Nietzsche
1850–1893	Guy de Maupassant
1859–1941	Henri Bergson
1862–1949	Maurice Maeterlinck
1870–1925	Pierre Louÿs
1871–1922	Marcel Proust

THE LATE 19th CENTURY

PARIS, LATE 19th CENTURY

If the dominant trend in the arts of the first half of the 19th century was that of the flight from reality, the tendency in the latter half was toward the facing of the artistic facts of life with greater frankness. Governments sought constitutional formulas that would strike a just balance between social rights and material progress; religious denominations were trying to reconcile time-honored Scriptural truths with the new scientific knowledge; social theories were concerned with how political liberalism could evolve side by side with religious orthodoxy; and philosophies were attempting a new resolution between the static absolutes of idealism and the dynamic thought underlying the theories of evolution. Architects were wondering how their work could still remain in the realm of the fine arts and yet make use of the new materials and technological methods at their command. Sculptors, such as Rodin, were asking whether the traditional mythological and historical themes could be replaced by more contemporary subjects. The realistic and impressionistic painters were seeking a formula for the incorporation of the new physical discoveries concerning the nature of light and its perception by the human eye into the accepted framework of the pictorial art. Novelists, such as Zola, were trying to establish an alliance between scientific and literary methods. Poets and playwrights, such as Mallarmé and Maeterlinck, were looking for a middle ground between the realities of the revolutionary age and the traditional limitations of poetic expression. And composers, such as Debussy, were endeavoring to harmonize the new acoustical discoveries involving the physics of sound with the accepted concepts of tonality and musical form.

In this process governments and rulers settled down from high-flown heroics and histrionics into the drab but necessary routine of bureaucratic officialdom. The energies of artists were diverted from historical and exotic subjects into everyday life and seemingly trivial occurrences. The social criticism in the novels of Balzac and Dickens and the content of pictures like Daumier's *Legislative Body* (Fig. 18:15) were often highly critical of existing customs and conventions. Their use of the ugly and the violence of their shock techniques, however, were calculated to arouse but not to insult or alienate to the point where their patrons would stop buying their novels and pictures. Some artists, however, found life such a disillusionment that their art became the sole compensation for the miseries of their existence. This group of painters and poets eventually severed their ties with their middle-class potential patrons altogether. They retreated into a private world of art, where the painters painted pictures for a limited audience of other painters of similar persuasion, and the poets put down their inspirations only for the eyes and ears of other poets. They thus led the insecure lives of an underprivileged social group and tended to band together in a desperate little society within society. In general, however, the artists turned toward the new world of the great city for their material and inspiration. The artificial replaced the natural, and urban entertainments eclipsed the delights of nature. The usual was dominant over the unusual, description replaced narration, and the here-and-now was definitely in the ascendancy over the there-and-then.

PAINTING

About the middle of the 19th century the most important younger painters began to look about for a means of avoiding the grandiose, the heroic, the glorification of the past, and soaring flights of artistic imagination. Gustave Courbet was in the vanguard of a group who styled themselves "realists," defined painting as a physical language, and ruled out the abstract and invisible as outside its province. The saints and miracles of the 19th century, according to Courbet, were mines, machines, and railroad stations. With a keen eye and a desire to record accurately what he saw about him, he consciously set out to build an art on the commonplace. His painting was concerned with the present not the past, with the momentary not the permanent, with bodies not souls, and with materiality not spirituality. His nudes suggested no nymphs or goddesses; they were merely the models who posed in his studio. Courbet, however, sometimes got almost as passionate about the ugly as his predecessors did about the beautiful. Both Courbet and his younger colleague, Edouard Manet, who came under his influence, were sometimes betrayed into an emotional interest in their subjects in spite of themselves; they even tried at times to induce shock reactions from their audiences much in the manner of the novelists Balzac and Dickens.

The generation of painters who followed Courbet were much less concerned with their subjects than he was. Like the realists they took their easels out of doors and tried to do as much of their painting on the spot as possible rather than to work from sketches in their studios. They were strictly against a picture carrying any moral, any message, or any literary associations whatsoever, and they cultivated a calculated indifference toward the content of their pictures. They even carried their optical realism to the point where they tried to separate visual experience from memory and thus avoid the associational values the mind contributes to it. In 1874 Claude Monet exhibited a picture called *Impression—Sunrise*, which gave the new movement its name. At first *impressionism* was picked up as a term of critical derision. But the word has a certain appropriateness, implying as it does something unfinished, incomplete, an affair of the moment, an act of instantaneous vision, a sensation rather than a cognition.

It is impossible, of course, to substantiate any claim of a direct cause-and-effect relationship between science and art in this period, or any formal connection between optical physics and painting. On the other hand there is equally no valid reason to deny that painters were unaware of or indifferent to such things as the invention of the camera, the scientific discoveries about the nature of light, and the new knowledge about the physiology of the eye. Joint researches of Daguerre and Niepce on the making of photographic images on prepared metal plates, which resulted in the Daguerreotype process, had been published as early as 1839. The revelation that visual imagery was primarily dependent on minute gradations of light intensity was bound to make an impression on painters. Physicists, such as Helmholtz and others, made discoveries about the component prismatic parts of white light, and pointed out that the sensation of color has more to do with a retinal reaction in the eye than with objects themselves. The color wheel also demonstrated that two separate hues on a disk that was at rest were fused by the eye into a third when the disk was in rapid rotation.

Painters also did some speculation of their own on the nature of the visual experience. Form and space, they maintained, are not actually seen but implied from varying intensities of light and color. Objects are not so much entities in themselves as they are agents for the absorption and refraction of light. Hard outlines, indeed line itself, do not exist in nature.

Shadows, they maintained, are not black but tend to take on a color complementary to that of the objects which cast the reflections. The concern of the painter, they concluded, should therefore be with light and color more than with objects and substances. A painting should consist of a breakdown of sunlight into its component parts, and brilliance can be achieved by the use of the primary colors that make up the spectrum. Instead of a green mixed by the painter on his palette, separate daubs of yellow and blue should be placed close together and the mixing left to the spectator's eye. What seems confusion at close range is clarified at the proper distance. By thus trying to step up the luminosity of their canvases so as to convey the illusion of sunlight seen through a prism, they achieved a veritable carnival of color in which the eye seems to join in a dance of vibrating light intensities. As a result of this re-examination of their technical procedures, the impressionists discovered a new method of visual representation. Since, however, it was concerned so exclusively with the world of appearances, impressionism was more the ultimate phase of realism than a new style in itself.

Manet's *Rue de Berne* (Fig. 19:1) was painted late in his career with the impressionistic theory in mind. In it he builds a cityscape out of a con-

Fig. 19:1. Manet. *Rue de Berne*. 1878. Jakob Goldschmidt Collection, New York

figuration of interrelated planes. By his subtle use of color intensities rather than by linear perspective, he achieves the effect of recession and depth. Other versions show some roadmenders in the foreground, and the choice of such a casual street scene is in keeping with the general preference for subjects that can be taken in at a glance, rather than those that must be studied carefully and in detail. It also exemplifies the conscious cultivation of the accidental—the random scene in which emotional involvement with the subject is impossible.

More than any other painter, however, Claude Monet was the central figure of impressionism, and his picture the *Old San Lazare Station* (Fig. 19:2) is among his most typical works. The rendering of the humid atmosphere, the mixture of steam and smoke, the hazy sunlight filtering in from the open background and the transparent roof, the contrast between the open spaces and the closed forms of the engines and railroad cars are the things that concern him most. There is no hustle and bustle, no drama of arriving or departing people, no crowds or excitement, no interplay of men and machines, such as one might expect in such a setting. Instead his people merely file from the waiting room toward the train, and the workmen go about their tasks in a matter-of-fact manner. The picture therefore tends to become an atmospheric study in blues and greens.

The full development of Monet's broken-color technique is even more clearly discernible in the *Garden at Giverny* (Fig. 19:3), his suburban home. In it he breaks his light up into a spectrum of bright colors that delights the eye by forming shimmering patterns in and around the leaves and lilies. Water imagery repeatedly recurs in impressionistic painting. Its iridescence, its fluidity, its surface reflections, the perpetual play of changing light, make it an ideal medium for conveying the conception of the insubstantial, impermanent, fleeting nature of visual experience. This is but one of many versions Monet painted of the same subject. It was his habit to do the same scene over and over again, and it is evident that subject matter was of little concern to him. With scientific detachment he tries to maintain the constancy of his subject matter so as to focus the interest on the variables of light and atmosphere. Each version varies according to the season, day or hour. Monet might even be called the weather man of painting, were it not that his genuine admiration for nature usually overcame his objective detachment in spite of himself.

Impressionism is clearly an art of the urban man who sees himself in terms of temporal flow, mounting tensions, and sudden change. His volatile life is ruled by impermanent rather than permanent forces, and becoming is more real to him than being. Impressionistic painters purposely

Fig. 19:2 (above). Monet. *The Old San Lazare Station*. 31½″ x 23½.″ 1877. Art Institute, Chicago. Fig. 19:3 (below). Monet. *Garden at Giverny*. 35″ x 39″. Art Institute, Chicago

chose everyday subjects, such as street scenes, children playing, or dancing in a night café. When they did go to the country it was to the suburbs in the manner of city folk on a holiday. As a result, the general effect of the style is bright, cheerful, and lighthearted rather than heavy or somber. They were intoxicated by light rather than life, and they saw the world as a myriad of mirrors that refracted a constantly changing kaleidoscope of color and varying intensities of light. They lived therefore in a visual world of reflections rather than substances, and one in which visual values replaced the tactile. In order to reproduce the fugitive atmospheric effects they desired, they had to work directly from nature. This led to a speeding-up in the process of painting to a point where working with oils approached the technique of water colors. The criticism of hasty work and careless craftsmanship that they incurred from their contemporaries was sometimes fully justified. In general, however, there was no lack of technical skill on the part of its most important practitioners when their intentions are fully taken into account. They wanted their paintings to seem improvised and to have an unfinished fragmentary look. Beauty, like color, they felt was in the eye of the beholder, not in the picture itself. They intended in fact to paint not so much what is seen but how it is seen. Instead of composing, which implies a placing together, they sought to isolate one aspect of experience and explore it to the utmost. Their art therefore becomes one of analysis more than synthesis, sensation more than perception, sight more than insight. As such the cool objectivity of impressionism represents the triumph of technique over expression.

In their total immersion in the two-dimensional world of appearances, the impressionists consciously neglected the other dimensions of psychological depth and emotional involvement. As a consequence they soon began to chafe under the arbitrary limitations of such an overrefined, one-sided theory. And their audiences also were not happy with the role of innocent bystander that had been assigned to them. Both artist and spectator had, in effect, resigned their active roles in the scheme of things for that of the aloof observer of life who lets the river of experience go by without attempting to divert its flow in any significant direction. In scarcely more than a dozen years after Monet had shown his *Impression—Sunrise*, the movement had worked itself into a dead end. Even though no one painted an "Impression—Sunset" to commemorate the event, the movement in its pristine form was to all intents and purposes at an end with the last impressionist exhibit in 1886. Many of the discoveries that were made, however, survived in variously modified forms in the work of the post-impressionistic painters who had come under its influence.

Fig. 19:4. Seurat. *Sunday Afternoon on the Island of La Grande Jatte.* 81″ x 220⅜″. 1884–1886. Art Institute, Chicago

Fig. 19:5. Gauguin. *Mahana No Atua (Day of the God).* 26″ x 34½″. 1894. Art Institute, Chicago

Sunday Afternoon on the Island of La Grande Jatte (Fig. 19:4) by Georges
Seurat shows how the impressionistic theory was carried to its logical conclusion. Light, shadow, and color are still the major concern, and the subject is also that of the relaxed atmosphere of a group of middle-class
Parisians on a Sunday outing. Instead of being dashed off out of doors in
a single afternoon, however, Seurat worked on his large canvas in his
studio over a period of years. Instead of informal casual arrangements, all
seems as set as in an old-fashioned family portrait. Instead of misty nebulous forms, such details as a bustle, a parasol, or a plug hat are as stylized
and geometrical as in a Renaissance composition. Finally, instead of hastily
painted patches of broken color, Seurat has now evolved a formula called
pointillism in which the gradations of color intensities are controlled by
applying each dot with the most minute care. What seems to be a colored
cloud dissolves on closer inspection into a rainbow of multicolored con-
fettilike spots, all carefully graduated in shades from warm to cool.

Gauguin's *Mahana No Atua* (Fig. 19:5), or *Day of the God*, shows how the
brilliant color of the impressionists can be adapted to make quiet, two-
dimensional decorative designs. Van Gogh's *Starry Night* (Fig. 19:6), on
the other hand, demonstrates how the same colors can be used to achieve
intensely expressive effects. The deep purple sky, the yellow light of the

Fig. 19:6. Van Gogh. *Starry Night.* 29″ x 36¼″. 1889. Collection Museum of
Modern Art, New York

stars, the green upward-curling silhouette of the cypress tree all stem from impressionism. The broken color, however, has here become a myriad of dark swirling vertiginous lines that are used as a means toward the revelation of an inner ecstatic vision.

In the 1870's Paul Cézanne was also using the prismatic color palette of the impressionists. He soon discovered the expressive limitations of the theory, and his solution of some of the pictorial problems it posed became a turning point in the history of painting. For him the superficial beauty of impressionism did not provide a solid-enough base on which to build a significant art. The delight in the transitory tended too much to exclude the more permanent values. Instead of severing connections with the past, he said that he wanted "to make of impressionism something solid like the art of the museums." Poussin was the old master he chose to emulate, and his expressed desire was to recreate Poussin in the light of nature (*vivifier Poussin sur nature*). The cultivation of instantaneous vision, according to Cézanne, ruled out the participation of too many other important faculties. His pictures, unlike those of the impressionists, were not meant to be grasped immediately, and their meaning is never obvious. A painting for Cézanne should be not only an act of the eye, but also of the mind. If painting aimed only at the senses, any deeper probing of human psychology would be ruled out. Light is important in itself, but it can also be used to achieve inner illumination. Color as such is paramount, but it is also a means of describing masses and volumes, revealing form, creating relationships, separating space into planes, and producing the illusion of projection and recession. Primary colors produce brilliance, but judicious mixtures can run a whole gamut of subtle effects. Both light and color are therefore retained as the basis of his art, but not to the extent of eliminating the need for line and geometrical organization. Cézanne's interests are not so much in the specific or the particular as they are in the general. Analysis is necessary for simplification and the reduction of a picture to its bare essentials, but the primary process of the pictorial art for Cézanne is still that of composition and synthesis. His canvases therefore tend to be more austere than voluptuous, more sinuous than lush. His pictures have order, repose, and a serene color harmony, yet are capable of rising to high points of tension and grandeur. In one landscape everything may be cool and shadowy, while in another the heat of the southern sun seems almost to burn the canvas.

The forms he chooses are those of his daily experience—apples, mountains, houses, trees—constants by which it is possible to measure the extent of his spiritual growth. Mont Ste.-Victoire, a rising rocky mass near his

Fig. 19:7 (above). Cézanne. *Mont Ste.-Victoire.* 25⅝″ x 31⅞″. 1885–1887. Metropolitan Museum, New York. Fig. 19:8 (below). Cézanne. *Mont Ste.-Victoire.* 27⅞″ x 36⅛″. 1904. George W. Elkins Collection, Philadelphia Museum of Art

home in Aix-en-Provence, was for Cézanne a recurring motive. Just as Goethe wrote his *Faust* throughout his entire creative career, so Cézanne paints his mountain again and again until it becomes a kind of symbol of his ambitions and aspirations. The contrast of an early and late version provides an interesting index to his artistic growth. The first picture, subtitled *Landscape with Viaduct* (Fig. 19:7), dates between 1885 and 1887. The second version, called simply *Mont Ste.-Victoire* (Fig. 19:8), was done between 1904 and 1906. Both are landscapes organized by means of color into a pattern of planes. Both show his way of achieving perspective not by converging lines but by intersecting and overlapping planes of color. In the first version there is a complementary balance between the vertical rise of the trees and the horizontal line of the viaduct. In the second such details are omitted in favor of a balance achieved by the dense green foliage of the lower foreground against the purple and light green jagged mass of the mountain in the background. In the early picture such details as the road, houses, and shrubs are readily recognizable. In the later one all is reduced to the barest essentials, and only such formal contours as the cones, cubes, and slanting surfaces remain. In one the mountain descends in a series of gently sloping lines; in the other it plunges precipitously downward. Both, however, are landscapes viewed through the same sensitive and highly individual temperament. Both show his lifelong desire to mold nature into a coherent pattern in order to bridge the inanimate world of things and the animate world of the human mind.

In a still life, such as *Basket of Apples* (Fig. 19:9), Cézanne works in a more intimate vein. The search for pure formal values, however, still obtains. In one of his letters he said that nature reveals itself in the forms of the cylinder, the sphere, and the cone. Here his cylinders are the horizontally arranged biscuits; his spheres are in the form of apples; and his cone, the vertically rising bottle. They are balanced in this instance by the forward-tilting ellipse of the basket and the receding plane of the table top. An almost imperceptible feeling of diagonal motion is induced by the distribution of the fruit from the upper left to the lower right, which is brought to an equally imperceptible stop by means of the pear-shaped apple at the extreme right. Such a simple geometrical arrangement of familiar forms imparts a feeling of comfort as well as one of order and clarity. Cézanne often painted these still life compositions so slowly and carefully that he sometimes found it necessary to use artificial flowers and fruits so that he could study their arrangement for weeks at a time. While he treats his cones and cubes as abstractions, his warm color saves them from frigidity, and he never fails to relate them in a subtle and expressive way to living forms.

Fig. 19:9 (above). Cézanne. *Still Life: Basket of Apples.* 24⅜″ x 31″. 1890–1894. Art Institute, Chicago. Fig. 19:10 (below). Cézanne. *Card Players.* 25⅝″ x 31⅞″. 1890–1892. Stephen C. Clark Collection, New York

Cézanne never overlooked the human values in his art, and the stolid peasants he found in the cafés of his native Provence often served him as models. His *Card Players* (Fig. 19:10) are every bit as impassive and monumental in their way as are his mountains. They are posed with the same stability and equilibrium as his still lifes; and their lines, volumes, masses, and textures are conceived with the same simplicity as one of his landscapes. Cézanne sets himself such severe limitations that his pictures fall mainly within the classifications of landscapes, still life, figure compositions, and portraits. Even within these categories, he keeps his themes constant so that each picture can be treated as a separate experiment. By such means he tried to bring form and stability into a visual world where everything was change and transition. If he succeeded only at times and failed at others, it must be equated with the immensity of the task that Cézanne set for himself. Like all great masters, he realized in his mature years that he had made only a beginning, and he once remarked that he would forever be the primitive of the method he had discovered. His historical position may indeed be just this, and his work can be said to form the bridge between impressionism and modern painting.

SCULPTURE

Among the sculptural exhibits at the Paris Salon of 1877 was a statue of a nude youth called the *Bronze Age*. So astonishingly natural and lifelike it seemed, rumors soon began to be circulated that the sculptor was trying to pass off as a statue a cast taken from a living model. The stories were given sufficient credence in official quarters to warrant its hasty withdrawal. The artistry of Auguste Rodin, however, did not have to wait long for recognition, and the figure, with explanations and apologies, was again exhibited the following year. A short while later it was bought by the state for placement in the Luxembourg Gardens. Such was the gulf, however, between a work of art and life, between a statue and a living being, between a monument and reality, that in academic circles it was actually a disgrace if a statue looked too real or believable.

Like his forward-looking contemporaries in other fields, Rodin had veered away from the heroic and toward the natural. Though he admired Gothic sculpture and even wrote a book about it, his work contains no sermons in stone. Though he admired Dante and drew practically all his later subjects from an early project for the *Gates of Hell*, his conceptions show little of the escapism that animated his immediate predecessors. For Rodin, the process of forming supersedes that of form itself. The *Hand of*

Fig. 19:11. Rodin. *Hand of God.* Marble. 29″ high. 1898. Metropolitan Museum, New York

Fig. 19:12. Rodin. *Orpheus and Eurydice Emerging from the Gates of Hell.* Marble. 50″ x 30″. *c.*1893. Metropolitan Museum, New York

God (Fig. 19:11) exemplifies this both in the method of execution as well as in the subject itself. Out of an indefinite mass of uncut stone, symbolic of the formless void, the hand of the Creator arises. Divine omnipotence is suggested by the scale of the hand in relation to those of the human figures that are emerging from a lump of uncarved marble. The significance of the work was caught by the philosopher Henri Bergson, author of *Creative Evolution*, who called it "the fleeting moment of creation, which never stops." It is the implication that nothing is ever quite complete, that everything takes place in the flow of time, that matter is the womb which is continuously giving birth, that creation is a never-ending process rather than an accomplished fact—in short, the acceptance of the theory and philosophy of evolution—that gives Rodin's conception its daring quality.

Rodin always acknowledges his material frankly, seeking neither to disguise it nor to escape from it. Other figures and groups, such as his *Orpheus and Eurydice* (Fig. 19:12), also seem to be barely emerging out of their original stone or clay state. This is not, however, the mighty Michelangelesque struggle of man against his material bonds. Rather it is a sensuous love of material as such, a reveling in the flesh or stone, and a desire to explore all its possibilities and potentialities. If Michelangelo left his figures incomplete and still dominated by their material medium, it was largely because he lacked the time to finish them. With Rodin the incompleteness is a conscious and calculated part of his expressive design. Like the symbolist poets, the novelist Proust, and the dramatist Maeterlinck, Rodin went one step beyond mere description. For Rodin, as with his literary contemporaries, events were nothing in themselves. Only when conjured up later in memory did they acquire the necessary subjective coloration; and only then, paradoxically, could the artist treat them with the needed objective detachment. Rodin always preferred to work from a memory image rather than directly from a model in the flesh. When he did work with one, it was usually to make a quick sketch or an impression in soft clay. He could then allow his figures to take plastic shape in this preliminary stage at the moment of inspiration and thus promote the feeling that they were the product of improvisation. All the arduous labor of transferring them into marble or bronze was left until the forms had been refined in memory and had assumed a more subjective and personal quality.

Rodin defined sculpture as an art of hollows and projections; or, as he put it in less fastidious moments, the art of the hole and the lump. Light and shadow thus become the principal means of animating his material. His figures do not displace volume as much as they cast shadows, and they seem to exist more in time than in space. His choice of subjects also reveals this preoccupation with the transitory—*Dawn, Eternal Springtime, Awakening, The Kiss, The Wave, The Tempest,* and *Twilight.* The surface play of light, and his greater concern with the atmosphere that envelops his forms than with the figures themselves, links his art with that of the impressionistic painters. It sometimes seems that his intentions are really closer to the two-dimensional pictorial art, and that oil and canvas would really have been the proper medium for his transitory and impermanent visions. Through memory and introspection, however, Rodin was able to give his compositions some three-dimensional plausibility, and by the projection of some psychological depth into his work, he saved his art from becoming commonplace.

ARCHITECTURE

Throughout the 19th century there was a sharp division of thought about the work of an architect. Was he primarily an artist or a builder? A designer or engineer? Should he concern himself more with decoration or with structure? Was his place in a studio making drawings or in the field working with his materials? The champions of the pictorial viewpoint achieved such virtuosity that they could produce a design based on any known building from the past at practically a moment's notice. Late in the century all the historical styles had been so carefully catalogued and documented that the range of choices was almost unlimited. What had begun as the revival of special periods had now been broadened to include them all. The term for such a freedom of choice is *eclecticism*, and if a name is to be chosen for the style of the period this is the only one possible. The sole limitation on this eclecticism was based on a general acceptance of the appropriateness of the styles of certain periods to special situations. The classical was considered best for commemorative buildings and monuments; but classicism now could be anything from Mycenean Greek to late imperial Roman. Medieval was the preference for churches, but again this might mean Byzantine, Romanesque, early or late Gothic. For public buildings Renaissance was thought most suitable, though here again the choice was anything from the 15th century on.

The industrial age, on the other hand, had produced new methods and materials that opened up entirely new possibilities. The potentialities of cast iron, for instance, were perceived by engineers and industrialists long before architects began to speculate on the creative applications that could be made to their art. The structural use of iron actually dates from the latter part of the 18th century. However, it was found at first in bridges, cotton mills, and other utilitarian buildings; and in this early stage it was usually combined with brick, stone, or timber or else used as a substitute for one or more of them. Nevertheless the first steps toward a revolution in the art of building had been taken. The century was eventually to see the spanning of broader widths, the enclosure of more cubic space, and projections toward greater heights than had hitherto been thought possible. The new materials and structural principles were both a threat and challenge to the traditional pictorial designers, and the more they were incorporated into building plans, the more progressive the architecture became.

It has already been noted how iron columns and girders had been used quite openly by John Nash in the exotic Brighton Pavilion (Fig. 18:17), marking one of the first instances of their use in a large residential building. In Paris, Gau also had used iron to reinforce the vaults of his Gothic Revival Church of Ste.-Clotilde (Fig. 18:14), but it had been masked by stone facing. In his Library of St. Genevieve, however, Henri Labrouste went one step further and achieved an even more penetrating insight into the possibilities of the new material at his command. A first glance at its exterior (Fig. 19:13) reveals simply a well-executed Renaissance revival building—as such it is indebted to a 15th-century Italian church in Rimini designed by Alberti—with the usual festoons of garlands adorning the space above its seriated windows. A closer inspection, however, will show that the first floor is conceived more as a solid space, while the bold arcade of windows above gives promise of light and air within. Since this is a library building, there is a working relationship between the closed storage space for the books below and the open reading room above. This is as far as the exterior goes toward a unity of means and ends, however, and the stone on the outside gives no hint that the interior is constructed of iron.

By utilizing the strength of metal, Labrouste was able to replace the massive masonry ordinarily required for such a large reading room (Fig. 19:14) and at the same time provide for a maximum of open space and brilliant illumination. The roof is vaulted by means of girders, cast in the form of arches, spanning the room crosswise and dividing it into two parallel barrel vaults. An open foliated pattern related to the classical acanthus leaf is used as a decorative motive, and the vaults are supported by tall, thin, fluted Corinthian colonettes, also made of iron. Labrouste has thus managed his material so that he brings out its full structural possibilities. By allowing his iron colonettes to assume a form associated with carved stone, however, he compromises with tradition and lets the expressive potentialities lag somewhat behind.

Fig. 19:13 (above). Labrouste. *Library of St. Genevieve*. 1843–1850. Paris (Courtesy French Government Tourist Office). Fig. 19:14 (below). Reading Room (Archives Photographiques)

Fig. 19:15. Labrouste. *National Library*, Stacks. 1858–1868. Paris (Archives Photographiques)

What Labrouste had begun with the Library of St. Genevieve, however, reached an even more brilliant fulfillment later in his masterwork, the stacks of the Bibliothèque Nationale (Fig. 19:15). This storage space for books is conceived as the very heart of the library, and it is now brought out into the open alongside the reading room itself. Though closed to the public, a full view of it is obtained through a glass-enclosed archway. All superfluous ornamentation is now omitted in favor of the function for which it was designed. Except for the bookcases and the glass ceiling, everything is of cast iron. By dividing his space into five stories, four above and one below the ground level, Labrouste provided for the housing of almost a million volumes. The floors are of open grillwork, which permits a free flow of light to reach all levels. Frequent stairways provide rapid communication between the floors, and the strategically placed bridges permit freedom of access between the two wings. As a composition they present a pleasing visual pattern of vertical and horizontal intersecting planes. In both these libraries it is evident that Labrouste has taken a bold stride toward the realization of the potentialities of the new materials that were available to him, and his work as a whole represents a positive contribution to the development of a new architecture.

The same year that Labrouste was completing his first library, a new and original structure was going up in London that made no pretensions whatsoever of being either a Roman bath or a Renaissance palace. The London *Times* referred to it as Mr. Paxton's "monstrous greenhouse"; and, to be sure, it was conceived and carried out by a landscape gardener skilled in the construction of conservatories and nurseries. The occasion was that of The Great Exhibition of the Works of Industry of All Nations, and the latest mechanical inventions as well as raw materials were to be brought together there with the finished products of industry. Machinery of all sorts was to take its place beside the manufactured arts and crafts that were being turned out by the new factories. The Crystal Palace (Fig. 19:16), as it was eventually called, that Joseph Paxton constructed to house the exposition was destined to eclipse the exhibits themselves and to find for itself a unique place in the history of modern architecture. His light and airy structure was rectangular in shape, 408 feet in width and—with a neat bit of symbolism to coincide with the year of the exhibition—1851 feet in length. It rose by means of a skeleton of cast-iron girders and wrought-iron trusses and supports, all bolted together with mathematical precision. Its walls and roof enclosed 33 million cubic feet of space in a transparent sheath of glass. The rapidity of its construction was no less remarkable than its form. The whole structure was accurately analyzed into a multiplicity of prefabricated parts, and so well planned that 18,000 panes of glass could be put in place by 80 workmen in a week. Begun the end of September 1850, it was easily ready for the grand opening, May 1, 1851.

The building, contrary to expectations, turned out to be a thing of surprising beauty and brilliance, as inexpensive in its construction as it was daring in its use of materials. No applied decoration of any sort marred the forthright character of the exterior; and while the iron columns of the interior paid lip service to their classical ancestors, the enormous scale made such details incidental. At the inauguration ceremonies (Fig. 19:17) Albert, the Prince Consort, stood by Osler's crystal fountain and restated the purpose of the exhibition, which was to present "a living picture of the point of development at which the whole of mankind had arrived, . . . and a new starting point from which all nations will be able to direct their further exertions." Nothing seemed impossible to the machine age, and the engineers were indeed the prophets of the new order. Everything now seemed set for Victorian man to step out of his self-created pseudo-Gothic gloom into the new and shining age of industrial prosperity. Mr. Paxton and his greenhouse, however, had to wait more than half a century before the architects fully caught up with them.

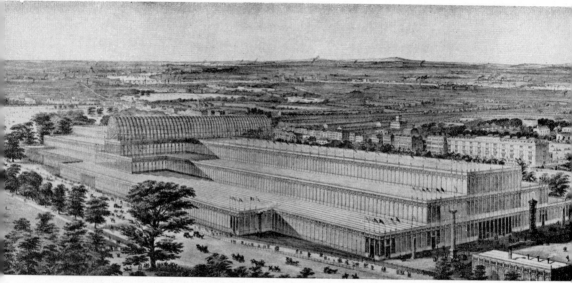

Fig. 19:16 (above). Paxton. *Crystal Palace*. 1851. London. Fig. 19:17 (below). Paxton. *The Foreign Pavilion*. 1851. London. Prints from Nash, Haghe, and Roberts. *The Great Exhibition* (Courtesy British Information Services)

Across the channel meanwhile, Georges-Eugène Haussmann was re-planning the city of Paris on a scale commensurate with its growth into one of the first of the great 19th-century industrial cities. The new method of cast-iron construction, the need for wide and long streets to facilitate the flow of traffic, and the accessibility of railroad stations were all taken into account in his designs. If the taste of his patron, Napoleon III, ran somewhat to festoons of floral garlands and bulbous terra-cotta statuary, they were only a camouflage for the really fundamental changes that were going on beneath the surface. The expositions devoted to the wonders of modern industry, which were held at regular intervals, reached a climax in the International Exhibition of 1889. Its Gallery of Machines, by employing steel and glass, achieved a span of 375 feet, the widest ever made up to that time. Even more spectacular, however, was the tower that soared more than 1000 feet above the ground. Gustave Eiffel, an engineer who had made his reputation in bridges and industrial buildings, was entrusted with a contract for this unprecedented structure that he conceived as a bridge into the sky. It was to be built by means of an assembly of small machine-manfactured parts riveted together with precision down to a tenth of a millimeter. In just 17 months he was able to boast that he had engineered a structure that would stand forever against earth, wind, and weather.

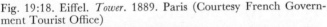

Fig. 19:18. Eiffel. *Tower.* 1889. Paris (Courtesy French Government Tourist Office)

From its four foundation members, the Eiffel Tower (Fig. 19:18) makes a series of three spectacular upward leaps to a platform 984 feet above the ground, where all of its elegant lines converge. A lantern then carries the height still further to a point over 1000 feet in the sky. A spiral staircase and a system of elevators corresponding to the above stages allow visitors to mount as far as the base of the lantern. Except for a few nonfunctional decorations about the base, Eiffel's design is a masterpiece of structural integrity and honest use of material. Before it was built, however, a violent protest in the form of a petition was received by the exposition authorities. "We the writers, painters, sculptors, and architects," it began, "come in the name of French good taste and of this menace to French history to express our deep indignation that there should stand in the heart of our capital this unnecessary and monstrous Eiffel Tower." What was to have been but a temporary exhibition building, however, turned out to be such a rousing success that it was assured a permanent place in the Parisian scheme of things. Uses for it quite unanticipated at the time it was built were found. Successively and simultaneously it has served as a lookout point, a weather observation post, a beacon tower for air traffic, a radio tower, and television sending station. It was at once the prototype of the modern steel skyscraper and a symbol of the modern metropolis.

LITERATURE AND MUSIC

The desire on the part of writers to come to terms with their own world rather than explore the avenues of escape was responsible for the literary movements known as realism and naturalism. In some cases writers cultivated a kinship with the scientific materialism that dominated the thought of the period following the February Revolution. In others, notably with Zola and Ibsen, they allied themselves with sociology and wrote their novels and plays much as a social worker might handle a case history. Somewhat earlier Balzac had proved himself far too sophisticated a writer to see much beyond the ignorance and poverty of the Middle Ages and rustic village life and was able to write glowingly of the beauty of factories and big cities. The subject matter of his novels was drawn from the complex moral and psychological problems of middle-class life in the large cities that he knew. This did not imply complete acceptance of the bourgeois image of man; on the contrary, it often meant violent opposition to the values he accepted. Attitudes toward their writing varied with the temperaments of individual writers. Flaubert, for instance, felt it necessary to withdraw from life in order to describe it with the necessary objectivity;

and he was convinced that such scientific detachment alone qualified the artist as well as the scientist. Zola, on the other hand, could not write without a passionate self-identification with the oppressed subjects of his novels. In the spirit of a reformer he found it a necessity to bring social sores out into the sunlight of public exposure in order to effect a cure. With him the novelist becomes a social research worker, and the novel a documentary case history.

This method was obviously better adapted to the writing of novels than to the needs of poetry or music. Some realism, to be sure, can be found in the vivid instrumentation of Berlioz; and his unfinished opera, *Benvenuto Cellini*, had included a forging song. Wagner's *Ring of the Nibelungs* includes a scene which calls for anvils to be hammered backstage, while the fire glows and sparks fly during the forging of a sword. In spite of its exotic setting, Bizet's conception of the character of Carmen was realistic enough to cause a certain sensation when it was first performed; while sometime later the whir of sewing machines could be heard in Charpentier's opera *Louise*. In general, however, music as well as poetry found a far more congenial sphere of operation in the more intangible realm of the imagination. Thus another movement arose in the 1880's under the leadership of the poet Mallarmé, which tried to give freer reign to the imaginative process through a new use of symbolism.

The art of the symbolist was one of the fleeting moment; everything rushes past in an accelerated panorama. With the metaphor as a starting point, a symbolist prose poem flows by in a sequence of images that sweeps the reader along on a swift current of words with a minimum of slowing down to ponder on their meaning. Like the impressionistic painters the symbolists reveled in sense data, and like the realistic novelists they looked for their material among the seemingly inconsequential occurrences of daily life. But in their endeavor to endow such happenings with profundity, and in their effort to attach to them a deeper symbolic significance, they went one step beyond their colleagues. While the painters had found a new world in the physics of light, and the novelists another in the social sciences, the symbolists looked to the new discoveries in psychology. By purposely leaving their poetry in an inconclusive and fragmentary state, they were making use of the psychological mechanism of reasoning from part to whole. Since the whole was not defined by the poets, the reader's imagination was allowed full scope. Just as the impressionistic painters had left the mixing of color to the eye of the observer, and the relationship of the subject matter to the viewer's mind, so Mallarmé and the symbolists left the connection, order, and form of their verbal still lifes to be completed by the reader. They also found a new world to explore in listening to colors, looking at sounds, savoring perfumes, and in all such mixtures of separate sensations known to psychology as synaesthesia. Debussy's piano prelude, *Sounds and Perfumes on the Evening Air*, is an attempt to capture this sort of thing in the tonal medium. They pushed outward to the threshold limits of perception in order to develop more delicate sensibilities and stimulate the capacities for new and peripheral experiences. They moved about in a twilight zone where sensation ends and ideation begins. The very word *symbolism*, however, implies that their images are revelations of something surpassing the senses. And it is here that they parted company with the objective techniques of realism and impressionism, which were largely content with careful description.

Maurice Maeterlinck made an interesting attempt to translate the aims of the symbolist poets into dramatic form. His *Pelléas et Mélisande*, a play first performed in 1892, makes use of the uniquely atmospheric method he devised to effect a synthesis between the material world and that of the imagination. In it he denies the external aspects of life, and his symbols are but the outward and visible signs of an inward and spiritual reality. They function like links between the visible and invisible, the momentary and the eternal. The tangible fragments of common experience, the seemingly trivial everyday occurrences, however, furnish clues to the more decisive stuff of life. "Beneath all human thoughts, volitions, passions, actions," he writes in one of his essays, "there lies the vast ocean of the Unconscious, the unknown source of all that is good, true and beautiful. All that we know, think, feel, see and will are but bubbles on the surface of this vast sea." This sea, then, is the symbol of the absolute toward which all life is reaching out but can never quite grasp. What is heard is only the ripples on the surface. "The shallows murmur," as Maeterlinck puts it, "while the deeps are dumb." A play by its very nature must unfold through the medium of speech, but Maeterlinck felt that "it is in silence that true life lies." [1]

In his drama the sea, the forest, the fountain, the abyss, are the *dramatis personae* in a more profound sense than the human characters, who at best are but shadowy reflections of real people. In spite of the settings in which they appear, Maeterlinck's characters belong neither to the past nor the future but hover in a kind of extended now. They seem to have no spatial existence, no volume, but function more as creatures of duration. They grope their way through the impenetrable forest of symbols that surrounds them and mysteriously controls their destinies. Daytime is never more than a shadowy twilight, and at night even the moon is veiled and its light pale. Maeterlinck is the master of the enigmatic, the indefinite, and paradoxical.

Wise old Arkel is blind, but he is the only one in the cast who can "see" what is going on. Philosophical profundities flow more naturally from the child Yniold than from the more "mature" members of the family. And on her deathbed Mélisande declares sonorously that she was never in better health. A book without a subject had once been projected by Flaubert, but it was never written. *Pelléas and Mélisande*, however, comes perilously close to being a play without a plot. So little is externalized that the progress of what plot there is seems to unfold within the characters. One overhears rather than hears the dialogue, and so little happens in the ordinary sense that a kind of dramatic vacuum is created which can be filled only by the imaginations of the spectators. Just as the eye must mix the colors in an impressionistic painting, so the observer's imagination in a Maeterlinck play must connect the metaphors, must unite the separate tableaux into a flow of images, must fill each pregnant pause with projections from his own experience, and must supply the emotional depth to its surface play of symbols.

Such a fragile philosophy is too flimsy a foundation on which to build a very substantial dramatic art, and it is not too surprising that Maeterlinck's audiences were somewhat baffled. A period that knew Zola's realistic novels and Ibsen's problem plays found it hard to enter into this crepuscular world of the spirit. Maeterlinck's good fortune, even though he never quite realized it, was to find a composer who could fill his silences with the necessary nebulous sounds, who could give voice to the "murmur of eternity on the horizon," and who could write the music that provided the link from dream to dream. It was, indeed, as if the music of Claude Debussy had been created for the very purpose of providing the tonal envelope to enclose Maeterlinck's "ominous silence of the soul." Debussy was able to make the sea sing "the mysterious chant of the infinite." In his score the references to the ocean on which all the characters are floating toward their unknown destinies are handled with special sensitivity. Its waters in one guise or another are present in practically every scene, either in the fragmentary form of a spring in the forest, a well in a courtyard, a fountain in a park, or the stagnant fetid pools of underground caverns. This ever-present water imagery is used as the symbol of the flowing, fleeting nature of experience. As an unstable medium without form of its own, it becomes the means of capturing vague atmospheric effects and reflecting subtle changes of mood. The course of Mélisande's life is conveyed by means of these changing waters. She comes from over the sea, is found by a dark pool in the forest, discovers her love for Pelléas at a fountain in the park, and as she dies she asks that the window be opened so that she can once more be with the sea.

Other symbols likewise play their appointed parts. Mélisande weeps in the first scene because of the loss of a golden crown, symbolic of her happier state of childhood innocence. Later when she tosses her wedding ring up and down beside the fountain, one knows that she is taking her wedding vows lightly. When it falls into the bottomless well and disappears, it means that her marriage has dissolved. Only the circles on the surface of the water remain, and as they expand they tell of larger things to come.[2]

Pelléas and Mélisande, Act II, Scene 1   Debussy

Ce n'est plus el-le. Elle est per-due... per-du-e!
'Tis not my ring.— The ring is lost... 'Tis lost!—

Il n'y a plus qu'un grand cercle sur l'eau...
Nought but a cir-cle of wa-ter re-mains...

When her husband Golaud is hurt in the forest, his wound is more spiritual than physical. In the tower scene with Pelléas, so reminiscent of the balcony scene in *Romeo and Juliet*, Mélisande's hair cascades downward like water, catching the gleam of the moonlight, enveloping Pelléas and symbolizing their union. Debussy does this through a descending passage of seventh chords, which tumble downward in a ladder of whole tones.

In the meantime, two turtle doves, symbolic of the lovers' souls, fly

Pelléas and Mélisande, Act III, Scene 1   Debussy

While thus leaning out her hair suddenly turns over and envelopes Pelleas.

mes che-veux descendent de la tour!.. ____

All my hair has fallen down the tower!.. ____

Retenu

più f   *ff*   *p subito*

outward from the tower and are lost in darkness. And love, the ultimate
symbol of happiness, the most fleeting and impermanent of them all, is
the one force that all the characters conspire in spite of themselves to
destroy, and by so doing are destroyed. This is the true tragedy, truer than
the murder of Pelléas and the death of Mélisande. Neither Pelléas nor
Mélisande struggle or protest. They founder like leaky vessels on the sea of
life and are slowly but inevitably submerged. Arkel, of whom Debussy
spoke as one belonging to a "world beyond the grave," makes this poign-
antly clear as he intones his final monologue: "She was a poor little being,
mysterious, like everybody. . . ." The key words are: "like everybody."
But everything still goes on in a continuous flux and every end is but
another beginning, a momentary pause in the eternal duration. The final
words are directed to Mélisande's child—"now it is the turn of the poor
little one. . . ." The orchestral postlude becomes the prelude to silence,
and to another beginning. . . .

Debussy was conversant with the literary figures and developments of
his time, especially the work of Mallarmé and Pierre Louÿs. He had entered into their discussions and sought the technical means of translating
their poetic theories into the medium of music. His style first took shape in
the songs he wrote on texts by the symbolist poets, but Maeterlinck's
drama provided him with the necessary lyric material to ripen it and bring
it to maturity. Like the poets, his musical methods were in many ways the
opposite of conventional operatic techniques. He followed Wagner in
giving the orchestra the main task of carrying on the sequence of the

drama; and, as a result, his work became more of a symphonic poem with running commentary by the singers than a conventional opera. With his characteristic insight, Debussy saw that melody, in the sense of a set operatic aria, impeded rather than promoted the dramatic progress. "I wished—intended, in fact—that the action should never be arrested; that it should be continuous, uninterrupted," he commented. "Melody is, if I may say so, almost anti-lyric, and powerless to express the constant change of emotion or life. Melody is suitable only for song (chanson), which confirms a fixed sentiment." [3]

In thus considering recitative as the most important element of the lyric drama, he allies himself with his illustrious predecessors Lully and Rameau. But while their characters spoke in the highly inflected accents of Baroque grandiloquence, Debussy's speak in cadences more closely approximating modern French. His prosody, in contrast to theirs, is more spoken than declaimed; and it comes closer to conversational than to theatrical French. "The characters in this drama endeavor to sing like real persons," the composer wrote; and by bringing their language closer to everyday speech, and allowing the flow of dramatic action to proceed without interruption, his opera assumes a plausibility seldom achieved in such a highly artificial medium. By using modes other than the traditional major and minor, his recitative takes on the flexible character of psalmodic chant. The rhythms are free, and the absence of regular accentuation allows the words to flow with elasticity. Debussy's motives parallel the literary symbols and are often just broken fragments of melody, which suggest rather than define atmospheric effects or are associated with the mood of a character. While used with greater subtlety, they nevertheless are much closer to Wagner's system of leitmotifs than Debussy was willing to admit. His harmonic method likewise was well suited to the rendition of the ambiguities and obscurities of the symbolist poets. His key centers lose their boundaries; progressions move about freely in tonal space; the predominance given to the tritone interval accents the indefinite drift; and everything is in a state of flux, always on its way but never arriving. Debussy's sensitivity to the timbre of sounds borders on the uncanny. He thought of Mélisande's voice as "soft and silky"; the woodwinds dominate the orchestral coloration with their peculiarly poignant and penetrating quality; and while the shimmering strings are usually divided, they are always present. Above all, performers must know how to make this intangible music live and breathe, how to render its rhythms with the proper elasticity, and how to fill its silences with meaning.

Debussy's evocation of Maeterlinck's pallid world is one of those rare instances of the indissoluble union of literature and music that makes it impossible for later generations to think of them as separate entities. Debussy worked on the score over a period of ten years and was constantly worrying about the audience reaction to his fragile lyric drama. The play had not been a success, and in a letter dated August 1894, Debussy anxiously asks a friend, "how will the world get along with these two poor little beings?" In an obvious reference to the popularity of Zola's writing, he goes on to express his hatred of "crowds, universal suffrage, and tricolored phrases." Even after the opera had been accepted for performance in 1897 and rehearsals had begun, he withdrew it again for another five years of revision. Contrary to expectation, however, the opera was a success and was widely performed. His elusive music ultimately proved its capacity to cast a spell over the most indifferent of audiences. After this it dropped out of sight for a while, but recent revivals have assured it a permanent place in the international repertory.

IDEAS

Any interpretation of the complex interplay of forces that underlies and motivates the divergent tendencies of the latter part of the 19th century is fraught with the usual danger of oversimplification. Two of the most salient ideas, however, are chosen principally because they provide significant insights into the relationship of the several arts. These are the influence of the scientific method on the arts, and the interpretation of experience in terms of time.

The Alliance of Art and Science

Artists in all fields were aware of the extraordinary success of the scientific method. Realism and impressionism brought a new objective attitude into the arts, together with an emphasis on the technical side of the crafts and a tendency for artists to become specialists pursuing but one aspect of their various media. Architects began to look toward the engineers for the more advanced developments in building. Each painting for an impressionist was a kind of experiment, an adventure in problem-solving. Cézanne thought of each picture as a type of visual research problem. In sculpture Rodin was seeking for a new synthesis of matter and form. The literary realists were cultivating a scientific detachment in their writing and developing a technique that would enable them to record the details of their minute observations of everyday life with accuracy and precision. Zola, by means of his experimental novel, introduced a modified scientific technique to fiction. In addition to his poetic dramas Maeterlinck wrote popular nature studies, such as his *Life of the Bee* and the *Magic of the Stars*.

Debussy, when writing to a friend about some of his compositions, spoke of them as his "latest discoveries in musical chemistry."

Many of the actual discoveries of scientific research opened up new vistas in the various arts. Experiments in optical physics revealed some secrets of light and color that painters could explore. New chemical syntheses provided them with more luminous pigments for their canvases. Increased knowledge of the physiology of the eye and the psychology of perception led to a re-examination of how an observer looks at a picture and what he perceives. New metal alloys and processes of casting were a boon to sculptors. The theories of evolution gave Rodin some poetic ideas on how form emerges from matter, the animate from the inanimate. Helmholtz' book *On the Sensation of Tone as a Physiological Basis for the Theory of Music* stirred Debussy and other composers to speculate on the relation of tone to overtone and consonance to dissonance, in their harmonic procedures.

The impressionistic painters were convinced that pictures were made with color, not line and form; the symbolists claimed that poetry was made with words, not ideas; and composers felt that music should be a play of varied sonorities, rather than a means of evoking programmatic associations. By pursuing this general line of thought, Monet revealed a new concept of light; Rodin, an atmospheric extension of three-dimensional form; the symbolists, a new world of poetry; Debussy, a new concept of sound; and Paxton and Eiffel, by incorporating light and air into their designs, achieved a new architectural relationship between inner and outer space. This mechanistic phase, however, could lead just so far, and artists were soon trying to push beyond it into paths that would lead to deeper psychological insights. Each of the post-impressionists in his own way was probing to see how the new discoveries could be used as a means toward new modes of expression. Cézanne's path led into a new concept of pictorial geometry. Maeterlinck attempted to humanize science and describe it in poetical terms. In his case the result was a kind of animism in which stones, fountains, and objects spoke a language and felt a soul life of their own. In an essay on the "Intelligence of Flowers" he tried to establish more sympathetic ties between man and nature. In his stage fantasy *The Bluebird*, Sugar and Bread are among the live characters. Cézanne also felt the living force of the objects he placed in his still lifes, and in a conversation with a friend spoke warmly of the "soul" of a sugar bowl. The symbolists also tried to effect a synthesis between the phenomenal world and that of the creative imagination. Their metaphors were material in the sense that they received expression through the senses, but they hinted at the existence of a more profound ideational world and were definitely based on a view that life was something more than the sum of its molecular parts. Debussy also veered away from the exploration of the physical elements of sound toward the deeper psychological implications of tonal symbolism.

Continuous Flux

The arts of the late 19th century are also bound together by their common tendency toward the interpretation of experience in terms of time. Progress was an idea which was carried over from the late 18th century. Material progress continued to be an indisputable fact, but it was rapidly becoming apparent that it did not go hand in hand with moral, spiritual, and aesthetic progress. With industrialization came a specialization in which men were concerned more with fragments than wholes. Industrial man was rapidly forfeiting to the machine his place as the primary productive unit. With this loss of control came a corresponding shift from a rational world view toward an increasingly irrational one. With industrialization also came a capitalistic economy in which the lives of workers were controlled by intangible forces outside themselves, such as the fluctuations in foreign markets and on the stock exchange. Two centuries previously Baroque man had been shaken by the Copernican revolution in which the notion of a static earth in the center of the universe was replaced by that of a freely moving satellite around the sun. Late 19th-century man was similarly rocked by the Darwinian and other evolutionary theories, which taught that creation was an ever-continuing process rather than an accomplished fact. As a result of such forces and ideas the onward-and-upward notion of progress was revised downward to one of continuous flux and change.

The literary and visual realists concentrated on the momentary, the fragmentary, the everyday occurrence. Even when they planned their works in more comprehensive schemes, the effect was more that of a broad cross section than a coherent three-dimensional structure. For 20 years Balzac worked on parts of his *Human Comedy*, Wagner on his Ring cycle, Rodin on his *Gates of Hell*, and Proust on his *Remembrance of Things Past*. None, however, is a systematic, organic, or logical whole, or a single perfected masterpiece. Instead of an all-embracing unity, they are easily broken down into a collection of fragments, motives, genre scenes, scraps, and pieces. The late 19th century produced no grandiose metaphysical systems, such as those of Thomas Aquinas, Leibniz, Kant, or Hegel, each of whom tried to encompass all experience in a single universal structure.

The thinker who came the closest to making a coherent picture of this turbulent age was Henri Bergson, a lecturer at the École Normale in Paris. His point of departure was a remark made by the pre-Socratic philosopher Heraclitus, who had said that one cannot step into the same river twice.

Bergson cited him in support of his theory that time was more real than space, the many closer to experience than the one, and that becoming was closer to reality than being. Bergson was critical of the intellect because it tended to reduce reality to immobility. He therefore ranked intuition as a higher faculty than reason, because through it the perception of the flow of duration was possible, and through it static quantitative facts were quickened into the dynamic qualitative values of motion and change. Existence is never static but a transition between states and between moments of duration. Experience, he taught, is durational, "a series of qualitative changes, which melt into and permeate one another, without precise outlines. . . ." Art for Bergson is the force that sets man free and through which he can grasp "certain rhythms of life and breath," which compel him even against his will "to fall in with it, like passers by who join in a dance. And thus they compel us to set in motion, in the depth of our being, some secret chord which was only waiting to thrill."

Bergson was thus convinced that reality is mobility, tendency, or "incipient change of direction." Looking at or listening to a work of art is to perceive the mobile qualities of the objects or sounds presented. The aesthetic experience is essentially temporal and involves an "anticipation of movement," which permits the spectator or auditor in various ways "to grasp the future in the present." His theory of art is based on what he calls his "spiritualistic materialism" by which finely perceived material activity elicits spiritual echoes. All is based on the "uniqueness of the moment"; and perception of the temporal flow is synonymous with an awareness of the pulsation of life, something that is quite apart from the mechanical or inert matter. Past, present, and future are molded into an organic whole as "when we recall the notes of a tune melting, so to speak, into one another." Time, therefore, is "the continuous progress of the past, which gnaws into the future and which swells as it advances." Bergson's concept of time, however, is not clock time with its divisions into seconds, minutes, hours, nor is it concerned with the usual groupings of past, present, and future. These are just arbitrary conveniences, like the points on a watch past which the hands move. Time cannot be spatialized and measured in such a quantitative way; it is a quality, not a substance.

The application of Bergson's theory of time to the arts of the late 19th century can be very illuminating. The philosopher often cited the motion picture as an example of what he meant by the perception of duration. The pictures in themselves are static, but through mobility the separate states are melted together by the mind into a continuous temporal flow. So also are the separate colors on an impressionistic canvas, the separate metaphors in a symbolist poem, the separate scenes in a Maeterlinck play, the separate chords in a Debussy progression, molded by the mind into a temporal continuum. In visual impressionism the eye mixes the colors; in a symbolist poem the mind supplies the connecting verbs for the nominal fragments; in a Maeterlinck play the imagination makes the irrelevancies of speech and action into a dramatic sequence; and in Debussy's music the ear bridges over the silences.

In all the arts this ceaseless flux leads toward the improvisatory, the consciously incomplete; and each work tries to be a product of inspiration rather than calculation. With the visual impressionists all pictorial substance is atomized into an airy mixture of color sprays, fleeting shadows, and momentary moods. Cézanne sometimes paints so thinly that parts of the canvas are actually bare, and at other times the texture is so thin as to be almost transparent. Rodin likewise leaves parts of the stone surrounding his figures uncut; and it is by no means an accident that some of the most important buildings of the time were open to the air and sky and were conceived as temporary exposition structures, such as the Crystal Palace, the Gallery of Machines, and the Eiffel Tower. In *Pelléas et Mélisande* the characters are only outlined or sketched out, and what they really feel has to be inferred by the spectator. The imagination actually supplies the emotional depth to what is but a surface play of forms. In all instances the audience, through perception, imagination, and memory actively participates in the creative activity.

Both the awareness of science and the accentuation of the temporal flow became important means by which the arts at the end of the century established the basis for the transition to the various modern styles. Cézanne has with justification been called the first great modern master; the functional architecture of Labrouste, Paxton, and Eiffel has become the foundation stone of contemporary architecture; Rodin's convex and concave surfaces and his preoccupation with the atmospheric problems of light and shadow have led to important new developments in sculpture; the fragmentary style of the symbolists anticipated the "stream-of-consciousness" and other techniques of modern literature; and Debussy's concept of relative rather than absolute tonality together with his harmonic experimentation have for their part pointed toward some of the significant musical developments of the 20th century.

CHAPTER

CHRONOLOGY: 20th Century Panorama *

General Events

1891	Wainwright Building in St. Louis, the first skyscraper, built by Louis Sullivan
	The "Kinetescopic Camera" for motion pictures patented by Thomas Edison, who had previously developed the process of sound recording
1903	Aviation age began as Wright brothers made successful flights at Kitty Hawk, N. C.
1905	Einstein published first article on theory of relativity
1908	Model T (touring car) introduced by Henry Ford, beginning era of mass production and assembly line
1909	Wireless radio transmission developed by Marconi
1914–1918	World War I
1917	Russian Revolution began
1922	Fascist Revolution in Italy
1929	Collapse of New York Stock Market heralded the beginning of the depression
1933	Nazi Revolution in Germany
1936–1939	Spanish Civil War
1939–1945	World War II
1945	First atomic bomb exploded

Architecture

1856–1924	Louis Sullivan
1869–	Frank Lloyd Wright
1883–	Walter Gropius
1886–	Miës van der Rohe
1888–	Le Corbusier
1890–	J. J. P. Oud

Painting

1844–1910	Henri Rousseau (le douanier)
1866–1944	Vasily Kandinsky
1869–1954	Henri Matisse
1870–1954	John Marin
1871–	Giacomo Balla
1871–	Georges Rouault
1872–1944	Piet Mondrian
1879–1940	Paul Klee
1881–1955	Fernand Léger
1881–	Pablo Picasso
1882–	Georges Braque
1883–1949	Jose Clemente Orozco
1884–1920	Amadeo Modigliani
1886–	Diego Rivera
1886–	Oskar Kokoschka
1887–	Marc Chagall
1887–	Marcel Duchamp
1888–	Giorgio de Chirico
1889–	Thomas Hart Benton
1892–1942	Grant Wood
1893–	Joan Miro
1897–1946	John Stewart Curry
1898–	Charles Burchfield
1904–	Salvador Dali

Sculpture

1861–1944	Aristide Maillol
1874–1946	Charles Despiau
1876–	Constantin Brancusi
1883–	Ivan Mestrovic
1885–	Paul Manship
1888–	Hans (Jean) Arp
1898–	Henry Moore

Literature and Philosophy

1856–1939	Sigmund Freud
1856–1950	George Bernard Shaw
1863–1938	Gabriele d'Annunzio
1869–1951	André Gide
1871–1945	Paul-Ambroise Valéry
1874–1946	Gertrude Stein
1875–1955	Thomas Mann
1878–	Carl Sandburg
1882–1941	James Joyce
1885–1951	Sinclair Lewis
1887–	Robinson Jeffers
1888–1953	Eugene O'Neill
1888–	T. S. Eliot
1889–	Jean Cocteau
1896–	André Breton
1897–	William Faulkner
1899–	Ernest Hemingway
1905–	Jean Paul Sartre

Music

1860–1911	Gustav Mahler
1862–1918	Claude Debussy
1864–1949	Richard Strauss
1866–1925	Erik Satie
1872–1915	Alexander Scriabin
1873–1943	Sergei Rachmaninoff
1874–1951	Arnold Schoenberg
1875–1937	Maurice Ravel
1876–1946	Manuel de Falla
1881–1945	Bela Bartok
1882–	Igor Stravinsky
1885–1935	Alban Berg
1891–1953	Serge Prokofieff
1892–	Darius Milhaud
1892–1955	Arthur Honegger
1895–	Paul Hindemith
1898–1937	George Gershwin
1899–	François Poulenc

20

THE 20th CENTURY

THE AGE OF 'ISMS

When a 20th-century man gets into conversation, opens his newspaper, tunes in his radio, turns on his television set, or reads a book, it will not be long before he encounters an 'ism of one sort or another. Someone will be speaking, gesticulating, or writing for or against liberalism or conservatism, internationalism or nationalism, socialism or capitalism, individualism or collectivism, parliamentarianism or totalitarianism. Like big black flies 'isms buzz through the air waves in swarms and light on the printed page. The Greeks once went to war for the beauty of Helen of Troy; the Middle Ages went on crusades to try to keep the sepulcher of Christ out of the hands of the infidels; the Baroque period shed its blood over religious dogmas; but the 20th century fights its revolutions and wars over the conflicting ideologies expressed in its multiplicity of 'isms. In the early years there were the struggles of rival colonialisms; in the wake of World War I came the Russian revolution, which let Bolshevism and communism out of Pandora's box; then fascism came to Italy, Nazism to Germany, a civil war to Spain, and a second world war. Yet the struggle still goes on, with the 'isms being hurled back and forth as weapons in a never-ending psychological war, the temperature of which fluctuates between cold and hot depending on the emotional responses people and countries make to the various 'isms. The late 19th century was somehow able to contain the opposing forces of democracy and dictatorship, liberty and authority, freedom of individual enterprise and economic monopoly, the advances of science and orthodox religious beliefs, freedom of thought and anti-

---

* It is obviously impossible to include a comprehensive list of the men and events that have influenced the 20th century. This Chronology is therefore confined to the major developments and personalities who are mentioned in the following chapter.

intellectual tendencies, diversity and conformity, innovation and stand-ardization. In our century, however, the equilibrium has been upset with revolutions and wars as one of its expressions, and a variety of art move-ments as another. In spite of all the disagreeable clangor and confusion, the many strident voices of our age can be heard speaking through these 'isms as each clamors to be heard.

Since the arts are forms of action, artists as well as social reformers and revolutionists shout their battle cries, issue their manifestoes and white papers, and formulate their own 'isms. In the late 19th century such rela-tively simple aesthetic creeds as realism, naturalism, symbolism, and im-pressionism had their faithful flocks of followers. By comparison the 20th century is an angry Tower of Babel, in which one hears such terms being bandied about as orphism, associationism, purism, syntheticism, kineticism, complementarism, plastic dynamism, parallelism, neo-plasticism, suprem-atism, divisionism, and physical transcendentalism. Like great gaudy moths they come out of their chrysalises, flutter around briefly in the lime-light, and soon are seen and heard no more. Some brave philologist has yet to compile a dictionary of these glittering abstractions. Then there are those that linger on, such as constructivism, expressionism, cubism, prim-itivism, and surrealism, which are forces still to be reckoned with even though they too have often been productive of more heat than light.

The groups responsible for these 'isms have rarely talked or written about them very sensibly. The only thing that really matters, however, is whether their pictures, pieces, or poems are worth looking at, listening to, or read-ing. These organized art movements have generally been too busy begetting doctrines to be prime producers. Their principal purpose is fulfilled in provoking lively discussions, formulating ideas, getting themselves talked about, and arranging for exhibitions, concerts, and publications. It is a historical truism that committees seldom create anything; for that it takes an individual. The painters Paul Klee and Pablo Picasso, the writers James Joyce and T. S. Eliot, the composers Igor Stravinsky and Paul Hindemith, for instance, have all been claimed by the surrealists at one time or another. In spite of the affinity of some of their work to the move-ment, they never signed the manifestoes or had any close connection with the group. The most resourceful artists have always refused to become the prisoner of any one theory, particularly those which offered the solitary confinement of a fanatical adherence to a single 'ism. Instead they have instinctively preserved their freedom of choice and have continuously searched for stimulating ideas wherever they may be found.

While still within the 20th century, it is most difficult to see the forest for the trees. Yet, now that the halfway mark has been passed, it should at least be possible to group the trees into something resembling clumps. The complexity of the problem, however, should never be minimized, and care should always be taken that these clumps are not confused with the forest. It is possible, for instance, to localize some movements in geographical terms, such as the Americans who fall into the regional schools. One knows certain aspects of the small Middle Western town through Sinclair Lewis' novels, Illinois through Carl Sandburg's poetry, the Deep South through William Faulkner's books, and New England through Eugene O'Neill's plays. One sees Iowa through Grant Wood's eyes, Missouri through Thomas Benton's, Kansas through John Stewart Curry's, upstate New York through Charles Burchfield's, and the Maine coast through John Marin's. One can also hear the rhythms and melodies of these regions through the folk-song collectors and adapters. It is possible to identify the early phases of expressionism with Germany prior to 1933; abstractionism with Russia and Holland up to 1921; futurism with Italy before World War I; cubism, the mechanical style, and surrealism with Paris; and the international style of architecture with Germany, France, and Holland. Yet any very strict localization of arts, styles, and ideas is impossible in such a mobile period. The foremost architect of the century, Frank Lloyd Wright, found that his ideas were accepted in Europe and the Orient before his own United States discovered him. American artists have gone abroad to study in Paris and other European centers, while established European artists, because of political upheavals in their native countries, have come to the United States to continue their careers and to teach.

From the temporal point of view, the 20th century has been marked by events that have colored many of its works of art. The aftermath of World War I brought about the bitter disillusionment that gave birth to the nihilistic movement called dadaism. The Mexican social revolution that culminated in the 1920's gave rise to the school of muralists, which includes Rivera, Orozco, and Siqueiros. The depression of the 1930's brought forth many forms of violent protest and social comment. The Spanish civil war, which began in 1936, was directly responsible for Picasso's great mural *Guernica* and for Ernest Hemingway's novel *For Whom the Bell Tolls*. The ideational wars and intellectual revolutions, which also affect the arts, do not obey such strict temporal laws and are therefore spread over wider intervals.

In approaching the art of the 20th century, one must keep many things in mind. All art has to be understood first and foremost in terms of its own frame of reference. No man, whether artist or criminal, should be condemned for what he was not attempting to do. When, however, his intentions are known, then his acts can be judged honorable or otherwise depending on whether his aims are valid, and how well he has realized them. The contemporary artist, contrary to the expectations of a substantial segment of his potential audience, does not necessarily aim to please. The customer, in his considered opinion, is not always right. His motives may be to delight or irritate, to exhort or castigate, to surprise or excite, to soothe or shock. A painter may have deliberately planned a picture as a visual sock in the eye. A composer may have contrived a composition as aural assault and battery. Judging by the reactions to some of Picasso's early exhibits and the riot that greeted the first performance of Stravinsky's ballet *The Rites of Spring* (1913), one knows they have sometimes succeeded beyond their wildest expectations, since it is also the audience's privilege to accept or reject.

The matter of an artist's honest convictions must also be taken into consideration. When a sculptor comes to the conclusion that he inhabits a misshapen and deformed world, can he be blamed if he does not portray it in symmetrical contours? If a novelist feels that life is ugly and cruel, would common candor permit him to suppress his convictions? If a composer is convinced that his age is marked by dissonance, would he be truthful if he wrote about it in saccharine harmonies? When all artists observe the current informality of dress and manners, and the absence of ceremony and protocol, should they be blamed because their works lack the formal organization characteristic of previous centuries? At times an artist may find a tight organization necessary for his purpose, at others it might be served better by deliberately contrived chaos. Sometimes the contemporary artist's work has meaning; often the act of painting or writing is a substitute for meaning. Just as some abstract painters have tried to eliminate subject matter from their pictures, writers, such as James Joyce and Gertrude Stein, have at times written without a subject. In the absence of such a normal focus their work becomes extremely difficult to read, and much of it must inevitably remain enigmatic. Some conservative composers, such as Rachmaninoff, continue to write in the lush emotional vein of the late 19th century. Others, such as Stravinsky and Hindemith, write music that is intentionally nonexpressive. Schoenberg, in order to avoid sounding Romantic, often went to such extreme lengths that he became highly Romantic about his antiromanticism. The problem of understanding such a complex picture is therefore far from simple.

When new resources are being developed in commercial fields, and when technological processes in communications and engineering have undergone such radical changes, 20th-century artists would be remiss in their duties if they were not carrying on active experimentation in new materials and methods in their own areas. The architects who are aware of such possibilities, and who accept the machine age with all its processes and problems, can hardly be blamed when they point out the absurdity of people going to football games in Roman colosseums, catching trains in Roman baths, working in Renaissance office buildings, putting their money in Doric temples, hearing operas in Baroque theaters, living in English Tudor houses, and on Sunday going to Gothic churches. Such architecture is the heritage of 19th-century eclecticism, which has been called with considerable justification, façade-making. Yet it cannot be denied that the Romans solved the colosseum problem, and that the Gothic style is still the most appropriate for the liturgies of some churches. While such eclecticism is still an architectural force, there is, however, a noticeable trend away from it.

The representational convention in painting, like eclecticism in architecture, still survives. It is found, however, principally in the popular media, and the most important lines of development have followed the courses set by the three principal figures of post-impressionism. Van Gogh's overwhelming emotionalism led to expressionism; Gauguin's attempt to go native in pursuit of values he believed lost to civilization pointed the way toward neo-primitivism; and Cézanne's imposition of geometrical forms on nature was the taking off point for cubism and abstract design. Developments in 20th-century sculpture have, on the whole, lagged behind those in the other arts. Such a solid and static medium presupposes a larger spatial environment and a more unhurried command of leisure time for contemplation than is available to modern man. In an age of rapid locomotion, a more fleeting experience of space and a swifter flow of images seem to be in order. This is a demand that the more ponderous three-dimensional art has found some difficulty in supplying. Some significant experiments have been made to mobilize modern sculpture for service in this turbulent century, but its principal developments have followed along with those of painting. While the traditional narrative techniques and literary methods are still in use, the most advanced developments have evolved from the fragmentary style of the symbolists. Each sight, sound, and fleeting image is recorded, and the union of the fragments is left to the mind of the reader. Modern musical practices have taken up where Richard Wagner left off, and moved in either pro- or anti-Wagnerian directions. Some composers, such as Richard Strauss, have continued along the lines of the music drama; others, such as Gustav Mahler, have adapted the style for symphonic purposes; while still others, such as Schoenberg, have extended the techniques and taken them into the field of chamber music. French and Russian composers, such as Ravel and Stravinsky, however, after their initial Wagnerian intoxication, have sobered up in the direction of the more dry and austere forms of contemporary neo-classicism.

There are in the main two distinct and recognizable trends that have had a coherent aesthetic inception and are leading in clearly discernible directions—*expressionism* and *constructivism*. The first grows out of the subjective viewpoint and implies a rather strong emotional involvement in the aesthetic process. The second stems from the objective approach in which logical and analytical considerations are dominant. Both movements run concurrently and are by no means mutually exclusive. Some artists have developed but one side, others have successfully combined both. Expressionism implies an exploration of the world of emotions and psychological states as well as the protests against existing conditions in the external world. In its broad sense expressionism embraces not only such movements as neo-primitivism, dadaism, surrealism, and the various forms of social comment but also the individualistic but warmly human spatialized dreams of Frank Lloyd Wright. Constructivism includes such developments as cubism and its various modifications, futurism, the mechanical style, and abstract design in painting and sculpture; new modes of literary presentation, such as the stream-of-consciousness technique; the 12-tone method of musical composition; and the strict functionalism of the international style in architecture.

It can readily be seen that the 20th century presents no unified picture, and that the contemporary artist is confronted with an almost infinite range of choices. A multiplicity of styles rather than any over-all unity seems to be most characteristic. Those who fear that our age has been overtaken by creeping conformity need look only to the architects, painters, sculptors, writers, and musicians who have dared to be different. Anything that is merely modern, however, will last only until the novelty has worn off. The wild experimentation that characterized the period just before and after World War I is now definitely a thing of the past. The blind alleys have been discovered and blocked off, and the number of choices has narrowed down. The liberating theories that have stood the test of time and proved productive have been retained. Yet when they become the accepted principles of today, there is always the implied danger that they will become the basis of a new and perhaps sterile academicism of tomorrow.

EXPRESSIONISM

The sparks that ignited the conflagration of 20th-century expressionism were struck by the discovery of the primitive arts of the South Sea islanders and the wood carvings of the African Negro tribes, the psychological probings of Sigmund Freud, the imaginative fantasies of individual artists, and the various reactions to the political, social, and economic conditions that came about when artists, authors, and composers were drawn into the flames fed by wars, revolutions, dictatorships, and economic depressions.

The term *neo-primitivism* as used here is limited to the conscious adaptation by sophisticated artists of authentic specimens of primitive art, such as that of the natives of the South Seas and the aboriginal tribes of Africa. The first major artist to employ the colorful Polynesian patterns and motives in his woodcuts and paintings was Paul Gauguin. Such pictures as his *Day of the God* (Fig. 19:5), which were painted during his extended sojourn in Tahiti clearly reflect the native influence. Examples of Polynesian craftsmanship, such as oars, arrows, and harpoons, had been collected by traders on their voyages and were shown in the Paris expositions of 1878 and 1889. Later when expeditions were made into the interior of the dark continent, wooden objects carved by African tribesmen came to light. Ethnological museums were founded in Paris and Dresden to house these collections, and they commanded considerable interest on the part of scholars, artists, and the general public. Soon articles and books on African sculpture began to appear in Germany and France. What the harems of Algiers had been to Delacroix and the Japanese prints to the impressionists, African sculpture became to the artists of the early 20th century. Meanwhile Sir James Frazer had been publishing *The Golden Bough*, a monumental 12-volume compendium of primitive customs and beliefs, folk lore, magical practices, and taboos, which became one of the most influential works of the century. This primitive art, with its complete negation of the notion of progress, seemed like the promise of a new beginning. Particularly impressive was the animistic attitude of the primitive carvers who divined the spirit of their wood and stone and revealed it in the grain and textures of their materials. The German expressionists were fascinated by its strange weird forms and its anti-intellectualism. In it the French artists found a new wealth of decorative motives and a justification for their abstract designs in its simplified geometrical forms.

New discoveries were also being made by Sigmund Freud when he brought the psychological world of the subconscious to light and exposed some of its dark drives, hidden terrors, and mysterious motivations. Beginning with his *Interpretations of Dreams* in 1900, the books of Freud and his associates were destined to affect the pictorial, literary, and musical expression of the 20th century. Artists are well aware that they inhabit a number of complex overlapping worlds. They also know that there are worlds to be explored that are not seen by the eye and that are not subject to the same type of logical organization. The expressionistic painter, for instance, is perfectly aware of the world he sees through his eyes, but he is interested in a form of vision for which he must close his eyes so that he can paint his dream fantasies. Accordingly he has departed from the classical notion of art as an imitation of nature, and moved into the worlds of the mind, spirit, and imagination, which demand new psychological insights and symbols. These intangible worlds are much more difficult to see and write about than the one that comes through the organs of sense perception alone. The results of these excursions into the subconscious may be very uneven, but the artist's passport to such nether region is quite valid.

Neo-Primitivism

The *Young Ladies of Avignon* (Fig. 20:1), which Picasso finished in 1907, is one of the pivotal pictures of the century. From his sketches it is known to have started out as an allegory. A man in the midst of fruit and women was to have symbolized Vice, while his counterpart entering on the left with a skull in his hands was to have represented Virtue. While it was in its preliminary stages, however, Picasso was greatly impressed by an exhibit of some pre-Roman sculpture of Spain. As in most primitive art, the human body was sharply angular and reduced to a severe geometrical pattern. The girl on the left, who is pulling back some curtains, is thus represented as a system of overlapping planes and geometrically arranged contours. Picasso had also a short while later been stimulated by some Negro sculpture that he had seen in the Trocadero Museum in Paris, and he had started a collection of his own, which contained some specimens from the west coast of Africa.

The resemblance of the *Mask* from Itumba in the French Congo (Fig. 20:2) to the head of the figure in the upper right of Picasso's picture is most striking. The head of the young woman just below and the profile of the figure on the left also show this African influence. The drawings Picasso made just before this picture was finished reveal his interest in the oval-shaped heads, the long noses, small mouths, and angular bodies that characterize the sculpture of the Ivory Coast. Under these African influences

Fig. 20:1 (above). Picasso. *Les Demoiselles d'Avignon* (*Young Ladies of Avignon*). 96″ x 92″. 1907. Collection Museum of Modern Art, New York. Fig. 20:2 (below left). *Wooden Mask* from Itumba, French Congo. 14″ high. Collection Museum of Modern Art, New York. Fig. 20:3 (below right). Modigliani. *Head*. Stone 22¼″ high. *c.*1915. Collection Museum of Modern Art, New York. Gift of Mrs. John D. Rockefeller, Jr.

Picasso turned entirely away from the pathos of his early period toward a stricter formalism. The original allegorical plan in this case was abandoned, and the female figures, the drapery in the background, and the still life below were all blended together into an abstract design. The title of the picture is relatively unimportant and seems to have come from the suggestion of a friend rather than the artist himself. The color with its spectrumlike blending of bright shades one into another contributes the effect of an emotional crescendo, while the formal arrangement of the figures suggests the angular rhythms of a primitive dance. The *Young Ladies of Avignon* became one of the epoch-making monuments of modern art, and Picasso and others continued to explore the expressive possibilities of primitive forms.

The impact of this primitive art was felt in many other fields. When the young Italian painter Modigliani came to Paris in 1906, he fell so completely under the spell of African Negro sculpture that for a while he traded the brush for the chisel. One of his works in this medium, *Head* (Fig. 20:3), is in the same Ivory Coast style that Picasso had adopted. Afterward in his paintings he continued to use the stylized oval faces and elongated forms. The sculpture of Matisse, Brancusi, and Henry Moore at various times also came under the African influence.

Knowledge of non-European musical systems had likewise increased rapidly during the late 19th century. The orchestrations of Debussy and Ravel had been influenced by the strange and exotic sounds of the gamelan orchestras from Java, which they heard at the International Exposition of 1889. By far the strongest of these influences, however, was that of American jazz music, which had its beginnings in New Orleans and Chicago and which was heard in Europe through the traveling Negro bands. In his group of piano pieces called *The Children's Corner* (1908), Debussy included a number called "Golliwog's Cake Walk." The Golliwog was an eccentric comic-strip character in the Paris newspapers who was born out of an ink blot. Obviously a popularization of the interest in primitivism, he delighted grown-ups as well as children with his antics. The cake walk was, of course, a favorite dance in the American Negro minstrel shows and one of the ancestors of the fox trot.

Igor Stravinsky included a Moor in his ballet *Petrouchka* (1911), although the music he gives him is quasi-Oriental. Two years later, however, in the *Rites of Spring*, Stravinsky achieves the primitive musical counterpart of Picasso's *Young Ladies of Avignon*. Subtitled "Scenes from Pagan Russia," the opening "Dance of the Adolescents" uses repetitive rhythms and syncopated accents similar to those of American jazz. The sharply angular melodies, the complex polyrhythmic textures, the brutal accentuations, and the geometrical movements of the dancers are a masterly realization of the spirit of savagery.

"Dance of the Adolescents" from *The Rites of Spring*   Stravinsky

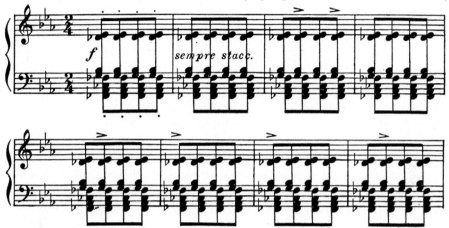

The primitive hypnotic repeated rhythms first exploited by Stravinsky, though without the jazz element, are found in the familiar "Ritual Fire Dance" from Manuel de Falla's ballet, *Love the Sorcerer* (*El Amor Brujo*, 1915). The culmination, however, is reached in Ravel's *Bolero* (1928), in which the dance tune is repeated in the same key 18 times. The vast dynamic crescendo and heavy use of a battery of percussion instruments invariably incites an audience to a thoroughly primitive state of frenzy. The entrance of jazz idioms into serious musical forms is also one of the familiar patterns of contemporary music. Stravinsky published some ragtime music for piano in 1922, with a cover designed by Picasso; and George Gershwin's *Rhapsody in Blue* (1924) and his jazz opera *Porgy and Bess* (1935) have achieved a wide popular success.

Wild Animals, Blue Riders, and Operatic Uproars

Expressionism in painting was at first one of the several reactions to the cool atmospheric effects, objective detachment, and vague vapidities of impressionism. The expressionist looks inward to a world of emotions and psychological states rather than outward at a world of colored reflections. He deals with intensities of feeling rather than intensities of light. He presents subjective reactions rather than represents objective realities. His world is felt more than it is seen, and he therefore needs to cultivate an inner eye to look at his materials. The heat of creation supersedes the coldness of imitation. His distorted pictures seek a psychological rather than a mathematical focus. He reasserts the supremacy of the human imagination over the impersonality of nature. The most immediate influence was Van Gogh, whose frenzied canvases, passionate pictorial outbursts, saturated colors, and evangelical fervor first showed the way. Such a painting as the *Starry Night* (Fig. 19:6) with the dark green flames of the cypress trees, the rolling rhythms of the hills, and the cosmic explosion of the milky way was enough to set imaginations on fire. The barbaric splendor of Gauguin's color harmonies was also adopted as a useful means in establishing lively emotional responses. More distantly the imaginative invention of Romanesque sculpture and the luminous colors of medieval stained glass also played their part. So also did the primitive arts of Polynesia and Africa.

The violent color clashes and visual distortions of the French painters of the expressionistic persuasion earned for them the critical designation of *Les Fauves*, or the Wild Animals. The early work of Matisse was so classified, though in retrospect it is difficult to understand why. If there was ever anything "wild" about Matisse at all, it has to be found in his reveling in brilliant color for its own sake, a subtle resourcefulness of invention, and a quality of Oriental splendor, which make him at least a *fauve* devoid of ferocity. To Matisse, expression did not apply to the content of his canvases or to the communication of an emotional message but rather to the entire formal management of his pictorial pattern. "Expression to my way of thinking," he once remarked, "does not consist of the passion mirrored upon a human face or betrayed by a violent gesture. The whole arrangement of my picture is expressive. . . ." [1]

The *Blue Window* (Fig. 20:4), which he painted in 1911, shows his concern with formal aesthetic problems, vibrant color harmonies, and arabesquelike decorative motives. The picture is composed as an abstract still-life study merging subtly into a stylized landscape. The hatpins in the cushion on the left unite with an empty vase behind them; the flowers in the other vase grow into the foliage and the roof of the painter's studio outside; the ancient idol in the axial center leads the eye to the vertical division of the casement window, while the lines formed by the contours of the lamp continue with those of the tree trunk in the garden. The bedroom table and its objects are thus united with the trees and sky beyond, and the interior and exterior elements become parts of one design. Depth and recession are suggested only by a slight lessening of the color intensities. In this picture Matisse came close to realizing his dream of an "art of balance, of purity and serenity devoid of depressing subject matter."

Fig. 20:4. Matisse. *Blue Window.* 51½″ x 35⅝″. *c.*1911. Collection Museum of Modern Art, New York

Fig. 20:5. Kandinsky. *Improvisation No. 30.* 43¼″ x 43¾″. 1913. Art Institute, Chicago

As a formal term, *expressionism* was first employed in Germany where several groups of painters were occupied with the exploitation of its various possibilities. Kandinsky, an international figure who painted in Germany and France as well as in his native Russia, was associated prior to World War I with the so-called Blue Rider group in Munich. His *Improvisation No. 30* (Fig. 20:5) shows what can be done with pure line, color, and form. In his rather complete commentary on this work, the artist states that its content is "what the spectator *lives* or *feels* while under the effect of the *form and color combinations* of the picture." This would coincide with the aesthetics of projecting the observer's own inner states and emotions into the picture, which may or may not coincide with what the artist had in mind when he painted it. This feeling-into process is what the psychologists call empathy. In more candid moments Kandinsky has also referred to this picture as an *Improvisation on a Warlike Theme*, and he tells us that he painted it "subconsciously in a state of strong tension." On close inspection the wandering lines, contrasting colors, and vague shapes resolve themselves in the lower right into two cannons belching forth some billowing clouds of smoke and possibly some toppling buildings in the center, all of which would fit into the rumors of war current at the time it was painted in 1913. Kandinsky, like the Russian composer Alexander Scriabin, was a theosophist and a mystic. He believed that a pictorial composition should approach the abstract quality of absolute music, which creates its own forms without any reference to natural objects. Hence he uses the titles "composition" and "improvisation" depending on whether the pictures are carefully worked out or done spontaneously.

Some of the earliest and most violent outbursts of musical expressionism are found in Richard Strauss' operas *Salome* (1905) and *Electra* (1909). Taking off from the music dramas of Richard Wagner, Strauss makes an operatic excursion into the realm of abnormal psychology. In *Salome* he makes highly effective use of a simultaneous attraction-repulsion principle by using a rainbow of radiant orchestral colors to illuminate the horrifying subject matter. The sensational nature of Oscar Wilde's libretto, together with the sensuous "Dance of the Seven Veils," and Salome's soliloquy to the severed head of John the Baptist, caused the opera to be banned at first in New York, Boston, and London. *Elektra* is a dramatically effective version of Hugo von Hofmannsthal's play, filled with mounting emotional tensions, blood-curdling shrieks, and lurid orchestral sounds.

This tendency continues in Arnold Schoenberg's expressionistic song cycle *Pierrot Lunaire* (1912) and in the monodrama *The Lucky Hand* (*Die Glückliche Hand*, 1913) in which the dissonances of the musical score are reinforced by crescendos of colored lights. Something of a climax is achieved in Alban Berg's opera *Wozzeck* (1925), a musical dramatization of big-city low life in which a ballet of beggars, drunkards, and street-girls pursue the murderer as he vainly tries to escape from himself. Whereas Wagner had worked up his climaxes over a considerable period of time, generally starting low in pitch and volume and mounting upward in an extended melodic, harmonic, and dynamic crescendo, Schoenberg and Berg telescope the process. Their music became all climax, with the extremes of low and high, soft and loud, following each other suddenly and by leap instead of in a gradual progression. Dissonances with Wagner existed in chains of sequences that eventually resolved. To Schoenberg and Berg dissonance exists freely for its own sake with little or no relation to consonance.

Dream Fantasies

Giorgio de Chirico's *Melancholy and Mystery of a Street* (Fig. 20:6) takes expressionism into an introspective dream world full of free associations. "Everything," according to this artist, "has two aspects: the current aspect, which we see nearly always and which ordinary men see, and the ghostly and metaphysical aspect, which only rare individuals may see in moments of clairvoyance and metaphysical abstraction." On a visit to the Versailles Palace, for instance, he says he realized that "every corner of the palace, every column, every window possessed a spirit, an impenetrable soul. . . . At that moment I grew aware of the mystery which urges men to create strange forms." [2] His intention was to break down the barriers of childhood and adulthood, the sleeping and waking state, the unbelievable and the believable, the illogical and the logical, the fantastic and the familiar. This picture is filled with an ominous silence and an all-pervading emptiness that are heightened by the mystery of deep perspective. *Nostalgia of the Infinite, Disquieting Muses, Enigma of an Autumn Afternoon* are the deliberately ambiguous but evocative titles of some of Chirico's other pictures. They are filled with sundials casting lengthened shadows, the paradoxical juxtapositions of ancient ruins and modern factory buildings, and spacious Italian city squares populated only with strange statues. These elusive fantasies are based on Chirico's memories of his own youth in Greece and Italy and are painted with a meticulous academic brush technique.

The melancholy empty spaces of Chirico's dream world find a remarkable parallel in Thomas Mann's short novel *Death in Venice* (1913), and Gustav Mahler's *Song of the Earth* (1911). In them there is the same attempt to synthesize the contradictory tendencies of the time, the same juxtaposition of banal and fanciful elements, the same weary lyricism, the same

Fig. 20:6 (above). Chirico. *Melancholy and Mystery of a Street*. 33½″ x 27¼″. 1914. Stanley R. Resor Collection. Fig. 20:7 (below left). Klee. *Herzog Leiter Nicht Allein (Duke Ladder Not Alone)*. Oil and tempera on paper. 13½″ x 19⅛″. Art Institute, Chicago. Fig. 20:8 (below right). *Personages with Star*. 78¼″ x 97½″. 1933. Art Institute, Chicago

longing for the unattainable, the same vision of the ineffable hovering elusively on the distant horizon. Chirico and Chagall, who was also painting in Paris at the same time and in a similar vein, were later hailed as prophets of surrealism, which did not get under way as a conscious movement until 1924.

Paul Klee is rapidly coming to be regarded as one of the most significant pictorial talents of our time. Such pictures as *Duke Ladder Not Alone* (Fig. 20:7) have caused many to dismiss him lightly with a shrug, a scoff, or a smile. His disarming childlike innocence, however, is a highly deceptive simplicity and usually a mask for infinitely subtle meaning. His inventiveness outdoes even Picasso in its endless variety. He can delight the eye, tickle the fancy, or repel the observer with images straight out of nightmares. *Apparatus for Magnetic Treatment of Plants*, *The Twittering Machine*, *A Cookie Picture*, *Moonplay*, *Idol for Housecats*, *Child Consecrated to Suffering*, *A Phantom Breaks Up*, so the titles run. Because of this wide range, a whole exhibit or picture book is needed to convey an adequate idea of his highly imaginative art.

Klee consciously set out to look at the world through the eyes of a child in order to achieve a spontaneity untroubled by reason. "I want to be as though new-born, knowing nothing," as he put it. By experimenting with hypnotic suggestion and psychic automatism, his drawings acquire the casual quality of doodles or the impulsiveness of improvisations. His mastery of line is so complete, however, that his work should never be confused with carelessness. By sticking mainly to small forms, and to the techniques of water color and ink, pencil and crayon drawings, he produces pictures with a refreshing unpretentiousness. He also has an element of genial humor that is notably missing in so much of modern art.

Dadaism and Surrealism

Dadaism was the direct product of the disillusionment and defeatism of World War I. At that time the anguished artists felt that the civilization which had brought about such horrors should be swept away forthwith and a new beginning made. It was a nihilistic movement, particularly distrustful of reason; a protest, a challenge to polite society, and against everything including the prevailing forms of art. These artists had finally evolved an 'ism to end all 'isms. They concocted nonsense for the sake of nonsense, wrote manifestoes against manifestoes, and their political expression came close to anarchy. Their painters produced rubbish pictures compounded out of the contents of waste baskets. The principal value of the movement was in the bitter but humorous iconoclasm that helped to clear the postwar atmosphere. Fortunately it did not last very long, and many of the same artists and ideas were absorbed into surrealism, its logical successor, which has aptly been called the "dadaism of the successful."

Surrealism, or superrealism, followed dadaism as the next episode in expressionism. The term was coined by the French critic and playwright Guillaume Apollinaire to describe an exhibit of Chagall's pictures during the Paris season of 1911–1912. The group who adopted it as their motto, however, dates from 1924, the year of the surrealist manifesto. "It is pure psychic automatism," wrote its author André Breton, "by means of which one sets out to express verbally, in writing or in any other manner, the real functioning of thought without any control by reason or any aesthetic or moral preoccupation." Members of the group believed in the superior reality of the dream to the waking state, fantasy thought to that directed by reason, the subconscious to the conscious mind. Breton also spoke of the "convulsive beauty" of dreams, and the surrealists developed a psychological symbolism in the Freudian manner, especially the Freud of the *Interpretation of Dreams* (1900). The painter Salvador Dali associated himself with the group in 1929 and became one of its leading advocates. He described his pictures as "hand-painted dream photographs," and they were adorned with symbols of assorted phobias, delusions, complexes, and other trappings of abnormal psychology. The work of great artists who experimented with fantasy in the past, such as Bosch, Dürer, Brueghel, Hogarth, Goya, William Blake, and Daumier, were cited as precedents. Among the living painters, Klee, Picasso, Chagall, and Chirico were all claimed as kindred spirits by the surrealists.

Miro comes closer perhaps than any of the other surrealistic painters to realizing an art of the imagination existing outside logic or reason. His *Personages with Star* (Fig. 20:8) uses the technique of automatic drawing in a trancelike state and is obviously influenced by Kandinsky. While so much of surrealism is morbid, Miro lightens his fantasies with a touch of gay humor. Some of his other pictures, which bear such fanciful titles as *Persons Magnetized by the Stars Walking on the Music of a Furrowed Landscape*, teem with abstract insects that buzz silently and geometrical worms that squirm statically. This Catalonian painter was with the surrealists only five years and is now working independently in his own highly individualistic style.

The attempts by the surrealists themselves to work in the mediums of sculpture, literature, and music have not been so successful as their painting. Only by going outside the movement can significant parallels be found. James Joyce and Gertrude Stein both tried to establish a method for subconscious or automatic writing as a way of tapping the reservoir of the subconscious mind. The result was the stream-of-consciousness technique, which is most notably exemplified in James Joyce's *Ulysses* (1922).

The more irreverent iconoclastic tendencies of surrealism find their musical counterpart in such things as Erik Satie's three piano pieces of 1913. Entitled *Dessicated Embryos*, they have semisarcastic expression marks, such as the one which calls upon the pianist to play a melody "like a nightingale with the toothache." There is also the biting satire of Prokofieff's brilliant fairy tale opera *The Love of Three Oranges* (1921) and the weird symbolism of Bela Bartok's legendary opera *Bluebeard's Castle* (1922). Paul Klee's world of childhood fantasy finds a charming lyrical counterpart in Maurice Ravel's opera *The Child and the Sorceries* (*L'Enfant et les Sortilèges*) of 1925. In Colette's libretto a child breaks some bric-a-brac and toys in a temper tantrum. The objects then come to life in a dreamlike sequence in order to seek revenge. A Wedgewood teapot and a china cup, appropriately enough, carry on a conversation in broken English and dance a fox trot; a little old man pops up out of nowhere and sings arithmetic problems with erroneous answers; two cats sing a hilarious meowing duet; and all that is left of the fairy princess in the story book is "a golden hair and the debris of a dream." Ravel's ingenious orchestration is made up of the usual instruments with the addition of whistles, wood-blocks, and friction instruments, including cheese graters for certain bizarre effects.

Neo-classical Interlude

One of the constantly recurring phases of Western art ever since the days of antiquity has been a periodic bow before the shrines of Greece and Rome. No century would therefore be complete without a neo-classical episode of some sort. While works of this kind can be found in each year of the present century, the movement both in regard to some notable collaborative efforts as well as individual works comes to its sharpest focus in the 1920's. Interestingly enough the emotional extremes of pictorial expressionism and such neo-primitive outbursts as Stravinsky's *Rites of Spring* served the purpose of stirring things up in the comparative calm before the storm of World War I. After the conflict, however, an interlude of order and clarity seemed more important than violent expression, just as it had been after the stresses of the French Revolution and the Napoleonic wars.

In 1917 Picasso made a trip to Italy where he was impressed by the Pompeiian wall paintings and stimulated by meetings in Rome with

Stravinsky and Serge Diaghileff, who was there with his Russian ballet company. One of the direct results was their collaboration on a ballet with song called *Pulcinella*, which was first performed in Paris in 1920. Stravinsky's score was based on the form of the classical dance suite of the early 18th century with music adapted from Pergolesi. Picasso designed the costumes in the manner of the stylized *commedia dell' arte* characters, Pierrot, Harlequin, and so on. His scenery included a backdrop full of angular distortions showing a street in Naples with a view of the bay and a moonlit Mount Vesuvius. In 1922 an adaptation of Sophocles' *Antigone* by Jean Cocteau was mounted in Paris. Picasso designed the scenery and masks, while the incidental music for harp and oboe was supplied by Arthur Honegger. An opera called *The Eumenides* by Darius Milhaud based on Paul Claudel's translation of the tragedy by Aeschylus was written in the same year. *Mercury* was the title of still another ballet brought out by the Diaghileff company in 1924, with music by Erik Satie and costumes and scenery by Picasso. Three years later Stravinsky completed his opera-oratorio *Oedipus Rex*. Diaghileff again was the producer, and Jean Cocteau's text, which was based on Sophocles' tragedy, was translated into Latin so that it would be in a "petrified" language and would thus be reduced mere syllabic material. The motionless stance of the actors was intended to make them as static as Greek columns, and the chorus was placed back of a bas relief where only their heads were visible. Such productions continued sporadically throughout the 1930's where Stravinsky is again found collaborating with André Gide on a work for orchestra, chorus, and tenor called *Persephone* (1934).

This neo-classicism is also reflected in Picasso's pictures of these years, such as *Three Graces* (Fig. 20:9). Elegance of line, sculpturesque modeling of the bodies, and a reduction of pictorial elements to the barest essentials characterize this aspect of his work. Others, such as *The Pipes of Pan* (1923), are beach scenes in which the figures appear against geometrically organized backgrounds and chaste colors of white and blue. After the *Three Graces* his painting took another tack, but his many book illustrations show that the classical current still continued. Picasso had long admired the linear technique of Ingres, especially the pencil drawings. His etchings for such publications as the new edition of Ovid's *Metamorphoses* of 1930 and Gilbert Seldes' new version of Aristophanes' *Lysistrata* of 1934 show his capacity for effective expression even in this austere medium.

The statues of Maillol and Despiau, which reassert the expressive importance of the nude human figure both in the round and in relief, are the

Fig. 20:9. Picasso. *Three Graces*. Oil and charcoal. 78⅞″ x 59″.
1924. Collection the Artist. Courtesy Museum of Modern Art,
New York

sculptural counterpart of this movement in France; while the ballet and
many purely instrumental works reveal the musical aspect of this movement. The list would include such works as Debussy's *Six Épigraphes Antiques* (1914) for two pianos, the first of which is an "Invocation to Pan";
Ravel's revival of the French classical piano suite in the *Tomb of Couperin*
(1918); and Prokofieff's well-known *Classical Symphony*, which is consciously
patterned after the symphonic style of the 18th century and has a finale in
the Haydn manner. Stravinsky adopted the style in a way that is marked by
more cerebration than inspiration in such works as his *Duo Concertante*
(1932), which contains movements labeled "Eclogue" and "Dithyramb"
that the composer says are tributes to the pastoral poets of antiquity.

One of the most consistent patterns in contemporary literature, especially in France, is the reinterpretation of Greek myths in highly sophis-

ticated terms as a subtle device for pointing out modern moralistic or
political parallels. This tendency runs regularly through the works of
André Gide from his early *Prometheus Drops His Chains* of 1899 to his autobiographical story *Theseus* of 1946. Other instances can be found in Franz
Werfel's antiwar play, *The Trojan Women* (1914) and Jean Paul Sartre's
The Flies (1943). The latter was played in Paris during the Nazi occupation
and the allusion to the plague of flies that sucked the blood of Orestes in
Aristophanes' bitter comedy could have escaped no one. Poets have sometimes found classical subjects a convenient way of leaving their work unfinished like the ruins of antiquity. Paul-Ambroise Valéry's trilogy of 1922,
for instance, contains a poem called "Fragments of Narcissus." T. S.
Eliot's *Sweeny Agonistes* (1932), in which he contrasts the grandeur of the
past with the banality of the present, is also incomplete and bears the subtitle "Fragments of an Aristophanic Melodrama." Freud's use of such
characters from Greek literature as Oedipus, Electra, and Narcissus to
symbolize recurrent subconscious drives in the human psychology has also
found its way into literature.

James Joyce's novels *The Portrait of the Artist as a Young Man* (1916) and
Ulysses (1922) both use classical allusions as a frame of reference, but avoid
the logic and order of Greek forms. The author's admitted inspiration for
Ulysses was Homer's *Odyssey*. With the adoption of the stream-of-consciousness technique the classical molds became convenient devices to hold the
nebulous dreamlike sequences in some semblance of unity. They also serve
to provide the bewildered reader with a few straws to grasp when he begins
to founder on the sea of such an unfamiliar style of writing. The entire
action of *Ulysses* occurs in a single 24-hour period, though this unity of time
and place is not from Homer. The plot, however, has to do with a wanderer
who voyages through the terrors and temptations of the labyrinth of
Dublin's streets while on his way home to his wife and son, which is
reminiscent of Odysseus' search for Penelope and Telemachus. In the
larger sense it has to do with man's eternal quest to find a meaning for life.
The titles of the chapters in Joyce's manuscript originally were based on
quotations from the *Odyssey*, but they were omitted at the time it was
printed. Most of the work is obscure and cryptic, but the juxtaposition of
the heroic past helps to heighten the squalid picture that he is painting of
the present.

Such classical allusions are useful to the 20th-century writer in a number
of different ways. The myths can be a means of endowing trivial daily
occurrences with the solemnity of eternal truths. As a psychology in symbols
they can show the eternal recurrence of basic human problems, such as

love, war, and the conflict of man's desires with the forces of fate and nature. As dramatic devices the plots of Greek plays increase the sense of tragedy because their outcome is already known to the audience. The adroit juxtaposition of past and present can be an effective means of drawing poignant parallels. A mythological plot, stripped as it is down to its bare essentials, can allow for the presentation of a maximum of seemingly irrelevant detail without becoming chaotic. Finally the refuge into the safety of time-honored symbols can become a convenient way of avoiding censorship.

Forms of Protest

This Will Be the Last, Little Father (Fig. 20:11) is the title of a print by Georges Rouault that describes the heartbreaking farewell of a son as he leaves for war and almost certain death. Rouault, who like Matisse was identified at the beginning of his career with *Les Fauves*, declared that the search of a painter is for "sincere and fitting means of expression" according to his individual temperament and gifts. Among Rouault's many gifts is a capacity for passionate protest against the conditions that degrade man and womankind. His pictures often mirror the grimacing masks of those who presume to sit in judgment on their fellow men, and the insensitive countenances of people in positions of power who are indifferent to human suffering. The prolific number of his prints richly continues the graphic arts tradition established by Hogarth, Goya, Daumier, and Toulouse-Lautrec. His series of 100 etchings and aquatints for two projected portfolios entitled *Miserere* (Have Mercy on Us) and *Guerre* (War), with texts by one of his literary friends, occupied him intermittently during the years following World War I. Though the series was never published as such, some 58 large prints have been issued separately. The title page of the volume on war in which this print was to have appeared read: "They Have Ruined Even the Ruins."

In his *Guernica* (Fig. 20:10) Picasso uses expressionistic techniques as a violent protest against a cruel and inhuman act by some modern barbarians. The occasion that lighted the fuse which set off this pictorial explosion of carnage and terror was the first saturation air raid of the century. This macabre "experiment" was carried out by the German air force against the defenseless Basque town of Guernica, an incident in General Franco's successful rebellion against the legally elected government of the Spanish Republic. Picasso, a Spaniard himself and a partisan of the Loyalist side, had already been commissioned to paint a mural for the Spanish Pavilion of the Paris World's Fair of 1937. He began working on it just two days

Fig. 20:10. Picasso. *Guernica*. 11′ 6″ x 25′ 8″. 1937. Collection the Artist. Courtesy Museum of Modern Art, New York

Fig. 20:11 (left). Rouault. *This Will Be the Last, Little Father*. Etching from *Miserere et Guerre*. 23⅛″ x 16⅞″. 1927. Collection Museum of Modern Art, New York. Fig. 20:12 (above). Mestrovic. *Job*. Bronze. 4′ high. 1946. Syracuse University Collection.

after the news of the bombing had reached Paris. *Guernica* is thus one of those rare coincidences of the right artist painting the right picture at the right time.

Besides recalling the Apocalyptic visions of Romanesque Last Judgments, it is a work of sociological expressionism in the tradition of Hogarth, Goya, and Daumier. Its purpose was frankly propagandistic and its intention was to horrify. The huge canvas took up one whole wall of the Spanish building where it made an unforgettable impression on the thousands who saw it. The attention it attracted, and the measure of understanding accorded to it have, for once, been in proportion to its value as one of the most important paintings of the century.

The principal action of the picture begins in the lower right where a woman dashes forward clutching her hands in an attitude of despair. The triangular composition then mounts to its apex at the point where the lamp, horse's head, and the eye of day with the electric bulb of night as its pupil, all converge. From this climax the eye moves downward to the head of the dismembered warrior in the lower left. According to Picasso himself, the picture is symbolic, though much of it is still to be explained. The sculptured warrior grasping the broken sword in his severed hand represents the Spanish people. The horse with the spear in his back, the inevitable victim of every bullfight, here signifies the Spanish Republic. Above, an arm reaches outward holding the lamp of truth over the gruesome scene. The bull, symbol of brute force, is the only triumphant figure in this allegorical struggle between the forces of darkness and light, barbarism and civilization.

The *Guernica* appeared at a time when many of the earlier pictorial experiments could be combined. It employs all the exaggerations, distortions, and shock techniques developed by expressionistic drawing, but omits the lurid coloration in favor of the somber shades of mourning—black, white, and gradations of gray. The abstract design, the overlapping planes on a two-dimensional surface, and the absence of modeling, all derive from cubism. So also is the simultaneous principle of the day-and-night symbol; the head of the bull, which is seen both from the front and the side at the same time; and the sensation of inner and outer space by which the observer is at once both inside and outside the burning buildings. The elongation of the heads to express headlong motion coincides with the photography of movement made with stroboscopic cameras. The screaming nightmarish subject matter is similar to that of surrealism, but the 100 preliminary sketches Picasso made before he began to paint show that it is a carefully worked-out composition rather than a hasty effort of psychic automatism.

Picasso usually paints so rapidly and prolifically that he often has difficulty resisting the temptations of his own facile technique. Much of his work is consequently uneven. Here, however, he worked in a disciplined and selective manner that shows his complete command of his medium. The successful synthesis of all these divergent 20th-century techniques, as well as the vivid dramatization of his subject, have thus given powerful expression to the chaos and conflicts of this tortured century.

The eminent Jugoslav sculptor Ivan Mestrovic characteristically looks to the human figure as a way of achieving a similar result with an even greater economy of means. *Job* (Fig. 20:12), after he has lost his family and flocks, sits down among the ashes and cries out, "Let the day perish wherein I was born, and the night in which it was said, There is a man child conceived." (Job: 3:3.) By this allusion to the age-old personification of human misery, and by the twisted and tortured posture of the emaciated body, Mestrovic creates a symbol of the plight of mankind crying out to the heavens in a protest against needless suffering.

Organic Architecture

Unlike the more nebulous and explosive forms that are possible to painting, poetry, and music, successful expression in architecture must always accept the sobering discipline of sound structure. Fragile dream fantasies in glass have been proposed from time to time by the surrealists and others, but seldom have they been either practical or structurally above reproach. The buildings of Frank Lloyd Wright, on the other hand, are charged with emotional warmth but tempered by sound engineering principles. His personality is that of a fiery Old Testament prophet, determined to save the world from the lust of landlords, the rapaciousness of real estate interests, and the pettifoggery of the politicians who make the rigid building codes of large cities. His weapons in this lifelong struggle have been his staunch individualism; his daring architectural imagination; a technique that has earned him the reputation of being one of the greatest engineers of modern times; and the living example of the more than 600 houses, churches, factories, and office buildings that he has constructed over his long lifespan.

"Organic architecture" is his own designation for the expressive ideals and structural methods of his art. He accepts the dictum of his master Louis Sullivan that form follows functions, but Wright carries it further to the point where "form and function are one." People and the land in his conception are united by means of buildings. A house and the contours of its site must exist in an intimate relationship, and the architect must merge a building and the landscape into a humanized form of spatial harmony. Wright welcomes the use of local materials derived from the surrounding region as a means of uniting a building and its environment. Hence one of his houses may have granite floors from the local quarry, and another unfinished timbered ceilings hewn from a nearby forest. Wright is interested in the rooms of his houses more than their façades, and such interior space in his opinion should provide freedom of movement and not confinement. Wright's conception of space is three-dimensional, not so much in the sense of mass and thickness but in the sense of voids and spatial depth. Hence he has developed the principle of the flexible ground plan. The out of doors, he feels, should be invited inside, and the indoor space must go outside. He has therefore used the cantilever principle to move the building supports inward so as to leave the corners open. The corner window, one of Wright's best-known innovations, was for him an opportunity to "destroy the box," so dear to the cubist-minded architects of the international style and which Wright considers as the prison cells of the human spirit. He also opposes the extreme structural purity of the buildings of the international school, with their skeletal anatomy left open for all the world to see and their bleak avoidance of all decorative detail. Wright's style embraces inspiration for architectural forms based on those derived from nature, such as the shell, flower, or tree. His creative freedom also allows for decorative motives to grow organically out of his basic designs and materials, such as the relation of masses and voids, the fenestration, the grains of wood, the texture of the stone, and patterns molded in poured concrete.

Skyscrapers, according to Wright, should not be built in congested city areas. They should be built out in the open where they can breathe and have plenty of room to cast shadows, and an 18-story skyscraper is now under construction in the small town of Bartlesville, Oklahoma, in which the floors are cantilevered outward from a central trunk as branches from a tree. Wright's philosophy of architecture is that of a liberating force. Through his masterly articulation, space for living and working comes to life and begins to breathe. Architectural designs must embrace human purposes as well as building materials and structural principles. "Nothing is complete in itself," he observes, "but is only complete as the part is merged into the larger expression of the whole."

Falling Water (Fig. 20:13), which Wright built for Mr. Edgar J. Kaufmann at Bear Run, Pennsylvania, is an expressive combination of reinforced concrete material, cantilevered construction, and a dramatic site. It is characteristic of Wright's warm sense of humanity that he should have

Fig. 20:13. Wright. *Falling Water*. Reinforced concrete and stone. 1937–1939. Country house of Edgar J. Kaufmann, Bear Run, Pa. (Hedrich-Blessing)

Fig. 20:14. Wright. *Solomon R. Guggenheim Museum*. Redesigned 1951. New York

begun his career building houses in the Chicago of the 1890's. Human needs with him are always foremost, and the first thing he thinks of when building a house is the people who are going to live in it. For Wright a house must express a sense of shelter. Then there are the other considerations, like the manner of living, the region, the site, the availability of materials, and so on. His ingenious solutions for dwelling places have been highly influential both in his own country and abroad. In this case, Wright's client loved the waterfall and wanted to live near it. The house therefore embraces both the stream and the falling water; and by means of the cantilevered slabs that project from the rock embankment on which they rest, he carries the living space outward over the waterfall. Like all his buildings it is intimately related to the site. The two ledges of natural rock below, for instance, are paralleled by the two concrete shelves jutting out into the open space above them. The horizontal planes of these porches in turn are balanced by the vertical volumes of the chimney mass. The local stone used in this section is related both in color and texture to the natural rock of the river bank. The cantilevering here allows the several stories the independence to develop their own fluid floor plans. As on the outside, the inside space also radiates around the central core, with advancing and receding areas promoting what Wright calls the "freedom of interior and exterior occupation."

It is somehow fitting that at the end of his notable career the nation's largest city should at last get around to awarding a commission to the dean of American architects. It finally came in the form of a project for a modern art gallery to house the abstract painting and sculpture collection of the Guggenheim Museum (Fig. 20:14). To Wright a museum should not be a group of boxlike compartments but a continuous flow of floor space in which the eye encounters no obstructions. Cantilever construction is used here to get a circular spiraling structure, so that the space can be released into a flowing continuity which Wright has likened to an unbreaking wave on the seashore. The visitor enters and follows a ramp three-quarters of a mile long, but which rises so gradually (about 1 foot in 4) that he climbs six stories without becoming aware of it. The pictures are hung along the walls of the spiral ramp, which is punctuated from time to time by pedestals for the sculpture and which is lighted from a central well covered by a glass dome at the top.

Because of the inflammatory nature of its subject matter, the violent color clashes of its painting, the twisted bodies of its sculpture, the lacerations of its literary soul, the strident dissonances of its music, and the individualistic approach of its architecture, an expressionistic work of art cannot be disregarded by the public. The challenge to society was made and accepted, sides were chosen, and the heated discussions that followed have, in general, led to a better understanding than has been the case with abstract art. Not too surprisingly the constructivist art, which rests on a rational basis, has on the whole been less intelligible generally than that which is built on emotion.

CONSTRUCTIVISM

The heat generated by the contemporary psychological and political revolutions was felt in expressionism, but the light of the new intellectual viewpoints is mirrored in the various forms of constructivism. In the early years of the century, physicists were at work formulating a fundamental new view of the universe, which resulted in the concepts of space-time and relativity. In the visual arts there were new conquests of space; and in literature and music there were new ways of presenting materials in the temporal dimension. In painting, for instance, there was the development of the cubist canon of multiple-visual viewpoints, in which all sides of an object could be seen at the same time. In sculpture a new theory of volume was worked out whereby open holes or gaps in the surface suggested the simultaneous existence of the third dimension by stimulating the imagination to visualize what is on the other side. Similarly the architects of the international style, by the use of steel and glass, were able to incorporate the simultaneous experience of outer and inner space in their buildings. In literature the stream-of-consciousness technique was developed, in which objective description and the subjective flow of images in the mind were merged. In music the so-called atonal method of composition was formulated so that the 12 possible tones were related only to one another rather than to an absolute key center. Such novel organizations of space and time demand new ways of thinking about the world, new ways of looking at it, reading about it, and listening to it. Constructivism therefore indicates the many abstract turns the various arts have taken, and it is essentially an architectural concept—whether it applies to building, painting, sculptural, literary, or musical situations.

Cubism

As a pictorial style, cubism made several significant departures from generally accepted practices. A strong shove in the direction of abstraction was received from the large retrospective exhibit of Cézanne's paintings that was held in Paris in 1907. Many of the impressionable young painters who saw it were struck by Cézanne's pictorial architecture. They also noticed in the catalogue a quotation from one of the master's letters in which he remarked that all nature can be reduced to the forms of the cylinder, the sphere, and the cone. Art, they reasoned, was not an imitation of nature in the usual sense but an imposition upon nature of geometrical categories derived from the human mind. As a result cubist painting becomes a play of planes and angles on a flat surface. Cézanne's famous sentence, moreover, never mentioned cubes at all. His cylinders, spheres, and cones are all rounded forms presupposing curvilinear drawing; while cubist drawing, on the contrary, is mainly rectilinear.

The Renaissance ideal was the complete description of a pictorial situation from one point of view. Another viewpoint would imply another picture. The cubist theory of vision is predicated on the fact that in a fast-moving age objects are perceived hastily and casually, as, for instance, from moving vehicles. The world is therefore seen in fragments and from several points of view, rather than as a whole and from a single viewpoint. To continue to paint in the static Renaissance manner, the cubists thought, was incompatible with the dynamics of the modern age, and the results in any case would be a falsification of the visual facts of their time. They therefore undertook a new definition of pictorial space in which objects are represented simultaneously from many visual angles, in wholes or in parts, opaque and transparent. Just as the Crystal Palace and the Eiffel Tower had pointed the way to the interpenetration of the inner and outer aspects of architectural space, cubism undertook to move inside as well as outside an object, below and above it, in and around it.

One of the earliest instances of this new approach can be seen in Picasso's *Young Ladies of Avignon* (Fig. 20:1), where the faces of the second and third figures from the left are seen frontally, but their noses appear in profile. The cubists were also convinced that pictorial space, limited as it is by the two-dimensions of the flat canvas, was something quite apart from natural space. From the Renaissance onward the accepted formula was to produce the illusion of three-dimensionality by some form of linear perspective derived from the principles of Euclidean geometry. The cubist painter, however, approaches his canvas as an architect in order to construct his picture. He accepts the limitations of his medium; and, instead of trying to create the illusion of depth, he builds his pictorial architecture on the straight lines of the triangle and T-square by which he defines the planes of his surface. The expression of volume, as achieved by the modeling of objects in light and shade, was also abandoned, and with it went the tactile emphasis and structural solidity of Renaissance painting. Instead

Fig. 20:15 (above). Picasso. *Three Musicians*. 80″ x 74″. 1921. A. E. Gallatin Collection, Philadelphia Museum of Art. Fig. 20:16 (below left). Picasso. *Accordionist*. 51¼″ x 35″. 1911. Solomon R. Guggenheim Museum, New York. Fig. 20:17 (below right). Picasso. *Woman's Head*. Bronze. 16¼″ high. *c.*1909. Albright Art Gallery, Buffalo, N. Y.

of representing objects in the round, the cubists analyzed them into their basic geometrical forms, broken up into a series of planes, then collected, reassembled, tilted at will into a new complex pictorial pattern of inter-penetrating surfaces and planes. The emphasis is therefore on design, texture, and forms rather than on the representation of objects as such. The technique in its earliest stage can again be observed in the *Young Ladies of Avignon* in the way Picasso renders the bodies of the figures on the extreme left and upper right. His *Accordionist* (Fig. 20:16) shows it in a more de-veloped form after all the rules had been worked out.

Cubism was mainly associated with Picasso and Braque in the decade between 1907 and 1917. Actually its paternity is not to be attributed to any one man; it is rather the collective brain child of the 20th century. In its early doctrinaire stages, the pictures tended to be rather cold, im-personal studies in abstract design. After it had run its course in this pure state, various modifications began to appear on all sides, such as Picasso's *Three Musicians* (Fig. 20:15). The flat two-dimensional arrangement of cubism is retained, but the bright coloration gives the canvas a gaiety not found in the more studied aspects of the style. The three masked figures sitting at a table are the same *commedia dell' arte* figures that regularly recur on Picasso's canvases, cubist or otherwise. They come from his love of circus and theatrical performances in which the clowns and other per-formers dress in gay carnival costumes. The figure on the left playing a violin is a Harlequin, the central one with the clarinet is a Pierrot, while the more solemn monk on the right plays what appears to be an accordion.

Just as the discovery of the rules of linear perspective had revolutionized the expression of the Florentine Renaissance, cubism brought about a new way of looking at things in the 20th century, and its influence was felt directly in architecture and sculpture, as well as indirectly in literature and music. Picasso's *Woman's Head* (Fig. 20:17) is a translation by one of its leading exponents of cubist principles into the three-dimensional medium of sculpture. It presents a geometrical analysis of the structure of the human face and emphasizes its most important planes and surfaces. By this process of disintegration the head can be organized into a number of different facets, each of which can cast its own shadow and thus bring variety and a sense of movement to the composition.

Constantin Brancusi's *Bird in Space* (Fig. 20:18) presents one of the modi-fications of the stricter canons of cubism. His work is characterized by a direct and honest approach to the individual qualities of his materials. He accepts marble for its smoothness or roughness, and metal for its hardness or softness. Whatever the material, he tries to divine its nature and realize

its potentialities without forcing it to simulate something else. In this case
he is dealing with a bronze that has such a high copper content it approaches the brilliance of gold. By molding it into a graceful curvilinear
form and giving it a high polish, he releases the metal medium into a form
of energy. It is the abstraction of a movement, a feather in flight. Brancusi
has sometimes tried to increase the sense of motion in sculpture by placing
his figures on slowly rotating turntables. In this way his glistening surfaces
catch the light and his forms seem to float through space.

The musical aspect of this new concept of space-time is found in the
breaking up of traditional tonality as well as in the search for new musical
resources and mediums of expression. Stravinsky, as a strict adherent of
the principles of order, had said that "tonal elements become musical only
by virtue of their being organized." The 12-tone system of musical composition that Schoenberg evolved around 1915 was an answer to the need
for a new order of things, and one of the stricter forms of tonal organization. Schoenberg, who preferred to be called a constructor rather than a
composer, begins a work by setting forth a basic row of 12 different tones.
This row can be played in normal order, upside down by melodic inversion,
backward in retrograde motion, and upside down once more in retrograde
inversion. Furthermore it can be presented successively in sequences, or
simultaneously as in the various species of counterpoint. It can also be
played vertically as in a chord or tone cluster, or horizontally as in a
melody. A row can be used either as a whole, or it can be fragmented into
shorter themes or motives. It has been estimated that around half a billion
different combinations are possible, which certainly is no limitation on its
possibilities. As a system it provides a wealth of material as well as a certain
freedom within an orderly framework. The 12-tone method has generally
been referred to as atonality. Schoenberg himself called it simply a method
of composing with 12 tones that are related only with one another. Tonality
is thus relative rather than an absolute, since there is no single tonal center.
Tonality in the usual sense, however, is not excluded; rather it is encompassed and transcended.

Abstract Design

Piet Mondrian's *N:12 Blue Square* (Fig. 20:19) arrives at the end of the
rational road of cubism, just as Kandinsky had found the end of the emotional trail of expressionism. In both cases the artists found themselves up
a nonobjective blind alley, since abstraction could be pushed just so far
and no farther. Mondrian, who began his career by painting landscapes
in his native Holland, also tried in turn the techniques of impressionism,

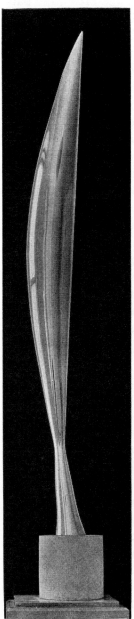

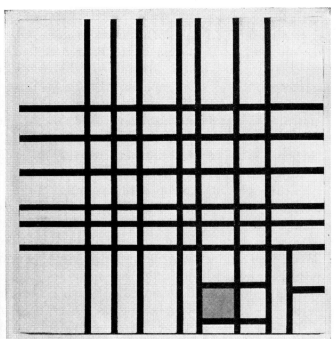

Fig. 20:19. Mondrian. *N:12 Blue Square.* 24″ x 24″. Harry Holtz-man Collection, New York

Fig. 20:18. Brancusi. *Bird in Space.* Bronze. 54″ high. 1919. Collection Museum of Modern Art, New York

Fig. 20:20. Arp. *Relief.* Wood. 19¾″ x 19¾″. 1938–1939. Collection Museum of Modern Art, New York

expressionism, and cubism. Mondrian's tastes ran to the criss-cross patterns of city streets, the cleanliness of an architect's blueprints, the gaunt open appearance of the structural steel skeletons of skyscrapers under construction, and the simplicity of the façades of the buildings of the international modern style. He eventually came to feel that the raw materials of nature and all references to the "primitive animal nature of man" should be rigidly excluded in order to reveal "true human nature." He hoped to approach a state of universality in his pictures by using "only a single neutral form: the rectangular area in varying dimensions." He even carries his abstraction to the realm of color by the use of black lines of various widths on a white background, relieved occasionally by a "climax" of one of the primary colors—red, blue, or yellow—in as pure a state as possible. In his opinion a work of art should be constructed; and he approached a canvas with all the objectivity of a draftsman making a blueprint. The results of this pictorial engineering were the series of chaste, two-dimensional spatial studies for which he became known. His visual patterns have a repose that rests on a precise balance of horizontal and vertical elements, and they are clean to the point of being prophylactic. His pictures are far more complex than meets the casual eye; and they have had a greater influence on advertising layouts, posters, interior designs, even linoleum, than is generally realized.

Hans Arp, who was a member of both the dadaist and surrealist movements, has also been associated with the medium of abstract sculpture. His *Relief* (Fig. 20:20) represents this phase of his work in wood, which he cuts with a jig-saw. In the manner of the African Negro carvers, he accepts the nature of wood with its curved shapes, knots, grain, and other distinguishing characteristics. Then he sets himself the problem of bringing out its beauty by varying its contours and by cutting and refining its surfaces and textures.

Futurism and the Mechanical Style

The movement known as futurism was begun in Italy under the leadership of the poet and dramatist Marinetti prior to World War I. Agreeing with Nietzsche, who said that history was the process by which the dead bury the living, Marinetti's *Manifesto* of 1909 said that futurism was being founded to "deliver Italy from its plague of professors, archeologists, tourist guides and antique dealers." They wanted to destroy the museums, libraries, academies, and universities in order to make way for their particular wave of the future. "A roaring motor-car, which runs like a machine gun," they said, "is more beautiful than the Winged Victory of Samothrace." Theirs was a vision of a state ruled by a mechanical superman, in which the people would be reduced to cogs in the gigantic wheel of a fully mechanized society. War was praised as "a motor for art," and their social thinking was completely antidemocratic. Mussolini himself frankly acknowledged his indebtedness to the group for some of the ideas and symbols that were later incorporated into his fascist movement.

"We go out. We swallow fog. The city is full of phantoms. Men cloaked in the mist walk silently. The canals exhale vapors." So goes in part a poem by Gabriele d'Annunzio, who was claimed by the movement, although he managed to remain on the fringe of the charmed circle. In architecture futurists admired factories, skyscrapers, grain elevators, railway terminals, and triple-decked bridges. A Manifesto on the "Aesthetics of Machinery" was written by one of the painters to celebrate the beauty and spiritual qualities of gears, pulleys, pistons, locomotives, steam shovels, fly-wheels, and pinions. Above all they admired the motion, force, velocity, and strength of mechanical forms. They wanted most of all to include the dynamic sensation of motion in their pictures. A galloping horse, they said, has not four legs but twenty. Giacomo Balla, in a picture called *Leash in Motion*, paints a dog with each of its legs in several positions spreading out fanwise. As a composite photographic painting of moving bodies, his *Swifts: Paths of Movement and Dynamic Sequences* (Fig. 20:21) shows the same principle applied to mechanical motion.

Fig. 20:21. Balla. *Swifts: Paths of Movement and Dynamic Sequences.* ' 38⅛" x 47¼". 1913. Collection Museum of Modern Art, New York

Fig. 20:22. Leger. *Mechanical Elements.* 83⅛" x 66⅛". 1918–1923. Private Collection, Paris

Their musical manifesto was issued in 1913, and the following year a program entitled "Networks of Noises" was presented in Milan. The numbers included such gems as *Awakening of Capital* and *Meeting of Automobiles and Aeroplanes.* An "orchestra" of 19 noise instruments was conducted by their inventor Luigi Russolo. It consisted of three bumblers, two exploders, three thunderers, three whistlers, two rufflers, two gurglers, one fricasseur, two stridors, and one snorer. Futurism burst upon the international scene in 1912 by way of a picture exhibition in Paris, but it was not until 1921 that its equivalent in concert form took place. The movement was influential chiefly in the formation of the so-called mechanical style. The futurists were a bit too noisy and exhibitionistic to be very enduring, and their productivity ran more to manifestoes than to significant works of art. As a result their future was all too soon behind them.

By taking some of the ideas developed by the cubists and others by the futurists, Fernand Léger developed an individual style of his own. *Mechanical Elements* (Fig. 20:22) shows his delight with the precision of machine forms, and he makes his compositions hum like well-oiled motors. He loved crankshafts, cylinder blocks, and pistons, which he painted in gleaming colors of enamellike brightness. Taking Cézanne's statement about cylinders, spheres, and cones far more literally than the cubists did, he made his lines curvilinear rather than rectilinear, and he modeled his forms in light and shade. His buildings are structural steel skeletons populated by robots with spheres for heads, cylinders for legs, pipes for arms, and tubes for fingers. There is no room in Léger's world for sentiment; and such human forms as do occur are introduced by the artist only for their "plastic value" and for this reason remain "purposely inexpressive." In 1924 he made an abstract film called *Ballet Méchanique*, in which machine forms and motorized movements replaced human beings and their activities.

Stravinsky, meanwhile, had composed an *Étude for Pianola* in 1917; and the French composer Arthur Honegger, using the normal symphonic complement, gave voice in 1924 to the triumphant song of the machine in his symphonic movement called *Pacific 231*. The name is an allusion to that year's model of an American locomotive, and the sounds were designed to evoke the atmosphere of a song of the rails, complete with the grinding of the wheels and the shriek of the steam whistle.

Industrial Design and Utilitarian Music

When Walter Gropius was called upon to reorganize the art school at Weimar, Germany, just after World War I, he renamed it the Bauhaus and made it over into a technical school of design with special emphasis on the industrial arts and the study of modern materials. All the visual arts were included in the curriculum, with none of the usual separations into a hierarchy of fine as opposed to the applied arts. By making furniture designing and photography as respectable as architecture and painting, he hoped to break down the snobbish distinction between artist and craftsman. In the 19th century Ruskin and Morris had made a similar effort to bring the world of art and the world of work back together again, but in their Romanticism they thought only in terms of handicrafts and shunned the machine. The constructivism of Gropius, however, regarded the machine as another new tool to be mastered and as a force that is made to serve rather than enslave. His objective was a marriage of beauty to utility within the framework of the machine age.

The exploration of materials and industrial processes led to many new approaches in printing, pottery, metalwork, weaving, and stagecraft. The students were taught never to forget the purposes their products were designed to serve. The results of the new movement were soon felt in new furniture designs, such as the tubular steel chairs, indirect-lighting fixtures, streamlined appliances, posters and advertising layouts, many of which are all too familiar today. In order to counterbalance the utilitarian side, however, Gropius added to his distinguished faculty the painters Kandinsky, Klee, and Lyonel Feininger in order to uphold the expressive and creative aspects of drawing and painting. Their work in this sane atmosphere did much to dispel the current confusions brought about by such movements as futurism and dadaism.

While the Bauhaus was primarily a school for the visual arts, the constructive new line of thinking was felt in other fields as well. A movement generally known as *Gebrauchsmusik*, which can be rendered either as utilitarian music or workaday music, got under way in Germany. The composers who adopted its principles tried to establish a new relationship between the producers and consumers of music wherever they were to be found. It was mainly identified with the composers Paul Hindemith and Kurt Weill, who wrote vocal music for school situations, marches for special occasions, and pieces for amateur rather than professional performance. As such, *Gebrauchsmusik* tried to counteract the distinction between the art music of the Romantics and the reality of situations where music could serve a functional purpose. It also implied a coming to terms with the new media of radio and moving pictures. Technical proficiency was considered more important than inspiration. By writing music only on order, its espousers eventually got bogged down over the problem of whether the work creates the demand or the demand the work.

Contemporary Architecture and the International Style

Among the earliest and boldest instances of modern architecture is the skyscraper. It came out of the American Middle West as an answer to the need for commercial centralization. In the hands of Louis Sullivan, who put up the Wainwright Building in St. Louis in 1891, the skyscraper was a "proud and soaring thing," reflecting the pride of the businessman in his work. As such, more new engineering ideas and new materials have gone into the construction of skyscrapers than any other modern architectural form—except such engineering feats as suspension bridges and highway construction. The principal drawback to skyscrapers as an architectural form, however, is their contribution to congestion in already overcrowded areas. From a human viewpoint their value has thus far been somewhat less spectacular than their engineering.

Sullivan's slogan that "form follows function" is subject to a variety of interpretations, but the line of thought it provoked led to an important re-evaluation of architectural forms in relation to human activities, and to a re-examination of basic architectural methods, materials, and purposes.

Modern building had to wait until structural steel was available in units of sufficient length and at a reasonable cost. As long as architecture remained an art of masonry, it had to use either the post-and-lintel or the arch methods of construction. The methods of cantilevering and suspension, both of which had long been known in principle, could be effectively employed on a large scale only with materials as strong as steel and reinforced concrete. The cantilever is simply the horizontal architectural member that extends, tablelike, outward over its vertical supports. Sullivan's disciple Frank Lloyd Wright, and the architects identified with the international style, accepted the principle that stone should behave like stone, wood like wood, and steel like steel; and that design must be modified in relation to its materials and purposes. Their lines of development, however, have led in divergent directions.

The international style crystallized in France with the work of Le Corbusier, in Holland with J. J. P. Oud, and in Germany with Miës van der Rohe and Walter Gropius. Open structures, such as the Bauhaus Machine Shop (Fig. 20:23) and Lever House in New York (Fig. 20:24), are the lineal descendants of the Crystal Palace and the Eiffel Tower. Walter Gropius in 1914 was building steel and glass factories that could easily be taken for 1954. When the Bauhaus moved from Weimar to Dessau in 1925, he designed its studios, machine shops, administrative offices, and professors' houses into a single masterly space composition. As an exponent of the international style, he started with the open box as the basic unit of space, varied its volume, and grouped several of them in a related pattern of cubes. The Machine Shop (Fig. 20:23) shows how the building is treated as an open volume rather than as a closed mass. By the method of cantilevering Gropius allowed the building to project several feet outward over its site. The horizontal emphasis thus established is then carried out in the concrete base and repeated at the roof level. Between these parallel lines hang the glass-curtained walls that bear no structural weight. This transparency permits details, such as the spiral staircase and the skeletal structure of the interior, to remain open and visible from the exterior. By thus allowing the interior and exterior of the building to be seen at the same time, Gropius achieved the architectural equivalent of the cubist painters, who presented the front view and the profile of a human face or several different sides of an object simultaneously. The Bauhaus group has proved to be one of the most important and influential buildings of its decade.

The steel, glass, and concrete creations of Gropius were absorbed directly into the international modern style. One of the most recent examples is

Fig. 20:23 (above). Gropius. *Bauhaus Machine Shop*. 1926. Dessau, Germany. Courtesy Museum of Modern Art

Fig. 20:24. Skidmore, Owings and Merrill. *Lever House*. 1952. New York

the Lever Brothers building in New York (Fig. 20:24). Unlike the pronounced vertical tendency of the earlier skyscrapers, it is balanced by a horizontal base. The lower part then becomes a pedestal for the skyscraper to stand on. Here again the building is cantilevered outward beyond the substructure—a device that, together with the glass walls, contributes notably to the effect of spaciousness and openness. By omitting the ground floor and reducing the supporting steel shafts to a minimum, he created an open passageway for pedestrians. Le Corbusier was the first to design domestic houses on steel stilts, but the Lever Brothers building became the first instance of their use on a large scale.

The international style is thus mainly identified with the cantilevered steel skeleton enclosed in a transparent sheath of glass. Frank Lloyd Wright has sharply criticized this emphasis on structural openness, which he characterizes as "indecent exposure." Le Corbusier's definition of a house as a "machine for living" likewise reveals certain mechanistic limitations of the style in its approach to human problems. While the internationalists have succeeded in breaking down the distinction between architecture and engineering, they have in their zeal sometimes failed to realize that the construction of bridges and viaducts is one thing, and that the building of domestic dwellings, apartment houses, and offices for human living and working situations is quite another. By their insistent use of the vocabulary of steel, glass, and concrete and the principle of cantilevering to the point where they have become commonplace stereotypes, they have added them for better or worse to the accepted architectural language of today. By employing new methods and materials just because they are new, however, they have often neglected to make a critical appraisal of just why they are being used. Technological inventiveness alone is never an adequate foundation on which to build a permanent style. Now that the novelty has worn off, and the devices have been so often repeated, they have the dubious distinction of having become clichés. It cannot be denied, however, that the international style is one of the few aspects of contemporary art to achieve wide popular acceptance.

RELATIVISM

The only thing that is permanent is change. This paradoxical statement points its finger at the very heart of 20th-century thought, whether expressed in philosophical, scientific, or aesthetic terms. No static unchanging absolute can possibly provide a satisfactory view of the moving world of today. Even the firmest dogmas of religious faiths and political doctrines are subject to far more commentary and modification from time to time than their devotees would care to admit. The shift from a static world order to the present dynamic view of the universe, which began with Galileo and Copernicus, has swept all before it. Those who believe in orderly progress toward some definable objective interpret this flux as some form of evolution; those who accept it at face value, as most scientists do, believe simply in change. Both would agree with Nietzsche when he said that truth has never yet hung on the arm of an absolute; both must of necessity describe the world in relative terms. In his observations of physical phenomena, Albert Einstein saw that in a world where everything was moving, any calculation or prediction, in order to be valid, had to be based on the relative position of the observer. Newton's absolute space, which was immovable, and his absolute time, which flowed on uniformly— both of which were "unrelated to any outward circumstances"—had to be discarded and replaced by the theory of relativity. All space in the modern view has to be measured by mobility and change of relative position, and all time by the duration of movement. In the modern scientific view, therefore, the world is a spacio-temporal continuum, in which all events are related in the four dimensions of space-time.

The study of the life and customs of primitive tribes by anthropologists has shown how ethical considerations are relative to traditions, social organizations, and economic conditions. In Tibet, for instance, one woman may have several husbands, because the men are so poor they cannot support a whole wife individually. In some African tribes, on the other hand, a rich man may have as many wives as he can afford. The pragmatic philosophers William James and John Dewey took a long look at history and a wide view of the world and came to the conclusion that when an idea was useful and effective it was true; and when it no longer works, it is soon discarded for one that does.

Such a relative world, in which all things appear differently to each person depending on his history, geographical position, educational back-ground, system of values, psychological constitution, and so on, can only be understood in terms of many frames of reference. Any absolutism—a totalitarian society such as Plato's *Republic* for instance—insists on a maximum of conformity; while a relativism—such as that of a modern democracy—allows for many competing images of man and thus for a maximum of diversity. This relative world, moreover, is populated by men who see themselves in multiple images and express themselves in a multiplicity of styles. In it can be found Marx's proletarian man, speaking in some of the forms of social protest and bent on bringing about the ultimate triumph of the working classes and masses. Darwin's jungle man is there too, beating on his neo-primitive tom-toms and discoursing in an existentialist vocabulary on the survival of the fittest. Nietzche's superman, determined to impose his mighty will on an unwilling world, has been thwarted in two world wars. The voice of Freud's psychological man is heard coming from couches and canvases as he generously tries to share his surrealistic nightmares with the world at large. Mechanical man, the spawn of the Industrial Revolution and the machine age, walks robotlike among us, thinking mechanistic thoughts in his electronic brain and expressing futuristic principles in his mechanical style. There is also Einstein's man of relativity, drawing abstract pictures of his space-time world in slashing angular lines organized by the multifocus perspective of cubism. Modern art as the mirror of this relativistic world thus assumes many shapes and reflects a multiplicity of human images.

Small wonder then that this world, which has produced scientists who analyze and synthesize, and physicists who work with fission and fusion, has also given birth to revolutionists who want to destroy a social order so that they can reconstruct it in a different way; warring nations who hope to break down one international order so as to build up a new balance of power; and iconoclasts who feel compelled to tear down the images men live by so they can remake the world in their own image. In this relative world, then, the cubist disintegrates the objects in his paintings so that he can reintegrate them in patterns of his own choosing. Since each picture creates its own spatial relationships, space is relative to the mind and mood of the painter rather than an absolute as in Euclidean geometry. It is both impossible and undesirable to make any precise analogy between cubist principles and the mathematics of space-time. A relationship, however unsystematic though it is, can nevertheless be found in the cubist concept of the simultaneity of several viewpoints, in the presentation of objects from many sides at once, in the use of multifocus perspective, and in the symbolic emphasis on abstract geometrical forms. By representing bodies at rest or in successive stages of motion, such a picture as Duchamp's *Nude Descending the Staircase* sets up a space-time continuum of its own. By showing a figure frontally and from the side, clothed and in the nude, opaque and transparent as in an X-ray view, Picasso in the *Girl Before a Mirror* (Fig. 20:25) creates his own pictorial theory of relativity.

Concurrently with this new conquest of two-dimensional space, architecture developed many new ways of molding its three-dimensional equivalent. Frank Lloyd Wright ruled out such self-contained absolutes as the Greek temple in favor of an architecture specifically related to the changing

Fig. 20:25. Picasso. *Girl Before a Mirror.* 63¾″ x 51¼″. 1932. Collection Museum of Modern Art, New York

aspects of human living and working space. He thus evolved the flexible floor plan with its advancing and receding areas, and its freedom of interior and exterior occupation. The international stylists also came up with their version of the simultaneous perception of inner and outer space by means of the glass-curtain wall and the organizing of such multibuilding complexes as apartment houses and the United Nations group into systems of related cubes of varying volumes.

In music the experience of dissonance is emancipated from its dependence on consonance so that it demands neither preparation, anticipation, nor resolution. The absolutes of tonality, rhythmical regularity, and musical form have yielded to a host of tonal relativisms. Instead of an insistent reiteration of a single meter, a modern musical score can use polymetrical sequences in which a measure of $\frac{4}{8}$ is succeeded by one of $\frac{7}{8}$, then $\frac{2}{8}$, $\frac{9}{8}$, and so on. The same principle can be used simultaneously with several rhythms going on at the same time, as in the polyrhythmical textures of Stravinsky's *Rites of Spring*. Instead of organizing a work around a single key center, some composers have employed two tonalities simultaneously in the technique known as bitonality, while others have gone one step farther into polytonality. This, in turn, led to Schoenberg's method of composing with 12 tones that are related only with one another. Within the internal organization of the work, the sequence of tones known as the row can be played forward or backward, normally or upside down, simultaneously as in a chord, or fragmented into shorter motives. The 12-tone method emphasizes change and discourages repetition, and the principle of constant variation in a perpetual state of tonal flux is its ideal.

James Joyce found the answer in his *Ulysses* by making a simultaneous cross section of the life of a city. In this labyrinthine literary space-time continuum, all events, whether memories of the past or premonitions of the future, flow together into a kind of extended now. As in a dream there is no distinction between before and after. Actually the reader can begin at almost any place in the book and the continuity would not be broken. The series of fleeting images are simply recorded, and the door to the dream world of free association of words and thoughts is left open so that the reader can move in and supply the transitions between moods, the union of the fragments, and thus in turn create his own relative order.

Many of the forms of expressionism are also relative to the individual psychology of the artist, just as a Frank Lloyd Wright building is relative to the need of the human situation. Expressionism presupposes the free associational techniques of psychological relativism. Somewhat like the romantic revolt of a century earlier, the expressionistic artist reasserts the primacy of the imagination over the intellect, and takes flight from reality in order to find a superior reality in the world of mystery and fantasy. The tendency is anti-intellectual in the extreme, though the symbols and vocabulary are evolved by highly rationalistic procedures. The emotional content poured on their canvases, pages, and musical scores all takes place within the human imagination and hence is relative to the infinite number of unsolved conflicts and suppressed passions of many different private worlds.

Historical relativism has provided the modern artist with an unparalleled number of choices of styles and techniques from the past as well as the present. The artist of the 20th century is the heir of all the ages. A Picasso exhibit or a Stravinsky concert can mean a bewildering assortment of styles. Inspiration for one can be drawn from ancient Iberian sculpture, Oriental textiles, Romanesque wall frescoes, medieval illuminated manuscripts as well as from contemporary sources. His media may include pencil drawings; collages constructed of cloth and paper; ceramics, and woodcuts as well as oils and water colors. Sources for the other may be drawn from the free rhythms of Gregorian chant, the dissonant counterpoint of the 14th century, the operas of Mozart, or the polyrhythmic practices of the African aborigines. When Picasso said, "I do not search, I find," he implied that his freedom of approach was unlimited. He can accept for the moment any style that comes along without becoming its dogmatic prisoner. Both Picasso and Stravinsky have repeatedly demonstrated that a new work can be based on an aesthetic theory diametrically opposed to the one that preceded it. This does not mean, however, that they must repudiate or burn up that which has gone before. To these master craftsmen historical relativism provides a complete freedom of choice without the necessity of sacrificing either their originality or their principles.

Philosophers of history, such as Spengler and Toynbee, through their sweeping historical panoramas have shown that the past still exists within the living present. From the point of view of historical relativity, tradition is usually a more potent factor than innovation, and at all times including the present, evolution has been a stronger force than revolution. Most 20th-century ideas and problems are variations on old themes that have bothered men from the 5th century B. C. to the present day. Those that have led to such sharp dissonances in the past were never really resolved; instead, they have become outmoded, outgrown, temporarily forgotten, or else bypassed or circumvented in one way or another. "Ideas have never conquered the world as ideas," as Romain Rolland has said, "but only by the force they represent. They do not grip men by their intellectual contents, but by the radiant vitality which is given off from them at certain periods in history. . . . The loftiest and most sublime idea remains ineffective until the day when it becomes contagious, not by its own merits, but by the merits of the groups of men in whom it becomes incarnate by the transfusion of their blood." [3] Much more important than the solutions or lack of them have been the emotional forces they have generated and the good fruits they have yielded, since all the ideas have ultimately been embodied in the buildings men erect to house their activities, the statues and pictures that reflect their images, the words that express their innermost thoughts, and the music that gives voice to their strivings and aspirations.

FOOTNOTES

CHAPTER 1

[1] Homer. *Odyssey*, VII, 80–81. Translated by Samuel H. Butcher and Andrew Lang in *The Complete Works of Homer*. New York, Modern Library, 1935. P. 99.

[2] Plato. *Sophist*, 223. Jowett translation.

[3] Plutarch. *Lives of the Noble Grecians and Romans*, XIII, 1. Translated by John Dryden. New York, Modern Library, 1932. P. 192.

[4] Aristophanes. *Lysistrata*, 254–304. Translator anonymous. In *The Complete Greek Drama*. Edited by Whitney J. Oates and Eugene O'Neill, Jr. New York, Random House, 1938. Vol. II, p. 821.

[5] Commissioner's Report of 409 B. C. Quoted from G. P. Stevens *et al. The Erechtheum*. Cambridge, Harvard University Press, 1927. P. 481.

[6] Homer. *Iliad*, II, 546–551. In *Complete Works. Op. cit.* Pp. 34–35.

[7] By W. B. Dinsmoor. *The Architecture of Ancient Greece*. London, B. T. Batsford, 1950.

[8] *Ibid.* P. 193.

[9] Plutarch. *Op. cit.* Pp. 192–193.

[10] Quintilian. *Institutes of Oratory*, XII, X, 9. Translated by H. E. Butler. London, W. Heinemann; New York, G. P. Putnam's Sons (Loeb Classical Library), 1921.

[11] Plato. *Republic*, X, 601. Jowett translation.

[12] *Ibid.* III, 398. Translated by Paul Shorey. London, W. Heinemann; New York, G. P. Putnam's Sons (Loeb Classical Library), 1930. Vol. I.

[13] *Ibid.*, III, 424. Jowett translation.

[14] Friedrich Nietzsche. *Birth of Tragedy*. Translated by William A. Haussmann. In *The Complete Works of Friedrich Nietzsche*, Vol. I, p. 69. New York, Macmillan Co., 1924.

[15] This fragment was found in Vienna in 1892. A transcription of the notation is included in Curt Sachs. *Rise of Music in the Ancient World*. New York, W. W. Norton & Co., 1943. P. 244.

[16] Nietzsche. *Op. cit.* P. 69.

[17] Euripides. *The Bacchae*. Translated by Gilbert Murray. London, George Allen and Unwin, Ltd. The only currently available American edition is in *The Complete Greek Drama. Op. cit.* Vol. II, pp. 227–288.

[18] Plato. *Republic*. VII, 530. Jowett translation.

[19] Plato. *Phaedo*, 61. Jowett translation.

[20] Aristotle. *Poetics*, Ch. VI. Translated by

Samuel H. Butcher. London, Macmillan & Co., 1902.

[21] Plato. *Republic*, III. 401. Jowett translation.

[22] *Ibid.*, III, 400.

[23] *Ibid.*, X, 602.

[24] Plato. *Sophist*, 236. Jowett translation.

[25] Plato. *Republic*, X, 602. Jowett translation.

[26] *Ibid.*, III, 401.

[27] *Ibid.*, V, 472.

[28] Aristotle. *Poetics. Op. cit.*, 1448a.

CHAPTER 2

[1] Polybius. VI, 31:10. Quoted from F. Haverfield. *Ancient Town-Planning*. Oxford, England, Clarendon Press, 1913. P. 55.

[2] Most of the information about Pergamon comes from the monumental series of monographs entitled *Altertümer von Pergamon*, published during the latter part of the 19th century by Staatliche Museen zu Berlin. The most complete publication on the city in English is Esther V. Hansen. *The Attalids of Pergamon*. Ithaca, N. Y., Cornell University Press, 1947, Volume 29 of Cornell Studies in Classical Philology.

[3] Plato. *Republic*, III, 399. Jowett translation.

[4] Aristotle. *Politics*, VIII, Ch. VII, 1342b. Jowett translation.

[5] Cyril Bailey. *Epicurus*. Oxford, England, Clarendon Press, 1926. P. 169.

CHAPTER 3

[1] Edward Gibbon. *The Decline and Fall of the Roman Empire*. New York, Modern Library, 1932. Vol. I, p. 70.

[2] *Ibid.* Vol. I, p. 1.

[3] Pliny. *Letters*, Book IX, Epistle VII. Translated by William Melmoth. London, W. Heinemann; New York, G. P. Putnam's Sons (Loeb Classical Library), 1927. Vol. 2, p. 189.

[4] *Ibid.* Book III, Epistle VI. Vol. I, p. 205.

[5] *Ibid.* Book X, Epistle XXIV. Vol. II, p. 307.

[6] Quintilian. *Institutes of Oratory*, I, X, 14. Translated by H. E. Butler. London, W. Heinemann; New York, G. P. Putnam's Sons (Loeb Classical Library), 1921.

[7] *Ibid.* I, X, 25.

[8] Letter to Septitius Clarus. *Ibid.* P. 211.

[9] Pliny. *Op. cit.* Vol. I, p. 205.

[10] Athenaeus. *Deipnosophistai (Sophists at Dinner)*,

Book VI. Translated by Charles B. Gulick for
Loeb Classical Library. Quoted from Oliver
Strunk, editor. *Source Readings in Music History.*
New York, W. W. Norton & Co., 1950. Pp. 53–54.

[11] Gibbon. *Op. cit.* Vol. I, p. 68.

[12] Vergil. *Aeneid*, Book VI. J. W. Mackail
translation.

CHAPTER 4

[1] Sidonius Apollinaris. *Epistolae*, 1:5. Quoted
from E. Hutton. *Ravenna.* London, Dent, 1913.
See also W. B. Anderson's edition of Sidonius.
Cambridge, England, University Press, 1936.
P. 382.

[2] *The Letters of Cassiodorus.* Translated by
Thomas Hodgkin. London, Henry Frowde, 1886.
P. 148.

[3] Oliver Strunk, editor. *Source Readings in Music
History.* New York, W. W. Norton & Co., 1950.
P. 86.

[4] *The Letters of Cassiodorus. Op. cit.* P. 194.

[5] For a transcription of part of this fragment,
see Curt Sachs. *The Rise of Music in the Ancient
World.* New York, W. W. Norton & Co., 1943.
P. 246.

[6] *St. Augustine's Confessions*, Book IX, Ch. 7.
Translated by William Watts. London, W. Heinemann (Loeb Classical Library), 1925. Vol. 2,
p. 31.

[7] Strunk. *Op. cit.* P. 70.

[8] Martin Gerbert. *De Cantu et musica sacra.* 2
vols., 1774. As quoted in Gustave Reese. *Music in
the Middle Ages.* New York, W. W. Norton & Co.,
1940. P. 104.

CHAPTER 5

[1] Epistle 1:20. Quoted from Joan Evans.
Cluniac Art of the Romanesque Period. Cambridge,
England, Cambridge University Press, 1950.
Pp. 1–2.

[2] Gilon. *Vita St. Hugonis.* In M. Marrier.
Bibliteca Cluniensis. Paris, 1614. Quoted in Evans.
Op. cit. P. 29.

[3] Hildebert, Bishop of Le Mans. In Marrier.
Op. cit. VI, col. 432.

[4] *A Medieval Garner.* Translated by G. G.
Coulton. London, Constable & Co., 1910. Pp.
70–71.

[5] Elizabeth Gilmore Holt, editor. *Literary
Sources of Art History.* Princeton, Princeton University Press, 1947. P. 16.

[6] An English translation is in Oliver Strunk,
editor. *Source Readings in Music History.* New York,
W. W. Norton & Co., 1950. Pp. 103–116.

[7] *Ibid.* P. 104.

[8] Guido of Arezzo. *Prologus antiphonarii sui*
(*c.*1025). In Strunk. *Op. cit.* P. 125.

[9] *Ibid.* Pp. 118–119.

[10] *Ibid.* P. 125.

[11] *Scholia enchiriadis.* In Strunk. *Op. cit.* Pp. 126–
138.

[12] As quoted in P. H. Lang. *Music in Western
Civilization.* New York, W. W. Norton & Co.,
1941. P. 80.

[13] Evans. *Op. cit.* P. 24.

CHAPTER 6

[1] References to panels indicate divisions normally found in complete presentations of the
Tapestry. Scenes included in the illustrations are
designated by the usual term, Figure.

[2] Quoted from Henry Adams. *Mont-St. Michel
and Chartres.* Boston and New York, Houghton
Mifflin Co., 1904. P. 19.

[3] This and the following quotations are from
the translation by Isabel Butler. Boston and New
York, Houghton Mifflin Co., 1904.

[4] *Flamenca*, 11, 583 ff. Quoted from H. J.
Chayton. *The Provençal Chanson de Geste.* London,
Oxford University Press, 1946. Pp. 13–14.

[5] Adams. *Op. cit.* Pp. 21–22.

CHAPTER 7

[1] Henry Adams. *Mont-St. Michel and Chartres.*
Boston and New York, Houghton Mifflin Co.,
1904. Pp. 104–105. The Adams translation is also
quoted in E. G. Holt, editor. *Literary Sources of Art
History.* Princeton, Princeton University Press,
1947. Pp. 45–46.

[2] Quoted from Cecil Headlam. *The Story of
Chartres.* London, Dent, 1922. P. 141.

[3] Quoted from David M. Robb. *History of
Painting.* New York, Harper & Bros., 1951. P. 85.
Another translation appears in Erwin Panofsky.
Abbot Suger on the Abbey of St.-Denis. Princeton,
Princeton University Press, 1946. P. 21.

CHAPTER 8

[1] Paul Sabatier. *Life of St. Francis of Assisi.* New
York, Charles Scribner's Sons, 1894. P. 338.

[2] Ernest F. Henderson, editor. *Select Historical
Documents of the Middle Ages.* London, G. Bell &
Sons, 1896. Pp. 344–349.

[3] St. Bonaventura. *Life of St. Francis*, Ch. XII,
par. 3. Translated by E. Gurney Salter. London,
Dent (Temple Classics), 1904.

[4] *Ibid.*, Ch. II, par. 4.

[5] *Ibid.*, Ch. XIV, par. 6.

[6] *Rerum Italicarum Scriptores*, XVI, Part 6, pp.
555–556. Quoted from Millard Meiss. *Painting in
Florence and Siena after the Black Death.* Princeton,
Princeton University Press, 1951. P. 65.

[7] Translated by Anna Hume. Quoted from
Sonnets, Triumphs and Other Poems of Petrarch. New

York, T. Y. Crowell & Co., no date given. Part I, p. 316.

[8] Boccaccio. *Decameron*, "Introduction to the First Day." Translated by J. M. Rigg. New York, E. P. Dutton & Co., 1928.

[9] Hume translation. *Op. cit.*

[10] Walter Scott. *Lay of the Last Minstrel*, Canto VI, XXXI.

[11] Translation by Matthew Arnold.

[12] Dante. Preface to *Divine Comedy*. Charles A. Dinsmore. *Aids to the Study of Dante*. Boston and New York, Houghton Mifflin Co., 1903. P. 270.

[13] *Ibid.* P. 270.

[14] *Ibid.* P. 272.

CHAPTER 9

[1] For the full text of the motet, see Gugliemo Dufay. *Opera Omnia*. Vol. 2, *Motetti*, pp. 70–76. Edited by Gugliemus de Van. Rome, American Institute of Musicology, 1948. Another edition is in *Denkmäler der Tonkunst in Oesterreich*. Vol. 53, Jahrgang 25.

The four-part motet *Nuper Rosarum* is divided so that the two upper parts, the *cantus* and *contra-tenor*, are sung by the choir over the two isorhythmic tenor lines that function as a ground bass. The isorhythms are managed so that the chant *"Terribilis est locus iste"* appears at first in triple or perfect time with dotted whole notes; in the second strophe, it is in duple or imperfect time in plain whole notes; in the third, also imperfect, it is in half notes; while in the fourth strophe, it returns to perfect time in dotted halves. It thus begins and ends with a perfect triple rhythm, and the decrease in rhythmic values has the effect of quickening the pace and giving the work a sense of moving toward a climax.

Isometrically the proportions work out so that the second strophe represents a reduction of the rhythmic values of the first by one third; part three is one half of part two; while part four is one half of part one; thus making the proportions work out in the ratio of 6:4:2:3. The form is thus as perfectly rounded out in its way as that of Brunelleschi's dome.

[2] Jefferson B. Fletcher. *Literature of the Italian Renaissance*. New York, Macmillan Co., 1934. P. 132.

[3] For the remainder of the fragment, see *Denkmäler*, etc. *Op. cit.* Vol. 14, Jahrgang 1. P. 41.

[4] Complete text and music is in *ibid.* P. 44.

CHAPTER 10

[1] Jacob Burckhardt. *Civilization of the Renaissance in Italy*. New York, Oxford University Press, 1945. P. 235.

[2] *Michelangelo, a Record of His Life as Told in His Own Letters and Papers*. Translated and edited by Robert W. Carden. London, Constable & Co., 1913. Quoted in Elizabeth Gilmore Holt, editor. *Literary Sources of Art History*. Princeton, Princeton University Press, 1947. P. 185.

[3] Translated by Creighton Gilbert. Quoted in *Ibid.* P. 199.

[4] Giorgio Vasari. *Lives of the Most Eminent Painters, Sculptors and Architects*. Translated by Mrs. Jonathan Foster. London, Bohn, 1859. Preface to Part I.

[5] Charles de Tolnay. *The Sistine Chapel*. Princeton, Princeton University Press, 1945. P. 20.

[6] *Ibid.*

[7] Plato. *Timaeus*, 90a. Jowett translation.

[8] Michael Angelo Buonarroti. *His Sonnets*. Translated by John Addington Symonds. London, privately printed, 1895. P. xv.

[9] Cosimo Bartoli. *Ragionamenti accademici . . . sopra alcuni luoghi difficili di Dante*. Venice, 1567. Translated by Alexander H. Krappe, Roger H. Sessions, and Oliver Strunk. Quoted from Alfred Einstein. *The Italian Madrigal*. Princeton, Princeton University Press, 1949. Vol. I, pp. 21–22.

[10] Henricus Glareanus. *Dodecachordon*. Basel, 1547. P. 241. Quoted from Leo Schrade. *Monteverdi, Creator of Modern Music*. New York, W. W. Norton & Co., 1950. P. 24.

[11] Josquin des Pres. *Werken*. Edited by A. Smijers. Leipzig and Amsterdam, 1921. Introduction to Vol. I.

[12] Oliver Strunk, editor. *Source Readings in Music History*. New York, W. W. Norton & Co., 1950. P. 358.

CHAPTER 11

[1] *The Architecture of A. Palladio, in Four Books*. Translated by G. Leoni. London, 1742. Book III, Ch. XX.

[2] *Ibid.*

[3] *Ibid.*

[4] *Ibid.* Book IV, Preface.

[5] E. MacCurdy, editor. *Notebooks of Leonardo da Vinci*. New York, Reynal & Hitchcock, 1938. Vol. II, p. 437.

[6] Giorgio Vasari. *Lives of the Most Eminent Painters, Sculptors and Architects*. Translated by Mrs. Jonathan Foster. Edited and annotated by E. H. and E. W. Blashfield and A. A. Hopkins. New York, Charles Scribner's Sons, 1896. Vol. III, p. 348.

[7] Pietro Caliari. *Paolo Veronese*. Rome, 1888. Pp. 102 ff. Quoted from Elizabeth Gilmore Holt, editor. *Literary Sources of Art History*. Princeton, Princeton University Press, 1947. Pp. 245–248.

[8] Dated April 7, 1540.

[9] *Relacioni degli Ambasciatori Veneti al Senato rac-*

colte. Eugenio Alberti, editor. Florence, 1839. Series I, Vol. I, pp. 11–12. Quoted from Leo Schrade. *Monteverdi, Creator of Modern Music.* New York, W. W. Norton & Co., 1951. P. 32.

[10] This literal translation is original.

[11] The numbering of the measures follows the score as published by G. Schirmer, Inc., New York (Octavo N. 4452); and Example 11:1 is quoted by permission of that firm as copyright owners. Another edition is to be found in Archibald T. Davison and Willi Apel, editors. *Historical Anthology of Music.* Cambridge, Mass., Harvard University Press, 1949. Vol. I, pp. 175–178. Recordings are available, such as the one by the Harvard Glee Club, Radcliffe Choral Society, Boston Symphony Brass Choir, E. Power Biggs, organist, G. Wallace Woodworth, conductor (Victor Album 928).

CHAPTER 13

[1] See Rudolph Wittkower. *Bernini's Bust of Louis XIV.* London, Oxford University Press, 1951. 19 pages.

CHAPTER 14

[1] Henry Peacham. *The Compleat Gentleman.* Reprinted in 1906 by Oxford University Press from the edition of 1632.

[2] Francis Pilkington. *First Booke of Ayres of 4 Parts: With Tablature for the Lute or Orpherian, with the Violl de Gamba.* 1605. Example 14:1 and Fig. 14:13 reproduced by permission of the Huntington Library, San Marino, Calif.

CHAPTER 15

[1] John Dryden. "Prologue Spoken at the Opening of the New House." March 26, 1674.

[2] John Dryden. Preface to *Albion and Albianus.* In *Dramatic Works of John Dryden,* edited by J. Saintsbury. Edinburgh, William Paterson, 1882. Vol. VII, pp. 228–229.

[3] *Ibid.* P. 279.

[4] The best edition is that by Edward J. Dent. Copyright, 1925, by Oxford University Press. Example 15:2 quoted by permission.

CHAPTER 16

[1] The numbering of the arias follows the excellent English version of the libretto by Edward J. Dent. New York, Edwin F. Kalmus.

[2] Letter of September 26, 1781. In *The Letters of Mozart and His Family.* 3 vols. Translated by Emily Anderson. London, Macmillan & Co., 1938. Vol. III, p. 114.

CHAPTER 17

[1] Robert J. Goldwater and Marco Treves, editors. *Artists on Art.* New York, Pantheon Books, 1947. P. 196.

[2] Romain Rolland. *Beethoven the Creator.* Translated by Ernest Newman. New York, Harper & Bros., 1929. P. 86.

[3] P. B. Shelley. Preface to *Prometheus Unbound.*

[4] Alfred Einstein. *Gluck.* Translated by Eric Blom. London, J. M. Dent & Sons; New York, E. P. Dutton & Co., 1926. P. 98, p. 99.

CHAPTER 18

[1] Théophile Gautier. *Histoire de Romanticisme,* 1868. Translation is original.

[2] Entry for December 24, 1853. In *The Journal of Eugène Delacroix.* Translated by Walter Pach. New York, Crown Publishers, Inc., 1938.

[3] *Dictionaire raisonné de l'architecture française du XIe au XVIe siècle.* 1854–1869.

[4] Victor Hugo. Preface to *Cromwell.* In *Prefaces and Prologues to Famous Books.* Vol. 39 of The Harvard Classics. Edited by Charles W. Eliot. New York, P. F. Collier & Son, 1910. P. 365.

[5] Victor Hugo. *Après une lecture de Dante.* 1837. Translation is original.

[6] Victor Hugo. *Selected Poems.* From Edition Definitive translated by David Tolmie. Philadelphia, George Barrie & Son, 1897. Vol. I, pp. 7–13.

[7] Goethe. *Faust.* Swanick translation. Lines 3672–3675.

[8] *Memoirs of Hector Berlioz.* Translated by Rachel and Eleanor Holmes. Edited by Ernest Newman. New York, Alfred A. Knopf, 1932.

[9] Victor Hugo. Preface to *Cromwell. Op. cit.* P. 372.

CHAPTER 19

[1] Quotations are from Maeterlinck's essay *The Treasure of the Humble.* Translated by Alfred Sutro. New York, Dodd, Mead & Co., 1903.

[2] Permission for reprint granted by Durand et Cie., Paris, France, copyright owners; Elkan-Vogel Co., Inc., Philadelphia, Pa., agents.

[3] Lawrence Gilman. *Debussy's Pelléas et Mélisande.* New York, G. Schirmer, Inc., 1907. P. 51.

CHAPTER 20

[1] Robert J. Goldwater and Marco Treves, editors. *Artists on Art.* New York, Pantheon Books, 1945. P. 410.

[2] *Ibid.* P. 440.

[3] Romain Rolland. *Jean-Christophe.* New York, Modern Library, 1910. Pp. 174–175.

INDEX

Certain features of a Glossary are combined with the Index. When technical terms are defined in the text a page reference is given; in other instances, a short definition is included in parentheses after the entry. In all cases Figure references are cited in **bold face** type, so that terms may be clarified by looking at the illustrations. Works of art are listed by title as well as by artist. Buildings will be found under their respective cities in addition to title and architect. Birth and death dates as well as general events will be found in the Chronologies at the beginnings of Chapters and have not been indexed.